Reserved Word L

ACCEPT	COMP-3	
ACCESS	COMP-4	
ACTUAL	COMPUTATIONAL	DELIMITED
ADD	COMPUTATIONAL-1	DELIMITER
ADDRESS	COMPUTATIONAL-2	DEPENDING
ADVANCING	COMPUTATIONAL-3	DEPTH
AFTER	COMPUTATIONAL-4	DESCENDING
ALL	COMPUTE	DESTINATION
ALPHABETIC	CONFIGURATION	DETAIL
ALPHANUMERIC	CONSOLE	DISABLE
ALPHANUMERIC-EDITED	CONSTANT	DISP
ALSO	CONTAINS	DISPLAY
ALTER	CONTROL	DISPLAY-ST
ALTERNATE	CONTROLS	DISPLAY-n
AND	COPY	DIVIDE
APPLY	CORE-INDEX	DIVISION
ARE	CORR	DOWN
AREA	CORRESPONDING	DUPLICATES
AREAS	COUNT	DYNAMIC
ASCENDING	CSP	EGI
ASSIGN	CURRENCY	EJECT
AT	CURRENT-DATE	ELSE
AUTHOR	CYL-INDEX	EMI
BASIS	CYL-OVERFLOW	ENABLE
BEFORE	C01	END
BEGINNING	C02	END-OF-PAGE
BLANK	C03	ENDING
BLOCK	C04	ENTER
BOTTOM	C05	ENTRY
BY	C06	ENVIRONMENT
CALL	C07	EOP
CANCEL	C08	EQUAL
CBL	C09	EQUALS
CD	C10	ERROR
CF	C11	ESI
CH	C12	ETI
CHANGED	DATA	EVERY
CHARACTER	DATE	EXAMINE
CHARACTERS	DATE-COMPILED	EXCEPTION
CLOCK-UNITS	DATE-WRITTEN	EXCEEDS
CLOSE	DAY	EXHIBIT
COBOL	DE	EXIT
CODE	DEBUG	EXTEND
CODE-SET	DEBUG-CONTENTS	EXTENDED-SEARCH
COLLATING	DEBUG-ITEM	FD
COLUMN	DEBUG-LINE	FILE
COM-REG	DEBUG-NAME	FILE-CONTROL
COMMA	DEBUG-SUB-1	FILE-LIMIT
COMMUNICATION	DEBUG-SUB-2	FILE-LIMITS
COMP	DEBUG-SUB-3	FILLER
COMP-1	DEBUGGING	FINAL
COMP-2	DECIMAL-POINT	FIRST

ADVANCED COBOL

ADVANCED COBOL

KENT T. FIELDS
Auburn University

CLAUDE SIMPSON
Northeast Louisiana University

JOHN A. BONNO
Texas A & I University

JOHN WILEY & SONS

New York · Chichester · Brisbane · Toronto · Singapore

Library of Congress Cataloging in Publication Data:

Fields, Kent T.
    Advanced COBOL.

    Includes index.
    1. COBOL (Computer program language)   I. Simpson,
Claude L.   II. Bonno, John A.   III. Title.
QA76.73.C25F5   1987   005.13′3   86-28996
ISBN 0-471-88020-5

Printed in the United States of America

10 9 8 7 6 5 4 3 2 1

Cover Design by Sheila Granda
Computer Graphic by Marjory Dressler

Preface

Objectives of the Book

This book is intended to be used by students who have had previous coursework in the COBOL language. The first chapter provides a set of refresher materials for those students who have not used the language recently. This review material is not exhaustive but is intended to represent the basic background material on which the remainder of the text is based.

The topics in the book represent advanced concepts that are not generally covered in a first course in COBOL, but which are commonly used in commercial applications. Although structured concepts are stressed throughout the book, some features of the language which do not support structured concepts are introduced as an aid to those students who might otherwise be faced with these features in the process of maintaining work done by someone else.

Throughout the text the assumption is made that the student will be applying the concepts in a commercial environment—the approach is a "real-world" approach.

Organization of the Book

The book is organized into four basic parts.

- The first two chapters review language and structured programming concepts.
- Chapters 3 through 6 and Chapter 11 address file-processing topics. Chapter 3 covers sequential file-processing procedures. Chapters 4, 5, and 6 present material on processing information stored on disk. Chapters 4 and 5 are concerned with indexed files, and Chapter 7 treats relative file organization. Chapter 11 covers table-handling techniques. Some introductory courses in COBOL incorporate table handling so some instructors may choose to omit this material or to assign it as review material following Chapter 1. Others may wish to include the material and to assign it following Chapter 7.
- Chapters 7 through 10 present material which should be entirely new to most students: new PROCEDURE DIVISION entries such as ACCEPT, CALL, and STRING (Chapter 7); the SORT feature (Chapter 8); the REPORT WRITER feature (Chapter 8); and techniques for on-line processing (Chapter 9).

• The appendices provide reference material such as statement formats (Appendix A) and technical discussions of disk and tape storage (Appendices E and F). Appendix B is a unique feature of this book. It is a "rogues' gallery" of COBOL features that may be encountered by a commercial programmer, possibly in the process of maintaining or adapting older operational programs. The undesirable or controversial features of the language are presented separately from the desirable features in order to emphasize those characteristics which make their incorporation in programs undesirable.

Instructor's Manual

This book is accompanied by an *Instructor's Resource Manual*, which contains suggested solutions to the end-of-chapter materials and also includes additional assignments and sample solutions which are structured so that overhead projector transparencies or other visual aids may be prepared from them.

Uses for the Book

This text is intended for use at the two- or four-year college level in a second-semester or third-quarter course in COBOL programming. The illustrative materials have been tested on IBM or DEC-VAX computers. Features that are non-standard are described in sections enclosed within "NON-STANDARD FEATURE" or "IBM ONLY" borders. Similarly, features available only for the 1968 COBOL standard are bordered with "1968-1968-1968," and those unique to the 1974 standard are bordered with "1974-1974-1974-1974."

Kent T. Fields
Claude L. Simpson
John A. Bonno

Acknowledgments

We would like to express our thanks to our editors, Gene Davenport and Carol Beasley, for their support. We are grateful to the many people who have contributed to the development of the book. We gratefully acknowledge the assistance of J. D. Penn, Winfred Jones, N. Gajendar, and Raju Duppatla of the Grambling State University Computer Center; Ron Gillet of the Coastal Corporation; and Lynda Huggins, Dean Van McGraw, and Gloria Brantley of Northeast Louisiana University. We would also like to thank Geneva Harvey, who typed the original manuscript, and Dean Tsegai Emmanuel of Grambling University, and Robert Rogow and Wayne Alderman of Auburn University, who have been unfailingly supportive of our efforts. We are especially grateful to Jack V. Breglio of Santa Ana, John F. Buck of Indiana University, Richard Fisher of Miami University, Donald Golden of Cleveland State University, and Phillip Heeler of Northwest Missouri State University who reviewed the manuscript and have made invaluable suggestions for its improvement. Naturally, any remaining shortcomings of the manuscript are our sole responsibility.

COBOL is an industry language and is not the property of any company or group of companies, or of any organization or group of organizations.

No warranty, expressed or implied, is made by any contributor or by the CODASYL Programming Language Committee as to the accuracy and functioning of the programming system and language. Moreover, no responsibility is assumed by any contributor, or by the committee, in connection therewith.

The authors and copyright holders of the copyrighted material used herein

FLOW-MATIC (trademark of Sperry Rand Corporation), Programming for the UNIVAC® I and II, Data Automation Systems copyrighted 1958, 1959, by Sperry Rand Corporation; IBM Commercial Translator Form No. F 28-8013, copyrighted 1959 by IBM; FACT, DSI 27A5260-2760, copyrighted 1960 by Minneapolis-Honeywell

have specifically authorized the use of this material in whole or in part, in the COBOL specifications. Such authorization extends to the reproduction and use of COBOL specifications in programming manuals or similar publications.

K. T. F.
C. L. S.
J. A. B.

Contents

Preface   v
Acknowledgments   vii

CHAPTER 1   REVIEW OF COBOL PRINCIPLES   1

Section 1   History of COBOL   1
Section 2   The Structure of the Language   2
   Separators   2
   COBOL Words   3
   User-Created Words   3
Section 3   The Structure of a COBOL Program   3
Section 4   The IDENTIFICATION DIVISION   4
   PROGRAM-ID   5
   AUTHOR   5
   INSTALLATION, DATE-WRITTEN, DATE-COMPILED,
   SECURITY   5
Section 5   The ENVIRONMENT DIVISION   5
   File-Control Entries   6
   I-O-CONTROL   6
Section 6   The DATA DIVISION   6
   FILE SECTION   7
   File Description Entry   7
   Record Description Entries   7
   WORKING-STORAGE SECTION   8
Section 7   The PROCEDURE DIVISION   8
Section 8   Arithmetic Statements   9
   The ADD Statement   9
   The COMPUTE Statement   10
   The DIVIDE Statement   10
   The MULTIPLY Statement   11
   The SUBTRACT Statement   12
Section 9   Input/Output Instructions   12
   The OPEN Statement   12
   The CLOSE Statement   13
   The ACCEPT Statement   13
   The DISPLAY Statement   14

ix

The READ Statement (Sequential)   14
The READ Statement (I-O)   15
The WRITE Statement (Sequential)   15
The WRITE Statement (Nonsequential)   16
The REWRITE Statement   16
The START Statement   16
The DELETE Statement   17
The STOP Statement   17
Section 10   Logical Statements   17
The PERFORM...UNTIL Statement   18
Section 11   Transfer of Control Statements   18
The ALTER Statement   18
The GO TO Statement   18
The IF Statement   19
The PERFORM Statement   19
Section 12   Everything Else   20
The CALL Statement   20
The INSPECT Statement   20
The MOVE Statement   20
The SET Statement   21
Section 13   Shorthand Notation for COBOL Statements   21
Section 14   Exercises and Problems   21

CHAPTER 2   A REVIEW OF STRUCTURED PROGRAMMING AND DOCUMENTATION STANDARDS

                                                                      23

Section 1   The Basic Objectives of Program Coding   23
Section 2   Basic Program Structures   24
Section 3   Structured Program Style   25
Section 4   Implementation of Sequence Structures in COBOL   26
Section 5   Implementation of Selection and CASE Structures in
            COBOL   27
Section 6   Implementation of Repetition Structures in COBOL   29
Section 7   Programming Standards—Identification and Use of
            Blank Lines   30
Section 8   Shorthand Notation for COBOL Implementation of
            Basic Program Structures   31
Section 9   Characteristics of Well-Designed Modules   31
   Top-Down Design   32
   Cohesion   32
   Coupling   36
   Span of Control   37
Section 10   Sample Program Illustrating Structured Concepts   38
Section 11   Sample Program Illustrating Unstructured Code   39
Section 12   Questions and Problems   40

CHAPTER 3   SEQUENTIAL FILE PROCESSING

                                                                      51

Section 1   General Concepts of Sequential File Update   51
Section 2   Sequential File-Processing Requirements   52
   Retention Cycle   53
Section 3   Master File Maintenance Program Concepts   54
   Sequence Checking   54
   Data Validation   55

Audit Reports 57
Error Listing 57
Section 4 The Relationship of the Transaction File Key to the
Master File Key 58
Additions 58
Copies or Passes 58
Deletions and Changes 58
Section 5 End-of-File Processing 59
Section 6 An Illustration of Update Concepts 60
Section 7 Structured Program Design for a Sequential Update 61
Section 8 ENVIRONMENT DIVISION Entries for a Sequential
Update 65
Section 9 DATA DIVISION Entries 66
FILE SECTION Entries 66
WORKING-STORAGE SECTION Entries 67
Section 10 PROCEDURE DIVISION Entries 67
000-VM-CONTROL-MODULE. 67
100-INITIALIZE-TOTALS-ETC. 68
200-UPDATE-MASTER-FILE. 69
210-COMPARE-KEYS. 70
220-ADD-MASTER. 70
230-COPY-MASTER. 71
240-DELETE-MASTER. 72
250-CHANGE-MASTER. 72
300-PRINT-AUDIT. 72
400-PRINT-AUDIT-TOTALS. 74
500-READ-MASTER. 75
600-READ-TRANSACTION. 76
Section 11 An Examination of Inputs, Processes, and Outputs 76
Section 12 Sample Program for Sequential File Processing 80
Section 13 Questions and Problems 88

CHAPTER 4 DISK UTILIZATION: INDEXED ACCESS METHODS
AND CONCEPTS   93

Section 1 The File Structure 94
Section 2 Example Problem Illustrating Indexed Organization 95
Section 3 Creation of an Indexed File 95
Section 4 ENVIRONMENT DIVISION Entries for Creating
Indexed Files 96
Section 5 DATA DIVISION Entries for Creating Indexed Files 97
Section 6 PROCEDURE DIVISION Entries for Creating
Indexed Files 98
Section 7 Updating Master File Concepts 99
Section 8 ENVIRONMENT DIVISION Entries for Updating
Indexed Files 100
Section 9 DATA DIVISION Entries for Updating Indexed Files 101
Section 10 PROCEDURE DIVISION Entries for Updating an
Index File 105
000-MAIN-MODULE. 105
100-INITIALIZE-TOTALS-ETC. 105
200-UPDATE-MASTER-FILE. 105
220-ADD-MASTER. 106
240-DELETE-MASTER. 107

```
                     250-CHANGE-MASTER,                              108
                     260-IDENTIFY-ERROR,                            109
                     300-PRINT-AUDIT,                               109
                     400-PRINT-AUDIT-TOTALS,                        109
                     500-READ-TRANSACTION,                          110
                     600-READ-MASTER,                               110
```
Section 11   An Examination of the Program Inputs and
                     Outputs   110
    The Outputs   113
Section 12   Sample COBOL Program   116
Section 13   Questions, Problems, and Exercises   122

CHAPTER 5   OTHER INDEXED APPLICATIONS   125

Section 1   Introduction   125
Section 2   An Example Problem   125
Section 3   Hierarchy Chart   128
Section 4   The Structure of the Files   128
Section 5   ENVIRONMENT DIVISION Entries for the Sample
                     Program   129
Section 6   DATA DIVISION Entries for the Sample Program   130
Section 7   Some New PROCEDURE DIVISION Statements   130
    The START Verb   130
    The READ NEXT Statement   131
Section 8   PROCEDURE DIVISION Entries for the Sample
                     Program   131
    000-CONTROL-CHECK-PRINT,   131
    100-HOUSEKEEPING,   132
    200-PRINT-CHECKS,   133
Section 9   The START Verb and Use of Alternate Key   134
    210-START-INVOICE-FILE,   134
    220-PROCESS-INVOICES,   135
    230-WRITE-CHECK,   135
    232-STUB-TOTAL,   135
    233-WRITE-CHECK-RECORD,   136
    300-DISPLAY-TOTALS,   136
    800-READ-INVOICE,   136
Section 10   An Examination of Inputs and Outputs   137
    Inputs   137
    Outputs   138
Section 11   The Sample Program Listing   139
Section 12   An Example of Using Indexed Files to Process
                     Inverted Lists   144
Section 13   Questions and Exercises   146

CHAPTER 6   DISK UTILIZATION: RELATIVE FILES   149

Section 1   The Concept of a Relative File   149
Section 2   ENVIRONMENT DIVISION Entries for Relative Files   150
Section 3   PROCEDURE DIVISION Commands for Relative
                     Files   151
    The OPEN Statement   151
    The READ Statement for Sequential Access   152

The RANDOM READ Statement for RANDOM or DYNAMIC
ACCESS MODE   152
The Sequential READ Statement for DYNAMIC ACCESS MODE   153
The START Statement   154
The Sequential WRITE Statement for Relative Files   155
The RANDOM or DYNAMIC WRITE Statement for a Relative File   155
The REWRITE Statement   156
The DELETE Statement   158
Section 4   The Concept of Hashing   159
Section 5   The Concept of Pointers   162
Section 6   An Example of an Inverted List Using a Relative
File   164
Section 7   Questions and Exercises   172

CHAPTER 7   SOME SPECIAL STATEMENTS   **175**

Section 1   The ACCEPT Statement   175
Format 1   176
Format 2   176
Section 2   The DISPLAY Statement   177
Section 3   The EXAMINE Statement   178
Section 4   The INSPECT Statement   183
Section 5   The UNSTRING Command   183
Section 6   The STRING Statement   186
Section 7   GO TO DEPENDING ON   188
Section 8   The CALL Statement   189
The USING Option of the CALL Statement   191
Section 9   The COPY Feature   192
Section 10   Using Variable-Length Records   194
Section 11   The SET, SEARCH, and SEARCH ALL Statements   195
Section 12   The EJECT or New Page Feature   198
Section 13   Sample Program   199
Section 14   Exercises and Problems   202

CHAPTER 8   THE COBOL SORT FEATURE   **207**

Section 1   The Need for Sequenced Data   207
Section 2   The SD Entry   210
Section 3   The SELECT Statement for SORT Files   211
Section 4   The SORT Command   211
Section 5   The INPUT PROCEDURE   216
Section 6   The OUTPUT PROCEDURE   218
Section 7   The SORTING Process   224
Section 8   The COBOL Program   225
Section 9   Questions and Exercises   227

CHAPTER 9   THE REPORT WRITER FEATURE   **229**

Section 1   Testing for Control Breaks   229
Section 2   Headings   230
Section 3   Footings   230

Section 4   Page Control   230
Section 5   Line Control   231
Section 6   Totaling—Subtotals and Grand Totals   231
Section 7   Detail Lines   231
Section 8   REPORT WRITER Features in the DATA DIVISION   233
Section 9   The 01 Entries in the REPORT WRITER   243
Section 10   Developing Totals—Manual Methods and the Sum
             Clause   250
Section 11   FILE SECTION Entries in the ENVIRONMENT
             DIVISION   253
Section 12   PROCEDURE DIVISION Entries   253
             DECLARATIVES   254
             Using DECLARATIVES for INVALID KEY and End of File   255
             Other REPORT WRITER PROCEDURE DIVISION Commands   256
Section 13   Sample COBOL Program   258
Section 14   Questions and Exercises   267

CHAPTER 10   ON-LINE TRANSACTION PROCESSING   **269**

Section 1   Menus and Screens   270
Section 2   The MASTER MENU Program (APMENU)   272
             Run-Time Library Calls   273
             DISPLAY and ACCEPT Statements   274
             The Main Menu Program   274
             000-MAIN.   274
             200-GET-ANSWER.   276
             CALL-1, CALL-2, etc.   277
             800-PAINT-MENU.   277
Section 3   The Chart of Accounts Maintenance Submenu   278
             100-HANDLE-REQUEST.   281
             210-ADD-AN-ACCOUNT.   281
Section 4   Questions and Exercises   282

CHAPTER 11   TABLE-HANDLING CONCEPTS AND TECHNIQUES   **285**

Section 1   Introduction   285
             Table Terms and Concepts   285
Section 2   Classification of Tables   288
             Internal versus External Tables   288
             Static versus Volatile Tables   288
             Table Organization Methods   289
             Sequential Table Organization   289
             Positional Organization   289
             Levels of Tables (Dimensions)   290
Section 3   Table-Retrieval Methods   291
             Serial Search of a Table   291
             Serial Search with Early Exit   292
             Binary Table Search   292
             Relative Retrieval of Table Entries   293
Section 4   Processing Table Data in COBOL   294
             Table Construction   294
             Input-Loaded Table   295
             Data Retrieval from Tables   296
             Sequential Table Search Using PERFORM VARYING   296
             Sequential Search with Early Exit   299

The SEARCH Statement 300
The Binary Table Search—SEARCH ALL 300
Direct Retrieval from a Table 301
Two-Dimension Tables 302
000-MAIN. 305
100-INITIALIZE. 306
200-READ-AND-ACCUMULATE. 306
450-PRINT-TABLE. 307
Three-Dimension Tables 308
DATA DIVISION Entries for Three-Dimension Tables 310
Section 5 Questions and Problems 311

APPENDIX A ANSI STANDARD COBOL FORMAT WITH
IBM EXTENSIONS 317

APPENDIX B A ROGUES' GALLERY OF COBOL FEATURES 343

Section 1 The GO TO Statements—Unconditional Branching 343
Section 2 The ALTER Statement 344
Section 3 The CORRESPONDING Option 347
Section 4 77-Level Entries in WORKING-STORAGE 349
Section 5 88-Level Definition of Condition Names 350
Section 6 A Sample Program 352
Inputs to the Sample Program 352
The Sample Program 352
Outputs from the Sample Program 354

APPENDIX C FILE STATUS KEY VALUES 355

APPENDIX D CREATING AN INDEXED FILE FROM A
SEQUENTIAL FILE 357

APPENDIX E MAGNETIC TAPE OPERATIONS 361

Section 1 Characteristics of Magnetic Tape 361
Section 2 How Data Are Stored on Tapes 362
Tape Density 364
Section 3 Blocking 364
Section 4 Tape Labels 365

APPENDIX F CHARACTERISTICS OF DISK STORAGE DEVICES 367

Section 1 Rigid Disk—A Single Surface View 367
Section 2 Rigid Disk—Multiple Surfaces 371
Section 3 Flexible Disk 371

INDEX 373

1

Review of COBOL Principles

COBOL (COmmon Business Oriented Language) is an English oriented, procedure-based programming language. The language is designed principally for the development of programs that are oriented toward business applications.

Each computer manufacturer has developed its own COBOL compiler. However, through the efforts of all in the industry, the basic characteristics of each of these versions of the language are similar. Most differences are to be found in the ENVIRONMENT DIVISION. This virtual uniformity makes COBOL extremely transportable from one brand of computer to another.

This book covers certain "advanced" COBOL concepts and it is assumed that the reader is familiar with the basic structure and the principles of coding the language. The material in this chapter is presented so that the reader may review the basic features of the language, if needed, and to outline the basic elements, which are considered to be "given" throughout the remainder of the text. If some of the structures, rules, and commands discussed in this chapter are not familiar to the reader it may be necessary to briefly review a COBOL principles book.

SECTION 1
History of COBOL

The development of COBOL has been a continuous process over the years under the direction of the Conference on Data Systems Languages (CODASYL). This committee is composed of representatives from the computer manufacturing group and from the computer users group of the American National Standards Institute (ANSI).

COBOL-60, the first version published by CODASYL, was released in 1960. Subsequent versions of the language have extended or changed the language, with COBOL-74 being the latest version. COBOL-8x has been specified by the standards committee and, if approved by the various user's groups, may be released at any time. Most COBOL installations support COBOL-74, but some still implement the COBOL-68 compiler. In this book we cover the 1974 standards but we also provide coverage of the 1968 standards in those circumstances where the two differ. In such cases discussion which relates to the 1974 standard alone will be highlighted with a border of "1974.1974.1974---1974" and material for which only the 1968 standard is applicable will be similarly marked with a border of "1968.1968...," etc.

SECTION 2
The Structure of the Language

COBOL is a highly structured language with many rules that must be followed precisely. A character is the smallest recognizable element in the COBOL language. The legitimate characters that may be used in COBOL are:

Numbers	0–9
Letters	A–Z
Punctuation	ƀ , ; . * " ( )
Special characters	< > + −* / = $

Note: Throughout this book the character "ƀ" will be used to indicate a blank space.

Some of these COBOL characters may be combined to form a COBOL word. A COBOL word may not exceed 30 characters in length and may be made up of any combination of letters, numbers, and hyphens (note that no special characters other than hyphens are allowed) so long as

- at least one alphabetic character (letter) is included in the word, and
- the word does not either begin or end with a hyphen.

COBOL words may be grouped to form COBOL sentences, which in turn may be combined to form COBOL paragraphs.

As indicated above, COBOL is an English oriented language. Just as there are rules for the spelling of words and the formation of sentences (syntax) in English, so there are rules for the spelling of words and for syntax in COBOL. A programmer must understand these rules thoroughly in order to effectively develop programs using COBOL. There are also some rules for the proper development of any program, whether in COBOL or in other high-level languages. These Structured Programming concepts, although not a part of the COBOL language itself, are essential to the process of doing a good job of programming. A review of Structured Programming concepts is presented in Chapter 2. If you have not previously been exposed to this material you should cover it prior to writing any advanced programs in COBOL. All the example programs in this book are structured.

Separators

A separator is a string of one or more punctuation characters. The rules for the formation of separators are as follows:

1. One or more spaces may be used as a separator. When a space appears it is a separator.

2. A comma, period, or semicolon is a separator when it is immediately followed by a space. The use of these values must meet explicit permission requirements. For example, a period may be placed only at the end of a sentence, paragraph, or section. These symbols contribute to the readability of COBOL. It is, effectively, the space which follows the comma or colon which is the separator. The period, however, has certain syntactical meanings of its own.

3. Parentheses are separators. They must be in matched pairs.

4. Quotes are separators. They also must be in matched pairs.

COBOL Words

A COBOL word is made up of a string of not more than 30 characters. These words may be user-created or are provided by the COBOL language as reserved words. See the inside covers of this book for a list of COBOL reserved words.

User-Created Words

User-created words are composed of the combination of alphabetic characters, digits, and the hyphen (the hyphen may not be used to begin or end a word) and must contain at least one alphabetic character. User-created words may be used for:

Program-names: A program-name identifies the source and object programs. Usually, COBOL compilers use only the first few characters (usually six or eight) of the program-name for identity purposes.

File-names: File-names are the internal names that the source program uses to access the file. File-names must be unique.

Record-names: Record-names are used to define and distinguish between records within a file.

Data-names: A data-name is used to name an elementary or higher level data-item.

Paragraph-names: A paragraph-name is used to identify the beginning of a set of COBOL procedure statements.

Section-names: A section-name identifies the beginning of a set of paragraphs which are grouped so that structuring of the program is enhanced.

SECTION 3
The Structure of a COBOL Program

A COBOL program is composed of four divisions. These divisions are:

```
IDENTIFICATION DIVISION
ENVIRONMENT DIVISION
DATA DIVISION
PROCEDURE DIVISION
```

All four divisions are required and all must be included in your program in the sequence indicated previously.

The ENVIRONMENT, DATA, and PROCEDURE divisions may be divided into SECTIONS. In the ENVIRONMENT and DATA divisions, these sections are defined by COBOL reserved words called *section headers*. In the PROCEDURE division, sections are user-defined and are very helpful as an aid in following the program code.

Sections are divided into paragraphs. In the IDENTIFICATION and ENVIRON-MENT divisions, paragraphs begin with COBOL reserved words called *paragraph headers*. Paragraph names in the PROCEDURE DIVISION are user defined.

Paragraphs may be subdivided into sentences. A COBOL sentence consists of one or more COBOL statements, which are terminated by the use of a period.

A paragraph is composed of statements. The COBOL statements are of three types: compiler-directing, conditional, and imperative. All COBOL statements begin with a verb that determines the COBOL statement type.

A compiler-directing statement is a command to the COBOL compiler to complete some task during compile time. An example of such a statement is the eject command (discussed in Chapter 7).

A conditional statement tests the truth-value of a statement and then provides for action based on whether the statement is true or not. The conditional statements are:

IF

READ with AT END or INVALID KEY

WRITE with INVALID KEY

DELETE

REWRITE

START with INVALID KEY

any arithmetic statement with ON SIZE ERROR

PERFORM UNTIL

SEARCH AT END with WHEN

GO TO with DEPENDING ON

EXHIBIT CHANGED

RETURN with AT END

All other statements are imperative statements. Discussion of these imperative statements may be further classified as Input/Output statements or arithmetic statements for convenience of exposition, but the reader should understand that they are still imperative statements.

SECTION 4
The IDENTIFICATION DIVISION

The purpose of the IDENTIFICATION DIVISION is to provide identifying information in both the source and object programs.

The general format of the IDENTIFICATION DIVISION is as follows:

IDENTIFICATION DIVISION.

PROGRAM-ID. program-name.

[AUTHOR. [comment.]...]

[INSTALLATION. [comment.]...]

[DATE-WRITTEN. [comment.]...]

[DATE-COMPILED. compiler generated.]

[SECURITY. [comment.]...]

Only the first two entries are required by the COBOL compiler. Since one of the strengths of COBOL is that it has some excellent self-documenting features, some, or all, of these entries are normally included in the IDENTIFICATION DIVISION.

PROGRAM-ID

The program-name assigned in the PROGRAM-ID entry is user-determined and usually may not exceed six or eight characters. One of these characters must be alphabetic. The program-name is normally used to identify both the source and object programs and all listings generated by the COBOL compiler. PROGRAM-ID is the only required paragraph in the IDENTIFICATION DIVISION.

AUTHOR

Although AUTHOR is not required in the IDENTIFICATION DIVISION, it should be included to help in the internal documentation procedures of most organizations.

INSTALLATION, DATE-WRITTEN, DATE-COMPILED, SECURITY

These paragraphs are also optional but their inclusion is most helpful in documentation.

SECTION 5
The ENVIRONMENT DIVISION

The ENVIRONMENT DIVISION, which must be included in any COBOL program, describes:

- the hardware configuration of the compiling computer, the configuration of the executing computer, and
- the relationship between the files and the input/output media.

The general form of the ENVIRONMENT DIVISION is as follows:

ENVIRONMENT DIVISION.

CONFIGURATION SECTION.

SOURCE-COMPUTER. name.

OBJECT-COMPUTER. name.

[SPECIAL-NAMES. special names entry]

[INPUT-OUTPUT SECTION.

FILE-CONTROL. paragraph.

[I-O-CONTROL. paragraph.]]

Note: [] denotes that these are optional entries. The full format designation for the ENVIRONMENT DIVISION is given in Appendix A. The CONFIGURATION

SECTION deals with the characteristics of the source and object computers. The three paragraphs that may be included in this section are:

SOURCE-COMPUTER, (name of the compiling computer)

OBJECT-COMPUTER, (name of the executing computer)

SPECIAL-NAMES, (relates user-defined names to COBOL names)

The INPUT-OUTPUT SECTION assigns names to the files that the program is going to work with and relates those file-names to specific devices. This section also provides information required for the transmission and handling of data during the execution of the object program. The section consists of the FILE-CONTROL and I-O CONTROL paragraphs.

FILE-CONTROL *Entries*

The purpose of the FILE-CONTROL paragraph is to name and associate files with external media. The content of the FILE-CONTROL entry is dependent upon the organization of the file that is named. The basic file organization types are: (1) sequential, (2) indexed, and (3) relative.

Indexed, relative, and sequential files will be covered in Chapters 2 through 6.

I-O-CONTROL

The I-O-CONTROL paragraph defines special control techniques to be used in the object program and sets up the area of memory that is to be shared by different files.

SECTION 6
The DATA DIVISION

In order to process data, these data must first be brought into the computer's memory. The data may come from an external source, such as a disk or tape, or may be generated internally by the program. Data that come from an external source are brought into the area defined by a COBOL program's FILE SECTION. Similarly, data that are generated internally are usually stored within the area defined in the WORKING-STORAGE SECTION of the DATA DIVISION. One function of the DATA DIVISION is, then, to provide for allocation of space for data storage.

Another purpose of the DATA DIVISION is to describe the size and types of data-items that are contained within its boundaries.

A third purpose of the DATA DIVISION is to provide an area to store data to be linked to another program if this object program CALLs another program and contains a USING statement. This section is called the LINKAGE SECTION.

The DATA DIVISION may also be used to provide an area for a description of reports when the REPORT WRITER feature is used. This section is called the REPORT SECTION. The REPORT WRITER feature, including REPORT SECTION entries, is discussed in detail in Chapter 9.

The general format of the DATA DIVISION is as follows:

```
DATA DIVISION,
[FILE SECTION,
    [file description entries]
    [record description entries]]
```

```
[WORKING-STORAGE SECTION.
    [record description entries]]
[LINKAGE SECTION.
    [record description entries]]
[REPORT SECTION.
    [report description entries]]
```

FILE SECTION

The FILE SECTION describes the characteristics of the files that are first named by the select statement(s) in the ENVIRONMENT DIVISION. For each file the records are described using record description entries (discussed later). The FD (file description) entry is used to describe the files that were named within the SELECT statement. There will be one FD in the FILE SECTION for each of the SELECT statements included in the FILE-CONTROL paragraph of the ENVIRONMENT DIVISION.

The FILE SECTION also describes the records contained within the files through the use of a record description entry.

File Description Entry

The general format of the FD is as follows:

```
[FD file-name
[BLOCK CONTAINS [integer-1 TO] integer-2 {RECORDS    }]
                                         {CHARACTERS }
[RECORD CONTAINS [integer-3 TO] integer-4 [CHARACTERS]

LABEL {RECORD IS   }{STANDARD}
      {RECORDS ARE }{OMITTED }
[VALUE OF implementor-name-1 IS {data-name-1}
                               {literal-1  }
    [implementor-name-2 IS {data-name-2}
                           {literal-2  }
[DATA {RECORD is   } data-name-3 [data-name-4] ...]
      {RECORDS ARE }
```

Only the FD with its associated file-name and LABEL statement is required in the file description entry. Indeed, in some compilers even the LABEL statement is not required. However, the other entries should be included for documentation purposes.

One or more record description entries should follow each FD.

Record Description Entries

Record description entries are indicated by an 01 level number in Margin A. There will be one record description entry for each record type contained in the file. These record entries all share the same physical area of memory no matter how they are described.

The record description may be subdivided into group items or elementary items, as dictated by the necessities of the processing logic.

An elementary item is a data-item that is not subdivided based on level numbers. (Legitimate level numbers are 01-49) A group item is subdivided into fields of data containing level numbers greater than the level number of the group item itself. For example:

```
01 RECORD-NAME,
    05  EMPLOYEE-NAME,                   [group item
        10 LAST-NAME   PIC X(20),
        10 FIRST-NAME  PIC X(10), ] elementary items
        10 MIDDLE-INIT PIC X,
```

The data description entry also defines the size and characteristics of a data field. The general format is as follows:

$$
\begin{aligned}
&\text{level-number} \begin{Bmatrix} \text{data-name-1} \\ \underline{\text{FILLER}} \end{Bmatrix} \\
&\quad [\underline{\text{REDEFINES}}\ \text{data-name-2}] \\
&\quad \left[\begin{Bmatrix} \underline{\text{PICTURE}} \\ \underline{\text{PIC}} \end{Bmatrix} \text{IS]}\ \text{character string} \right] \\
&\quad \left[[\text{USAGE} \begin{Bmatrix} \underline{\text{COMPUTATIONAL}} \\ \underline{\text{COMP}} \\ \underline{\text{COMPUTATIONAL-1}} \\ \underline{\text{COMP-1}} \\ \underline{\text{COMPUTATIONAL-3}} \\ \underline{\text{COMP-3}} \\ \underline{\text{DISPLAY}} \\ \underline{\text{INDEX}} \end{Bmatrix} \right] \\
&\quad \left[\underline{\text{OCCURS}} \begin{Bmatrix} \text{integer-1 TO integer-2 TIMES } \underline{\text{DEPENDING}}\ \text{ON data-name-3} \\ \text{integer-2 TIMES} \end{Bmatrix} \right] \\
&\qquad [\underline{\text{INDEXED}}\ \text{BY index-name-1, [...]]} \\
&\qquad \left[\begin{Bmatrix} \underline{\text{ASCENDING}} \\ \underline{\text{DESCENDING}} \end{Bmatrix} \text{KEY IS data-name-4 [data-name-5]...} \right] \\
&\quad \left[\begin{Bmatrix} \underline{\text{SYNCHRONIZED}} \\ \underline{\text{SYNC}} \end{Bmatrix} \begin{Bmatrix} \underline{\text{LEFT}} \\ \underline{\text{RIGHT}} \end{Bmatrix} \right] \\
&\quad \left[\begin{Bmatrix} \underline{\text{JUSTIFIED}} \\ \underline{\text{JUST}} \end{Bmatrix} [\underline{\text{RIGHT}}] \right] \\
&\quad [\text{BLANK WHEN ZERO}] \\
&\quad [\text{VALUE IS literal}].
\end{aligned}
$$

The record description clauses may be written in almost any order, except that data-name-1 or FILLER must immediately follow the level number, and the RE-DEFINES clause, when used, must immediately follow the complete description of the record being defined.

For a detailed description of all these entries, see an introductory COBOL text. (For example: *Structured COBOL* by Stern and Stern [Wiley, 1985]).

WORKING-STORAGE SECTION

The purpose of the WORKING-STORAGE SECTION is to define temporary storage for the description of fields that are not part of input or output.

SECTION 7
The PROCEDURE DIVISION

The PROCEDURE DIVISION is the place in the COBOL program where the commands which actually cause data to be manipulated are specified. Execution starts with the first statement in the first paragraph and continues sequentially to the end of the program unless a sequence-altering instruction is encountered (IF, PER-FORM, GO TO etc.).

The general format of the PROCEDURE DIVISION is one of the following:

PROCEDURE DIVISION [USING data-name-1 [data-name-2]...].
[DECLARATIVES.
[{section-name SECTION [segment-number].
                           declarative statements.
[paragraph-name.[sentence]}]
END DECLARATIVES.]
{section-name SECTION [segment-number].
[paragraph-name. [sentence]]}
[END PROGRAM].

or

    PROCEDURE DIVISION [USING data-name-1 [data-name-2...]
    {paragraph-name. [sentence.]...}

The DECLARATIVES (discussed in Chapter 9, on the REPORT WRITER) may contain no more than 49 sections. Segment numbers are integers that usually range from 0 through 127. Also, the DECLARATIVES section must be at the beginning of the PROCEDURE DIVISION. A COBOL procedure is referenced either by its paragraph-name or section-name. These procedures are broken down into statements or instructions. The classes of instructions in the PROCEDURE DIVISION are: arithmetic, input/output, logical, transfer, and general.

SECTION 8
Arithmetic Statements

The arithmetic statements in COBOL are: ADD, COMPUTE, DIVIDE, MULTIPLY, and SUBTRACT.

The ADD *Statement*

The ADD statement causes the summation and storage of two or more operands. The three formats of the ADD instruction are as follows:

Format 1

    ADD {dentifier-1}{,identifier-2} TO identifier-m [ROUNDED]
        [ON SIZE ERROR any imperative statement]

Format 2

$$\text{ADD} \begin{Bmatrix} \text{identifier-1} \\ \text{literal-1} \end{Bmatrix} \begin{Bmatrix} \text{identifier-2} \\ \text{literal-2} \end{Bmatrix} \begin{bmatrix} \text{identifier-3} \\ \text{literal-3} \end{bmatrix}$$

        GIVING identifier-n [ROUNDED]
          [ON SIZE ERROR any imperative statement]

Format 3

    ADD {CORRESPONDING} {identifier-1 TO identifier-2 ROUNDED
        [ON SIZE ERROR imperative statement]

In the first format, the values of the data-items that precede the word TO are added together and their sum is added to the current value of the data-name, following the word TO. The contents of the data-items preceding the word TO remain as they were prior to the execution of the ADD statement. In the second format, the data-items preceding the word GIVING are added together and their sum is moved to the data-item named following the word GIVING. Notice that the word TO does *not* appear in the second format type.

The ROUNDED phrase serves to round off values according to this rule:

After decimal point alignment, the result of the addition is rounded up by 1 if the value to be truncated is ≥ 5.

The ON SIZE ERROR phrase causes the ADD statement to become a conditional statement. If, after decimal alignment, the absolute value of the result exceeds the PICTURE size of the data-item, the imperative statement following ON SIZE ERROR is executed.

The ADD CORRESPONDING option is not a standard COBOL feature. It is an extension to the language which is supported by a number of compilers, including those of IBM. Since there is some controversy concerning the use of this feature we have included discussion of it in the Rogues' Gallery-Appendix B.

The COMPUTE *Statement*

The COMPUTE statement assigns the value of an arithmetic expression to a data-item. This statement is *not* algebraic; for example, COMPUTE N = N + 1 is a legal COBOL statement, but it violates the rules of algebra. Obviously, and by definition, under the rules of algebra [N] cannot be equal to [N] + 1. However, the COMPUTE statement does follow the order of execution of algebraic notation. The COMPUTE statement has the capability of combining all types of arithmetic statements into a single arithmetic expression. For example:

```
COMPUTE A = B * C / D + U - R
```

The symbols used in the COMPUTE statement and the order of hierarchy of execution are:

( )	highest hierarchical level
** exponentiation	executed first
* multiplication	middle level hierarchy
/ division	middle level hierarchy
+ addition	lowest level of hierarchy
− subtraction	lowest level of hierarchy

The order of execution can be altered through the use of parentheses.

The ROUNDED and ON SIZE ERROR options may be included in the COMPUTE statement.

The DIVIDE *Statement*

The DIVIDE statement divides one numeric data-item into another and stores the result. There are two basic formats of the DIVIDE instruction and they are as follows:

Format 1

```
DIVIDE {identifier-1}  INTO  identifier-2[ROUNDED]
       {literal-1   }
                          [identifier-3[ROUNDED]]...
            [ON SIZE ERROR  any imperative statement]
```

Format 2

$$\underline{DIVIDE} \begin{Bmatrix} \text{identifier-1} \\ \text{literal-1} \end{Bmatrix} \underline{INTO} \begin{Bmatrix} \text{identifier-2} \\ \text{literal-2} \end{Bmatrix}$$
$$\underline{GIVING} \text{ identifier-3 } [\underline{ROUNDED}]$$
$$[\underline{ON} \ \underline{SIZE} \ \underline{ERROR} \text{ any imperative statement}]$$

Format 3

$$\underline{DIVIDE} \begin{Bmatrix} \text{identifier-1} \\ \text{literal-1} \end{Bmatrix} \underline{BY} \begin{Bmatrix} \text{identifier-2} \\ \text{literal-2} \end{Bmatrix}$$
$$\underline{GIVING} \text{ identifier-3 } [\underline{ROUNDED}]$$
$$[\underline{ON} \ \underline{SIZE} \ \underline{ERROR} \text{ any imperative statement}]$$

In Format 1 the value of the second data-item listed is divided by the value of the first data-item (or literal) listed and the quotient replaces the second data-item. The value of the first data-item remains unchanged as a result of the DIVIDE instruction.

In the second format the division is the same but the initial value of the dividend (the second data-name listed) is retained. The data-name you specify following GIVING is the receiving field for the quotient.

The third format operates quite differently from the first two. If you use this format, without the GIVING option, the value of the first data-item is divided by the value of the second and the quotient replaces the first data-item. In effect, you are using the "mirror image" of Format 1. If you utilize the GIVING option with the DIVIDE BY, the value of the first data-item will be preserved and the quotient will be stored at the third data location—identifier-3.

There is a nonstandard feature implemented by many compilers that allows you to preserve the remainder of a division. You may use it by adding this clause to any of the preceding formats:

[REMAINDER identifier-4]

It is possible that this feature may not be available on the computer you are using.

The MULTIPLY *Statement*

The MULTIPLY statement multiplies the values of numeric data-items and stores the results. There are two forms of the MULTIPLY statement.

Format 1

$$\underline{MULTIPLY} \begin{Bmatrix} \text{identifier 1} \\ \text{literal-1} \end{Bmatrix} \underline{BY} \{\text{identifier-2}\} [\underline{ROUNDED}]$$
$$[\text{identifier-3 } [\underline{ROUNDED}]]...$$
$$[\underline{ON} \ \underline{SIZE} \ \underline{ERROR} \text{ any imperative statement}]$$

Format 2

$$\underline{MULTIPLY} \begin{Bmatrix} \text{identifier-1} \\ \text{literal-1} \end{Bmatrix} \underline{BY} \begin{Bmatrix} \text{identifier-2} \\ \text{literal-2} \end{Bmatrix}$$
$$\underline{GIVING} \text{ identifier-3 } [\underline{ROUNDED}]$$
$$[\text{identifier-4 } [\underline{ROUNDED}]]...$$
$$[\underline{ON} \ \underline{SIZE} \ \underline{ERROR} \text{ any imperative statement}$$

In the first format the two numeric items specified are multiplied together and the result is stored at the location specified following BY. The product of the multiplication replaces the second data-item listed (the one following BY) but the value of the first data-item listed remains unchanged.

In the second format you provide a storage location for the product of the multiplication (the data-item following GIVING), and the values of the multiplier and multiplicand remain unchanged.

The SUBTRACT Statement

The SUBTRACT statement is used to subtract one value from another and to store the result. Alternately, it may be used to (1) sum two or more numeric data-items and (2) subtract this sum from another data-item, and (3) store the results. The general formats of the SUBTRACT statement are as follows:

Format 1

$$\underline{\text{SUBTRACT}} \begin{Bmatrix} \text{identifier-1} \\ \text{literal-1} \end{Bmatrix} \begin{bmatrix} \text{identifier-2} \\ \text{literal-2} \end{bmatrix} ..$$
$$\quad\quad \underline{\text{FROM}}\ \text{identifier-n}\ [\underline{\text{ROUNDED}}]$$
$$\quad\quad \underline{\text{ON}}\ \underline{\text{SIZE}}\ \underline{\text{ERROR}}\ \text{any imperative statement}]$$

Format 2

$$\underline{\text{SUBTRACT}} \begin{Bmatrix} \text{identifier-1} \\ \text{literal-1} \end{Bmatrix} \begin{bmatrix} \text{identifier-2} \\ \text{literal-2} \end{bmatrix} ...$$
$$\underline{\text{FROM}}\ \{\text{identifier-m}\}$$
$$\underline{\text{GIVING}}\ \{\text{identifier-n}\}\ \underline{\text{ROUNDED}}]$$
$$\quad\quad [\text{identifier-o}\ [\underline{\text{ROUNDED}}]]...$$
$$\underline{\text{ON}}\ \underline{\text{SIZE}}\ \underline{\text{ERROR}}\ \text{any imperative statement}]$$

In the first format the values of the identifiers or literals preceding the word FROM are added together and the result subtracted from the identifier following FROM; the result is stored at the identifier following GIVING. Only the value of identifier-n is changed as a result of the execution of this statement.

The second format works the same way, except that the result is moved to identifier-n and the contents of identifier-m remain unchanged as a result of the execution of this instruction.

SECTION 9
Input/Output Instructions

The input/output instructions used in COBOL are OPEN, CLOSE, ACCEPT, READ, DISPLAY, WRITE, REWRITE, START, DELETE, and STOP. The function of these statements is to allow or cause the transfer data from some input/output device to the computer's memory or vice versa.

The OPEN Statement

The execution of the OPEN statement by a COBOL object program checks for the availability of a file and makes a record area that is associated with the file available to the program. If a file is not present and the mode of operation is OUTPUT, a file is created.

The general format of the OPEN verb is:

```
       ⎧ INPUT  file-name-1 [WITH NO REWIND][REVERSED] ⎫
       ⎪ OUTPUT file-name-2 [WITH NO REWIND][REVERSED] ⎪
OPEN   ⎨ I-O    file-name-3                            ⎬
       ⎪ EXTEND file-name-4                            ⎪
       ⎩                                               ⎭
```

A file must be successfully OPENed in order for a program to process data for the file. The execution of the OPEN statement does *not* transfer data. It merely makes the file ready for input/output operations.

The phrases that may be included in the OPEN statement have the following purposes:

INPUT   Positions the current record pointer to the first record in the file. Data may only be READ from this file.

OUTPUT   At the time of execution of the OPEN statement, a file is created with no data in it. If an existing file is OPENed in the OUTPUT mode, the data in that file may be destroyed.

EXTEND   When the EXTEND phrase is specified, the OPEN statement positions the current record pointer to the position following the last record in the file. Subsequent WRITE instructions cause records to be added to the end of the file.

I-O   The execution of the OPEN statement in the I-O mode causes the opening of a mass storage device for INPUT or OUTPUT operations. The file must exist in order for the READ or WRITE instructions to be successfully executed.

The REWIND and NO REWIND options, which are included in the full format descriptions in Appendix A, refer to magnetic tape operations. A card, disk, or printer file would not contain this clause.

The CLOSE Statement

The CLOSE statement provides for the orderly termination of input/output operations on a file or a set of files. If a file was OPENed for output, an end-of-file indicator is written at the end of the file on execution of a CLOSE statement.

The general format of the CLOSE command is as follows:

```
CLOSE   file-name-1   [file-name-2]...
```

The ACCEPT Statement

The purpose of the ACCEPT statement, which is discussed in detail in Chapter 7, is to transfer low-volume data from a terminal to the computer's memory without specifying a file (FD) for the data. The ACCEPT statement executes the transfer of data in accordance with the rules of the MOVE statement. The programmer should be aware that these statements may not work well on some equipment. Conceptual data-items such as DATE, DAY, and TIME can be ACCEPTed from the computer's operating system and require no program definition. For example:

```
ACCEPT PROGRAM-DATE FROM DATE,
ACCEPT PROGRAM-TIME FROM TIME,
ACCEPT PROGRAM-DAY FROM DAY,
```

Other low-volume data may be ACCEPTed as follows:

```
ACCEPT data-name-1.
```

Data-name-1 is defined in the DATA DIVISION of the executing program.

Some computer systems allow you to ACCEPT data from specific lines and positions on that line; see your local computer center for specifics. One example might be as follows:

```
ACCEPT CUST-NAME FROM LINE 1 POSITION 35,
```

where CUST-NAME is a data-item.

The DISPLAY Statement

The DISPLAY statement, discussed in detail in Chapter 7, causes low-volume data-items to be displayed on a specified terminal or the system console. Again, as in the case of the ACCEPT statement, there is no necessity for file setup procedures. You may DISPLAY items from WORKING-STORAGE without having to specify an FD in the FILE SECTION. On some computer systems the DISPLAY command allows the specification of the format of the data that are to be DISPLAYED.

The general format of the DISPLAY statement is as follows:

$$\underline{\text{DISPLAY}} \begin{Bmatrix} \text{identifier-1} \\ \text{literal-1} \end{Bmatrix} \begin{bmatrix} \text{identifier-2} \\ \text{literal-2} \end{bmatrix} [\underline{\text{UPON}} \text{ device-name}]$$

The DISPLAY statement causes the values of the operand identifier-1 to be transferred to the display unit in accordance with the form of the DISPLAY statement. Identifier-1 must be in the USAGE DISPLAY format.

The phrases which follow are not included in the preceding standard format. They are available as nonstandard features of many compilers but they are hardware dependent, so some may not be available on the machine you are using.

UNIT   selects a unit other than the executing unit upon which to display the data.

LINE   selects the line on the CRT to display the data.

POSITION   selects a column within the LINE to begin displaying data.

SIZE   specifies the size of the data-item to be displayed and overrides the DATA DIVISION definition for the field.

ERASE   causes the CRT screen to be erased prior to data display.

HIGH/LOW   causes display to be bright or half bright.

REVERSE   causes the displayed data to appear in reverse video.

The READ Statement (Sequential)

The READ command obtains the next logical record from a file. In order to execute the READ statement, the file must have previously been opened as I-O or INPUT.

The general format of the READ statement is as follows:

```
READ file-name [INTO identifier-1]
     [AT END any imperative statement]
```

The INTO phrase causes the record that is being read to be moved to the area of memory specified by the specified data-name. The record that has been read will then be available both in the record area associated with the file and in the area specified by identifier-1.

The AT END phrase, in effect, causes the READ statement to include a logic statement. If the end-of-file condition is detected when the READ statement is executed, the specified imperative statement is executed. Also, after the end condition is detected, no more READ statements can be issued to that file unless the file is first closed then opened again.

The READ *Statement* (I-O)

The use of the READ statement and other COBOL features for processing records stored in direct access mode is discussed in detail in Chapters 4, 5, and 6. The general formats for the READing of data from mass storage devices are as follows:

Format 1

```
READ file-name [NEXT] RECORD [INTO identifier-1]
     [AT END any imperative statement]
```

Format 2

```
READ file-name RECORD [INTO identifier-1]
     [KEY IS data-name]
     [INVALID KEY any imperative statement]
```

Format 1 is used for the retrieval of data from a mass storage device where the *sequential* access mode is specified. The NEXT phrase is included for files where DYNAMIC is specified and records are to be retrieved sequentially.

Format 2 is used for random access files that are to be retrieved randomly. The KEY phrase must be specified for files whose organization is INDEXED. The data-name for KEY must be one of the data-items that is specified in the record description for that file.

The INVALID KEY return indicates procedures to be followed if no record is found in the file for the value of the specified key.

If the organization of the file is RELATIVE then no KEY is specified in the READ statement since RELATIVE KEY is stipulated in the SELECT statement for such files.

The execution of the READ statement causes the retrieval of a record based on the value of the KEY or RELATIVE key at the time the statement is executed.

The AT END phrase is specified only for Format 1 and causes the execution of the imperative statement when the end-of-file condition is detected.

The information presented here should be sufficient for purposes of review. These concepts are addressed in more detail in the chapters on indexed access methods (Chapters 4 and 5) and on relative files (Chapter 6).

The WRITE *Statement (Sequential)*

The WRITE statement causes the release of the next logical record to an output file. Also, the statement may be used for vertical positioning in a printer file.

The format is:

```
WRITE record-name [FROM identifier-1]
      [ {BEFORE[ADVANCING]} {identifier-2} [LINE ]]
      [ {AFTER  [ADVANCING]} {integer   } [LINES]]
```

The FROM phrase works as if a MOVE statement has been executed prior to the WRITE.

After the successful execution of a WRITE statement the record is no longer available in the record area.

The WRITE Statement (Nonsequential)

The WRITE statement in this form causes the release of a logical record or output of a physical record to an I/O file.

The general format of the instruction is:

```
WRITE record-name [FROM identifier]
      [INVALID KEY any imperative statement]
```

After the successful execution of a WRITE statement the record is no longer available in the record area.

If the file is RELATIVE, the specified RELATIVE KEY must not be a part of the record (defined in WORKING STORAGE) to be written and must be determined by the programmer's logic prior to the execution of the WRITE statement.

The INVALID KEY return indicates one of the following conditions:

1. A key has a value not greater than the value of the previously written key on an indexed file being accessed sequentially.
2. A key for an indexed file OPENed as OUTPUT or I-O already exists.
3. An item already exists for a record which you are attempting to write to a RELATIVE file.
4. You are out of file space.

The REWRITE Statement

The REWRITE statement causes the logical replacement of an existing record in a mass storage file. Before a REWRITE statement may be executed, a successful READ to that file must have been previously executed.

The general form of the REWRITE statement is as follows:

```
REWRITE record-name [FROM identifier]
        [INVALID KEY any imperative statement]
```

If the FROM option is specified in the command, the identifier and record-name must not refer to the same memory area. Also, the lengths of both areas must be the same.

The INVALID KEY must be specified for files that are not opened in the sequential access mode. The INVALID KEY phrase specifies what is to be done if you try to replace a record that does not exist. Obviously, this is usually caused by not reading the file prior to issuing the REWRITE command or by replacing the values in the KEY areas.

The START Statement

The START statement causes a positioning of the current record pointer at some desired point in an indexed file for the purpose of sequential processing of that file beginning at the selected point.

The general format of the START statement is as follows:

$$
\text{START file-name } \left[\underline{\text{KEY}} \left\{ \begin{array}{l} \text{IS } = \\ \text{IS NOT} \\ \text{IS } > \end{array} \right\} \text{data-name} \right]
$$
$$
\text{[INVALID KEY any imperative statement]}
$$

The access mode specified for the referenced file must be DYNAMIC (see Chapter 5) or SEQUENTIAL. The organization type may be RELATIVE (see Chapter 6),

SEQUENTIAL, or INDEXED (see Chapter 4). The file must be OPENed in the INPUT or I-O mode.

The INVALID KEY return indicates that the logical starting point cannot be determined.

The DELETE *Statement*

The DELETE statement *logically* removes a record from a mass storage file. The DELETE command may not be implemented on some systems, so the programmer must check the instruction set for the computer in use.

The format of the DELETE verb is:

DELETE file-name [INVALID KEY any imperative statement]

The STOP *Statement*

The STOP statement causes a temporary or permanent cessation of the execution of an object program.

We have included the STOP comment in the interest of completeness. We discourage use of this command because it may stop processing on your computer system, thereby incurring the wrath of other users. If you have an application which seems to require the use of a STOP statement, check with the operations people in your center before using the feature. STOP RUN affects only the execution of your program, so use it as you see fit.

The format of the STOP command is as follows:

STOP {literal}
     {RUN}

If STOP literal is specified, the value of the literal is displayed and program execution is suspended. STOP RUN causes the program execution to be terminated.

SECTION 10
Logical Statements

The purpose of the logical commands in a COBOL program is to test for the existence of a condition by comparison of values and by testing the result of that comparison.

An AT END clause or an INVALID KEY clause associated with input/output instructions are logical instructions. They test for an exception, and provide for the processing to be done when that exception exists, by causing the imperative statement included after the AT END or INVALID KEY phrases to be executed.

The ON SIZE ERROR phrase included as part of an arithmetic statement is also a type of logical instruction. It tests for an exceptional condition, and if that condition exists, the imperative statement included with the phrase is executed.

The GO TO ...DEPENDING ON... statement (if your shop standard allows the use of this statement) is also a logical command. The value of the specified identifier is tested and a branch occurs depending on the value of that identifier. The GO TO with DEPENDING ON is discussed in Chapter 7.

The IF statement, however, is the principal logical statement in COBOL. This statement causes a specified condition to be evaluated. The action taken by the object program depends upon whether the condition evaluated is true or false.

The general form of the IF verb is:

$$\underline{IF} \quad condition \begin{Bmatrix} statement\text{-}1 \\ \underline{NEXT}\ \underline{SENTENCE} \end{Bmatrix} \begin{Bmatrix} \underline{ELSE}\ statement\text{-}2 \\ \underline{ELSE}\ \underline{NEXT}\ \underline{SENTENCE} \end{Bmatrix}$$

In this general format, statement-1 or statement-2 may take the form of other conditional statements or imperative statements. If the tested condition is true, then statement-1 is executed, if specified, or if no condition is specified, then the NEXT SENTENCE is executed. The ELSE, if specified, is ignored when the tested condition is true.

If the condition tested is false, statement-2 is executed or, if no statement-2 is specified, the NEXT SENTENCE is executed.

The PERFORM...UNTIL *Statement*

The UNTIL phrase, when used with a PERFORM statement, is also a logical construct. See the discussion of the PERFORM instruction in a COBOL principles book for particulars.

SECTION 11
Transfer of Control Statements

COBOL statements are executed in sequence one after the other in the sequence they are written in unless a sequence-altering instruction is encountered. Some of the sequence-altering instructions may be destructive of structured code. We present them here in the interest of completeness, since you may encounter them in code which has been written by someone else. Of the three presented here, the PERFORM statement (in its many forms) will be used frequently since it implements structured concepts. The ALTER statement, on the other hand, should not be used at all—but you should know what it does since you may encounter it (heaven forbid) in doing maintenance work on someone else's program. The GO TO statements are a special case. There is general agreement that the use of these statements should be, at best, infrequent. Many believe that any unconditional branching (use of GO TO) is destructive of good structured programming technique. Indeed, many refer to structured programming as GOTOless programming. Others assert that there are unusual conditions in which the use of a forward-pointing GO TO will improve the legibility of the code. In any event such conditions would be extremely rare. You should avoid the use of GO TO statements. The conditions in which their use is permitted (if at all) will be outlined in the shop standards or class standards where you work or go to school. The following discussions address the sequence-altering instructions.

The ALTER *Statement*

Do not use the ALTER statement; everyone will think you are a dummy or will hate you or, more probably, both. The use of this statement is so destructive of proper coding that virtually all data processors, who rarely agree on anything, are convinced that it should not be used. There are still some programs, written prior to this consensus or coded by one of the few who still use this statement, which incorporate the ALTER statement. For this reason we have included a discussion of the statement in the Rogues' Gallery—Appendix B.

The GO TO *Statement*

The GO TO statement alters the sequence of statement execution by transferring control to another part of the PROCEDURE DIVISION.

Format 1

GO TO procedure-name-1.

Format 2

GO TO procedure-name-1[,procedure-name-2]...,[procedure-name-n]
   DEPENDING ON identifier-1

In Format 1, control is transferred to the point in the program identified by procedure-name. In Format-2 the value of identifier-1 (which must be defined with an unedited numeric integer PICTURE) is evaluated, and control is transferred to the point in the program identified by procedure-name-1 (if the value of identifier-1 is a 1), or to procedure-name-2 (if the value of identifier-1 is a 2), and so forth.

The IF *Statement*

The IF statement is a sequence-altering instruction when:

- the statement contains an ELSE clause that is executed, or
- the statement contains GO TO that is executed, or
- the statement contains a PERFORM statement that is executed.

The PERFORM *Statement*

The PERFORM statement is used to temporarily transfer control to one or more procedures and then to return control to the statement following the PERFORM statement when the execution of the specified procedure(s) is complete.

Format 1

PERFORM procedure-name-1 [THRU procedure-name-2]

Format 2

PERFORM procedure-name-1 [THRU procedure-name-2] $\left\{\begin{array}{l}\text{identifier-1}\\\text{integer}\end{array}\right\}$ TIMES

Format 3

PERFORM procedure-name-1 [THRU procedure-name-2] UNTIL condition-1

Format 4

PERFORM procedure-name-1   [(THRU) procedure-name-2]

VARYING $\left\{\begin{array}{l}\text{identifier-1}\\\text{index-name-1}\end{array}\right\}$ FROM $\left\{\begin{array}{l}\text{identifier-3}\\\text{index-name-2}\\\text{literal-1}\end{array}\right\}$

BY $\left\{\begin{array}{l}\text{identifier-4}\\\text{literal-2}\end{array}\right\}$ UNTIL condition-1

$\left[\text{AFTER}\right.$ $\left\{\begin{array}{l}\text{identifier-5}\\\text{index-name-3}\end{array}\right\}$ FROM $\left\{\begin{array}{l}\text{identifier-6}\\\text{index-name-4}\\\text{literal-3}\end{array}\right\}$

BY $\left\{\begin{array}{l}\text{identifier-7}\\\text{literal-4}\end{array}\right\}$ UNTIL condition-2

$\left[\text{AFTER}\right.$ $\left\{\begin{array}{l}\text{identifier-8}\\\text{index-name-5}\end{array}\right\}$ FROM $\left\{\begin{array}{l}\text{identifier-9}\\\text{index-name-6}\\\text{literal-5}\end{array}\right\}$

BY $\left\{\begin{array}{l}\text{identifier-10}\\\text{literal-6}\end{array}\right\}$ UNTIL condition-3$\left.\vphantom{\begin{array}{l}a\\b\end{array}}\right]\left.\vphantom{\begin{array}{l}a\\b\end{array}}\right]$

Format 1 is the basic PERFORM statement that causes execution of the procedure(s) specified and transfers control to the next executable statement following that PERFORM statement. The procedures being executed may contain other valid PERFORM statements.

Format 2 causes the specified procedure(s) to be executed the number of TIMES indicated by identifier-1 or integer-1. If more than one procedure-name is specified, each set of procedures is executed in sequence until the number of TIMES specified is exhausted. For example, the instruction

```
PERFORM FIND-NAME 16 TIMES,
```

would cause the execution of

```
FIND NAME    )
FIND-NAME    |
FIND-NAME    |
   •          }   16  sets
   •          |
   •          |
FIND-NAME    )
```

Format 3 is the conditional form of the PERFORM statement. In structured program logic this statement is equivalent to the DO...UNTIL... structure. The procedure(s) are executed until a specified condition is met, then control is returned as in Format 1.

See Appendix A for the particulars on Format 4.

SECTION 12
Everything Else

The CALL Statement

The purpose of the CALL statement is to transfer control from one object program to another.

The format of this instruction is:

$$\underline{CALL} \quad \begin{Bmatrix} \text{identifier-1} \\ \text{literal-1} \end{Bmatrix} \quad [\underline{USING} \text{ data-name-1}[,\text{data-name-2}]...]$$

An example is:

CALL "PROGRAM2" where PROGRAM2 is another accessible object program. This instruction is covered in more detail in Chapter 7.

The INSPECT Statement

The INSPECT statement, discussed in detail in Chapter 7, provides the ability to tally, replace, or both tally and replace either a character or a group of characters within a data-item.

The MOVE Statement

The MOVE statement transfers data from one data area to another. The data that are being MOVEd are transferred in accordance with the edit rules.

The general form is:

Format 1

$$\text{\underline{MOVE}} \quad \begin{Bmatrix} \text{identifier-1} \\ \text{literal} \end{Bmatrix} \quad \text{\underline{TO}} \quad \text{identifier-2[,identifier-3]}...$$

Format 2

$$\text{\underline{MOVE}} \quad \begin{Bmatrix} \text{CORRESPONDING} \\ \text{CORR} \end{Bmatrix} \quad \text{identifier-1} \quad \text{\underline{TO}} \quad \text{identifier-2}$$

The SET *Statement*

The SET statement establishes reference points for table searching, and other table-handling operations. There are two forms of the command:

$$\text{\underline{SET}} \quad \begin{Bmatrix} \text{identifier-1} \\ \text{index-name-1} \end{Bmatrix} \begin{bmatrix} \text{identifier-2}... \\ \text{index-name-2} \end{bmatrix} \quad \text{\underline{TO}} \quad \begin{Bmatrix} \text{identifier-3} \\ \text{index-name-3} \\ \text{integer-1} \end{Bmatrix}$$

$$\text{\underline{SET}} \quad \text{index-name-4 [index-name-5]}... \begin{Bmatrix} \text{\underline{UP BY}} \\ \text{\underline{DOWN} BY} \end{Bmatrix} \begin{Bmatrix} \text{identifier-4} \\ \text{integer-2} \end{Bmatrix}$$

See Chapter 7 for the SEARCH command, to be used in conjunction with the SET command.

SECTION 13
Shorthand Notation for COBOL Statements

A complete list of the general formats for the COBOL language is in Appendix A. The formats of all the statements discussed in this chapter are included.

SECTION 14
Exercises and Problems

1. What are the four divisions of a COBOL program?
2. List the purpose of each of the COBOL divisions.
3. Which section of the ENVIRONMENT DIVISION is the FILE-CONTROL paragraph in?
4. What is the purpose of the FILE-CONTROL paragraph?
5. What is the purpose of the FILE SECTION of the DATA DIVISION? WORKING-STORAGE SECTION?
6. How many record description entries can you have in a single FD entry?
7. List the arithmetic statements available in the COBOL language.
8. What is the purpose of the OPEN statement?
9. In what ways may a file be OPENed in a COBOL program?
10. What is the purpose of the DISPLAY statement?
11. What is the purpose of the ACCEPT statement?

12. How must a file be OPENed in order to use the REWRITE statement?
13. What is the purpose of the REWRITE statement?
14. What is the purpose of the START statement?
15. What is the purpose of the DELETE statement?
16. Do you DELETE file-name or record-name?
17. How many STOP statements can you have in a COBOL program?
18. What is the purpose of the IF statement?
19. What is the purpose of the CALL statement?
20. What is the purpose of the SET statement?

2

A Review of Structured Programming and Documentation Standards

There are many ways in which a particular problem may be addressed when coding a program in COBOL, or any other programming language. There are some standard objectives that should be considered in any situation. By keeping these objectives in mind, the overall efficiency of operations may be optimized.

SECTION 1
The Basic Objectives of Program Coding

There are three basic objectives that should be achieved if you are to have a well-written program.

1. The code should do the things which the program/system specifications require. It should include all the features outlined in the program specifications and should be free of logic and programming errors. In short, the program should "get the job done."

2. The program should be written in such a way that any informed reader of the code be able to easily understand the logical structure of the program. One of the major tasks of data processing organizations is program maintenance—the procedures through which unforeseen errors are corrected and postimplementation program changes are made. It is unrealistic to expect that any one individual who codes a program will be available, perhaps years later, to perform maintenance. Furthermore, independent auditors, internal auditors, and investigators from regulatory agencies may be called upon to review program code. The program should include an internal "audit trail," which allows these, and other knowledgeable individuals, to follow the program logic.

3. The cost of developing the program should be optimized. Obviously, the programmer should attempt to minimize the cost of coding and testing the program, but this must be done in a way which is consistent with other objectives. In many cases, it is best (i.e., easiest and cheapest) to recode a program that is poorly structured and poorly documented, difficult or impossible to maintain, or unsuited to audit.

More and more data processing organizations are implementing standards which require well-structured, well-documented programs. Even though the initial cost of early planning and imposition of standards may be relatively high, the long-run cost savings usually offset these earlier costs.

SECTION 2
Basic Program Structures

There are basically three different structures that should appear in any well-written program. These three basic structures may be combined to form rather complex program segments. The more commonly used terms and a brief discussion of each are outlined in the following paragraphs and are illustrated by flow diagrams in Figure 2-1 even though there is no standard nomenclature for these structures at the present time.

Figure 2–1
Program structures.

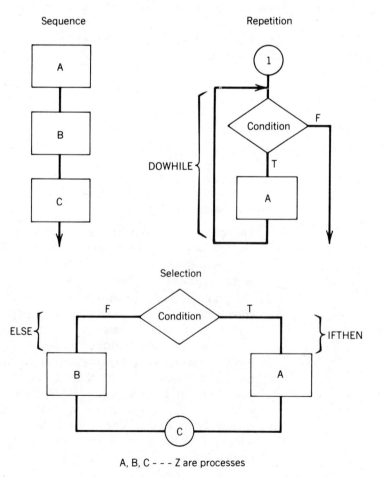

A, B, C - - - Z are processes

Sequence structures, also known as "simple sequence structures," provide for the execution of instructions in the order (or sequence) in which they are listed in the program. This sequential order of execution is changed only when one of the other structures is encountered. Since you are already a COBOL programmer, you have seen that this structure is the default structure in COBOL.

Selection structures have other, more colorful, names, of which IFTHENELSE is probably the most common. This structure provides that a "set of code" will be executed if, and only if, certain conditions are met (IF, THEN) and, in the event those conditions are not met, a different specific "set of code" will be executed (ELSE). Some authorities separate one special form of selection structure (the CASE structure) as a separate type of program structure and some programmers oppose the use of CASE structures altogether. There are some circumstances, however, in which the authors believe that CASE meets the basic objectives of a well-written program better than any other structure.

A well-structured program will incorporate combinations of these structures. Figure 2-2 is a flow diagram for a program which combines (or compounds, or nests) these structures.

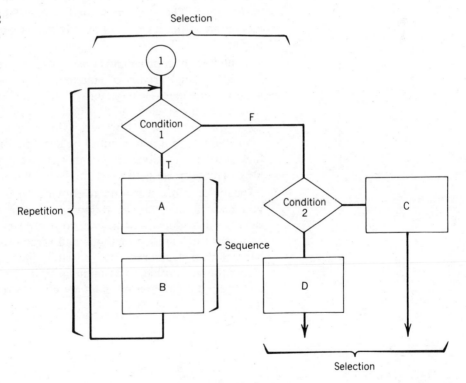

Figure 2–2
Nested program structures.

SECTION 3
Structured Program Style

A major purpose of a well-written program is to provide for readability of the code. There are no absolute rules for coding a structured program; rather there are certain basic guidelines that should be applied rationally in order to achieve the best possible balance of the objectives listed in Section 1. Some of these guidelines are:

1. Minimize (and wherever possible, eliminate) unconditional branches in the code. Unconditional transfers are implemented in COBOL by the various GO TO statements. Some data processing installations attempt to address the serious problems represented by the uncontrolled use of GO TO statements by eliminating them. So-called GOTOless coding conventions should not be confused with structured programming style, however, since the latter term is much more comprehensive. Be extremely wary of the use of GO TO statements in COBOL. The authors believe that there are a very limited number of circumstances where the conservative use of unconditional branches is warranted. However, these circumstances are extremely rare and we have relegated discussion of GO TO statements, and others that are destructive of structured style, to Appendix B, which we have captioned "A Rogues' Gallery of COBOL Features."

2. Practice "top-down" program design. The structure of the program should allow any reader of the program code to progress naturally from the top of the listing to the bottom of the listing, without the need to refer back to earlier code. The effort expended in the planning of the code and the segmentation of the logic pays big dividends when the actual coding process begins.

3. The modules of code should consist of short, self-contained, easily read, and logically related groups of statements. A common rule of thumb for the length of modules is a maximum of 50 lines of code. The rule allows the code to appear on a single page of program listing, so you don't have flip a lot of pages when you read. However, if the code which you write is a little longer than 50 lines, or if works out to be considerably shorter, then logic dictates that you leave it alone. Remember, these guidelines are just that—guidelines. The purpose is to meet the basic objectives discussed earlier.

4. Expend the effort necessary to provide for a well-documented program. If you code a GOTOless, top-down program with well-designed, properly structured modules, but neglect to use descriptive data-names and utilize haphazard indentation methods and forego the use of notes, then you will have a well-structured, but possibly incomprehensible, program which meets the basic objectives minimally, if at all. Some methods for proper documentation of your program are discussed in the latter part of this chapter.

SECTION 4
Implementation of Sequence Structures in COBOL

The basic structures are easily implemented in COBOL. Indeed, the basic organization of COBOL is sequential, and in the absence of any intervening selection or repetition structures, the program will follow the sequence in which statements are written the the PROCEDURE DIVISION.

Implementation of Selection and CASE Structures in COBOL

The selection structure is ordinarily implemented through the use of the IF statement with the THEN and ELSE options. These structures may be nested. Figure 2-3 is a flow diagram illustrating grade assignments for a class in programming.

The code would be:

```
IF AVERAGE-GRADE > 89
    THEN MOVE "A" TO COURSE-GRADE
ELSE IF AVERAGE-GRADE > 79
    MOVE "B" TO COURSE-GRADE
ELSE IF AVERAGE-GRADE > 69
    MOVE "C" TO COURSE-GRADE
ELSE IF AVERAGE-GRADE > 59
    MOVE "D" TO COURSE-GRADE
ELSE MOVE "F" TO COURSE-GRADE.
PERFORM 206-WRITE-NEW-GRADE-RECORD.
```

The code structure in the preceding example was beginning to get a little repetitious, even with only five conditions (or cases) to handle. Selection structures which test a relatively large number of conditions may be considered to represent a special class of selection structure—the CASE structure. (The CASE structure is present when three or more nested conditions exist.) If, for example, grades are assigned on the basis of A+, A, A−, B+, etc., where 100 through 97 represents A+, 96 through 93 represents an A, 92 through 90 represents an A−, and so on, then the coding would become relatively more complex using the IFTHENELSE code. The extended grade example for a case structure is diagrammed in Figure 2-4.

The COBOL statement which implements the CASE structure is the GO TO statement with the DEPENDING ON clause. Many authorities are so sensitive to very real problems associated with the use of GO TO (in any form) that they recommend that GO TO *never* be used. We believe that the judicious use of GO TO allows for programming efficiency without being destructive to structured programming. The use of GO TO with DEPENDING ON to implement the CASE structure is one of those rare circumstances in which, we believe, the benefits of an unconditional branch outweigh the disadvantages. The GO TO DEPENDING ON statement is discussed more fully in Chapter 7. A full discussion of other forms of GO TO has been included in Appendix B, "A Rogues' Gallery of COBOL Features." As is emphasized in that appendix, no unconditional branch should appear in any COBOL program unless all of the following conditions can be met:

- No more efficient way of coding the instruction exists.
- The branch is "forward looking." You may not branch to a part of the code which is earlier in the sequence than the point of the branch. Also, the branch cannot cross a level in the module being controlled by its control module.
- There may be *no* nested branches. The code to which a branch refers may not even contain a PERFORM statement.

The CASE structure meets all these requirements. Obviously, if your instructor or management of the data center where you work oppose the use of the GO TO in

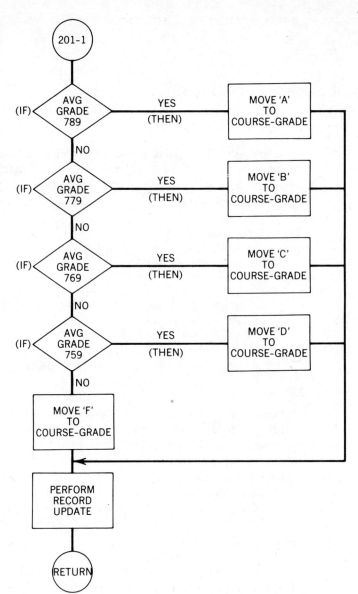

Figure 2-3
IFTHENELSE for course grades.

Figure 2-4
Case structure for course grades.

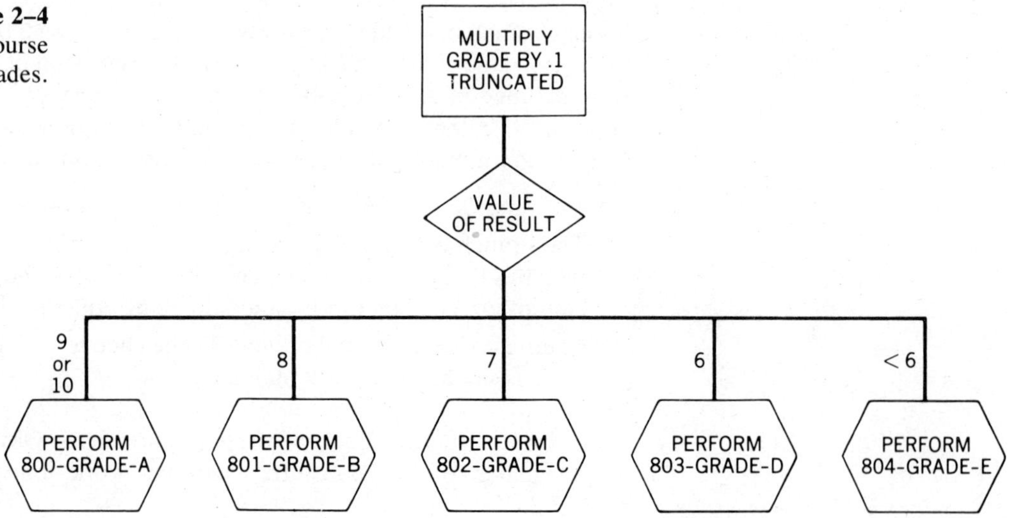

any form (a common and creditable practice) then your duty is clear: Implement CASE structures though the use of IFTHENELSE.

SECTION 6
Implementation of Repetition Structures in COBOL

Repetition structures are implemented using the PERFORM statement with the UNTIL option. Suppose you are looking at an airline's set of records that contain information about flights to different destinations. The records are sequenced by hour within date, beginning one week from today. You want to catch the next available plane to, say, Tahiti.

The DOWHILE (Figure 2-1) is implemented indirectly in the COBOL language through the use of a PERFORM with the (you guessed it) UNTIL option. A set of code is performed so long as the test condition is false.

```
PERFORM 205-SEARCH-FLIGHTS
    UNTIL DESTINATION IS EQUAL TO "TAHITI".
DISPLAY "FOUND IT "
    DEPARTURE-TIME
    FLIGHT-NUMBER
    FARE.
        o
        o
        o
205-SEARCH-FLIGHTS.
    READ FLIGHTS-FILE, AT END DISPLAY "SEARCH FAILURE",
                            MOVE 1 TO EOF-FLIGHTS.
    IF DESTINATION IS EQUAL TO "TAHITI" NEXT-SENTENCE
        ELSE
    DISPLAY "THAT'S NOT IT " DESTINATION.
```

The DOWHILE may not be implemented directly in COBOL since the PERFORM using the UNTIL option tests the condition *before* the specified procedure is PERFORMed. You can simulate the DOWHILE, however, by changing the state of the test condition within the PERFORMed procedure. For example, our Tahiti trip program could be written:

```
PERFORM 205-SEARCH-FLIGHTS
    UNTIL FOUNDIT-FLAG IS NOT EQUAL TO ZERO.
DISPLAY 'FOUND IT'
    DEPARTURE-TIME
    FLIGHT-NUMBER
    FARE.
        o
        o
        o
205-SEARCH-FLIGHTS.
    READ FLIGHTS-FILE, AT END MOVE 1 TO EOF-FLIGHTS.
    IF DESTINATION IS EQUAL TO 'TAHITI'
        MOVE 1 TO FOUNDIT-FLAG
            ELSE
    DISPLAY "THAT'S NOT IT "
        DESTINATION.
```

SECTION 7

Programming Standards—Identification and Use of Blank Lines

Even in a well-structured program, the readability of the code is affected by the number of white spaces in the code, by the way in which the statements and phrases of statements are indented, by the descriptiveness of data-names, paragraph-names, and section-names assigned by the programmer, and by the effective use of explanatory notes inserted into the code.

Some suggestions for improving the readability of your programs are outlined below.

1. You have no control over the placement of paragraph- and section-names. Since they must begin in Margin A, let this be the starting point for your indentation standards. Any entry beginning in Margin A is (by definition) a paragraph- or section-name, and no other code should be included on the same line.

2. Begin all sentences in column 12.

3. Include no more than one statement on each line and indent connecting options. For example:

```
IF TYPE-CODE = "SALE"
        THEN PERFORM 205-SALES-FUNCTION
ELSE
        PERFORM 210-ERROR-ON-SALE.
```

4. Follow a consistent pattern of indentation—commonly four spaces.

5. When a statement includes multiple functions, group similar functions by use of indentation and use a separate line for each function. For example:

```
OPEN INPUT    TRANSACTIONS
              ADDRESSES
     I/O      MASTER-FILE
              OPEN-ITEMS.
```

6. Skip lines in the code when doing so improves readability.

7. When coding options associated with verbs are used, code the option on a separate line and indent so that it is clear that the option is being used. For example:

```
PERFORM 512-INTEREST-CALCULATION
      VARYING INTEREST-RATE
          FROM STARTING-INTEREST-RATE
          BY INTEREST-INCREMENT
              UNTIL INTEREST-RATE IS GREATER THAN
              PRIME-RATE.
```

8. Use notes liberally so that any reader who scans your program may easily determine what you have done with the code.

9. One of the more common difficulties in discovering errors in programs is associated with a misplaced or misidentified period. There are two ways to minimize this difficulty, one of which is followed in this text and one of which is not.

   • Eliminate the use of commas in the code since they may be confused with periods and are used only as editing symbols—they have no effect on the actual operation of the program. Furthermore, the function of commas can be replaced by blank spaces, indentions, use of new lines, and other standards listed previously.

- Place all periods on a line by themselves and in a predetermined column of the code, say, column 12. Although this standard is not used in this text, it has many adherents and does, indeed, make location of end-of-sentence conditions much easier. An example of the application of this standard is:

```
READ INPUT-FILE
      AT END PERFORM 666-ENDFILE-HOUSEKEEPING
             STOP RUN
   .
IF IN-DEPARTMENT = 77
      MOVE IN-SALES TO
             SALE-AMOUNT OF EXCEPTION-REPORT
      PERFORM 111-EXCEPTION-REPORTING
   .
PERFORM 105-SALES-REPORT-SETUP
   .
PERFORM 107-SALES-REPORTING
   .
```

SECTION 8
Shorthand Notation for COBOL Implementation of Basic Program Structures

$$\text{IF condition THEN} \begin{Bmatrix} \text{NEXT SENTENCE} \\ \text{statement-1} \end{Bmatrix} \text{ELSE \{statement-2\}}$$

$$\text{PERFORM procedure-name-1} \left[\begin{Bmatrix} \text{THROUGH} \\ \text{THRU} \end{Bmatrix} \text{procedure-name-2} \right] \text{UNTIL condition}$$

SECTION 9
Characteristics of Well-Designed Modules

In practice, the basic design of a program may be produced as a part of structured system design methods. In many instances, including assignments in a class environment, you may be called upon to determine the basic components of the program design. The process is one of decomposition of the program problem into a series of relatively simple subtasks. This process may be done in such a way as to enhance the efficiency of the programming process.

Some of the topics associated with this process of module design are: the concept of top-down design, task decomposition, charting of the decomposition, intramodule cohesion, intermodule coupling, and span of control.

Top-Down Design

Several years ago some programmers designed a tongue-in-cheek programming language and sent writeups of this joke to all their friends. The name of the "language" varied depending on the local revision, but one of the names was SUPERCODE. The language was purported to be ultimately powerful (remember, this whole thing was a joke), and a program written in this code might look like this:

DO TODAY'S STUF.   (notice that even misspellings are accepted)

The authors of SUPERCODE did two things for us:

- They indicated the starting point for a top-down system (or program design) and
- They completely bypassed the difficult task of problem decomposition. Indeed, the popularity of the joke is possibly an indication of the importance, and difficulty, of breaking a problem down into its component parts.

Top-down design is not synonymous with structured design, although the terms are often used interchangeably. Top-down design is simply the process of decomposing a problem, beginning with its most important level. In a business environment, the highest level might be, as implied by the SUPERCODE example above, to take care of all the daily tasks necessary to run the business today and levels subordinate to that might be defined as long-range planning, manufacturing, marketing, financial activities, and so on. Theoretically, top-down design will begin at a very strategic level, but as a practical matter, most designs begin at a relatively lower level than is implied here. For example, the planning of this book began with the strategic level "design an advanced COBOL book." The chapter topics represent a further level of decomposition from that strategic beginning and the section and subsection materials represent a further refinement in two levels.

Another important mechanical procedure associated with module design is the charting of the decomposition process. There are several techniques for charting the structures of modules. The method used here is the hierarchy chart or visual table of contents (VTOC).

Figure 2-5 is a partial hierachy chart of the textbook project. The chart will be used later to illustrate the span of control concept. Figure 2-6 charts the components of this chapter and Figure 2-7 outlines the elements of this section of the chapter.

Cohesion

A well-designed module will exhibit the quality of intramodular cohesion, which means that the procedures included in any particular module are related to each other in some way. The more closely bound the elements are to one another, the stronger the cohesion. There are several different kinds of cohesion, some of which are superior to others in a programming context. These types are listed and then discussed, in increasing order of strength, next:

- coincidental
- logical
- temporal
- procedural
- communicational
- sequential
- functional

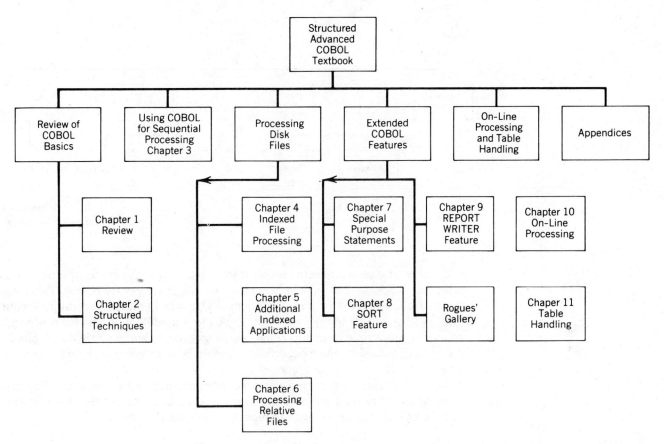

Figure 2–5
VTOC for textbook project.

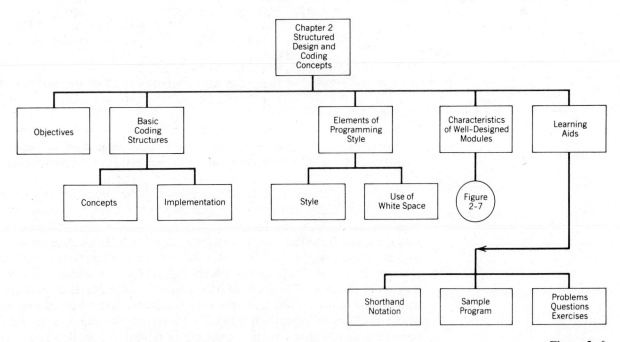

Figure 2–6
VTOC for Chapter 2.

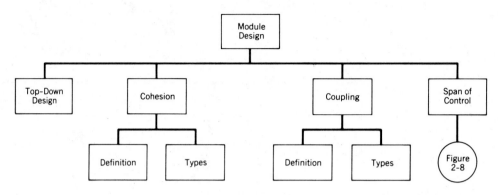

Figure 2–7
VTOC for module design.

Coincidental cohesion is the weakest form and may really be considered not to represent cohesion at all, since the internal elements are poorly bound. This form results from a random or illogical process. The way in which you prepare your "things I have to do today" list is analogous to a module with this form of weak cohesion. From time to time you may see a module coded in COBOL which has this form of cohesion. Such occurrences should be rare and you should avoid this form in the design of your programs.

Logical cohesion is achieved when the elements included in a module all belong to some class but do not contribute to a single task. For example, the following code is logically cohesive even though it is poor module design:

```
999-PRINT-ROUTINES:
    IF LAST-DIVISION = 'WOOD PRODUCTS'
        MOVE 'WOOD PRODUCTS' TO DIVISIONX OF OUTRECORD
        WRITE OUTFILE AFTER ADVANCING 1 LINES
            ELSE
    IF LAST-DIVISION = 'FOUNDRY'
        MOVE 'FOUNDRY     ' TO DIVISIONX OF OUTRECORD
        WRITE OUTFILE AFTER ADVANCING 1 LINES
            ELSE
    IF LAST-DIVISION = 'RETAIL SALES'
        MOVE 'RETAIL SALES ' TO DIVISIONX OF OUTRECORD
        WRITE OUTFILE AFTER ADVANCING 1 LINE,
```

The elements in the module are related, but only in the sense that each is a statement to print a line of output. Such organization does not contribute to maintainability, clarity, or module independence as do the stronger forms of cohesion.

Temporal cohesion is based on a grouping of functions which are related in terms of time. Although this is a moderately weak form, it is often included in programs in the form of otherwise unrelated "housekeeping" chores. A module with the name `001-INITIALIZE-NUMERIC-FIELDS` is an example of a module with temporal cohesion and illustrates the weakness of this form of cohesion. If it is necessary to initialize numeric fields before performing arithmetic operations, it may seem reasonable to do it all before you do anything else (perhaps so you won't forget to do it). Indeed, this is a classic approach in programming. But think of the problems this approach may cause someone else who is assigned to maintain the program later. Another example of temporal cohesion is a "wrap-up" module at the end of a program. The requirement that all files be closed prior to the end of a COBOL program results in `CLOSE` statements coupled with the `END RUN` statement in temporal cohesion.

You will see a lot of programs which have modules exhibiting *procedural cohesion*—if you are assigned maintenance of some older programs. Prior to the introduction of structured techniques in the early 1970s most programs were organized on the basis of sequential processes. Programs were coded on the basis of sequential flowcharts, and as a consequence modules were defined in terms of program procedure rather than the functions of a particular problem. Procedural cohesion includes all the processes necessary to accomplish a task, so functional divisions are difficult to identify.

The tertiary form of cohesion in the hierarchy of strength is *communicational cohesion*. This level occurs when all elements included in a module operate on the same input or output data-item. The emphasis here is on data, rather than process flows. An example of a communicationally cohesive module is:

```
612-FORMAT-PRINT-LINE.
     MOVE IN-CUST-NUMBER TO OUT-CUST-NUMBER.
     MOVE IN-CUST-NAME TO OUT-CUST-NAME.
     MOVE IN-INVOICE TO OUT-INVOICE.
     ADD IN-AMOUNT TO IN-BALANCE-FORWARD GIVING
          OUT-BALANCE-DUE.
```

This is a relatively strong form of cohesion and it is commonly encountered in COBOL programs. Hopefully, each of the paragraphs in this section exhibit communicational cohesion—each addressing as input a type of cohesion and all elements in the paragraph relating to that input.

Sequential cohesion is generally considered to be the second-strongest form. Central to the definition of this type is the idea that the "output" from one element in a module represents the "input" to the next. Thus, the module has an assembly line quality.

```
CALCULATION-OF-NET-PAY.
     SUBTRACT UNION-DUES FROM GROSS-PAY
          GIVING TEMP-BALANCE.
     SUBTRACT WITHHOLDING-TAX FROM TEMP-BALANCE.
     SUBTRACT FICA-TAX FROM TEMP-BALANCE.
     SUBTRACT HEALTH-INSURANCE-CONTRIBUTION FROM
          TEMP-BALANCE GIVING NET-PAY.
```

The strongest form of cohesion is the one which most fully achieves complete functional decomposition of a problem. That form is called *functional cohesion* and it is achieved when a module addresses a specific task. A module which exhibits functional cohesion by definition exhibits no cohesive weakness: it has none of the characteristics of the other six forms of cohesion. A functionally cohesive COBOL paragraph is one that might have been written by an unusually single-minded user of the output of the module.

```
CALCULATE-GROSS-PAY-THRU-CURRENT-PD.
     ADD GROSS-PAY-YTD TO CURRENT-GROSS-PAY
          GIVING GROSS-THRU-CURRENT-PD.
CALCULATE-FICA-TAX.
     IF GROSS-PAY-YTD > FICA-MAXIMUM
          MOVE ZERO TO FICA-TAX
               ELSE
```

```
       IF GROSS-THRU-CURRENT-PD > FICA-MAXIMUM
            SUBTRACT GROSS-PAY-YTD FROM GROSS-THRU-CURRENT-PD
                GIVING BASIS-FOR-FICA
            MULTIPLY BASIS-FOR-FICA BY FICA-RATE
                GIVING FICA-TAX
                  ELSE
            MULTIPLY CURRENT-GROSS-PAY BY FICA-RATE
                GIVING FICA-TAX.
                      0
                      0
                      0
   CALCULATION-OF TOTAL-DEDUCTIONS.
        ADD UNION-DUES
             WITHHOLDING-TAX
             FICA-TAX
             HEALTH-INSURANCE-CONTRIBUTIONS
                 GIVING
             TOTAL-DEDUCTIONS.
   CALCULATION-OF-NET-PAY.
        SUBTRACT TOTAL-DEDUCTIONS FROM CURRENT-GROSS-PAY
             GIVING NET-PAY.
```

Coupling

Whereas cohesion has to do with an *intra*modular characteristic, *coupling* is a concept related to a *inter*modular characteristic. Coupling is a measure of the degree of dependency between modules. A high degree of dependence between modules, or high coupling, is undesirable. You should attempt to achieve low coupling in the design of your programs. Coupling can occur in several ways. The source of the dependency between modules indicates the type of coupling. The types of coupling are:

- content
- common
- external
- control
- stamp
- data

There is no hierarchy of these types and they may occur in combination.

Content coupling occurs when one module *directly* references or modifies the instructions in the other. There are not many ways to achieve this type of coupling in COBOL without using some of the features included in the Rogues' Gallery, Appendix B. The most notorious of these features, and the one which most clearly illustrates the concept of content coupling, is the ALTER statement.

Common coupling occurs when data areas are shared by modules within the program. In COBOL this type of coupling is the rule rather than the exception since all data areas in the DATA DIVISION are global, or common, data areas. The effect of common coupling can be reduced through the incorporation of subprograms and the use of the CALL statement. In our opinion this type of coupling is not a significant problem in most business applications.

External coupling is really a version of common coupling. The difference between the two is that common coupling occurs when the modules share data records and external coupling occurs when they share at the field level. Again, we believe that this is not a significant concern in most COBOL programs.

Control coupling occurs when one module passes data to another *and* the passed data is intended to influence the internal logic of the receiving module. These passed data are typically referred to as switches or flags. Whenever possible, such coupling should be avoided. However, in many cases the sparing use of flags and switches contribute to improved structuring of programs. Control of end-of-file conditions is an example of a circumstance in which coupling is a trade-off for improved structuring.

The last two types of coupling are related in that they refer to nonglobal data. In COBOL such restricted data are available only when subprograms and the CALL statement are used. *Stamp coupling* occurs when two subprograms access the same data at the record level and *data coupling* occurs when two subprograms access the same data at the data element or field level.

When designing programs, you should make them as loosely coupled as possible. The modules in a program are, by definition, dependent—they are a part of the same problem solution. However, you should try to minimize dependence that will result in the situation where a change in one module will require a change to be made in another.

Span of Control

The notion of limiting span of control in a program is based on the fact that, being human, we cannot handle a very large number of things at the same time. The average person is most efficient when dealing with two to seven problems (concepts, ideas, situations, *modules*) at a time. In the decomposition of a programming problem, no level should have more than about seven members (the *maximum* in unusual circumstances should be nine) and no level except the highest should have fewer than two members. To illustrate, remember the hierachy chart for the first and second levels of the design of an advanced COBOL book. The first version looked like the one in Figure 2-8. The number of modules, 11, constitutes a too wide span of control. The solution is to slow the decomposition process and add another level of the chart (actually to add another level to the manner of seeing the problem which is reflected in the chart) as in Figure 2-5.

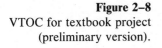

Figure 2–8
VTOC for textbook project
(preliminary version).

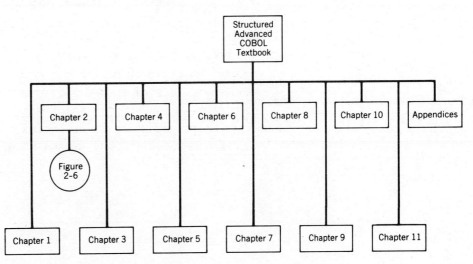

SECTION 10
Sample Program Illustrating Structured Concepts

The next program, Figure 2-9, may be contrasted with the one in Section 11, which performs the same tasks but is poorly structured.

Figure 2–9
Structured program.

```
IDENTIFICATION DIVISION.
PROGRAM-ID.
    'CLUNKER'.
AUTHOR,
    MARTY KOTLAR.
ENVIRONMENT DIVISION.
CONFIGURATION SECTION.
SOURCE-COMPUTER. IBM3033.
OBJECT-COMPUTER. IBM3033.
SPECIAL-NAMES.
    C01 IS PAGE-TOP.
INPUT-OUTPUT SECTION.
FILE-CONTROL.
    SELECT PARTS-FILE
        ASSIGN TO INFILE.
    SELECT PRINTFILE
        ASSIGN TO PRINTER.
DATA DIVISION.
FILE SECTION.
FD  PARTS-FILE
    LABEL RECORDS ARE STANDARD.
01  INPUT-PARTS-RECORD.
    05 PART-NUMBER          PICTURE IS 9(5).
    05 SALES                PICTURE IS S9(4)V99.
    05 FILLER               PICTURE IS X(69).
FD  PRINTFILE
    LABEL RECORDS ARE OMITTED.
01  PRINT-RECORD.
    05 FILLER               PICTURE IS X(30).
    05 PRINT-PART           PICTURE IS 9(5).
    05 FILLER               PICTURE IS X(5).
    05 EDITED-TOTAL         PICTURE IS ZZZ,ZZZ.99.
    05 FILLER               PICTURE IS X(83).
WORKING-STORAGE SECTION.
01  PART-NUMBER-HOLD        PICTURE IS 9(5)        VALUE IS ZERO.
01  TOTAL-SALES             PICTURE IS S9(6)V99    VALUE IS ZERO.
01  EOF-SWITCH              PICTURE IS 9           VALUE IS ZERO.
PROCEDURE DIVISION.
000-MAINLINE.
    PERFORM 100-INITIALIZE.
    PERFORM 200-ACCUMULATE-TOTALS.
    PERFORM 300-TEST-FOR-CONTROL-BREAKS UNTIL EOF-SWITCH > 1.
    PERFORM 320-PRINT-DETAIL.
    CLOSE PARTS-FILE PRINTFILE.
    STOP RUN.
100-INITIALIZE.
    OPEN INPUT PARTS-FILE OUTPUT PRINTFILE.
    PERFORM 310-READ-PART-FILE.
    MOVE PART-NUMBER TO PART-NUMBER-HOLD.
200-ACCUMULATE-TOTALS.
    ADD SALES TO TOTAL-SALES.
300-TEST-FOR-CONTROL-BREAKS.
    PERFORM 310-READ-PART-FILE.
    IF PART-NUMBER IS NOT EQUAL TO PART-NUMBER-HOLD
        PERFORM 320-PRINT-DETAIL
        ELSE
        ADD SALES TO TOTAL-SALES.
310-READ-PART-FILE.
    READ PARTS-FILE AT END MOVE 2 TO EOF-SWITCH.
320-PRINT-DETAIL.
    MOVE PART-NUMBER-HOLD TO PRINT-PART.
    MOVE TOTAL-SALES TO EDITED-TOTAL.
    WRITE PRINT-RECORD AFTER ADVANCING 1 LINE.
    MOVE SALES TO TOTAL-SALES.
    MOVE PART-NUMBER TO PART-NUMBER-HOLD.
```

SECTOPM 11
Sample Program Illustrating Unstructured Code

The program in Figure 2-10 is presented so that you may get an idea of the problems associated with writing or, even worse, trying to maintain an unstructured program. It performs the same tasks as the structured program in Section 10 and it actually works, but you will unquestionably have difficulty in following the logic. We call this program the "spaghetti" version: we think that after you try to follow the logic you'll agree that the name is appropriate.

Figure 2–10
Unstructured program.

```
IDENTIFICATION DIVISION.
PROGRAM-ID.
    'CLUNKER'.
AUTHOR.
    MARTY KOTLAR.
REMARKS.
    THIS PROGRAM PERFORMS THE SAME FUNCTIONS AS THE LAST PROGRAM
    BUT DOES SO IN A MOST INEFFICIENT WAY.  IT IS A COMPLETELY
    UNSTRUCTURED PROGRAM - IN THE VERNACULAR IT IS A SPAGHETTI
    PROGRAM.  THIS PROGRAM IS PRESENTED AS AN EXAMPLE OF METHODS
    WHICH YOU SHOULD NOT USE.
    TRY READING THROUGH THE TEXT OF THE STRUCTURED VERSION THEN
    READ THROUGH THIS VERSION AND WE THINK YOU'LL AGREE THAT THE
    STRUCTURED IS BETTER.
ENVIRONMENT DIVISION.
CONFIGURATION SECTION.
SOURCE-COMPUTER. IBM3033.
OBJECT-COMPUTER. IBM3033.
SPECIAL-NAMES.
    C01 IS PAGE-TOP.
INPUT-OUTPUT SECTION.
FILE-CONTROL.
    SELECT PARTS-FILE
        ASSIGN TO INFILE.
    SELECT PRINTFILE
        ASSIGN TO PRINTER.
DATA DIVISION.
FILE SECTION.
FD  PARTS-FILE
    LABEL RECORDS ARE STANDARD.
01  INPUT-PARTS-RECORD.
    05 PART-NUMBER            PICTURE IS 9(5).
    05 SALES                  PICTURE IS S9(4)V99.
    05 FILLER                 PICTURE IS X(69).
FD  PRINTFILE
    LABEL RECORDS ARE OMITTED.
01  PRINT-RECORD.
    05 FILLER                 PICTURE IS X(30).
    05 PRINT-PART             PICTURE IS 9(5).
    05 FILLER                 PICTURE IS X(5).
    05 EDITED-TOTAL           PICTURE IS ZZZ,ZZZ.99.
    05 FILLER                 PICTURE IS X(83).
WORKING-STORAGE SECTION.
01  PART-NUMBER-HOLD          PICTURE IS 9(5)      VALUE IS ZERO.
01  TOTAL-SALES               PICTURE IS S9(6)V99  VALUE IS ZERO.
01  EOF-SWITCH                PICTURE IS 9         VALUE IS ZERO.
01  FIRST-RECORD              PICTURE IS 9         VALUE IS ZERO.
PROCEDURE DIVISION.
INITIALIZE.
    OPEN INPUT PARTS-FILE OUTPUT PRINTFILE.
    READ PARTS-FILE AT END MOVE 2 TO EOF-SWITCH.
    MOVE PART-NUMBER TO PART-NUMBER-HOLD.
ACCUMULATE-TOTALS.
    ADD SALES TO TOTAL-SALES.
TEST-FOR-CONTROL-BREAKS.
    READ PARTS-FILE AT END MOVE 2 TO EOF-SWITCH.
    IF EOF-SWITCH IS EQUAL TO 2 GO TO WRAPUP.
    IF PART-NUMBER IS NOT EQUAL TO PART-NUMBER-HOLD
        GO TO PRINT-DETAIL
            ELSE
            ADD SALES TO TOTAL-SALES.
    GO TO TEST-FOR-CONTROL-BREAKS.
PRINT-DETAIL.
    MOVE PART-NUMBER-HOLD TO PRINT-PART.
    MOVE TOTAL-SALES TO EDITED-TOTAL.
    WRITE PRINT-RECORD AFTER ADVANCING 1 LINE.
    MOVE SALES TO TOTAL-SALES.
    MOVE PART-NUMBER TO PART-NUMBER-HOLD.
    GO TO TEST-FOR-CONTROL-BREAKS.
WRAPUP.
    MOVE PART-NUMBER-HOLD TO PRINT-PART.
    MOVE TOTAL-SALES TO EDITED-TOTAL.
    WRITE PRINT-RECORD AFTER ADVANCING 1 LINE.
    CLOSE PARTS-FILE, PRINTFILE.
    STOP RUN.
```

SECTION 12
Questions and Problems

I. Questions

1. What are the advantages and disadvantages of structured coding?
2. What are the basic objectives of program coding?
3. What are the constructs used in structured coding?
4. How is the CASE construct implemented in COBOL?
5. How is the repetition construct implemented in COBOL?
6. What are the seven types of cohesion?
7. What are the rule-of-thumb limits of span of control?
8. Why is a limited span of control important to the process of problem decomposition?

II. Problems

1. You have been asked to review the following program, which has been in use for several years. It is designed to take inputs which look like this:

60	122	128	131	134	136
61	125	131	134	137	139
62	128	134	137	140	141
63	132	141	141	144	145
64	136	144	145	148	149

and to produce a report which looks like this:

HEIGHT	AGES: 20-24	25-29	30-39	40-49	50-59
60	122	128	131	134	136
61	125	131	134	137	139
62	128	134	137	140	141
63	132	141	141	144	145
64	136	144	145	148	149

Required:
a. Critique the program for compliance with good structured programming techniques. Cite specific paragraphs, line, or ranges of lines to support your criticisms.
b. Rewrite the program in a proper manner.

```
010010   IDENTIFICATION DIVISION.
010020   PROGRAM-ID.  WEIGHTS.
010030   AUTHOR.  ERNESTO TREVINO JR.
010040   INSTALLATION.  MANHATTAN HIGH.
010050   DATE-WRITTEN.  15 JULY 1980.
010060   DATE-COMPILED.  JUL 25,1980.
010070   SECURITY.  NONE
010080   REMARKS.  BASED ON A FOUR YEAR STUDY OF 50,000,000 PERSONS.
010090             THE FIGURES REPRESENT WEIGHTS IN ORDINARY INDOOR
010100             CLOTHING AND SHOES, AND HEIGHTS WITH SHOES.
020010   ENVIRONMENT DIVISION.
020020   CONFIGURATION SECTION.
```

```
020030     SOURCE-COMPUTER. IBM-360-50.
020040     OBJECT-COMPUTER. IBM-360-50.
020050     SPECIAL-NAMES.  CO1 IS TO-NEW-PAGE.
020060     INPUT-OUTPUT SECTION.
020070     FILE-CONTROL.
020080         SELECT INFO-CARDS ASSIGN TO UR-S-INPUT.
020090         SELECT REPORT-O ASSIGN TO UR-S-OUTPUT.
020100     DATA DIVISION.
030010     FILE SECTION.
030020     FD INFO-CARDS.
030030         LABEL RECORDS ARE OMITTED.
030040     01 CARDS-IN.
030050         02 HEIGHT          PICTURE 99.
030060         02 FILLER          PICTURE X(5).
030070         02 20X-24X         PICTURE 999.
030080         02 FILLER          PICTURE X(5).
030090         02 25X-29X         PICTURE 999.
030100         02 FILLER          PICTURE X(5).
040010         02 30X-39X         PICTURE 999.
040020         02 FILLER          PICTURE X(5).
040030         02 40X-49X             PICTURE 999.
040040         02 FILLER          PICTURE X(5).
040050         02 50X-59X         PICTURE 999.
040060         02 FILLER          PICTURE X(38).
040070     FD REPORT-O.
040080         LABEL RECORDS ARE OMITTED.
040090     01 LINE-OUT PICTURE IS X(133).
040100     WORKING-STORAGE SECTION.
050010     77   TOTAL-H-W          PICTURE 9(3) VALUE ZERO.
050020     77   TOTAL-HEIGHT       PICTURE 9(3) VALUE ZERO.
050030     77   TOTAL-W-1          PICTURE 9(3) VALUE ZERO.
050040     77   TOTAL-W-2          PICTURE 9(3) VALUE ZERO.
050050     77   TOTAL-W-3          PICTURE 9(3) VALUE ZERO.
050060     77   TOTAL-W-4          PICTURE 9(3) VALUE ZERO.
050070     77   TOTAL-W-5          PICTURE 9(3) VALUE ZERO.
050080     77   INPUT-FLAG         PICTURE XXX VALUE 'YES'.
050090     01 HEADING-1.
050100         02 FILLER           PICTURE X(46) VALUE SPACE.
060010         02 WORDSX           PICTURE X(41) VALUE 'AVERAGE WEIGHT AND
060020-        'HEIGHT OF AMERICAN MEN'
060030         02 FILLER           PICTURE X(47) VALUE SPACE.
060040     01 HEADING-2.
060050         02 FILLER           PICTURE X.
060060         02 HEIGHT-1         PICTURE X(6) VALUE IS 'HEIGHT'.
060070         02 FILLER           PICTURE X(5) VALUE SPACE.
060080         02 20-24-X          PICTURE X(11) VALUE IS 'AGES: 20-24'.
060090         02 FILLER           PICTURE X(13) VALUE SPACE.
060100         02 25-29-X          PICTURE X(5) VALUE IS '25-29'.
070010         02 FILLER           PICTURE X(13) VALUE SPACE.
070020         02 30-39-X          PICTURE X(5) VALUE IS '30-39'.
070030         02 FILLER           PICTURE X(13) VALUE SPACE.
070040         02 40-49-X          PICTURE X(5) VALUE IS '40-49'.
070050         02 FILLER           PICTURE X(13) VALUE SPACE.
070060         02 50-59-X          PICTURE X(5) VALUE IS '50-59'.
070070         02 FILLER           PICTURE X(38) VALUE SPACE.
070080     01 DATA-LINE.
070090         02 FILLER           PICTURE X.
070100         02 FILLER           PICTURE X(1) VALUE SPACE.
```

```
080010        02 HEIGHT-O          PICTURE 99.
080020        02 FILLER            PICTURE X(15) VALUE SPACE.
080030        02 20X-24X-O         PICTURE 999.
080040        02 FILLER            PICTURE X(15) VALUE SPACE.
080050        02 25X-29X-O         PICTURE 999.
080060        02 FILLER            PICTURE X(15) VALUE SPACE.
080070        02 30X-39X-O         PICTURE 999.
080080        02 FILLER            PICTURE X(15) VALUE SPACE.
080090        02 40X-49X-O         PICTURE 999.
080100        02 FILLER            PICTURE X(15) VALUE SPACE.
090010        02 50X-59X-O         PICTURE 999.
090020        02 FILLER            PICTURE X(39) VALUE SPACE.
090030   01 AVERAGE-LINE.
090040        02 FILLER            PICTURE X.
090050        02 FILLER            PICTURE X(1) VALUE SPACE.
090060        02 AVE-H-O           PICTURE 99.
090070        02 FILLER            PICTURE X(15) VALUE SPACE.
090080        02 AVE-W-1           PICTURE 999.
090090        02 FILLER            PICTURE X(15) VALUE SPACE.
090100        02 AVE-W-2           PICTURE 999.
100010        02 FILLER            PICTURE X(15) VALUE SPACE.
100020        02 AVE-W-3           PICTURE 999.
100030        02 FILLER            PICTURE X(15) VALUE SPACE.
100040        02 AVE-W-4           PICTURE 999.
100050        02 FILLER            PICTURE X(15) VALUE SPACE.
100060        02 AVE-W-5           PICTURE 999.
100070        02 FILLER            PICTURE X(39) VALUE SPACE.
100080   PROCEDURE DIVISION.
100090        OPEN INPUT INFO-CARDS
100100             OUTPUT REPORT-O.
110010   WRITE-HEADINGS.
110020        MOVE HEADING-1 TO LINE-OUT.
110030        WRITE LINE-OUT FROM HEADING-1 AFTER ADVANCING TO-NEW-PAGE.
110040        MOVE HEADING-2 TO LINE-OUT.
110050        WRITE LINE-OUT FROM HEADING-2 AFTER ADVANCING 2 LINES.
110060        READ INFO-CARDS AT END DISPLAY 'ERROR NO CARDS'.
110070        PERFORM READ-PARAGRAPH THRU SUMS UNTIL INPUT-FLAG = 'NO'.
110080        PERFORM CALCULATE-AVERAGES.
110090        STOP RUN.
110100   READ-PARAGRAPH.
120010        MOVE HEIGHT TO HEIGHT-O.
120020        MOVE 20X-24X TO 20X-24X-O.
120030        MOVE 25X-29X TO 25X-29X-O.
120040        MOVE 30X-39X TO 30X-39X-O.
120050        MOVE 40X-49X TO 40X-49X-O.
120060        MOVE 50X-59X TO 50X-59X-O.
120070        MOVE DATA-LINE TO LINE-OUT.
120080        WRITE LINE-OUT FROM DATA-LINE AFTER ADVANCING 2 LINES.
120090   SUMS.
120100        ADD HEIGHT TO TOTAL-HEIGHT.
130010        ADD 20X-24X TO TOTAL-W-1.
130020        ADD 25X-29X TO TOTAL-W-2.
130030        ADD 30X-39X TO TOTAL-W-3.
130040        ADD 40X-49X TO TOTAL-W-4.
130050        ADD 50X-59X TO TOTAL-W-5.
130060        ADD 1 TO TOTAL-H-W.
130070        READ INFO-CARDS AT END MOVE 'NO' TO INPUT-FLAG.
130080   CALCULATE-AVERAGES.
```

```
130090      DIVIDE TOTAL-HEIGHT BY TOTAL-H-W GIVING AVE-H-O.
130100      DIVIDE TOTAL-W-1 BY TOTAL-H-W GIVING AVE-W-1.
140010      DIVIDE TOTAL-W-2 BY TOTAL-H-W GIVING AVE-W-2.
140020      DIVIDE TOTAL-W-3 BY TOTAL-H-W GIVING AVE-W-3.
140030      DIVIDE TOTAL-W-4 BY TOTAL-H-W GIVING AVE-W-4.
140040      DIVIDE TOTAL-W-5 BY TOTAL-H-W GIVING AVE-W-5.
140050      WRITE LINE-OUT FROM AVERAGE-LINE AFTER ADVANCING 2 LINES.
140060      STOP RUN.
```

2. Your company is in the process of reviewing programs which have been in use for more than 5 years. The program which follows qualifies for such review and you have been asked to conduct it. A program listing, the form of the inputs to the program, and and an example of the desired report is provided for you.

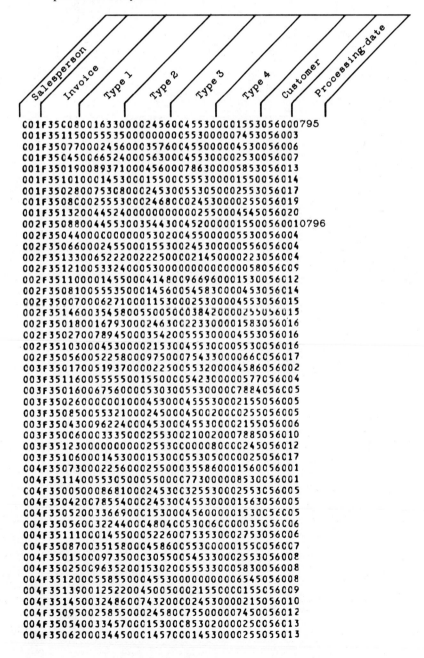

```
                        INTERNATIONAL TOYS, INC.
                        MONTHLY SALES REPORT
                            JULY , 1995
```

SALES-SALESPERSON 001	INVOICE NUMBER	CUSTOMER NUMBER	TYPE1 SALES	TYPE2 SALES	TYPE3 SALES	TYPE4 SALES	TOTAL SALES
	F35008	05600	163.30	24.55	455.30	15.53	658.69
	F35115	05600	555.35	.00	553.00	74.53	1,182.88
	F35077	05600	24.56	35.76	455.00	45.30	560.62
	F35045	05600	665.24	56.30	455.30	25.30	1,202.14
	F35019	05601	893.71	45.60	786.30	58.53	1,784.14
	F35101	05601	14.53	15.50	555.30	15.50	600.83
	F35028	05601	753.08	24.53	553.05	25.53	1,356.19
	F35080	05601	255.53	24.68	24.53	2.55	307.29
	F35132	05602	445.34	.00	2.55	45.45	493.24
TOTAL SALESPERSON 1			3,770.54	226.93	3,840.33	308.2	8,146.02

SALES-SALESPERSON 002	INVOICE NUMBER	CUSTOMER NUMBER	TYPE1 SALES	TYPE2 SALES	TYPE3 SALES	TYPE4 SALES	TOTAL SALES
	F35088	05600	445.53	354.43	452.00	15.50	1,267.46
	F35044	05600	.00	53.02	455.00	55.30	563.32
	F35066	05600	24.55	15.53	245.30	5.56	290.94
	F35133	05600	652.22	222.50	21.45	2.23	898.40
	F35121	05600	533.24	53.00	.00	.58	586.82
	F35110	05601	14.55	41.48	966.96	15.30	1,038.29
	F35081	05601	555.35	14.56	545.83	4.53	1,120.27
	F35007	05601	62.71	11.53	25.30	45.53	145.07
	F35146	05601	354.58	550.05	38.42	2.55	945.60
	F35018	05601	167.93	24.63	223.30	15.83	431.69
	F35027	05601	789.45	35.42	555.30	45.53	1,425.70
	F35103	05601	45.30	21.53	455.30	55.30	577.43
	F35056	05601	522.58	97.50	754.33	6.60	1,381.01
TOTAL SALESPERSON 2			4,167.99	1,495.13	4,738.49	270.3	10,672.00

SALES-SALESPERSON 003	INVOICE NUMBER	CUSTOMER NUMBER	TYPE1 SALES	TYPE2 SALES	TYPE3 SALES	TYPE4 SALES	TOTAL SALES
	F35017	05600	519.37	2.25	553.20	45.86	1,120.68
	F35116	05600	555.55	155.00	542.30	5.77	1,258.62
	F35016	05600	675.60	53.03	553.00	78.84	1,360.47

			555.55	55.85	542.30		
		05601	745.66	25.63	530.02		
	F35021	05601	290.39	45.63	.00	15.56	
	F35131	05601	545.52	.00	34.56	44.23	624.31
TOTAL SALESPERSON 9			2,227.57	221.77	2,779.20	229.8	5,458.34

SALES-SALESPERSON 010	INVOICE NUMBER	CUSTOMER NUMBER	TYPE1 SALES	TYPE2 SALES	TYPE3 SALES	TYPE4 SALES	TOTAL SALES
	F35047	05600	863.24	45.30	788.50	15.53	1,712.57
	F35020	05600	912.50	24.53	2.45	45.85	985.33
	F35046	05600	574.44	25.30	455.30	55.30	1,110.34
	F35068	05600	21.45	57.83	553.30	2.55	635.13
	F35151	05600	325.53	453.00	455.00	2.55	1,236.08
	F35148	05600	354.58	552.08	585.22	5.53	1,497.41
	F35150	05600	545.55	450.00	553.00	2.14	1,550.69
	F35152	05600	325.63	753.00	553.00	.00	1,631.63
	F35029	05601	145.63	24.53	550.03	78.82	799.01
	F35122	05601	545.53	15.60	.02	4.53	565.68
	F35009	05601	60.21	14.53	133.00	25.83	233.57
	F35055	05601	33.63	25.30	863.30	2.50	924.73
	F35149	05601	555.24	585.50	852.33	2.45	1,995.52
TOTAL SALESPERSON 10			5,263.21	3,024.50	6,344.45	243.5	14,877.74

Required:

a. Critique the program for compliance with good structured programming techniques. Cite specific paragraphs, line, or ranges of lines to support you criticisms.

b. Rewrite the program in a proper manner.

```
010010 IDENTIFICATION DIVISION.
010020 PROGRAM-ID.
010030     'TOY-SALES-REPORT'.
010040 AUTHOR.  TERRI JOHNSON.
010050 INSTALLATION. WILDER TECH.
010060 DATE-WRITTEN.  FEB 27,1975.
010070 DATE-COMPILED. JUL 24,1980.
```

```
010080 REMARKS. THIS PROGRAM GENERATES A REPORT FOR A COMPANY.
010090         THE REPORT IS BASED UPON EACH SALESPERSON'S RECEIPTS
010100         ON A MONTHLY BASIS.
020010 ENVIRONMENT DIVISION.
020020 CONFIGURATION SECTION.
020030 SOURCE-COMPUTER. IBM-360.
020040 OBJECT-COMPUTER. IBM-360.
020050 SPECIAL-NAMES.
020060      C01 IS TO-NEXT-PAGE.
020070 INPUT-OUTPUT SECTION.
020080 FILE-CONTROL.
020090      SELECT INPUT-RECORD ASSIGN UR-S-INPUT.
020100      SELECT PRINTED-OUTPUT ASSIGN UR-S-PRINTER.
030010 DATA DIVISION.
030020 FILE SECTION.
030030 FD   INPUT-RECORD
030040      LABEL RECORDS ARE OMITTED
030050      DATA RECORD IS SALES-INFORMATION.
030060 01   SALES-INFORMATION.
030070      02 SALESPERSON PICTURE 999.
030080      02 INVOICE     PICTURE X(6).
030090      02 TYPE1       PICTURE 9(5)V99.
030100      02 TYPE2       PICTURE 9(5)V99.
040010      02 TYPE3       PICTURE 9(5)V99.
040020      02 TYPE4       PICTURE 9(5)V99.
040030      02 CUSTOMER    PICTURE 9(5).
040040      02 PROCESSING-DATE  PICTURE 9999.
040050      02 FILLER      PICTURE X(34).
040060 FD   PRINTED-OUTPUT
040070      LABEL RECORDS ARE OMITTED.
040080 01   PRINTER-LINE   PICTURE X(132).
040090 WORKING-STORAGE SECTION.
040100 77   COUNTER            PICTURE 9 VALUE ZERO.
050010 77   LINE-COUNT         PICTURE 99 VALUE ZERO.
050020 77   DETAIL-LINE-TOTAL PICTURE 9(7)V99 VALUE ZERO.
050030 77   SALESPERSON-NUMBER PICTURE 999 VALUE ZERO.
050040 77   TOTAL-TYPE1        PICTURE 9(6)V99 VALUE ZERO.
050050 77   TOTAL-TYPE2        PICTURE 9(6)V99 VALUE ZERO.
050060 77   TOTAL-TYPE3        PICTURE 9(6)V99 VALUE ZERO.
050070 77   TOTAL-TYPE4        PICTURE 9(6)V99 VALUE ZERO.
050080 77   SUBTOTAL-TYPE1     PICTURE 9(8)V99 VALUE ZERO.
050090 77   SUBTOTAL-TYPE2     PICTURE 9(8)V99 VALUE ZERO.
050100 77   SUBTOTAL-TYPE3     PICTURE 9(8)V99 VALUE ZERO.
060010 77   SUBTOTAL-TYPE4     PICTURE 9(8)V99 VALUE ZERO.
060020 77   SUBDETAIL-LINE-TOTAL PICTURE 9(9)V99 VALUE ZERO.
060030 77   TOTALDETAIL-LINE-TOTAL PICTURE 9(7)V99 VALUE ZERO.
060040 01   DATES.
060050      02 MONTH        PICTURE 99      VALUE 1.
060060      02 YEAR         PICTURE 99      VALUE 1.
060070 01   MONTHS-OF-THE-YEAR.
060080      02 ALL-THE-MONTHS.
060090         03 FILLER PIC A(9)   VALUE '  JANUARY'.
060100         03 FILLER PIC A(9)   VALUE ' FEBRUARY'.
070010         03 FILLER PIC A(9)   VALUE '    MARCH'.
070020         03 FILLER PIC A(9)   VALUE '    APRIL'.
070030         03 FILLER PIC A(9)   VALUE '      MAY'.
070040         03 FILLER PIC A(9)   VALUE '     JUNE'.
070050         03 FILLER PIC A(9)   VALUE '     JULY'.
```

```
070060              03 FILLER PIC A(9)   VALUE '   AUGUST'.
070070              03 FILLER PIC A(9)   VALUE 'SEPTEMBER'.
070080              03 FILLER PIC A(9)   VALUE '  OCTOBER'.
070090              03 FILLER PIC A(9)   VALUE ' NOVEMBER'.
070100              03 FILLER PIC A(9)   VALUE ' DECEMBER'.
080010      02 MONTHLIST REDEFINES ALL-THE-MONTHS.
080020          03 MONTHTABLE OCCURS 12 TIMES PIC A(9).
080030 01   TYPE-REPORT-HEADING.
080040      02 FILLER          PICTURE X(53) VALUE SPACE.
080050      02 WORD-1    PICTURE X(24) VALUE 'INTERNATIONAL TOYS, INC.'.
080060      02 FILLER    PICTURE X(55) VALUE SPACE.
080070 01   TYPE-PAGE-HEADING.
080080      02 FILLER    PICTURE X(55) VALUE SPACE.
080090      02 WORD-2    PICTURE A(20) VALUE 'MONTHLY SALES REPORT'.
080100      02 FILLER    PICTURE X(57) VALUE SPACE.
090010 01   DATE-HEADING.
090020      02 FILLER    PICTURE X(56) VALUE SPACE.
090030      02 MONTH-OUT PICTURE A(9).
090040      02 YEAR-1    PICTURE X(4) VALUE ', 19'.
090050      02 YEAR-OUT  PICTURE 99.
090060      02 FILLER    PICTURE X(61) VALUE SPACE.
090070 01   TYPE-CONTROL-HEADING1.
090080      02 FILLER    PICTURE X(10) VALUE SPACE.
090090      02 WORD-3    PICTURE X(19) VALUE 'SALES-SALESPERSON 1'.
090100      02 SALE-PERSON PICTURE 999.
100010      02 FILLER    PICTURE X(6) VALUE SPACE.
100020      02 WORD-4    PICTURE X(7) VALUE 'INVOICE'.
100030      02 FILLER    PICTURE X(7) VALUE SPACE.
100040      02 WORD-5    PICTURE X(8) VALUE 'CUSTOMER'.
100050      02 FILLER    PICTURE X(7) VALUE SPACE.
100060      02 WORD-6    PICTURE X(5) VALUE 'TYPE1'.
100070      02 FILLER    PICTURE X(7) VALUE SPACE.
100080      02 WORD-7    PICTURE X(5) VALUE 'TYPE2'.
100090      02 FILLER    PICTURE X(7) VALUE SPACE.
100100      02 WORD-8    PICTURE X(5) VALUE 'TYPE3'.
110010      02 FILLER    PICTURE X(7) VALUE SPACE.
110020      02 WORD-9    PICTURE X(5) VALUE 'TYPE4'.
110030      02 FILLER    PICTURE X(7) VALUE SPACE.
110040      02 WORD-10   PICTURE X(5) VALUE 'TOTAL'.
110050      02 FILLER    PICTURE X(12) VALUE SPACE.
110060 01   TYPE-CONTROL-HEADING2.
110070      02 FILLER    PICTURE X(39) VALUE SPACE.
110080      02 WORD-11   PICTURE X(6) VALUE 'NUMBER'.
110090      02 FILLER    PICTURE X(8) VALUE SPACE.
110100      02 WORD-12   PICTURE X(6) VALUE 'NUMBER'.
120010      02 FILLER    PICTURE X(8) VALUE SPACE.
120020      02 WORD-13   PICTURE X(5) VALUE 'SALES'.
120030      02 FILLER    PICTURE X(7) VALUE SPACE.
120040      02 WORD-14   PICTURE X(5) VALUE 'SALES'.
120050      02 FILLER    PICTURE X(7) VALUE SPACE.
120060      02 WORD-15   PICTURE X(5) VALUE 'SALES'.
120070      02 FILLER    PICTURE X(7) VALUE SPACE.
120080      02 WORD-16   PICTURE X(5) VALUE 'SALES'.
120090      02 FILLER    PICTURE X(7) VALUE SPACE.
120100      02 WORD-17   PICTURE X(5) VALUE 'SALES'.
130010      02 FILLER    PICTURE X(12) VALUE SPACE.
130020 01   LINE-OF-DATA.
130030      02 FILLER    PICTURE X(39) VALUE SPACE.
```

```
130040      02 INVOICE-DATA   PICTURE X(6).
130050      02 FILLER    PICTURE X(9) VALUE SPACE.
130060      02 CUSTOMER-DATA PICTURE 9(5).
130070      02 FILLER    PICTURE X(4) VALUE SPACE.
130080      02 TYPE1-DETAIL PICTURE ZZ,ZZZ.99.
130090      02 FILLER    PICTURE X(3) VALUE SPACE.
130100      02 TYPE2-DETAIL PICTURE ZZ,ZZZ.99.
140010      02 FILLER    PICTURE X(3) VALUE SPACE.
140020      02 TYPE3-DETAIL PICTURE ZZ,ZZZ.99.
140030      02 FILLER    PICTURE X(3) VALUE SPACE.
140040      02 TYPE4-DETAIL PICTURE ZZ,ZZZ.99.
140050      02 FILLER    PICTURE X(4) VALUE SPACE.
140060      02 LINE-TOTAL PICTURE ZZ,ZZZ.99.
140070      02 FILLER    PICTURE X(24) VALUE SPACE.
140080 01   TYPE-CONTROL-SALESPERSON.
140090      02 FILLER    PICTURE X(16) VALUE SPACE.
140100      02 WORD-A    PICTURE X(18) VALUE 'TOTAL SALESPERSON'.
150010      02 SALESPERSON-OLD PICTURE ZZZ.
150020      02 FILLER    PICTURE X(25) VALUE SPACE.
150030      02 TYPE1-TOTAL PICTURE ZZZ,ZZZ.99.
150040      02 FILLER    PICTURE X(2) VALUE SPACE.
150050      02 TYPE2-TOTAL PICTURE ZZZ,ZZZ.99.
150060      02 FILLER    PICTURE X(2) VALUE SPACE.
150070      02 TYPE3-TOTAL PICTURE ZZZ,ZZZ.99.
150080      02 FILLER    PICTURE X(2) VALUE SPACE.
150090      02 TYPE4-TOTAL PICTURE ZZZ,ZZZ.99.
150100      02 FILLER    PICTURE X(2) VALUE SPACE.
160010      02 TOTAL-TOTAL PICTURE ZZZZ,ZZZ.99.
160020      02 FILLER    PICTURE X(21) VALUE SPACE.
160030 01   TYPE-CONTROL-FOOTING-FINAL.
160040      02 FILLER    PICTURE X(10) VALUE SPACE.
160050      02 WORD-8    PICTURE X(23) VALUE 'TOTAL SALES COMPANYWIDE'.
160060      02 FILLER    PICTURE X(21) VALUE SPACE.
160070      02 FINAL-TOTAL1 PICTURE ZZZZ,ZZZ.99.
160080      02 FILLER    PICTURE X(3) VALUE SPACE.
160090      02 FINAL-TOTAL2 PICTURE ZZZZ,ZZZ.99.
160100      02 FILLER    PICTURE X(3) VALUE SPACE.
170010      02 FINAL-TOTAL3 PICTURE ZZZZ,ZZZ.99.
170020      02 FILLER    PICTURE X(3) VALUE SPACE.
170030      02 FINAL-TOTAL4 PICTURE ZZZZ,ZZZ.99.
170040      02 FILLER    PICTURE X(3) VALUE SPACE.
170050      02 FINAL-TOTAL PICTURE ZZZZ,ZZZ.99.
170060      02 FILLER    PICTURE X(21) VALUE SPACE.
170070 PROCEDURE DIVISION.
170080 START-UP.
170090     OPEN INPUT INPUT-RECORD, OUTPUT PRINTED-OUTPUT.
170100     MOVE TYPE-REPORT-HEADING TO PRINTER-LINE.
180010     WRITE PRINTER-LINE AFTER ADVANCING TO-NEXT-PAGE.
180020     ADD 4 TO LINE-COUNT.
180030     READ INPUT-RECORD AT END GO TO STOP-THIS.
180040     MOVE PROCESSING-DATE TO DATES.
180050     MOVE TYPE-PAGE-HEADING TO PRINTER-LINE.
180060     WRITE PRINTER-LINE AFTER ADVANCING 1 LINES.
180070     ADD 1 TO LINE-COUNT.
180080     MOVE MONTHTABLE (MONTH) TO MONTH-OUT.
180090     MOVE YEAR TO YEAR-OUT.
180100     MOVE DATE-HEADING TO PRINTER-LINE.
190010     WRITE PRINTER-LINE AFTER ADVANCING 1 LINES.
```

```
190020      ADD 1 TO LINE-COUNT.
190030      PERFORM WRITE-HEADING2 THRU EXIT-1.
190040 READ-RECORD.
190050      READ INPUT-RECORD AT END GO TO SUM-SUBTOTAL.
190060      IF LINE-COUNT > 60 MOVE ZEROES TO LINE-COUNT, PERFORM
190070      WRITE-HEADING MOVE SPACES TO PRINTER-LINE
190080      WRITE PRINTER-LINE AFTER ADVANCING 2 LINES ADD 2 TO
190090       LINE-COUNT.
190100 BEGIN-COMPARE.
200010      IF SALESPERSON NOT = 10 TO SALESPERSON-NUMBER GO TO ADD-TOTAL.
200020 START-CALCULATE.
200030      MOVE INVOICE TO INVOICE-DATA.
200040      MOVE CUSTOMER TO CUSTOMER-DATA.
200050      MOVE TYPE1 TO TYPE1-DETAIL.
200060      ADD TYPE1 TO TOTAL-TYPE1.
200070      ADD TYPE1 TO SUBTOTAL-TYPE1.
200080      MOVE TYPE2 TO TYPE2-DETAIL.
200090      ADD TYPE2 TO TOTAL-TYPE2.
200100      ADD TYPE2 TO SUBTOTAL-TYPE2.
210010      MOVE TYPE3 TO TYPE3-DETAIL.
210020      ADD TYPE3 TO TOTAL-TYPE3.
210030      ADD TYPE3 TO SUBTOTAL-TYPE3.
210040      MOVE TYPE4 TO TYPE4-DETAIL.
210050      ADD TYPE4 TO TOTAL-TYPE4.
210060      ADD TYPE4 TO SUBTOTAL-TYPE4.
210070      ADD TYPE1, TYPE2, TYPE3, TYPE4 GIVING DETAIL-LINE-TOTAL.
210080      ADD DETAIL-LINE-TOTAL TO TOTAL DETAIL-LINE-TOTAL.
210090      ADD DETAIL-LINE-TOTAL TO SUBDETAIL-LINE-TOTAL.
210100      MOVE DETAIL-LINE-TOTAL TO LINE-TOTAL.
220010      MOVE LINE-OF-DATA TO PRINTER-LINE.
220020      WRITE PRINTER-LINE AFTER ADVANCING 1 LINES.
220030      MOVE ZEROES TO DETAIL-LINE-TOTAL.
220040      ADD 1 TO LINE-COUNT.
220050 EXIT-2.
220060      EXIT.
220070 GO-TO-PARAGRAPH.
220080      GO TO READ-RECORD.
220090 ADD-TOTAL.
220100      MOVE SALESPERSON-NUMBER TO SALESPERSON-OLD.
230010      MOVE TOTAL-TYPE1 TO TYPE1-TOTAL.
230020      MOVE TOTAL-TYPE2 TO TYPE2-TOTAL.
230030      MOVE TOTAL-TYPE3 TO TYPE3-TOTAL.
230040      MOVE TOTAL-TYPE4 TO TYPE4-TOTAL.
230050      MOVE TOTALDETAIL-LINE-TOTAL TO TOTAL-TOTAL.
230060      MOVE TYPE-CONTROL-SALESPERSON TO PRINTER-LINE.
230070      WRITE PRINTER-LINE AFTER ADVANCING 1 LINES.
230080      ADD 1 TO LINE-COUNT.
230090      MOVE ZEROES TO SALESPERSON-NUMBER.
230100      MOVE ZEROES TO TOTAL-TYPE1.
240010      MOVE ZEROES TO TOTAL-TYPE2.
240020      MOVE ZEROES TO TOTAL-TYPE3.
240030      MOVE ZEROES TO TOTAL-TYPE4.
240040      MOVE ZEROES TO TOTALDETAIL-LINE-TOTAL.
240050 EXIT-3.
240060      EXIT.
240070 PERFORM-PARAGRAPH.
240080      PERFORM WRITE-HEADING2 THRU EXIT-1.
240090 SUM-SUBTOTAL.
```

```
240100       PERFORM ADD-TOTAL THRU EXIT-3.
250010       MOVE SUBTOTAL-TYPE1 TO FINAL-TOTAL1.
250020       MOVE SUBTOTAL-TYPE2 TO FINAL-TOTAL2.
250030       MOVE SUBTOTAL-TYPE3 TO FINAL-TOTAL3.
250040       MOVE SUBTOTAL-TYPE4 TO FINAL-TOTAL4.
250050       MOVE SUBDETAIL-LINE-TOTAL TO FINAL-TOTAL.
250060       MOVE TYPE-CONTROL-FOOTING-FINAL TO PRINTER-LINE.
250070       WRITE PRINTER-LINE AFTER ADVANCING 22 LINES.
250080       GO TO STOP-THIS.
250090 WRITE-HEADING.
250100       MOVE TYPE-PAGE-HEADING TO PRINTER-LINE.
260010       WRITE PRINTER-LINE AFTER ADVANCING TO-NEXT-PAGE.
260020       ADD 3 TO LINE-COUNT.
260030       MOVE MONTHTABLE (MONTH) TO MONTH-OUT.
260040       MOVE YEAR TO YEAR-OUT.
260050       MOVE DATE-HEADING TO PRINTER-LINE.
260060       WRITE PRINTER-LINE AFTER ADVANCING 1 LINES.
260070       ADD 1 TO LINE-COUNT.
260080 WRITE-HEADING2.
260090       MOVE SALESPERSON TO SALESPERSON-NUMBER.
260100       MOVE SALESPERSON TO SALE-PERSON.
270010       MOVE TYPE-CONTROL-HEADING1 TO PRINTER-LINE.
270020       WRITE PRINTER-LINE AFTER ADVANCING 3 LINES.
270030       ADD 3 TO LINE-COUNT.
270040       MOVE TYPE-CONTROL-HEADING2 TO PRINTER-LINE.
270050       WRITE PRINTER-LINE AFTER ADVANCING 1 LINES.
270060       ADD 1 TO LINE-COUNT.
270070       IF COUNTER > 0 GO TO BEGIN-COMPARE ELSE ADD 1 TO COUNTER
270080        PERFORM START-CALCULATE THRU EXIT-2.
270090 EXIT-1.
270100       EXIT.
280010 STOP-THIS.
280020       CLOSE INPUT-RECORD, PRINTED-OUTPUT.
280030       STOP RUN.
280040
```

3

Sequential File Processing

In the past, sequential organization of files was the most commonly used organization type. In recent years, emphasis has passed from this organizational method to relative and indexed methods. There are, however, many applications in which the use of sequentially organized data is appropriate. Furthermore, a large number of users still use sequential files, particularly in those centers which are oriented to tape processing as opposed to disk processing.

SECTION 1
General Concepts of Sequential File Update

The process of updating a sequential master file usually requires the inclusion of four files. The systems flowchart in Figure 3-1 indicates the four files that are typically included in the update process.

The files included in the program and their reason for inclusion are:

File	Reason and/or Use
Transaction file	The transaction file contains activities that need to be included in the master file. This information is typically in the form of additions, deletions, replacements for, or changes to certain data-items that are included in the master file. For example, a customer's credit status may change, or a customer may no longer do business with your organization, or new customers may need to be added to the master file.
Master file	This file contains permanent or semipermanent information that must be retained by the organization for legal or transactional purposes. For example, your company could maintain a vendor master file that might include information such as the vendor's name, address, and amount of purchases made from a specific vendor in an accounts payable system.

Figure 3–1
Basic sequential file update.

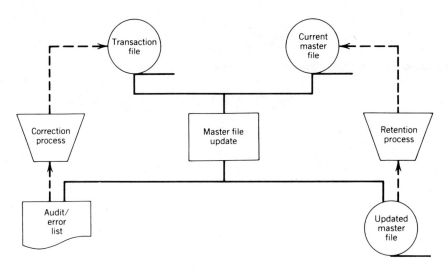

Audit/error list	This listing usually indicates the disposition of the changes that are included in the transaction file. Any errors that are encountered are indicated in order that corrections may be made. Also, included in the listing are totals that are used for audit purposes to verify that all the master and transaction records have been read and processed.
Updated master file	This file contains a combination of the activities from the transaction file and from the old master file.

Four files are required because:

- the current master file cannot have records inserted between existing records;
- there is no provision for erasing or deleting records that are no longer used;
- there is no way to back up and rewrite the record after it has been read and changes have been made to the record.

SECTION 2
Sequential File-Processing Requirements

Before the actual sequential master file maintenance can take place, certain requirements have to be fulfilled. These are:

1. The master file must be arranged or SORTed in a specific order based on the value of a specified field, called the *key field*. This key field might be, for example, student number in a student master file, customer number in a customer master file, or vendor number in a vendor master file.
2. The transaction file must be arranged or SORTed in the same sequence and based on the value of the same key field used to sequence the master file.

The revised system flowchart including these requirements is presented in Figure 3-2.

Figure 3–2
Sequential file update—with
SORTING.

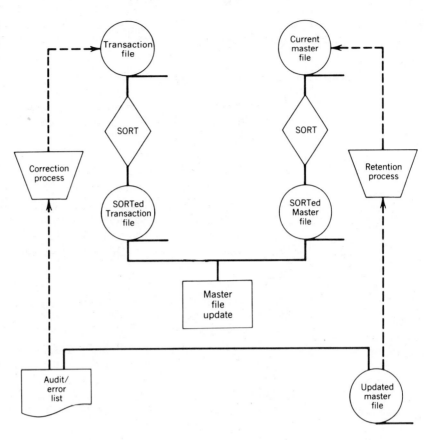

Retention Cycle

If care is not exercised when working with magnetic tape, the wrong master file can be used as input into the update process. In most computer sites this sort of error is controlled (usually sucessfully) in the tape library by data clerks or tape librarians and through operating system functions which control the "generations" of each file.

In reference to Figures 3-1 and 3-2 notice that when the master file maintenance process is successfully completed there are two versions of the "master file." We call these the "old master file" and the "updated master file." From an external point of view, these two files may appear to be identical when in fact they contain quite different information. If care is not exercised and the "old master file" is reentered in the next update cycle, the changes included in the first update cycle are lost.

The controls over this type of error are typically of two types:

the use of retention dates, or

the use of generations.

In a date retention system, an expiration date is set up and the tape is maintained until that date has expired. Most computer operating systems check the expiration date that is included in the tape label of the file. A message will then be displayed indicating whether the file's expiration date is or is not exceeded.

In a generation oriented retention system, the tape librarian keeps track of the number of generations of a certain file that are to be retained and continually numbers and updates those generations.

SECTION 3
Master File Maintenance Program
Concepts

There are certain functions that are performed in almost all master file maintenance programs. The following section addresses the functions generally performed in updating a sequential master file.

Sequence Checking

As noted earlier, one of the requirements of a sequential update is that the master file and the transaction file be sequenced on the same key field. In order to properly process the transaction file against the master file, the sequence of the records in both files must be checked to assure that this requirement is met. Processing is usually aborted if an out-of-sequence condition is detected on either file.

The process of sequence checking involves comparing the key value of the record being processed against the key value of the previous record of that same file. If the sequence mode is ascending sequence, the comparison result must be that the key value of the record being processed must be greater than the previous key value. In the case of descending sequence, the comparison result must be that the current key value must be less than the previous key value. Figure 3-3 illustrates this concept.

In order to start the process, the value of the previous key is initialized to LOW-VALUES in the case of ascending sequence (HIGH-VALUES will be used for a descending sequence) in order that a valid comparison will result for the record. The value of the key for the first record in Figure 3-3 is 1357. Since there is no previous key to compare to 1357 must be the highest key encountered thus far. So we can get the process started by comparing 1357 to LOW VALUES, move 1357 to PREVIOUS-KEY, process the record, get a new key value (1386) and we are under way. Subsequent processing requires the movement of the current key value to a WORKING-STORAGE previous key area prior to reading the next record from that file. Notice that when the current key value of 1208 is compared to the previous key value of 1611 an out-of-sequence condition is detected and one of two processing actions may be taken:

1. Flag the out-of-sequence record on the audit/error list and continue processing.
2. Flag the out-of-sequence record on the audit/error list or terminal and discontinue processing.

The latter situation is most commonly encountered.

Figure 3–3 Results of sequence-checking sequential file.	Current Key Values	Previous Key values	Result of Compare
	1357	Low-values	greater than
	1386	1357	greater than
	1402	1386	greater than
	1507	1402	greater than
	1611	1507	greater than
	1208	1611	Less than--file out of sequence
	1724		
	1729		

Figure 3–4
Sequential file update—with
EDIT.

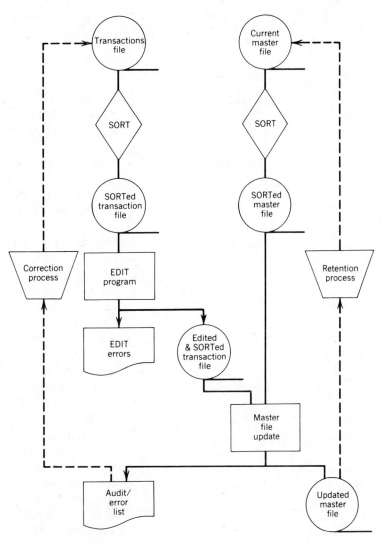

Data Validation

Data validation must be done at some point in the processing cycle. Some systems are designed so that the validation or editing is accomplished in the master file maintenance program. Other systems have a separate edit program in the system that runs prior to the actual update of the master file. Figure 3-4 illustrates the inclusion of an edit program in the system as a separate processing step.

In the example(s) used in this text a minor number of editing functions will be handled for purposes of illustration only, because in "real-life" situations Murphy's law is assumed to be in supreme dominance and everything that can be validated to ensure correctness will be (or should be) validated. Therefore, the degree of editing required in any actual situation should certainly be more extensive than anything we do here.

Some few of the typical types of validation tests are as follows:

Type	Validation
Character Testing	
Class test	Determines whether the data are numeric, alphabetic, or alphanumeric.

| Sign test | Detemines whether the data are positive, negative, or unsigned. |

Field Testing

Presence test	Determines if data are missing from a specific field. These are fields that are required for processing.
Absence test	Ensures that fields are blank that are supposed to be.
Range test	Usually applied to coded data to assure that these data are in a specific range. For example, student classification codes might range from 1 through 8. A code of less than 1 or greater than 8 is an error condition.
Limit test	Checks for a value that is greater than a minimum or maximum value. For example, automatic bank teller systems usually restrict cash withdrawals to a maximum of $200, therefore, a limit test of $200 might be made by programs that handle such transactions.
Reasonableness test	Identifies abnormal or exceptional situations. They may be correct, but they should be flagged on an audit/error report for checking.
Consistency test	Uses two or more data fields in order to establish whether or not a situation is consistent.
Date tests	Typically dates are tested to assure validity. In most data processing systems, date is carried in the form YYMMDD and checks are made to ensure that the year is appropriate, that the month is in the range of 1 to 12, and that the date is appropriate for that month: for example, the day cannot be less than 01 or greater than 31 for May. Also, leap year tests are made for February 29 by dividing the year by 4, and if there is no remainder, the 29th of February for that year is valid. (Note: There are a couple of exceptions to this rule.)

Account Number Tests

Modulus 11 check digits and other numbering schemes are used to ensure that an account number has been entered correctly. These schemes check for transcription and transposition errors.

For example, the modulus 11 check digit is the most frequently used method and has three different approaches: arithmetic progression, geometric progression, and prime number weighting. An illustration of the prime number weighting method is as follows:

Account number   2 4 6 8 7
$$x\ x\ x\ x\ x$$
Multiply by prime 1713 7 5 3

Add results 34 52 42 40 21=189

Subtract result from next highest multiple of 11. 198 - 189 = 9, or divide 189 by 11 and subtract remainder from 11. The check digit is 9. This method was developed by the Friden Company and detects all transposition and transcription errors.

The account number with its check digit is 246879.

Please note that in a modulus 11 situation the result of the calculation may be 10. Since check digits are only one character in length, special handling must be provided when the result is 10. The usual treatment is to assign no identification number for which the check digit will be 10.

Audit Reports

Audit trails provide information that help ensure the integrity of the data that are being processed. Some systems refer to the audit trail report as the audit totals.

Usually, the audit totals are printed as a separate part of the audit/error report. The content of this portion of the report varies from situation to situation, but typically includes these items:

- total transactions read
- total adds to file
  total adds processed
  total adds rejected
- total changes
  total changes processed
  total changes rejected
- total deletes
  total deletes processed
  total deletes rejected
- total master records read
- total master records written

These totals are used to balance the transaction data against the master file data or to assure that the updated master file includes all the information that it should contain and that it contains no extraneous data.

Error Listing

The error list is a listing of the disposition of the records contained in the transaction file. Each record contained in the transaction file must be listed on the audit/ error report, and some indication of the disposition of that record, together with a notation for any errors detected for that record during the data-editing process.

In out-of-sequence situations there will be at least two items of information printed or displayed. The first will indicate the key value of the previous record read and the second will indicate the key value of the record being processed when the out-of-sequence condition was encountered. Naturally, there will also be an error message indicating that an out-of-sequence condition has been encountered, and an indication of whether the error is associated with the master file or the transaction file.

SECTION 4
The Relationship of the Transaction File Key to the Master File Key

The critical logic in the master file maintenance program is the comparison of the value of the transaction file key to the value of the master file key. The result of this comparison determines the action that will be taken for that set of records. The comparison of the keys will result in one of the following conditions:

Result of Comparison	**Indication**
1. Transaction file key is less than the master file key.	The transaction is an ADDITION
2. Transaction file key is greater than master file key.	There is no activity this period for the master file record (PASS).
3. Transaction file key is equal to master file key.	The transaction is a CHANGE or DELETE.

Please note in our example there cannot be more than one transaction in the transaction file for a specific master file record. This is not usually true in batch processing systems but is used here to minimize the complication of our update program.

Logically, in all sequential update programs these conditions and the meaning associated with each will always be the same and actions taken will be the same as discussed below. The actions to be taken are as follows.

Additions

When the transaction file key is less than the master file key this means that you must have an add transaction. If you are using transaction codes to indicate the transaction type, this code must be the add code. If the code is not an add code, then the record must be written to the audit/error list with an indication of the error condition (inconsistency between record compare and transaction code). The record is not written to the updated master file.

If the record "passes" the code test, then the transaction must be written to the updated master file after all the appropriate edit tests have been made and the transaction record passes these tests. The data in the added record should also be written to the audit/error report in order to provide documentation of the addition.

After the transaction record has been written to the updated master file, the next transaction record is read from the transaction file and the comparison logic continues. Notice that there is no read of the master file at this point.

Copies or Passes

When the transaction key is greater than the master key, this means that the master file contains a record for which there is no processing activity on the transaction file. This old master file record must be written to the updated master file. No record of this activity is made on the audit/error list.

After the record is written to the updated master file, another record is read from the old master file (but not from the transaction file,) and processing continues.

Deletions and Changes

When the transaction key is equal to the master key, this means that you have either a delete transaction or a change transaction. If you are using transaction codes and you have an add code, an error has occurred and the following steps should be taken:

1. Print the master file record on the audit/error list.
2. Print the transaction file record on the audit report.
3. Print the appropriate error message.
4. Read the next record from both the old master file and the transaction file.

If the transaction record passes the code validation test just indicated, the next step is to determine whether the transaction is a delete or a change. If you are *not* using transaction codes this is accomplished by comparing the transaction record (with the exception of the key field) to spaces. If a true condition occurs for the comparison, you have a delete transaction. If there is nothing to change then the transaction must be a delete.

In order to delete a record, simply read the next records from both the old master file and the transaction file and *do not* write to the updated master file. Of course, an entry must be made on the audit/error report that a record has been deleted.

To process changes the following steps should be taken:

1. Compare each field in the transaction record to spaces. If the field does not contain spaces, move the field from the transaction record to the appropriate field in the master record.
2. After all fields have been tested and changed fields have been moved to the old master record, the old master record should be written to the updated master file.
3. The next record should be read from both the old master file and the transaction file, and processing continued.

SECTION 5
End-of-File Processing

The most difficult part of programming a sequential file update program is ensuring that all records from both input files have been processed.

There are three possible end-of-file conditions:

1. You may reach the end of both files simultaneously. The last record on the master file may have a change or a delete transaction associated with it or there may be an error.
2. You may reach an AT END condition on the transaction file and not AT END on the old master file.
3. You may reach an AT END condition on the master file and not AT END on the transaction file.

It is highly unlikely that you will finish processing the records from both the transaction file and the old master file at the same point. Although this is possible, one of the other two conditions is more likely to occur.

If you are AT END on the old master file and have records remaining on the transaction file, this means that all the remaining records should be additions and need to be processed accordingly.

If you encounter an end of file on the transaction file while there are still records on the master file, these master file records must be passed from the old master file to the updated master file.

SECTION 6
An Illustration of Update Concepts

Figure 3-5 presents an example of the updating process discussed in the preceding sections.

The processing steps for file maintenance using the data in Figure 3-5 are as follows:

1. Read a record from both the transaction file and old master file.
2. Compare the values of the keys—1:2.
3. The result is that the transaction key is greater than the master key, therefore the old master record is written to the updated master file.
4. Read the next record from the old master file and compare this to the transaction key—3:2.
5. The transaction key is less than the master key and the transaction code is an A, therefore the transaction is added to the updated master file and written to the audit/error list.
6. Read the next record from the transaction file and compare to the old master key—3:7.
7. The transaction key is greater than the master key, therefore the old master record whose key value is 3 is written to the updated master file.
8. The next record is read from the old master file and compared to the transaction key—7:7.
9. The result is an equal compare, therefore determine whether the transaction is a delete or change. It is a delete. Write a record to the audit/error list and read a record from both the transaction file and the old master file and compare keys—7:9.

Figure 3–5
Results of sequential file update.

Key Values Old Master File	Key Values/Transaction Codes Transaction File
1	2A
3	7D
7	9A
8	12C
12	
14	
20	A=Add C=Change D=Delete

Key Values Updated Master File	Audit/error list
1	2 added
2	7 deleted
8	9 added
9	
12	12 changed
14	
20	

10. The transaction key is greater than the old master key. Write the master record to the updated master, read the old master file and compare keys—12:9.

11. The transaction key is less than the master key and the code is add, therefore the transaction record is written to the updated master file and the audit/error list.

12. Read the next record from the transaction file and compare keys—12:12.

13. The keys are equal. Determine whether the transaction is a delete or change. It is a change. Change the appropriate fields and add the record to the updated master file. This assumes no duplicates.

14. Read a record from both the transaction file and the master file and compare keys—4:eof.

15. We are at end of file on the transaction file, therefore all records remaining on the old master file must be passed through the system to the updated master file.

SECTION 7
Structured Program Design for a Sequential Update

There are no special features of a sequential file process other than the ORGANIZATION and ACCESS MODE clauses of the ENVIRONMENT DIVISION discussed in the following section. The remainder of this chapter is an extended discussion of an example program.

The inputs for the master file to be updated in this example are:

```
OLD-VENDOR-MASTER-FILE
000115ABC MFG. CO.                        123 EL ST.                         MONROE      LA712900000000(
000126CADDY SHACK                         147 OAK LANE       P. O. BOX 148   RUSTON      LA712700000000(
000188RUSTON OFFICE SUPPLY CO.            210 SOUTH TRENTON                  RUSTON      LA712700000000(
004075SPIVEY'S FRIED CHICKEN             HWY 149                            GRAMBLING   LA712450000000(
004099ELECTRONIC SPECIALTY PRODUCTS 615R S MONROE                           RUSTON      LA712700000000(
005763EVANS BARBER SUPPLY               1305 E LINE AVE.                    RUSTON      LA712700000000(
005984MID-STATE WOOD PRESERVERS INC HWY 80                                  GRAMBLING   LA712450000000(
006666LINCOLN STORAGE SYSTEMS INC.      HWY 150 W                           GRAMBLING   LA712450000000(
007777KELLY'S CLEANERS                   MAIN STREET                        GRAMBLING   LA712450000000(
007779GRAY'S INSURANCE                   MAIN STREET                        GRAMBLING   LA712450000000(
008478DON DURRETT CONSTRUCTION CO.      HWY 563                             GRAMBLING   LA712450000000(
```

The following file additions (A), changes (C), and deletions (D) are to be processed:

```
TRANSACTION-FILE
000188                                                                        0009500(061483C
004075                      SOUTH HWY 149                                     00000 0(00000 C
005763                                                                        00000 0(00000 D
007778COLLEGIATE SHOPPE     MAIN STREET                           GRAMBLING   LA712450000000(000000A
```

Following the discussion of the example program, there is a comparison of these inputs and the outputs generated by the program (Figure 3-24). The hierarchy chart for this program is Figure 3-6 and the record layouts and report layouts are given in Figures 3-7 through 3-10.

A full listing of the program is presented in Section 12. Parts of the program are reproduced as they relate to the discussion. Take a few minutes to glance at the full program in Section 12 before you continue.

This program should not be considered a complete example of all that is involved in a sequential file update. For one thing, this program assumes that there can be no more than one transaction for a master file record, and for another, that the editing process can be envisioned by the student.

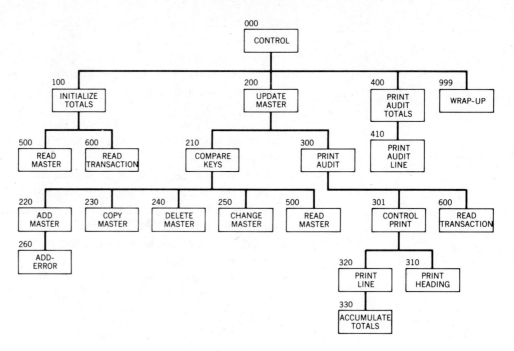

Figure 3–6
Structure diagram—update
sequential master file.

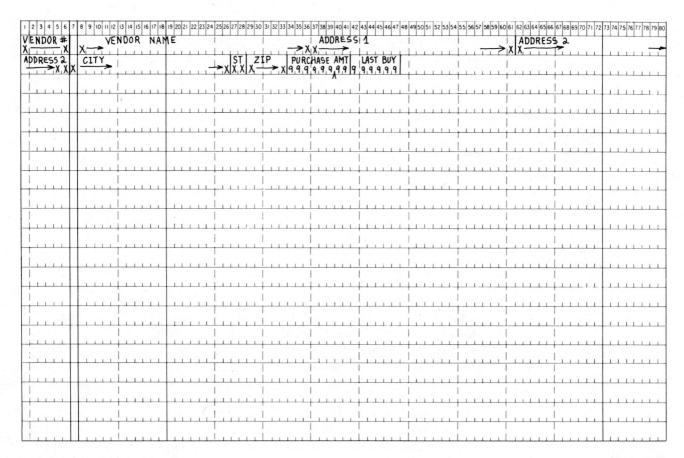

Figure 3–7
Record layout—old master.

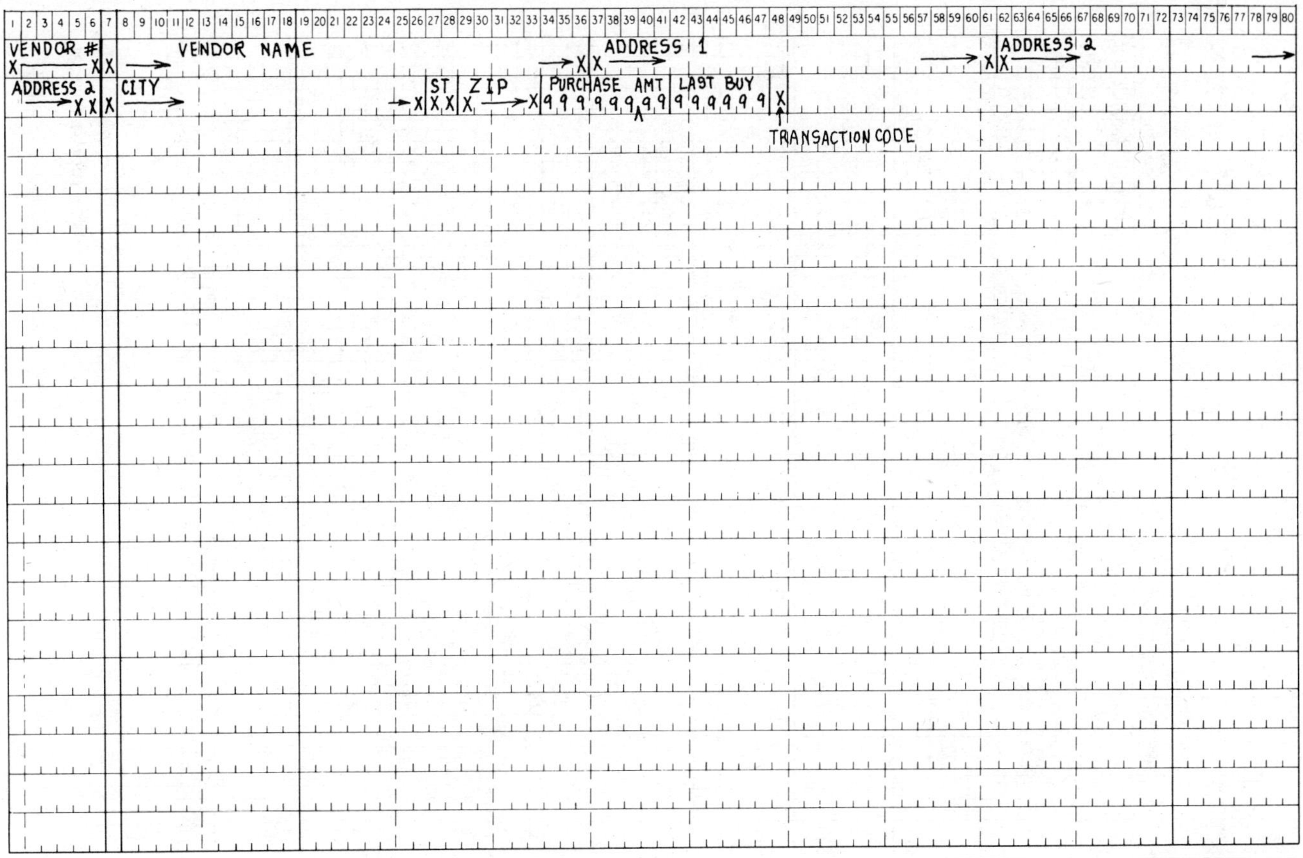

VENDOR # · VENDOR NAME · ADDRESS 1 · ADDRESS 2
ADDRESS 2 · CITY · ST · ZIP · PURCHASE AMT · LAST BUY · TRANSACTION CODE

Figure 3-8
Record layout—transaction file.

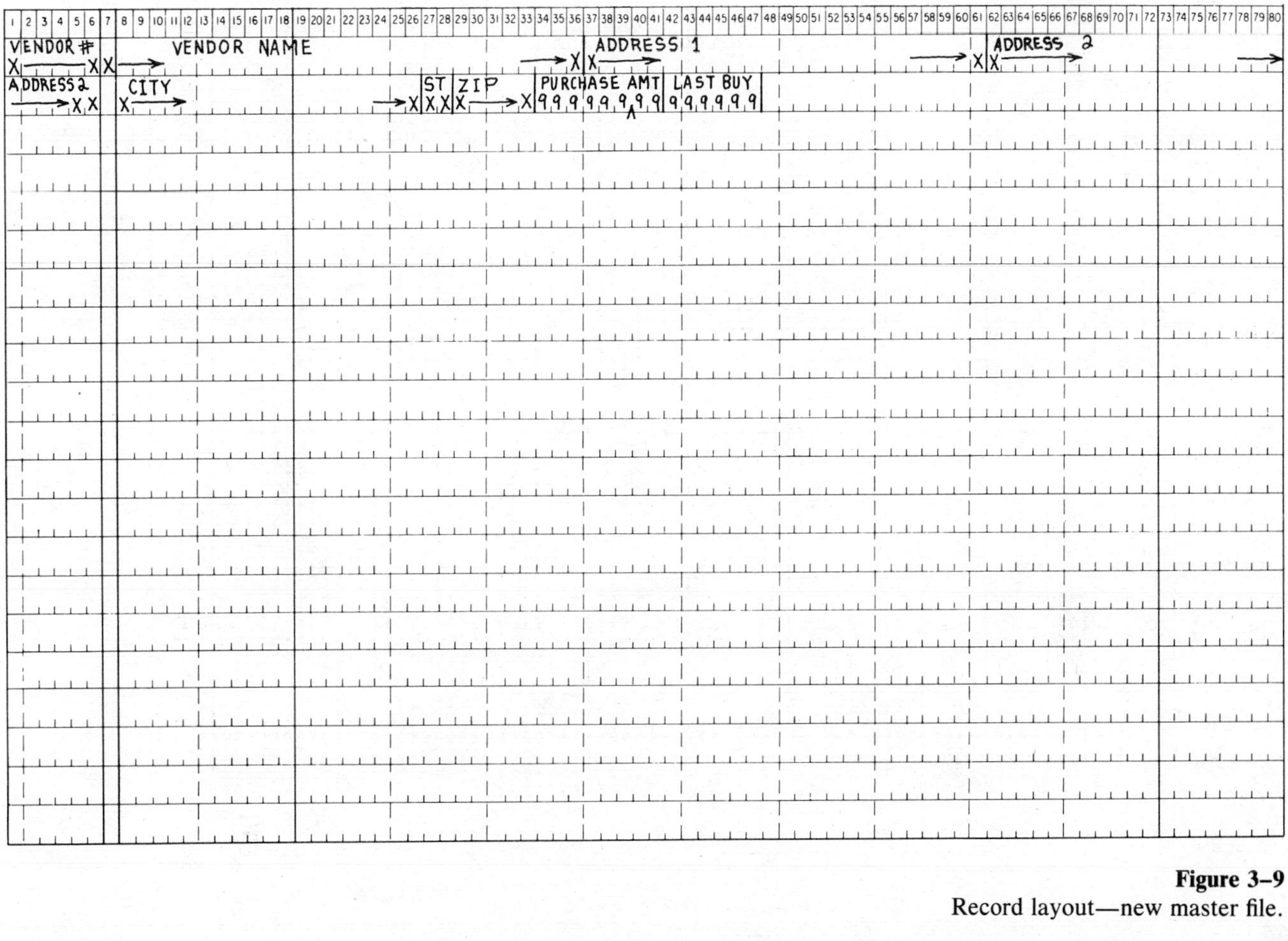

VENDOR # · VENDOR NAME · ADDRESS 1 · ADDRESS 2
ADDRESS 2 · CITY · ST · ZIP · PURCHASE AMT · LAST BUY

Figure 3-9
Record layout—new master file.

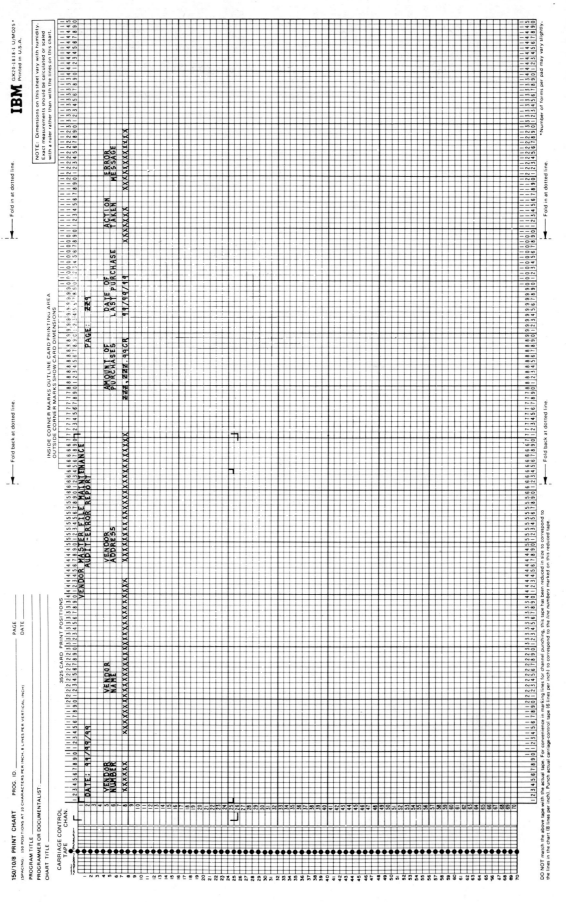

Figure 3–10 Audit/error report format.

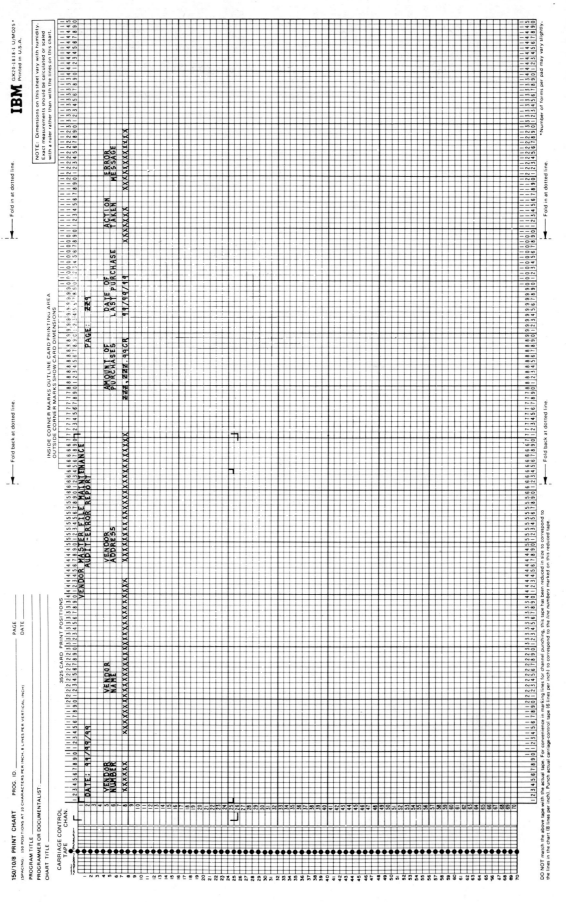

Figure 3–10 Audit/error report format.

SECTION 8
ENVIRONMENT DIVISION Entries for a
Sequential Update

As in any COBOL program, the four files that are used in this sequential update program must include a SELECT statement and be ASSIGNed to an external device or file.

The four files that are used in the program and were described before are:

1. OLD-VENDOR-MASTER-FILE
2. VENDOR-TRANSACTION-FILE
3. NEW-VENDOR-MASTER-FILE
4. VENDOR-AUDIT-ERROR-LIST

The ENVIRONMENT DIVISION entries necessary to this program are as follows:

```
ENVIRONMENT DIVISION.
    .
    .
    .
INPUT-OUTPUT SECTION.
FILE-CONTROL.
    SELECT OLD-VENDOR-MASTER-FILE
        ASSIGN TO "VENDMX"
        ORGANIZATION IS SEQUENTIAL
        ACCESS MODE IS SEQUENTIAL.
*
    SELECT VENDOR-TRANSACTION-FILE
        ASSIGN TO "VENDTR"
        ORGANIZATION IS SEQUENTIAL
        ACCESS MODE IS SEQUENTIAL.
*
    SELECT NEW-VENDOR-MASTER-FILE
        ASSIGN TO "NEWVEN"
        ORGANIZATION IS SEQUENTIAL
        ACCESS MODE IS SEQUENTIAL.
*
    SELECT VENDOR-AUDIT-ERROR-LIST
        ASSIGN TO "VENLST".
```

The ORGANIZATION and ACCESS MODE clauses are not necessary in this program (or any program whose organization structure is sequential) because the default option is sequential. They have been included here for two purposes:

1. to introduce these concepts, and
2. for documentation purposes.

Although these clauses are not strictly required, we do recommend their inclusion for documentation purposes—especially if you are using a number of files where there are mixed organization types.

The purpose of the ORGANIZATION clause is to tell the COBOL compiler that, in this case, the file is organized in a sequential manner. The purpose of the ACCESS MODE clause is to indicate that the records in this file are to be retrieved or accessed in a sequential fashion. Again, if the ORGANIZATION and ACCESS MODE clauses are omitted, the ORGANIZATION is assumed to be sequential and the ACCESS MODE is assumed to be sequential. You will note that we have specified sequential mode and sequential access for the error list file by default.

SECTION 9
DATA DIVISION Entries

FILE SECTION and WORKING-STORAGE SECTION entries are included in this program. The discussion here will center on the entries necessary to handle the update of our vendor master file example.

FILE SECTION *Entries*

Files are defined in the SELECT statements and then described in the file description (FD) entries of the FILE SECTION of the DATA DIVISION. Some programmers choose to define the detail of data-items in the FILE SECTION and others choose to do this in the WORKING-STORAGE SECTION. In this example, the detail of data-items is described in the WORKING-STORAGE SECTION.

One FD is required for each file SELECTed in the FILE-CONTROL paragraph. The FD entries for each of these files are as follows:

```
DATA DIVISION
FILE SECTION.
FD   OLD-VENDOR-MASTER-FILE
     RECORD CONTAINS 127 CHARACTERS
     LABEL RECORDS ARE STANDARD.
01   OLD-VENDOR-RECORD.
     05 FILLER                          PIC X(127).
FD   VENDOR-TRANSACTION-FILE
     RECORD CONTAINS 128 CHARACTERS
     LABEL RECORDS ARE STANDARD.
01   VENDOR-TRANSACTION-RECORD.
     05 FILLER                          PIC X(128).
FD   NEW-VENDOR-MASTER-FILE
     RECORD CONTAINS 127 CHARACTERS
     LABEL RECORDS ARE STANDARD.
01   NEW-VENDOR-RECORD.
     05 FILLER                          PIC X(127).
FD   VENDOR-AUDIT-ERROR-LIST
     RECORD CONTAINS 132 CHARACTERS
     LABEL RECORDS ARE OMITTED.
01   VENDOR-REPORT-LINE.
     05 FILLER                          PIC X(132).
```

Each of these files uses the RECORD CONTAINS clause. Although this clause is not required, it helps in the program and system documentation and should be included in all programs. Some IBM systems require the BLOCK CONTAINS clause *if* records are blocked and the blocking factor is other than a standard default factor incorporated in the operating system. In most systems, IBM or not, the absence of the BLOCK CONTAINS clause causes a default to the specifications of the JCL. If the JCL indicates a block size, then the records are considered to be blocked at the specified size. If the JCL specifies no blocking information then the records are considered to be unblocked.

The LABEL RECORD clause is specified as STANDARD for all files except the printer file, which is specified as OMITTED since there are no label records on printer files.

WORKING-STORAGE SECTION *Entries*

The WORKING-STORAGE SECTION contains entries for:

1. switches
2. sequence control fields
3. total areas
4. report headings
5. record descriptions for files
6. general edit areas
7. general working areas

The term "switch" is a carryover from the time when computer operators were required to set switches physically on the computer console to indicate certain processing conditions. The contemporary use of the term relates to WORKING-STORAGE variables that indicate certain processing conditions based on their value. Examples of the use of the conditions switches are:

1. Indication of end of file on a specific file. There is one switch for each input file.
2. Indication of whether or not the input record(s) have passed the edit process.

Sequence control entries are used to check the sequence of the OLD-VENDOR-MASTER-FILE and the VENDOR-TRANSACTION-FILE to assure that they are in ascending sequence on the control field, which, in this case, is the vendor number.

The total area of the WORKING-STORAGE is used to tally the number of records read/written in specific categories. There are also totals for the number of lines printed on a page and the number of pages written in the VENDOR-AUDIT-ERROR-LIST report.

The report headings are described in the WORKING-STORAGE SECTION.

There are four record description entries—one for each of the records contained in the four files. Although it is possible to have multiple record types for each of the files, the handling of such a situation is not included in this example program.

SECTION 10
PROCEDURE DIVISION Entries

The coding for the PROCEDURE DIVISION follows the hierarchy chart in Figure 3-6. The full listing of the PROCEDURE DIVISION is contained in Section 12 of this chapter. Each section of code in the division is discussed in detail in this section.

000-VM-CONTROL-MODULE.

This module, the first in the PROCEDURE DIVISION, is the primary module in the structured update program for our example. Its purpose is to cause the execution

Figure 3–11
Mainline module for example
program.

```
**********************
* PROCEDURE DIVISION
* BEGINS HERE
**********************
 PROCEDURE DIVISION.
*
*
 000-VM-CONTROL-MODULE.
*
    OPEN INPUT          OLD-VENDOR-MASTER-FILE
                        VENDOR-TRANSACTION-FILE
         OUTPUT         NEW-VENDOR-MASTER-FILE
                        VENDOR-AUDIT-ERROR-LIST.
    PERFORM 100-INITIALIZE-TOTALS-ETC.
    PERFORM 200-UPDATE-MASTER-FILE
          UNTIL WS-OMF-EOF-SW = "X"
          AND   WS-TF-EOF-SW = "X".
    PERFORM 400-PRINT-AUDIT-TOTALS.
    CLOSE    OLD-VENDOR-MASTER-FILE
             VENDOR-TRANSACTION-FILE
             NEW-VENDOR-MASTER-FILE
             VENDOR-AUDIT-ERROR-LIST.
    STOP RUN.
```

of the modules on the next level of the program. Figure 3-11 contains the statements in this module.

The first statement in the module causes all of the files in the program to be OPENed for input or output operations. Remember that the input files are:

```
OLD-VENDOR-MASTER-FILE
VENDOR-TRANSACTION-FILE
```

and the output files are:

```
NEW-VENDOR-MASTER-FILE
VENDOR-AUDIT-ERROR-LIST
```

The three PERFORM statements cause the execution of the three main modules in the program. The statement:

```
PERFORM 200-UPDATE-MASTER-FILE
    UNTIL WS-OMF-EOF-SW = "X"
    AND WS-TF-EOF-SW = "X",
```

is of special significance. The switches WS-OMF-EOF-SW and WS-TF-EOF-SW indicate an end-of-file condition on both the old master file and the transaction file. Processing of this paragraph and paragraphs that it controls is to continue until the end-of-file condition is reached on both files. This prevents stopping the processing of data on either file if records still remain on one file and the other file is out of records.

The CLOSE statement is executed after all processing in the program is complete and is a standard handling of CLOSE.

The final statement in the control module is a standard STOP RUN statement.

100-INITIALIZE-TOTALS-ETC,

Figure 3-12 contains the statements that initialize certain fields within the WORK-ING-STORAGE SECTION of the DATA DIVISION.

The first command initializes the end-of-file switches for the old master file and the transaction file to spaces. In the logic of this program an end-of-file switch that

Figure 3–12
Initialization procedures for
example program.

```
**************************
* THIS MODULE INITIALIZES
*  TOTALS, SWITCHES, ETC
**************************
 100-INITIALIZE-TOTALS-ETC.
     MOVE SPACES TO            WS-OMF-EOF-SW
                               WS-TF-EOF-SW
                               WS-PASSED-EDIT-SW.
     MOVE ZEROS TO             WS-TOTALS
                               WS-PAGE-NUMBER.
     MOVE 51 TO WS-LINE-COUNT.
     ACCEPT DATE-IN FROM DATE.
     MOVE LOW-VALUES TO        WS-OLD-MASTER-KEY
                               WS-TRANSACTION-KEY.
     PERFORM 500-READ-MASTER.
     PERFORM 600-READ-TRANSACTION.
```

contains a space indicates that the referenced file is not at the end and a switch that contains the letter "X" means that it is out of data. The WS-PASSED-EDIT-SW is used to indicate whether or not a record from the transaction file has passed the edits that are required by the program. If the switch contains a space, the record has passed the edits. If the switch has an "X" in it, the transaction record has flunked the edit tests.

The MOVE ZEROS statement initializes the total areas used by the program to zeros. Refer to the totals area logic in the WORKING-STORAGE SECTION. Notice that WS-TOTALS is an 01 entry. This one MOVE statement sets all totals subentries to zeros. Also, the MOVE ZEROS statement initializes the page count to zeros so that when you add 1 to the page counter, the first page of the report will be numbered 1.

The MOVE 51 command moves the numeric literal 51 to WS-LINE-COUNT, which is the control field for the number of lines that are printed on each page of the report.

The ACCEPT statement is used to move the system DATE from memory to a field in the WORKING-STORAGE SECTION called DATE-IN. This field is then moved to the heading area of the report to have the date that the report was executed included in the report listing.

The MOVE LOW-VALUES statement moves the lowest character configuration recognizable to the computer into the fields WS-OLD-MASTER-KEY and WS-TRANSACTION-KEY. These two fields are used as sequence control fields for the old master file and the transaction file. Moving LOW-VALUES to these fields helps prevent an inadvertent sequence error when checking sequence on the first record read from each file.

The final two statements in the module, the PERFORM statements, are what are commonly referred to in the programming trade as "pump priming." Most structured programmers include similar logic in their programs to avoid duplication of output of the last record contained in one of the files.

PERFORMing these two read paragraphs causes the program to read a transaction record and an old master record and sets up the areas necessary to perform the compare logic.

200-UPDATE-MASTER-FILE.

Figure 3-13 contains the statements in the 200-UPDATE-MASTER-FILE module.

This module is PERFORMed from the control module. Its purpose is to check to see if both files have reached the end-of-file state. If these files are completed, the IF statement causes a branch to the imputed exit point and the control module

Figure 3–13
End of processing test for
example program.

```
*********************
* THIS MODULE DETERMINES
* IF THE EOF PROCESS IS
* COMPLETE.
***********************
 200-UPDATE-MASTER-FILE.
*
        IF WS-OMF-EOF-SW = "X"
            AND WS-TF-EOF-SW = "X"
                    NEXT SENTENCE
            ELSE
            PERFORM 210-COMPARE-KEYS.
        PERFORM 300-PRINT-AUDIT.
```

takes over and completes the remaining logic in the program. If not, then the module causes the execution of 210-COMPARE-KEYS and 300-PRINT-AUDIT.

210-COMPARE-KEYS.

This module is the critical module in the program as far as the determination of the update process(es) required is concerned. Figure 3-14 contains the commands included in the module.

As you recall from the section on comparison of key values, when comparing the transaction key to the old master key, the meanings of these comparisons are:

- transaction key < old master key = addition
- transaction key > old master key = copy forward
- transaction key = old master key = change or delete

The series of IF statements included in the module determine this and PER-FORM the appropriate paragraphs based on the logic. The 220-ADD-MASTER is PERFORMed if the transaction is to be added to the updated master file. The 230-COPY-MASTER is executed if there is no activity for this old master file record. The 240-DELETE-MASTER is executed if the old master file record is not to be included in the updated master file. Finally, the 250-CHANGE-MASTER is executed if the transaction record contains data that are to be included in the updated master file for an existing old master file record.

220-ADD-MASTER.

The 220-ADD-MASTER module moves the record from the transaction file to the updated master file record area and then writes the record to the updated master file. Figure 3-15 shows the statements included in the module.

The IF statement checks to see if the transaction code included in the transaction record is indeed an add. (an "A" indicates add, "C" indicates changes, "D"

Figure 3–14
Test for type of change to file.

```
*****************************
* THIS MODULE DETERMINES
* ADD, DELETE OR CHANGE
*****************************
 210-COMPARE-KEYS.
*
    IF TF-VENDOR-NUMBER IS LESS THAN OM-VENDOR NUMBER
        PERFORM 220-ADD-MASTER
    ELSE IF TF-VENDOR-NUMBER IS GREATER THAN OM-VENDOR-NUMBER
        PERFORM 230-COPY-MASTER
    ELSE IF TF-CODE IS EQUAL TO "D"
        PERFORM 240-DELETE-MASTER
    ELSE IF TF-CODE = "A"
        PERFORM 260-ADD-ERROR
    ELSE PERFORM 250-CHANGE-MASTER.
```

Figure 3–15
Vendor master file ADD
procedure.

```
*************************
* THIS MODULE ADDS A
* RECORD TO THE NEW
* VENDOR MASTER FILE
*************************
 220-ADD-MASTER.
*
     IF TF-CODE NOT = "A"
          PERFORM 260-ADD-ERROR.
     MOVE "X" TO WS-AUDIT-SW.
     IF WS-PASSED-EDIT-SW = "X"
          ADD 1 TO TOTAL-MASTER-WRITTEN
          MOVE "ADDED" TO WS-ACTION
          MOVE TF-VENDOR-NUMBER TO NV-VENDOR-NUMBER
          MOVE TF-VENDOR-NAME TO NV-VENDOR-NAME
          MOVE TF-VENDOR-ADDRESS1 TO NV-VENDOR-ADDRESS1
          MOVE TF-VENDOR-ADDRESS2 TO NV-VENDOR-ADDRESS2
          MOVE TF-VENDOR-CITY TO NV-VENDOR-CITY
          MOVE TF-VENDOR-STATE TO NV-VENDOR-STATE
          MOVE TF-VENDOR-ZIP TO NV-VENDOR-ZIP
          MOVE TF-VENDOR-BUYS TO NV-VENDOR-BUYS
          MOVE TF-VENDOR-LAST-DATE TO NV-VENDOR-LAST-DATE
          MOVE " " TO WS-PASSED-EDIT-SW
          WRITE NEW-VENDOR-RECORD FROM NV-WORK-RECORD.
```

indicates delete). If the code is not "A" then the 260-ADD-ERROR paragraph is performed.

The WS-AUDIT-SW is used by another module to determine if a transaction record is to be included in the audit/error report. By moving an "X" to the switch we have turned it "on" to indicate a transaction to be processed.

The MOVE statements are moving the data from the transaction record to the updated master files work record area.

The final IF statement in the module tests the edit switch, WS-PASSED-EDIT-SW, to see if the transaction is to be included in the updated master file. If the switch is equal to " " then the transaction has passed the edit and is to be written to the updated master file; if not, the record is excluded.

Note: The authors are well aware of the use of 88's. However, the programming standards of most data processing organizations that we have worked in forbade the use of 88's and we have relegated them, we believe appropriately, to the Rogues' Gallery in Appendix B.

230-COPY-MASTER,

The 230-COPY-MASTER module is a simple module that copies the old master file record for which there is no activity to the updated master file. After the record is written, another record is read from the old master file. Figure 3-16 shows the logic for this module. Notice that WS-AUDIT-SW is not set on because there is no activity to be recorded on the audit report list.

Figure 3–16
Save of unchanged record.

```
******************************
* THIS MODULE COPIES A
* MASTER RECORD FROM THE
* OLD MASTER TO THE NEW MASTER
******************************
 230-COPY-MASTER.
*
     WRITE NEW-VENDOR-RECORD FROM OLD-VENDOR-RECORD.
     PERFORM 500-READ-MASTER.
     ADD 1 TO TOTAL-MASTERS-WRITTEN.
```

240-DELETE-MASTER.

240-DELETE-MASTER causes the noninclusion of a record from the old master file in the updated master file. This is accomplished simply by not writing a record to the updated master file that is on the old master file. The WS-AUDIT-SW is set on to cause the printing of the transaction record on the audit report. The message "DELETED" is moved to the WS-ACTION message to indicate the disposition of the record on the audit report.

After these statements are executed, a record is read from the old master file. From the description of the logic in the previous section of this chapter, it was indicated that the transaction file was also read. Notice that there is not a PERFORM of the paragraph that reads the transaction file in this module. The reason this is not included here is that the printing of the transaction record will be out of step. In other words, if we read the transaction record at this point, we would be printing a copy of the wrong record on the audit report list. Therefore, the read of the transaction record is included in the audit report logic.

Figure 3-17 shows the simple logic in the delete module.

250-CHANGE-MASTER.

The change module exists for the purpose of changing specified fields in the old master file record and then to write that changed record to the updated master file. Figure 3-18 illustrates the logic used in this program to accomplish this task.

The WS-AUDIT-SW is turned on and the message "CHANGED" is moved to the action taken message area of the audit report line.

The IF statements check to see if each of the transaction record fields are not blank: if they are, then that field is moved to the old master record field. After all fields are moved to the old master record then that record is written to the updated master file and another master record is read.

300-PRINT-AUDIT.

After the primary update logic is performed the audit report logic is handled. Figure 3-19 reproduces the program section which implements this logic.

There is only one statement in the 300-PRINT-AUDIT module. It controls whether or not the print process is to take place. The program logic calls for the printing of the transaction records only. If the logic is processing an old master record for which there is not an activity record, then that old master file record is not included in the audit report. Only transaction records are written in the audit report. The WS-AUDIT-SW is used to control this process. If the switch contains an "X" it is turned on and the audit report record is printed. Notice that the paragraph 320-PRINT-LINE contains the PERFORM of the transaction read module. Again, this causes the synchronization of the printing of the audit report line and the reading of the transaction record. Some programmers include the reading of the transaction record in the change, add, and delete logic paragraphs. This is accomplished by moving the transaction record to a hold area and then printing the audit report line from the hold area.

Figure 3–17
Vendor master file DELETE
procedure.

```
*********************
*THIS MODULE DELETES
*THE OLD MASTER RECORD
*********************
 240-DELETE-MASTER.
*
     MOVE "X" TO WS-AUDIT-SW.
     MOVE "DELETED" TO WS-ACTION.
     PERFORM 500-READ-MASTER.
```

Figure 3–18
Vendor master file CHANGE
procedure.

```
**********************
*THIS MODULE CHANGES
*DATA IN THE OLD MASTER
**********************
 250-CHANGE-MASTER.
*
      MOVE "X" TO WS-AUDIT-SW.
      MOVE "CHANGED" TO WS-ACTION.
      IF TF-VENDOR-NAME NOT EQUAL TO SPACES
          MOVE TF-VENDOR-NAME TO OM-VENDOR-NAME.
      IF TF-VENDOR-ADDRESS1 NOT EQUAL TO SPACES
          MOVE TF-VENDOR-ADDRESS1 TO OM-VENDOR-ADDRESS1.
                    .
                    .
                    .
      IF WS-PASSED-EDIT-SW = "X"
          ADD 1 TO TOTAL-MASTERS-WRITTEN
          WRITE NEW-VENDOR-RECORD FROM OM-WORK-RECORD.
      PERFORM 500-READ-MASTER.
```

Figure 3–19
Audit report print module.

```
**********************
* THIS MODULE PRINTS
* THE AUDIT REPORT
**********************
300-PRINT-AUDIT.
          IF WS-AUDIT-SW = "X"
                    PERFORM 301-CONTROL-PRINT.
*
301-CONTROL-PRINT.
          IF WS-LINE-COUNT > 50
                    PERFORM 310-PRINT-HEADINGS.
          PERFORM 320-PRINT-LINE.
*
310-PRINT-HEADINGS.
          MOVE ZEROS TO WS-LINE-COUNT.
          ADD 1 TO WS-PAGE-NUMBER.
          MOVE DATE-IN TO HEAD2-DATE.
          MOVE WS-PAGE-NUMBER TO HEAD2-PAGE-NUMBER.
          WRITE VENDOR-REPORT-LINE FROM HEAD1 AFTER PAGE.
          WRITE VENDOR-REPORT-LINE FROM HEAD2 AFTER 1.
          WRITE VENDOR-REPORT-LINE FROM HEAD3 AFTER 2.
          WRITE VENDOR-REPORT-LINE FROM HEAD4 AFTER 1.
*
320-PRINT-LINE.
          MOVE TF-VENDOR-NUMBER TO DL-VENDOR-NUMBER.
          MOVE TF-VENDOR-NAME TO DL-VENDOR-NAME.
          MOVE TF-VENDOR-ADDRESS1 TO DL-VENDOR-ADDRESS.
          MOVE TF-VENDOR-BUYS TO DL-VENDOR-BUYS.
          MOVE TF-VENDOR-LAST-DATE TO DL-VENDOR-LAST-DATE.
          MOVE WS-ACTION TO DL-ACTION.
          MOVE WS-ERROR-MESSAGE TO DL-ERROR-MESSAGE.
          WRITE VENDOR-REPORT-LINE FROM DL-VENDOR-LINE AFTER 2.
          MOVE SPACES TO DL-VENDOR-LINE.
          MOVE TF-VENDOR-ADDRESS2 TO DL-VENDOR-ADDRESS.
          WRITE VENDOR-REPORT-LINE FROM DL-VENDOR-LINE AFTER 1.
          MOVE TF-VENDOR-CITY TO DL-VENDOR-ADDRESS.
          WRITE VENDOR-REPORT-LINE FROM DL-VENDOR-LINE AFTER 1.
          ADD 4 TO WS-LINE-COUNT.
          PERFORM 330-ACCUMULATE-TOTALS.
          MOVE " " TO WS-AUDIT-SW.
          MOVE SPACES TO WS-ACTION
                        WS-PASSED-EDIT-SW
                        WS-ERROR-MESSAGE.
          PERFORM 600-READ-TRANSACTION.
```

Figure 3–19 (continued)

```
*
330-ACCUMULATE-TOTALS.
*
        IF TF-CODE = "A"
                PERFORM 331-ACCUMULATE-ADDS.
        IF TF-CODE = "C"
                PERFORM 332-ACCUMULATE-CHANGES.
        IF TF-CODE = "D"
                PERFORM 333-ACCUMULATE-DELETES.
*
331-ACCUMULATE-ADDS.
        ADD 1 TO WS-TOTAL-ADDS.
        IF WS-PASSED-EDIT-SW = "X"
                ADD 1 TO WS-ADDS-REJECTED
        ELSE
                ADD 1 TO WS-ADDS-PROCESSED.
*
332-ACCUMULATE-CHANGES.
        ADD 1 TO WS-TOTAL-CHANGES.
        IF WS-PASSED-EDIT-SW = "X"
                ADD 1 TO WS-CHANGES-REJECTED
        ELSE
                ADD 1 TO WS-CHANGES-PROCESSED.
*
333-ACCUMULATE-DELETES.
        ADD 1 TO WS-TOTAL-DELETES.
        IF WS-PASSED-EDIT-SW = "X"
                ADD 1 TO WS-DELETES-REJECTED
        ELSE
                ADD 1 TO WS-DELETES-PROCESSED.
```

Also included in the module is the logic to accumulate the totals for the audit report. This can be seen in paragraphs 330-ACCUMULATE-TOTALS through 333-ACCUMULATE-DELETES.

400-PRINT-AUDIT-TOTALS.

The primary level in the structure chart shows that the 400-PRINT-AUDIT-TOTALS is one of the last series of instructions to be executed in the program. Indeed, the logic in this module is executed only after the update of the files is accomplished. Figure 3-20 depicts the logic used to cause the printing of the audit totals portion of the audit/error report.

The first instruction, PERFORM-310-PRINT-HEADINGS, causes the report to skip to a new page and print heading lines. The next PERFORM instruction causes line description entries and totals to be moved from the WORKING-STORAGE SECTION and printed on the audit report. This is accomplished with the use of the PERFORM VARYING statement.

Figure 3–20
Totals print procedure.

```
**************************
*THIS MODULE PRINTS
*TOTALS ACCUMULATED
*DURING THE UPDATE
**************************
 400-PRINT-AUDIT-TOTALS.
*
        PERFORM 310-PRINT-HEADINGS.
        PERFORM 410-PRINT-AUDIT-LINE
            VARYING I FROM 1 BY 1
            UNTIL I IS GREATER THAN 12.
*
 410-PRINT-AUDIT-LINE.
        MOVE WS-AUDIT-MESSAGE (I) TO AL-MESSAGE.
        MOVE WS-TOTAL-VALUES (I) TO AL-AMOUNT.
        WRITE VENDOR-REPORT-LINE FROM AUDIT-LINE AFTER 1.
```

```
500-READ-MASTER.
```

The program includes only one read statement for the old master file and it is included in this module. It is:

```
READ OLD-VENDOR-MASTER-FILE INTO OM-WORK-RECORD
     AT END MOVE "X" TO WS-OMF-EOF-SW
            MOVE HIGH-VALUES TO WS-MASTER-KEY.
```

The READ statement reads a record from the old master file and moves it to the work area, OM-WORK-RECORD, in the WORKING-STORAGE SECTION of the program.

If an end of file is encountered, the end-of-file switch, WS-OMF-EOF-SW, is turned on by moving an "X" to the switch. Also, HIGH-VALUES is moved to the WS-OLD-MASTER-KEY to cause records that might remain on the transaction file to be added to the updated master file.

The statement

```
IF OM-VENDOR-NUMBER IS NOT > WS-OLD-MASTER-KEY
     PERFORM 510-ABORT-RUN.
```

checks the vendor number of the current record against the vendor number of the previous record. If the vendor number of the current record is not greater than the vendor number of the previous record, the run is aborted. Figure 3-21 illustrates the logic used in this program to accomplish this task.

In the 510-ABORT RUN paragraph the message that the master file is out of sequence is displayed on the user's terminal or on the operator's console together with the values of the keys for the current master record and the previous master record. After the messages are displayed, the files are closed and the process is terminated.

Figure 3–21
READ procedure (old master file).

```
***************************
*THIS MODULE READS THE
* OLD VENDOR MASTER FILE
***************************
 500-READ-MASTER.
*
     READ OLD-VENDOR-MASTER-FILE INTO OM-WORK-RECORD
          AT END MOVE "X" TO WS-OMF-EOF-SW
                 MOVE HIGH-VALUES TO OM-VENDOR-NUMBER.
     ADD 1 TO WS-MASTERS-READ.
     IF OM-VENDOR-NUMBER NOT > WS-OLD-MASTER-KEY
          PERFORM 510-ABORT-RUN.
     MOVE OM-VENDOR-NUMBER TO WS-OLD-MASTER-KEY.
*
 510-ABORT-RUN.
*
     DISPLAY "VENDOR MASTER FILE OUT OF SEQUENCE".
     DISPLAY "PREVIOUS KEY = " WS-OLD-MASTER-KEY.
     DISPLAY "CURRENT KEY = " OM-VENDOR-NUMBER.
     PERFORM 900-END-ROUTINE.
               o
               o
               o
*
 900-END-ROUTINE.
*
     CLOSE     OLD-VENDOR-MASTER-FILE
               VENDOR-TRANSACTION-FILE
               NEW-VENDOR-MASTER-FILE
               VENDOR-AUDIT-ERROR-LIST.
     STOP RUN.
```

Figure 3–22
READ procedure (transactions file).

```
************************
* THIS MODULE READS
* TRANSACTION FILE
************************
 600-READ-TRANSACTION.
*
     READ VENDOR-TRANSACTION-FILE INTO TF-WORK-RECORD
          AT END MOVE "X" TO WS-TF-EOF-SW
               MOVE HIGH-VALUES TO TF-VENDOR-NUMBER.
     IF TF-VENDOR-NUMBER IS NOT GREATER THAN WS-TRANSACTION-KEY
               PERFORM 610-ABORT-RUN.
     MOVE TF-VENDOR-NUMBER TO WS-TRANSACTION-KEY.
     ADD 1 TO WS-TRANSACTIONS-READ.
     PERFORM 620-EDIT-TRANSACTION.
*
 610-ABORT-RUN.
*
     DISPLAY "TRANSACTION FILE OUT OF SEQUENCE"
     DISPLAY "PREVIOUS KEY = " WS-TRANSACTION-KEY.
     DISPLAY "CURRENT KEY = " TF-VENDOR-NUMBER.
     PERFORM 900-END-ROUTINE.
```

600-READ-TRANSACTION.

Figure 3-22 shows the logic involved in the reading of records from the vendor transaction file. These statements are very similar to those included in the 500-READ-MASTER module.

The READ statement causes a transaction record to be moved to the TF-WORK-RECORD area in WORKING-STORAGE. The AT END clause of the READ statement causes an "X" to be moved to the WS-TF-EOF-SW when an end-of-file condition is detected. Also, HIGH-VALUES are moved to TF-VENDOR-NUMBER to cause any remaining records on the old master file to be written to the updated master file.

Notice that the statement

```
IF TF-VENDOR-NUMBER NOT > WS-TRANSACTION-KEY
     PERFORM 610-ABORT-RUN.
```

precludes the possibility of having multiple transactions, which is one of the basic assumptions of this example program.

Sequence is checked in the same fashion as in 500-READ-MASTER.

The PERFORM 620-EDIT-TRANSACTION command causes the edit of the transactions, to see whether they are valid. In this program this module is null.

SECTION 11
An Examination of Inputs, Processes, and Outputs

Contrasting of the inputs to and the outputs from the above listed program with the results of processing is probably helpful at this point. Figure 3-23 shows the contents of the input files and the contents of the output files for the example program.

The records in the input file with the following vendor numbers:

000115

000126

004099

005984

006666

007777

007779

008478

have no activity on the transaction file and are copied forward to the updated master file. Notice that these records are included in the updated master file exactly as they appear in the old master file.

There were two records on the transaction file which contained information to change fields in the old master file. These records are for vendor numbers 000188 and 004075. Notice that the fields in the old master file have been changed to incorporate the information in the transaction file as we intended.

There was one record to be deleted from the old master file—the record for vendor number 005763. Notice that this record is not contained in NEW-VENDOR-MASTER-FILE, the updated master file, just as we intended.

Vendor number 007778 was to be added to the updated master file and placed between records 007777 and 007779. Notice that the updated master file contains this record in the appropriate position.

Figure 3-24 is the listing of the transactions from the transaction file and an indication of the disposition of each of the records. Other audit information is also included in the report.

```
OLD-VENDOR-MASTER-FILE
000115ABC MFG. CO.                          123 EL ST.                          MONROE      LA712900000000-(
000126CADDY SHACK                           147 OAK LANE      P. O. BOX 148      RUSTON      LA712700000000-(
000188RUSTON OFFICE SUPPLY CO.              210 SOUTH TRENTON                   RUSTON      LA712700000000-(
004075SPIVEY'S FRIED CHICKEN                                                   GRAMBLING   LA712450000000-(
004099ELECTRONIC SPECIALTY PRODUCTS 615R S MONROE                              RUSTON      LA712700000000-(
005763EVANS BARBER SUPPLY                   1305 E LINE AVE.                    RUSTON      LA712700000000-(
005984MID-STATE WOOD PRESERVERS INC HWY 80                                     GRAMBLING   LA712450000000-(
006666LINCOLN STORAGE SYSTEMS INC.   HWY 150 W                                 GRAMBLING   LA712450000000-(
007777KELLY'S CLEANERS                      MAIN STREET                         GRAMBLING   LA712450000000-(
007779GRAY'S INSURANCE                      MAIN STREET                         GRAMBLING   LA712450000000-(
008478DON DURRETT CONSTRUCTION CO.    HWY 563                                   GRAMBLING   LA712450000000-(


TRANSACTION-FILE
000188                                                                                      0009500-(061483C
004075                             SOUTH HWY 149                                            00000 0-(00000 C
005763                                                                                      00000 0-(00000 D
007778COLLEGIATE SHOPPE           MAIN STREET                           GRAMBLING   LA712450000000-(000000A
```

Figure 3–23 (page 1)
Inputs to the sample program.

```
CHAPTER III
OUTPUT FROM THE SAMPLE PROGRAM
NEW-VENDOR-MASTER-FILE
000115ABC MFG. CO.                          123 EL ST.                          MONROE      LA712900000000-(
000126CADDY SHACK                           147 OAK LANE      P. O. BOX 148      RUSTON      LA712700000000-(
000188RUSTON OFFICE SUPPLY CO.              210 SOUTH TRENTON                   RUSTON      LA712700009500-(061483
004075SPIVEY'S FRIED CHICKEN                SOUTH HWY 149                       GRAMBLING   LA712450000 0-(00000
004099ELECTRONIC SPECIALTY PRODUCTS 615R S MONROE                              RUSTON      LA712700000000-(
005984MID-STATE WOOD PRESERVERS INC HWY 80                                     GRAMBLING   LA712450000000-(
006666LINCOLN STORAGE SYSTEMS INC.   HWY 150 W                                 GRAMBLING   LA712450000000-(
007777KELLY'S CLEANERS                      MAIN STREET                         GRAMBLING   LA712450000000-(
007778COLLEGIATE SHOPPE                     MAIN STREET                         GRAMBLING   LA712450000000-(000000
007779GRAY'S INSURANCE                      MAIN STREET                         GRAMBLING   LA712450000000-(
008478DON DURRETT CONSTRUCTION CO.    HWY 563                                   GRAMBLING   LA712450000000-(
```

Figure 3–23 (page 2)
New vendor master file.

Figure 3–23 (page 3)
Audit/error report.

DATE: 83/06/15

VENDOR MASTER FILE MAINTENANCE
AUDIT-ERROR REPORT

VENDOR NUMBER	VENDOR NAME	VENDOR ADDRESS
000188		
004075		SOUTH HWY 149
005763		
007778	COLLEGIATE SHOPPE	MAIN STREET
		GRAMBLING

VENDOR MASTER FILE MAINTENANCE
AUDIT-ERROR REPORT

DATE: 83/06/15

VENDOR NUMBER	VENDOR NAME	VENDOR ADDRESS
TRANSACTIONS READ	5	
TOTAL ADDS	1	
PROCESSED	0	
REJECTED	0	
TOTAL DELETES	1	
PROCESSED	1	
REJECTED	0	
TOTAL CHANGES	2	
PROCESSED	2	
REJECTED	0	
MASTERS READ	12	
MASTERS WRITTEN	0	

PAGE: 1

AMOUNT OF PURCHASES	DATE OF LAST PURCHASE	ACTION TAKEN	ERROR MESSAGE
950.00	061483	CHANGED	
.00	00000	CHANGED	
.00	00000	DELETED	
.00	000000	ADDED	

PAGE: 2

AMOUNT OF PURCHASES	DATE OF LAST PURCHASE	ACTION TAKEN	ERROR MESSAGE

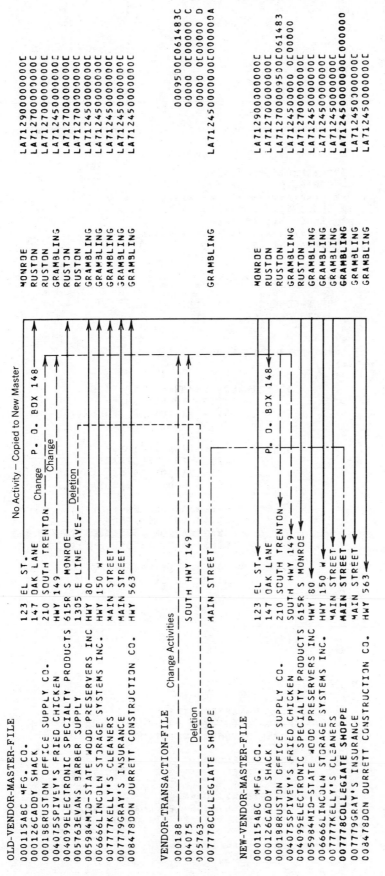

Figure 3-24
Disposition of file update activities.

SECTION 12
Sample Program for Sequential File Processing

A complete copy of the sequential file processing program is presented as Figure 3-25.

Figure 3–25
Sample program—sequential update of a master file.

```
IDENTIFICATION DIVISION.
PROGRAM-ID. VENDMAIN.
******************************
* SEQUENTIAL UPDATE OF A
* VENDOR MASTER FILE
******************************
ENVIRONMENT DIVISION.
*
*
CONFIGURATION SECTION.
*
SOURCE-COMPUTER. VAX-11.
OBJECT-COMPUTER. VAX-11.
*
*
INPUT-OUTPUT SECTION.
*
FILE-CONTROL.
        SELECT OLD-VENDOR-MASTER-FILE
                ASSIGN TO "VENDMX"
                ORGANIZATION IS SEQUENTIAL
                ACCESS MODE IS SEQUENTIAL.
*
        SELECT VENDOR-TRANSACTION-FILE
                ASSIGN TO "VENDTRAN"
                ORGANIZATION IS SEQUENTIAL
                ACCESS MODE IS SEQUENTIAL.
*
        SELECT NEW-VENDOR-MASTER-FILE
                ASSIGN TO "NEWVEND"
                ORGANIZATION IS SEQUENTIAL
                ACCESS MODE IS SEQUENTIAL.
*
        SELECT VENDOR-AUDIT-ERROR-LIST
                ASSIGN TO "VENDLI.LST".
/
*
*
*
DATA DIVISION.
**
*
FILE SECTION.
*
*
FD  OLD-VENDOR-MASTER-FILE
        RECORD CONTAINS 127 CHARACTERS
        LABEL RECORDS ARE STANDARD.
*
01  OLD-VENDOR-RECORD.
        05  FILLER            PIC X(127).
*
FD  VENDOR-TRANSACTION-FILE
        RECORD CONTAINS 128 CHARACTERS
        LABEL RECORDS ARE STANDARD.
*
01  VENDOR-TRANSACTION-RECORD.
        05  FILLER            PIC X(128).
*
*
```

Figure 3-25 (continued)

```
                      FD  NEW-VENDOR-MASTER-FILE
                            RECORD CONTAINS 127 CHARACTERS
                            LABEL RECORDS ARE STANDARD.
                      *
                      01  NEW-VENDOR-RECORD.
                            05  FILLER                PIC X(127).
                      *
                      *
                      FD  VENDOR-AUDIT-ERROR-LIST
                            RECORD CONTAINS 132 CHARACTERS
                            LABEL RECORDS ARE OMITTED.
                      *
                      01  VENDOR-REPORT-LINE.
                            05  FILLER                PIC X(132).
                      *
                      *
                      WORKING-STORAGE SECTION.
                      ********************************
                      * RECORD WORK AREAS
                      ********************************
                      01  OM-WORK-RECORD.
                            05  OM-VENDOR-NUMBER      PIC X(06).
                            05  OM-VENDOR-NAME        PIC X(30).
                            05  OM-VENDOR-ADDRESS1    PIC X(25).
                            05  OM-VENDOR-ADDRESS2    PIC X(25).
                            05  OM-VENDOR-CITY        PIC X(20).
                            05  OM-VENDOR-STATE       PIC X(02).
                            05  OM-VENDOR-ZIP         PIC X(05).
                            05  OM-VENDOR-BUYS        PIC S9(6)V99.
                            05  OM-VENDOR-LAST-DATE   PIC 9(6).
                      *
                      01  TF-WORK-RECORD.
                            05  TF-VENDOR-NUMBER      PIC X(06).
                            05  TF-VENDOR-NAME        PIC X(30).
                            05  TF-VENDOR-ADDRESS1    PIC X(25).
                            05  TF-VENDOR-ADDRESS2    PIC X(25).
                            05  TF-VENDOR-CITY        PIC X(20).
                            05  TF-VENDOR-STATE       PIC X(02).
                            05  TF-VENDOR-ZIP         PIC X(05).
                            05  TF-VENDOR-BUYS        PIC S9(6)V99.
                            05  TF-VENDOR-MONEY REDEFINES TF-VENDOR-BUYS PIC X(8).
                            05  TF-VENDOR-LAST-DATE.
                                10   TF-MONTH         PIC 9(02).
                                10   TF-DAY           PIC 9(02).
                                10   TF-YEAR          PIC 9(02).
                            05  TF-CODE               PIC X(01).
                      *
                      01  NV-WORK-RECORD.
                            05  NV-VENDOR-NUMBER      PIC X(06).
                            05  NV-VENDOR-NAME        PIC X(30).
                            05  NV-VENDOR-ADDRESS1    PIC X(25).
                            05  NV-VENDOR-ADDRESS2    PIC X(25).
                            05  NV-VENDOR-CITY        PIC X(20).
                            05  NV-VENDOR-STATE       PIC X(02).
                            05  NV-VENDOR-ZIP         PIC X(05).
                            05  NV-VENDOR-BUYS        PIC S9(6)V99.
                            05  NV-VENDOR-LAST-DATE   PIC 9(06).
                      *
                      01  DL-VENDOR-LINE.
                            05  FILLER                PIC X(02) VALUE SPACES.
                            05  DL-VENDOR-NUMBER      PIC X(06).
                            05  FILLER                PIC X(05) VALUE SPACES.
                            05  DL-VENDOR-NAME        PIC X(30).
                            05  FILLER                PIC X(05) VALUE SPACES.
                            05  DL-VENDOR-ADDRESS     PIC X(25).
                            05  FILLER                PIC X(06) VALUE SPACES.
                            05  DL-VENDOR-BUYS        PIC ZZZ,ZZZ.99CR.
                            05  FILLER                PIC X(04).
                            05  DL-VENDOR-LAST-DATE   PIC 99/99/99.
                            05  FILLER                PIC X(06).
```

```
          05   DL-ACTION                    PIC X(07).
          05   FILLER                       PIC X(03) VALUE SPACES.
          05   DL-ERROR-MESSAGE             PIC X(12).
     ********************************
     *   HEADING LINES
     ********************************
     01   HEAD1.
          05   FILLER     PIC X(39) VALUE SPACES.
          05   FILLER     PIC X(20) VALUE "VENDOR MASTER FILE M".
          05   FILLER     PIC X(10) VALUE "AINTENANCE".
     *
     01   HEAD2.
          05   FILLER     PIC X(07) VALUE " DATE: ".
          05   HEAD2-DATE PIC 99/99/99.
          05   FILLER     PIC X(30) VALUE SPACES.
          05   FILLER     PIC X(18) VALUE "AUDIT-ERROR REPORT".
          05   FILLER     PIC X(25) VALUE SPACES.
          05   FILLER     PIC X(07) VALUE "PAGE: ".
          05   HEAD2-PAGE-NUMBER   PIC ZZ9.
     *
     01   HEAD3.
          05   FILLER     PIC X(20) VALUE " VENDOR             ".
          05   FILLER     PIC X(20) VALUE " VENDOR             ".
          05   FILLER     PIC X(20) VALUE "         VENDOR     ".
          05   FILLER     PIC X(20) VALUE "                    ".
          05   FILLER     PIC X(20) VALUE "AMOUNT OF      DATE ".
          05   FILLER     PIC X(20) VALUE "OF         ACTION  E".
          05   FILLER     PIC X(04) VALUE "RROR".
     *
     01   HEAD4.
          05   FILLER     PIC X(20) VALUE " NUMBER             ".
          05   FILLER     PIC X(20) VALUE " NAME               ".
          05   FILLER     PIC X(20) VALUE "         ADDRESS    ".
          05   FILLER     PIC X(20) VALUE "                    ".
          05   FILLER     PIC X(20) VALUE "PURCHASES      LAST P".
          05   FILLER     PIC X(20) VALUE "URCHASE    TAKEN   ME".
          05   FILLER     PIC X(05) VALUE "SSAGE".
     *
     01   AUDIT-LINE.
          05   FILLER                    PIC X(01) VALUE SPACES.
          05   AL-MESSAGE                PIC X(19).
          05   FILLER                    PIC X(02) VALUE SPACES.
          05   AL-AMOUNT                 PIC ZZ,ZZ9.
     *
     01   WS-TOTAL-DESCRIPTIONS.
          05   FILLER             PIC X(18) VALUE " TRANSACTIONS READ".
          05   FILLER             PIC X(18) VALUE " TOTAL ADDS       ".
          05   FILLER             PIC X(18) VALUE "     PROCESSED    ".
          05   FILLER             PIC X(18) VALUE "     REJECTED     ".
          05   FILLER             PIC X(18) VALUE " TOTAL DELETES    ".
          05   FILLER             PIC X(18) VALUE "     PROCESSED    ".
          05   FILLER             PIC X(18) VALUE "     REJECTED     ".
          05   FILLER             PIC X(18) VALUE " TOTAL CHANGES    ".
          05   FILLER             PIC X(18) VALUE "     PROCESSED    ".
          05   FILLER             PIC X(18) VALUE "     REJECTED     ".
          05   FILLER             PIC X(18) VALUE " MASTERS READ     ".
          05   FILLER             PIC X(18) VALUE " MASTERS WRITTEN  ".
     01   WS-AUDIT-DESCRIPTIONS REDEFINES WS-TOTAL-DESCRIPTIONS.
          05   WS-AUDIT-MESSAGE OCCURS 12 TIMES PIC X(18).
     ********************************
     *   TOTALS
     *        AREA
     ********************************
     01   WS-TOTALS.
          05   WS-TRANSACTIONS-READ         PIC 9(05).
          05   WS-TOTAL-ADDS                PIC 9(05).
```

Figure 3-25 (continued)

Figure 3–25 (continued)

```
                       05   WS-ADDS-PROCESSED              PIC 9(05).
                       05   WS-ADDS-REJECTED               PIC 9(05).
                       05   WS-TOTAL-DELETES               PIC 9(05).
                       05   WS-DELETES-PROCESSED           PIC 9(05).
                       05   WS-DELETES-REJECTED            PIC 9(05).
                       05   WS-TOTAL-CHANGES               PIC 9(05).
                       05   WS-CHANGES-PROCESSED           PIC 9(05).
                       05   WS-CHANGES-REJECTED            PIC 9(05).
                       05   WS-MASTERS-READ                PIC 9(05).
                       05   WS-MASTERS-WRITTEN             PIC 9(05).
               01   WS-RECORD-COUNTS REDEFINES WS-TOTALS.
                       05   WS-TOTAL-VALUES OCCURS 12 TIMES PIC 9(05).
               *
               01   WS-LINE-COUNT                          PIC 9(02) VALUE 51.
               01   WS-PAGE-NUMBER                         PIC 9(03) VALUE ZEROS.
               ************************
               *   GENERAL
               *        EDIT
               *             REQUIREMENTS
               ************************

               ************************
               *
               *    SWITCHES
               ************************
               01   WS-OMF-EOF-SW                          PIC X VALUE " ".
               01   WS-TF-EOF-SW                           PIC X VALUE " ".
               01   WS-PASSED-EDIT-SW                      PIC X VALUE " ".
               01   WS-AUDIT-SW                            PIC X VALUE " ".
               ************************
               *   GENERAL WORKING-STORAGE
               *      VALUES
               ************************
               01   DATE-IN                                PIC 9(06).
               01   WS-ACTION                              PIC X(07).
               01   WS-ERROR-MESSAGE                       PIC X(12).
               01   I                                      PIC 9(02).
               ************************
               *  SEQUENCE CONTROL FIELDS
               ************************
               01   WS-OLD-MASTER-KEY                      PIC X(06).
               01   WS-TRANSACTION-KEY                     PIC X(06).
               ************************
               *
               *    PROCEDURE DIVISION
               *       BEGINS HERE
               ************************
               PROCEDURE DIVISION.
               *
               *
               000-VM-CONTROL-MODULE.
               *
                       OPEN INPUT OLD-VENDOR-MASTER-FILE
                                  VENDOR-TRANSACTION-FILE
                            OUTPUT  NEW-VENDOR-MASTER-FILE
                                    VENDOR-AUDIT-ERROR-LIST.
                       PERFORM 100-INITIALIZE-TOTALS-ETC.
                       PERFORM 200-UPDATE-MASTER-FILE
                               UNTIL WS-OMF-EOF-SW = "X"
                               AND   WS-TF-EOF-SW = "X".
                       PERFORM 400-PRINT-AUDIT-TOTALS.
                       CLOSE  OLD-VENDOR-MASTER-FILE
                              VENDOR-TRANSACTION-FILE
                              NEW-VENDOR-MASTER-FILE
                              VENDOR-AUDIT-ERROR-LIST.
                       STOP RUN.
```

Figure 3–25 (continued)
```
*************************
* THIS MODULE INITIALIZES
*    TOTALS, SWITCHES, ETC
*************************
100-INITIALIZE-TOTALS-ETC.
        MOVE SPACES TO WS-OMF-EOF-SW
                       WS-TF-EOF-SW
                       WS-PASSED-EDIT-SW.
        MOVE ZEROS TO   WS-TOTALS
                        WS-PAGE-NUMBER.
        MOVE 51 TO WS-LINE-COUNT.
        ACCEPT DATE-IN FROM DATE.
        MOVE LOW-VALUES TO     WS-OLD-MASTER-KEY
                              WS-TRANSACTION-KEY.

        PERFORM 500-READ-MASTER.
        PERFORM 600-READ-TRANSACTION.
*************************
* THIS MODULE DETERMINES
* IF THE EOF PROCESS IS
* COMPLETE.
*************************
200-UPDATE-MASTER-FILE.
*
        IF WS-OMF-EOF-SW = "X"
                AND WS-TF-EOF-SW = "X"
                          NEXT SENTENCE
                ELSE
                PERFORM 210-COMPARE-KEYS.
                PERFORM 300-PRINT-AUDIT.
*************************
* THIS MODULE DETERMINES
* ADD, DELETE OR CHANGE
*************************
210-COMPARE-KEYS.
*
        IF TF-VENDOR-NUMBER IS LESS THAN OM-VENDOR-NUMBER
                PERFORM 220-ADD-MASTER
        ELSE IF TF-VENDOR-NUMBER IS GREATER THAN OM-VENDOR-NUMBER
                PERFORM 230-COPY-MASTER
        ELSE IF TF-CODE IS EQUAL TO "D"
                PERFORM 240-DELETE-MASTER
        ELSE PERFORM 250-CHANGE-MASTER.
*************************
* THIS MODULE ADDS A
* RECORD TO THE NEW
* VENDOR MASTER FILE
*************************
220-ADD-MASTER.
        IF TF-CODE NOT = "A"
                PERFORM 260-ADD-ERROR.
        MOVE  "X" TO WS-AUDIT-SW.
        MOVE "ADDED" TO WS-ACTION.
        MOVE TF-VENDOR-NUMBER TO NV-VENDOR-NUMBER.
        MOVE TF-VENDOR-NAME TO NV-VENDOR-NAME.
        MOVE TF-VENDOR-ADDRESS1 TO NV-VENDOR-ADDRESS1.
        MOVE TF-VENDOR-ADDRESS2 TO NV-VENDOR-ADDRESS2.
        MOVE TF-VENDOR-CITY TO NV-VENDOR-CITY.
        MOVE TF-VENDOR-STATE TO NV-VENDOR-STATE.
        MOVE TF-VENDOR-ZIP TO NV-VENDOR-ZIP.
        MOVE TF-VENDOR-BUYS TO NV-VENDOR-BUYS.
        MOVE TF-VENDOR-LAST-DATE TO NV-VENDOR-LAST-DATE.
        IF WS-PASSED-EDIT-SW = " "
                WRITE NEW-VENDOR-RECORD FROM NV-WORK-RECORD.
*************************
* THIS MODULE COPIES A
* MASTER RECORD FROM THE\
```

Figure 3–25 (continued)
```
* OLD MASTER TO NEW MASTER
**********************
230-COPY-MASTER.
*
        WRITE NEW-VENDOR-RECORD FROM OLD-VENDOR-RECORD.
        PERFORM 500-READ-MASTER.
*********************
* THIS MODULE DELETES
* THE OLD MASTER RECORD
*********************
240-DELETE-MASTER.
        MOVE "X" TO WS-AUDIT-SW.
        MOVE "DELETED" TO WS-ACTION.
        PERFORM 500-READ-MASTER.
************************
* THIS MODULE CHANGES
* DATA IN THE OLD MASTER
************************
250-CHANGE-MASTER.
*
        MOVE "X" TO WS-AUDIT-SW.
        MOVE "CHANGED" TO WS-ACTION.
        IF TF-VENDOR-NAME NOT EQUAL SPACES
                MOVE TF-VENDOR-NAME TO OM-VENDOR-NAME.
        IF TF-VENDOR-ADDRESS1 NOT EQUAL SPACES
                MOVE TF-VENDOR-ADDRESS1 TO OM-VENDOR-ADDRESS1.
        IF TF-VENDOR-ADDRESS2 NOT EQUAL SPACES
                MOVE TF-VENDOR-ADDRESS2 TO OM-VENDOR-ADDRESS2.
        IF TF-VENDOR-CITY NOT EQUAL SPACES
                MOVE TF-VENDOR-CITY TO OM-VENDOR-CITY.
        IF TF-VENDOR-STATE NOT EQUAL SPACES
                MOVE TF-VENDOR-STATE TO OM-VENDOR-STATE.
        IF TF-VENDOR-ZIP NOT EQUAL SPACES
                MOVE TF-VENDOR-ZIP TO OM-VENDOR-ZIP.
        IF TF-VENDOR-MONEY NOT EQUAL TO SPACES
                MOVE TF-VENDOR-BUYS TO OM-VENDOR-BUYS.
        IF TF-VENDOR-LAST-DATE NOT EQUAL SPACES
                MOVE TF-VENDOR-LAST-DATE TO OM-VENDOR-LAST-DATE.
        IF WS-PASSED-EDIT-SW = " "
                WRITE NEW-VENDOR-RECORD FROM OM-WORK-RECORD.
        PERFORM 500-READ-MASTER.
*
260-ADD-ERROR.
        MOVE "X" TO WS-PASSED-EDIT-SW.
        MOVE "CODE ERROR" TO WS-ERROR-MESSAGE.
*********************
* THIS MODULE PRINTS
* THE AUDIT REPORT
*********************
300-PRINT-AUDIT.
        IF WS-AUDIT-SW = "X"
                PERFORM 301-CONTROL-PRINT.
*
301-CONTROL-PRINT.
        IF WS-LINE-COUNT > 50
                PERFORM 310-PRINT-HEADINGS.
        PERFORM 320-PRINT-LINE.
*
310-PRINT-HEADINGS.
        MOVE ZEROS TO WS-LINE-COUNT.
        ADD 1 TO WS-PAGE-NUMBER.
        MOVE DATE-IN TO HEAD2-DATE.
        MOVE WS-PAGE-NUMBER TO HEAD2-PAGE-NUMBER.
        WRITE VENDOR-REPORT-LINE FROM HEAD1 AFTER PAGE.
        WRITE VENDOR-REPORT-LINE FROM HEAD2 AFTER 1.
        WRITE VENDOR-REPORT-LINE FROM HEAD3 AFTER 2.
```

Figure 3–25 (continued)

```
                            WRITE VENDOR-REPORT-LINE FROM HEAD4 AFTER 1.
             *
             320-PRINT-LINE.
                     MOVE TF-VENDOR-NUMBER TO DL-VENDOR-NUMBER.
                     MOVE TF-VENDOR-NAME TO DL-VENDOR-NAME.
                     MOVE TF-VENDOR-ADDRESS1 TO DL-VENDOR-ADDRESS.
                     MOVE TF-VENDOR-BUYS TO DL-VENDOR-BUYS.
                     MOVE TF-VENDOR-LAST-DATE TO DL-VENDOR-LAST-DATE.
                     MOVE WS-ACTION TO DL-ACTION.
                     MOVE WS-ERROR-MESSAGE TO DL-ERROR-MESSAGE.
                     WRITE VENDOR-REPORT-LINE FROM DL-VENDOR-LINE AFTER 2.
                     MOVE SPACES TO DL-VENDOR-LINE.
                     MOVE TF-VENDOR-ADDRESS2 TO DL-VENDOR-ADDRESS.
                     WRITE VENDOR-REPORT-LINE FROM DL-VENDOR-LINE AFTER 1.
                     MOVE TF-VENDOR-CITY TO DL-VENDOR-ADDRESS.
                     WRITE VENDOR-REPORT-LINE FROM DL-VENDOR-LINE AFTER 1.
                     ADD 4 TO WS-LINE-COUNT.
                     PERFORM 330-ACCUMULATE-TOTALS.
                     MOVE " " TO WS-AUDIT-SW.
                     MOVE SPACES TO WS-ACTION
                                    WS-PASSED-EDIT-SW
                                    WS-ERROR-MESSAGE.
                     PERFORM 600-READ-TRANSACTION.
             *
             330-ACCUMULATE-TOTALS.
             *
                     IF TF-CODE = "A"
                             PERFORM 331-ACCUMULATE-ADDS.
                     IF TF-CODE = "C"
                             PERFORM 332-ACCUMULATE-CHANGES.
                     IF TF-CODE = "D"
                             PERFORM 333-ACCUMULATE-DELETES.
             *
             331-ACCUMULATE-ADDS.
                     ADD 1 TO WS-TOTAL-ADDS.
                     IF WS-PASSED-EDIT-SW = "X"
                             ADD 1 TO WS-ADDS-REJECTED
                     ELSE
                             ADD 1 TO WS-ADDS-PROCESSED.
             *
             332-ACCUMULATE-CHANGES.
                     ADD 1 TO WS-TOTAL-CHANGES.
                     IF WS-PASSED-EDIT-SW = "X"
                             ADD 1 TO WS-CHANGES-REJECTED
                     ELSE
                             ADD 1 TO WS-CHANGES-PROCESSED.
             *
             333-ACCUMULATE-DELETES.
                     ADD 1 TO WS-TOTAL-DELETES.
                     IF WS-PASSED-EDIT-SW = "X"
                             ADD 1 TO WS-DELETES-REJECTED
                     ELSE
                             ADD 1 TO WS-DELETES-PROCESSED.
             ************************
             * THIS MODULE PRINTS
             * TOTALS ACCUMULATED
             * DURING THE UPDATE
             ************************
             400-PRINT-AUDIT-TOTALS.
             *
                     PERFORM 310-PRINT-HEADINGS.
                     PERFORM 410-PRINT-AUDIT-LINE
                             VARYING I FROM 1 BY 1
                             UNTIL I IS GREATER THAN 12.
             *
             410-PRINT-AUDIT-LINE.
```

Figure 3–25 (continued)

```
                     MOVE WS-AUDIT-MESSAGE (I) TO AL-MESSAGE.
                     MOVE WS-TOTAL-VALUES (I) TO AL-AMOUNT.
                     WRITE VENDOR-REPORT-LINE FROM AUDIT-LINE AFTER 1.
*****************************
*  THIS MODULE READS THE
*  OLD VENDOR MASTER FILE
*****************************
500-READ-MASTER.
                     READ OLD-VENDOR-MASTER-FILE INTO OM-WORK-RECORD
                            AT END MOVE "X" TO WS-OMF-EOF-SW
                                    MOVE HIGH-VALUES TO OM-VENDOR-NUMBER.
                     ADD 1 TO WS-MASTERS-READ.
                     IF OM-VENDOR-NUMBER IS NOT > WS-OLD-MASTER-KEY
                            PERFORM 510-ABORT-RUN.
                     MOVE OM-VENDOR-NUMBER TO WS-OLD-MASTER-KEY.
*
510-ABORT-RUN.
*
                     DISPLAY "VENDOR MASTER OUT OF SEQUENCE".
                     DISPLAY "PREVIOUS KEY = " WS-OLD-MASTER-KEY.
                            DISPLAY "CURRENT KEY = " OM-VENDOR-NUMBER.
                     PERFORM 520-ABORT-CLOSE.
*
520-ABORT-CLOSE.
                     CLOSE   OLD-VENDOR-MASTER-FILE
                             VENDOR-TRANSACTION-FILE
                             NEW-VENDOR-MASTER-FILE
                             VENDOR-AUDIT-ERROR-LIST.
                     STOP RUN.
*********************
*  THIS MODULE READS
*  TRANSACTIONS FILE
*********************
600-READ-TRANSACTION.
*
                     READ VENDOR-TRANSACTION-FILE INTO TF-WORK-RECORD
                            AT END
                                    MOVE "X" TO WS-TF-EOF-SW
                                    MOVE HIGH-VALUES TO TF-VENDOR-NUMBER.
                     IF TF-VENDOR-NUMBER IS NOT > WS-TRANSACTION-KEY
                            PERFORM 610-ABORT-RUN.
                     MOVE TF-VENDOR-NUMBER TO WS-TRANSACTION-KEY.
                     ADD 1 TO WS-TRANSACTIONS-READ.
                     PERFORM 620-EDIT-TRANSACTION.
*
610-ABORT-RUN.
                     DISPLAY "TRANSACTION FILE OUT OF SEQUENCE".
                     DISPLAY "PREVIOUS KEY = " WS-TRANSACTION-KEY.
                     DISPLAY "CURRENT KEY = " TF-VENDOR-NUMBER.
                     PERFORM 520-ABORT-CLOSE.
*******************
*  THIS MODULE EDITS
*  TRANSACTION RECORDS
*  NULL FOR THIS PROGRAM
*******************
620-EDIT-TRANSACTION.
                     EXIT.
```

SECTION 13
Questions and Problems

I. Questions

1. How many files are usually included in a sequential update program? Why are each of these files required?

2. Give the general names of the files that are usually included in a sequential update.

3. What sequence must each of the input files be in?

4. Is it imperative that a transaction code be included in the transaction records? Why or why not?

5. Describe what activities will take place in a sequential update when the following key comparison results exist in a sequential update program:

   a. The master file key is greater than the transaction file key.

   b. The master file key is less than the transaction file key.

   c. The master file key is equal to the transaction file key.

6. Describe the types of data validations that are usually required in a sequential update program.

7. What is an audit/error report and why are they used in sequential update programs? What items are usually included in such a report? Why?

8. Assume that you have a PERSONNEL MASTER file for SOMEBODY UNIVERSITY that you wish to update. Code the required ENVIRONMENT DIVISION entries. Include the ORGANIZATION and ACCESS MODE statements in your code.

9. What field in the PERSONNEL MASTER that is listed below do you think should be the key field? Why?

Columns	Content
1-9	social security number
10-30	name
31-49	address
50-65	city
66-67	state
68-76	zip code
77-80	highest degree
81-90	title/rank code
91-92	hire date
93-99	salary 9(5)v99

10. Based on the data presented in Question 9, is it possible to develop the FILE SECTION entries for a sequential update of the PERSONNEL MASTER? Why or why not? If possible, code these entries.

II. Problems and Exercises

1. Modify the example program included in the chapter material to incorporate the edits discussed in the chapter.

2. Modify the example program included in the textual example to provide for multiple transactions to the same master file record.

3. A sequential customer master file is to be updated with input customer transaction records. The transaction file may be assumed to be in the same sequence as the customer master file. Your program should provide for the following:

   Input Files:

   customer master file

   customer transaction file

   Output Files:

   updated customer master file

   audit/error list

   The format of the customer master file, the updated customer master file, and the transaction file is as follows:

Field Name	Location	Data Type
customer number	1-5	alphanumeric [key]
customer name	6-25	alphanumeric
address	26-50	alphanumeric
city name	51-70	alphanumeric
state	71-72	alphanumeric
zip code	73-81	numeric
credit limit	82-87	numeric S9(4)v99
balance	88-93	numeric S9(4)v99
transaction code	94	alphanumeric [included in transaction file only]

   The format of the output audit/error list is left to the student's discretion but should include the following features:

   - a listing of all the data items
   - an indication of the disposition of the transaction record
   - an error message, if any
   - appropriate record counts

4. The Somebody University PERSONNEL MASTER FILE is to be updated with personnel transaction records. The transaction file and master file may be assumed to be in sequence on the appropriate key field.

   Write a COBOL program that will provide for the following:
   a. Edit as follows:
      1. Salary cannot be changed to exceed 65550.99.
      2. Rank cannot be changed to ASSOCPROF or PROF unless the high degree field contains PHD, EDD, DBA, LLD, or DSC. Please notice that if the rank is being changed then title can be changed at the same time.
   b. Create and update personnel master file.

   Input Files:

   personnel master file

   personnel transaction file

Output Files:

update personnel master file

audit/error list

The format of the personnel master file, updated personnel master file, and transaction file is as follows:

Columns	transaction code [for transaction file only]
Columns	**Content**
1-9	social security number [key field]
10-30	name
31-49	address
50-65	city
66-67	state
68-76	zip code
77-80	highest degree
81-90	title/rank code
91-92	hire date
93-99	salary 9(5)v99
100	transaction code [for transaction file only]

The format of the audit/error list is left to the student's imagination, but should minimally include the following items:

- a listing of all the data items in the record
- an indication of the disposition of the transactions
- appropriate record counts

5. The Simple-Gillet Company inventory master file is to be updated with inventory transaction records. The transaction file and master file may be assumed to be in sequence on the part number field [the key].

Write a COBOL program that will update the inventory master file given:

input files:

inventory master file

output files:

updated inventory master file
audit/error report

The format of the inventory master file, the inventory transaction file, and the updated inventory master file is as follows:

Columns	Content
1-15	part number [key field]
16-40	part name
41-45	bin location
46-51	quantity on hand
52-57	reorder point
58-63	maximum quantity
64-70	cost
71-78	retail price

79-95	supplier name
96-101	economic order quantity
102-107	safety stock
108-113	quantity on order
114	transaction code [for transaction file only]

The format of the audit/error report is left to the student's discretion, but should minimally include the following:

- a listing of all the data-items included in the transaction record
- an indication of the disposition of the transaction
- appropriate record counts

4

Disk Utilization: Indexed Access Methods and Concepts

The previous chapter introduced sequential access methods. There are a number of disadvantages to the use of sequential files. Chief among these disadvantages is that the update of a master file is relatively slow because each record on the existing master file must be processed regardless of the amount of change activity. Furthermore, when processing data that are stored in sequential form, no record can be accessed directly. In order to find a specific record in the sequential file, each record in the file must be read until the desired record is found.

The use of indexed access methods is one way to overcome these problems. These methods incorporate the indexed sequential (ISAM) and the virtual storage (VSAM) methods, and other methods which incorporate the use of a file index. The data that are stored in a file using an indexed method can be accessed in either a random or sequential manner. Obviously, this leads to some time savings for the user of indexed access methods.

There are also some disadvantages associated with the use of indexed methods. Many believe the primary disadvantage to be that the use of indexed methods increases the amount of disk space consumed when compared to the disk space used when sequential or relative access methods are used. Also, the time required to randomly retrieve a record from an indexed file is greater than the time required to retrieve a record from a relative file (see Chapter 6). Even though there are disadvantages associated with the use of the indexed methods, they continue to be one of the most popular of all the organizational methods used with disk files. The primary reason for this popularity is the capability of accessing the data in an indexed file either randomly or sequentially. We will use the problem introduced in Chapter 3 to illustrate the concepts of maintaining indexed files. First, however, let us discuss the indexed file structure.

SECTION 1
The File Structure

Although it isn't absolutely essential that you know all the details of the physical layout of an indexed file (the operating system takes care of addressing the records for you), you should be able to visualize the processing of these files if you have a basic understanding of their physical structure. You may want to refer to Appendix F if you don't know how disk devices work.

Although indexed files are maintained in sequential order they differ from sequential files in several respects, one of the more important of which is that indexed files are made up of several parts. The two major parts are the index and the data storage area, each of which may be subdivided further. The location of any data-item stored on disk may be accessed if its "address" on the disk pack can be established. On the original creation of a file the data are stored in an area of the file called the *prime data area* or the *primary data area* and some of the keys are stored in another part of the file called the *index*. The reason that only part of the keys are included in the index is that only the keys for the first or the last record on a particular area (cylinder or track) are included. Depending on the size of the file, the index may be a low-level or partial index (an index for tracks) or a higher-level index (an index for cylinders). If the file resides entirely within a single cylinder, then the higher-level index is not necessary. If the file resides on several cylinders, then the higher-level index is probably used.

For a simple example of these concepts, consider the data in the vendor master file that we have been using.

| | **Cylinder Index** |
Cylinder	**Vendor Number**
4	001245
5	056732
6	107389

| | **Track Index for Cylinder 5** |
Surface	**Vendor Number**
1	012345
2	024560
3	029567
4	030678
5	039894
6	041093
7	044575
8	049877
9	051036
10	056732

In the preceding example, the high vendor number is indicated for a specific cylinder. In a retrieval process the system would first determine which cylinder contains a specific record by comparing the value of the key of the record sought to the high (or low) key value for that cylinder. If you are looking for vendor 035457 you know that the record, if it exists, is stored on cylinder 5 because 1245 < 35457 < 107389. Each cylinder has a low-level track index. As you can see, such a scan would reveal that 035457 is located on track 5. Each record on track 5 of cylinder 5 would be compared to the value 035457 until the record is found or, if there is no record with a key of 035457, not found.

This process is faster, on average, than looking at every record in a file until the specific record is found.

Remember, an indexed file is a sequential file with indexes that allow you more flexible access to a file than you can have with a sequential file.

In the subsequent sections of this chapter, we will be discussing the updating of the vendor master file discussed in Chapter 3 and created through the use of the program presented earlier in that chapter. But we will be using indexed, rather than sequential, methods.

SECTION 2
Example Problem Illustrating Indexed Organization

You will recall that in the problem covered in Chapter 3 we updated a sequential master file and that the master file contained master data concerning the vendors in an accounts payable system. Also recall that the data in the master file and the transaction file had to be in the same sequence on the same key field in order to update the sequential master file.

For our discussion in this chapter, we will create and maintain a similar vendor master file using indexed access methods. What is required to do this? It may sound to you as if more programming activity is required than was required for the sequential maintenance program and that the level of such programming is more complex. This not true—in fact, the indexed update program is much less difficult to write and maintain than the sequential update program.

The systems flowchart for this operation is presented in Figure 4-1.

Notice that no sorting operation is required for the indexed file update and that it is not necessary to create a "new" master file. The updated vendor master file is simply updated—the changes are added to the same physical file. In other words, there is no need to copy the contents of the vendor master file to the new master file during the update process. Also, though not explicitly stated, there is no sequence requirement on the vendor transaction file.

Figure 4-1
System flowchart—indexed file update.

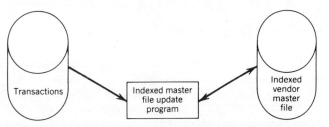

SECTION 3
Creation of an Indexed File

At some point in time an indexed file has to come into existence. Usually, the indexed file is created from a *sorted* sequential file. Although the possibility of randomly accessing records from an indexed file exists, the records in the file are maintained in that file in a sequential fashion based on the contents of a field called the *key field*. Therefore, the file from which the indexed file is to be created must be in ascending sequence on the appropriate key field.

There are two ways to create an indexed file:

1. Write a program that reads the sequential file and writes the indexed file.
2. Use specialized software provided by the manufacturer to create the indexed file and load the contents of the sequential file into the new indexed file.

Of these methods, the use of the specialized software is the most efficient. An example of the use of such software to create the INDEXED-VENDOR-MASTER is presented in Appendix F. We are using the first method here in order to introduce some of the concepts of indexed files that should make these concepts clearer.

The systems flowchart for the creation of the INDEXED-VENDOR-MASTER is presented in Figure 4-2.

Figure 4–2
System flowchart—indexed file creation.

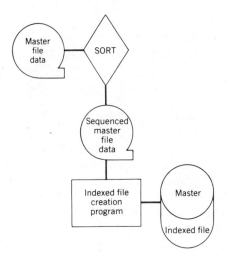

SECTION 4
ENVIRONMENT DIVISION Entries for Creating Indexed Files

Two files are used in the creation program: the input file, which we have named SEQUENTIAL MASTER, and the output file, called INDEXED-VENDOR-MASTER. The ENVIRONMENT DIVISION entries for sequential file processing were discussed in Chapter 3; if you have any question concerning these entries, please refer to that chapter.

The SELECT statement for the INDEXED-VENDOR-MASTER is as follows:

```
SELECT INDEXED-VENDOR-MASTER
      ASSIGN TO "INVENDM.DAT"          Note: These entries are for
      ORGANIZATION IS INDEXED                the DEC VAX system
      ACCESS MODE IS SEQUENTIAL
      RECORD KEY IS IVM-VENDOR-NUMBER.
```

As you know, the SELECT and ASSIGN phrases give the file a name and assign that name to an external device or file: in our case the device is a disk file called IVENDM.DAT. The ORGANIZATION clause specifies that the organizational characteristics of this file are INDEXED in nature. The ACCESS MODE IS SEQUENTIAL indicates that the records are to be accessed (in this case written) sequentially. The RECORD KEY phrase identifies the data field in the indexed file that is the key field. The key field specified in our example is IVM-VENDOR-NUMBER. The records that are written to the INDEXED-VENDOR-MASTER file will be arranged in either ascending sequence or descending sequence, based on the values of the key field IVM-VENDOR-NUMBER. For most manufacturers' COBOL compilers, the record key must be specified as an alphanumeric data-item. The record key must also be a part of the record.

SECTION 5
DATA DIVISION Entries for Creating
Indexed Files

The DATA DIVISION entries for the program that creates an indexed file are no different than the DATA DIVISION entries for a sequential file. Figure 4-3 gives the DATA DIVISION entries for our creation program.

Notice that the key field, IVM-VENDOR-NUMBER, is contained within the record and that it is specified as an alphanumeric data item of six characters.

Figure 4-3
DATA DIVISION for creation
of indexed file.

```
FILE SECTION.
*
FD   SEQUENTIAL-MASTER
              LABEL RECORDS ARE STANDARD.
01   SM-VENDOR-RECORD.
         05   SM-VENDOR-NUMBER               PIC X(06).
         05   SM-VENDOR-NAME                 PIC X(30).
         05   SM-VENDOR-ADDRESS1             PIC X(25).
         05   SM-VENDOR-ADDRESS2             PIC X(25).
         05   SM-VENDOR-CITY                 PIC X(20).
         05   SM-VENDOR-STATE                PIC X(02).
         05   SM-VENDOR-ZIP                  PIC X(05).
         05   SM-VENDOR-BUYS                 PIC S9(06)V99.
         05   SM-VENDOR-LAST-DATE            PIC 9(06).
         05   SM-VENDOR-CODE                 PIC X(01).
*
FD   INDEXED-VENDOR-MASTER
              LABEL RECORDS ARE STANDARD.
*
01   IVM-VENDOR-RECORD.
         05   IVM-VENDOR-NUMBER              PIC X(06).
         05   IVM-VENDOR-NAME                PIC X(30).
         05   IVM-VENDOR-ADDRESS1            PIC X(25).
         05   IVM-VENDOR-ADDRESS2            PIC X(25).
         05   IVM-VENDOR-CITY                PIC X(20).
         05   IVM-VENDOR-STATE               PIC X(02).
         05   IVM-VENDOR-ZIP                 PIC X(05).
         05   IVM-VENDOR-BUYS                PIC S9(06)V99.
         05   IVM-VENDOR-LAST-DATE           PIC 9(06).
         05   IVM-VENDOR-CODE                PIC X(01).
*
*
WORKING-STORAGE SECTION.
*
01   EOF-SW                                  PIC X(01).
01   INPUT-RECORDS                           PIC 9(04).
01   OUTPUT-RECORDS                          PIC 9(04).
01   HOLD-KEY                                PIC X(06).
*
*
*
```

SECTION 6
PROCEDURE DIVISION Entries for
Creating Indexed Files

Figure 4-4 contains the PROCEDURE DIVISION entries to create the indexed master file that we will use in the update example in subsequent sections of this chapter.

The 100-INITIALIZE module contains the OPEN statement for the indexed file. It is:

```
OPEN OUTPUT INDEXED-VENDOR-MASTER.
```

Figure 4–4
PROCEDURE
DIVISION—indexed
file-creation program.

```
*
*
*
PROCEDURE DIVISION.
000-MAIN-MODULE.
        PERFORM 100-INITIALIZE.
        PERFORM 200-PROCESS-RECORDS
                UNTIL EOF-SW = "X".
        DISPLAY "RECORDS READ = " INPUT-RECORDS.
        DISPLAY "RECORDS WRITTEN = " OUTPUT-RECORDS.
        CLOSE   SEQUENTIAL-MASTER
                INDEXED-VENDOR-MASTER.
        STOP RUN.
*
100-INITIALIZE.
        OPEN INPUT SEQUENTIAL-MASTER
                OUTPUT INDEXED-VENDOR-MASTER.
        MOVE LOW-VALUES TO HOLD-KEY.
        MOVE " " TO EOF-SW.
        MOVE ZEROS TO   INPUT-RECORDS
                        OUTPUT-RECORDS.
        PERFORM 300-READ-SEQUENTIAL.
*
200-PROCESS-RECORDS.
        MOVE SM-VENDOR-NUMBER TO IVM-VENDOR-NUMBER.
        MOVE SM-VENDOR-NAME TO IVM-VENDOR-NAME.
        MOVE SM-VENDOR-ADDRESS1 TO IVM-VENDOR-ADDRESS1.
        MOVE SM-VENDOR-ADDRESS2 TO IVM-VENDOR-ADDRESS2.
        MOVE SM-VENDOR-CITY TO IVM-VENDOR-CITY.
        MOVE SM-VENDOR-STATE TO IVM-VENDOR-STATE.
        MOVE SM-VENDOR-ZIP TO IVM-VENDOR-ZIP.
        MOVE SM-VENDOR-BUYS TO IVM-VENDOR-BUYS.
        MOVE SM-VENDOR-LAST-DATE TO IVM-VENDOR-LAST-DATE.
        MOVE SM-VENDOR-CODE TO IVM-VENDOR-CODE.
        WRITE IVM-VENDOR-RECORD
                    INVALID KEY
                        DISPLAY "ERROR IN WRITE TO INDEXED FILE"
                        DISPLAY "RUN ABORTED"
                        MOVE "X" TO EOF-SW.
        ADD 1 TO OUTPUT-RECORDS.
        PERFORM 300-READ-SEQUENTIAL.
*
300-READ-SEQUENTIAL.
        READ SEQUENTIAL-MASTER
                    AT END MOVE "X" TO EOF-SW
                    MOVE HIGH-VALUES TO HOLD-KEY.
        IF EOF-SW NOT = "X" ADD 1 TO INPUT-RECORDS.
        IF SM-VENDOR-NUMBER NOT > HOLD-KEY AND EOF-SW NOT = "X"
                        DISPLAY "INPUT FILE OUT OF SEQUENCE"
                        DISPLAY "RUN ABORTED"
                        MOVE "X" TO EOF-SW.
        MOVE SM-VENDOR-NUMBER TO HOLD-KEY.
```

The OPEN statement signifies to the compiler that the file is to be opened for output procedures only. This allows the program to check for a number of conditions that will be presented in the discussion of the FILE STATUS procedure.

The 200-PROCESS-RECORDS paragraph moves the data fields from the sequential master record area to the indexed master record area and then WRITEs the indexed record to disk.

The WRITE command differs somewhat from those you have used to create printed output or other sequential files. The WRITE command is:

```
WRITE IVM-VENDOR-RECORD
     INVALID KEY
          DISPLAY "ERROR IN WRITE TO INDEXED FILE"
          DISPLAY "RUN ABORTED"
          MOVE "X" TO EOF-SW.
```

The WRITE specifies that the record is to be written in the same way as in a sequential file. The INVALID KEY clause specifies action to be taken if an error condition is encountered. In this case, we DISPLAY an error message and set the end-of-file switch to "on," which in turn, will cause the execution of the program to stop.

The conditions that can cause the INVALID KEY return are:

1. The current RECORD KEY contents are not greater that the previous RECORD KEY contents. The "sequential" file is not in ascending order.
2. The current RECORD KEY contents duplicate a RECORD KEY previously written to the file. Record keys are not unique.
3. There is a boundary violation—out of disk space.

If it is useful to be able to detect the type of error from the choices given above, we may use the FILE STATUS option to determine this. Our program is written so that this kind of error detection is not necessary. We want to abort the run in any of the three cases listed above. The FILE STATUS option will be explained in a subsequent section of this chapter.

In the 300-READ-SEQUENTIAL module we read the sequential master file, testing for high sequence and accumulating a count of the number of records read. If the sequence of the current record key is not greater than the previous key, the program is aborted after a message is displayed on the terminal.

SECTION 7
Updating Master File Concepts

Once you have created the indexed master file you have the capability to update or maintain that file randomly.

Recall from the sequential update process that, when you use *sequential* organization, the master and the transaction file must be in the same sequence. Also recall that the results of a comparison of the keys had certain meanings as far as the update process is concerned. This is not true in the maintenance of an indexed file since the keys are not compared as a result of instructions coded in your program.

The primary logic steps involved in the maintenance of an indexed file are as follows:

1. Read the transaction file.
2. Move the key from the transaction record to the master record.
3. Randomly read the indexed file.
4. If the INVALID KEY return is received on the read, the record does not exist on the master file and the transaction record must be an add.
5. If a valid record is retrieved from the master file, the transaction record must be either a deletion or change. A deletion is easily detected by comparing the transaction record, with the exception of the key field to SPACES. If an equal compare results, the record is to be deleted. The deletion is accomplished by the use of the DELETE command. If the record is a change, then the individual fields in the record are tested and moved to the master record, and then the master record, as appropriate, is REWRITEn to disk.
6. The end-of-job routines are initiated when an end of file is detected on the transaction file.

The process appears to be easy—and it is, insofar as your program is concerned. Most of the tedious tasks are taken care of by the computer's operating system.

SECTION 8
ENVIRONMENT DIVISION Entries for
Updating Indexed Files

The ENVIRONMENT DIVISION entries necessary to update the INDEXED-VENDOR-MASTER are as follows:

```
ENVIRONMENT DIVISION.
CONFIGURATION SECTION.
SOURCE-COMPUTER. VAX-11.
OBJECT-COMPUTER. VAX-11.
INPUT-OUTPUT SECTION.
FILE-CONTROL.
    SELECT INDEXED-VENDOR-MASTER
        ASSIGN TO "INVENDM.DAT"          (for DEC VAX system)
        ORGANIZATION IS INDEXED
        ACCESS MODE IS RANDOM
        RECORD KEY IS IVM-VENDOR-NUMBER
        FILE STATUS IS WS-FILE-STATUS.
    SELECT TRANSACTION-FILE
        ASSIGN TO "VENDTR".              (for DEC VAX system)
    SELECT AUDIT-ERROR-LIST
        ASSIGN TO "AUDLST.LST".          (for DEC VAX system)
```

The SELECT statement for the INDEXED-VENDOR-MASTER is the only statement that is radically different from the statements that you are familiar with from the sequential update of this same file. There may always be variations in the structure of the ASSIGN statement, which is dependent on the compiler in use. The ORGANIZATION clause contains the phrase IS INDEXED. This indicates to the COBOL compiler that the INDEXED-VENDOR-MASTER is of the indexed file organization type.

The possibilities for the ACCESS MODE clause are:

SEQUENTIAL

RANDOM

DYNAMIC

The value selected for this program is RANDOM. What is communicated to the compiler is that the records that form the INDEXED-VENDOR-MASTER are to be retrieved randomly. Had we selected the SEQUENTIAL option, the records would have to be retrieved sequentially. If the DYNAMIC option had been selected, records in the INDEXED-VENDOR-MASTER could be accessed either sequentially or randomly. Use of the DYNAMIC option is the subject of Chapter 5 of this text.

The selection of the RANDOM access option has an effect on the READ and WRITE statements that are included in the program for the INDEXED-VENDOR-MASTER file. In most compilers these statements require the inclusion of the INVALID KEY clause. This is discussed in a subsequent section of this chapter.

The RECORD KEY clause is used (and must be included) to indicate the field in the record that is the key field for random access to the file.

The FILE STATUS clause may be included in programs that are compiled under the COBOL-74 compiler. This is an extremely useful feature because its inclusion allows the programmer more control over the INVALID KEY clause on I/O operations than is otherwise possible. The clause provides that a two-digit alphanumeric field be specified in the WORKING-STORAGE SECTION. Each time there is a READ or WRITE to the file, one of the values specified in Appendix C is stored in FILE STATUS. Any code of 90 or above is a manufacturer's code. In the example used here these codes are for the DEC-VAX-11 system. Even so, a considerable degree of standardization in the 90-level codes seems to occur from one manufacturer to another. A full listing for possible file status codes for the DEC VAX-11 and IBM systems is presented in Appendix C.

SECTION 9
DATA DIVISION Entries for Updating Indexed Files

Figure 4-5 contains the DATA DIVISION entries for our update program. There are two facts worth noting:

1. These entries are not significantly different from the sequential update program's DATA DIVISION entries.
2. The RECORD KEY (IVM-VENDOR-NUMBER) is contained within the record. Also note that the key has an alphanumeric PICTURE clause. Most compilers require that this be the case, although some some compilers do allow numeric PICTURE clauses.

Figure 4–5
DATA DIVISION entries for
update of an indexed file.

```
*
DATA DIVISION.
**
*
FILE SECTION.
*
*
FD  INDEXED-VENDOR-MASTER
                LABEL RECORDS ARE STANDARD.
*
01  IVM-VENDOR-RECORD.
        05  IVM-VENDOR-NUMBER           PIC X(06).
        05  IVM-VENDOR-NAME             PIC X(30).
        05  IVM-VENDOR-ADDRESS1         PIC X(25).
        05  IVM-VENDOR-ADDRESS2         PIC X(25).
        05  IVM-VENDOR-CITY             PIC X(20).
        05  IVM-VENDOR-STATE            PIC X(02).
        05  IVM-VENDOR-ZIP              PIC X(05).
        05  IVM-VENDOR-BUYS             PIC S9(06)V99.
        05  IVM-VENDOR-LAST-DATE        PIC 9(06).
        05  IVM-VENDOR-CODE             PIC X(01).
*
FD  TRANSACTION-FILE
                LABEL RECORDS ARE STANDARD.
*
01  TRANSACTION-RECORD.
        05  TF-VENDOR-NUMBER            PIC X(06).
        05  TF-VENDOR-NAME              PIC X(30).
        05  TF-VENDOR-ADDRESS1          PIC X(25).
        05  TF-VENDOR-ADDRESS2          PIC X(25).
        05  TF-VENDOR-CITY              PIC X(20).
        05  TF-VENDOR-STATE             PIC X(02).
        05  TF-VENDOR-ZIP               PIC X(05).
        05  TF-VENDOR-BUYS              PIC S9(6)V99.
        05  TF-VENDOR-MONEY REDEFINES TF-VENDOR-BUYS PIC X(8).
        05  TF-VENDOR-LAST-DATE.
            10  TF-MONTH                PIC 9(02).
            10  TF-DAY                  PIC 9(02).
            10  TF-YEAR                 PIC 9(02).
        05  TF-VENDOR-CODE              PIC X(01).
*
FD  AUDIT-ERROR-LIST
                LABEL RECORDS ARE OMITTED.
*
01  VENDOR-REPORT-LINE                  PIC X(132).
*
```

Figure 4–5 (continued)

```
      *
      WORKING-STORAGE SECTION.
      *
      01   DL-VENDOR-LINE.
              05   FILLER                          PIC X(02) VALUE SPACES.
              05   DL-VENDOR-NUMBER                PIC X(06).
              05   FILLER                          PIC X(05) VALUE SPACES.
              05   DL-VENDOR-NAME                  PIC X(30).
              05   FILLER                          PIC X(05) VALUE SPACES.
              05   DL-VENDOR-ADDRESS               PIC X(25).
              05   FILLER                          PIC X(06) VALUE SPACES.
              05   DL-VENDOR-BUYS                  PIC ZZZ,ZZZ.99CR.
              05   FILLER                          PIC X(04).
              05   DL-VENDOR-LAST-DATE             PIC 99/99/99.
              05   FILLER                          PIC X(06).
              05   DL-ACTION                       PIC X(07).
              05   FILLER                          PIC X(03) VALUE SPACES.
              05   DL-ERROR-MESSAGE                PIC X(12).
      *****************************
      *    HEADING LINES
      *****************************
      01   HEAD1.
              05   FILLER                  PIC X(39) VALUE SPACES.
              05   FILLER          PIC X(20) VALUE "VENDOR MASTER FILE M".
              05   FILLER          PIC X(10) VALUE "AINTENANCE".
      *
      01   HEAD2.
              05   FILLER          PIC X(07) VALUE " DATE: ".
              05   HEAD2-DATE      PIC 99/99/99.
              05   FILLER          PIC X(30) VALUE SPACES.
              05   FILLER          PIC X(18) VALUE "AUDIT-ERROR REPORT".
              05   FILLER          PIC X(25) VALUE SPACES.
              05   FILLER          PIC X(06) VALUE "PAGE: ".
              05   HEAD2-PAGE-NUMBER    PIC ZZ9.
      *
      01   HEAD3.
              05   FILLER          PIC X(20) VALUE "   VENDOR           ".
              05   FILLER          PIC X(20) VALUE " VENDOR            ".
              05   FILLER          PIC X(20) VALUE "         VENDOR     ".
              05   FILLER          PIC X(20) VALUE "                    ".
              05   FILLER          PIC X(20) VALUE "AMOUNT OF     DATE  ".
              05   FILLER          PIC X(20) VALUE "OF          ACTION E".
              05   FILLER          PIC X(04) VALUE "RROR".
      *
      01   HEAD4.
              05   FILLER          PIC X(20) VALUE "  NUMBER            ".
              05   FILLER          PIC X(20) VALUE " NAME              ".
              05   FILLER          PIC X(20) VALUE "         ADDRESS    ".
              05   FILLER          PIC X(20) VALUE "                    ".
              05   FILLER          PIC X(20) VALUE "PURCHASES     LAST P".
              05   FILLER          PIC X(20) VALUE "URCHASE   TAKEN   ME".
              05   FILLER          PIC X(05) VALUE "SSAGE".
      *
      01   AUDIT-LINE.
              05   FILLER                  PIC X(01) VALUE SPACES.
              05   AL-MESSAGE              PIC X(19).
              05   FILLER                  PIC X(02) VALUE SPACES.
              05   AL-AMOUNT               PIC ZZ,ZZ9.
```

```
*
01  WS-TOTAL-DESCRIPTIONS.
        05  FILLER              PIC X(18) VALUE " TRANSACTIONS READ".
        05  FILLER              PIC X(18) VALUE "   TOTAL ADDS     ".
        05  FILLER              PIC X(18) VALUE "    PROCESSED     ".
        05  FILLER              PIC X(18) VALUE "     REJECTED     ".
        05  FILLER              PIC X(18) VALUE "  TOTAL DELETES   ".
        05  FILLER              PIC X(18) VALUE "    PROCESSED     ".
        05  FILLER              PIC X(18) VALUE "     REJECTED     ".
        05  FILLER              PIC X(18) VALUE "  TOTAL CHANGES   ".
        05  FILLER              PIC X(18) VALUE "    PROCESSED     ".
        05  FILLER              PIC X(18) VALUE "     REJECTED     ".
01  WS-AUDIT-DESCRIPTIONS REDEFINES WS-TOTAL-DESCRIPTIONS.
        05  WS-AUDIT-MESSAGE OCCURS 10 TIMES PIC X(18).
***************************
*   TOTALS
*       AREA
***************************
01  WS-TOTALS.
        05  WS-TRANSACTIONS-READ        PIC 9(05).
        05  WS-TOTAL-ADDS               PIC 9(05).
        05  WS-ADDS-PROCESSED           PIC 9(05).
        05  WS-ADDS-REJECTED            PIC 9(05).
        05  WS-TOTAL-DELETES            PIC 9(05).
        05  WS-DELETES-PROCESSED        PIC 9(05).
        05  WS-DELETES-REJECTED         PIC 9(05).
        05  WS-TOTAL-CHANGES            PIC 9(05).
        05  WS-CHANGES-PROCESSED        PIC 9(05).
        05  WS-CHANGES-REJECTED         PIC 9(05).
01  WS-RECORD-COUNTS REDEFINES WS-TOTALS.
        05  WS-TOTAL-VALUES OCCURS 10 TIMES PIC 9(05).
*
01  WS-LINE-COUNT                       PIC 9(02) VALUE 51.
01  WS-PAGE-NUMBER                      PIC 9(03) VALUE ZEROS.
***************************
*   GENERAL
*       EDIT
*           REQUIREMENTS
***************************


***************************
*
*   SWITCHES
***************************
01  WS-AUDIT-SW                         PIC X VALUE " ".
***************************
*   GENERAL WORKING-STORAGE
*       VALUES
***************************
01  DATE-IN                            PIC 9(06).
01  WS-ACTION                          PIC X(07).
01  WS-ERROR-MESSAGE                   PIC X(12).
01  I                                  PIC 9(02).
01  WS-FILE-STATUS                     PIC X(02).
01  WS-EOF-SWITCH                      PIC X(01).
/
***************************
*
```

Figure 4–5 (continued)

SECTION 10

PROCEDURE DIVISION Entries for
Updating an Indexed File

In this section, the entries that are peculiar to an indexed process are discussed on a module-by-module basis.

000-MAIN-MODULE.

The statements contained in 000-MAIN-MODULE are as follows:

```
000-MAIN-MODULE.
    OPEN INPUT      TRANSACTION-FILE
         OUTPUT     AUDIT-ERROR-LIST
         I-O        INDEXED-VENDOR-MASTER.
    PERFORM 100-INITIALIZE-TOTALS-ETC.
    PERFORM 200-UPDATE-MASTER-FILE
         UNTIL WS-EOF-SWITCH = "X".
    PERFORM 400-PRINT-AUDIT-TOTALS.
    CLOSE      TRANSACTION-FILE
               AUDIT-ERROR-LIST
               INDEXED-VENDOR-MASTER.
    STOP RUN.
```

The OPEN statement, as you can see, is a little different from the OPEN statement for the sequential update process. Notice that the phrase for the INDEXED-VENDOR-MASTER is:

```
I-O INDEXED-VENDOR-MACTER.
```

When the ACCESS MODE for a file is RANDOM or DYNAMIC, the file *must* be OPENed as I-O. This means that the file can have the capability of both input and output operations in this file.

100-INITIALIZE-TOTALS-ETC.

The module for initializing the switches, totals, and other fields is as follows:

```
100-INITIALIZE-TOTALS-ETC.
    MOVE SPACES TO WS-EOF-SWITCH.
    MOVE ZEROS TO WS-TOTALS
                  WS-PAGE-NUMBER.
    MOVE 51 TO WS-LINE-COUNT.
    ACCEPT DATE-IN FROM DATE.
    PERFORM 500-READ-TRANSACTION.
```

The only difference between this module for the update of a sequential file and the update of the indexed file is that a READ of the TRANSACTION-FILE is PERFORMed in this module as a "pump priming" operation.

200-UPDATE-MASTER-FILE.

The statements included in the update module are as follows:

```
200-UPDATE-MASTER-FILE.
    PERFORM 600-READ-MASTER.
```

```
    IF WS-FILE-STATUS = "23"
        AND TF-VENDOR-CODE = "A"
        PERFORM 220-ADD-MASTER.
 ELSE IF (WS-FILE-STATUS = "00"
        AND TF-VENDOR-CODE = "D")
            PERFORM 240-DELETE-MASTER
 ELSE IF (WS-FILE-STATUS = "00"
        AND TF-VENDOR-CODE = "C")
            PERFORM 250-CHANGE-MASTER.
 ELSE PERFORM 260-IDENTIFY-ERROR.
 PERFORM 300-PRINT-AUDIT.
 PERFORM 500-READ-TRANSACTION.
```

This module contains the primary update logic for the program.

The first statement, PERFORM 600-READ-MASTER, can only be executed after a TRANSACTION-RECORD has been read. This is shown in the 600-READ-MASTER paragraph which is discussed below. After a valid master record is retrieved, the IF statements determine whether the record is addition, deletion, or change.

Notice that the field, WS-FILE-STATUS, is being tested to help determine this. Refer to Appendix C. Notice that a status code of "00" indicates a successful access of the INDEXED-VENDOR-MASTER. Also notice that a status code of "23" indicates that the record is not in the file. This status value is important to the logic of our program.

If the status value is "23" from the READ of the master file, means the TRANSACTION-FILE contains a value that is not in the INDEXED-VENDOR-MASTER. Therefore, the transaction record must be an addition. If you are using update codes, the update code and the status code must be "A" and "23" in order for the add process to transpire.

If the status code return is "00", this means that we have a successful access of the INDEXED-VENDOR-MASTER. In other words, the value of the key on the transaction file produced a record on the master file. The next step, at this point, is to determine if the record on the transaction file is a deletion or a change. In the example contained here, we use codes to do this although it is not necessary. A status code of "00" and a transaction code of "D" indicates that the record is to be deleted. A status code of "00" and a transaction code of "C" indicates that the transaction record contains information that is to be changed in the master record.

The final clause in the IF statement, ELSE PERFORM 260-IDENTIFY-ERROR, is used to identify whatever else may have happened in the process. The possibilities are many. If you refer to Appendix C, you can get an idea of the number of possibilities for error.

The next statement, PERFORM 300-PRINT-AUDIT, causes the transaction record to be included in the AUDIT-ERROR-LIST.

The last statement in the module, PERFORM 500-READ-TRANSACTION, causes the next transaction record to be read from the transaction file.

The remainder of this chapter discusses the submodules of the program.

220-ADD-MASTER.

200-ADD-MASTER is executed when a record is read on the transaction file and there is no corresponding record on the INDEXED-VENDOR-MASTER. The logic in the module is as follows:

```
  220-ADD-MASTER.
        IF TF-VENDOR-CODE NOT = "A"
            MOVE "CODE ERROR " TO WS-ERROR-MESSAGE
```

```
    ELSE
        MOVE "ADDED" TO WS-ACTION
        MOVE TF-VENDOR-NUMBER TO IVM-VENDOR-NUMBER
        MOVE TF-VENDOR-NAME TO IVM-VENDOR-NAME
        MOVE TF-VENDOR-ADDRESS1 TO IVM-VENDOR-ADDRESS
        MOVE TF-VENDOR-ADDRESS2 TO IVM-VENDOR-ADDRESS2
        MOVE TF-VENDOR-CITY TO IVM-VENDOR-CITY
        MOVE TF-VENDOR-STATE TO IVM-VENDOR-STATE
        MOVE TF-VENDOR-ZIP TO IVM-VENDOR-ZIP
        MOVE TF-VENDOR-BUYS TO IVM-VENDOR-BUYS
        MOVE TF-VENDOR-LAST-DATE TO IVM-VENDOR-LAST-DATE
        PERFORM 700-WRITE-MASTER
        ADD 1 TO WS-ADDS-PROCESSED.
```

The first statement determines that the transaction code is not present, and an error message is indicated.

The statement

```
MOVE "ADDED" TO WS-ACTION
```

is used to indicate the disposition of the record from the transaction file on the AUDIT-ERROR-LIST.

The remainder of the MOVE statements are moving the values of the fields in the transaction record to the INDEXED-VENDOR-MASTER record.

The statement

```
PERFORM 700-WRITE-MASTER.
```

causes the record to be written to the INDEXED-VENDOR-MASTER.

The final statement

```
ADD 1 TO WS-ADDS-PROCESSED.
```

counts the number of additions that are made to the vendor master file.

240-DELETE-MASTER.

240-DELETE-MASTER is executed when all of the following conditions are met:

1. The key value in the transaction record is moved to the key field of the indexed master and the indexed master is read.
2. The status code returned by the program is "00".
3. The transaction code is "D".

The statements contained in this module are as follows:

```
240-DELETE-MASTER.
    DELETE INDEXED-VENDOR-MASTER
        INVALID KEY
            DISPLAY "NOT ABLE TO DELETE RECORD"
            DISPLAY "VENDOR NUMBER = " TF-VENDOR-NUMBER
            STOP RUN.
    ADD 1 TO WS-DELETES-PROCESSED.
    MOVE "DELETED" TO WS-ACTION.
```

The first statement is a little different from most statements that you have encountered to this point. In fact, it differs between COBOL-68 and COBOL-74.

The DELETE statement causes the removal of the record from the INDEXED-VENDOR-MASTER.

The DELETE statement is a little different in another respect. You are accustomed to reading files and writing records. At first blush, the DELETE command looks a lot like a write statement. First-time users and beginning students usually want to DELETE a record-name. The DELETE syntax statement requires that you DELETE a file-name.

Also inherent in the DELETE logic is the fact that you must first successfully read a record from the file in order to delete a record from that file.

The INVALID KEY option is used to indicate that you have not previously read a record from the indexed file or that you have somehow "fiddled" with the key in the interim between reading the record and the deletion operation.

The statement

```
ADD 1 TO WS-DELETES-PROCESSED.
```

causes the program to count the number of records that were deleted from the INDEXED-VENDOR-MASTER.

The next statement

```
MOVE "DELETED" TO WS-ACTION.
```

is used to indicate the disposition of the record from the transaction file on the AUDIT-ERROR-LIST.

250-CHANGE-MASTER.

250-CHANGE-MASTER is executed for transaction records that are identified as being legitimate changes to the master file.

The statements included in this module are as follows:

```
250-CHANGE-MASTER.
    MOVE "CHANGED" TO WS-ACTION.
    IF TF-VENDOR-NAME NOT EQUAL SPACES
        MOVE TF-VENDOR-NAME TO IVM-VENDOR-NAME.
    IF TF-VENDOR-ADDRESS1 NOT EQUAL SPACES
        MOVE TF-VENDOR-ADDRESS1 TO IVM-VENDOR-ADDRESS1.
        MOVE TF-VENDOR-ADDRESS2 TO IVM-VENDOR-ADDRESS2.
    IF TF-VENDOR-CITY NOT EQUAL SPACES
        MOVE TF-VENDOR-CITY TO IVM-VENDOR-CITY.
    IF TF-VENDOR-STATE NOT EQUAL SPACES
        MOVE TF-VENDOR-STATE TO IVM-VENDOR-STATE.
    IF TF-VENDOR-ZIP NOT EQUAL SPACES
        MOVE TF-VENDOR-ZIP TO IVM-VENDOR-ZIP.
    IF TF-VENDOR-MONEY NOT EQUAL TO SPACES
        MOVE TF-VENDOR-BUYS TO IVM-VENDOR-BUYS.
    IF TF-VENDOR-LAST-DATE NOT EQUAL SPACES
        MOVE TF-VENDOR-LAST-DATE TO
IVM-VENDOR-LAST-DATE.
    REWRITE IVM-VENDOR-RECORD
        INVALID KEY
            DISPLAY "REWRITE ERROR"
            DISPLAY "VENDOR NUMBER = " TF-VENDOR-NUMBER
            STOP RUN.
    ADD 1 TO WS-CHANGES-PROCESSED.
```

The first statement

```
MOVE "CHANGED" TO WS-ACTION.
```

is used to indicate the disposition of the transaction record in the AUDIT-ERROR-LIST.

The IF statements contained in the module are used to see if the transaction record fields are blank and, if they are not, to move the contents of the field to the appropriate field in the master record.

The REWRITE statement is used to write the changed record back to the indexed master file.

If the key is not the same as it was when you read the record the INVALID KEY clause is invoked.

Notice that we are REWRITEing the record-name. The syntax of the REWRITE statement requires the use of a record-name rather than a file-name. The statement

```
ADD 1 TO WS-CHANGES-PROCESSED.
```

counts the number of records that were changed on the indexed master file.

260-IDENTIFY-ERROR.

As we indicated in Chapter 3, the logic in the example programs of this text are for purposes of exposition only. Most working programs in the "real world" will be considerably larger and more complex than these examples. One of the areas of complexity is the error identification process. Nothing would be gained, insofar as the exposition of indexed file access methods is concerned, by including a detailed module here. For this reason the module is presented in null form.

```
260-IDENTIFY-ERROR.
    EXIT.
```

300-PRINT-AUDIT.

The logic for the printing of the AUDIT-ERROR-LIST is as follows:

```
********************
*THIS MODULE PRINTS
*THE AUDIT REPORT
********************
300-PRINT-AUDIT.
        IF WS-LINE-COUNT > 50
            PERFORM 310-PRINT-HEADINGS.
        PERFORM 320-PRINT-LINE.
*
```

There is nothing in this logic that is markedly different from the similar logic of the program in Chapter 3.

400-PRINT-AUDIT-TOTALS.

The logic to print the totals accumulated during the processing of the data is as follows:

```
400-PRINT-AUDIT-TOTALS.
    PERFORM 310-PRINT-HEADINGS.
    PERFORM 410-PRINT-AUDIT-LINE
        VARYING I FROM 1 BY 1
        UNTIL I IS GREATER THAN 10.
```

```
410-PRINT-AUDIT-LINE.
    MOVE WS-AUDIT-MESSAGE (I) TO AL-MESSAGE.
    MOVE WS-TOTAL-VALUES (I) TO AL-AMOUNT.
    WRITE VENDOR-REPORT-LINE FROM AUDIT-LINE AFTER 1.
```

Again this logic is essentially the same as the logic presented in Chapter 3.

500-READ-TRANSACTION.

The logic required to read the records from the TRANSACTION-FILE is as follows:

```
500-READ-TRANSACTION.
    READ TRANSACTION-FILE
        AT END MOVE "X" TO WS-EOF-SWITCH.
    IF WS-EOF-SWITCH NOT = "X"
        ADD 1 TO WS-TRANSACTIONS-READ.
```

The READ statement is an ordinary sequential READ and the AT END option sets the end-of-file switch. The AT END condition determines that the update of the indexed master file is complete. If there are no more transaction records in the TRANSACTION-FILE there is nothing else to do to the INDEXED-VENDOR-MASTER except CLOSE it.

600-READ-MASTER.

The first statement

```
MOVE ZEROS TO WS-FILE-STATUS.
```

is probably not necessary, but old habits die hard.
The next statement

```
MOVE TF-VENDOR-NUMBER TO IVM-VENDOR-NUMBER.
```

is critical. This moves the value of the key from the transaction file to the record area in the INDEXED-VENDOR-MASTER. This value is used to search the cylinder and track indexes to locate the record on the prime data area for the file. The READ statement uses the key value for comparison purposes. If the READ is successful, the WS-FILE-STATUS is set to "00". If unsuccesful, one of the status codes presented in Appendix C will be returned to WS-FILE-STATUS.

SECTION 11
An Examination of the Program Inputs and Outputs

A printout of the input files is presented in Figure 4-6.

Figure 4-7 is the program used to print the vendor master file.

Please notice that there are several differences between the program to randomly update the master file and this program, which processes the records sequentially. A summary of these differences follows on page 113:

```
VENDOR-MASTER-FILE

000115ABC MFG. CO.                     123 EL ST.          MONROE      LA71290000000000{
000126CADDY SHACK                      147 OAK LANE        RUSTON      LA71270000000000{
000188RUSTON OFFICE SUPPLY CO.         210 SOUTH TRENTON   RUSTON      LA71245000000000{
004075SPIVEY'S FRIED CHICKEN           HWY 149             GRAMBLING   LA71270000000000{
004099ELECTRONIC SPECIALTY PRODUCTS    615R S MONROE       RUSTON      LA71270000000000{
005763EVANS BARBER SUPPLY              1305 E LINE AVE.    RUSTON      LA71245000000000{
005984MID--STATE WOOD PRESERVERS INC   HWY 80              GRAMBLING   LA71245000000000{
006666LINCOLN STORAGE SYSTEMS INC.     HWY 150 W           GRAMBLING   LA71245000000000{
007777KELLY'S CLEANERS                 MAIN STREET         GRAMBLING   LA71245000000000{
007779GRAY'S INSURANCE                 MAIN STREET         GRAMBLING   LA71245000000000{
008478DON DURRETT CONSTRUCTION CO.     HWY 563             GRAMBLING   LA71245000000000{

                                                                                   X 148


TRANSACTION-FILE-

000188                  SOUTH HWY 149                      0009500{061483C
004075                                                     00000 0{00000 D
005763                  MAIN STREET                        00000 0{00000 A
007778COLLEGIATE SHOPPE MAIN STREET     GRAMBLING   LA71245000000000{000000A
```

Figure 4-6

Inputs to the indexed program.

Figure 4–7
Program to print indexed
vendor master file.

```
IDENTIFICATION DIVISION.
PROGRAM-ID. INDXMA.
AUTHOR. CSIMPSON.
INSTALLATION. GRAMBLING STATE UNIVERSITY.
**************************
*INDEXED SEQUENTIAL UPDATE
* VENDOR MASTER FILE
**************************
ENVIRONMENT DIVISION.
*
*
CONFIGURATION SECTION.
*
SOURCE-COMPUTER. VAX-11.
OBJECT-COMPUTER. VAX-11.
*
*
INPUT-OUTPUT SECTION.
*
FILE-CONTROL.
        SELECT INDEXED-VENDOR-MASTER
                ASSIGN TO "IVENDM.DAT"
                ORGANIZATION IS INDEXED
                ACCESS MODE IS SEQUENTIAL
                RECORD KEY IS IVM-VENDOR-NUMBER
                FILE STATUS IS WS-FILE-STATUS.
*
*
*
DATA DIVISION.
**
*
FILE SECTION.
*
*
FD  INDEXED-VENDOR-MASTER
                LABEL RECORDS ARE STANDARD.
*
01  IVM-VENDOR-RECORD.
        05  IVM-VENDOR-NUMBER           PIC X(06).
        05  IVM-VENDOR-NAME             PIC X(30).
        05  IVM-VENDOR-ADDRESS1         PIC X(25).
        05  IVM-VENDOR-ADDRESS2         PIC X(25).
        05  IVM-VENDOR-CITY             PIC X(20).
        05  IVM-VENDOR-STATE            PIC X(02).
        05  IVM-VENDOR-ZIP              PIC X(05).
        05  IVM-VENDOR-BUYS             PIC S9(06)V99.
        05  IVM-VENDOR-LAST-DATE        PIC 9(06).
        05  IVM-VENDOR-CODE             PIC X(01).
WORKING-STORAGE SECTION.
01  WS-FILE-STATUS                      PIC X(02).
01  WS-EOF-SWITCH                       PIC X(01).
/
**************************
*
*   PROCEDURE DIVISION
*      BEGINS HERE
**************************
PROCEDURE DIVISION.
*
*
000-MAIN-MODULE.
        OPEN
                        I-O         INDEXED-VENDOR-MASTER.
```

```
          PERFORM 100-INITIALIZE-TOTALS-ETC.
          PERFORM 200-UPDATE-MASTER-FILE
                  UNTIL WS-EOF-SWITCH = "X".
          CLOSE

                  INDEXED-VENDOR-MASTER.
          STOP RUN.
  ***********************
  * THIS MODULE INITIALIZES
  *   TOTALS, SWITCHES, ETC
  ***********************
  100-INITIALIZE-TOTALS-ETC.
          MOVE SPACES TO  WS-EOF-SWITCH.
          READ INDEXED-VENDOR-MASTER AT END MOVE "X" TO WS-EOF-SWITCH.
  *******************
  * THIS MODULE DETERMINES
  * THE UPDATE PROCESS
  ******************
  200-UPDATE-MASTER-FILE.
  *
          DISPLAY IVM-VENDOR-RECORD.
          READ INDEXED-VENDOR-MASTER AT END MOVE "X" TO WS-EOF-SWITCH.
```

Figure 4–7 (continued)

```
000115ABC MFG. CO.              123 EL ST.                         MONROE       LA712200000000C
000126CADDY SHACK               147 OAK LANE      P. O. BOX 148    RUSTON       LA712700000000C
000188RUSTON OFFICE SUPPLY CO.  210 SOUTH TRENTON                 RUSTON       LA712700009500C061483
004075SPIVEY'S FRIED CHICKEN    SOUTH HWY 149                      GRAMBLING    IA712450000 0C00000
004099ELECTRONIC SPECIALTY PRODUCTS  615R S MONROE                RUSTON       IA712700000000C
005984MID-STATE WOOD PRESERVERS INC  HWY 80                       GRAMBLING    LA712450000000C
006666LINCOLN STORAGE SYSTEMS INC.   HWY 150 W                    GRAMBLING    LA712450000000C
007777KELLY'S CLEANERS          MAIN STREET                       GRAMBLING    LA712450000000C
007778COLLEGIATE SHOPPE         MAIN STREET                       GRAMBLING    LA712450000000C000000
007779GRAY'S INSURANCE          MAIN STREET                       GRAMBLING    IA712450000000C
008478DON DURRETT CONSTRUCTION CO.   HWY 563                      GRAMBLING    LA712450000000C
```

Figure 4–8
Indexed file after update.

1. The SELECT statement's ACCESS MODE is presented as being SEQUENTIAL because the indexed file is accessed in a sequential fashion.
2. The OPEN statement opens the indexed file for sequential operations as follows:

```
OPEN INPUT INDEXED-VENDOR-MASTER.
```

3. The READ statement does not contain an INVALID KEY clause but does contain an AT END clause. This is necessary to process the file in a sequential manner.

The Outputs

The program in Figure 4-7 was used to print the master file after the update process had been completed. The output from the program is presented in Figure 4-8.

Notice that there are differences in the master file prior to the update and after the update. The printout of the master file after the update incorporates the changes that were included in the TRANSACTION-FILE. The changes to the file are the same as in Chapter 3. Figure 4-9 illustrates the changes.

Figure 4-10 depicts the AUDIT-ERROR-LIST that resulted from the execution of the indexed update program.

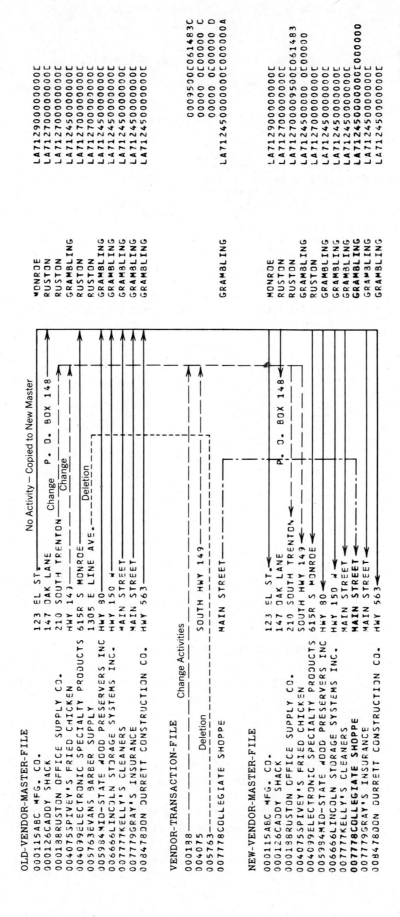

Figure 4–9 Distribution of file update activities.

VENDOR MASTER FILE MAINTENANCE
AUDIT—ERROR REPORT

PAGE: 1

VENDOR NUMBER	VENDOR NAME	VENDOR ADDRESS	AMOUNT OF PURCHASES	DATE OF LAST PURCHASE	ACTION TAKEN	ERROR MESSAGE
000188		SOUTH HWY 149	950.00	061483	CHANGED	
004075			.00	00000	CHANGED	
005763			.00	00000	DELETED	
007778	COLLEGIATE SHOPPE	MAIN STREET GRAMBLING	.00	000000	ADDED	

VENDOR MASTER FILE MAINTENANCE
AUDIT—ERROR REPORT

PAGE: 2

VENDOR NUMBER	VENDOR NAME	VENDOR ADDRESS	AMOUNT OF PURCHASES	DATE OF LAST PURCHASE	ACTION TAKEN	ERROR MESSAGE

```
TRANSACTIONS READ    5
  TOTAL ADDS         1
    PROCESSED        1
    REJECTED         0
  TOTAL DELETES      1
    PROCESSED        1
  * REJECTED         0
  TOTAL CHANGES      2
    PROCESSED        2
    REJECTED         0
MASTERS READ        12
MASTERS WRITTEN      0
```

Figure 4-10
Audit/error list—indexed file
update.

SECTION 12
Sample COBOL Program

Figure 4-11 contains the complete indexed master file update program used in this chapter.

Figure 4–11
Indexed master file update
listing.

```
IDENTIFICATION DIVISION.
PROGRAM-ID. INDXMA.
AUTHOR. CSIMPSON.
INSTALLATION. GRAMBLING STATE UNIVERSITY.
**************************
*INDEXED SEQUENTIAL UPDATE
* VENDOR MASTER FILE
**************************
ENVIRONMENT DIVISION.
*
*
CONFIGURATION SECTION.
*
SOURCE-COMPUTER. VAX-11.
OBJECT-COMPUTER. VAX-11.
*
*
INPUT-OUTPUT SECTION.
*
FILE-CONTROL.
        SELECT INDEXED-VENDOR-MASTER
                ASSIGN TO "IVENDM.DAT"
                ORGANIZATION IS INDEXED
                ACCESS MODE IS RANDOM
                RECORD KEY IS IVM-VENDOR-NUMBER
                FILE STATUS IS WS-FILE-STATUS.
        SELECT TRANSACTION-FILE
                ASSIGN TO "VENDTR".
*
        SELECT AUDIT-ERROR-LIST
                ASSIGN TO "AUDLST.LST".
/
*
*
*
DATA DIVISION.
**
*
FILE SECTION.
*
*
FD  INDEXED-VENDOR-MASTER
                LABEL RECORDS ARE STANDARD.
*
01  IVM-VENDOR-RECORD.
        05  IVM-VENDOR-NUMBER        PIC X(06).
        05  IVM-VENDOR-NAME          PIC X(30).
        05  IVM-VENDOR-ADDRESS1      PIC X(25).
        05  IVM-VENDOR-ADDRESS2      PIC X(25).
        05  IVM-VENDOR-CITY          PIC X(20).
        05  IVM-VENDOR-STATE         PIC X(02).
        05  IVM-VENDOR-ZIP           PIC X(05).
        05  IVM-VENDOR-BUYS          PIC S9(06)V99.
        05  IVM-VENDOR-LAST-DATE     PIC 9(06).
        05  IVM-VENDOR-CODE          PIC X(01).
*
FD  TRANSACTION-FILE
                LABEL RECORDS ARE STANDARD.
*
```

```
Figure 4-11 (continued)  01  TRANSACTION-RECORD.
                             05  TF-VENDOR-NUMBER          PIC X(06).
                             05  TF-VENDOR-NAME            PIC X(30).
                             05  TF-VENDOR-ADDRESS1        PIC X(25).
                             05  TF-VENDOR-ADDRESS2        PIC X(25).
                             05  TF-VENDOR-CITY            PIC X(20).
                             05  TF-VENDOR-STATE           PIC X(02).
                             05  TF-VENDOR-ZIP             PIC X(05).
                             05  TF-VENDOR-BUYS            PIC S9(6)V99.
                             05  TF-VENDOR-MONEY REDEFINES TF-VENDOR-BUYS PIC X(8).
                             05  TF-VENDOR-LAST-DATE.
                                 10   TF-MONTH             PIC 9(02).
                                 10   TF-DAY               PIC 9(02).
                                 10   TF-YEAR              PIC 9(02).
                             05  TF-VENDOR-CODE            PIC X(01).
                        *
                        FD  AUDIT-ERROR-LIST
                                    LABEL RECORDS ARE OMITTED.
                        *
                        01  VENDOR-REPORT-LINE             PIC X(132).
                        *
                        *
                        WORKING-STORAGE SECTION.
                        *
                        01  DL-VENDOR-LINE.
                             05  FILLER                    PIC X(02) VALUE SPACES.
                             05  DL-VENDOR-NUMBER          PIC X(06).
                             05  FILLER                    PIC X(05) VALUE SPACES.
                             05  DL-VENDOR-NAME            PIC X(30).
                             05  FILLER                    PIC X(05) VALUE SPACES.
                             05  DL-VENDOR-ADDRESS         PIC X(25).
                             05  FILLER                    PIC X(06) VALUE SPACES.
                             05  DL-VENDOR-BUYS            PIC ZZZ,ZZZ.99CR.
                             05  FILLER                    PIC X(04).
                             05  DL-VENDOR-LAST-DATE       PIC 99/99/99.
                             05  FILLER                    PIC X(06).
                             05  DL-ACTION                 PIC X(07).
                             05  FILLER                    PIC X(03) VALUE SPACES.
                             05  DL-ERROR-MESSAGE          PIC X(12).
                        ******************************
                        *   HEADING LINES
                        ******************************
                        01  HEAD1.
                             05  FILLER              PIC X(39) VALUE SPACES.
                             05  FILLER      PIC X(20) VALUE "VENDOR MASTER FILE M".
                             05  FILLER      PIC X(10) VALUE "AINTENANCE".
                        *
                        01  HEAD2.
                             05  FILLER      PIC X(07) VALUE " DATE: ".
                             05  HEAD2-DATE  PIC 99/99/99.
                             05  FILLER      PIC X(30) VALUE SPACES.
                             05  FILLER      PIC X(18) VALUE "AUDIT-ERROR REPORT".
                             05  FILLER      PIC X(25) VALUE SPACES.
                             05  FILLER      PIC X(06) VALUE "PAGE: ".
                             05  HEAD2-PAGE-NUMBER   PIC ZZ9.
                        *
                        01  HEAD3.
                             05  FILLER      PIC X(20) VALUE "  VENDOR            ".
                             05  FILLER      PIC X(20) VALUE " VENDOR             ".
                             05  FILLER      PIC X(20) VALUE "          VENDOR    ".
                             05  FILLER      PIC X(20) VALUE "                    ".
                             05  FILLER      PIC X(20) VALUE "AMOUNT OF      DATE ".
                             05  FILLER      PIC X(20) VALUE "OF          ACTION  E".
                             05  FILLER      PIC X(04) VALUE "RROR".
                        *
                        01  HEAD4.
                             05  FILLER      PIC X(20) VALUE "  NUMBER            ".
                             05  FILLER      PIC X(20) VALUE " NAME               ".
                             05  FILLER      PIC X(20) VALUE "         ADDRESS    ".
                             05  FILLER      PIC X(20) VALUE "                    ".
                             05  FILLER      PIC X(20) VALUE "PURCHASES    LAST P".
```

117

```
                05  FILLER        PIC X(20) VALUE "URCHASE   TAKEN   ME".
                05  FILLER        PIC X(05) VALUE "SSAGE".
*
01   AUDIT-LINE.
                05  FILLER                 PIC X(01) VALUE SPACES.
                05  AL-MESSAGE             PIC X(19).
                05  FILLER                 PIC X(02) VALUE SPACES.
                05  AL-AMOUNT              PIC ZZ,ZZ9.
*
01   WS-TOTAL-DESCRIPTIONS.
                05  FILLER                 PIC X(18) VALUE " TRANSACTIONS READ".
                05  FILLER                 PIC X(18) VALUE " TOTAL ADDS      ".
                05  FILLER                 PIC X(18) VALUE "    PROCESSED     ".
                05  FILLER                 PIC X(18) VALUE "    REJECTED      ".
                05  FILLER                 PIC X(18) VALUE " TOTAL DELETES   ".
                05  FILLER                 PIC X(18) VALUE "    PROCESSED     ".
                05  FILLER                 PIC X(18) VALUE "    REJECTED      ".
                05  FILLER                 PIC X(18) VALUE " TOTAL CHANGES   ".
                05  FILLER                 PIC X(18) VALUE "    PROCESSED     ".
                05  FILLER                 PIC X(18) VALUE "    REJECTED      ".
01   WS-AUDIT-DESCRIPTIONS REDEFINES WS-TOTAL-DESCRIPTIONS.
                05  WS-AUDIT-MESSAGE OCCURS 10 TIMES PIC X(18).
**************************
*   TOTALS
*        AREA
**************************
01   WS-TOTALS.
                05  WS-TRANSACTIONS-READ    PIC 9(05).
                05  WS-TOTAL-ADDS           PIC 9(05).
                05  WS-ADDS-PROCESSED       PIC 9(05).
                05  WS-ADDS-REJECTED        PIC 9(05).
                05  WS-TOTAL-DELETES        PIC 9(05).
                05  WS-DELETES-PROCESSED    PIC 9(05).
                05  WS-DELETES-REJECTED     PIC 9(05).
                05  WS-TOTAL-CHANGES        PIC 9(05).
                05  WS-CHANGES-PROCESSED    PIC 9(05).
                05  WS-CHANGES-REJECTED     PIC 9(05).
01   WS-RECORD-COUNTS REDEFINES WS-TOTALS.
                05  WS-TOTAL-VALUES OCCURS 10 TIMES PIC 9(05).
*
01   WS-LINE-COUNT                         PIC 9(02) VALUE 51.
01   WS-PAGE-NUMBER                        PIC 9(03) VALUE ZEROS.
**************************
*   GENERAL
*        EDIT
*             REQUIREMENTS
**************************

**************************
*
*   SWITCHES
**************************
01   WS-AUDIT-SW                           PIC X VALUE " ".
**************************
*   GENERAL WORKING-STORAGE
*     VALUES
**************************
01   DATE-IN                               PIC 9(06).
01   WS-ACTION                             PIC X(07).
01   WS-ERROR-MESSAGE                      PIC X(12).
01   I                                     PIC 9(02).
01   WS-FILE-STATUS                        PIC X(02).
01   WS-EOF-SWITCH                         PIC X(01).
/
**************************
*
```

Figure 4–11 (continued)

Figure 4-11 (continued)

```
*   PROCEDURE DIVISION
*      BEGINS HERE
**********************
PROCEDURE DIVISION.
*
*
000-MAIN-MODULE.
        OPEN INPUT      TRANSACTION-FILE
        DISPLAY "OPENED TF".
        OPEN     OUTPUT AUDIT-ERROR-LIST
        DISPLAY "OPENED AEL".
        OPEN     I-O    INDEXED-VENDOR-MASTER.
        DISPLAY "OPENED IVM".
        PERFORM 100-INITIALIZE-TOTALS-ETC.
        PERFORM 200-UPDATE-MASTER-FILE
                UNTIL WS-EOF-SWITCH = "X".
        PERFORM 400-PRINT-AUDIT-TOTALS.
        CLOSE    TRANSACTION-FILE
                 AUDIT-ERROR-LIST
                 INDEXED-VENDOR-MASTER.
        STOP RUN.
**********************
* THIS MODULE INITIALIZES
*   TOTALS, SWITCHES, ETC
**********************
100-INITIALIZE-TOTALS-ETC.
        MOVE SPACES TO WS-EOF-SWITCH.
        MOVE ZEROS TO   WS-TOTALS
                        WS-PAGE-NUMBER.
        MOVE 51 TO WS-LINE-COUNT.
        ACCEPT DATE-IN FROM DATE.
        PERFORM 500-READ-TRANSACTION.
**********************
* THIS MODULE DETERMINES
* THE UPDATE PROCESS
**********************
200-UPDATE-MASTER-FILE.
*
        PERFORM 600-READ-MASTER.
        IF WS-FILE-STATUS = "23"
                PERFORM 220-ADD-MASTER
        ELSE IF (WS-FILE-STATUS = "00" AND TF-VENDOR-CODE = "D")
                PERFORM 240-DELETE-MASTER
        ELSE IF (WS-FILE-STATUS = "00" AND TF-VENDOR-CODE = "C")
                PERFORM 250-CHANGE-MASTER
        ELSE PERFORM 260-IDENTIFY-ERROR.
        PERFORM 300-PRINT-AUDIT.
        PERFORM 500-READ-TRANSACTION.
**********************
*THIS MODULE ADDS A
* RECORD TO THE INDEXED
* MASTER FILE
**********************
220-ADD-MASTER.
*
        IF TF-VENDOR-CODE NOT = "A"
                PERFORM 270-ADD-ERROR.
        MOVE "ADDED" TO WS-ACTION.
        MOVE TF-VENDOR-NUMBER TO IVM-VENDOR-NUMBER.
        MOVE TF-VENDOR-NAME TO IVM-VENDOR-NAME.
        MOVE TF-VENDOR-ADDRESS1 TO IVM-VENDOR-ADDRESS1.
        MOVE TF-VENDOR-ADDRESS2 TO IVM-VENDOR-ADDRESS2.
        MOVE TF-VENDOR-CITY TO IVM-VENDOR-CITY.
        MOVE TF-VENDOR-STATE TO IVM-VENDOR-STATE.
        MOVE TF-VENDOR-ZIP TO IVM-VENDOR-ZIP.
        MOVE TF-VENDOR-BUYS TO IVM-VENDOR-BUYS.
```

```
                  MOVE TF-VENDOR-LAST-DATE TO IVM-VENDOR-LAST-DATE.
                  PERFORM 700-WRITE-MASTER.
                  ADD 1 TO WS-ADDS-PROCESSED.
       ************************
       *THIS MODULE DELETES
       *A MASTER RECORD
       ************************
       240-DELETE-MASTER.
       *
                  ADD 1 TO WS-DELETES-PROCESSED.
                  MOVE "DELETED" TO WS-ACTION.
                  DELETE INDEXED-VENDOR-MASTER
                         INVALID KEY
                                DISPLAY "NOT ABLE TO DELETE RECORD"
                                DISPLAY "VENDOR NUMBER = " TF-VENDOR-NUMBER.
       ************************
       * THIS MODULE CHANGES
       * DATA IN THE OLD MASTER
       ************************
       250-CHANGE-MASTER.
       *
                  MOVE "CHANGED" TO WS-ACTION.
                  IF TF-VENDOR-NAME NOT EQUAL SPACES
                         MOVE TF-VENDOR-NAME TO IVM-VENDOR-NAME.
                  IF TF-VENDOR-ADDRESS1 NOT EQUAL SPACES
                         MOVE TF-VENDOR-ADDRESS1 TO IVM-VENDOR-ADDRESS1.
                  IF TF-VENDOR-ADDRESS2 NOT EQUAL SPACES
                         MOVE TF-VENDOR-ADDRESS2 TO IVM-VENDOR-ADDRESS2.
                  IF TF-VENDOR-CITY NOT EQUAL SPACES
                         MOVE TF-VENDOR-CITY TO IVM-VENDOR-CITY.
                  IF TF-VENDOR-STATE NOT EQUAL SPACES
                         MOVE TF-VENDOR-STATE TO IVM-VENDOR-STATE.
                  IF TF-VENDOR-ZIP NOT EQUAL SPACES
                         MOVE TF-VENDOR-ZIP TO IVM-VENDOR-ZIP.
                  IF TF-VENDOR-MONEY NOT EQUAL TO SPACES
                         MOVE TF-VENDOR-BUYS TO IVM-VENDOR-BUYS.
                  IF TF-VENDOR-LAST-DATE NOT EQUAL SPACES
                         MOVE TF-VENDOR-LAST-DATE TO IVM-VENDOR-LAST-DATE.
                  REWRITE IVM-VENDOR-RECORD
                         INVALID KEY
                                DISPLAY "REWRITE ERROR"
                                DISPLAY "VENDOR NUMBER = " TF-VENDOR-NUMBER.
                  ADD 1 TO WS-CHANGES-PROCESSED.
       ************************
       *THIS MODULE IS A DUMMY
       *IF IT WERE HERE IT WOULD
       *DETERMINE THE ERROR TYPE
       *FROM THE FILE STATUS CODE
       ************************
       260-IDENTIFY-ERROR.
       *
                  EXIT.
       ************************
       *THIS MODULE ILLUSTRATES
       *AN ERROR IN THE TRANSACTION
       *CODE AND MOVES VALUES
       ************************
       270-ADD-ERROR.
       *
                  MOVE "CODE ERROR" TO WS-ERROR-MESSAGE.
       ************************
       * THIS MODULE PRINTS
       * THE AUDIT REPORT
       ************************
       300-PRINT-AUDIT.
                  IF WS-LINE-COUNT > 50
```

Figure 4–11 (continued)

120

Figure 4–11 (continued)

```
                                  PERFORM 310-PRINT-HEADINGS.
                              PERFORM 320-PRINT-LINE.
           *
           310-PRINT-HEADINGS.
                   MOVE ZEROS TO WS-LINE-COUNT.
                   ADD 1 TO WS-PAGE-NUMBER.
                   MOVE DATE-IN TO HEAD2-DATE.
                   MOVE WS-PAGE-NUMBER TO HEAD2-PAGE-NUMBER.
                   WRITE VENDOR-REPORT-LINE FROM HEAD1 AFTER PAGE.
                   WRITE VENDOR-REPORT-LINE FROM HEAD2 AFTER 1.
                   WRITE VENDOR-REPORT-LINE FROM HEAD3 AFTER 2.
                   WRITE VENDOR-REPORT-LINE FROM HEAD4 AFTER 1.
           *
           320-PRINT-LINE.
                   MOVE TF-VENDOR-NUMBER TO DL-VENDOR-NUMBER.
                   MOVE TF-VENDOR-NAME TO DL-VENDOR-NAME.
                   MOVE TF-VENDOR-ADDRESS1 TO DL-VENDOR-ADDRESS.
                   MOVE TF-VENDOR-BUYS TO DL-VENDOR-BUYS.
                   MOVE TF-VENDOR-LAST-DATE TO DL-VENDOR-LAST-DATE.
                   MOVE WS-ACTION TO DL-ACTION.
                   MOVE WS-ERROR-MESSAGE TO DL-ERROR-MESSAGE.
                   WRITE VENDOR-REPORT-LINE FROM DL-VENDOR-LINE AFTER 2.
                   MOVE SPACES TO DL-VENDOR-LINE.
                   MOVE TF-VENDOR-ADDRESS2 TO DL-VENDOR-ADDRESS.
                   WRITE VENDOR-REPORT-LINE FROM DL-VENDOR-LINE AFTER 1.
                   MOVE TF-VENDOR-CITY TO DL-VENDOR-ADDRESS.
                   WRITE VENDOR-REPORT-LINE FROM DL-VENDOR-LINE AFTER 1.
                   ADD 4 TO WS-LINE-COUNT.
                   MOVE " " TO WS-AUDIT-SW.
                   MOVE SPACES TO WS-ACTION
                                     WS-ERROR-MESSAGE.

           **********************
           * THIS MODULE PRINTS
           * TOTALS ACCUMULATED
           * DURING THE UPDATE
           **********************
           400-PRINT-AUDIT-TOTALS.
           *
                   PERFORM 310-PRINT-HEADINGS.
                   PERFORM 410-PRINT-AUDIT-LINE
                       VARYING I FROM 1 BY 1
                       UNTIL I IS GREATER THAN 10.
           *
           410-PRINT-AUDIT-LINE.
                   MOVE WS-AUDIT-MESSAGE (I) TO AL-MESSAGE.
                   MOVE WS-TOTAL-VALUES (I) TO AL-AMOUNT.
                   WRITE VENDOR-REPORT-LINE FROM AUDIT-LINE AFTER 1.
           **************************
           *THIS MODULE READS THE
           *TRANSACTION FILE
           **************************
           500-READ-TRANSACTION.
           *
                   READ TRANSACTION-FILE
                       AT END MOVE "X" TO WS-EOF-SWITCH.
                   ADD 1 TO WS-TRANSACTIONS-READ.
           ***************************
           *THIS MODULE READS THE
           *INDEXED MASTER FILE
           ***************************
           600-READ-MASTER.
           *
                   MOVE ZEROS TO WS-FILE-STATUS.
                   MOVE TF-VENDOR-NUMBER TO IVM-VENDOR-NUMBER.
                   READ INDEXED-VENDOR-MASTER
                       INVALID KEY
```

Figure 4–11 (continued)

```
                                        DISPLAY "FOR YOU INFO ONLY"
                                        DISPLAY "INVALID KEY = "  TF-VENDOR-NUMBER.
        ****************************
        *THIS MODULE WRITES  A
        *MASTER RECORD
        ****************************
        740-WRITE-MASTER.
        *
                MOVE ZEROS TO WS-FILE-STATUS.
                WRITE IVM-VENDOR-RECORD
                        INVALID KEY
                                MOVE "WRITE FAIL " TO WS-ERROR-MESSAGE.
```

SECTION 13
Questions, Problems, and Exercises

I. Questions

1. What are the advantages of using indexed update procedures, as opposed to sequential update procedures? What are the disadvantages?
2. What files are typically included in an indexed update procedure?
3. How are indexed files initially created? Describe the specialized software method(s) used on your computer system.
4. Assume that you have been assigned the task of converting a sequential master file to an indexed master file that will contain the same data. How would you go about this process? Explain your reasoning.
5. The Somebody University PERSONNEL MASTER FILE is an indexed file whose key is SOCIAL SECURITY NUMBER. Code the SELECT statement entries necessary to access this file for the following:

    - sequential operations
    - random operations
    - random and/or sequential operations

6. In what sequence must the transaction file be arranged in order to update an indexed file in a random manner? Why?
7. What is the purpose of the FILE-STATUS entry? Change your entries in Question 5 to provide for FILE-STATUS.
8. Describe how the OPEN, READ, and WRITE statements used for indexed files differ from these statements when used for sequential files.

II. Problems and Exercises

1. Write a program to create an indexed customer master file from the sequential master file described in Exercise II-3 in Chapter 3.
2. Write a program to create an indexed personnel master file from the sequential personnel master file described in Exercise II-4 in Chapter 3.
3. Use the software routines provided with your computer system to create an indexed customer master file from the sequential master file described in Exercise II-3 in Chapter 3.
4. Use the software routines provided with your computer system to create an indexed personnel master file from the sequential master file described in Exercise II-4 in Chapter 3.

5. Write a COBOL program to read the file you have created in Exercises 1 or 3 preceding to sequentially read the indexed customer master file and print each record on a line printer.

6. Write a COBOL program to read the indexed file you have created in Exercises 2 or 4 preceding to sequentially read the indexed personnel master file and print each record read on a line printer.

7. Using the indexed customer master file created in 1 or 3 preceding together with the transaction file described in Exercise II-4 of Chapter 3, write a COBOL program to randomly update the customer master file described in Exercise II-3 of Chapter 3. Also create the same audit/error list described in Exercise II-3 of Chapter 3.

8. Using the indexed personnel master file created in Exercises 2 or 4 together with the transaction file described in Exercise II-4 of Chapter 3, write a COBOL program to randomly update the personnel master file. Also create the same audit/error list described in Exercise II-4 of Chapter 3.

9. Using the inventory master file from Exercise II-5 of Chapter 3 as the input file, write a COBOL program that will create an indexed inventory master file.

10. Write a COBOL program to read the indexed inventory master file you have created in Exercise 9 preceding and print each record read on a line printer.

11. Using the indexed inventory master file from Exercise 9 preceding and the transaction file described in Exercise II-5 of Chapter 3, write a COBOL program to randomly update the indexed inventory master file.

5

Other Indexed Applications

SECTION 1
Introduction

As you have seen, the indexed file organization structure is a versatile organization method that allows a programmer to minimize programming effort and to increase processing capability. It is a method that also allows the system developers to minimize the use of special-purpose software programs (such as utility sort packages) in processing. This is explained in further detail in subsequent sections of this chapter.

The inclusion of certain features that are peculiar to indexed files allows the programmer to perform tasks such as:

1. Access an indexed file, either sequentially or randomly, within a single program.
2. Implement an inverted list structure with indexed files.
3. Start processing data of an indexed file at a specific point within the file.

The purpose of this chapter is to illustrate some of the important features of indexed files that were not presented in Chapter 4. This chapter will include the three features mentioned in the previous list.

SECTION 2
An Example Problem

Most of the examples in this book to this point have dealt with the techniques required to update or maintain a master file. Not all applications in a data processing function include a master file update. In fact, most data processing systems focus on the processing of transactions. Nonetheless, the advantages of continuing our illustration of rather complex material through the use of a familiar situation seems to outweigh the disadvantage of possibly giving you the wrong impression of "real-world" operations. We will continue with another part of an accounts payable system as an illustrative example.

At some point in an accounts payable system, the need to write a check payable to the appropriate vendor arises: the focus in this chapter is on the checkwriting program in an accounts payable system.

The method that we have chosen to present our selected techniques probably would *not* be implemented in a real accounts payable system. The example program is, however, adequate for our discussion.

The systems flowchart for our example problem is presented in Figure 5-1. The inputs to the example program are:

```
VENDOR-MASTER-FILE

INVOICE-MASTER

CHECK-MASTER-FILE
```

The outputs of the example program are:

```
CHECK-LIST (the printed checks)

CHECK-MASTER-FILE

VENDOR-MASTER-FILE
```

The VENDOR-MASTER-FILE contains the vendor's names and addresses used by the program for inclusion on the check.

The INVOICE-MASTER contains invoices that are received from the various vendors and that have been selected for payment. This file has as its primary key a field called "transaction number." The primary key may be used in applications other than ours to retrieve or write records, but for the purposes of our present program this field has no utility. Fortunately, the file is organized with an ALTERNATE RECORD KEY, which, in this case, is the vendor's name. This ALTERNATE KEY allows us to access this file using a path other than the primary key path. This is a powerful tool in our case specifically, and in many other applications, since the necessity of sorting a file in the same sequence as the VENDOR-MASTER-FILE has been eliminated.

The CHECK-MASTER-FILE is used for two purposes in the example problem. First, the CHECK-MASTER-FILE is used to retrieve the check number of the last check written on the file during the previous processing. Second, the

Figure 5–1
Checkwriter system flowchart.

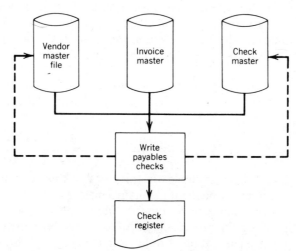

`CHECK-MASTER-FILE` contains a record of all checks that have been written but have not yet cleared the bank.

The `CHECK-LIST` file will contain records from which the checks will actually be printed. An automated accounts payable system usually uses a preprinted check form, which typically includes a stub on which invoice data may be printed. In our example, a maximum of 14 vendor invoices may be included on the stub. (See Figure 5-2 for a sample accounts payable check).

In real life, an accounts payable system will provide for the payment of an unlimited number of invoices from a specific vendor. Our sample program does not make this provision, because our focus is on indexed organization methods in COBOL rather than on a complete system design. We implied before that the checks that are written in this system are written so that all invoices for a specific

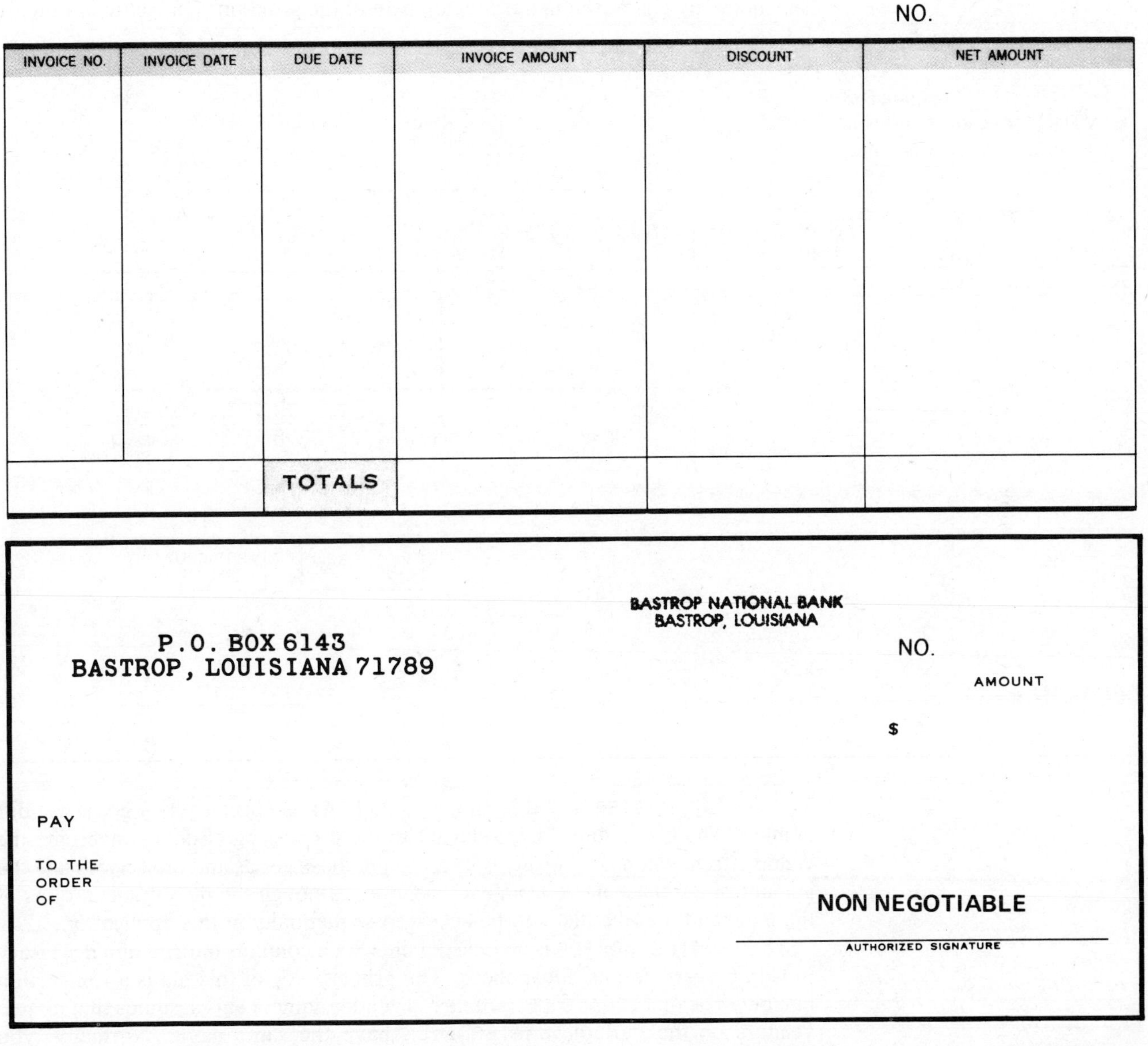

NO.

INVOICE NO.	INVOICE DATE	DUE DATE	INVOICE AMOUNT	DISCOUNT	NET AMOUNT
		TOTALS			

BASTROP NATIONAL BANK
BASTROP, LOUISIANA

P.O. BOX 6143
BASTROP, LOUISIANA 71789

NO.

AMOUNT

$

PAY

TO THE
ORDER
OF

NON NEGOTIABLE

AUTHORIZED SIGNATURE

Figure 5–2
Preprinted check form.

vendor will be paid in one check. Also notice that the VENDOR-MASTER-FILE is in sequence on the vendor number and that the INVOICE-MASTER is in sequence on the transaction number. How, then, is it possible to link these files together and produce one check to a vendor without sorting the two files in sequence on the vendor's name? The alternate path provided by the ALTERNATE RECORD KEY is the feature of COBOL which allows this. Details of the use of this feature are included in Sections 5 and 8.

SECTION 3
Hierarchy Chart

The hierarchy chart used in the development of the program is presented in Figure 5-3.

Figure 5–3
VTOC for accounts payable checkwriter.

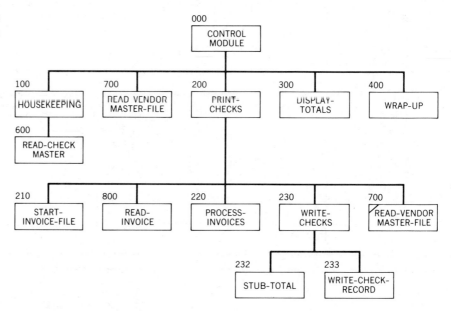

SECTION 4
The Structure of the Files

The VENDOR-MASTER-FILE is an indexed file whose primary key is the vendor number. The file contains data relevant to the processing of data concerning the vendors from whom a company is likely to purchase goods and/or services and the amount of purchase made from each vendor. Although the file organization is of the indexed type, the file is to be accessed sequentially in this application.

The INVOICE-MASTER is an indexed file which contains information necessary to help prepare an individual check. The primary key of this file is a transaction number. The ALTERNATE RECORD KEY is vendor name. (This assumes that no two vendors on the VENDOR-MASTER-FILE have the same name. Normally, you would use a key—whether primary or alternate—that is unique. In the example case you would typically use the vendor number as the ALTERNATE RECORD KEY, but we want to illustrate that you can use a name as a key). This alternate path is sometimes called an *inverted list,* particularly when duplicates are allowed to exist in the alternate path. You should see Section 12 of this chapter or a data structures text for a more complete discussion of inverted lists. The file is STARTed randomly, beginning with a particular vendor. Then the file is accessed sequentially until the vendor name changes.

The CHECK-MASTER-FILE is an indexed file whose primary key is check number. The file is accessed sequentially to retrieve the last check number used during previous processing and then accessed randomly to write the images of the current checks that are being written to the file.

SECTION 5
ENVIRONMENT DIVISION Entries for the Sample Program

The ENVIRONMENT DIVISION entries (using DEC-VAX computer) for the files included in the example program are as follows:

```
        SELECT VENDOR-MASTER-FILE
            ASSIGN TO "IVENDM.DAT"
            ORGANIZATION IS INDEXED
            ACCESS MODE IS DYNAMIC
            RECORD KEY IS VM-VENDOR-NUMBER.
  *
        SELECT INVOICE-MASTER
            ASSIGN TO "INVMF.DAT"
            ORGANIZATION IS INDEXED
            ACCESS MODE IS DYNAMIC
            RECORD KEY IS IR-TRANSACTION-NUMBER
            ALTERNATE RECORD KEY IS IR-VENDOR-NAME
                WITH DUPLICATES.
  *
        SELECT CHECK-LIST
            ASSIGN TO "CHECKS.LST".
  *
        SELECT CHECK-MASTER
            ASSIGN TO "CHECK.DAT"
            ORGANIZATION IS INDEXED
            ACCESS MODE IS DYNAMIC
            RECORD KEY IS CM-CHECK-NUMBER.
```

The VENDOR-MASTER-FILE, INVOICE-MASTER, and the CHECK-MASTER all have an ORGANIZATION IS INDEXED clause because these files are all indexed. The files use the same ACCESS MODE of DYNAMIC. As indicated in Chapter 4, the three ACCESS MODE options are:

SEQUENTIAL

RANDOM

DYNAMIC

The DYNAMIC ACCESS mode allows the programmer to access the file either sequentially, randomly, or both, in the same program, with one OPEN statement for the file.

A major difference among the ENVIRONMENT DIVISION entries occurs with the entry for the INVOICE-MASTER. Notice that the following clause occurs immediately after the RECORD KEY clause:

```
ALTERNATE RECORD KEY IS IR-VENDOR-NAME
    WITH DUPLICATES.
```

This clause establishes the existence of an alternate path through the invoice file which may be used in lieu of the primary key path. This file was created and maintained through one or more other programs in the system: when the file is maintained, the alternate key path is also maintained. Furthermore, when the file is created with the ALTERNATE RECORD KEY, a second index is created and associated with the file. Obviously, this adds to the disk overhead required for such a file. If a file contains an alternate path, the fact that this path exists must be described in the ENVIRONMENT DIVISION of any program that uses the file—whether or not the alternate path is being used. Having more than one access path available to you when you use such a file compensates for this additional bother.

Because we use the vendor's name as the alternate path in the example and since a number of invoices for a specific vendor may exist in the file, the WITH DUPLICATES option is specified for this file. If only one invoice were allowed per vendor then the WITH DUPLICATES option would not be specified.

SECTION 6
DATA DIVISION Entries for the Sample Program

The DATA DIVISION entries are included in the program listing at the end of this chapter. There are not any noteworthy differences from anything you have seen to this point in the book.

SECTION 7
Some New PROCEDURE DIVISION Statements

The PROCEDURE DIVISION contains some statements that are radically different from the statements you have seen to this point. After a brief description of their functions, these statements will be presented in the context of their functional use.

The START Verb

The general format of the START verb is as follows:

```
START file-name
            ⎧ IS =                  ⎫
            ⎪ IS EQUAL TO           ⎪
      [KEY  ⎨ IS NOT <              ⎬  data-name]
            ⎪ IS NOT LESS THAN      ⎪
            ⎪ IS >                  ⎪
            ⎩ IS GREATER THAN       ⎭
      [INVALID KEY any imperative statement]
```

The purpose of the START verb is to randomly locate the point in an indexed file at which record(s) for a specific key begin. The file can be processed beginning with a key whose value is equal to, less than, or greater than the value of a specified data-name. The START verb does not READ records—it only postions a pointer so that the record may be accessed.

The data-name serves the purpose of specifying the path through the file that the programmer wishes to follow. In our case, the path selected could be either IR-TRANSACTION-NUMBER or IR-TRANSACTION-NAME.

The INVALID KEY provides the programmer with an option if the value of the key is not on the file.

The READ NEXT *Statement*

The format of the READ NEXT statement is as follows:

```
READ file-name NEXT
    AT END any imperative statement.
```

The purpose of the READ NEXT statement in this chapter is to sequentially read an indexed file whose ACCESS MODE IS DYNAMIC. Since DYNAMIC files may be accessed either randomly or sequentially, there must be some indication of your intent. When you invoke the NEXT clause in a READ statement you implicity dictate sequential access. As always, when you access a file sequentially, the AT END statement must be specified.

The READ...NEXT statement is used after a file's record pointer has been positioned to a selected point. The READ...NEXT statement then reads the indexed file as if it were a sequential file from the point of selection.

SECTION 8
PROCEDURE DIVISION Entries for the Sample Program

000-CONTROL-CHECK-PRINT

The instructions included in the control module are as follows:

```
000-CONTROL-CHECK-PRINT,
      PERFORM 100-HOUSEKEEPING,
      MOVE LOW-VALUES TO VM-VENDOR-NUMBER,
      START VENDOR-MASTER-FILE
          KEY > VM-VENDOR-NUMBER
          INVALID KEY MOVE "X" TO CHECK-MASTER-EOF-SW,
      PERFORM 700-READ-VENDOR-MASTER,
      PERFORM 200-PRINT-CHECKS
          UNTIL CHECK-MASTER-EOF-SW = "X",
      PERFORM 300-DISPLAY-TOTALS,
      PERFORM 400-FINISH,
      STOP RUN,
```

In this paragraph the START verb is used to locate the first record on the VENDOR-MASTER-FILE. In this case the "first" record is defined as the one with the lowest vendor number. Finding the first record is accomplished in two steps.

1. The statement

```
MOVE LOW-VALUES TO VM-VENDOR-NUMBER.
```

moves low values to the key field for the VENDOR-MASTER-FILE so that all the records in the file have vendor numbers higher than this starting point.

2. The statement

```
START VENDOR-MASTER-FILE
      KEY IS > VM-VENDOR-NUMBER
      INVALID KEY
           MOVE "X" TO CHECK-MASTER-EOF-SW.
```

finds the first record on the file whose key field contains a value greater than LOW-VALUES. The INVALID KEY path would be taken if there are no records on the file in our example.

Even though our particular test was for a "greater than" condition for the START, you are not prohibited from STARTing processing on a "not less than" or an "equal" condition. In our example we want to START the VENDOR-MASTER-FILE at the first record on the file and to continue to read that file sequentially to its end. The purpose of the START verb is to *find* the starting point from which to begin reading the file. It is important to note that the START verb *does not* cause a record to be READ. It positions the file pointer at the selected location to begin reading the file. In actual practice, ACCESS MODE IS SEQUENTIAL might have been used instead of this approach, but we wished to illustrate the use of DYNAMIC and START in an indexed file.

100-HOUSEKEEPING.

The 100-HOUSEKEEPING module first OPENS the files then READs the CHECK-MASTER-FILE in a pump-priming operation for the 600-READ-CHECK-MASTER module. The purpose of the 600-READ-CHECK-MASTER module is to retrieve the number of the last check written in the system in order to use this number as an input in the checkwriting function.

The next two statements increment the check number by 1 and move the date from memory to the WORKING-STORAGE. The last statement in the module is to reset the end-of-file switch to the null state in order that it can be used in subsequent modules of this program.

Also included in the 100-HOUSEKEEPING routine is a START verb for the CHECK-MASTER file. As discussed before, the purpose of this START command is to position the file record pointer to the beginning of the CHECK-MASTER file for sequential retrieval of data.

The statements contained in 100-HOUSEKEEPING are:

```
100-HOUSEKEEPING.
     OPEN I-O  VENDOR-MASTER-FILE
               INVOICE-MASTER
               CHECK-MASTER
          OUTPUT
               CHECK-LIST.
     MOVE ZEROS TO  WS-DISCOUNT-AMOUNT
                    WS-NET-AMOUNT
                    WS-TOTAL-GROSS
                    WS-TOTAL-DISCOUNT
                    WS-TOTAL-NET.
```

```
        MOVE LOW-VALUES TO CM-CHECK-NUMBER.
        START CHECK-MASTER
            KEY > CM-CHECK-NUMBER
            INVALID KEY MOVE "X" TO CHECK-MASTER-EOF-SW.
        READ CHECK-MASTER NEXT
            AT END MOVE "X" TO CHECK-MASTER-EOF-SW.
        PERFORM 600-READ-CHECK-MASTER
            UNTIL CHECK-MASTER-EOF-SW = "X".
        ADD 1 TO HOLD-CHECK-NUMBER.
        ACCEPT HOLD-DATE FROM DATE.
        MOVE SPACES TO CHECK-MASTER-EOF-SW.
```

200-PRINT-CHECKS

The purpose of the 200-PRINT-CHECKS module is to control the actual check-printing function.

```
    200-PRINT-CHECKS.
        PERFORM 210-START-INVOICE-FILE.
        IF INVOICE-PRESENT-SW = "X"
            PERFORM 800-READ-INVOICE
            MOVE HOLD-CHECK-NUMBER TO CHECK-LINE-NUMBER
            WRITE CHECK-LINE FROM CHECK-NUMBER-LINE AFTER 8
            PERFORM 220-PROCESS-INVOICES
                UNTIL VM-VENDOR-NAME NOT EQUAL
                    IR-VENDOR-NAME
            MOVE " " TO INVOICE-MASTER-EOF-SW
            PERFORM 230-WRITE-CHECK.
        PERFORM 700-READ-VENDOR-MASTER.
```

When the program enters this module a vendor record has been read from the VENDOR-MASTER-FILE. The module then PERFORMS the 210-START-INVOICE-FILE paragraph, which returns a value in the INVOICE-PRESENT-SW to indicate whether or not there are any invoices on the INVOICE-MASTER for the vendor NUMBER read from the INVOICE-MASTER-FILE. If invoices are present, the INVOICE-PRESENT-SW contains an "X" and processing continues; if not, then it is necessary to bypass further processing of this vendor and get another vendor number from the VENDOR-MASTER-FILE. In short, we want to not do the remainder of the statements in the paragraph. There are several approaches which may be taken here, and we have taken this opportunity to illustrate one of those options.

After the invoice file is STARTed, the statement

```
    PERFORM 800-READ-INVOICE
```

causes the first invoice record for a specific vendor to be READ from the invoice master file. (Please remember that the START verb did not read the first invoice record for this vendor).

The following statements

```
    MOVE HOLD-CHECK-NUMBER TO CHECK-LINE-NUMBER.
    WRITE CHECK-LINE FROM CHECK-NUMBER-LINE AFTER 8.
```

are for the purposes of printing the check number on the check in the appropriate position. These positioning values will vary from program to program, depending on the layout of the check form.

The statement

```
PERFORM 220-PROCESS-INVOICES
      UNTIL VM-VENDOR-NAME NOT EQUAL IR-VENDOR-NAME.
```

is an important logic control statement in this program. Since the invoice master may contain a number of invoices for the same vendor, the program must retrieve all invoices for a specific vendor. The modular logic, to this point, has

1. read a record from the vendor master file;
2. used this vendor name to randomly START the invoice file at this particular vendor, if records exist for the vendor;
3. read the first record for the specified vendor from the invoices file.

The PERFORM statement now processes the stub information for the remaining invoice records. The PERFORM UNTIL function compares the name from the vendor master to the name retrieved from the invoice master and terminates processing for this module if the names are unequal.

The statement

```
MOVE " " TO INVOICE-MASTER-EOF-SW.
```

is important, since we are accessing the INVOICE-MASTER sequentially, and it is probable that at some point we will get an end-of-file return for one of the vendors on the invoice master file even though we are not at end on the VENDOR-MASTER-FILE. MOVE " " TO INVOICE-MASTER-EOF-SW causes the switch to be reset, in order that we may continue to process invoices for the remaining vendors on the VENDOR-MASTER-FILE.

The PERFORM 230-WRITE-CHECK statement will cause the printing of the negotiable check portion of the accounts payable check.

The last statement in this module causes the reading of the next record from the vendor master file.

SECTION 9
The START Verb and Use of Alternate Key

```
210-START-INVOICE-FILE.
```

The statements in 210-START-INVOICE-FILE are as follows:

```
210-START-INVOICE-FILE.
     MOVE VM-VENDOR-NAME TO IR-VENDOR-NAME.
     MOVE "X" TO INVOICE-PRESENT-SW.
     START INVOICE-MASTER
           KEY = IR-VENDOR-NAME
           INVALID KEY
                MOVE " " TO INVOICE-PRESENT-SW.
```

The START command, as used in this module, serves the following purposes:

1. Using the IR-VENDOR-NAME as the key field specifies that we will use the alternate path.

2. By specifying "KEY =" we are looking for a particular vendor.
3. By using the INVALID KEY option we can set a switch to indicate whether there are invoices for the vendor name that we have specified (when the "switch" has a value of blank) or not (when the "switch" value is "X").

The START verb moves the pointer to the place in the INVOICE-MASTER where the first invoice for the specified vendor exists. Again, the START verb does not read the first invoice record for this vendor.

220-PROCESS-INVOICES.

The statements in 220-PROCESS-INVOICES are as follows (a reminder: IR=invoice record; DL=detail line; WS=WORKING-STORAGE):

```
220-PROCESS-INVOICES.
    MOVE IR-INVOICE-NUMBER TO DL-INVOICE-NO.
    MOVE IR-INVOICE-DATE TO DL-INV-DATE.
    MOVE IR-INVOICE-AMOUNT TO DL-INVOICE-AMT.
    IF IR-TERMS-CODE = "P"
        MULTIPLY IR-TERMS-AMOUNT BY IR-INVOICE-AMOUNT
            GIVING WS-DISCOUNT-AMOUNT
    ELSE
        MOVE IR-TERMS-AMOUNT TO WS-DISCOUNT-AMOUNT.
    SUBTRACT WS-DISCOUNT-AMOUNT FROM IR-DISCOUNT-AMOUNT
        GIVING WS-NET-AMOUNT.
    MOVE WS-DISCOUNT-AMOUNT TO DL-DISCOUNT.
    MOVE WS-NET-AMOUNT TO DL-NET-AMOUNT.
    ADD IR-INVOICE-AMOUNT TO WS-TOTAL-GROSS.
    ADD WS-DISCOUNT-AMOUNT TO WS-TOTAL-DISCOUNT.
    ADD WS-NET-AMOUNT TO WS-TOTAL-NET.
    ADD 1 TO STUB-COUNT.
    PERFORM 800-READ-INVOICE.
```

The purpose of this module is to process the invoices read from the INVOICE-MASTER and to write the appropriate invoice information on the check stub. The statements in this module also calculate the amount of discount that is due on an invoice. The IF statement determines whether the discount is a percentage or an absolute amount and then calculates the discount in accordance with that determination.

The last statement in the module reads another record from the INVOICE-MASTER. Remember from the preceding modules that this module is PERFORMed UNTIL the vendor name on the invoice master is no longer equal to the vendor name on the vendor master.

230-WRITE-CHECK.

After a check stub is printed, the stub total is printed, and then the negotiable portion of the check is printed from the values calculated during the printing of the stub information. Also the name and address values from the VENDOR-MASTER-FILE are used in printing the check. The logic for this paragraph is demonstrated in the complete program at the end of the chapter. There is nothing in this module that you not have seen before.

232-STUB-TOTAL.

As the invoices are printed on the stub, the total amount of discounts, the total gross amount, and the total net amount of the invoices for a particular vendor are also calculated. These totals are then printed as the last line on the check stub. The statements in this module are:

```
232-STUB-TOTAL.
     MOVE WS-TOTAL-GROSS TO DL-INVOICE-AMT.
     MOVE WS-TOTAL-DISCOUNT TO DL-DISCOUNT.
     MOVE WS-TOTAL-NET TO DL-NET-AMOUNT.
     WRITE CHECK-LINE FROM DETAIL-LINE AFTER 1.
```

233-WRITE-CHECK-RECORD.

233-WRITE-CHECK-RECORD creates a disk record of the data included on each printed check so that the same data may be used for processing in other parts of an accounts payable system. The WRITE process is an indexed WRITE with an INVALID KEY clause. The INVALID KEY return occurs only if there are duplicate check numbers. The module includes:

```
233-WRITE-CHECK-RECORD.
     MOVE HOLD-CHECK-NUMBER TO CM-CHECK-NUMBER.
     MOVE VM-VENDOR-NAME TO CM-VENDOR-NAME.
     MOVE HOLD-DATE TO CM-CHECK-DATE.
     MOVE WS-TOTAL-NET TO CM-CHECK-AMOUNT.
     ADD 1 TO HOLD-CHECK-NUMBER.
     WRITE CHECK-RECORD
         INVALID KEY
               DISPLAY "DUPLICATE CHECK NUMBER"
               MOVE "X" TO CHECK-MASTER-EOF-SW.
```

By setting the CHECK-MASTER-EOF-SW on we cause processing to cease. This is probably a good idea, because a duplicate check number in an accounts payable system is a serious problem that usually requires further investigation before processing can continue.

300-DISPLAY-TOTALS.

The purpose of the 300-DISPLAY-TOTALS routine is to provide part of the audit trail. As checks are written in the preceding modules, totals are accumulated for the gross amount, discount amount, and net amount. These totals are displayed at the end of job in order to provide a documentary audit trail for comparison with balances created in other accounting processes.

```
300-DISPLAY-TOTALS.
     MOVE GT-GROSS TO DISPLAY-AMOUNT.
     DISPLAY "GROSS AMOUNT = " DISPLAY-AMOUNT.
     MOVE GT-DISCOUNT TO DISPLAY-AMOUNT.
     DISPLAY "DISCOUNT AMOUNT = " DISPLAY-AMOUNT.
     MOVE GT-NET TO DISPLAY-AMOUNT.
     DISPLAY "NET AMOUNT = " DISPLAY-AMOUNT.
```

800-READ-INVOICE.

The only other module of the program that deserves special notice is the 800-READ-INVOICE module. The READ retrieves the next invoice in sequence from the invoice master and, if the file is AT END, sets the INVOICE-MASTER-EOF-SW "on." If the "switch" is on, HIGH-VALUES are moved to IR-VENDOR-NAME to cause a break on vendor name in the 200-PRINT-CHECKS module.

Since the `INVOICE-MASTER` is a dynamic file, which is read sequentially in this application, we indicate that records are retrieved sequentially through the use of the `NEXT` clause in the `READ` statement.

SECTION 10
An Examination of Inputs and Outputs

The inputs and outputs to the program are contained in Figures 5-4 and 5-5.

Inputs

The records contained in the `VENDOR-MASTER-FILE` are the same records you are acquainted with from Chapters 3 and 4.

The `INVOICE-MASTER` contains invoice records for four of the vendors on the `VENDOR-MASTER-FILE`. These are:

    RAY'S INSURANCE

    RUSTON OFFICE SUPPLY CO.

    KELLY'S CLEANERS

    CADDY SHACK

This means that checks should be written for only these four vendors. There are three invoices on the `INVOICE-MASTER` for the `RUSTON OFFICE SUPPLY CO.` Even though we are only going to write one check to this vendor, the check should have three invoices listed on the stub.

```
000115ABC MFG. CO.              123 ELM ST.                      MONROE     LA7129000000000+000000
000126CADDY SHACK               147 OAK LANE     P. O. BOX 148   RUSTON     LA7127000010000+101383
000188RUSTON OFFICE SUPPLY CO.  210 SOUTH TRENTON                RUSTON     LA7127000000000+000000
004075SPIVEY'S FRIED CHICKEN    SOUTH HWY 149                    GRAMBLING  LA7124500000000+000000
004099ELECTRONIC SPECIALTY PRODUCTS 615R S MONROE                RUSTON     LA7127000000000+000000
005984MID-STATE WOOD PRESERVERS INC HWY 80                       GRAMBLING  LA7124500000000+000000
006666LINCOLN STORAGE SYSTEMS INC.  HWY 150W                     GRAMBLING  LA7124500000000+000000
007777KELLY'S CLEANERS          MAIN STREET                      GRAMBLING  LA7124500000000+000000
007778COLLEGIATE SHOPPE         MAIN STREET                      GRAMBLING  LA7124500000000+000000
007779GRAY'S INSURANCE          MAIN STREET                      GRAMBLING  LA7124300000500+102183
008478DON DURRETT CONSTRUCTION CO.  HWY 563                      GRAMBLING  LA7124500000000+000000
```

VENDOR-MASTER-FILE

```
10138301 GRAY'S INSURANCE          23   00000100+P10118310218310318300015000+02101.0   000005000+POLICY A      102.0
10138302 RUSTON OFFICE SUPPLY CO.  345  00010000+A10028310128310318300002350+01235.55  000002350+PAPER        102.0
10138303 KELLY'S CLEANERS          55   00000200+P10138310238311058300004477+02335.00  000004077+333.01       7
10138304 RUSTON OFFICE SUPPLY CO.  88   00000200+P101383   11038300013450+03200.0      000002350+PENS         205.0
10138305 CADDY SHACK               98   00000200+P10088310188311088300002275+01101.0   000002275+UNIFORM RENT 205.0
10148301 RUSTON OFFICE SUPPLY CO.  107  00000200+P10148310248311138300002975+01101.0   000002975+PENS         205.0
```

INVOICE-MASTER (PARTIAL)

```
000200ABC MFG. CO.       101383000000000+
```

CHECK-MASTER

Figure 5–4
Inputs to the sample program.

Figure 5-5
Outputs from the sample
program.

```
000200ABC MFG. CO.              111383000000000+
000201CADDY SHACK               831125000002230+
000202RUSTON OFFICE SUPPLY CO.   831125000018347+
000203KELLY'S CLEANERS           831125000004388+
000204GRAY'S INSURANCE           831125000014850+
```

CHECK-MASTER (POST PROCESSING)

NO. **000202**

INVOICE NO.	INVOICE DATE	DUE DATE	INVOICE AMOUNT	DISCOUNT	NET AMOUNT
345	10 02 83		23.50	1.00	22.50
88	10 13 83		134.50	2.69	131.81
107	10 14 83		29.75	.59	29.16
		TOTALS	187.75	4.28	183.47

```
JOHNSON TRUCKING COMPANY          BASTROP NATIONAL BANK
        P.O. BOX 6143                 BASTROP, LOUISIANA
   BASTROP, LOUISIANA 71789                              NO. 000202
                                                            AMOUNT
        83 11 25                                   $ ******183.47


PAY

TO THE
ORDER
OF    RUSTON OFFICE SUPPLY CO.      JOHNSON TRUCKING COMPANY
      210 SOUTH TRENTON                  NON NEGOTIABLE

      RUSTON           LA  71270         AUTHORIZED SIGNATURE
```

Figure 5-5 (continued)

The CHECK-MASTER contains only one record in this example: a check that was written to the ABC MFG. CO. The number of that check was 000200. This check record should appear in the updated version of the CHECK-MASTER file.

Outputs

The outputs created in this program are the CHECK-LIST and CHECK-MASTER files and audit displays.

CHECK-LIST contains one check for each of the four vendors that are in the INVOICE-MASTER. Four checks were written and Figure 5-5 shows the check for RUSTON OFFICE SUPPLY CO. as an example of the printed output. Notice that the three invoices included in the INVOICE-MASTER appear on the stub portion of the check and that only this one check was written to this vendor.

As a result of the execution of this program, CHECK-MASTER contains the combination of the check(s) that were present prior to the execution of this run and the checks written during this run.

SECTION 11
The Sample Program Listing

Figure 5-6 is the listing of the program used as the example program in this chapter.

Figure 5–6
Example program.

```
IDENTIFICATION DIVISION.
PROGRAM-ID. PRINTCKS.
AUTHOR. CSIMPSON.
INSTALLATION. GRAMBLING STATE UNIVERSITY.
*
*DEMONSTRATION OF START VERB
*AND ALTERNATE KEYS.
*
*
ENVIRONMENT DIVISION.
*
*
CONFIGURATION SECTION.
*
SOURCE-COMPUTER. VAX-11.
OBJECT-COMPUTER. VAX-11.
*
*
INPUT-OUTPUT SECTION.
*
FILE-CONTROL.
        SELECT VENDOR-MASTER-FILE
                ASSIGN TO "IVENDM.DAT"
                ORGANIZATION IS INDEXED
                ACCESS MODE IS DYNAMIC
                RECORD KEY IS VM-VENDOR-NUMBER.
    *
        SELECT INVOICE-MASTER
                ASSIGN TO "INVMF.DAT"
                ORGANIZATION IS INDEXED
                ACCESS MODE IS DYNAMIC
                RECORD KEY IS IR-TRANSACTION-NUMBER
                ALTERNATE RECORD KEY IS IR-VENDOR-NAME
                        WITH DUPLICATES.
    *
        SELECT CHECK-LIST
                ASSIGN TO "CHECKS.LST".
    *
        SELECT CHECK-MASTER
                ASSIGN TO "CHECK.DAT"
                ORGANIZATION IS INDEXED
                ACCESS MODE IS DYNAMIC
                RECORD KEY IS CM-CHECK-NUMBER
                FILE STATUS IS XX-XX.
    *
    *
    *
DATA DIVISION.
*
*
FILE SECTION.
*
*
FD VENDOR-MASTER-FILE
        LABEL RECORDS ARE STANDARD.
*
01  VENDOR-MASTER-RECORD.
        05  VM-VENDOR-NUMBER      PIC X(06).
        05  VM-VENDOR-NAME        PIC X(30).
        05  VM-VENDOR-ADDRESS1    PIC X(25).
        05  VM-VENDOR-ADDRESS2    PIC X(25).
        05  VM-VENDOR-CITY        PIC X(20).
        05  VM-VENDOR-STATE       PIC X(02).
```

Figure 5-6 (continued)

```
                            05  VM-VENDOR-ZIP           PIC X(05).
                            05  VM-VENDOR-BUYS          PIC S9(06)V99.
                            05  VM-VENDOR-DATE          PIC 9(06).
                    *
                    FD  INVOICE-MASTER
                            LABEL RECORDS ARE STANDARD
                            RECORD CONTAINS 87 TO 407 CHARACTERS.
                    *
                    01  INVOICE-RECORD.
                            05  IR-TRANSACTION-NUMBER       PIC X(09).
                            05  IR-VENDOR-NAME             PIC X(30).
                            05  IR-INVOICE-NUMBER          PIC X(10).
                            05  IR-TERMS-AMOUNT            PIC S9(04)V9999.
                            05  IR-TERMS-CODE             PIC X(01).
                            05  IR-INVOICE-DATE            PIC X(06).
                            05  IR-TERMS-END             PIC X(06).
                            05  IR-DUE-DATE             PIC X(06).
                            05  IR-INVOICE-AMOUNT          PIC S9(07)V99.
                            05  IR-INDEX                 PIC 9(02).
                            05  IR-DISTRIBUTION-DATA
                                    OCCURS 1 TO 10 TIMES
                                    DEPENDING ON IR-INDEX.
                                    10  IR-ACCOUNT-NUMBER   PIC X(08).
                                    10  IR-DIST-AMOUNT     PIC S9(7)V99.
                                    10  IR-DESCRIPTION     PIC X(15).
                    *
                    FD  CHECK-LIST
                            LABEL RECORDS ARE OMITTED.
                    *
                    01  CHECK-LINE                        PIC X(132).
                    *
                    FD  CHECK-MASTER
                                    LABEL RECORDS ARE STANDARD.
                    *
                    01  CHECK-RECORD.
                            05  CM-CHECK-NUMBER           PIC X(06).
                            05  CM-VENDOR-NAME            PIC X(30).
                            05  CM-CHECK-DATE             PIC X(06).
                            05  CM-CHECK-AMOUNT           PIC S9(07)V99.
                    *
                    *
                    WORKING-STORAGE SECTION.
                    *
                    *AREA FOR SWITCHES
                    *
                    01  EOF-SW2              PIC X(01) VALUE SPACES.
                    01  EOF-SW              PIC X(01) VALUE SPACES.
                    01  INVOICE-PRESENT-SW  PIC X(01) VALUE SPACES.
                    *
                    *
                    *AMOUNTS AND HOLD AREA
                    *
                    *
                    01  XX-XX               PIC X(02).
                    01  WS-DISCOUNT-AMOUNT  PIC S9(6)V99.
                    01  WS-NET-AMOUNT       PIC S9(6)V99.
                    01  WS-TOTAL-GROSS      PIC S9(6)V99.
                    01  WS-TOTAL-DISCOUNT   PIC S9(6)V99.
                    01  WS-TOTAL-NET        PIC S9(6)V99.
                    01  STUB-COUNT          PIC 99 VALUE ZEROS.
                    01  I                   PIC 99 VALUE ZEROS.
                    01  GT-GROSS            PIC S9(7)V99 VALUE ZEROS.
                    01  GT-DISCOUNT         PIC S9(7)V99 VALUE ZEROS.
                    01  GT-NET              PIC S9(7)V99 VALUE ZEROS.
                    01  HOLD-CHECK-NUMBER   PIC 9(06).
                    01  DISPLAY-AMOUNT      PIC $Z,ZZZ,ZZZ.99CR.
```

Figure 5–6 (continued)
```
01  HOLD-DATE              PIC X(06).
*
*
*PRINT LINES AND HEADINGS AREA
*
*
01  CHECK-NUMBER-LINE.
        05  FILLER PIC X(22) VALUE "CLAUDE L. SIMPSON, JR.".
        05  FILLER PIC X(41) VALUE SPACES.
        05  CHECK-LINE-NUMBER PIC X(7).
01  AMOUNT-LINE.
        05  FILLER              PIC X(4) VALUE SPACES.
        05  AL-DATE             PIC XXBXXBXX.
        05  FILLER              PIC X(46) VALUE SPACES.
        05  AL-AMOUNT           PIC *,***,***.99.
01  ADDRESS-LINE.
        05  FILLER              PIC X(10) VALUE SPACES.
        05  AL-ADDRESS          PIC X(30).
        05  AL-ADD-CITY REDEFINES AL-ADDRESS.
                10  AL-CITY     PIC X(20).
                10  FILLER      PIC X.
                10  AL-STATE    PIC XX.
                10  FILLER      PIC XX.
                10  AL-ZIP      PIC X(5).
01  DETAIL-LINE.
        05  DL-INVOICE-NO       PIC X(8).
        05  FILLER              PIC X(01) VALUE SPACES.
        05  DL-INV-DATE         PIC XXBXXBXX.
        05  FILLER              PIC X(01) VALUE SPACES.
        05  DL-DUE-DATE         PIC XXBXXBXX.
        05  DL-INVOICE-AMT      PIC Z,ZZZ,ZZZ.99CR.
        05  FILLER              PIC X(04) VALUE SPACES.
        05  DL-DISCOUNT         PIC ZZ,ZZZ.99CR.
        05  FILLER              PIC X(01) VALUE SPACES.
        05  DL-NET-AMOUNT       PIC Z,ZZZ,ZZZ.99CR.
*
*
*PROCEDURE DIVISION BEGINS HERE
*
*
PROCEDURE DIVISION.
*
000-CONTROL-CHECK-PRINT.
        PERFORM 100-HOUSEKEEPING.
        MOVE LOW-VALUES TO VM-VENDOR-NUMBER.
        START VENDOR-MASTER-FILE KEY > VM-VENDOR-NUMBER
                INVALID KEY MOVE "X" TO EOF-SW.
        PERFORM 700-READ-VENDOR-MASTER.
        PERFORM 200-PRINT-CHECKS THRU 200-PRINT-EXIT
                UNTIL EOF-SW = "X".
        PERFORM 300-DISPLAY-TOTALS.
        PERFORM 400-FINISH.
        STOP RUN.
100-HOUSEKEEPING.
        OPEN I-O            VENDOR-MASTER-FILE
                            INVOICE-MASTER
                            CHECK-MASTER
             OUTPUT         CHECK-LIST.
        MOVE ZEROS TO       WS-DISCOUNT-AMOUNT
                            WS-NET-AMOUNT
                            WS-TOTAL-GROSS
                            WS-TOTAL-DISCOUNT
                            WS-TOTAL-NET.
        MOVE LOW-VALUES TO CM-CHECK-NUMBER.
        START CHECK-MASTER KEY > CM-CHECK-NUMBER
                INVALID KEY MOVE "X" TO EOF-SW.
```

Figure 5-6 (continued)

```
                               READ CHECK-MASTER NEXT AT END MOVE "X" TO EOF-SW.
                               PERFORM 600-READ-CHECK-MASTER
                                       UNTIL EOF-SW = "X".
                               ADD 1 TO HOLD-CHECK-NUMBER.
                               ACCEPT HOLD-DATE FROM DATE.
                               MOVE SPACES TO EOF-SW.
                       200-PRINT-CHECKS.
                               PERFORM 210-START-INVOICE-FILE THRU 210-EXIT.
                               IF INVOICE-PRESENT-SW = "X"
                                       NEXT SENTENCE
                               ELSE
                                       PERFORM 700-READ-VENDOR-MASTER
                                       GO TO 200-PRINT-EXIT.
                               PERFORM 800-READ-INVOICE.
                               MOVE HOLD-CHECK-NUMBER TO CHECK-LINE-NUMBER.
                               WRITE CHECK-LINE FROM CHECK-NUMBER-LINE AFTER 8.
                               PERFORM 220-PROCESS-INVOICES
                                       UNTIL VM-VENDOR-NAME NOT EQUAL IR-VENDOR-NAME.
                               MOVE " " TO EOF-SW2.
                               PERFORM 230-WRITE-CHECK.
                               PERFORM 700-READ-VENDOR-MASTER.
                       200-PRINT-EXIT.  EXIT.
                       210-START-INVOICE-FILE.
                               MOVE VM-VENDOR-NAME TO IR-VENDOR-NAME.
                               START INVOICE-MASTER
                                       KEY = IR-VENDOR-NAME
                                       INVALID KEY
                                               MOVE " " TO INVOICE-PRESENT-SW
                                               GO TO 210-EXIT.
                               MOVE "X" TO INVOICE-PRESENT-SW.
                       210-EXIT.  EXIT.
                       220-PROCESS-INVOICES.
                               MOVE IR-INVOICE-NUMBER TO DL-INVOICE-NO.
                               MOVE IR-INVOICE-DATE TO DL-INV-DATE.
                               MOVE IR-INVOICE-AMOUNT TO DL-INVOICE-AMT.
                               IF IR-TERMS-CODE = "P"
                                       MULTIPLY IR-TERMS-AMOUNT BY IR-INVOICE-AMOUNT
                                               GIVING WS-DISCOUNT-AMOUNT
                               ELSE
                                       MOVE IR-TERMS-AMOUNT TO WS-DISCOUNT-AMOUNT.
                               SUBTRACT WS-DISCOUNT-AMOUNT FROM IR-INVOICE-AMOUNT
                                       GIVING WS-NET-AMOUNT.
                               MOVE WS-DISCOUNT-AMOUNT TO DL-DISCOUNT.
                               MOVE WS-NET-AMOUNT TO DL-NET-AMOUNT.
                               ADD IR-INVOICE-AMOUNT TO WS-TOTAL-GROSS.
                               ADD WS-DISCOUNT-AMOUNT TO WS-TOTAL-DISCOUNT.
                               ADD WS-NET-AMOUNT TO WS-TOTAL-NET.
                               WRITE CHECK-LINE FROM DETAIL-LINE AFTER 1.
                               ADD 1 TO STUB-COUNT.
                               PERFORM 800-READ-INVOICE.
                       230-WRITE-CHECK.
                               PERFORM 231-LINE-SKIP
                                       VARYING I FROM STUB-COUNT BY 1
                                       UNTIL I > 14.
                               MOVE ZEROS TO STUB-COUNT.
                               PERFORM 232-STUB-TOTAL.
                               MOVE HOLD-CHECK-NUMBER TO CHECK-LINE-NUMBER.
                               WRITE CHECK-LINE FROM CHECK-NUMBER-LINE AFTER 7.
                               MOVE HOLD-DATE TO AL-DATE.
                               MOVE WS-TOTAL-NET TO AL-AMOUNT.
                               WRITE CHECK-LINE FROM AMOUNT-LINE AFTER 4.
                               MOVE VM-VENDOR-NAME TO AL-ADDRESS.
                               WRITE CHECK-LINE FROM ADDRESS-LINE AFTER 5.
                               MOVE VM-VENDOR-ADDRESS1 TO AL-ADDRESS.
                               WRITE CHECK-LINE FROM ADDRESS-LINE AFTER 1.
                               MOVE VM-VENDOR-ADDRESS2 TO AL-ADDRESS.
```

Figure 5–6 (continued)

```
            WRITE CHECK-LINE FROM ADDRESS-LINE AFTER 1.
            MOVE VM-VENDOR-CITY TO AL-CITY.
            MOVE VM-VENDOR-STATE TO AL-STATE.
            MOVE VM-VENDOR-ZIP TO AL-ZIP.
            WRITE CHECK-LINE FROM ADDRESS-LINE AFTER 1.
            PERFORM 233-WRITE-CHECK-RECORD
            ADD WS-TOTAL-GROSS TO GT-GROSS.
            ADD WS-TOTAL-DISCOUNT TO GT-DISCOUNT.
            ADD WS-TOTAL-NET TO GT-NET.
            MOVE ZEROS TO WS-TOTAL-GROSS
                          WS-TOTAL-DISCOUNT
                          WS-TOTAL-NET.
231-LINE-SKIP.
            MOVE SPACES TO DETAIL-LINE.
            WRITE CHECK-LINE FROM DETAIL-LINE AFTER 1.
232-STUB-TOTAL.
            MOVE WS-TOTAL-GROSS TO DL-INVOICE-AMT.
            MOVE WS-TOTAL-DISCOUNT TO DL-DISCOUNT.
            MOVE WS-TOTAL-NET TO DL-NET-AMOUNT.
            WRITE CHECK-LINE FROM DETAIL-LINE AFTER 1.
233-WRITE-CHECK-RECORD.
            MOVE HOLD-CHECK-NUMBER TO CM-CHECK-NUMBER.
            MOVE VM-VENDOR-NAME TO CM-VENDOR-NAME.
            MOVE HOLD-DATE TO CM-CHECK-DATE.
            MOVE WS-TOTAL-NET TO CM-CHECK-AMOUNT.
            WRITE CHECK-RECORD
                    INVALID KEY
                            DISPLAY "DUPLICATE CHECK NUMBER"
                            MOVE "X" TO EOF-SW.
300-DISPLAY-TOTALS.
            MOVE GT-GROSS TO DISPLAY-AMOUNT.
            DISPLAY "GROSS AMOUNT = " DISPLAY-AMOUNT.
            MOVE GT-DISCOUNT TO DISPLAY-AMOUNT.
            DISPLAY "DISCOUNT AMOUNT = " DISPLAY-AMOUNT.
            MOVE GT-NET TO DISPLAY-AMOUNT.
            DISPLAY "NET AMOUNT = " DISPLAY-AMOUNT.
400-FINISH.
            CLOSE   VENDOR-MASTER-FILE
                    INVOICE-MASTER
                    CHECK-LIST
                    CHECK-MASTER.
600-READ-CHECK-MASTER.
            MOVE CM-CHECK-NUMBER TO HOLD-CHECK-NUMBER.
            READ CHECK-MASTER NEXT
                    AT END MOVE "X" TO EOF-SW.
700-READ-VENDOR-MASTER.
            READ VENDOR-MASTER-FILE NEXT
                    AT END MOVE "X" TO EOF-SW.
800-READ-INVOICE.
            READ INVOICE-MASTER NEXT
                    AT END MOVE "X" TO EOF-SW2.
            IF EOF-SW2 = "X"
                    MOVE HIGH-VALUES TO IR-VENDOR-NAME.
```

SECTION 12
An Example of Using Indexed Files to Process Inverted Lists

Suppose a business has a requirement to obtain a listing of the invoices due a certain vendor prior to the checkwriting process. You could read the invoice master file sequentially and select all records whose vendor name matches the desired vendor name. However, it would be more rational to invert the file on vendor name through the use of an ALTERNATE RECORD KEY on vendor name and allow duplicates in the ALTERNATE KEY path.

The indexed file may then be STARTed at the desired point and the file READ until there are no more records for the selected vendor.

Figures 5-7 through 5-9 present the program, the input, and the listing for your consideration.

Figure 5–7
Program using an INDEXED file to PROCESS an inverted list.

```
IDENTIFICATION DIVISION.
PROGRAM-ID. PRTINV.
AUTHOR. CSIMPSON.
INSTALLATION. GRAMBLING STATE UNIVERSITY.
*
*DEMONSTRATION OF INVERTED LISTS
*USING ALTERNATE RECORD KEYS
*
*
ENVIRONMENT DIVISION.
CONFIGURATION SECTION.
SOURCE-COMPUTER. VAX-11.
OBJECT-COMPUTER. VAX-11.
INPUT-OUTPUT SECTION.
FILE-CONTROL.
      SELECT INVOICE-MASTER
          ASSIGN TO "INVMF.DAT"
          ORGANIZATION IS INDEXED
          ACCESS MODE IS DYNAMIC
          RECORD KEY IS IR-TRANSACTION-NUMBER
          ALTERNATE RECORD KEY IS IR-VENDOR-NAME
               WITH DUPLICATES.
      SELECT PRINT-FILE ASSIGN TO "INVOICE.LST".
DATA DIVISION.
FILE SECTION.
FD  INVOICE-MASTER
          LABEL RECORDS ARE STANDARD
          RECORD CONTAINS 87 TO 407 CHARACTERS.
01  INVOICE-RECORD.
      05  IR-TRANSACTION-NUMBER          PIC X(09).
      05  IR-VENDOR-NAME                 PIC X(30).
      05  IR-INVOICE-NUMBER              PIC X(10).
      05  IR-TERMS-AMOUNT                PIC S9(04)V9999.
      05  IR-TERMS-CODE                  PIC X(01).
      05  IR-INVOICE-DA                  PIC X(06).
      05  IR-TERMS-END                   PIC X(06).
      05  IR-DUE-DATE                    PIC X(06).
      05  IR-INVOICE-AMOUNT              PIC S9(07)V99.
      05  IR-INDEX                       PIC 9(02).
      05  IR-DISTRIBUTION-DATA
          OCCURS 1 TO 10 TIMES
          DEPENDING ON IR-INDEX.
          10  IR-ACCOUNT-NUMBER          PIC X(08).
          10  IR-DIST-AMOUNT             PIC S9(07)V99.
          10  IR-DESCRIPTION             PIC X(15).
```

Figure 5–7 (continued)

```
FD  PRINT-FILE
        LABEL RECORDS ARE OMITTED.
01  PRINT-LINE PIC X(132).
WORKING-STORAGE SECTION.
01  EOF-SW      PIC X(01) VALUE SPACES.
01  WS-VENDOR      PIC X(30).
01  X-ANSWER      PIC X(01) VALUE SPACES.
01  WS-LINE-COUNT PIC 9(02) VALUE 50.
01  H1.
        05  FILLER PIC X(31) VALUE SPACES.
        05  FILLER PIC X(15) VALUE "XYZ CORPORATION".
01  H2.
        05  FILLER PIC X(21) VALUE "INVOICE        VENDOR".
        05  FILLER PIC X(25) VALUE SPACES.
        05  FILLER PIC X(15) VALUE "INVOICE     DUE".
01  H3.
        05  FILLER PIC X(23) VALUE " NUMBER            NAME".
        05  FILLER PIC X(23) VALUE SPACES.
        05  FILLER PIC X(16) VALUE "AMOUNT      DATE".
01  DETAIL-LINE.
        05  DL-INVOICE                 PIC X(09).
        05  FILLER       PIC X(04) VALUE SPACES.
        05  DL-VENDOR                  PIC X(30).
        05  FILLER       PIC X(01) VALUE SPACES.
        05  DL-AMOUNT               PIC Z,ZZZ,ZZZ.99CR.
        05  FILLER       PIC X(01) VALUE SPACES.
        05  DL-DATE      PIC XXBXXBXX.
PROCEDURE DIVISION.
000-MAIN.
        OPEN I-O    INVOICE-MASTER
            OUTPUT PRINT-FILE.
001-CYCLE.
        DISPLAY "ENTER VENDOR NAME TO DISPLAY".
        ACCEPT WS-VENDOR.
        IF WS-VENDOR = "END" GO TO 900-END.
        MOVE WS-VENDOR TO IR-VENDOR-NAME.
        START INVOICE-MASTER KEY = IR-VENDOR-NAME
            INVALID KEY DISPLAY "NO INVOICES FOR VENDOR"
            DISPLAY "PRESS ANY KEY TO CONTINUE"
            ACCEPT X-ANSWER
            GO TO 001-CYCLE.
        READ INVOICE-MASTER NEXT
            AT END MOVE "X" TO EOF-SW.
        PERFORM 200-READ-PRINT
            UNTIL IR-VENDOR-NAME NOT = WS-VENDOR.
        GO TO 001-CYCLE.
200-READ-PRINT.
        ADD 1 TO WS-LINE-COUNT.
        IF WS-LINE-COUNT > 50
            PERFORM 300-PRINT-HEADINGS.
        MOVE IR-INVOICE-NUMBER TO DL-INVOICE.
        MOVE IR-VENDOR-NAME TO DL-VENDOR.
        MOVE IR-INVOICE-AMOUNT TO DL-AMOUNT.
        MOVE IR-DUE-DATE TO DL-DATE.
        WRITE PRINT-LINE FROM DETAIL-LINE AFTER 1.
        READ INVOICE-MASTER NEXT
            AT END MOVE HIGH-VALUES TO WS-VENDOR.
300-PRINT-HEADINGS.
        MOVE ZEROS TO WS-LINE-COUNT.
        WRITE PRINT-LINE FROM H1 AFTER PAGE.
        WRITE PRINT-LINE FROM H2 AFTER 1.
        WRITE PRINT-LINE FROM H3 AFTER 1.
        MOVE SPACES TO DETAIL-LINE.
        WRITE PRINT-LINE FROM DETAIL-LINE AFTER 1.
900-END.
        CLOSE INVOICE-MASTER.
        CLOSE PRINT-FILE.
        STOP RUN.
```

Figure 5–8
Input to inverted list program.

```
10118301 RUSTON OFFICE SUPPLY CO.        12      1107830000100001
10118302 RUSTON OFFICE SUPPLY CO.        33      1108830000050001
10118303 ABC MANUFACTURING CO.           66      1109830000030001
```

Figure 5–9
Output from inverted list program.

```
                         XYZ CORPORATION

INVOICE       VENDOR                    INVOICE      DUE

NUMBER         NAME                     AMOUNT       DATE


 12            RUSTON OFFICE SUPPLY CO.     100.00   11 07 83

 33            RUSTON OFFICE SUPPLY CO.       5.00   11 08 83
```

SECTION 13
Questions and Exercises

I. Questions

1. What are the three allowable ACCESS modes for indexed files? What is the purpose of each?
2. What is the purpose of the START verb?
3. What is the purpose of the READ...NEXT statement and how is it used?
4. What is the purpose of the ALTERNATE RECORD KEY? When should an ALTERNATE KEY be used? Can you think of any obvious disadvantages of using an ALTERNATE RECORD KEY? What are they?

II. Problems and Exercises

1. Assume that you have a customer master file and an invoice file. Further assume that you wish to delete a customer from the master file but the record may not be deleted if invoices exist for that customer on the invoice file. Describe how you think the START verb can be used to help in this procedure.
2. This exercise uses the customer master file created in II-1 of Problem 3 from Chapter 4 and an invoice master which is described next to create a customer statement of account.

    Input Files:

    customer master file (from Chapter 4)
    invoice master file

    Output files:

    updated customer master file
    customer statement

    Program operations:

    a. Sequentially read each record from the indexed customer master file.

b. For each record read from the customer master file, determine if there are invoices for that customer (use the START verb)—if there are, prepare a monthly statement of account in the format described following. If no invoices exist for the customer, check the BALANCE field to see if it is non-zero—if it is, prepare a statement for the customer showing the unpaid balance. If there are no invoices for the customer and the balance due field is zero, skip the statement preparation process
for the customer.

c. After each invoice record has been processed, DELETE each invoice record from the INVOICE MASTER FILE.

d. After each statement is prepared for a customer, update the customer master file with the new balance (use the REWRITE statement).

e. Print a message on the statement if the credit limit has been exceeded.

The format for the records included in the INVOICE MASTER FILE is as follows:

Field Name	Location	Comments
invoice number	1–7	record key
customer number	8–12	alternate key
transaction type	13–14	CH=charge sale
		PA = payment
		CA = cash sale
		CM = credit memo
invoice amount	15–20	S9(4)V99
invoice date	21–26	

The format for the customer's monthly statement of account appears on page 148.

**ENSLEY LUMBER
AND SUPPLY, INC.
P.O. DRAWER 662
ENSLEY, AZ 54390**

PH. (602) 555-9807

001003
STATEMENT

ACCOUNT	DATE

MONTH ENDING

PLEASE RETURN
THIS PORTION
WITH YOUR
REMITTANCE

$ —————————————
REMITTANCE

DATE	INVOICE NO. CREDIT MEMO NO.	CHARGES	CREDITS	BALANCE
			PREVIOUS BALANCE ➡	

PLEASE PAY THIS AMOUNT

Preprinted statement form.

6

Disk Utilization: Relative Files

The previous two chapters addressed concepts of INDEXED file organizations. These chapters introduced you to some relatively efficient means of dealing with business data processing activities.

This chapter will deal with the RELATIVE file organization, which allows the programmer even more creative and efficient approaches to dealing with these business activities.

SECTION 1
The Concept of a Relative File

Relative files are only permitted on direct access storage devices such as magnetic disks and, usually, they must be of the fixed-length type. In the organization of a relative file, the records are arranged in sequence in the file based on a *relative position number*. This means that each record in the file must have a unique relative record number.

Records stored in, and retrieved from, a relative file must be stored or retrieved based on the relative record number. Technically, the first record in a file—the one to which all others relate—is the "zero" record, and the second is record 1. The third record in the file (again relative to the starting record) is record 3, and so on. If, as is often the case, the very first record in the file is used for header information, then the first *data* record would have the relative address of record 1, the second record a relative record number of 2, and so forth. The relative record number is the record's position in the file *relative* to the beginning of the file.

As was the case for indexed files, relative files may be accessed sequentially or randomly. When records from a relative file are accessed sequentially, the records are retrieved or written beginning at relative position 1 and continuing to the end of the file. Note should be made that not all relative record positions will contain a record. Different computer systems handle a vacant or inactive relative record area differently. The computer's operating system usually handles this type of situation; it is not normally something a programmer need be concerned with in the sequential access of this file organization type.

Relative files may also be accessed randomly. In this case, the relative record number for the record desired is moved to the RELATIVE KEY area in the WORK-ING-STORAGE section, and then the file uses this RELATIVE KEY to access the file randomly.

You can access relative files sequentially and randomly within the same program (just as you could with indexed files) through the use of the ACCESS MODE IS DYNAMIC capability. The commands that are used to accomplish this in a relative file are almost identical to the commands used in the access of INDEXED files.

The approach used in this chapter is a little different from the approach used in the previous chapters. We will cover the ENVIRONMENT DIVISION entries first, the DATA DIVISION entries second, and the commands that can be used in the PROCEDURE DIVISION with relative files will be presented third. Finally, a number of examples that illustrate the implementation of certain file structures will be presented.

SECTION 2
ENVIRONMENT DIVISION Entries for Relative Files

The ENVIRONMENT DIVISION entries in the FILE-CONTROL paragraph for relative files are very similar to the entries for INDEXED files. A FILE-CONTROL entry for a relative file is as follows:

```
INPUT-OUTPUT SECTION.
FILE-CONTROL.
    SELECT file-name
        ASSIGN TO device
        ORGANIZATION IS RELATIVE
                        ┌SEQUENTIAL┐
        ACCESS MODE IS  ┤RANDOM    ├
                        └DYNAMIC   ┘
        RELATIVE KEY IS data-name1
        [FILE STATUS IS data-name2.]
```

There are two differences from an INDEXED file. These differences are:

- ORGANIZATION IS RELATIVE
- RELATIVE KEY IS ...

The ORGANIZATION IS RELATIVE clause tells the compiler that we wish to work with a relative file. This clause must be specified for all files whose organization type is relative. This clause serves to specify that each record in the file is to be assigned a unique and clearly defined record position within the file.

The RELATIVE KEY clause is required when the ACCESS MODE IS DYNAMIC or RANDOM. The RELATIVE KEY that is designated as data-name1 *must be* an unsigned integer data-item whose description does not contain a PICTURE symbol of "P". Also, data-name1 *must be* described in the WORKING-STORAGE SECTION of the program. In other words, the RELATIVE KEY as designated by data-name1 may not be a part of the record. It must be a separate data-item.

Again, the possible ACCESS MODEs for relative files are as follows:

- SEQUENTIAL
- RANDOM
- DYNAMIC

The sequential ACCESS MODE allows for the sequential writing or retrieval of records to or from a relative file. This is no different from the discussion of sequential access discussed in previous chapters.

When the ACCESS MODE is DYNAMIC, records can be accessed from the file either sequentially or randomly. When the ACCESS MODE IS RANDOM the records in the file can be accessed randomly based on their relative record numbers. The contents of data-name1 give the relative record numbers. As indicated before, data-name1 must be an unsigned integer value.

The FILE STATUS values that can be returned by an OPEN, CLOSE, READ, WRITE, REWRITE, DELETE, or START verb are the same as those contained in Appendix C.

SECTION 3
PROCEDURE DIVISION Commands for
Relative Files

Just as in the case for indexed files, a relative file has certain PROCEDURE DIVISION verbs that are different from the I/O commands for sequential files.
The commands that are (or may be) used with relative files are as follows:

- OPEN
- READ
- WRITE
- REWRITE
- DELETE
- START

Each of these commands will be discussed in the sequence just listed.

The OPEN Statement

The general form for the OPEN statement is as follows:

$$
\text{OPEN} \left\{ \begin{array}{l} \text{INPUT file-name} \\ \text{OUTPUT file-name} \\ \text{I-O file-name} \\ \text{EXTEND file-name} \end{array} \right\}
$$

If the relative file is to be accessed sequentially, the SELECT statement usually specifies that the ACCESS MODE IS SEQUENTIAL. If we are reading data from the file then the OPEN mode is INPUT. This OPEN mode also indirectly dictates the form of the READ statement that will be used when READing records from the file.

When records are to be written to the file, the OUTPUT mode is specified. In the initial creation of a relative file, the OPEN mode will be OUTPUT. You should remember that when an OPEN command is given in the OUTPUT mode, any records that existed in that file are destroyed. If you wish to make subsequent additions to the file then OPEN EXTEND should be used.

If the ACCESS MODE is either RANDOM or DYNAMIC then the OPEN mode should be I-O. This form of the OPEN mode also indirectly stipulates the form of the READ statement when taken in conjunction with the ACCESS MODE statement and the type of operation being performed on the file.

The READ Statement for Sequential Access

If a more detailed explanation of the sequential READ is needed please see an introductory COBOL text (such as Stern and Stern cited in Chapter 1).

The use of a sequential READ to a relative file is coupled with the OPEN INPUT statement. The general form of this statement is:

```
READ file-name [INTO identifier]
     AT END  any imperative statement.
```

The first successful READ of the file accesses the first *active* record in the file. Remember that there are unused record positions (empty or inactive) within a relative file. The READ statement only accesses the active records within the file from the first active record to the last active record. The AT END condition is set after the last active record is retrieved from the file. If your installation still supports the 1968 ANSI standard for COBOL you will retrieve deleted records along with valid records and you must incorporate code to ensure that you do not process these invalid data.

The RANDOM READ Statement for
RANDOM or DYNAMIC ACCESS MODE

If the ACCESS MODE is RANDOM or DYNAMIC and records are to be retrieved from the file randomly, then the random form of the READ statement must be used. The general form for this statement is as follows:

```
READ file-name [INTO identifier]
     INVALID KEY any imperative statement.
```

The RELATIVE KEY was specified in the SELECT statement and the name of the key is an unsigned integer data-item in the WORKING-STORAGE SECTION of the program.

In order to retrieve a record from the file, a value must first be moved to the RELATIVE KEY area then the READ statement is executed. If the record exists, the normal return will be taken. If not, the INVALID KEY return will be taken. If the FILE STATUS clause is being used, the codes retrieved will be those contained in Appendix C. Consider the following example:

```
FILE-CONTROL.
     SELECT EMPLOYEE-MASTER
          ASSIGN TO "RELFIL.DAT"
          ORGANIZATION IS RELATIVE
          ACCESS MODE IS RANDOM
          RELATIVE KEY IS WS-EMPLOYEE-NUMBER.
               o
               o
               o
DATA DIVISION.
FILE SECTION.
```

```
FD  EMPLOYEE-MASTER
        LABEL RECORDS ARE STANDARD.
01  EMPLOYEE-RECORD        PIC X(104).
                    o
                    o
                    o
WORKING-STORAGE SECTION.
01  WS-EMPLOYEE-NUMBER       PIC 9(9).
                    o
                    o
                    o
PROCEDURE DIVISION.
000-MAIN-MODULE.
      OPEN I-O EMPLOYEE-MASTER.
                    o
                    o
                    o
200-RETRIEVE.
      DISPLAY "ENTER EMPLOYEE NUMBER".
      ACCEPT WS-EMPLOYEE-NUMBER.
      READ EMPLOYEE-MASTER
          INVALID KEY
              DISPLAY "NO SUCH EMPLOYEE".
                    o
                    o
                    o
```

In this example the file, EMPLOYEE-MASTER, is a relative file whose RELATIVE KEY is the employee's number. In order to retrieve the record for an employee the program DISPLAYs a message to enter the employee's number. That number is ACCEPTed from the system default device, in this case a terminal, and the record for the employee is READ from the relative file. If there is no active record on the file for this employee number (relative record number), then the INVALID KEY return is taken.

The Sequential READ *Statement for* DYNAMIC ACCESS MODE

To READ a record sequentially from a relative file whose ACCESS MODE is specified as DYNAMIC the following form of the READ statement is used:

```
READ file-name NEXT [INTO] identifier]
    [AT END  any imperative statement.]
```

The file-name specified in this form of the READ statement must have ACCESS MODE IS DYNAMIC specified. The file must have been opened as INPUT or as I-O.

The AT END statement must be specified unless the USE statement is declared in the DECLARATIVES (discussed in Chapter 9). The AT END statement is executed if the READ statement is issued and there are no more active records in the relative file. Once the AT END option is taken, another READ NEXT statement may not be issued to the same file unless:

• the file has been CLOSEd in the interim;
• a START command has been issued for the file;
• a random READ has been issued in the interim.

The START *Statement*

As was the case for indexed files, the START verb is issued for relative files to position the logical record pointer within the file for subsequent access of the file from that position. Remember that the START verb does not read a record: it merely positions the logical record pointer.

The general form of the START verb is as follows:

$$\text{START file-name} \left[\text{KEY IS} \left\{ \begin{array}{c} = \\ \text{NOT} < \\ > \end{array} \right\} \text{data name} \right]$$

INVALID KEY any imperative statement.

The file that is specified in the START verb must be a file whose access mode is sequential or dynamic. The data-name indicated in the general form is the name of the field that was specified in the SELECT statement as the RELATIVE KEY. The file must also have been OPENed as INPUT or I-O.

Consider the following logic:

```
FILE-CONTROL.
    SELECT EMPLOYEE-MASTER
        ASSIGN TO "RELFIL.DAT"
        ORGANIZATION IS RELATIVE
        ACCESS MODE IS DYNAMIC
        RELATIVE KEY IS WS-EMPLOYEE-NUMBER.
                o
                o
                o
DATA DIVISION.
FILE SECTION.
FD  EMPLOYEE-MASTER
    LABEL RECORDS ARE STANDARD.
01  EMPLOYEE-RECORD          PIC X(104).
WORKING-STORAGE SECTION.
01  WS-EMPLOYEE-NUMBER       PIC 9(04).
                o
                o
                o
PROCEDURE DIVISION.
000-MAIN-MODULE.
    OPEN I-O EMPLOYEE-MASTER.
    DISPLAY "ENTER BEGINNING EMPLOYEE NUMBER"
    ACCEPT WS-EMPLOYEE-NUMBER.
    START EMPLOYEE-MASTER
        KEY = WS-EMPLOYEE-NUMBER
        INVALID KEY MOVE "X" TO EOF-SW.
    PERFORM 600-READ-RELATIVE.
    PERFORM 200-PROCESS-EMPLOYEES
        UNTIL EOF-SW = "X".
    CLOSE EMPLOYEE-MASTER.
    STOP RUN.
200-PROCESS-EMPLOYEES.
    DISPLAY WS-EMPLOYEE-NAME WS-SALARY.
    PERFORM 600-READ-RELATIVE.
600-READ-RELATIVE.
    READ EMPLOYEE-MASTER NEXT INTO WS-RECORD
        AT END MOVE "X" TO EOF-SW.
```

In this example we are retrieving records sequentially from the EMPLOYEE-MASTER, beginning at some starting point and continuing to the point where there are no more active records.

The program requests the starting point through the use of a set of DISPLAY and ACCEPT statements. The logical record pointer is positioned to this starting point and the records are retrieved sequentially by the use of the READ NEXT statement unless the START verb gave an INVALID KEY return.

The Sequential WRITE Statement for Relative Files

Records may be written sequentially to a relative file. However, the WRITE statement must have an INVALID KEY clause as specified in the general form:

```
WRITE record-name [FROM identified]
      INVALID KEY  any imperative statement.
```

The SELECT statement must have specified ACCESS MODE IS SEQUENTIAL. In this case the RELATIVE KEY is optional.

Each issue of the WRITE command causes a successive relative record to be written to the file. That is, the first record is written in relative record location 1, the second in relative record locations 2, and so forth. If the WRITE is unsuccessful the INVALID KEY statement is executed. If this option is executed this frequently means that you have a file boundary violation.

The OPEN mode for this type of WRITE is OUTPUT. Remember, once you have opened a file as OUTPUT, you may not again open the file in the OUTPUT mode without destroying the records in the file. If you want to place records at the end of such a file, then consider the OPEN EXTEND option.

The RANDOM or DYNAMIC WRITE Statement for a Relative File

The general form for this statement is as follows:

```
WRITE record-name [FROM identifier]
      INVALID KEY  any imperative statement.
```

This statement is used for a random WRITE to a relative file whose ACCESS MODE is DYNAMIC or RANDOM. The specified file must be opened as I-O or OUTPUT. The ORGANIZATION mode must be RELATIVE and the RELATIVE KEY must be present and set to the value of the relative record number that is to be written to the file.

The INVALID KEY return will be taken for one of these two cases.

• An attempt is made to write a record that is already on the file.
• An attempt is made to write past the boundary for the file.

If the FILE STATUS is present the appropriate codes as specified in Appendix C are set.

Consider the following partial program code:

```
FILE-CONTROL.
     SELECT EMPLOYEE-MASTER
          ASSIGN TO "RELFIL.DAT"
          ORGANIZATION IS RELATIVE
```

```
                    ACCESS MODE IS DYNAMIC
                    RELATIVE KEY IS WS-EMPLOYEE-NUMBER.
                           o
                           o
                           o
        DATA DIVISION.
        FILE SECTION.
        FD  EMPLOYEE-MASTER
            LABEL RECORDS ARE STANDARD.
        01  EMPLOYEE-RECORD           PIC X(104).
                           o
                           o
                           o
        WORKING-STORAGE SECTION.
        01  WS-EMPLOYEE-NUMBER        PIC 9(04).
                           o
                           o
                           o
        PROCEDURE DIVISION.
        000-MAIN-MODULE.
            OPEN I-O EMPLOYEE-MASTER.
                           o
                           o
                           o
        200-PROCESS-EMPLOYEES.
            MOVE WS-EMPLOYEE-RECORD TO EMPLOYEE-RECORD.
            MOVE TF-EMPLOYEE-NUMBER TO WS-EMPLOYEE-NUMBER.
            PERFORM 700-WRITE-RELATIVE.
            PERFORM 600-READ-TRANSACTION.
                           o
                           o
                           o
        700-WRITE-RELATIVE.
            WRITE EMPLOYEE-RECORD
                INVALID KEY
                DISPLAY "UNABLE TO WRITE THIS EMPLOYEE"
                DISPLAY "EMPLOYEE NUMBER = " WS-EMPLOYEE-NUMBER
                MOVE "X" TO EOF-SW.
```

In this partial program, we are reading a record from a transaction file, setting the record up in WORKING-STORAGE in an area called WS-EMPLOYEE-RECORD, then writing this record to the relative file. Notice that the employee number is moved to RELATIVE KEY location in the statement:

```
MOVE TF-EMPLOYEE-NUMBER TO WS-EMPLOYEE-NUMBER.
```

After the RELATIVE KEY is set to the value of the employee number, the WRITE statement is set up and the record is written to the EMPLOYEE-MASTER--if there is not a duplication of employee number or if we are not past an externally defined file boundary.

The REWRITE Statement

The REWRITE statement for sequential access to a relative file is as follows:

```
REWRITE record-name [FROM identifier]
        INVALID KEY any imperative statement.
```

The REWRITE statement can only be issued after a successful read to the same file. Also, there can be no manipulation of the key such that the value of the key is changed between the time of the READ and REWRITE. If the REWRITE is attempted in this circumstance the INVALID KEY clause is invoked. The REWRITE statement replaces the record on the random access device.

Consider the logic:

```
FILE-CONTROL.
     SELECT EMPLOYEE-MASTER
          ASSIGN TO "RELFIL.DAT"
          ORGANIZATION IS RELATIVE
          ACCESS MODE IS DYNAMIC
          RELATIVE KEY IS WS-EMPLOYEE-NUMBER.
               o
               o
               o
DATA DIVISION.
FILE SECTION.
FD  EMPLOYEE-MASTER
     LABEL RECORDS ARE STANDARD.
01  EMPLOYEE-RECORD              PIC X(104).
               o
               o
               o
WORKING-STORAGE SECTION.
01  WS-EMPLOYEE-NUMBER           PIC 9(04).
               o
               o
               o
01  WS-EMPLOYEE-RECORD.
               o
               o
               o
PROCEDURE DIVISION.
000-MAIN-MODULE.
     OPEN I-O EMPLOYEE-MASTER.
     DISPLAY "ENTER EMPLOYEE NUMBER".
     ACCEPT WS-EMPLOYEE-NUMBER.
     PERFORM 600-READ-RELATIVE.
     PERFORM 300-ENTER-NEW-DATA.
     PERFORM 400-REWRITE-RELATIVE.
     CLOSE EMPLOYEE-MASTER.
     STOP RUN.
300-ENTER-NEW-DATA.
*IN THIS MODULE, NEW DATA FOR THE EMPLOYEE MASTER RECORD
*ARE ACCEPTED FROM THE TERMINAL AND MOVED TO THE
*APPROPRIATE AREA IN THE RECORD AREA IN THE
*WORKING-STORAGE SECTION.
400-REWRITE-RELATIVE.
     REWRITE EMPLOYEE-RECORD
          FROM WS-EMPLOYEE-RECORD
          INVALID KEY
          DISPLAY "CANNOT REWRITE RECORD".
600-READ-RELATIVE.
     READ EMPLOYEE-MASTER INTO WS-EMPLOYEE-RECORD
          INVALID KEY
          DISPLAY "NO SUCH EMPLOYEE".
```

In this example, the program requests an employee number, reads that employee's record from the relative file, ACCEPTS change data from the terminal, and then REWRITEs the record to disk.

The DELETE Statement

The general form for the RANDOM or DYNAMIC DELETE statement is as follows:

```
DELETE file-name
          INVALID KEY any imperative statement.
```

In this situation the following environment must exist:

- file opened I-O
- ACCESS MODE-RANDOM or DYNAMIC
- RELATIVE KEY clause specified in SELECT statement
- placement of the relative record number for an active record in the RELATIVE KEY area

The successful execution of the DELETE command logically removes the record from the file. In other words, the record is changed from active to inactive status.

Note that the DELETE statement specifies the file-name, not the record-name, to be DELETEd.

If the record to be DELETEd is not an active record, then the INVALID KEY clause is invoked.

Consider this partial program:

```
FILE-CONTROL.
     SELECT EMPLOYEE-MASTER
          ASSIGN TO "RELFIL.DAT"
          ORGANIZATION IS RELATIVE
          ACCESS MODE IS DYNAMIC
          RELATIVE KEY IS WS-EMPLOYEE-NUMBER.
               o
               o
               o
DATA DIVISION.
FILE SECTION.
FD  EMPLOYEE-MASTER
     LABEL RECORDS ARE STANDARD.
01  EMPLOYEE-RECORD              PIC X(104).
               o
               o
               o
WORKING-STORAGE SECTION.
01  WS-EMPLOYEE-NUMBER           PIC 9(04).
               o
               o
               o
PROCEDURE DIVISION.
000-MAIN-MODULE.
     OPEN I-O EMPLOYEE-MASTER.
     DISPLAY "ENTER EMPLOYEE NUMBER TO DELETE".
     ACCEPT WS-EMPLOYEE-NUMBER.
```

```
DELETE EMPLOYEE-MASTER
    INVALID KEY
        DISPLAY "NO SUCH EMPLOYEE".
CLOSE EMPLOYEE-MASTER.
    STOP RUN.
```

In this example, the file EMPLOYEE-MASTER is OPENed as I-O, and then the employee number to be deleted from the file is accepted from the terminal into the RELATIVE KEY area named WS-EMPLOYEE-NUMBER. The DELETE command is then issued. If the record to be deleted is not an active record then the INVALID KEY return is taken.

The preceding discussion should have served to highlight the use of the various verbs associated with relative files. That exposition, however, gave no indication of the power of the relative file in certain circumstances. Subsequent sections of this chapter should give you an idea of the power of the relative file in implementing more complex data structures.

Many data structures textbooks apply the structure being discussed through some scientific language such as Pascal. These structures may also be implemented in COBOL.

Discussion of some of the concepts that are used in the implementation of these more advanced structures is necessary before getting to the details of coding. The following sections will highlight the concepts of hashing and pointers.

SECTION 4
The Concept of Hashing

In the previous examples we have been using a four-digit employee number as the relative key. This assumes that the employee number can take on values from 0001 to 9999. A large number of organizations do not use a special number for identification purposes. In fact, most agencies use the social security number as the key for identifying an individual.

There is a problem in using such a number as the relative record number: the key can take on values from 000 00 0001 to 999 99 9999. It doesn't take much imagination to see that we are out of random access storage before we start, because a relative file reserves one record position for each possible key. Some method has to be available to reduce this unreasonable amount of on-line storage. We need to be able to transform the key, in this case a social security number, into a relative record address that covers the maximum number of records we need for our files—not those for every possible social security number. A common technique used to make this key to address transformation is referred to as *hashing*.

There are a large number of hashing methods available to a programmer, and these methods are almost always included in a good data structures textbook. Some of the methods you are likely to encounter are:

- digit analysis
- division
- pseudorandom
- folding
- multiplication

These are just a few of the many techniques available to the programmer. You should study the benefits of each of them at some future point, if have not already. However, several studies have shown that the *division* method, especially by prime numbers, tends to give the best results in reducing collisions.

A *collision* is a situation where two or more keys are transformed into the same relative record number. There are a couple of problems that occur when the hashing algorithm yields the same relative record address. The first is *primary clustering*, in which the hashing algorithm does not spread the relative record addresses over a broad-enough range. This usually results from the collision solution algorithm, whereby when a collision occurs the record is placed in the next available sequential relative record address.

The other problem is *secondary clustering*, which results from another form of collision solution.

The collision solution that we recommend: Place the colliding record in the high part of the file above the possible high address for the record you are trying to place in the file. Use an address offset to reach this location.

For purposes of illustration, we will use a prime number division method to transform keys to relative record addresses. The prime number division method works, in our case, as follows:

- Determine the maximum number of records that can be contained in the file.
- Estimate the percentage of collisions that you think will occur.
- Select a prime number that is high enough to contain all the records you think will be in the file.
- Select another prime number that is large enough to handle the overflow from collisions. The sum of the two prime numbers is the total number of addresses that may be used.
- Divide the key by the first prime number using this form of the DIVIDE statement:

      DIVIDE data-name-1 BY prime-number-1
          GIVING integer-1 REMAINDER relative-key.

- Determine if there is a collision.
- If there is a collision, use the area between the first prime number and the sum of the two prime numbers as the collision overflow area.

This is not the world's greatest solution to the key collision problem, but it is commonly used in the business community because of its ease of application.

Let us consider an example of this method. First, the maximum number of employees that we can have in our master file is 1000. Therefore we choose the prime number 1009 from the table of prime numbers in Appendix D as the first prime number that we will use. Second, we estimate that we will have approximately a 10 percent collision rate. Therefore, we select another prime number that is about 100 numbers higher than the prime number. In this case we will use 101, a prime number that is large enough to accomodate the expected number of collisions. Table 6.1 gives the results of dividing some sample social security numbers by the prime numbers selected for hashing.

Notice that when dividing by the prime number, the remainder is in the range of 0 to 1008. The remainder from the prime number division is the relative record address.

In the preceding example, two keys resulted in the same relative record address in four different cases. These are, by definition, collisions!

Table 6.1

Prime Number Division Example

Key	Prime #	Relative Key	Overflow Key
000000082	1009	0882	—
000002100	1009	0882	1009
123456789	1009	0594	—
261889134	1009	0157	—
309557845	1009	0681	—
423581667	1009	0438	—
433581665	1009	0239	—
435106006	1009	0990	—
501672939	1009	0157	1010
515952831	1009	0681	1011
560582608	1009	0370	—
612663124	1009	0342	—
613176064	1009	0710	—
624593328	1009	0130	—
627598660	1009	0660	—
651396378	1009	0104	—
665423728	1009	0336	—
671393990	1009	0345	—
674876676	1009	0972	—
686533554	1009	0873	—
704923554	1009	0812	—
714168919	1009	0737	—
724558719	1009	0864	—
821745105	1009	0370	1012
888576433	1009	0583	—
896448625	1009	0557	—
955078747	1009	0743	—
957323685	1009	0629	—

In a COBOL program the procedure for determining a collision is:

- hash the key,
- read the relative file,
- determine whether a collision has occurred using the following decision rule:

      INVALID KEY return—no collision
      no INVALID KEY return—collision!!!!

In a collision situation we need to develop a procedure to place the records in the collision area, called the *overflow area,* of the file. In our example this would be relative record position 1009 to 1110. The simplest procedure, which has been followed in Table 6.1, is to place the first record that collides in relative record 1009, the second in 1010, and so on. Another approach is to use a second prime number to hash the overflow. The second number selected for overflow in the example was the prime number 101. In order to hash the overflow items, the key is divided by the *second* prime number and the result is added to the *first* prime number to yield the relative address. Thus, the addresses for the overflow items in Table 6.1 are as given in Table 6.2

Table 6.2

Key	Prime Number #2	Result	Prime Number #1	Address
000000082	101	082	1009	1091
501672939	101	081	1009	1090
515952831	101	088	1009	1096
821745105	101	015	1009	1024

The program used to create the data in Table 6.1 is as follows:

```
IDENTIFICATION DIVISION.
PROGRAM-ID. HASH.
AUTHOR. GEN MIXON.
ENVIRONMENT DIVISION.
CONFIGURATION SECTION.
SOURCE-COMPUTER. VAX-11.
OBJECT-COMPUTER. VAX-11.
DATA DIVISION.
WORKING-STORAGE SECTION.
01  IN-AREA    PIC 9(09)      VALUE ZEROES.
01  REL-KEY    PIC 9(04).
01  RESULT     PIC 9(05).
PROCEDURE DIVISION.
000-MAIN.
    PERFORM 100-PROCESS UNTIL IN-AREA = 999999999.
    STOP RUN.
000-PROCESS.
    DISPLAY "ENTER SSN".
    DISPLAY "IF YOU HAVE NO MORE TO PROCESS - ENTER"
        "999999999".
    ACCEPT IN-AREA.
    IF IN-AREA = 999999999 GO TO END-ROUTINE.
    DIVIDE IN-AREA BY 1009
        GIVING RESULT REMAINDER REL-KEY.
    DISPLAY IN-AREA " " 1009 " " REL-KEY.
```

Note: The program is for purposes of illustration and is not well structured. We use this expedient in order to accentuate the development of relative keys.

SECTION 5
The Concept of Pointers

A number of structures used with relative files require the use of pointers. A pointer is simply a relative record address that is a part of a record that shows where another record is located. Another way of looking at a pointer is as a *link* to another record, in that file or in another file.

There are a number of different types of pointers that can be used in working with linked files. Some of these are:

- first: points to the first record in the list
- last: points to the last record in the list

- next: points to the next record in the list or chain
- prior: points to the previous record in the list
- owner: points to the record that owns records in this set of records
- null: the last record in a list of records

Sometimes files that contain pointers are referred to as *linked lists*. Files that contain a number of these pointers are referred to as *multilinked lists*.

In the example that we have been using, the records for employees are stored in the file in relative record number sequence. This may create some problems when trying to handle the file in different sequences—for example, employee name. If the file needs to be processed in ascending employee name sequence (a realistic requirement), the file would have to be input into a sort program and another file created in ascending employee name sequence. (See Chapter 8 for the SORT verb).

A way around this is to include a pointer in the relative file that would maintain alphabetic sequence. Consider the data in Table 6.3.

Table 6.3

Relative Record	Name	Social Security Number
0002	Tolman, Hubert	000000002
0003	Emmanuel, Tsegai	000000003
0004	Foster, Robert	000000004
0005	Penn, J. D.	000000005
0006	Jones, Winfred	000000006
0007	Davis, Clifford	000000007

Notice that the records in the table are not in sequence on employee name.

The solution to the problem of processing this type of file in one or more sequences is to add a pointer field that maintains this sequence. In order to place the links in the file, another file must be created, or a header record needs to be placed in the file itself. That header contains a pointer that, in turn, points to the first record in the list. Let us assume, for our example, that relative record position 1 is reserved for the header. With the addition of the pointer to the record Table 6.4 is obtained.

The header record, record 1, points to the first record in the alphabetic sequence, record 7. The record for Clifford Davis contains a pointer that points to the next record in sequence, record 3—the record for Tsegai Emmanuel. This record in turn points to record 4, the record for Robert Foster, and so forth, until the record for Hubert Tolman is retrieved. This record contains a pointer with a special value that indicates that the end of the linked list has been reached.

Table 6.4

Employee Data with Embedded Pointers

Relative Record	Name	SSN	Pointer
0001	Header	null	0007
0002	Tolman, Hubert	000000002	0000
0003	Emmanuel, Tsegai	000000003	0004
0004	Foster, Robert	000000004	0006
0005	Penn, J. D.	000000005	0002
0006	Jones, Winfred	000000006	0005
0007	Davis, Clifford	000000007	0003

Obviously, updating relative files that contain pointers is a tedious process. A verbal description of this process follows:

For deletions

1. Sequentially search the chain for the record to be deleted while retaining the pointer for the previous record.
2. When the record to be deleted is found, save the pointer for this record.
3. Delete the record.
4. Replace the record pointer from the record that pointed to the deleted record with the pointer from the deleted record.
5. If the record to be deleted is the first record, change the header pointer to the value of the pointer from the first record.
6. If the record to be deleted is the last record, change the pointer in the record that pointed to the last record to the null pointer.

For additions

1. Sequentially search the chain for the record whose name is less than or equal to the name to be added to the list, saving the pointer from the previous record.
2. When a low or equal name compare results:
    a. Place the record to be added in its logical record position.
    b. Replace the pointer in the last record read with the value of the record that was just added to the file.
    c. Insert the pointer from the previous record in the record that is added to the file.
3. If the record to be added is now the first record in the chain:
    a. Move the pointer from the header record to the record to be added.
    b. Move the relative record number to the header record.
    c. Add the record to the file.
4. If the record to be added is now the last record in the file:
    a. Move the null pointer to the pointer area of the record to be added.
    b. Move the relative record number for the record to be added to the previously last record
    c. Add the record to the file.

Maintaining pointers that are embedded in a file is usually a slow and tedious process. Therefore, embedded pointers are not used unless the benefits of rapid retrieval outweigh this disadvantage.

SECTION 6
An Example of an Inverted List Using a Relative File

An inverted file is a file that uses pointers or indexes to maintain and retrieve records that have similar attributes. In the example that we have been using (concerning the employee master file), it is easy to utilize an inverted list to retrieve data concerning certain attributes of the employees contained in the file.

Let us assume that we need to be able to retrieve employees' records from the file, based on employee occupation. An employee master file is likely to contain a large number of employee records that have the same occupational classification. For example, if we wanted to be able to retrieve all the records for secretaries from a file we could search each record in the file, comparing the occupation contained in the file to the desired occupation (secretary) or we could have a file (an attributes file) associated with the EMPLOYEE-MASTER that contained all of the occupations that are contained within the EMPLOYEE-MASTER. There are generally two approaches to this inversion process:

- All pointers for a specific occupation are maintained in the attributes file.
- The attributes file contains the pointer to the first record in the EMPLOYEE-MASTER and the pointers for occupations are embedded in the EMPLOYEE-RECORD.

Since we discussed embedded pointers before, we will use an attributes file that includes all the pointers for a specific occupation in the attributes record.

In our example, the attributes file is an indexed file that uses the attribute (occupation) as the RECORD KEY. The ATTRIBUTE-RECORD is a variable-length record that contains the attribute name, the number of records with that attribute, and the relative record numbers of all the records in the EMPLOYEE-MASTER for that particular occupation. In order to retrieve all records for a specific attribute, one simply reads the attributes file for the desired attribute and then retrieves the records, based on the relative record numbers contained in the ATTRIBUTE-RECORD, from the EMPLOYEE-MASTER.

The inputs to the program are displayed in Figure 6-1. The EMPLOYEE-MASTER contains a record for each of the active records contained in the file. Notice that there is no indication in the DISPLAYed employee records of the relative record number. If you desire to know the relative record number of a specific record, you can either imbed the record number or you can hash the record key to derive that number. The keys for the records contained in the file and their relative record numbers are as follows:

SSN	Relative Record Number
000 00 0004	0004
000 00 0099	0099
100 10 1000	0128
000 99 1004	0166
410 41 4010	0233
200 20 2000	0256
411 41 4011	0315
300 30 3000	0384
412 41 4012	0397
409 49 4009	0440
408 48 4008	0448
407 47 4007	0456
406 46 4006	0464
405 45 4005	0472
413 41 4013	0479
404 44 4004	0480

403	43	4003	0488
402	42	4002	0496
401	41	4001	0504
400	40	4000	0512
000	00	1000	1000

The program that retrieves records from this partially inverted file (inverted on occupation) is presented in Figure 6-2.

Figure 6-2 is a very simple program that DISPLAYs a message asking for the occupation of the employees that you want to retrieve from the relative file, EMPLOYEE-MASTER. The program then ACCEPTs the occupation from the terminal and retrieves the record for the specified occupation from the ATTRIBUTES-FILE. The program then uses the pointers contained in the attributes record to retrieve all the records for the specified occupation.

The output from the program is presented in Figure 6-3. Notice that when the occupation for DEAN is specified, the three records for the deans are retrieved from the EMPLOYEE-MASTER and displayed on the terminal. Also observe that the VICE PRESIDENT records are retrieved when the occupation of VICE PRESIDENT is specified.

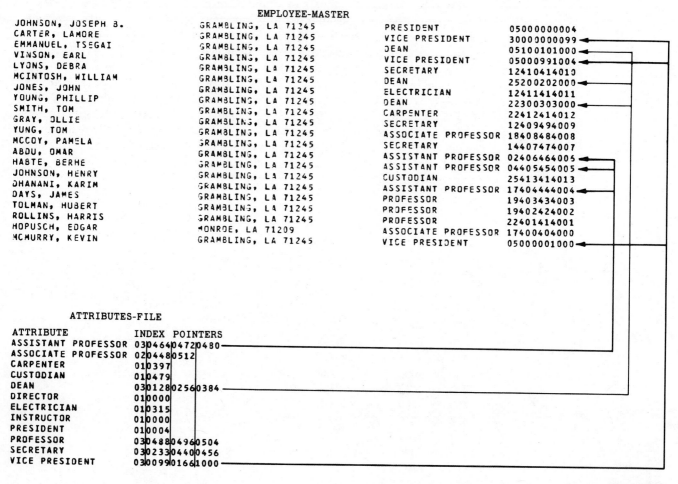

Figure 6-1
Inputs to relative file processing
example program.

Figure 6-2
Inquiry program.

```
IDENTIFICATION DIVISION.
PROGRAM-ID. PRINAT.
AUTHOR. CSIMPSON.
INSTALLATION. GRAMBLING STATE UNIVERSITY.
ENVIRONMENT DIVISION.
CONFIGURATION SECTION.
SOURCE-COMPUTER. VAX-11.
OBJECT-COMPUTER. VAX-11.
INPUT-OUTPUT SECTION.
FILE-CONTROL.
        SELECT ATTRIBUTES-FILE
                ASSIGN TO 'ATTRIB.DAT'
                ORGANIZATION IS INDEXED
                ACCESS MODE IS DYNAMIC
                RECORD KEY IS ATTRIBUTE.
        SELECT EMPLOYEE-MASTER
                ASSIGN TO 'RELFILE.DAT'
                ORGANIZATION IS RELATIVE
                ACCESS MODE IS DYNAMIC
                RELATIVE KEY IS WS-EMPLOYEE-NUMBER.
DATA DIVISION.
FILE SECTION.
FD   ATTRIBUTES-FILE
        LABEL RECORDS ARE STANDARD
        RECORD CONTAINS 26 TO 418 CHARACTERS.
01   ATTRIBUTE-RECORD.
        05   ATTRIBUTE             PIC X(20).
        05   AT-INDEX              PIC 9(02).
        05   ATTRIBUTE-POINTERS
             OCCURS 1 TO 99 TIMES DEPENDING ON AT-INDEX.
                10   EMPLOYEE-POINTER    PIC 9(04).
FD   EMPLOYEE-MASTER
        LABEL RECORDS ARE STANDARD.
01   EMPLOYEE-RECORD.
        05   EMPLOYEE-NAME         PIC X(30).
        05   EMPLOYEE-ADDRESS      PIC X(30).
        05   OCCUPATION            PIC X(20).
        05   YEARS-SVC             PIC 9(02).
        05   SOCIAL-SECURITY       PIC 9(09).
        05   FILLER                PIC X(13).
WORKING-STORAGE SECTION.
01   WS-EMPLOYEE-NUMBER            PIC 9(04).
01   I                            PIC 9(02) VALUE ZEROS.
01   END-SWITCH                    PIC X(01).
01   DISPLAY-LINE.
        05   DL-NAME               PIC X(30).
        05   FILLER                PIC X(02) VALUE SPACES.
        05   DL-YEARS              PIC 9(02).
        05   FILLER                PIC X(02) VALUE SPACES.
        05   DL-SSN                PIC 999B99B9999.
01   DISPLAY-HEAD.
        05   FILLER                PIC X(13) VALUE "EMPLOYEE NAME".
        05   FILLER                PIC X(16) VALUE SPACES.
        05   FILLER                PIC X(05) VALUE "YEARS".
        05   FILLER                PIC X(02) VALUE SPACES.
        05   FILLER                PIC X(03) VALUE "SSN".
```

Figure 6–2 (continued)

```
PROCEDURE DIVISION.
000-MAIN-MODULE.
        OPEN I-O ATTRIBUTES-FILE
                EMPLOYEE-MASTER.
        PERFORM 300-DISPLAY-ENTER.
        DISPLAY DISPLAY-HEAD.
        PERFORM 200-PROCESS THRU 200-EXIT
                UNTIL END-SWITCH = "X".
        CLOSE ATTRIBUTES-FILE
                EMPLOYEE-MASTER.
        STOP RUN.
200-PROCESS.
        IF ATTRIBUTE = "END"
                MOVE "X" TO END-SWITCH
                GO TO 200-EXIT.
        READ ATTRIBUTES-FILE
                INVALID KEY
                DISPLAY "NO SUCH OCCUPATION"
                GO TO 200-EXIT.
        PERFORM 210-PROCESS-EMPLOYEE THRU 210-EXIT.
        PERFORM 300-DISPLAY-ENTER.
        IF ATTRIBUTE NOT = "END"
                DISPLAY DISPLAY-HEAD.
200-EXIT. EXIT.
210-PROCESS-EMPLOYEE.
        IF AT-INDEX = 1
                AND EMPLOYEE-POINTER (1) = ZEROS
                GO TO 210-EXIT.
        PERFORM 220-DISPLAY-DATA THRU 220-EXIT
                VARYING I FROM 1 BY 1
                UNTIL I > AT-INDEX.
210-EXIT. EXIT.
220-DISPLAY-DATA.
        MOVE EMPLOYEE-POINTER (I) TO WS-EMPLOYEE-NUMBER.
        READ EMPLOYEE-MASTER
                INVALID KEY
                DISPLAY "INACTIVE RECORD"  WS-EMPLOYEE-NUMBER
                GO TO 220-EXIT.
        MOVE EMPLOYEE-NAME TO DL-NAME.
        MOVE YEARS-SVC TO DL-YEARS.
        MOVE SOCIAL-SECURITY TO DL-SSN.
        DISPLAY DISPLAY-LINE.
220-EXIT. EXIT.
300-DISPLAY-ENTER.
        DISPLAY "ENTER OCCUPATION".
        ACCEPT ATTRIBUTE.
        IF ATTRIBUTE = "END"
                MOVE "X" TO END-SWITCH.
```

Figure 6–3
Output from inquiry program.

```
DEAN
EMMANUEL, TSEGAI        05  100 10 1000
MCINTOSH, WILLIAM       25  200 20 2000
YOUNG, PHILLIP          22  300 30 3000
VICE PRESIDENT
CARTER, LAMORE          30  000 00 0099
VINSON, EARL            05  000 99 1004
MCMURTRY, KEVIN         05  000 00 1000
```

Figure 6-4 presents the program used to create the ATTRIBUTES-FILE. Notice that the file originally has no pointers contained in it and that the pointer field (1) contains zeros to indicate the null set.

Figure 6-5 presents the program used to create the EMPLOYEE-MASTER. After the employee's social security number is entered, the program hashes this and uses the remainder for the relative record number and then writes the record to the employee master file.

At some point in time the record addresses for the EMPLOYEE-MASTER must be posted to the pointer area of the ATTRIBUTES-FILE. In our example, we assume a one-time posting operation. A "real-world" situation would be handled on a continuing basis: therefore, this example is for the purpose of demonstration only.

Figure 6-6 contains the program that posts the relative record number to the ATTRIBUTES-FILE. The employee master file is read sequentially, the social security number is hashed, the occupation is used to retrieve the appropriate attribute record, the relative record number is placed in the proper pointer field, and then the record is rewritten to the ATTRIBUTES-FILE. The program logic continues in this fashion until the end-of-file condition is encountered on the EMPLOYEE-MASTER at which time the appropriate end-of-file action is taken.

Figure 6–4
Program to create attributes file.

```
IDENTIFICATION DIVISION.
PROGRAM-ID. CRATT.
AUTHOR. CSIMPSON.
INSTALLATION. GRAMBLING STATE UNIVERSITY.
ENVIRONMENT DIVISION.
CONFIGURATION SECTION.
SOURCE-COMPUTER. VAX-11.
OBJECT-COMPUTER. VAX-11.
INPUT-OUTPUT SECTION.
FILE-CONTROL.
        SELECT ATTRIBUTES-FILE
                ASSIGN TO "ATTRIB.DAT"
                ORGANIZATION IS INDEXED
                ACCESS MODE IS SEQUENTIAL
                RECORD KEY IS ATTRIBUTE.
DATA DIVISION.
FILE SECTION.
FD  ATTRIBUTES-FILE
        LABEL RECORDS ARE STANDARD
        RECORD CONTAINS 26 TO 418 CHARACTERS.
01  ATTRIBUTE-RECORD.
        05   ATTRIBUTE              PIC X(20).
        05   AT-INDEX               PIC 9(02).
        05   ATTRIBUTE-POINTERS
                OCCURS 1 TO 99 TIMES DEPENDING ON AT-INDEX.
                10  EMPLOYEE-POINTER    PIC 9(4).
WORKING-STORAGE SECTION.
01  ATTRIBUTE-IN                 PIC X(20).
01  I                           PIC 9(02) VALUE 1.
PROCEDURE DIVISION.
000-MAIN.
        OPEN OUTPUT ATTRIBUTES-FILE.
        PERFORM ENTER-ATTRIBUTES THRU EAX
                UNTIL ATTRIBUTE-IN = "END".
        CLOSE ATTRIBUTES-FILE.
        STOP RUN.
ENTER-ATTRIBUTES.
        DISPLAY "ENTER ATTRIBUTE".
        ACCEPT ATTRIBUTE-IN.
        IF ATTRIBUTE-IN = "END"
                GO TO EAX.
        MOVE I TO AT-INDEX.
        MOVE ZEROS TO EMPLOYEE-POINTER (1).
        MOVE ATTRIBUTE-IN TO ATTRIBUTE.
        WRITE ATTRIBUTE-RECORD
                INVALID KEY DISPLAY "DUPLICATE RECORD".
EAX. EXIT.
```

Figure 6–5

Program to create employee master file.

```
IDENTIFICATION DIVISION.
PROGRAM-ID. POSTAT.
AUTHOR. CSIMPSON.
INSTALLATION. GRAMBLING STATE UNIVERSITY.
ENVIRONMENT DIVISION.
CONFIGURATION SECTION.
SOURCE-COMPUTER. VAX-11.
OBJECT-COMPUTER. VAX-11.
INPUT-OUTPUT SECTION.
FILE-CONTROL.
        SELECT ATTRIBUTES-FILE
              ASSIGN TO "ATTRIB.DAT"
              ORGANIZATION IS INDEXED
              ACCESS MODE IS DYNAMIC
              RECORD KEY IS ATTRIBUTE.
        SELECT EMPLOYEE-MASTER
              ASSIGN TO "RELFILE.DAT"
              ORGANIZATION IS RELATIVE
              ACCESS MODE IS SEQUENTIAL
              RELATIVE KEY IS WS-EMPLOYEE-NUMBER.
DATA DIVISION.
FILE SECTION.
FD  ATTRIBUTES-FILE
        LABEL RECORDS ARE STANDARD
        RECORD CONTAINS 26 TO 362 CHARACTERS.
01  ATTRIBUTE-RECORD.
        05  ATTRIBUTE           PIC X(20).
        05  AT-INDEX            PIC 9(02).
        05  ATTRIBUTE-POINTERS
            OCCURS 1 TO 99 TIMES DEPENDING ON AT-INDEX.
                10  EMPLOYEE-POINTER    PIC 9(04).
FD  EMPLOYEE-MASTER
        LABEL RECORDS ARE STANDARD.
01  EMPLOYEE-RECORD.
        05  EMPLOYEE-NAME       PIC X(30).
        05  EMPLOYEE-ADDRESS    PIC X(30).
        05  OCCUPATION          PIC X(20).
        05  YEARS-SVC           PIC 9(02).
        05  SOCIAL-SECURITY     PIC 9(09).
        05  FILLER              PIC X(13).
WORKING-STORAGE SECTION.
01  WS-EMPLOYEE-NUMBER          PIC 9(04).
01  WS-RESULT                   PIC 9(06).
01  I                           PIC 9(02) VALUE ZEROS.
01  PRIME-NO                    PIC 9(04) VALUE 1009.
01  EOF-SW                      PIC X(01) VALUE SPACES.
```

Figure 6–6
Program to update relative file.

```
IDENTIFICATION DIVISION.
PROGRAM-ID. CREMP.
AUTHOR. CSIMPSON.
INSTALLATION. GRAMBLING STATE UNIVERSITY.
ENVIRONMENT DIVISION.
CONFIGURATION SECTION.
SOURCE-COMPUTER. VAX-11.
OBJECT-COMPUTER. VAX-11.
INPUT-OUTPUT SECTION.
FILE-CONTROL.
        SELECT EMPLOYEE-MASTER
            ASSIGN TO "RELFILE.DAT"
            ORGANIZATION IS RELATIVE
            ACCESS MODE IS DYNAMIC
            RELATIVE KEY IS WS-EMPLOYEE-NUMBER.
DATA DIVISION.
FILE SECTION.
FD  EMPLOYEE-MASTER
        LABEL RECORDS ARE STANDARD.
01  EMPLOYEE-RECORD                      PIC X(104).
WORKING-STORAGE SECTION.
01  WS-EMPLOYEE-RECORD.
        05  EMPLOYEE-NAME                PIC X(30).
        05  EMPLOYEE-ADDRESS             PIC X(30).
        05  OCCUPATION                   PIC X(20).
        05  YEARS-SERVICE                PIC 9(02).
        05  SOCIAL-SECURITY-NO           PIC 9(09).
        05  FILLER        PIC X(13).
01  WS-EMPLOYEE-NUMBER                   PIC 9(04).
01  WS-RESULT           PIC 9(06).
PROCEDURE DIVISION.
000-MAIN.
        OPEN OUTPUT EMPLOYEE-MASTER.
        PERFORM 100-PROCESS THRU 100-EXIT
            UNTIL EMPLOYEE-NAME = "END".
        CLOSE EMPLOYEE-MASTER.
        STOP RUN.
100-PROCESS.
        DISPLAY "ENTER NAME".
        ACCEPT EMPLOYEE-NAME.
        IF EMPLOYEE-NAME = "END"
            GO TO 100-EXIT.
        DISPLAY "ENTER ADDRESS".
        ACCEPT EMPLOYEE-ADDRESS.
        DISPLAY "ENTER OCCUPATION".
        ACCEPT OCCUPATION.
        DISPLAY "ENTER YEARS OF SERVICE".
        ACCEPT YEARS-SERVICE.
        DISPLAY "ENTER SSN".
        ACCEPT SOCIAL-SECURITY-NO.
        PERFORM 200-HASH.
        WRITE EMPLOYEE-RECORD FROM WS-EMPLOYEE-RECORD
            INVALID KEY DISPLAY "DUPLICATE RECORD" EMPLOYEE-NAME.
100-EXIT. EXIT.
200-HASH.
        DIVIDE SOCIAL-SECURITY-NO BY 1009
            GIVING WS-RESULT REMAINDER WS-EMPLOYEE-NUMBER.
```

Figure 6–6 (continued)

```
PROCEDURE DIVISION.
000-MAIN-MODULE.
        OPEN INPUT EMPLOYEE-MASTER
             I-O   ATTRIBUTES-FILE.
        PERFORM 700-READ-EMPLOYEE.
        PERFORM 200-PROCESS-RECORD
              UNTIL EOF-SW = "X".
        CLOSE  EMPLOYEE-MASTER
               ATTRIBUTES-FILE.
        STOP RUN.
200-PROCESS-RECORD.
        DIVIDE SOCIAL-SECURITY BY PRIME-NO
               GIVING WS-RESULT
               REMAINDER WS-EMPLOYEE-NUMBER.
        MOVE OCCUPATION TO ATTRIBUTE.
        PERFORM 750-READ-ATTRIBUTE.
        IF AT-INDEX > 1 ADD 1 TO AT-INDEX.
        IF AT-INDEX = 1
               AND EMPLOYEE-POINTER (1) NOT = ZEROS
               ADD 1 TO AT-INDEX.
        MOVE WS-EMPLOYEE-NUMBER TO EMPLOYEE-POINTER (AT-INDEX).
        REWRITE ATTRIBUTE-RECORD
               INVALID KEY DISPLAY "KEY FIDDLE!".
        PERFORM 700-READ-EMPLOYEE.
700-READ-EMPLOYEE.
        READ EMPLOYEE-MASTER
             AT END MOVE "X" TO EOF-SW.
750-READ-ATTRIBUTE.
        READ ATTRIBUTES-FILE
             INVALID KEY
             DISPLAY "NO SUCH OCCUPATION" OCCUPATION.
```

SECTION 7
Questions and Exercises

I. Questions

1. Explain the concept of relative record numbers.
2. How many relative records can be accessed at one time?
3. Give the ENVIRONMENT DIVISION entries for a relative file whose relative key is PERSONNEL-FILE-NUMBER, and that is to be read sequentially. Randomly. Both sequentially and randomly.
4. Can a relative key be an actual part of the record? Why or why not?
5. What data type must a relative key be?
6. What are the possible ACCESS MODEs for a relative file?
7. How may a relative file be OPENed?
8. If a relative file is to be READ sequentially, how should the file be OPENed?
9. Give the general form of the sequential READ of a relative file.
10. Does a sequential READ to a relative file access the unused (blank) areas of the relative file?
11. What must a programmer do prior to issuing a random READ to a relative file?
12. What is the difference between the sequential READ statement for a relative file whose ACCESS MODE is DYNAMIC and the same file whose ACCESS MODE is SEQUENTIAL?
13. Is there any difference in the use of a START verb for a relative file and the use of a START verb for an indexed file? If so, what?
14. Give the general form of the random WRITE to a relative file.
15. When a record is DELETEd from a relative file, is the record physically removed from the file? If not, what happens to the record?
16. What is hashing? Why is hashing important to the use of a relative file?

17. Name and give examples of two hashing methods.
18. Why is prime number division so commonly used as a hashing method?
19. What is a record "collision"? How are these collisions handled in a program that maintains a relative file?
20. What is primary clustering? Secondary clustering?
21. What is a pointer?
22. Name and illustrate the various types of pointers.
23. What is an inverted list? How may this structure be implemented in a COBOL program using relative files?
24. What is the difference between imbedded pointers and written an attributes file?

II. Exercises

1. Using the sequential customer master file from Exercise II-3 of Chapter 3 as input, create a relative file using the customer number as the field on which to hash in order to create the relative record address.
2. Using the personnel master file described in Exercise II-4 of Chapter 3, create a relative file using the social security number as the field on which to hash in order to create the relative record numbers for the file.
3. Use the relative customer master file as input to create another relative file containing records from the customer master file which is inverted on customer name. The format of this file is as follows.

Field name	Location	Data Type
see foregoing	1–94	same as foregoing
NAME-POINTER	95–98	unsigned integer 9(4)

   a. Write a COBOL program to access and print the records in this file sequentially on either record number or customer name.

   b. Write a COBOL program to maintain the records in this file. The transactions file from Exercise II-3 of Chapter 3 may be used as the input transactions file for this process.

4. Add an invoice pointer to the customer master file created in Exercise 3(b). The purpose of this invoice pointer is to indicate whether a customer contained in the customer master file has any invoice charges on the invoice master file. If the customer does not have activity on the invoice master file, the invoice pointer field in the customer master file will contain zeros. If the customer has invoices on the invoice master file, the invoice pointer field will have a relative address pointer to the first invoice that the customer has in the invoice master file. The first invoice record and subsequent invoice records for a specific customer will have imbedded pointers which indicate the location of the next invoice record for that customer. The last invoice in a set of invoices for a specific customer will have a pointer value of zeros. The record format for the invoice master file is as described in Exercise II-5 of Chapter 5, with the following exception:

Field Name	Location	Data Type
NEXT-POINTER	27–30	unsigned integer 9(04)

Prepare a statement of account for each customer using the statement form indicated below. Statements for customers with zero balances are not to be printed.

7

Some Special Statements

There are some COBOL features not previously discussed that deserve attention but are not typically covered in a first course in the language. Some of these features are not available on all compilers or are not allowed on some subset COBOL compilers. You will need to check a user's manual for your particular equipment and level of COBOL. In some cases the features discussed here are non-ANSI-standard.

SECTION 1
The ACCEPT Statement

The ACCEPT statement was discussed briefly in Chapter 1 and has been used in its basic form in several previous chapters. Here we discuss some additional uses of the verb.

The purpose of the ACCEPT statement is to make low-volume data available to an executing program.

There are two general forms of the ACCEPT statement. They are as follows:

FORMAT 1

```
ACCEPT  identifier-1 [FROM input-source]
        [AT END  any imperative statement  [END-ACCEPT]
```

FORMAT 2

```
ACCEPT  identifier-2  FROM  {DATE       }
                           {DAY        }
                           {DAY-OF-WEEK}
                           {TIME       }
```

```
VALUE OF INPUT               VALUE OF DATA-ITEMS AFTER INPUT
----- -- -----               ----- -- ---------- ----- -----
                             ITEM-A      ITEM-B      ITEM-C
                             ------      ------      ------
       HELLO                 HELLO       space       000
       SIGNON                HELLO       SIGNON      000
       602                   HELLO       SIGNON      602
       END          *        END         SIGNON      602

       *  No  Processing takes Place after END is ACCEPTed to be stored at
ITEM-A.
```

Figure 7–1
Results of ACCEPT illustration.

FORMAT 1

Format 1 ACCEPTs data from an input source, usually a terminal, and transfers the data ACCEPTed from the input source to identifier-1. The treatment of the data is as if they are alphanumeric, no matter what the definition. Some compilers require specification of FROM input source.

An example of the ACCEPT statement follows:

```
DATA DIVISION.
WORKING-STORAGE SECTION.
01   ITEM-A    PIC X(5)    VALUE SPACE.
01   ITEM-B    PIC X(6)    VALUE SPACE.
01   ITEM-C    PIC 9(3)    VALUE ZEROES.
PROCEDURE DIVISION.
     PERFORM ACCEPT-DATA
         UNTIL ITEM-A = "END".
     STOP RUN.
ACCEPT-DATA.
     ACCEPT ITEM-A.
     ACCEPT ITEM-B.
     ACCEPT ITEM-C.
     ACCEPT ITEM-A.
     ACCEPT ITEM-C.
     ACCEPT ITEM-C.
```

The results of the execution of the program are as presented in Figure 7-1.

FORMAT 2

The purpose of Format 2 is to enter the system date information into the program.
DATE is a six-digit field that contains the following, in the order listed:

YEAR

MONTH of the year

DAY of the year

A date of July 23, 1987 would go into memory as 870723.

DAY has two elements: year (two digits) and DAY of year (three digits) (Julian calendar day). If July 23, 1987 were to be ACCEPTed from DAY, the receiving field (identifier-2) would contain 87204.

TIME represents elapsed time on a 24-hour clock. TIME is an eight-digit field that consists of:

- HOURS
- MINUTES
- SECONDS
- HUNDREDTHS OF A SECOND

DAY-OF-WEEK is a one-digit field that represents the numerical day of the week. The range of values is from 1, for Monday, through 7, for Sunday.

SECTION 2
The DISPLAY Statement

The purpose of the DISPLAY statement is to transfer low-volume data from an executing program to a default output device or a specified device. The default device may be the terminal that is causing the program to execute the operator's console, the system printer, or any other device. Since there is a considerable variation in the default device definition from center to center, you should consult with data processing personnel at your center to determine this assignment or simply specify the device on which a DISPLAY is to occur. It may be redundant if you specify the default device but you won't have to worry about finding out what the default device is. If you want to DISPLAY on the line printer, then the device must be specified in the SPECIAL-NAMES paragraph of the FILE-CONTROL section of the DATA DIVISION.

The general form of the DISPLAY statement is as follows:

$$\underline{\text{DISPLAY}} \begin{Bmatrix} \text{identifier-1} \\ \text{literal-1} \end{Bmatrix} [\underline{\text{UPON}} \text{ output device}] [\text{WITH } \underline{\text{NO}} \text{ ADVANCING}]$$

Figure 7-2 is a simple program illustrating the use of the DISPLAY statement, and Figure 7-3 is the output from that program. The discussion of the EXAMINE verb later in this chapter includes several additional examples of the use of

Figure 7–2
Display program.

```
IDENTIFICATION DIVISION.
PROGRAM-ID. DISEXP.
AUTHOR. CSIMPSON.
INSTALLATION. GRAMBLING STATE UNIVERSITY.
ENVIRONMENT DIVISION.
SOURCE-COMPUTER. VAX-11.
OBJECT-COMPUTER. VAX-11.
DATA DIVISION.
WORKING-STORAGE SECTION.
01  AUTHOR-ONE        PIC X(14) VALUE "KENT T. FIELDS".
01  AUTHOR-TWO     PIC X(14) VALUE "CLAUDE SIMPSON".
01  AUTHOR-THREE   PIC X(10) VALUE "JOHN BONNO".
01  NUMERIC-VALUE  PIC 9(05) VALUE 12345.
PROCEDURE DIVISION.
000-MAIN-ROUTINE.
        DISPLAY AUTHOR-ONE.
        DISPLAY AUTHOR-TWO.
        DISPLAY AUTHOR-THREE.
        DISPLAY NUMERIC-VALUE.
        DISPLAY AUTHOR-ONE " " AUTHOR-TWO " " AUTHOR-THREE.
        DISPLAY 654321 " " NUMERIC-VALUE.
        STOP RUN.

Ready
```

DISPLAY. The WITH NO ADVANCING phrase causes the cursor to stay on the same line as the item(s) DISPLAYed after the execution of the DISPLAY statement.

Figure 7–3
Output from the display
program.

```
KENT T. FIELDS
CLAUDE SIMPSON
JOHN BONNO
12345
KENT T. FIELDS CLAUDE SIMPSON JOHN BONNO
654321 12345
```

SECTION 3
The EXAMINE Statement

The EXAMINE statement allows the programmer to replace and/or count the number of occurrences of a given character or string of characters in a data-item. The EXAMINE can merely replace characters, or can count them, or both. First let's look at the replacement function.

The general form of the statement is:

```
EXAMINE data-name REPLACING ALL literal BY literal.
EXAMINE data-name REPLACING LEADING literal BY literal.
EXAMINE data-name REPLACING UNTIL FIRST literal BY literal.
```

For example:

```
EXAMINE COST REPLACING ALL 'Ƀ' BY 'O'.
EXAMINE NAME REPLACING LEADING 'Ƀ' BY '-'.
EXAMINE VARIABLE REPLACING UNTIL FIRST '*' BY 'Ƀ'.
```

Probably the most common use of the EXAMINE statement is in the screening of numeric data-items replacing all blanks by zeros. This will allow a program to run that may otherwise terminate because of a data exception (imbedded or trailing blanks in a numeric field), although there may be some errors in the output from the program.

In order to show how the EXAMINE statements work we have written a program which shows a value being moved to a data-name (THISPLACE) and EXAMINEs it for various characters. The paragraph-names are descriptive of the option being illustrated, and the PROCEDURE DIVISION entries along with the DISPLAYed results are presented in Figure 7-4. The first eight paragraphs in the program illustrate the use of the REPLACING ALL option, the second seven show the use of the REPLACING UNTIL FIRST option, and the final seven paragraphs illustrate the use of the REPLACING LEADING option. As you can see, there are three forms of the REPLACING option. The ALL option would substitute all occurrences of a particular character with the replacing character. The LEADING option would substitute a particular character with a replacing character, but only at the start of the variable (if at all). "Leading" implies that the character being sought must begin the variable (and possibly continue) in order to be replaced. Once an intervening character is found, the replacement is stopped. The UNTIL FIRST option would substitute the replacing character for whatever was in the data-item up to the point where the particular character was found. It is probably easier to study the PROCEDURE DIVISION entries in Figure 7-4 and the output to see exactly what each option does.

Figure 7-4 (page 1)
EXAMINE with REPLACING
ALL option.

```
IDENTIFICATION DIVISION.
PROGRAM-ID. EXAMINE-STATEMENTS.
AUTHOR. DEBBIE ALRIDGE.
ENVIRONMENT DIVISION.
DATA DIVISION.
WORKING-STORAGE SECTION.                                    Data
    01 THISPLACE PICTURE XXXXX.                         Displayed
PROCEDURE DIVISION.                                          ↓
REPLACING-ALL-1.
    MOVE ' 8 4 ' TO THISPLACE.                             8 4
    DISPLAY THISPLACE.                                    08040
    EXAMINE THISPLACE REPLACING ALL SPACES BY ZEROES.
    DISPLAY THISPLACE.
REPLACING-ALL-2.
    MOVE 'AAAAA' TO THISPLACE.                            AAAAA
    DISPLAY THISPLACE.                                    XXXXX
    EXAMINE THISPLACE REPLACING ALL 'A' BY 'X'.
    DISPLAY THISPLACE.
REPLACING-ALL-3.
    MOVE 'AAABB' TO THISPLACE.                            AAABB
    DISPLAY THISPLACE.                                    XXXBB
    EXAMINE THISPLACE REPLACING ALL 'A' BY 'X'.
    DISPLAY THISPLACE.
REPLACING-ALL-4.
    MOVE 'BBABB' TO THISPLACE.                            BBABB
    DISPLAY THISPLACE.                                    BBXBB
    EXAMINE THISPLACE REPLACING ALL 'A' BY 'X'.
    DISPLAY THISPLACE.
REPLACING-ALL-5.
    MOVE 'BBBBB' TO THISPLACE.                            BBBBB
    DISPLAY THISPLACE.                                    BBBBB
    EXAMINE THISPLACE REPLACING ALL 'A' BY 'X'.
    DISPLAY THISPLACE.
REPLACING-ALL-6.
    MOVE 'BBAAA' TO THISPLACE.                            BBAAA
    DISPLAY THISPLACE.                                    BBXXX
    EXAMINE THISPLACE REPLACING ALL 'A' BY 'X'.
    DISPLAY THISPLACE.
REPLACING-ALL-7.
    MOVE 'ABABA' TO THISPLACE.                            ABABA
    DISPLAY THISPLACE.                                    XBXBX
    EXAMINE THISPLACE REPLACING ALL 'A' BY 'X'.
    DISPLAY THISPLACE.
REPLACING-ALL-8.
    MOVE 'BBCBA' TO THISPLACE.                            BBCBA
    DISPLAY THISPLACE.                                    BBCBX
    EXAMINE THISPLACE REPLACING ALL 'A' BY 'X'.
    DISPLAY THISPLACE.
```

Figure 7–4 (page 2)
EXAMINE with REPLACING
UNTIL FIRST option.

Data
Displayed
↓

```
REPLACING-UNTIL-FIRST-1.
    MOVE 'AAAAA' TO THISPLACE.                          AAAAA
    DISPLAY THISPLACE.                                  AAAAA
    EXAMINE THISPLACE REPLACING UNTIL FIRST 'A' BY 'Y'.
    DISPLAY THISPLACE.
REPLACING-UNTIL-FIRST-2.
    MOVE 'AAABB' TO THISPLACE.                          AAABB
    DISPLAY THISPLACE.                                  AAABB
    EXAMINE THISPLACE REPLACING UNTIL FIRST 'A' BY 'Y'.
    DISPLAY THISPLACE.
REPLACING-UNTIL-FIRST-3.
    MOVE 'BBABB' TO THISPLACE.                          BBABB
    DISPLAY THISPLACE.                                  YYABB
    EXAMINE THISPLACE REPLACING UNTIL FIRST 'A' BY 'Y'.
    DISPLAY THISPLACE.
REPLACING-UNTIL-FIRST-4.
    MOVE 'BBBBB' TO THISPLACE.                          BBBBB
    DISPLAY THISPLACE.                                  YYYYY
    EXAMINE THISPLACE REPLACING UNTIL FIRST 'A' BY 'Y'.
    DISPLAY THISPLACE.
REPLACING-UNTIL-FIRST-5.
    MOVE 'BBAAA' TO THISPLACE.                          BBAAA
    DISPLAY THISPLACE.                                  YYAAA
    EXAMINE THISPLACE REPLACING UNTIL FIRST 'A' BY 'Y'.
    DISPLAY THISPLACE.
REPLACING-UNTIL-FIRST-6.
    MOVE 'ABABA' TO THISPLACE.                          ABABA
    DISPLAY THISPLACE.                                  ABABA
    EXAMINE THISPLACE REPLACING UNTIL FIRST 'A' BY 'Y'.
    DISPLAY THISPLACE.
REPLACING-UNTIL-FIRST-7.
    MOVE 'BBCBA' TO THISPLACE.                          BBCBA
    DISPLAY THISPLACE.                                  YYYYA
    EXAMINE THISPLACE REPLACING UNTIL FIRST 'A' BY 'Y'.
    DISPLAY THISPLACE.
```

Figure 7–4 (page 3)
EXAMINE with REPLACING
LEADING option.

DATA
DISPLAYED
↓

```
REPLACING-LEADING-1.
    MOVE 'AAAAA' TO THISPLACE.
    DISPLAY THISPLACE.                                  AAAAA
    EXAMINE THISPLACE REPLACING LEADING 'A' BY 'Z'.
    DISPLAY THISPLACE.                                  ZZZZZ
REPLACING-LEADING-2.
    MOVE 'AAABB' TO THISPLACE.
    DISPLAY THISPLACE.                                  AAABB
    EXAMINE THISPLACE REPLACING LEADING 'A' BY 'Z'.
    DISPLAY THISPLACE.                                  ZZZBB
REPLACING-LEADING-3.
    MOVE 'BBABB' TO THISPLACE.
    DISPLAY THISPLACE.                                  BBABB
    EXAMINE THISPLACE REPLACING LEADING 'A' BY 'Z'.
    DISPLAY THISPLACE.                                  BBABB
REPLACING-LEADING-4.
    MOVE 'BBBBB' TO THISPLACE.
    DISPLAY THISPLACE.                                  BBBBB
    EXAMINE THISPLACE REPLACING LEADING 'A' BY 'Z'.
    DISPLAY THISPLACE.                                  BBBBB
REPLACING-LEADING-5.
    MOVE 'BBAAAT' TO THISPLACE.
    DISPLAY THISPLACE.                                  BBAAA
    EXAMINE THISPLACE REPLACING LEADING 'A' BY 'Z'.
    DISPLAY THISPLACE.                                  BBAAA
REPLACING-LEADING-6.
    MOVE 'ABABA' TO THISPLACE.
    DISPLAY THISPLACE.                                  ABABA
    EXAMINE THISPLACE REPLACING LEADING 'A' BY 'X'.
    DISPLAY THISPLACE.                                  XBABA
REPLACING-LEADING-7.
    MOVE 'BBCBA' TO THISPLACE.
    DISPLAY THISPLACE.                                  BBCBA
    EXAMINE THISPLACE REPLACING LEADING 'A' BY 'X'.
    DISPLAY THISPLACE.                                  BBCBA
```

Another type of EXAMINE statement uses the TALLYING option. The TALLY option counts the number of occurrences of a particular character in a data-item. COBOL provides for the automatic allocation of storage space for a signed numeric variable called TALLY. You need not (indeed, you may not) define this variable, since its inclusion is automatic. When you use the TALLYING option of EXAMINE, the result of the count will be stored at TALLY, which is initialized at zero each time the TALLYING option is invoked. The EXAMINE statement with the TALLYING option will then count the occurrence of a particular character and the total number of occurrences will be stored in the variable TALLY. You can then use TALLY in your program with such commands as:

```
MOVE TALLY TO TOTAL-COUNT.
IF TALLY IS GREATER THAN ZERO THEN...
```

The general form of the EXAMINE with the TALLYING option is:

```
EXAMINE data-item TALLYING ALL literal.
EXAMINE data-item TALLYING LEADING literal.
EXAMINE data-item TALLYING UNTIL FIRST literal.
```

For example:

```
EXAMINE GROUP-A TALLYING UNTIL FIRST "$".
EXAMINE GROUP-A TALLYING ALL "1".
EXAMINE GROUP-A TALLYING LEADING "b".
```

In order to show how the EXAMINE statement with the TALLYING option works we have written another series of statements that use this function. Figure 7-5 illustrates these statements and the results of the use of EXAMINE with TALLYING in a way similar to that used in Figure 7-4. A review of this material should be more instructive than a narrative discussion.

These statements are very similar to the ones with the REPLACING option, except that no replacing occurs. There is only a counting function. The special register TALLY will contain the relative position or the number of the occurrences of a specific character in the data-item.

The last form of the EXAMINE statement combines the TALLYING and the REPLACING options. That is, the EXAMINE statement can both count the occurrence of a particular character and, at the same time, replace it with some other character. Rather than attempt to show all the possible combinations, we have supplied Figure 7-6 to show some of the possibilities.

There are persuasive reasons to avoid the use of the EXAMINE statement and the similar INSPECT statement (discussed in Section 4) in the main body of a production program. It is generally preferable to include editing functions in a separate program and to provide only edited data to production programs. There should be procedures for the rejection of data which fail editing standards. It is equally important that there be procedural provisions that will assure that such rejected transactions are:

- reviewed by qualified personnel;
- corrected by qualified personnel;
- resubmitted for processing;
- processed

Figure 7-5

EXAMINE with TALLYING
option.

```
                                                          Data
                                                        Displayed    Tally
                                                           ↓           ↓
        TALLYING-ALL-1.
            MOVE ' 8 4 ' TO THISPLACE.
            DISPLAY THISPLACE.
            EXAMINE THISPLACE TALLYING ALL SPACES.          8 4
            DISPLAY THISPLACE ' ' TALLY.                     8 4       00003
        TALLYING-ALL-2.
            MOVE 'AAAAA' TO THISPLACE.
            DISPLAY THISPLACE.
            EXAMINE THISPLACE TALLYING ALL 'A'.             AAAAA
            DISPLAY THISPLACE '    ' TALLY.                 AAAAA      00005
        TALLYING-ALL-3.
            MOVE 'AAABB' TO THISPLACE.
            DISPLAY THISPLACE.
            EXAMINE THISPLACE TALLYING ALL 'A'.             AAABB
            DISPLAY THISPLACE '    ' TALLY.                 AAABB      00003
        TALLYING-ALL-4.
            MOVE 'BBABB' TO THISPLACE.
            DISPLAY THISPLACE.
            EXAMINE THISPLACE TALLYING ALL 'A'.             BBABB
            DISPLAY THISPLACE '    ' TALLY.                 BBABB      00001
        TALLYING-ALL-5.
            MOVE 'BBBBB' TO THISPLACE.
            DISPLAY THISPLACE.
            EXAMINE THISPLACE TALLYING ALL 'A'.             BBBBB
            DISPLAY THISPLACE '    ' TALLY.                 BBBBB      00000
        TALLYING-ALL-6.
            MOVE 'BBAAA' TO THISPLACE.
            DISPLAY THISPLACE.
            EXAMINE THISPLACE TALLYING ALL 'A'.             BBAAA
            DISPLAY THISPLACE '    ' TALLY.                 BBAAA      00003
        TALLYING-ALL-7.
            MOVE 'ABABA' TO THISPLACE.
            DISPLAY THISPLACE.
            EXAMINE THISPLACE TALLYING ALL 'A'.             ABABA
            DISPLAY THISPLACE '    ' TALLY.                 ABABA      00003
        TALLYING-ALL-8.
            MOVE 'BBCBA' TO THISPLACE.
            DISPLAY THISPLACE.
            EXAMINE THISPLACE TALLYING ALL 'A'.             BBCBA
            DISPLAY THISPLACE '    ' TALLY.                 BBCBA      00001
```

Figure 7-6

EXAMINE with REPLACING
and TALLY.

```
        IDENTIFICATION DIVISION.
        PROGRAM-ID. EXAMINE-STATEMENTS.
        AUTHOR. DEBBIE ALRIDGE.
        ENVIRONMENT DIVISION.
        DATA DIVISION.                                              DATA DISPLAYED
        WORKING-STORAGE SECTION.
            01 THISPLACE PICTURE XXXXX.
        PROCEDURE DIVISION.
        REPLACING-ALL-1.
            MOVE ' 8 4 ' TO THISPLACE.                    8 4
            DISPLAY THISPLACE.
            EXAMINE THISPLACE TALLYING ALL SPACES.
            EXAMINE THISPLACE REPLACING ALL SPACE BY ZEROES.
            DISPLAY THISPLACE '        ' TALLY 'SPACES WERE REPLACED'.   08040    00003SPACES WERE REPLACED
        REPLACING-ALL-2.
            MOVE 'AAAAA' TO THISPLACE.                    AAAAA
            DISPLAY THISPLACE.
            EXAMINE THISPLACE TALLYING ALL 'A';
            EXAMINE THISPLACE REPLACING ALL 'A' BY 'X'.
            DISPLAY THISPLACE '        ' TALLY '-A- WERE REPLACED'.      XXXXX    00005-A- WERE REPLACED
        REPLACING-ALL-3.
            MOVE 'AAABB' TO THISPLACE.                    AAABB
            DISPLAY THISPLACE.
            EXAMINE THISPLACE TALLYING ALL 'A';
            EXAMINE THISPLACE REPLACING ALL 'A' BY 'X'.
            DISPLAY THISPLACE '        ' TALLY '-A- WERE REPLACED'.      XXXBB    00003-A- WERE REPLACED
        REPLACING-ALL-4.
            MOVE 'BBABB' TO THISPLACE.                    BBABB
            DISPLAY THISPLACE.
            EXAMINE THISPLACE TALLYING ALL 'A';
            EXAMINE THISPLACE REPLACING ALL 'A' BY 'X'.
            DISPLAY THISPLACE '        ' TALLY '-A- WERE REPLACED'.      BBXBB    00001-A- WERE REPLACED
        REPLACING-ALL-5.
            MOVE 'BBBBB' TO THISPLACE.                    BBBBB
            DISPLAY THISPLACE.
            EXAMINE THISPLACE TALLYING ALL 'A'.
            EXAMINE THISPLACE REPLACING ALL 'A' BY 'X'.
            DISPLAY THISPLACE '        ' TALLY '-A- WERE REPLACED'.      BBBBB    00000-A- WERE REPLACED
        REPLACING-ALL-6.
            MOVE 'BBAAA' TO THISPLACE.                    BBAAA
            DISPLAY THISPLACE.
            EXAMINE THISPLACE TALLYING ALL 'A';
            EXAMINE THISPLACE REPLACING ALL 'A' BY 'X'.
            DISPLAY THISPLACE '        ' TALLY '-A- WERE REPLACED'.      BBXXX    00003-A- WERE REPLACED
        REPLACING-ALL-7.
            MOVE 'ABABA' TO THISPLACE.                    ABABA
            DISPLAY THISPLACE.
            EXAMINE THISPLACE TALLYING ALL 'A';
            EXAMINE THISPLACE REPLACING ALL 'A' BY 'X'.
            DISPLAY THISPLACE '        ' TALLY '-A- WERE REPLACED'.      XBXBX    00003-A- WERE REPLACED
        REPLACING-ALL-8.
            MOVE 'BBCBA' TO THISPLACE.                    BBCBA
            DISPLAY THISPLACE.
            EXAMINE THISPLACE TALLYING ALL 'A';
            EXAMINE THISPLACE REPLACING ALL 'A' BY 'X'.
            DISPLAY THISPLACE '        ' TALLY '-A- WERE REPLACED'.      BBCBX    00001-A- WERE REPLACED
        WRAPUP.
            STOP RUN.
```

SECTION 4
The INSPECT Statement

The INSPECT statement is very similar to the EXAMINE statement and, indeed, in versions of COBOL where one is found the other typically is not.

The INSPECT statement allows the programmer to replace and/or count the number of occurrences of a given character in a data-item. The general form of the statement is:

```
INSPECT data-name TALLYING some-counter FOR ALL literal.
INSPECT data-name TALLYING some-counter FOR ALL literal BEFORE INITIAL
        literal.
INSPECT data-name TALLYING some-counter FOR LEADING data-name AFTER
        INITIAL data-name.
INSPECT data-name REPLACING ALL literal BY literal BEFORE INITIAL literal.
INSPECT data-name REPLACING LEADING data-name BY data-name BEFORE
        INITIAL data-name.
```

For example:

```
INSPECT COST TALLYING SPACE-COUNTER FOR ALL SPACES.

INSPECT NAME TALLYING Z-COUNTER FOR ALL 'Z' BEFORE INITIAL 'A'.

INSPECT WORD TALLYING NUMBER-OF-NINES FOR LEADING NINES AFTER
INITIAL ONE.

INSPECT COST REPLACING ALL '.' BY '0'.

INSPECT NAME REPLACING ALL 'Z' BY 'Z' BEFORE INITIAL 'A'.
```

In the preceding examples the word ALL may be ALL, LEADING, or CHARAC-TERS. The word BEFORE may be BEFORE or AFTER and the word TALLYING may be TALLYING or REPLACING.

The function of the word TALLYING is to count the number of occurrences. The number should be stored in a data-name as specified after the word TALLY-ING. This data-name is programmer created and must be described in the DATA DIVISION.

The function of the word REPLACING is to substitute a specified character in place of a particular character being checked on in the data-name.

The word ALL can be ALL, LEADING, FIRST. The item—literal—can be a literal or a data-name. BEFORE may be BEFORE or AFTER.

The INSPECT statement may use the TALLYING and/or the REPLACING options. You may INSPECT a data-item and want to know how many times a specific character occurred (TALLYING) and also to change it to something else (REPLAC-ING).

The INSPECT statement is more powerful than the EXAMINE statement in that more than one character may be checked for and more than one counter can be used.

SECTION 5
The UNSTRING Command

The purpose of the UNSTRING command is to separate a contiguous data-item into two or more receiving fields.

The UNSTRING command is a very powerful instruction that allows for considerable character manipulation in your COBOL program. Not all the possibilities for the use of the statement can be shown here but an example will probably help illustrate the use and power of the command.

The general form of the UNSTRING command is as follows:

```
UNSTRING sending-field
        [DELIMITED BY [ALL] delimiter [OR [ALL] delimiter]...]
        INTO receiving-field[DELIMITER in receiving-field]
                [COUNT IN some-counter]
[WITH POINTER some-pointer]
[TALLYING IN some-tally]
[ON OVERFLOW any imperative statement [END-UNSTRING]
```

Obviously, from the general format, this statement has many forms and can be used to deconcentrate data according to multiple sets of UNSTRING rules, count, tally, or use a pointer to indicate where the search begins.

The program in Figure 7-7 is provided to aid you in your examination to the UNSTRING command for use in your programs. In the illustration we want to take some records containing people's names and be able to access the data on the basis of title or any of the two or three names of a particular individual. The way the UNSTRING works is to scan the series of (string) characters in a record until it encounters the character you have specified as a delimiter. This delimiter causes a grouping of the data encountered since the last occurrence of the delimiter to be

Figure 7–7
Illustration of UNSTRING.

```
IDENTIFICATION DIVISION.
PROGRAM-ID.  UNSTRING1.
AUTHOR.  CSIMPSON.
INSTALLATION. GRAMBLING STATE UNIVERSITY.
ENVIRONMENT DIVISION.
CONFIGURATION SECTION.
SOURCE-COMPUTER. VAX-11.
OBJECT-COMPUTER. VAX-11.
INPUT-OUTPUT SECTION.
FILE-CONTROL.
        SELECT OUT-FILE
                ASSIGN TO "NAMES.DAT".
DATA DIVISION.
FILE SECTION.
FD  OUT-FILE
        LABEL RECORDS ARE STANDARD.
01  NAME-RECORD.
        05  HONORARY-TITLE              PIC X(05).
        05  LAST-NAME                   PIC X(30).
        05  FIRST-NAME                  PIC X(15).
        05  MIDDLE-INITIAL              PIC X(01).
        05  ADDRESS-LINE                PIC X(34).
        05  CITY                        PIC X(20).
        05  STATE                       PIC X(02).
        05  ZIP-CODE                    PIC X(05).
WORKING-STORAGE SECTION.
*********************************
*PLEASE NOTE THAT THE ACCEPT
* AREA IS EXPANDED TO SIZE
* TO INCLUDE DELIMITER CHARACTER
*********************************
01  INPUT-DATA                          PIC X(114).
01  EOF-SW                              PIC X(01) VALUE SPACE.
01  POINTER1                            PIC 99   VALUE ZEROS.
01  TALLY1                              PIC 99   VALUE ZEROS.
01  COUNTER1                            PIC 99   VALUE ZEROS.
01  DESTIN-DELIM                        PIC XX   VALUE SPACES.
```

Figure 7–7 (continued)

```
PROCEDURE DIVISION.
000-MAIN-MODULE.
        PERFORM 100-INITIALIZE.
        PERFORM 200-CREATE-RECORD
                UNTIL EOF-SW = "X".
        CLOSE OUT-FILE.
        STOP RUN.
100-INITIALIZE.
        OPEN OUTPUT OUT-FILE.
        DISPLAY "ENTER DATA IN THE FOLLOWING FORMAT".
        DISPLAY "HONORARY TITLE/LAST/NAME/FIRST NAME/MI/ADDRESS/".
        DISPLAY "CITY/STATE/ZIPCODE".
        ACCEPT INPUT-DATA.
200-CREATE-RECORD.
        MOVE SPACES TO NAME-RECORD.
        UNSTRING INPUT-DATA DELIMITED BY "/"
                INTO    HONORARY-TITLE
                        LAST-NAME
                        FIRST-NAME
                        MIDDLE-INITIAL
                        ADDRESS-LINE
                        CITY
                        STATE
                        ZIP-CODE
                ON OVERFLOW DISPLAY "TOO MANY FIELDS".
        WRITE NAME-RECORD.
        DISPLAY NAME-RECORD.
        ACCEPT INPUT-DATA.
        IF INPUT-DATA = "99999/"
                MOVE "X" TO EOF-SW.
```

transferred to the receiving field. Then the process continues. In reading this sentence you are doing the same thing—you unstring the characters on the basis of blanks and (perhaps) commas, colons, semicolons, and periods. The purpose of the example program is to ACCEPT data from a terminal, UNSTRING the data into a record, then write the record to disk. The DISPLAY statements are included in the program so you may see the result of the UNSTRING operation.

Notice that the fields that are input on the terminal are separated by a "/" character. This character was chosen as our delimiter character, but there is nothing magic about it. You can use any character. The COUNT operation will count the number of characters that are included in the LAST-NAME field.

The POINTER phrase is used to give a starting point in the operation and must be initialized to a value of 01 or greater, but less than the maximum number of characters in the field. This is important! If the POINTER field of the DATA DIVISION is not greater than 0 or the field is not large enough to include the value of the largest record size, the UNSTRING operation will not work. Normally, in such circumstance the ON OVERFLOW clause will be executed and the "UNSTRING" operation aborted without an UNSTRING of the fields being accomplished. In our example the pointer (pointer1) is started at position 1 in the INPUT-DATA field and ends at position 115. Since the maximum size of the output record is 114 characters (including the eight delimiter characters required to separate the fields), this allows for all possible inputs.

The TALLYING option simply counts the number of fields that you UNSTRING; in our case there were 08.

The DELIMITER IN phrase causes the delimiter character to be stored in the field DESTIN-DELIM. This is useful if the program you are writing uses the "OR" option in the delimiter process and you need to know what the delimiting character was.

Figure 7-8 is a list of the inputs for the UNSTRING program and Figure 7-9 shows the outputs.

Figure 7-8
Inputs to the UNSTRING program.

```
MR/JONES/WINFRED/R/604 PLEASANT AVENUE/GRAMBLING/LA/71245
MR/PENN/JULIUS/D/1612 SNOWMOUND LANE/GRAMBLING/LA/71245
MS/ONEAL/GENIE//265 REGAL STREET/ASPREMONT/NC/84927
MRS/JOHNSON/ANGIE/R/P.O. BOX 62/SNOWMASS/CO/91457
MR/MORRIS/CASEY/A/7045 DUNDEE LANE/PORTLAND/TX/78305
MR/LACKEY/JAMES/T/743 AILSIE STREET/TAFT/TX/78390
```

Figure 7-9
Outputs from the UNSTRING program.

```
MR    JONES                    WINFRED          R604 PLEASANT
AVENUE            GRAMBLING          LA71245
MR    PENN                    JULIUS           D1612 SNOWMOUND
LANE             GRAMBLING          LA71245
MS    ONEAL                    GENIE            265 REGAL
STREET           ASPREMONT          NC84927
MRS   JOHNSON                 ANGIE            RP.O.BOX 62
                 SNOWMASS           CO91457
MR    MORRIS                  CASEY            A7045 DUNDEE
LANE             PORTLAND           TX78305
MR    LACKEY                  JAMES            T743 AILSIE
STREET           TAFT               TX78390
```

SECTION 6
The STRING Statement

Suppose that you have some data in the form shown in Figure 7-9 and that, in order to process the data, the fields should be in a different order and have no embedded blanks. For example, if you wanted to use the names in Figure 7-9 for addressing envelopes, the order of the data fields is not really appropriate to that purpose since the last name precedes the first name. Figure 7-10 is a program to reorganize the data into a form more suitable for the preparation of addresses. The program uses the STRING command to accomplish this purpose. Figure 7-11 is the output from the STRING program. Notice that the input records are in accordance with the record format NAME-RECORD. Now look at the line that was strung together. Notice that the honorary title is positioned before first name, which is followed in turn by middle initial and last name. Further note that spaces are interspersed at appropriate points and that middle initial has a " , " added that was not in the input record.

The DELIMITED BY " " stops the extraction of the data from the field when the first space is encountered. The " " DELIMITED BY SIZE phrase separates the various items in the line by a space. The " , " phrase that is included in the middle-initial portion causes a period to be inserted after the middle initial.

In situations in which a data-item actually includes the delimiting character, for example, VAN-STEE, the record should be built with a hyphen separating the names, then an INSPECT OUTPUT-NAME REPLACING ALL "-" BY " " coded so that the output will include the delimiter.

Figure 7–10
STRING program.

```
00001          IDENTIFICATION DIVISION.
00002          PROGRAM-ID. STRING1.
00003          AUTHOR. CSIMPSON.
00004          INSTALLATION. GRAMBLING STATE UNIVERSITY.
00005          ENVIRONMENT DIVISION.
00006          CONFIGURATION SECTION.
00007          SOURCE-COMPUTER. VAX-11.
00008          OBJECT-COMPUTER. VAX-11.
00009          INPUT-OUTPUT SECTION.
00010          FILE-CONTROL.
00011              SELECT IN-FILE
00012                  ASSIGN TO "NAMES.DAT".
00013          DATA DIVISION.
00014          FILE SECTION.
00015          FD  IN-FILE
00016              LABEL RECORDS ARE OMITTED.
00017          01  NAME-RECORD.
00018              05  HONORARY-TITLE       PIC X(05).
00019              05  LAST-NAME            PIC X(30).
00020              05  FIRST-NAME           PIC X(15).
00021              05  MIDDLE-INITIAL       PIC X(01).
00022              05  ADDRESS-LINE         PIC X(34).
00023              05  CITY                 PIC X(20).
00024              05  STATE                PIC X(02).
00025              05  ZIP-CODE             PIC X(05).
00026          WORKING-STORAGE SECTION.
00027          01  EOF-SW                   PIC X(01).
00028          01  OUTPUT-NAME                  PIC X(50).
00029          PROCEDURE DIVISION.
00030          000-MAIN-MODULE.
00031              PERFORM 100-INITIALIZE.
00032              PERFORM 200-BUILD-LINE
00033                  UNTIL EOF-SW = "X".
00034              CLOSE IN-FILE.
00035              STOP RUN.
00036          100-INITIALIZE.
00037              MOVE " " TO EOF-SW.
00038              OPEN INPUT IN-FILE.
00039              READ IN-FILE
00040                  AT END MOVE "X" TO EOF-SW.
00041          200-BUILD-LINE.
00042              MOVE SPACES TO OUTPUT-NAME.
00043              STRING          HONORARY-TITLE DELIMITED BY " "
00044                              " " DELIMITED BY SIZE
00045                              FIRST-NAME DELIMITED BY " "
00046                              " " DELIMITED BY SIZE
00047                              MIDDLE-INITIAL DELIMITED BY SIZE
00048                              ". " DELIMITED BY SIZE
00049                              LAST-NAME DELIMITED BY SIZE
00050                  INTO    OUTPUT-NAME.
00051              DISPLAY OUTPUT-NAME.
00052              READ IN-FILE
00053                  AT END MOVE "X" TO EOF-SW.
00054
```

Figure 7–11
Output from the STRING
program.

```
MR WINFRED R JONES
MR JULIUS D PENN
MS GENIE ONEAL
MRS ANGIE R JOHNSON
MR CASEY A MORRIS
MR JAMES T LACKEY
```

```
                         FIGURE 7-11
                 Output from the STRING Program
```

SECTION 7
GO TO DEPENDING ON

There is some controversy concerning the use of the GO TO DEPENDING ON statement. Since it results in an unconditional branch in the program logic, the objectives of a well-structured program are violated. It is, however, the statement which allows the implementation of the CASE structure in COBOL. We considered relegating the discussion of this statement to the Rogues' Gallery but decided that the usefulness of the CASE structure deserves attention here. Your instructor and/or the shop where you work may object to the use of GO TO in any form. As always, you should follow shop standards.

The GO TO DEPENDING ON statement has the general form:

```
GO TO par-1, par-2, par-3 DEPENDING ON data-name.
```

For example:

```
GO TO A, B, C, D, E DEPENDING ON TYPE-TRANSACTION.
GO TO STRAIGHT-LINE, SUM-OF-YEARS-DIGIT, DECLINING-BALANCE
    DEPENDING ON TYPE-OF-DEPRECIATION.
```

The computer will number the paragraph-name listed as number 1, number 2, number 3, etc., and then look at the value of the data-name. When data-name has the value 1, then control will be transferred to the first paragraph-name listed; when the data-name has the value 2, then control will be transferred to the second (number 2) paragraph-name listed. If the value of data-name is less than 1 or greater than the number of paragraph-names listed, the statement will be ignored and control will pass to the next statement in your program. Figure 7-12 contains a section of the PROCEDURE DIVISION for a magazine subscriptions program. In it there is a GO TO DEPENDING ON statement in the paragraph SUNDAY-SCHEDULE.

In the paragraph SUNDAY-SCHEDULE the GO TO DEPENDING ON statement will transfer control to either RATE-1, RATE-2, RATE-3, RATE-4, RATE-5, or RATE-6 or it will fall to the next command DEPENDING ON the value of TERM which is part of the record SUBSCRIPTIONS. Figure 7-13 contains segments of the DATA DIVISION for this program. The record contains information about the person who has the subscription, including the TERM of the subscription. It is the value of TERM which controls the transfer in the GO TO DEPENDING ON statement.

Figure 7-12

Program segment illustrating GO TO DEPENDING ON.

```
221-SUNDAY-SCHEDULE.
    GO TO 2210-RATE-1
          2211-RATE-2
               2212-RATE-3
                    2213-RATE-4
                         2214-RATE-5
                              2215-RATE-6
    DEPENDING ON TERM.
    MULTIPLY TERM BY 1.33 GIVING CHARGE.
2210-RATE-1.
    MOVE 1.50 TO CHARGE.
2211-RATE-2.
    MOVE 2.95 TO CHARGE.
2212-RATE-3.
    MOVE 4.25 TO CHARGE.
2213-RATE-4.
    MOVE 5.80 TO CHARGE.
2214-RATE-5.
    MOVE 6.75 TO CHARGE.
2215-RATE-6.
    MOVE 8.00 TO CHARGE.
```

Figure 7–13
Subscription program
(segment).

```
IDENTIFICATION DIVISION.
PROGRAM-ID. ROGUES-GALLERY.
AUTHOR. CHERYL J. SIDNEY.
REMARKS.
        THE WORLD EMPIRE PUBLISHING COMPANY PUBLISHES TWO MAGAZINES
        TODAY'S LIFE AND SPORTSMAN'S JOURNAL AND A DAILY
        NEWSPAPER THE EVENING PLANET. SUBSCRIPTION RATES VARY BY
        PUBLICATION AND THE TERM OF THE SUBSCRIPTION.
ENVIRONMENT DIVISION.
CONFIGURATION SECTION.
SOURCE-COMPUTER.   IBM-3033.
OBJECT-COMPUTER.   IBM-3033.
INPUT-OUTPUT SECTION.
FILE-CONTROL.
        SELECT INPUT-FILE ASSIGN TO INFILE.
        SELECT OUTPUT-FILE ASSIGN TO PRINTER.
DATA DIVISION.
FILE SECTION.
FD  INPUT-FILE
        LABEL RECORDS ARE OMITTED.
01  KEY-TO-PUBLICATION.
        02 PUBLICATION     PICTURE X.
        02 MONTH           PICTURE X(9).
        02 DAYS            PICTURE 99.
        02 YEAR            PICTURE 99.
        02 FILLER          PICTURE X(66).
01  SUBSCRIPTIONS.
        02 NAME-SUB        PICTURE X(15).
        02 ADDRESS-SUB     PICTURE X(15).
        02 CITY-SUB        PICTURE X(20).
        02 TERM            PICTURE 99.
        02 DAYS-PER-WEEK   PICTURE 9.
        02 FILLER          PICTURE X(27).
```

SECTION 8
The CALL Statement

Interprogram communication is accomplished through the use of the CALL statement. In order to use this COBOL feature, there is some terminology with which you should be familiar:

- Driver program: this term usually refers to the program that includes the CALL statement.
- Subprogram: this is the program that is CALLed. It may be incorporated in the driver program or may be a separate program. The subprogram may, in turn, CALL other subprograms.

Consider the following partial program segments:

```
IDENTIFICATION DIVISION.
PROGRAM-ID.
        DRIVER-PROG.
            o
            o
            o
            o
            o
            o
        STOP RUN.
```

```
IDENTIFICATION DIVISION.
PROGRAM-ID.
    PROG1.
          o
          o
          o
    CALL "PROG2"
          o
          o
          o
    EXIT PROGRAM.
IDENTIFICATION DIVISION.
PROGRAM-ID.
    PROG2.
          o
          o
          o
    EXIT PROGRAM.
```

There are number of points to be noted here:

1. DRIVER-PROG CALLs the subprogram PROG1, which is a *separately compiled* program. The term "separately compiled" means that it is not a part of any other program. In the preceding illustration DRIVER-PROG is compiled and a machine executable (object) program results. Similarly, the compilation of PROG1 results in a separate object program as is the case with the compilation of PROG2. The CALL of PROG1 which occurs within DRIVER-PROG is quite different than a PERFORM in that it accesses external object code.
2. DRIVER-PROG contains a STOP RUN, PROG1 and PROG2 do not.
3. PROG1 and PROG2 use a EXIT PROGRAM statement as the last executable statements in each of the programs.
4. Each of the three programs is a separately compiled program.

Some compilers also allow CALLed subprograms which are a part of the driver program. They are not separately compiled but are "nested" with the driver program.

```
IDENTIFICATION DIVISION.
PROGRAM-ID.
    DRIVER-PROG.
          o
          o
          o
    CALL "PROG1".
          o
          o
          o
    STOP RUN.
IDENTIFICATION DIVISION.
PROGRAM-ID.
    PROG1.
          o
          o
          o
```

```
        CALL "PROG2".
              o
              o
              o
        EXIT PROGRAM.
 IDENTIFICATION DIVISION.
 PROGRAM-ID.
        PROG2.
              o
              o
              o
        EXIT PROGRAM.
        END PROGRAM PROG2.
        END PROGRAM PROG1.
        END PROGRAM DRIVER-PROG.
```

In this example all the programs are part of a single run unit and are compiled as a unit. For this reason there must be additional statements in the program to indicate the limits of each call routine. The END PROGRAM statements do this. Note that there is an END PROGRAM statement for each of PROG1, PROG2, and DRIVER-PROG.

There must also be a statement that causes each of the CALLed modules to cease and to return control to the driver module. The EXIT PROGRAM statement does these things.

In the preceding examples, the driver program we named "DRIVER-PROG" called the subprogram we named "PROG1," which was executed until the EXIT PROGRAM statement is encountered, at which time control returns to DRIVER-PROG. Control returns to the statement immediately following the CALL in the driver program or module.

There is another form of the CALL in which a subprogram may have access to the DATA DIVISION of the driver program. Specification of the amount of DATA DIVISION accessible to the CALLed program and provision for access is accomplished through:

- the USING phrase
- the LINKAGE section of the DATA DIVISION of the CALLed program.

The USING *Option of the* CALL *Statement*

The USING option allows data to be passed to the CALLed program. Consider the following program segments:

```
 IDENTIFICATION DIVISION.
 PROGRAM-ID.
        CALLER.
              o
              o
              o
        DATA DIVISION.
 FILE SECTION.
              o
              o
              o
 01  RECORD1     PIC X(80).
              o
              o
              o
```

```
WORKING-STORAGE SECTION.
01  RECORD2     PIC X(80).
            o
            o
            o
PROCEDURE DIVISION.
000-MAIN.
            o
            o
            o
CALL "CALLED" USING RECORD1
                    RECORD2.
STOP RUN.
IDENTIFICATION DIVISION.
PROGRAM-ID.
    CALLED.
            o
            o
            o
DATA DIVISION.
FILE SECTION.
            o
            o
            o
LINKAGE SECTION.
01  TOM-BAT    PIC X(80).
01  WOM-BAT    PIC X(80).
PROCEDURE DIVISION USING TOM-BAT
                        WOM-BAT.
000-MAIN.
            o
            o
            o
    EXIT PROGRAM.
```

In the preceding example, the CALLed program can access the data contained in RECORD1 and RECORD2 of the CALLing program. The CALLed program refers to these two records as TOM-BAT and WOM-BAT. The actual internal storage space is the same for RECORD1 as for TOM-BAT. Similarly, reference to RECORD2 or to WOM-BAT points to the same 80 characters internally. The two programs share this space.

Different COBOL compilers provide additional CALL features which may be available to you.

SECTION 9
The COPY Feature

The COPY command is probably one of the most useful statements insofar as the programmer is concerned, because of the amount of work that it may eliminate. However, the COPY statement cannot be used unless someone else has previously done a considerable amount of work prior to the use of the COPY statement. The COPY statement searches the COBOL library for the file named in the COPY statement and makes a copy of what is there and returns it to your program as if you had included it in the program yourself. Before COPY can be used you must create the information and store it in the library. The process of creating the COBOL library varies from computer to computer and from manufacturer to manufacturer. For this book we will assume that the computer center personnel or your instructor will give you the statements necessary to create the COBOL library.

Let's assume that to put entries in the library all you have to do is:

```
ASSEMBLE IN LIBRARY UNDER NAME1.
    .  01   RECORD-1.
            05   NAME         PIC X(20).
            05   ADDRESS      PIC X(30).
            05   PHONE        PIC 9(10).
            05   EXTRA        PIC X(20).
END ASSEMBLE
```

Depending on the system you are using, the process of creating a COBOL library may be almost this simple. Now you would have in the library a series of entries under the title NAME1.

Then in your COBOL program you could have the following entry:

```
FD   CUSTOMER-INFORMATION
     LABEL RECORDS ARE STANDARD.
01   CUSTOMER-RECORD COPY NAME1.
```

The compiler would go to the library and bring back the library entries under NAME1 and insert them into your program just as if you had coded them yourself. The result would be to make the following an integral part of your program:

```
FD   CUSTOMER-INFORMATION
     LABEL RECORDS ARE STANDARD.
01   CUSTOMER-RECORD.
     05   NAME         PIC X(20).
     05   ADDRESS      PIC X(30).
     05   PHONE        PIC 9(10).
     05   EXTRA        PIC X(20).
```

In large data processing installations or in those dealing with complex processing activities there may be data files or data bases accessed by multiple programs. In these conditions there may be many programmers coding new programs or maintaining old programs that access these files, and standardization of data definition may be desirable. In addition to the control and efficiency factors, which make any type of standardization desirable, there is also an elimination of duplication of effort—only one programmer need define the file, the others will COPY the definition.

If there is an entry (data-name) in the library that does not precisely fit your program you can change it as it comes to your program (while not affecting what is in the library). This is done with the COPY command and the REPLACING option.

Assume that in the above example that the PHONE number is not sufficiently descriptive—the field is actually the customer's home phone number. You could change this entry by using:

```
01 CUSTOMER-RECORD COPY NAME1 REPLACING PHONE BY
HOME-PHONE.
```

The result would be:

```
FD   CUSTOMER-INFORMATION
     LABEL RECORDS ARE STANDARD.
01   CUSTOMER-RECORD.
     05   NAME       PIC X(20).
     05   ADDRESS    PIC X(30).
     05   HOME-PHONE PIC 9(10).
     05   EXTRA      PIC X(20).
```

SECTION 10
Using Variable-Length Records

Although variable-length records do not seem to be widely used in business data processing applications, their utility would seem to be unquestionable. For some reason, business programmers seem to utilize fixed-length records in many instances where variable-length records would seem to be a better "fit." The use of this option can speed the processing of records and reduce storage space requirements.

The employee records master file program discussed in Chapter 6 will be used to illustrate variable-length records. The file definition of one of the files used in that chapter was:

```
DATA DIVISION.
FILE SECTION.
FD   ATTRIBUTES-FILE
         LABEL RECORDS ARE STANDARD
         RECORD CONTAINS 26 TO 418 CHARACTERS.
```

Note that the RECORD CONTAINS clause is quite different than for a fixed-length record. As you will see, the variation in length is attributable to one or more fields in the record that may appear more than one time. The rest of the FD entry for ATTRIBUTES-FILE is:

```
01   EMPLOYEE-RECORD.
     05   ATTRIBUTE             PIC X(20).
     05   AT-INDEX              PIC 9(02).
     02   ATTRIBUTE-POINTERS
          OCCURS 1 TO 99 TIMES DEPENDING ON AT-INDEX.
               10 EMPLOYEE-POINTER    PIC 9(04).
```

Any given record may include up to 99 pointers for employees with a particular attribute. If only one employee with such an attribute is recorded, the record length will be 26 characters (attribute plus index plus one pointer or 20 + 2 + 4 = 26). If a record pointed to 40 different employee skills, then the record length would be of 182 characters length—attribute and index (22 characters) plus 40 pointers (40 x 4 characters).

In the example the value of the variable AT-INDEX will always indicate the number of variable elements included in the record. When you get ready to use the data in the variable-length record, you may "point" to any of the variable elements—taking care not to exceed the number of elements in the variable portion of the record. For example, in the employee master file program the portions dealing with the variable-length records were:

```
        READ ATTRIBUTES-FILE
            INVALID KEY .............
                o
                o
                o
210-PROCESS-EMPLOYEE.
    IF AT-INDEX =1
        AND EMPLOYEE-POINTER (1) = ZEROS
        GO TO 210-EXIT.
    PERFORM 220-DISPLAY-DATA THRU 220-EXIT
        VARYING I FROM 1 BY 1
        UNTIL I > AT-INDEX.
210-EXIT.  EXIT.
220-DISPLAY-DATA.
    MOVE EMPLOYEE-POINTER (I) TO WS-EMPLOYEE-NUMBER.
                o
                o
                o
    DISPLAY DISPLAY-LINE.
220-EXIT.  EXIT.
```

Notice that the "pointer" I is moved from one variable element to another. If you are maintaining the records and add another employee skill to the file you would increment AT-INDEX by 1, MOVE the new value to EMPLOYEE-POINTER (AT-INDEX) and WRITE (or REWRITE) the new record.

SECTION 11
The SET, SEARCH and SEARCH ALL Statements

The SET, SEARCH, and SEARCH ALL statements are used to retrieve data from tables.

The SEARCH statement is used to search a table sequentially. The SET statement is used to establish the initial value of a search index in conjunction with a SEARCH.

The following partial program will be used to illustrate the sequential search of a table. The illustration utilizes a "hard-coded" table in which the values are established with VALUE clauses, but the procedure is the same for a table of variable values.

```
IDENTIFICATION DIVISION.
PROGRAM-ID. SEQSRCH.
                o
                o
                o
```

```
          WORKING-STORAGE SECTION.
          01  WS-TABLE.
              05 FILLER PIC X(16)   VALUE "CACURRENT ASSETS".
              05 FILLER PIC X(16)   VALUE "ININVESTMENTS    ".
              05 FILLER PIC X(16)   VALUE "ITINTANGIBLES    ".
              05 FILLER PIC X(16)   VALUE "LILIABILITIES    ".
              05 FILLER PIC X(16)   VALUE "NWNET WORTH      ".
          01  BALANCE-SHEET-TABLE REDEFINES WS-TABLE.
              05 TABLE-ENTRIES OCCURS 5 TIMES INDEXED BY INDEX-1
                    ASCENDING KEY IS BS-ABBREVIATION.
                 10 BS-ABBREVIATION  PIC XX.
                 10 BS-TITLE         PIC X(14).
          01  INDEX-1                    PIC 99   VALUE ZERO.
                  o
                  o
                  o
          PROCEDURE DIVISION.
          000-MAIN.
                  o
                  o
                  o
              PERFORM 600-SEARCH-BS-TABLE.
                  o
                  o
                  o
          600-SEARCH-BS-TABLE.
              SET INDEX-1 TO 1.
              SEARCH TABLE-ENTRIES
                  AT END
                      PERFORM 670-ERROR-ROUTINE
                  WHEN RECORD-ABBREVIATION =
                      BS-ABBREVIATION (INDEX-1)
                      MOVE BS-TITLE (INDEX-1) TO DL-DESCRIPTION.
                  o
                  o
                  o
```

In this partial program we are taking a coded item from an input record (RECORD-ABBREVIATION) and looking for the description for this item in BALANCE-SHEET-TABLE.

Notice that we have not defined INDEX-1 in the WORKING-STORAGE SECTION. Definition is accomplished automatically when you use the INDEXED BY clause in the table description entries. The sequential search function is accomplished in the paragraph named 600-SEARCH-BS-TABLE. The first statement in this paragraph is:

```
SET INDEX-1 TO 1.
```

This statement initializes the index at 1 in this case. The SET command may be used to initialize the index to any value which is within the range of the table.

The next statement is the sequential table search. Notice that the SEARCH statement references the level of data description which contains the OCCURS clause (table entries) rather than the elementary data-items (BS-ABBREVIATION, for example). The AT END statement is processed if the table search does not result in a match with the input item. In the example, 670-ERROR-ROUTINE is performed if no match is found.

The WHEN clause sets up the search conditions to be performed—in this case, when the abbreviation code in the input record record is equal to the abbreviation code in the table. When there is a "match" the description of the item is moved to a print field.

The SEARCH ALL statement invokes a binary table search. Consider the following example, again in partial form, in which a search is made of a table which is "loaded" from an input file.

```
IDENTIFICATION DIVISION.
PROGRAM-ID.
     BINSRCH.
ENVIRONMENT DIVISION.
CONFIGURATION SECTION.
          o
          o
          o
INPUT-OUTPUT SECTION.
FILE-CONTROL.
     SELECT TABLE-FILE ASSIGN TO "TABFIL".
          o
          o
          o
DATA DIVISION.
FILE SECTION.
FD   TABLE-FILE
     LABEL RECORDS ARE STANDARD.
01   TABLE-RECORD.
     05 TABLE ABBREVIATION  PIC XX.
     05 TABLE DESCRIPTION   PIC X(14).
WORKING-STORAGE SECTION.
          o
          o
          o
01   BALANCE-SHEET-TABLE.
     05 TABLE-ENTRIES OCCURS 50 TIMES
          INDEXED BY INDEX-1.
     10 BS-ABBREVIATION    PIC XX.
     10 BS-DESCRIPTION     PIC X(14).
          o
          o
          o
PROCEDURE DIVISION.
000-MAIN.
     PERFORM 111-INITIALIZE.
          o
          o
          o
     PERFORM 611-SEARCH-TABLE.
111-INITIALIZE.
*   In this paragraph you would insert the code to "load"
*   the table from input records.
611-TABLE-SEARCH.
     SEARCH ALL TABLE-ENTRIES
          AT END
               PERFORM 670-ERROR-ROUTINE
          WHEN
               RECORD ABBREVIATION =
                   BS-ABBREVIATION (INDEX-1)
               MOVE BS-DESCRIPTION (INDEX-1) TO DL-TITLE.
```

This program performs essentially the same functions as the program in the previous example. There are, however, a few differences. Notice that the table in the above example is relatively large, which makes it a likely candidate for the use of the more efficient binary search. Also, although it is not apparent from the logic provided, the items loaded into the table must be in sequence on the search argument BS-ABBREVIATION. Another difference is that the SET command is used only with the SEARCH and not with SEARCH ALL.

Except for the few differences discussed in the last paragraph, SEARCH and SEARCH ALL are very similar in the way they are coded in a program. However, they are very different in the way they work. SEARCH is a sequential procedure and SEARCH ALL is a binary procedure.

The general form for SEARCH is:

$$
\begin{aligned}
&\text{SEARCH identifier-1}\ \left[\text{VARYING}\ \left\{\begin{array}{l}\text{identifier-2}\\ \text{index-name-1}\end{array}\right\}\right]\\
&\qquad\text{[AT END imperative-statement-1]}\\
&\qquad\text{WHEN condition-1}\left\{\begin{array}{l}\text{imperative-statement-2}\\ \text{NEXT\ \ SENTENCE}\end{array}\right\}\\
&\qquad\left[\text{WHEN condition-2}\left\{\begin{array}{l}\text{imperative-statement-3}\\ \text{NEXT\ \ SENTENCE}\end{array}\right\}\right]
\end{aligned}
$$

The general form for SEARCH ALL is:

$$
\begin{aligned}
&\text{SEARCH\ \ ALL identifier-1}\\
&\qquad\text{[AT END imperative-statement-1]}\\
&\qquad\text{WHEN}\ \left\{\begin{array}{l}\text{data-name-1}\ \{=\}\\ \text{condition-1}\end{array}\right\}\left\{\begin{array}{l}\text{identifier-3}\\ \text{literal-1}\\ \text{arithmetic-expression-1}\end{array}\right\}\\
&\qquad\left[\text{AND}\ \left\{\begin{array}{l}\text{data-name-2}\ \{=\}\\ \text{condition-2}\end{array}\right\}\left\{\begin{array}{l}\text{identifier-4}\\ \text{literal-2}\\ \text{arithmetic-expression-2}\end{array}\right\}\right]\ldots\\
&\qquad\left\{\begin{array}{l}\text{NEXT SENTENCE}\\ \text{imperative-statement-2}\end{array}\right\}
\end{aligned}
$$

SECTION 12
The EJECT or New Page Feature

There may be circumstances in which you will want to provide spaces in the source listing of your COBOL program. This is commonly done to make the program documentation more readable. The way to accomplish this is to put a "/" in column 7 at the point where you want the listing to skip to a new page. This EJECT instruction must be on a line by itself—don't combine it with any other statements. Consider the following partial program code:

```
IDENTIFICATION DIVISION.
PROGRAM-ID.
    EJECT.
/
ENVIRONMENT DIVISION.
```

When this program is compiled, the compiler will cause the printing of the source statements for the IDENTIFICATION DIVISION and the ENVIRONMENT DIVISION to appear on different pages.

SECTION 13
Sample Program

Figure 7-14 is a program which uses some of the features described in this chapter. Figure 7-15 presents the input data for the program and Figure 7-16 the output.

Figure 7-14

Program using some Chapter 7 features.

```
IDENTIFICATION DIVISION.
PROGRAM-ID.  CASE-STRUCTURE.
AUTHOR.  SUSAN KEYES.
REMARKS.
     THE WORLD EMPIRE PUBLISHING COMPANY PUBLISHES TWO MAGAZINES
     TODAY'S LIFE AND SPORTSMAN'S JOURNAL AND A DAILY
     NEWSPAPER THE EVENING PLANET. SUBSCRIPTION RATES VARY BY
     PUBLICATION AND THE TERM OF THE SUBSCRIPTION.
ENVIRONMENT DIVISION.
CONFIGURATION SECTION.
SOURCE-COMPUTER.   IBM-3033.
OBJECT-COMPUTER.   IBM-3033.
INPUT-OUTPUT SECTION.
FILE-CONTROL.
     SELECT INPUT-FILE ASSIGN TO INFILE.
     SELECT OUTPUT-FILE ASSIGN TO PRINTER.
DATA DIVISION.
FILE SECTION.
FD   INPUT-FILE
     LABEL RECORDS ARE OMITTED.
01   KEY-TO-PUBLICATION.
     02 PUBLICATION      PICTURE X.
     02 MONTH            PICTURE X(9).
     02 DAYS             PICTURE 99.
     02 YEAR             PICTURE 99.
     02 FILLER           PICTURE X(66).
01   SUBSCRIPTIONS.
     02 NAME-SUB         PICTURE X(15).
     02 ADDRESS-SUB      PICTURE X(15).
     02 CITY-SUB         PICTURE X(20).
     02 TERM-SUB         PICTURE 99.
     02 DAYS-PER-WEEK    PICTURE 9.
     02 FILLER           PICTURE X(27).
FD   OUTPUT-FILE
     LABEL RECORDS ARE OMITTED.
01   LISTING             PICTURE X(133).
WORKING-STORAGE SECTION.
01   LAST-PUBLICATION    PICTURE X             VALUE SPACE.
01   VALUEX              PICTURE S999          VALUE -1.
01   EOF-INFILE          PICTURE X             VALUE 'N'.
01   HEADING-1.
     02 FILLER           PICTURE X(36)         VALUE SPACES.
     02 PERIODICAL       PICTURE X(24)         VALUE SPACES.
     02 FILLER           PICTURE X(20)         VALUE SPACES.
     02 MONTH-OUT        PICTURE X(9)          VALUE SPACES.
     02 FILLER           PICTURE X             VALUE SPACES.
     02 DAYS-OUT         PICTURE Z9            VALUE ZEROES.
     02 FILLER           PICTURE X(4)          VALUE ', 19'.
     02 YEAR-OUT         PICTURE 99            VALUE ZEROES.
     02 FILLER           PICTURE X(35)         VALUE SPACES.
01   DETAIL-LIST.
     02 FILLER           PICTURE X(17)         VALUE SPACES.
     02 NAME-OUT         PICTURE X(15)         VALUE SPACES.
     02 FILLER           PICTURE X(10)         VALUE SPACES.
     02 ADDRESS-OUT      PICTURE X(15)         VALUE SPACES.
     02 FILLER           PICTURE X(10)         VALUE SPACES.
     02 CITY-OUT         PICTURE X(25)         VALUE SPACES.
     02 FILLER           PICTURE X(10)         VALUE SPACES.
     02 TERM-OUT         PICTURE 99            VALUE ZEROES.
     02 FILLER           PICTURE X             VALUE SPACE.
     02 DAYS-MONTHS      PICTURE X(6)          VALUE SPACE.
     02 CHARGE           PICTURE $ZZ.99.
     02 FILLER           PICTURE X(16)         VALUE SPACE.
```

Figure 7–14 (continued)

```
PROCEDURE DIVISION.
000-MAIN-PROCESS.
    OPEN INPUT INPUT-FILE OUTPUT OUTPUT-FILE.
    PERFORM 100-READ-SUBSCRIPTION.
    PERFORM 400-CONTROL-BREAKS.
    PERFORM 200-SELECT-PUBLICATION UNTIL EOF-INFILE = 'Y'.
    CLOSE INPUT-FILE OUTPUT-FILE.
    STOP RUN.
100-READ-SUBSCRIPTION.
    READ INPUT-FILE, AT END MOVE 'Y' TO EOF-INFILE.
200-SELECT-PUBLICATION.
    IF PUBLICATION IS NUMERIC PERFORM 400-CONTROL-BREAKS.
    PERFORM 410-MOVE-NAMES.
    IF LAST-PUBLICATION IS EQUAL TO '1'
        PERFORM 210-TODAYS-LIFE-SUBSCRIPTIONS,
            ELSE
    IF LAST-PUBLICATION IS EQUAL TO '2'
        PERFORM 220-PLANET-SUBSCRIPTIONS,
            ELSE
    IF LAST-PUBLICATION IS EQUAL TO '3'
        PERFORM 230-SPORTSMAN-SUBSCRIPTIONS,
            ELSE
            PERFORM 900-ERROR-ROUTINE.
    PERFORM 100-READ-SUBSCRIPTION.
400-CONTROL-BREAKS.
    IF PUBLICATION IS EQUAL TO '1'
        MOVE 'TODAYS LIFE        ' TO PERIODICAL
        MOVE 'MONTHS' TO DAYS-MONTHS
        PERFORM 300-WRITE-HEADINGS,
            ELSE
    IF PUBLICATION IS EQUAL TO '2'
        MOVE 'THE EVENING PLANET    ' TO PERIODICAL
        MOVE 'MONTHS' TO DAYS-MONTHS
        PERFORM 300-WRITE-HEADINGS,
            ELSE
    IF PUBLICATION IS EQUAL TO '3'
        MOVE 'SPORTSMANS JOURNAL     ' TO PERIODICAL
        MOVE 'WEEKS' TO DAYS-MONTHS
        PERFORM 300-WRITE-HEADINGS,
            ELSE
            PERFORM 900-ERROR-ROUTINE.
    MOVE PUBLICATION TO LAST-PUBLICATION.
    PERFORM 100-READ-SUBSCRIPTION.
410-MOVE-NAMES.
    MOVE NAME-SUB TO NAME-OUT.
    MOVE ADDRESS-SUB TO ADDRESS-OUT.
    MOVE CITY-SUB TO CITY-OUT.
    MOVE TERM-SUB TO TERM-OUT.
210-TODAYS-LIFE-SUBSCRIPTIONS.
    IF TERM-SUB = 12 MOVE 8.00 TO CHARGE,
        ELSE
    IF TERM-SUB = 24 MOVE 15.00 TO CHARGE,
        ELSE
    IF TERM-SUB = 36 MOVE 24.00 TO CHARGE,
    ELSE DISPLAY 'ERROR IN TERM'.
    PERFORM 400-WRITE-DETAIL.
220-PLANET-SUBSCRIPTIONS.
    IF DAYS-PER-WEEK = 1 PERFORM 221-SUNDAY-SCHEDULE
        THROUGH 2299-SUNDAY-EXIT.
    IF DAYS-PER-WEEK = 6 PERFORM 222-DAILY-SCHEDULE.
    MULTIPLY TERM-SUB BY 6.00 GIVING CHARGE.
    PERFORM 400-WRITE-DETAIL.
221-SUNDAY-SCHEDULE.
    EXAMINE TERM-SUB REPLACING ALL '0' BY '7'.
    EXAMINE TERM-SUB REPLACING ALL '8' BY '7'.
    EXAMINE TERM-SUB REPLACING ALL '9' BY '7'.
    GO TO 2210-RATE-1
            2211-RATE-2
                2212-RATE-3
                    2213-RATE-4
                        2214-RATE-5
                            2215-RATE-6
                                2216-ERROR
        DEPENDING ON TERM-SUB.
    MULTIPLY TERM-SUB BY 1.33 GIVING CHARGE.
```

Figure 7-14 (continued)

```
2210-RATE-1.
     MOVE 1.50 TO CHARGE.
2211-RATE-2.
     MOVE 2.95 TO CHARGE.
2212-RATE-3.
     MOVE 4.25 TO CHARGE.
2213-RATE-4.
     MOVE 5.80 TO CHARGE.
2214-RATE-5.
     MOVE 6.75 TO CHARGE.
2215-RATE-6.
     MOVE 8.00 TO CHARGE.
2216-ERROR.
     DISPLAY 'ERROR IN TERM OF SUBSCRIPTION ', TERM-SUB,
        'NOT ALLOWED - MUST BE NUMERIC 1 THROUGH 6'.
2299-SUNDAY-EXIT.
222-DAILY-SCHEDULE.
     IF TERM-SUB IS LESS THAN 6
        MULTIPLY TERM-SUB BY 4.50 GIVING CHARGE
               OTHERWISE
        MULTIPLY TERM-SUB BY 4.00 GIVING CHARGE.
230-SPORTSMAN-SUBSCRIPTIONS.
     IF TERM-SUB = 15 MOVE 8.00 TO CHARGE,
        ELSE
     IF TERM-SUB = 26 MOVE 13.50 TO CHARGE,
        ELSE
     IF TERM-SUB = 52 MOVE 24.00 TO CHARGE,
        ELSE
     DISPLAY 'ERROR IN TERM'.
     PERFORM 400-WRITE-DETAIL.
300-WRITE-HEADINGS.
     MOVE MONTH TO MONTH-OUT.
     MOVE DAYS TO DAYS-OUT.
     MOVE YEAR TO YEAR-OUT.
     WRITE LISTING FROM HEADING-1 AFTER ADVANCING 1.
     MOVE SPACES TO LISTING.
     WRITE LISTING AFTER ADVANCING 1 LINES.
400-WRITE-DETAIL.
     WRITE LISTING FROM DETAIL-LIST AFTER ADVANCING 1 LINES.
900-ERROR-ROUTINE.
     MOVE NAME-SUB TO NAME-OUT.
     MOVE ADDRESS-SUB TO ADDRESS-OUT.
     MOVE CITY-SUB TO CITY-OUT.
     MOVE TERM-SUB TO TERM-OUT.
     PERFORM 400-WRITE-DETAIL.
     CLOSE INPUT-FILE, OUTPUT-FILE.
     STOP RUN.
```

Figure 7-15
Input to the sample program.

```
3      JULY 0387
OLIVER MCGILL    30 POSSUM TROT KNOXVILLE, TENN.        15
JOHNSON CAIN     70126 EAGLE ST PEAK, N.M.              26
AL TEUTSCHLAND   123 20TH PL    PANTHER CITY, TEX.      11
FRED WIMPLE      8215 HARMONY   IDAHO, IDA.             52
EDDIE GARCIA     1234 EASYST    HAMMONDSBURG, PA.       52
JAI SUNG         2606 AVE G     HICKORY, N.C.           26
STIMSON CAMP     HWY 10 NORTH   SCURRY, OKLA.           15
1SEPTEMBER1587
JAMES TOWNWAY    245 GARRAR ST  WACO, TEXAS             12
ALICE RORARK     2914 RUGGLES   ITHICA N.Y.            24
MARY RAGLAND     APT 2 313 MAIN OWENSBORO, KY           11
AMY CRUEZ        3114 OAKLAND   OAKFIELD, CALIF         36
2      JUNE0787
SANDY PAPER      8854 HIGHWAY 41D.C.                    011
PAUL SALEM       54 AVE D       BELLEVILLE ILL          016
ALEX MARTINDALE399 OEACE ST    WATERLOO IOWA           018
SUSAN CROW       108 CROW       SAGINAW MICHIGAN        012
GARY FRENCH      252 DORAN      DULUTH MINNESOTA        087
2      MAY2487
BEN  BEENE       3414 RIDGE RD  HATTIESBURG, MS         101
JANE DURST       4105 NORTHBR   MEMPHIS, TN             206
TOM SLOVACEK     28 APPLE ST    SILVER CITY, NM         156
BOB WOOD         289 HANCOCK    CINCINNATI, OHIO        521
1SEPTEMBER2988
SILVIA GEORGE    2704 D MAIN    DALLAS, TX              12
PETER GROVES     89115 AVE A    SAN DIEGO, CALIF        24
```

```
           SPORTSMANS JOURNAL                              JULY   3, 1987
OLIVER MCGILL          30 POSSUM TROT      KNOXVILLE, TENN.        15 WEEKS $ 8.00
JOHNSON CAIN           70126 EAGLE ST      PEAK, N.M.             26 WEEKS $13.50
AL TEUTSCHLAND         123 20TH PL         PANTHER CITY, TEX.     11 WEEKS $13.50
FRED WIMPLE            8215 HARMONY        IDAHO, IDA.            52 WEEKS $24.00
EDDIE GARCIA           1234 EASYST         HAMMONDSBURG, PA.      52 WEEKS $24.00
JAI SUNG               2606 AVE G          HICKORY, N.C.          26 WEEKS $13.50
STIMSON CAMP           HWY 10 NORTH        SCURRY, OKLA.          15 WEEKS $ 8.00
           TODAYS LIFE                                  SEPTEMBER 15, 1987
JAMES TOWNWAY          245 GARRAR ST       WACO, TEXAS            12 MONTHS$ 8.00
ALICE RORARK           2914 RUGGLES        ITHICA N.Y.            24 MONTHS$15.00
MARY RAGLAND           APT 2 313 MAIN      OWENSBORO, KY          11 MONTHS$15.00
AMY CRUEZ              3114 OAKLAND        OAKFIELD, CALIF        36 MONTHS$24.00
           THE EVENING PLANET                            JUNE   7, 1987
SANDY PAPER            8854 HIGHWAY 41     D.C.                   01 MONTHS$26.00
PAUL SALEM             54 AVE D            BELLEVILLE ILL         01 MONTHS$ 6.00
ALEX MARTINDALE        399 OEACE ST        WATERLOO IOWA          01 MONTHS$ 6.00
SUSAN CROW             108 CROW            SAGINAW MICHIGAN       01 MONTHS$ 6.00
GARY FRENCH            252 DORAN           DULUTH MINNESOTA       08 MONTHS$48.00
           THE EVENING PLANET                            MAY 24, 1987
BEN  BEENE             3414 RIDGE RD       HATTIESBURG, MS        10 MONTHS$ 2.00
JANE DURST             4105 NORTHBR        MEMPHIS, TN            20 MONTHS$20.00
TOM SLOVACEK           28 APPLE ST         SILVER CITY, NM        15 MONTHS$90.00
BOB WOOD               289 HANCOCK         CINCINNATI, OHIO       52 MONTHS$12.00
           TODAYS LIFE                                  SEPTEMBER 29, 1988
SILVIA GEORGE          2704 D MAIN         DALLAS, TX             12 MONTHS$ 8.00
PETER GROVES           89115 AVE A         SAN DIEGO, CALIF       24 MONTHS$15.00
```

Figure 7–16
Output for the sample program.

SECTION 14
Exercises and Problems

I. Exercises

1. Give the PROCEDURE DIVISION commands(s) necessary to change any blanks which may be READ in from the data records to zeros. The record has (FILLER should not change):

1–5	account number
6–10	blank
11–15	an amount
16–20	blank
21–25	credit limit

2. Give the PROCEDURE DIVISION command(s) to tally the number of A's stored in the following data-item.

    ```
    05 RESPONSE-SEQUENCE    PIC X(30),
    ```

3. Give the command to tally the leading blanks in the following entry:

    ```
    05 NAME PIC    X(25),
    ```

4. Give the command to tally all of the 1's, replacing them with zeros in the entry:

    ```
    05 RANDOM-NUMBER      PIC 9(7)V99,
    ```

5. By use of the INSPECT statement, replace any *'s with a blank in:

    ```
    05 CUSTOMER-RECORD  PIC X(30),
    ```

6. Give the command which will go to either FIFO, LIFO, or NIFO, dependent upon the value of INVENTORY-CODE.
7. Give the FD and 01 entry for a file (UPDATE-CUSTOMER) which will use an existing file (CUSTOMER-INFO) from the COBOL library.
8. What is the purpose(s) of the ACCEPT statement?
9. What is the purpose(s) of the DISPLAY statement?
10. What is the purpose of the UNSTRING statement?
11. What is the purpose of the DELIMITER phrase in an UNSTRING command?
12. What is the purpose of the POINTER phrase in an UNSTRING command?
13. What is the purpose of the TALLYING phrase in an UNSTRING command?
14. What is the purpose of the STRING command?
15. What does the DELIMITED BY phrase accomplish in a STRING statement?
16. What command in COBOL allows the user to partially implement the CASE construct?
17. What is the purpose of a CALL statement?
18. What are the basic advantages for the use of the COPY statement?
19. What are the advantages of using variable-length records?
20. What is the basic difference between a SEARCH and SEARCH ALL command?

II. Program Exercises

1. You have a field in an inventory file named product name. The data-items in this field are reversed as follows:

   ```
   MARKER, FELT TIP
   ```

   Provide the entries necessary to reverse these items in an output report field to read:

   ```
   FELT TIP MARKER
   ```

2. Write a COBOL program to ACCEPT a user's name from a terminal and then DISPLAY back to the terminal operator the following message:

   ```
   WELCOME TO THIS COMPUTER SYSTEM, [user's name]
   ```

3. Write a COBOL program that uses the input file from Exercise II-3 from Chapter 3. Count the number of A's, B's, and C's that appear in the customer name field. Your output report should be a four-field report as follows:

Customer Name	No. A's	No. B's	No. C's
CHARLES B JOHNSON	1	1	1
JOSEPH J JIMPSON	0	0	0
BILLY B BACCON	1	3	2

4. Refer to Exercise 3 preceding. Change all A's to I's, all B's to T's, and C's to U's. The output report should appear as follows:

Customer Name In	Customer Name Out
CHARLES B JOHNSON	UHIRLES T JOHNSON
JOSEPH J JIMPSON	JOSEPH J JIMPSON
BILLY B BACCON	TILLY T TIUUON

5. Refer to Exercise II-3 from Chapter 3. Remove the `FD`, record, and field description entries. Put these items in a file named `CUSTFD`. Insert the `COPY` statement in your program at the point where the `FD`, etc., were removed and recompile your program.

6. Refer to Exercise II-4 in Chapter 6. Instead of including the invoices in a separate invoice master file, change the customer master file to include variable-length records. Provide for a maximum of 10 invoice records per customer. Write a COBOL program that uses the invoice master file as an input file together with the customer master file and create a variable-length customer master file.

7. Provide the COBOL logic necessary to sequentially search the following table based on state abbreviation.

Field Name	Location
state abbreviation	1–2
state name	3–30
population	35–42

8. Provide the COBOL logic necessary to binarily search the table in 7, preceding.

9. Reviewers III, Inc. maintains records for movies that they have reviewed for clients since beginning in business in 1923. The format for these records is:

pos 1–34	name of the movie (A)
pos 35–37	studio code (A)
pos 38–39	year of production (N)
pos 40	critical rating for direction (N)
pos 41	critical rating for production (N)
pos 42	critical rating for actor 1 (N)
pos 43	critical rating for actor 2 (N)
pos 44	critical rating for actor 3 (N)
pos 45–54	actor 1—last name (A)
pos 44–53	actor 2—last name (A)
pos 54–63	actor 3—last name (A)

The codes for critical ratings are provided by reviewers employed by the company and each is a numeric code (0-9) where, in effect—and in the reviewers opinion, a "9" indicates an award-winning performance and a "0" indicates (charitably) an extremely poor performance. The company plans to change the rating system to allow for an increased number of ratings. They plan to utilize an alphabetic rating scale, rather than the old numeric one, and must convert the existing records to the new format. The new equivalences for the old numeric codes are:

Old	New	
0	S	(presumably for "stinko")
1	P	
2	B	
3	L	
4	C	
5	N	
6	O	

7	G
8	T
9	A

a. Prepare a set of test data of 15 or more items using a representative sample of movies with which you are familar. You may use fictional studio codes and years of production. Include your own critical ratings but be sure that all possible codes (0-9) are represented in your test data.

b. Prepare a program to convert old critical ratings to new using either the EXAMINE or the INSPECT statement, whichever is available at your computer center. Your program should produce two listings: one of your test data prior to processing and one of the new version of the file incorporating the new codes.

c. Prepare a program as required in part (b) using the GO TO DEPENDING ON statement rather than EXAMINE or INSPECT.

8

The COBOL SORT Feature

The Need for Sequenced Data

In many data processing applications the order, or sequence, of the input information is important. For example, in order to make a sales report that is in part number order, it is often necessary that the input data be sequenced in part number order.

Let us assume you want a simplified report to show the part number and the total unit sales for each part. The report should appear as follows:

```
PART
NUMBER    SALES
  10       40
  11       70
  12       30
```

In order to generate such a report using sequential processing methods certain logical steps would be required. The PROCEDURE DIVISION for such a program is given in Figure 8-1.

Basically, the process in Figure 8-1 would be as follows:

- Read the first input record (to get the process started) save the part number, accumulate the unit sales, read another record, and compare the part number on this sales record with the part number for the first.

- If the part numbers match, then accumulate the sales and read another record and continue reading and accumulating until the part numbers do not match.

- If the part numbers (previous record compared to the latest record) do not match, then the part number and the total sales should be written (for the former part number), the total sales accumulator reset to the amount of the latest record read (effectively resetting to zero and then adding the current amount), and the process of saving the part number and accumulating sales (for the new part number) started over again.

- Additional records are read repeating the test for part number equality.

```
003800 PROCEDURE DIVISION.
003900 000-MAINLINE.
004000     PERFORM 100-INITIALIZE.
004100     PERFORM 200-ACCUMULATE-TOTALS.
004200     PERFORM 300-TEST-FOR-CONTROL-BREAKS UNTIL EOF-SWITCH > 1.
004300     PERFORM 320-PRINT-DETAIL.
004400     CLOSE PARTS-FILE PRINTFILE.
004500     STOP RUN.
004600 100-INITIALIZE.
004700     OPEN INPUT PARTS-FILE OUTPUT PRINTFILE.
004800     PERFORM 310-READ-PART-FILE.
004900     MOVE PART-NUMBER TO PART-NUMBER-HOLD.
005000 200-ACCUMULATE-TOTALS.
005100     ADD SALES TO TOTAL-SALES.
005200 300-TEST-FOR-CONTROL-BREAKS.
005300     PERFORM 310-READ-PART-FILE.
005400     IF PART-NUMBER IS NOT EQUAL TO PART-NUMBER-HOLD
005500         PERFORM 320-PRINT-DETAIL
005600             ELSE
005700         ADD SALES TO TOTAL-SALES.
005800 310-READ-PART-FILE.
005900     READ PARTS-FILE AT END MOVE 2 TO EOF-SWITCH.
006000 320-PRINT-DETAIL.
006100     MOVE PART-NUMBER-HOLD TO PRINT-PART.
006200     MOVE TOTAL-SALES TO EDITED-TOTAL.
006300     WRITE PRINT-RECORD AFTER ADVANCING 1 LINE.
006400     MOVE SALES TO TOTAL-SALES.
006500     MOVE PART-NUMBER TO PART-NUMBER-HOLD.
```

Figure 8–1
PROCEDURE DIVISION for
program to print SORTed data.

The input data for the program and the output when the part numbers are in order appear below:

INPUT		OUTPUT	
PART	SALES	PART	TOTAL
10	10	10	40
10	30	11	70
11	50	12	30
11	20		
12	30		

Now, try to run the same program with the data not in part number order. The input data for the program and the output might look like this:

INPUT		OUTPUT	
PART NUMBER	SALES	PART NUMBER	TOTAL
10	10	10	40
10	30	11	50
11	50	12	30
12	30	11	20
11	20		

Note that the second report lists part number 11 twice. This is caused by the data not being in numerical (part number) order. In sequential processing there is no way of knowing that record(s) at the front of the file would have matching part numbers somewhere else in the file (out of sequence). Therefore, the data must be sorted in order to process the file sequentially.

Let's look at another example. We have a data file that has the following format:

Cols. 1–5   salesperson's number
       6–24   salesperson's name
       27–28   division code
       30–35   invoice number
       36–42   amount of sale (dollars and cents)

The data for the first 24 records are given in Figure 8-2.

A program to read and accumulate totals for these salespeople with the sequence unaltered (from that given in Figure 8-2) would produce a report with somewhat meaningless results because the totals for each person would not be accumulated properly.

A partial report when the data are not sorted before the program analyzes the data would look like this:

```
ID        NAME        TOTAL
26241     JABLONSKI   $24.57
52546     DUNNIGAN     46.55
32400     RAMIREZ     167.27
42566     JOHNSON      34.50
32400     RAMIREZ      74.12
26241     JABLONSKI   186.76
42566     JOHNSON     139.70
77396     MORRIS       65.78
26421     JABLONSKI    15.13
32400     RAMIREZ      76.60
```

Since the ID numbers change randomly when dealing with unsorted data, the only way you can accumulate the sales amount by salesperson when processing a sequential file is to have, for example, all of Ramirez's records together, all of Jablonski's records together, and so on. You might also need to have each salesperson's sales grouped by division and other groupings.

Figure 8–2
Inputs to the SORT program.

```
70432WILKINSON        AB51K3900001527
32400RAMIREZ          SN51Z4130008117
77396MORRIS           AB52R5230001684
70432WILKINSON        AB52K9980017642
77396MORRIS           SN52S7270004569
77396MORRIS           AB52A6310002397
32400RAMIREZ          SN52N7790001593
70432WILKINSON        AB51G5860031985
70432WILKINSON        SN51P1930011159
70432WILKINSON        AB52H2560001969
77396MORRIS           AB51L4700002210
26421JABLONSKI        DA51R5170001513
32400RAMIREZ          SN51K5890007660
26421JABLONSKI        DA52A2600002457
52546DUNNIGAN         SN52F5360001027
52546DUNNIGAN         SN52W1090003628
32400RAMIREZ          SN52S1960016727
42566JOHNSON          AB53G0220003450
32400RAMIREZ          SN51O5610007412
26421JABLONSKI        DA51T4780018676
42566JOHNSON          AB51P6880005228
42566JOHNSON          AB52C6290006232
77396MORRIS           AB52V4200006578
32400RAMIREZ          SN51Y2100005157
```

One way of ordering the data in some desired order is to have it sorted before you use it. Depending on the storage medium it can be sorted by hand, by some mechanical device, by a specially written program or part of a program, or by the built-in SORT feature of COBOL.

To use the built-in COBOL SORT you must specify certain additional information in the ENVIRONMENT, DATA, and PROCEDURE DIVISIONs. The items that must be defined are:

1. ENVIRONMENT DIVISION: Specify a file where the sorted information can be saved.
2. DATA DIVISION: A description of the file that will be used to temporarily store the sorted records. This description is called an SD entry (SORT DESCRIPTION entry) If the file is to be permanently saved you will need another FD entry to describe the file to be used for this purpose.
3. PROCEDURE DIVISION: A command to start the sorting of a file, specification of the field or fields on which the sorting should take place, specification of the order (ascending or descending), and identification of the paragraphs in the program that should outline the sorting procedure.

SECTION 2
The SD Entry

When a file (the original file) is sorted, you will create a new file (the sorted file) but also you will save the original, unless you specify that it be destroyed. The sorted file must be described; this is done in an SD (SORT DESCRIPTION) entry. The SD is very similar to an FD entry except that the LABEL RECORDS clause is not required. The general form is:

```
SD  name-of-the-file [any of the options available
                      in an FD entry]
```

For example,

```
SD    SORT-TEMPORARY
      RECORD CONTAINS 39 CHARACTERS
```

Some compilers require the use of a DATA RECORD IS clause. We have followed this convention in the programs at the end of the chapter.

Each SD will also have an 01 entry describing the record either as a unit or by breaking it down into the various data-items. The sort keys to be used in the sort must be defined in the SD. Figure 8-3 contains the SD and 01 entry for our sort program.

Figure 8–3
SD entry.

```
DATA DIVISION.
FILE SECTION.
SD   SORT-TEMPORARY
     RECORD CONTAINS 39 CHARACTERS
     DATA RECORD IS SORT-RECORD.
01   SORT-RECORD.
     02   SALESMAN-NUMBER              PIC 9(5).
     02   SALESMAN-NAME                PIC X(19).
     02   DIVISION-CODE                PIC XX.
     02   INVOICE                      PIC X(6).
     02   SALE-AMOUNT                  PIC 9(5)V99.
```

SECTION 3
The SELECT Statement for SORT Files

Just as every FD has a corresponding entry in the ENVIRONMENT DIVISION so will SD entries be associated with ENVIRONMENT DIVISION entries. The form of the SELECT and ASSIGN statements are the same for sort files as for other disk or tape files. This entry is for the temporary sorted information file and not the original, which may be on cards, tape, disk, or other medium.

We have decided to put the temporary sorted file for our sales-processing application on disk and therefore have specified:

```
SELECT SORT-TEMPORARY ASSIGN TO SORTEMP.
```

The sorted file may be put on any medium that is supported by the processing center where you will run your program. If you use magnetic tape for a sort-work file (defined in the SD) you may actually use multiple physical tapes, typically three or more, and you will have to allow for this in the specification of any job control or run control statements. Nonetheless, the coding of the COBOL program treats the sort-work file as a single logical file, so you will have a single SD for each sort task regardless of the number of tapes employed.

In the ENVIRONMENT DIVISION you have specified the internal and external names of the files to be used. In the DATA DIVISION you have described the files and the fields which make up the records. Figure 8-4 gives the ENVIRONMENT DIVISION and the FILE SECTION for the sort program.

Figure 8–4
ENVIRONMENT DIVISION for
SORT program.

```
ENVIRONMENT DIVISION.
CONFIGURATION SECTION.
SOURCE-COMPUTER.
    IBM-370.
OBJECT-COMPUTER.
    IBM-370.
INPUT-OUTPUT SECTION.
FILE-CONTROL.
    SELECT SORT-TEMPORARY
        ASSIGN TO SORTWK1.
    SELECT OUTPUT-FILE
        ASSIGN TO PRINTER.
    SELECT SALES-FILE-INPUT
        ASSIGN TO SALES IN.
```

SECTION 4
The SORT Command

In addition to the normal statements you would have in a PROCEDURE DIVISION to generate a report, you will need some additional commands if you want the data sorted before you use it.

In order for data to be sorted you will need a SORT command. The general form of the SORT command is:

$$\underline{\text{SORT}} \text{ file-name-1 ON } \begin{Bmatrix} \underline{\text{ASCENDING}} \\ \underline{\text{DESCENDING}} \end{Bmatrix} \text{KEY data-name-1 [data-name-2]}$$

$$\begin{Bmatrix} \underline{\text{INPUT}} \text{ PROCEDURE IS section-name-1} \\ \underline{\text{USING}} \text{ file-name-2 [,file-name-3]...} \\ \underline{\text{OUTPUT}} \text{ PROCEDURE IS section-name-3} \\ \underline{\text{GIVING}} \text{ file-name-4} \end{Bmatrix}$$

For example:

```
SORT SORT-TEMPORARY ON DESCENDING KEY DIVISION-CODE
                    ON ASCENDING KEY SALESMAN-NUMBER
                    ON DESCENDING KEY INVOICE
        USING SALES-FILE-INPUT
        GIVING OUTPUT-FILE.
```

or:

```
SORT SORT-TEMPORARY ON DESCENDING KEY DIVISION-CODE
                    ON ASCENDING KEY SALESMAN-NUMBER
                    ON DESCENDING KEY INVOICE
        INPUT PROCEDURE IS SELECT-DIVISIONS-TO-PROCESS SECTION
        OUTPUT PROCEDURE IS PREPARE-REPORT SECTION.
```

Some compilers recognize that you are referring to a section-name implicitly. In those cases you need not use the word SECTION in the format above. Indeed, you may get an error message if you do. Also, the THROUGH option may be used with the INPUT PROCEDURE and the OUTPUT PROCEDURE clauses.

Let's look at the various parts of this SORT command. It begins with the word SORT. Following the word SORT is the name of the file that will hold the sorted information (the name of the file where the sorted information is stored). The data stored in this file are to be arranged in some order (sorted by some characteristic) as prescribed in the ON DESCENDING KEY clause or ON ASCENDING KEY clause.

If you have ON DESCENDING KEY DIVISION-CODE this tells the SORT PROCEDURE that you want the information sorted by DIVISION-CODE and that it should be in DESCENDING order. DESCENDING order for alphabetic information is from z to a and for numeric data is from high numbers to low numbers. ASCENDING order is from low numbers to high numbers and from a to z. If you have a project requiring the sort of special characters refer to Appendix G, which lists the complete collating sequence for COBOL.

If the data are to be sorted on more than one field, then the order in the SORT command also specifies the major and minor fields of the sort. The first item listed is the major field. The data will be sorted by this characteristic first. If additional sort fields are given then sorting occurs first by the major field and then within this field by the minor field.

A few examples will help to illustrate this concept. If you have data concerning cities and states and want it sorted you could specify:

```
ON ASCENDING KEY STATE
ON ASCENDING KEY CITY
```

The data would be organized by states in alphabetical order, and within each state the cities would also be in alphabetical order.

If the data to be sorted were:

```
ALABAMA         FOLEY
ALABAMA         BOAZ
DELAWARE        LEWES
ALABAMA         YORK
DELAWARE        DOVER
PENNSYLVANIA    YORK
```

and you have

```
ON ASCENDING KEY STATE
ON ASCENDING KEY CITY
```

the sorted file will be

```
ALABAMA          BOAZ
ALABAMA          FOLEY
ALABAMA          YORK
DELAWARE         DOVER
DELAWARE         LEWES
PENNSYLVANIA     YORK
```

If, on the other hand, you have

```
ON ASCENDING KEY CITY
ON ASCENDING KEY STATE
```

the sorted file will be

```
ALABAMA          BOAZ
DELAWARE         DOVER
ALABAMA          FOLEY
DELAWARE         LEWES
ALABAMA          YORK
PENNSYLVANIA     YORK
```

The first key states whether ASCENDING or DESCENDING is the major field on which the data are to be sorted. Any other keys given are intermediate and minor fields. You can sort on the entire record or on any field or fields. Each successive field to be sorted is always ordered within the previous field. That is, ON ASCENDING KEY STATE, ON ASCENDING KEY CITY means each city is to be in order within each state which is to be in order.

Probably the easiest sort is the one in which you specify the name of the file to be sorted, the fields on which to sort, and the name of the output file where the sorted information is to be stored. The effect will be to take the unsorted file and sort it and you will have two files—the sorted one and the original (unsorted) one. The sorted file may exist on a tape, a card deck, a disk file, or any other medium where data can be stored. Disk and tape files are very handy for further processing of the sorted data.

If what you want is a listing of the sorted file on the printer, the following PROCEDURE DIVISION will generate such a list where OUTPUT-FILE is defined as a printfile. The output will, of course, be unedited.

```
PROCEDURE DIVISION
    SORT SORT-TEMPORARY ON DESCENDING KEY DIVISION-CODE
                        ON ASCENDING KEY SALESMAN-NUMBER
                        ON DESCENDING KEY INVOICE
        USING SALES-FILE-INPUT
        GIVING OUTPUT-FILE.
    STOP RUN.
```

The output from this PROCEDURE DIVISION is given in Figure 8-5, along with the original data.

Figure 8-5
UNSORTed and SORTed data.

	70432WILKINSON	AB51K3900001527
	32400RAMIREZ	SN51Z4130008117
	77396MORRIS	AB52R5230001684
	70432WILKINSON	AB52K9980017642
	77396MORRIS	SN52S7270004569
	77396MORRIS	AB52A6310002397
	32400RAMIREZ	SN52N7790001593
	70432WILKINSON	AB51G5860031985
	70432WILKINSON	SN51P1930011159
	70432WILKINSON	AB52H2560001969
	77396MORRIS	AB51L4700002210
	26421JABLONSKI	DA51R5170001513
Original	32400RAMIREZ	SN51K5890007660
Data	26421JABLONSKI	DA52A2600002457
	52546DUNNIGAN	SN52F5360001027
	52546DUNNIGAN	SN52W1090003628
	32400RAMIREZ	SN52S1960016727
	42566JOHNSON	AB53G0220003450
	32400RAMIREZ	SN5105610007412
	26421JABLONSKI	DA51T4780018676
	42566JOHNSON	AB51P6880005228
	42566JOHNSON	AB52C6290006232
	77396MORRIS	AB52V4200006578
	32400RAMIREZ	SN51Y2100005157

	32400RAMIREZ	SN52S1960016727
	32400RAMIREZ	SN52N7790001593
	32400RAMIREZ	SN5105610007412
	32400RAMIREZ	SN51Z4130008117
	32400RAMIREZ	SN51Y2100005157
	32400RAMIREZ	SN51K5890007660
	52546DUNNIGAN	SN52W1090003628
	52546DUNNIGAN	SN52F5360001027
	70432WILKINSON	SN51P1930011159
	77396MORRIS	SN52S7270004569
	26421JABLONSKI	DA52A2600002457
	26421JABLONSKI	DA51T4780018676
Sorted	26421JABLONSKI	DA51R5170001513
Data	42566JOHNSON	AB53G0220003450
	42566JOHNSON	AB52C6290006232
	42566JOHNSON	AB51P6880005228
	70432WILKINSON	AB52K9980017642
	70432WILKINSON	AB52H2560001969
	70432WILKINSON	AB51K3900001527
	70432WILKINSON	AB51G5860031985
	77396MORRIS	AB52V4200006578
	77396MORRIS	AB52R5230001684
	77396MORRIS	AB52A6310002397
	77396MORRIS	AB51L4700002210

To see how the whole program fits together, refer to Figure 8-6 (a copy of the ENVIRONMENT, DATA, and PROCEDURE DIVISIONs).

The preceding example illustrates the easiest way to sort the data. This process sorted all of the records in the input file. The output file created by the GIVING OUTPUT-FILE entry could have been used further had we not directed it to the printer. Had the file gone to a disk, we could have opened it as input for the rest of the commands in the PROCEDURE DIVISION, or it could have been used as input to another program.

There will be occasions when you want to sort part, but not all, of the records in a file. So instead of releasing all of the records in the file to the sort, we can select the ones that we want and release only those selected to the sort.

The original file in the example contains records for three divisions of the company—AB, SN, DA. Let's assume that we want only those records from the divisions SN or AB (no DA division records). Figure 8-5 lists the records for the original file.

Figure 8-6
SORT program with USING and
GIVING options.

```
ENVIRONMENT DIVISION.
CONFIGURATION SECTION.
SOURCE-COMPUTER.
    IBM-370.
OBJECT-COMPUTER.
    IBM-370.
INPUT-OUTPUT SECTION.
FILE-CONTROL.
    SELECT SORT-TEMPORARY
        ASSIGN TO SORTWK1.
    SELECT OUTPUT-FILE
        ASSIGN TO PRINTER.
    SELECT SALES-FILE-INPUT
        ASSIGN TO SALESIN.
DATA DIVISION.
FILE SECTION.
SD  SORT-TEMPORARY
    RECORD CONTAINS 39 CHARACTERS.
01  SORT-RECORD.
    02 SALESMAN-NUMBER              PIC 9(5).
    02 SALESMAN-NAME                PIC X(19).
    02 DIVISION-CODE                PIC XX.
    02 INVOICE                      PIC X(6).
    02 SALE-AMOUNT                  PIC 9(5)V99.
FD  SALES-FILE-INPUT
    LABEL RECORDS OMITTED.
01  SALES-RECORD.
    02 FILLER                       PIC X(24).
    02 DIVISION-OF-INPUT-RECORD     PIC XX.
    02 FILLER                       PIC X(54).
FD  OUTPUT-FILE
    LABEL RECORDS OMITTED.
01  PRINT-LINE                      PIC X(133).
WORKING-STORAGE SECTION.
01  OTHER-WS.
    02 TOTAL         PIC 9(6)V99   VALUE ZERO.
    02 LAST-DIVISION PIC XX        VALUE SPACES.
    02 BLANKS        PIC X(133)    VALUE SPACES.
    02 END-SWITCH    PIC XXX       VALUE SPACES.
    02 EOF-SALES     PIC XXX       VALUE SPACES.
PROCEDURE DIVISION.
000-MAINLINE.
    SORT SORT-TEMPORARY ON DESCENDING KEY DIVISION-CODE
                        ON ASCENDING KEY SALESMAN-NUMBER
                        ON DESCENDING KEY INVOICE
        USING SALES-FILE-INPUT
        GIVING OUTPUT-FILE.
    CLOSE SALES-FILE-INPUT OUTPUT-FILE.
    STOP RUN.
```

SECTION 5
The INPUT PROCEDURE

In order to select the records from a file that we want to be sorted we must instruct the SORT as to which records are to be processed. Instead of the USING option we will use the INPUT PROCEDURE option. Compare the following two sort commands.

```
SORT SORT-TEMPORARY ON DESCENDING KEY DIVISION-CODE
                    ON ASCENDING KEY SALESMAN-NUMBER
                    ON DESCENDING KEY INVOICE
        USING SALES-FILE-INPUT
        GIVING OUTPUT-FILE
```

and

```
SORT SORT-TEMPORARY ON DESCENDING KEY DIVISION-CODE
                    ON ASCENDING KEY SALESMAN-NUMBER
                    ON DESCENDING KEY INVOICE
        INPUT PROCEDURE IS SELECT-DIVISIONS-TO-PROCESS
        GIVING OUTPUT-FILE.
```

Notice that the USING option has been replaced by the INPUT PROCEDURE option in the second example. The INPUT PROCEDURE defines the SECTION (series of paragraphs) to be used to select the records to be sorted. This means that in the PROCEDURE DIVISION there must be a SECTION known, in this case, as

```
SELECT-DIVISIONS-TO-PROCESS SECTION.
```

In this section we will develop the commands necessary to select the particular records that we desire. In our problem, these are records for divisions AB and SN. It could just as easily have been only those records with sales over $10,000 or any other characteristic.

If we only want records for the divisions AB or SN, we can find these by having an IF statement which checks on the division code. If the record is for the division we want we will move it to the record description that is part of the SD entry and then release it to the sorting routine. Figure 8-7 contains part of a PROCEDURE DIVISION which selects certain records to be released to the sort.

All of the commands should be familiar to you except RELEASE. The RELEASE statement transfers records from the INPUT PROCEDURE to the input phase of the sort operation. The RELEASE statement may only be used within the range of the INPUT PROCEDURE and the sort-record-name must be the name of a logical record in the SD entry. After a record is RELEASEd the logical record is no longer available. The general format for the RELEASE statement:

```
RELEASE record-name [FROM identifier]
```

For example:

```
IF DIVISION-OF-INPUT-RECORD IS EQUAL TO 'SN' OR
    DIVISION-OF INPUT-RECORD IS EQUAL TO 'AB'
        MOVE SALES-RECORD TO SORT-RECORD
        RELEASE SORT-RECORD.
```

Notice that the record-name that is RETURNed is the name of the record defined in the SD entry.

The SORT command causes the sorting process to begin. Since we have declared an INPUT PROCEDURE, it is the INPUT PROCEDURE which will dictate which records will be RELEASEd to the SORT. Since the SORT has an INPUT PROCEDURE specified, all of the statements in the INPUT PROCEDURE will be used to create the sorted file. It is as if the SORT command has a PERFORM statement where a paragraph or set of paragraphs are executed.

Figure 8-8 contains the output from this INPUT PROCEDURE along with the original file. Note that the DA division records are not part of the sorted file.

Figure 8-7
PROCEDURE DIVISION for
SORT with INPUT
PROCEDURE.

```
PROCEDURE DIVISION.
000-MAINLINE.
    SORT SORT-TEMPORARY ON DESCENDING KEY DIVISION-CODE
                        ON ASCENDING KEY SALESMAN-NUMBER
                        ON DESCENDING KEY INVOICE
            INPUT PROCEDURE IS SELECT-DIVISIONS-TO-PROCESS
            OUTPUT PROCEDURE IS PREPARE-REPORT.
    CLOSE SALES-FILE-INPUT OUTPUT-FILE.
    STOP RUN.
SELECT-DIVISIONS-TO-PROCESS SECTION.
    OPEN INPUT SALES-FILE-INPUT.
    READ SALES-FILE-INPUT AT END MOVE 'END' TO EOF-SALES.
    PERFORM READ-AND-SELECT
        UNTIL EOF-SALES IS EQUAL TO 'END'.
PREPARE-REPORT SECTION.
    OPEN OUTPUT OUTPUT-FILE.
    WRITE PRINT-LINE FROM HEADING-1 AFTER 1.
    WRITE PRINT-LINE FROM HEADING-2 AFTER 1.
    RETURN SORT-TEMPORARY AT END MOVE 'END' TO END-SWITCH.
    MOVE DIVISION-CODE TO LAST-DIVISION.
    PERFORM MOVE-AND-WRITE.
    PERFORM PROCESS-AFTER-FIRST
        UNTIL END-SWITCH IS EQUAL TO 'END'.
READ-AND-SELECT.
    IF DIVISION-OF-INPUT-RECORD IS EQUAL TO 'SN' OR
        DIVISION-OF-INPUT-RECORD IS EQUAL TO 'AB'
            MOVE SALES-RECORD TO SORT-RECORD
            RELEASE SORT-RECORD.
    READ SALES-FILE-INPUT AT END MOVE 'END' TO EOF-SALES.
PROCESS-AFTER-FIRST.
    RETURN SORT-TEMPORARY
        AT END PERFORM WRITE-TOTAL-LINE
            MOVE 'END' TO END-SWITCH.
    IF DIVISION-CODE IS NOT EQUAL TO LAST-DIVISION
        PERFORM WRITE-TOTAL-LINE MOVE DIVISION-CODE
            TO LAST-DIVISION
                ELSE
        PERFORM MOVE-AND-WRITE.
MOVE-AND-WRITE.
    MOVE SALESMAN-NAME TO SALESMAN-NAM.
    MOVE DIVISION-CODE TO DIVISION-RPT.
    MOVE INVOICE TO INVOICE-RPT.
    MOVE SALE-AMOUNT TO AMOUNT.
    MOVE SALESMAN-NUMBER TO SALESMAN-NUM.
    WRITE PRINT-LINE FROM DETAIL-LINE AFTER 1.
    MOVE DIVISION-CODE TO LAST-DIVISION.
    ADD SALE-AMOUNT TO TOTAL.
WRITE-TOTAL-LINE.
    MOVE LAST-DIVISION TO DIVISION-DTL.
    MOVE TOTAL TO TOTAL-DTL.
    MOVE ZERO TO TOTAL.
    WRITE PRINT-LINE FROM DIVISION-TOTAL-LINE AFTER 2.
    WRITE PRINT-LINE FROM BLANKS AFTER 3.
```

Figure 8–8
Inputs to SORT and selected
records using an INPUT
PROCEDURE.

Original
File

```
70432WILKINSON          AB 51K3900001527
32400RAMIREZ            SN 51Z4130008117
77396MORRIS             AB 52R5230001684
70432WILKINSON          AB 52K9980017642
77396MORRIS             SN 52S7270004569
77396MORRIS             AB 52A6310002397
32400RAMIREZ            SN 52N7790001593
70432WILKINSON          AB 51G5860031985
70432WILKINSON          SN 51P1930011159
70432WILKINSON          AB 52H2560001969
77396MORRIS             AB 51L4700002210
26421JABLONSKI          DA 51R5170001513
32400RAMIREZ            SN 51K5890007660
26421JABLONSKI          DA 52A2600002457
52546DUNNIGAN           SN 52F5360001027
52546DUNNIGAN           SN 52W1090003628
32400RAMIREZ            SN 52S1960016727
42566JOHNSON            AB 53G0220003450
32400RAMIREZ            SN 51O5610007412
26421JABLONSKI          DA 51T4780018676
42566JOHNSON            AB 51P6880005228
42566JOHNSON            AB 52C6290006232
42566JOHNSON            AB 51C2590002510
77396MORRIS             AB 52V4200006578
32400RAMIREZ            SN 51Y2100005157
```

Sorted
File
(DA Division
records
excluded)

```
32400RAMIREZ            SN 52S1960016727
32400RAMIREZ            SN 52N7790001593
32400RAMIREZ            SN 51Z4130008117
32400RAMIREZ            SN 51Y2100005157
32400RAMIREZ            SN 51O5610007412
32400RAMIREZ            SN 51K5890007660
52546DUNNIGAN           SN 52W1090003628
52546DUNNIGAN           SN 52F5360001027
70432WILKINSON          SN 51P1930011159
77396MORRIS             SN 52S7270004569
42566JOHNSON            AB 53G0220003450
42566JOHNSON            AB 52C6290006232
42566JOHNSON            AB 51P6880005228
42566JOHNSON            AB 51C2590002510
70432WILKINSON          AB 52K9980017642
70432WILKINSON          AB 52H2560001969
70432WILKINSON          AB 51K3900001527
70432WILKINSON          AB 51G5860031985
77396MORRIS             AB 52V4200006578
77396MORRIS             AB 52R5230001684
77396MORRIS             AB 51L4700002210
77396MORRIS             AB 52A6310002397
```

SECTION 6
The OUTPUT PROCEDURE

To this point we have shown two types of SORTs. The first example used the entire input file as data for the sort and also used the USING option. The second example used the INPUT PROCEDURE option where only certain records were sorted.

In both cases the output from the sort was directed to the printer and was not used in further processing. You may, however, want to write another series of statements that would use the sorted information to generate some kind of report.

One method for doing this is to utilize the OUTPUT PROCEDURE option rather than the GIVING option. The OUTPUT PROCEDURE is very similar to the INPUT PROCEDURE in that a series of commands will be executed with respect to the output desired rather than to the records to be released to the sort.

Let's say that we want a report with headings, footings, and totals. Figure 8-9 contains the DATA DIVISION for a program to generate such a report. Note that the FILE SECTION is the same as before and that the WORKING-STORAGE SEC-TION merely contains the description of the various lines we wish to take to the printer for our report.

In the PROCEDURE DIVISION we will want to read the records to be sorted and then use the sorted file to make the report.

Figure 8–9
DATA DIVISION for SORT
program.

```
DATA DIVISION.
FILE SECTION.
SD   SORT-TEMPORARY
     RECORD CONTAINS 39 CHARACTERS.
01   SORT-RECORD.
     02 SALESMAN-NUMBER              PIC 9(5).
     02 SALESMAN-NAME                PIC X(19).
     02 DIVISION-CODE                PIC XX.
     02 INVOICE                      PIC X(6).
     02 SALE-AMOUNT                  PIC 9(5)V99.
FD   SALES-FILE-INPUT
     LABEL RECORDS OMITTED.
01   SALES-RECORD.
     02 FILLER                       PIC X(24).
     02 DIVISION-OF-INPUT-RECORD     PIC XX.
     02 FILLER                       PIC X(54).
FD   OUTPUT-FILE
     LABEL RECORDS OMITTED.
01   PRINT-LINE                      PIC X(133).
WORKING-STORAGE SECTION.
01   HEADING-1.
     02 FILLER        PIC X(57) VALUE SPACES.
     02 FILLER        PIC X(20) VALUE 'AMBROISE AND COMPANY'.
     02 FILLER        PIC X(56) VALUE SPACES.
01   HEADING-2.
     02 FILLER        PIC X(57) VALUE SPACES.
     02 FILLER        PIC X(20) VALUE 'MONTHLY SALES REPORT'.
     02 FILLER        PIC X(56) VALUE SPACES.
01   DETAIL-LINE.
     02 FILLER             PIC X(15)   VALUE SPACES.
     02 SALESMAN-NUM       PIC 9(5)    VALUE ZERO.
     02 FILLER             PIC X(15)   VALUE SPACES.
     02 SALESMAN-NAM       PIC X(19)   VALUE SPACES.
     02 FILLER        PIC X(15)   VALUE SPACES.
     02 INVOICE-RPT    PIC X(6)    VALUE SPACES.
     02 FILLER        PIC X(15)   VALUE SPACES.
     02 DIVISION-RPT   PIC XX      VALUE SPACES.
     02 FILLER        PIC X(15)   VALUE SPACES.
     02 AMOUNT        PIC $ZZ,ZZZ.99.
     02 FILLER        PIC X(15)   VALUE SPACES.
01   DIVISION-TOTAL-LINE.
     02 FILLER        PIC X(48) VALUE SPACES.
     02 FILLER        PIC X(19) VALUE 'TOTAL FOR DIVISION'.
     02 DIVISION-DTL  PIC XX      VALUE SPACES.
     02 FILLER        PIC X(5)  VALUE SPACES.
     02 TOTAL-DTL     PIC $ZZZ,ZZZ.99.
     02 FILLER        PIC X(48) VALUE SPACES.
01   OTHER-WS.
     02 TOTAL         PIC 9(6)V99 VALUE ZERO.
     02 LAST-DIVISION PIC XX      VALUE SPACES.
     02 BLANKS        PIC X(133)  VALUE SPACES.
     02 END-SWITCH    PIC XX      VALUE SPACES.
     02 EOF-SALES     PIC XX      VALUE SPACES.
```

The first part of our PROCEDURE DIVISION, in which the SORT command specifies the sorting to be done and also provides details of an OUTPUT PROCEDURE, might look like this:

```
PROCEDURE DIVISION.
        SORT SORT-TEMPORARY ON DESCENDING KEY DIVISION-CODE
                            ON ASCENDING KEY SALESMAN-NUMBER
                            ON DESCENDING KEY INVOICE
            USING SALES-FILE-INPUT
            OUTPUT PROCEDURE IS PREPARE-REPORT SECTION.
```

Note that the OUTPUT PROCEDURE specifies that the section PREPARE-REPORT will contain the commands that will generate the report we desire. When the sort command is finished, control will be passed to the next command just as it is in other COBOL programs. The SORT command, however, specifies a series of activities to be accomplished and not just the actual sorting of the data.

Figure 8-10 contains the complete PROCEDURE DIVISION. All of the commands should be familiar to you, except for the RETURN.

Figure 8-10
Complete PROCEDURE
DIVISION for SORT program.

```
PROCEDURE DIVISION.
000-MAINLINE.
        SORT SORT-TEMPORARY ON DESCENDING KEY DIVISION-CODE
                            ON ASCENDING KEY SALESMAN-NUMBER
                            ON DESCENDING KEY INVOICE
            USING SALES-FILE-INPUT
            OUTPUT PROCEDURE IS PREPARE-REPORT.
        CLOSE SALES-FILE-INPUT OUTPUT-FILE.
        STOP RUN.
PREPARE-REPORT SECTION.
        OPEN OUTPUT OUTPUT-FILE.
        RETURN SORT-TEMPORARY AT END MOVE 'END' TO END-SWITCH.
        MOVE DIVISION-CODE TO LAST-DIVISION.
        PERFORM MOVE-AND-WRITE.
        PERFORM PROCESS-RECORDS
            UNTIL END-SWITCH IS EQUAL TO 'END'.
PROCEDURES-TO-PERFORM SECTION.
PROCESS-RECORDS.
        IF FIRST-RECORD IS EQUAL TO 1
            MOVE DIVISION-CODE TO LAST-DIVISION
            MOVE ZERO TO FIRST-RECORD.
        IF DIVISION-CODE IS EQUAL TO LAST-DIVISION
            PERFORM MOVE-AND-WRITE
                ELSE
            PERFORM WRITE-TOTAL-LINE
                MOVE DIVISION-CODE TO LAST-DIVISION
                PERFORM MOVE-AND-WRITE.
        RETURN SORT-TEMPORARY
            AT END PERFORM WRITE-TOTAL-LINE
                    MOVE 'END' TO END-SWITCH.
MOVE-AND-WRITE.
        MOVE SALESMAN-NAME TO SALESMAN-NAM.
        MOVE DIVISION-CODE TO DIVISION-RPT.
        MOVE INVOICE TO INVOICE-RPT.
        MOVE SALE-AMOUNT TO AMOUNT.
        MOVE SALESMAN-NUMBER TO SALESMAN-NUM.
        WRITE PRINT-LINE FROM DETAIL-LINE AFTER 1.
        ADD SALE-AMOUNT TO TOTAL.
WRITE-TOTAL-LINE.
        MOVE LAST-DIVISION TO DIVISION-DTL.
        MOVE TOTAL TO TOTAL-DTL.
        MOVE ZERO TO TOTAL.
        WRITE PRINT-LINE FROM DIVISION-TOTAL-LINE AFTER 2.
        WRITE PRINT-LINE FROM BLANKS AFTER 3.
```

A new statement (RETURN) in Figure 8-10 is in the command RETURN SORT-TEMPORARY, AT END PERFORM WRITE-TOTAL-LINE MOVE 'END' TO END SWITCH. The RETURN command operates in much the same way as a READ command. In order to use the sorted file (a temporary file) the language specifications require you to use the RETURN command rather than a READ command. The functions of the RETURN and the READ are very similar. Notice that the RETURN command has the AT END option just as READ commands do and that you RETURN a file-name just as you do with a READ. The RETURN statement that must be a part of an OUTPUT PROCEDURE has the following general format:

```
RETURN file-name RECORD [INTO identifier]
           AT END imperative-statement
```

For example:

```
RETURN SORT-TEMPORARY
        AT END MOVE 1 TO EOF-SORTED-DATA-INDICATOR,
```

or:

```
RETURN SORT-TEMPORARY INTO FORMATTED-RECORD
        AT END MOVE 1  TO EOF-SORTED-DATA-INDICATOR,
```

The RETURN INTO statement is similar to a READ INTO statement.

After the records have been sorted, in our example, it is necessary to get the first record from the sorted file (RETURN), save the DIVISION-CODE for checking later on, move the various data fields to the respective output areas, write a detail line on the printer, and then go back and get another record from the sorted file. If the next record is from the same division as the preceding one, then we should continue to process and accumulate various totals. However, if the next record is for a new division, then the subtotals for this division should be printed.

Figure 8-11 presents the output from this program. Note that the output does not have any headings. Even though we described them properly in the DATA DIVISION, our purpose was to discuss the SORT feature and in order to limit our discussion to the issue at hand we included no WRITE statements in the PROCEDURE DIVISION which would write headings. In the next example we include the WRITE commands necessary to do the headings just to finish the job. The last example is one in which we have both an INPUT PROCEDURE and an OUTPUT PROCEDURE. In this example we want to select certain records to be sorted (not the entire file) and also to specify the output desired (not merely a dump of the sorted file).

Figure 8-12 contains the PROCEDURE DIVISION for a program which selects specific records for the sort procedure and generates a report (like the one in the preceding example)

Figure 8-13 contains the output from the PROCEDURE DIVISION given in Figure 8-12. Notice that the headings came out this time.

32400	RAMIREZ	52S196	SN	$ 167.27
32400	RAMIREZ	52S196	SN	$ 167.27
32400	RAMIREZ	52N779	SN	$ 15.93
32400	RAMIREZ	510561	SN	$ 74.12
32400	RAMIREZ	51Z413	SN	$ 81.17
32400	RAMIREZ	51Y210	SN	$ 51.57
32400	RAMIREZ	51K589	SN	$ 76.60
52546	DUNNIGAN	52W109	SN	$ 36.28
52546	DUNNIGAN	52F536	SN	$ 10.27
70432	WILKINSON	51P193	SN	$ 111.59
77396	MORRIS	52S727	SN	$ 45.69
		TOTAL FOR DIVISION SN	$ 837.76	
26421	JABLONSKI	52A260	DA	$ 24.57
26421	JABLONSKI	51T478	DA	$ 186.76
26421	JABLONSKI	51R517	DA	$ 15.13
		TOTAL FOR DIVISION DA	$ 226.46	
42566	JOHNSON	53G022	AB	$ 34.50
42566	JOHNSON	52C629	AB	$ 62.32
42566	JOHNSON	51P688	AB	$ 52.28
70432	WILKINSON	52K998	AB	$ 176.42
70432	WILKINSON	52H256	AB	$ 19.69
70432	WILKINSON	51K390	AB	$ 15.27
70432	WILKINSON	51G586	AB	$ 319.85
77396	MORRIS	52V420	AB	$ 65.78
77396	MORRIS	52R523	AB	$ 16.84
77396	MORRIS	52A631	AB	$ 23.97
77396	MORRIS	51L470	AB	$ 22.10
		TOTAL FOR DIVISION AB	$ 809.02	

Figure 8-11
Output from SORT program with output procedure.

Figure 8-12
SORT program to print selected records.

```
PROCEDURE DIVISION.
000-MAINLINE.
    SORT SORT-TEMPORARY ON DESCENDING KEY DIVISION-CODE
                        ON ASCENDING KEY SALESMAN-NUMBER
                        ON DESCENDING KEY INVOICE
        INPUT PROCEDURE IS SELECT-DIVISIONS-TO-PROCESS
        OUTPUT PROCEDURE IS PREPARE-REPORT.
    CLOSE SALES-FILE-INPUT OUTPUT-FILE.
    STOP RUN.
SELECT-DIVISIONS-TO-PROCESS SECTION.
    OPEN INPUT SALES-FILE-INPUT.
    READ SALES-FILE-INPUT AT END MOVE 'END' TO EOF-SALES.
    PERFORM READ-AND-SELECT
        UNTIL EOF-SALES IS EQUAL TO 'END'.
PREPARE-REPORT SECTION.
    OPEN OUTPUT OUTPUT-FILE.
    WRITE PRINT-LINE FROM HEADING-1 AFTER PAGE-TOP.
    WRITE PRINT-LINE FROM HEADING-2 AFTER 1.
    PERFORM MOVE-AND-WRITE.
    PERFORM PROCESS-RECORDS
        UNTIL END-SWITCH IS EQUAL TO 'END'.
PROCEDURES-TO-PERFORM SECTION.
READ-AND-SELECT.
    IF DIVISION-OF-INPUT-RECORD IS EQUAL TO 'SN' OR
        DIVISION-OF-INPUT-RECORD IS EQUAL TO 'AB'
            MOVE SALES-RECORD TO SORT-RECORD
            RELEASE SORT-RECORD.
    READ SALES-FILE-INPUT AT END MOVE 'END' TO EOF-SALES.
PROCESS-RECORDS.
    IF FIRST-RECORD IS EQUAL TO 1
        MOVE DIVISION-CODE TO LAST-DIVISION
        MOVE ZERO TO FIRST-RECORD.
    IF DIVISION-CODE IS EQUAL TO LAST-DIVISION
        PERFORM MOVE-AND-WRITE
            ELSE
        PERFORM WRITE-TOTAL-LINE
            MOVE DIVISION-CODE TO LAST-DIVISION
            PERFORM MOVE-AND-WRITE.
    RETURN SORT-TEMPORARY
        AT END PERFORM WRITE-TOTAL-LINE
            MOVE 'END' TO END-SWITCH.
MOVE-AND-WRITE.
    MOVE SALESMAN-NAME TO SALESMAN-NAM.
    MOVE DIVISION-CODE TO DIVISION-RPT.
    MOVE INVOICE TO INVOICE-RPT.
    MOVE SALE-AMOUNT TO AMOUNT.
    MOVE SALESMAN-NUMBER TO SALESMAN-NUM.
    WRITE PRINT-LINE FROM DETAIL-LINE AFTER 1.
    MOVE DIVISION-CODE TO LAST-DIVISION.
    ADD SALE-AMOUNT TO TOTAL.
WRITE-TOTAL-LINE.
    MOVE LAST-DIVISION TO DIVISION-DTL.
    MOVE TOTAL TO TOTAL-DTL.
    MOVE ZERO TO TOTAL.
    WRITE PRINT-LINE FROM DIVISION-TOTAL-LINE AFTER 2.
    WRITE PRINT-LINE FROM BLANKS AFTER 3.
```

```
                        AMBROISE AND COMPANY
                        MONTHLY SALES REPORT
32400              RAMIREZ                    51Y210          SN          $      51.57
32400              RAMIREZ                    51Y210          SN          $      51.57
32400              RAMIREZ                    52S196          SN          $     167.27
32400              RAMIREZ                    52N779          SN          $      15.93
32400              RAMIREZ                    510561          SN          $      74.12
32400              RAMIREZ                    51Z413          SN          $      81.17
32400              RAMIREZ                    51Y210          SN          $      51.57
32400              RAMIREZ                    51K589          SN          $      76.60
52546              DUNNIGAN                   52W109          SN          $      36.28
52546              DUNNIGAN                   52F536          SN          $      10.27
70432              WILKINSON                  51P193          SN          $     111.59
77396              MORRIS                     52S727          SN          $      45.69

                      TOTAL FOR DIVISION SN     $       773.63


42566              JOHNSON                    53G022          AB          $      34.50
42566              JOHNSON                    52C629          AB          $      62.32
42566              JOHNSON                    51P688          AB          $      52.28
70432              WILKINSON                  52K998          AB          $     176.42
70432              WILKINSON                  52H256          AB          $      19.69
70432              WILKINSON                  51K390          AB          $      15.27
70432              WILKINSON                  51G586          AB          $     319.85
77396              MORRIS                     52V420          AB          $      65.78
77396              MORRIS                     52R523          AB          $      16.84
77396              MORRIS                     52A631          AB          $      23.97
77396              MORRIS                     51L470          AB          $      22.10

                      TOTAL FOR DIVISION AB     $       809.02
```

Figure 8–13
Output from program to print
selected records.

SECTION 7
The SORTING Process

Up to this time we have only said that the computer would sort the file and return a sorted file to you. How does the computer actually sort the information?

Computer manufacturers and the developers of some programming languages write software that provides the capability for sorting data. The process varies from one computer to another, but the basis for any sort is a comparison of data-items. The software associated with the SORT feature is very efficient, and you may expect speedy, accurate results which do not waste machine resources.

Some systems use what are known as *sort-work files*. These sort-work files are used to store the data as they are being sorted. Usually three or more sort-work files are used. As the data are received, they are immediately sent to one of the work files, depending on the value of the fields to be sorted. The computer will continue to send records to these sort-work files and then merge them into one sorted file. Figure 8-14 illustrates the way in which the original data file is used by a COBOL program and sorted yielding a sorted file, and the original file (unsorted).

Figure 8–14
System flowchart for SORT
processes.

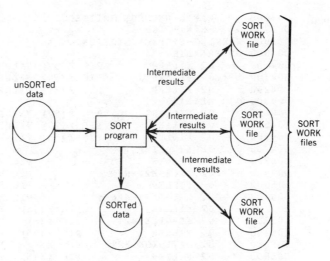

SECTION 8
Sample COBOL Program

The program presented in Figure 8-15 illustrates the use of the INPUT PROCEDURE
and also the OUTPUT PROCEDURE for a SORT.

Figure 8–15
Sample program.

```
000100 IDENTIFICATION DIVISION.
000200 PROGRAM-ID.
000300      'SORTER'.
000400      AUTHOR. ALBERT W. ROBBINS, JR.
000500 ENVIRONMENT DIVISION.
000600 CONFIGURATION SECTION.
000700 SOURCE-COMPUTER.
000800      IBM-370.
000900 OBJECT-COMPUTER.
001000      IBM-370.
001100 INPUT-OUTPUT SECTION.
001200 FILE-CONTROL.
001300      SELECT SORT-TEMPORARY
001400          ASSIGN TO SORTWK1.
001500      SELECT OUTPUT-FILE
001600          ASSIGN TO PRINTER.
001700      SELECT SALES-FILE-INPUT
001800          ASSIGN TO SALESIN.
001900 DATA DIVISION.
002000 FILE SECTION.
002100 SD   SORT-TEMPORARY
002200      RECORD CONTAINS 39 CHARACTERS.
002300 01   SORT-RECORD.
002400      02 SALESMAN-NUMBER           PIC 9(5).
002500      02 SALESMAN-NAME             PIC X(19).
002600      02 DIVISION-CODE             PIC XX.
002700      02 INVOICE                   PIC X(6).
002800      02 SALE-AMOUNT               PIC 9(5)V99.
002900 FD   SALES-FILE-INPUT
003000      LABEL RECORDS OMITTED.
003100 01   SALES-RECORD.
003200      02 FILLER                    PIC X(24).
003300      02 DIVISION-OF-INPUT-RECORD  PIC XX.
003400      02 FILLER                    PIC X(54).
003500 FD   OUTPUT-FILE
```

Figure 8–15 (continued)

```
003600          LABEL RECORDS OMITTED.
003700  01  PRINT-LINE                        PIC X(133).
003800  WORKING-STORAGE SECTION.
003900  01  HEADING-1.
004000      02 FILLER        PIC X(57) VALUE SPACES.
004100      02 FILLER        PIC X(20) VALUE 'AMBROISE AND COMPANY'.
004200      02 FILLER        PIC X(56) VALUE SPACES.
004300  01  HEADING-2.
004400      02 FILLER        PIC X(57) VALUE SPACES.
004500      02 FILLER        PIC X(20) VALUE 'MONTHLY SALES REPORT'.
004600      02 FILLER        PIC X(56) VALUE SPACES.
004700  01  DETAIL-LINE.
004800      02 FILLER                 PIC X(15)   VALUE SPACES.
004900      02 SALESMAN-NUM           PIC 9(5)    VALUE ZERO.
005000      02 FILLER                 PIC X(15)   VALUE SPACES.
005100      02 SALESMAN-NAM           PIC X(19)   VALUE SPACES.
005200      02 FILLER        PIC X(15)  VALUE SPACES.
005300      02 INVOICE-RPT   PIC X(6)   VALUE SPACES.
005400      02 FILLER        PIC X(15)  VALUE SPACES.
005500      02 DIVISION-RPT  PIC XX     VALUE SPACES.
005600      02 FILLER        PIC X(15)  VALUE SPACES.
005700      02 AMOUNT        PIC $ZZ,ZZZ.99.
005800      02 FILLER        PIC X(15)  VALUE SPACES.
005900  01  DIVISION-TOTAL-LINE.
006000      02 FILLER        PIC X(48) VALUE SPACES.
006100      02 FILLER        PIC X(19) VALUE 'TOTAL FOR DIVISION'.
006200      02 DIVISION-DTL  PIC XX    VALUE SPACES.
006300      02 FILLER        PIC X(5)  VALUE SPACES.
006400      02 TOTAL-DTL     PIC $ZZZ,ZZZ.99.
006500      02 FILLER        PIC X(48) VALUE SPACES.
006600  01  OTHER-WS.
006700      02 TOTAL         PIC 9(6)V99  VALUE ZERO.
006800      02 LAST-DIVISION PIC XX       VALUE SPACES.
006900      02 BLANKS        PIC X(133)   VALUE SPACES.
007000      02 END-SWITCH    PIC XX       VALUE SPACES.
007100      02 EOF-SALES     PIC XX       VALUE SPACES.
007200  PROCEDURE DIVISION.
007300  000-MAINLINE.
007400      SORT SORT-TEMPORARY ON DESCENDING KEY DIVISION-CODE
007500                          ON ASCENDING KEY SALESMAN-NUMBER
007600                          ON DESCENDING KEY INVOICE
007700          INPUT PROCEDURE IS SELECT-DIVISIONS-TO-PROCESS
007800          OUTPUT PROCEDURE IS PREPARE-REPORT.
007900      CLOSE SALES-FILE-INPUT OUTPUT-FILE.
008000      STOP RUN.
008100  SELECT-DIVISIONS-TO-PROCESS SECTION.
008200      OPEN INPUT SALES-FILE-INPUT.
008300      PERFORM READ-AND-SELECT
008400          UNTIL EOF-SALES IS EQUAL TO 'END'.
008500  PREPARE-REPORT SECTION.
008600      OPEN OUTPUT OUTPUT-FILE.
008700      WRITE PRINT-LINE FROM HEADING-1 AFTER 1.
008800      WRITE PRINT-LINE FROM HEADING-2 AFTER 1.
008900      RETURN SORT-TEMPORARY AT END MOVE 'END' TO END-SWITCH.
009000      MOVE DIVISION-CODE TO LAST-DIVISION.
009100      PERFORM MOVE-AND-WRITE.
009200      PERFORM PROCESS-AFTER-FIRST
009300          UNTIL END-SWITCH IS EQUAL TO 'END'.
009400  READ-AND-SELECT.
009500      READ SALES-FILE-INPUT AT END MOVE 'END' TO EOF-SALES.
009600      IF DIVISION-OF-INPUT-RECORD IS EQUAL TO 'SN' OR
009700          DIVISION-OF-INPUT-RECORD IS EQUAL TO 'AB'
009800              MOVE SALES-RECORD TO SORT-RECORD
009900              RELEASE SORT-RECORD.
010000  PROCESS-AFTER-FIRST.
010100      RETURN SORT-TEMPORARY
010200          AT END PERFORM WRITE-TOTAL-LINE
010300              MOVE 'END' TO END-SWITCH.
010400      IF DIVISION-CODE IS NOT EQUAL TO LAST-DIVISION
010500          PERFORM WRITE-TOTAL-LINE MOVE DIVISION-CODE
```

Figure 8–15 (continued)

```
010600                    TO LAST-DIVISION
010700                ELSE
010800            PERFORM MOVE-AND-WRITE.
010900    MOVE-AND-WRITE.
011000        MOVE SALESMAN-NAME TO SALESMAN-NAM.
011100        MOVE DIVISION-CODE TO DIVISION-RPT.
011200        MOVE INVOICE TO INVOICE-RPT.
011300        MOVE SALE-AMOUNT TO AMOUNT.
011400        MOVE SALESMAN-NUMBER TO SALESMAN-NUM.
011500        WRITE PRINT-LINE FROM DETAIL-LINE AFTER 1.
011600        MOVE DIVISION-CODE TO LAST-DIVISION.
011700        ADD SALE-AMOUNT TO TOTAL.
011800    WRITE-TOTAL-LINE.
011900        MOVE LAST-DIVISION TO DIVISION-DTL.
012000        MOVE TOTAL TO TOTAL-DTL.
012100        MOVE ZERO TO TOTAL.
012200        WRITE PRINT-LINE FROM DIVISION-TOTAL-LINE AFTER 2.
012300        WRITE PRINT-LINE FROM BLANKS AFTER 3.
```

SECTION 9
Review Questions and Exercises

I. Questions

1. Given the format of the records to be sorted, what are the basic elements of the SD entry?
2. What is the meaning of the term "ascending order"? "Descending order"?
3. Give the SD entry for a file (STUDENT-FILE) which contains information on students.

Cols.	Content
1 –20	name
25	classification code
27–29	semester hours completed
33–36	quality point average
38	gender code

4. Give the detailed record description for the preceding file.
5. Give the SORT command for the preceding file to sort the information in alphabetical order on the student name, (ascending order), on classification code (descending order), on the quality point average (ascending order), and on the gender code (descending). The sorted file should go to the printer.
6. Give the SORT command (under the same conditions as before) except that only those students who have quality point averages above 3.25 will be used in the sorted file. Transfer the sorted information to the printer.

II. Problems and Exercises

1. Prepare a COBOL program that uses the SORT feature to sort the customer master file from Exercise 3 of Chapter 3 in ascending customer name sequence.
2. Prepare a COBOL program that uses the SORT feature to sort the personnel master file in descending employee name sequence.
3. Prepare a COBOL program that uses the SORT feature to sort the invoice master file in ascending customer number sequence.

4. Prepare a COBOL program that uses the SORT feature to sort the inventory master file in ascending part name sequence.

5. Prepare a COBOL program that uses the SORT feature to select parts from the inventory master file that are supplied by ABC MANUFACTURING, INC. and sort these selected records in ascending part name sequence.

6. Prepare a COBOL program that uses the SORT verb to select ASSOC PROF's from the personnel master file, sorts them in ascending name sequence and lists the selected records on the line printer.

9

The REPORT WRITER Feature

Most business oriented programming will require that a report or listing of some type be produced. There are several tasks that may be required in a program that produces reports. Any one or combination of these tasks may be encountered in a particular application. They are:

1. testing for control breaks
2. headings
3. footings
4. page control
5. line control
6. totaling—subtotals and grand totals
7. detail lines

Even if you are already well acquainted with these concepts, it may be good idea to review briefly the meaning of the terms in the preceding list.

SECTION 1
Testing for Control Breaks

The term *control break* refers to a change in an important (or control) field during the processing of information. For example, if you are processing data accumulated over a calendar year and it is important to accumulate monthly totals or skip a few lines after reporting all the information for a particular month, the point at which the field indicating the month changes is called a control break. The dataname MONTH may be used for a CONTROL BREAK. For example:

```
02   MONTH PICTURE 99
```

may be used so that when the value stored in MONTH changes from 1 to 2 (etc.) certain subtotals will be printed.

You may have several control fields within a record. These fields are usually classified—according to their relative importance—as major, intermediate, or minor controls. If time is to be used to control the report, then a break between MONTHS will signal certain subtotals to be printed, whereas a break between YEARS will signal an intermediate break and yearly totals will be printed, and, finally, after all of the years are printed, grand totals will be printed.

SECTION 2
Headings

Headings are of three different types:

1. report headings
2. page headings
3. control (break) headings

Report headings are printed as the first item of the first page of a report, but on no other page. They will appear only once in a report but may appear anywhere on the first page and, indeed, may exceed a page, or many pages, in length. A page heading will be printed at the top of every page. It will, of course, follow the report heading (if any) on the first page. A control heading will appear prior to any information which may have control fields. On any control break a new control heading will appear before any of the information which created the break will appear.

SECTION 3
Footings

Footings are also of three different types:

1. report footings
2. page footings
3. control (break) footings

Report footings will appear only once, as the last line (or group of lines if you specify a multiple line footing) of the last page of a report. Page footings will appear as the last lines of every page of a report (except for the last page, where the report footing, if any, will be last). Control footings appear after every control break.

SECTION 4
Page Control

Page control refers to the processes which control:

• counting the number of lines which have been written on a page to make sure the desired number of lines (and no more) is printed;

- the printing of any required page footings;
- advancing to a new page;
- the printing of any required headings on the next page before further processing.

SECTION 5
Line Control

Line control refers to the process of counting the number of lines printed in order to provide for proper spacing of different types of lines on the page.

SECTION 6
Totaling—Subtotals and Grand Totals

Total accumulations are of two types:

1. grand totaling (final totals)
2. subtotaling

Grand totals are those that appear only once, at the end of the report. The data are summed as each record is read and accumulated for all of the records. For example, the process of adding the sales from each salesperson to an accumulator would result in a grand total.

Subtotals are those that are accumulated for specific parts of the report. These subtotals are interspersed throughout the report as control breaks are encountered. They are then set back to zero and the process is repeated so that the amount of sales will be accumulated and printed for each salesperson. Each time a new salesperson is encountered, the subtotal for the previous salesperson will be printed, the accumulators set back to zero, and the process started over.

In order to accumulate a grand total without using the REPORT WRITER, you simply add the appropriate data field to a total field each time a new record is accessed. The total field should be defined in WORKING-STORAGE. Subtotaling (control totaling) is a bit more complex. As each record is processed, you must code procedures to test for control breaks. On each control break the subtotal must be printed and the accumulator set back to zero and the process of accumulating totals started over for the new set of information. There must be a series of IF statements, ADD statements, MOVE statements, and others to accomplish this task. The logic involved can become quite tedious.

SECTION 7
Detail Lines

Detail lines are the actual lines of data that you are going to print between the various headings and footings.

Figure 9-1 has been prepared in order to show the various types of headings, footings, and so on. In this figure, a report program is used to total information concerning computer job accounting for a data processing class.

The REPORT WRITER feature is an extension of COBOL that is designed to provide a method for generating reports while providing for many of the tasks common to printed reports to be handled by the compiler rather than by the programmer. These "automatic" features require that you code certain special COBOL instructions. These appear in the DATA DIVISION, where you describe what the report will look like, and in the PROCEDURE DIVISION, where you dictate the conditions under which each line will be printed. The process of producing printed reports is much easier using the REPORT WRITER than using regular COBOL commands. The following sections illustrate how to use the REPORT WRITER features.

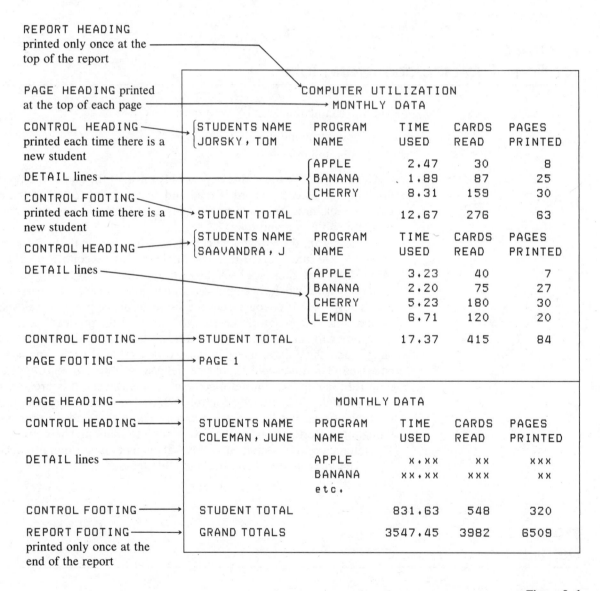

Figure 9–1
REPORT WRITER terminology.

SECTION 8
REPORT WRITER Features in the DATA DIVISION

Most of the writing of REPORT WRITER programs will be done in the DATA DIVISION. These entries are made in a special section—the REPORT SECTION. The words REPORT SECTION must begin in margin A and must follow all other sections in the DATA DIVISION. Figure 9-2 illustrates the new section in the DATA DIVISION.

At this point we should establish an illustrative problem to use as a guide as each feature is introduced. We will produce a sales report for a fictional company, INTERNATIONAL TOYS, INC. Figure 9-3 is a representation of the report to be printed. The report has been shortened here but the complete program and its inputs and outputs are given at the end of the chapter.

Examining the report you will note there are six operations to be accomplished. These are:

1. There is to be a heading which is to appear only on the first page of the report. The heading is to read:

   INTERNATIONAL TOYS, INC.

   This heading is to start on line 2.

Figure 9-2
REPORT SECTION for sample program.

```
REPORT SECTION.
RD  TOY-SALES-REPORT
    CONTROLS ARE FINAL, SALESPERSON
    PAGE LIMIT IS 60 LINES
    HEADING 2
    FIRST DETAIL 6
    LAST DETAIL 56
    FOOTING 59.
01  TYPE REPORT HEADING LINE IS 2.
    02 COLUMN 54 PIC X(24) VALUE 'INTERNATIONAL TOYS, INC.'.
01  TYPE PAGE HEADING.
    02 LINE IS 3 COLUMN 56
       PIC A(20) VALUE 'MONTHLY SALES REPORT'.
    02 LINE IS PLUS 1.
        03 COLUMN 57 PIC X(19) SOURCE IS MONTHTABLE (MONTH).
        03 COLUMN 67 PIC X(4) VALUE ', 19'.
        03 COLUMN 71 PIC 99 SOURCE IS YEAR.
01 TYPE CONTROL HEADING SALESPERSON.
    02 LINE IS PLUS 3.
        03 COLUMN 10  PIC X(19) VALUE 'SALES-SALESPERSON'.
        03 COLUMN 30  PIC 999    SOURCE SALESPERSON.
        03 COLUMN 39  PIC X(7)   VALUE 'INVOICE'.
        03 COLUMN 53  PIC X(8)   VALUE 'CUSTOMER'.
        03 COLUMN 68  PIC X(5)   VALUE 'TYPE1'.
        03 COLUMN 80  PIC X(5)   VALUE 'TYPE2'.
        03 COLUMN 92  PIC X(5)   VALUE 'TYPE3'.
        03 COLUMN 104 PIC X(5)   VALUE 'TYPE4'.
        03 COLUMN 115 PIC X(5)   VALUE 'TOTAL'.
    02 LINE IS PLUS 1.
        03 COLUMN 40  PIC X(6) VALUE 'NUMBER'.
        03 COLUMN 54  PIC X(6) VALUE 'NUMBER'.
        03 COLUMN 68  PIC X(5) VALUE 'SALES'.
        03 COLUMN 80  PIC X(5) VALUE 'SALES'.
        03 COLUMN 92  PIC X(5) VALUE 'SALES'.
        03 COLUMN 104 PIC X(5) VALUE 'SALES'.
        03 COLUMN 115 PIC X(5) VALUE 'SALES'.
```

Figure 9–2 (continued)

```
01  LINE-OF-DATA TYPE IS DETAIL LINE PLUS 1.
    02 COLUMN 39 PIC X(6) SOURCE IS INVOICE.
    02 COLUMN 54 PIC 9(5) SOURCE IS CUSTOMER.
    02 TYPE1-DETAIL COLUMN 64  PIC ZZ,ZZZ.99
           SOURCE IS TYPE1.
    02 TYPE2-DETAIL COLUMN 76  PIC ZZ,ZZZ.99
           SOURCE IS TYPE2.
    02 TYPE3-DETAIL COLUMN 88  PIC ZZ,ZZZ.99
           SOURCE IS TYPE3.
    02 TYPE4-DETAIL COLUMN 100 PIC ZZ,ZZZ.99
           SOURCE IS TYPE4.
    02 LINE-TOTAL COLUMN 111   PIC ZZ,ZZZ.99
           SOURCE DETAIL-LINE-TOTAL.
01 TYPE CONTROL FOOTING SALESPERSON LINE PLUS 1.
    02 COLUMN 17 PIC X(22) VALUE 'TOTAL SALESPERSON'.
    02 COLUMN 34 PIC ZZZ SOURCE SALESPERSON-OLD.
    02 TYPE1-TOTAL COLUMN 63  PIC ZZZ,ZZZ.99 SUM TYPE1.
    02 TYPE2-TOTAL COLUMN 75  PIC ZZZ,ZZZ.99 SUM TYPE2.
    02 TYPE3-TOTAL COLUMN 87  PIC ZZZ,ZZZ.99 SUM TYPE3.
    02 TYPE4-TOTAL COLUMN 99  PIC ZZZ,ZZZ.99 SUM TYPE4.
    02 TOTAL-TOTAL COLUMN 110 PIC Z,ZZZ,ZZZ.99
           SUM DETAIL-LINE-TOTAL.
01 TYPE CONTROL FOOTING FINAL.
    02 LINE IS 59.
       03 COLUMN 10  PIC X(23) VALUE 'TOTAL SALES COMPANYWIDE'.
       03 COLUMN 62  PIC Z,ZZZ,ZZZ.99 SUM TYPE1-TOTAL.
       03 COLUMN 74  PIC Z,ZZZ,ZZZ.99 SUM TYPE2-TOTAL.
       03 COLUMN 86  PIC Z,ZZZ,ZZZ.99 SUM TYPE3-TOTAL.
       03 COLUMN 98  PIC Z,ZZZ,ZZZ.99 SUM TYPE4-TOTAL.
       03 COLUMN 109 PIC ZZ,ZZZ,ZZZ.99 SUM TOTAL-TOTAL.
```

```
                    INTERNATIONAL TOYS, INC.
                    MONTHLY SALES REPORT
                      JANUARY , 1983
```

		INVOICE NUMBER	CUSTOMER NUMBER	TYPE1 SALES	TYPE2 SALES	TYPE3 SALES	TYPE4 SALES	TOTAL SALES
SALES-SALESPERSON	001	F35008	05600	163.30	24.56	455.30	15.53	658.69
		F35115	05600	555.35	.00	553.00	74.53	1,182.88
		F35077	05600	24.56	35.76	455.00	45.30	560.62
		F35045	05600	665.24	56.30	455.30	25.30	1,202.14
		F35019	05601	893.71	45.60	786.30	58.53	1,784.14
		F35101	05601	14.53	15.50	555.30	15.50	600.83
		F35028	05601	753.08	24.53	553.05	25.53	1,356.19
		F35080	05601	255.53	24.68	24.53	2.55	307.29
		F35132	05602	445.24	.00	2.55	45.45	493.24
TOTAL SALESPERSON	1			3,770.54	226.93	3,840.33	308.22	8,146.02

				TYPE1	TYPE2 SALES	TYPE3		TAL
...PERSON	002							
		F35...				530.02	55.5...	
		F35021		...53		.00	15.56	
		F35131			.00	34.56	44.23	62...
TOTAL SALESPERSON	9			221.77		2,779.20	229.80	5,458.5...

		INVOICE NUMBER	CUSTOMER NUMBER	TYPE1 SALES	TYPE2 SALES	TYPE3 SALES	TYPE4 SALES	TOTAL SALES
SALES-SALESPERSON	010	F35047	05600	863.24	45.30	788.50	15.53	1,712.57
		F35020	05600	912.50	24.53	2.45	45.85	985.33
		F35046	05600	574.44	25.30	455.30	55.30	1,110.34
		F35068	05600	21.45	57.83	553.30	2.55	635.13
		F35151	05600	325.53	453.00	455.00	2.55	1,236.08
		F35148	05600	354.58	552.08	585.22	5.53	1,497.41
		F35150	05600	545.55	450.00	553.00	2.14	1,550.69
		F35152	05600	325.63	753.00	553.00	.00	1,631.63
		F35029	05601	145.63	24.53	550.03	78.82	799.01
		F35122	05601	545.53	15.60	.02	4.53	565.68
		F35009	05601	60.21	14.53	133.00	25.83	233.57
		F35055	05601	33.68	25.30	863.30	2.50	924.78
		F35149	05601	555.24	585.50	852.33	2.45	1,995.52
TOTAL SALESPERSON	10			5,263.21	3,026.50	6,344.45	243.58	14,877.74
TOTAL SALES COMPANYWIDE				55,364.54	68,517.79	59,329.53	3,473.6	186,685.52

Figure 9–3
Output for REPORT WRITER
program.

234

2. There is to be a heading appearing on each page of the report starting on line 3 and reading:

SALES REPORT

(followed by a heading containing the date of the report).

JANUARY, 1985,

3. There is to be a subheading containing the sales information for each salesperson being reported. This line identifies the salesperson being reported on with the words:

SALES-SALESPERSON

and the salesperson's number, followed by column headings which identify the type of information being reported:

INVOICE NUMBER, CUSTOMER NUMBER, etc.

4. Following the subheading there will be one or more detail lines of information taken from the input records, along with a total calculated by the program.
5. At any time the salesperson number changes we are to print a footing which reports the total sales for the previous salesperson.
6. At the end of the report a line is to be printed to report the total of all sales.

The input to the program producing this report is a series of data records, each of which contains the information shown in Figure 9-4, as it is defined in an FD entry of the DATA DIVISION.

These data will be used to illustrate the elements of the REPORT WRITER feature as they are discussed.

In a program not using the REPORT WRITER feature, the heading, footing, and detail lines would probably be described in WORKING-STORAGE and the logic for deciding when each line would be produced would be written in the PROCEDURE DIVISION. These are logically simple tasks but they usually require many COBOL statements. For example, you may know that you want only 45 lines printed on a page. When not using the REPORT WRITER, you must describe a numeric line counter in WORKING STORAGE, initialize it to zero, increment it by one each time a line is printed, test to determine whether 45 lines have been printed and, if they have been, to start the entire process over. The report writer simplifies the writing of such tasks.

In the REPORT SECTION you will have RDs (report descriptions) which are similar to FDs (file descriptions). Each RD consists of two parts: the RD clause, which describes the general attributes of a report, and one or more 01 entries, which define the specific attributes of each type of line to be written.

In the RD you specify what you want each page to look like in general form. You decide how many lines are to be written on a page, on which lines the page is to begin and end, and other general characteristics.

The form of the RD for the toy program is shown in Figure 9-5.

We begin coding the RD entry by selecting a name for the report. This name is programmer supplied, must follow the rules for programmer-supplied names, and should be descriptive. In the illustrative program the report will be called

Figure 9–4
Input to the REPORT WRITER
program.

```
001F3500800163300002456004553000015530560001 83
001F351150055535000000000553000007453056003
001F3507700024560003576004550000045300560 06
001F3504500665240005630004553000025300560 07
001F3501900893710004560007863000058530560 13
001F3501010001453000155000555300000155005601 4
001F3502800753080002453005530500025530560 17
001F3508000255530002468000245300002550560 19
001F35132004452400000000000255000454505602 0
002F3508800445530035443004520000015500560 01
002F3504400000000005302004550000055300560 04
002F35066000245500015530024530000055605600 4
002F3513300652220022250002145000022305600 4
002F351210053324000530000000000000058056009
002F351100001455000414800966960001530056012
002F3508100555350001456005458300004530560 14
002F3500700062710001153000253000045530560 15
002F351460035458005500500003842000025505601 5
002F35018001679300024630022330000158305601 6
002F3502700789450003542005553000004553056016
002F35103000453000021530045530000553005601 6
002F3505600522580009750007543300006600560 17
003F350170051937000022500553200004586056002
003F351160055555001550000542300000577056004
003F3501600675600005303005530000078840560 05
003F3502600000010004530004553530002155056005
003F3508500553210002450004500200002550560 05
003F3504300962240004530004553000021550560 06
003F35006000333500025530021002000788505601 0
003F351230000000000025530000608000024505601 2
003F351060001453000153000553050000025056017
004F3507300022560002550003558600015600560 01
004F3511400553050005500007730000853005600 1
004F3500500086810002453003255300025530560 05
004F350420078554000245300455300001563056006
004F350520033669000153000456000015300560 05
004F35056003224400048040053006000003505600 6
004F351110001455000522600753530002753056006
004F3508700351580004586005530000015500560 07
004F35015000973500030550054533000255305600 8
004F3502500963520015302005553300058305600 8
004F351200055855000455300000000654505600 8
004F351390012522004500500021550000155056009
004F3514500324860074320000245300002150560 10
004F350950025855000245800755000007450560 12
004F3505400334570001530008530200002500560 13
004F3506200034450001457000145300002550550 13
004F350990002456000155000155530000250560 13
004F3508200532240002256007520000002250560 15
004F3513000744450002583000245500024550560 18
004F350590065542000486000025300000580056020
004F3510700024530001550004550000003250560 20
005F35072001235500021550001485000055305600 2
005F351110055236000000000885210007530560 02
005F3500400095015000215300303560002563056005
005F350780054235000458600500250004550560 05
005F351340065223002200500225530000253056005
005F350140001966000654100247530002253560 06
005F3502400750820015500005330200015530560 06
005F350900055525000547500853000001550560 06
005F351460055485550553000055630000021505600 6
005F351190052236003235800125000008520560 06
005F351420045555005520000021550000253056007
005F351440055635005353300024530000045305600 7
005F350500023378000215300775300001550560 08
005F35086003245600025580045500000253005600 8
005F350910054563003545600453000001530560 08
005F3509400155630000022005530000078300560 10
005F35098002456000155302563000024505601 1
005F351240045232000245500566530000025705601 1
```

Figure 9–4 (continued)

```
005F 3506 000865220001456000245300000220 56014
005F 3506 70002145000457500453300000245 056014
005F 3510 00000245000015500045530000253 0056014
005F 3512 60075532000255000530000000256 056014
005F 3512 90045532000215300225530005555 056017
005F 3504 10088654000453000453000001553 056019
006F 3500 30018852000225300255330000553 056003
006F 3504 80066744000153000712000001550 056004
006F 3507 60022235005830400021550005300 056004
006F 3551 30002445000145300126930002550 56004
006F 3514 00045533007520000214850000214 056004
006F 3504 00012345001563000545300001555 056007
006F 3504 90022556000143000785300001553 056007
006F 3513 70045533000255300215530000215 056007
006F 3501 30011522000256300430050000255 056009
006F 3503 90076518000254500455000005530 056011
006F 3509 60055542000345600455550007520 056012
006F 3509 20025563007552100455000000573 056015
006F 3510 20001553000155000453050005535 056015
006F 3512 70087855000215500134470003255 056015
006F 3510 50002145000145000552000074205 6019
006F 3514 7-055476007530000785830000255 056019
007F 3505 10034776000153000486300001550 056001
007F 3508 40032458000245800855300000253 56001
007F 3500 20079195000256300025300002550 056002
007F 3513 50055223000554500245500000255 56003
007F 3507 40002155000245800024550007200 056005
007F 3508 90045532001335800755000001550 056006
007F 3501 20036086000244500253000000000 56006
007F 3514 10055552400543200055530000255 056006
007F 3513 60045332000245500255300002550 056007
007F 3507 50003695009653000021450005550 056008
007F 3509 70003456000255300455300007686 056010
007F 3503 80000058000545300455300002565 056012
007F 3512 50025533000215300553000025500 56013
007F 3505 70054565000863000964300000730 056015
007F 3506 10088755000458600014530000000 056015
007F 3507 90032146000458600453060000255 56016
007F 3506 30002456000576000015300000255 056018
007F 3502 30063677001553000444000001553 056020
008F 3500 10003001000256300302450002553 056001
008F 3507 00000000000156500885500000256 056005
008F 3511 70085555000455200452000004500 056005
008F 3505 80085554000486000024660000257 056007
008F 3506 40002445000155000475800002450 56007
008F 3501 10083502000245500453000002550 056008
008F 3511 20044560002156005553000015500 56008
008F 3513 80000000005453000215500002152 15008
008F 3514 30055535007520000255330000245 50056008
008F 3505 30044355000214500553000000245 056010
008F 3503 70087533008631400455000005563 056013
008F 3508 30063324000258300453200000225 056016
008F 3509 30024563000022500553000005530 056016
008F 3510 80002155000255300455000003005 056016
008F 3512 80055445000215500132350005557 056016
008F 3502 20036741000443000253000001253 056018
008F 3510 40001455004530004785000000505 056018
009F 3507 10000000000455000430060000255 056004
009F 3501 00006890000246300545300002530 056005
009F 3510 90002155000245300696960004153 056005
009F 3511 80055555000558500542300004530 056006
009F 3508 60074566000256300530020005533 056016
009F 3502 10029039000456300C00000001556 056019
009F 3513 10054552000000003456004423 056019
010F 3504 70086324000453000788500001553 056005
010F 3502 00091250000245300002450004585 056006
010F 3504 60057440002530004553000055330 056006
010F 3506 80021450057830055330000255 056006
010F 3515 10032553004530000455000002550 56006
010F 3514 80035458005520800585220000553 056007
```

Figure 9–4 (continued)

```
010F35150005455500450000055300000214056007
010F35152003256300753000055300000000056009
010F35029001456300024530055003000788205601 0
010F35122005455300015600000002000045305601 0
010F35009000602100014530013300000258305601 3
010F35055000336800025300086330000025005601 6
010F35149005552400585500085233000024 5056018
```

Figure 9–5   **REPORT SECTION.**
The RD entry.   RD   TOY-SALES-REPORT
                        CONTROLS ARE FINAL, SALESPERSON
                        PAGE LIMIT IS 60 LINES
                        HEADING 2
                        FIRST DETAIL 6
                        LAST DETAIL 56
                        FOOTING 59.

TOY-SALES-REPORT. The statement begins in margin A with the report-name in margin B.

```
A    B
REPORT SECTION.
RD   TOY-SALES-REPORT
```

This is only part of the RD entry. Note that the word REPORT does not have to be part of the report-name; we could have called the report TOY-SALES, for example. Following the report-name are two additional clauses which we will use in this program. These are the CONTROLS ARE clause, and the PAGE LIMIT CLAUSE, which has five additional subparts.

The CONTROL clause will appear as:

```
CONTROL IS  control-name-1, control-name-2, etc.
```

or

```
CONTROLS  ARE  control-name-1, control-name-2, etc.
```

For example:

```
CONTROL IS FINAL, SALESPERSON
```

or

```
CONTROLS ARE FINAL, SALESPERSON
```

The word CONTROL or the word CONTROLS (with the optional use of IS or ARE) is followed by one or more control-names which define the control fields. These control-names are either data-names that are defined in the FILE SECTION or the word FINAL (a COBOL reserved word such as READ).

When you specify that a data-name is a control field, the REPORT WRITER feature will automatically check this field for a change in its value. A change indicates a control break and headings, footings, and so on will be printed. The data-names are for control breaks that appear throughout the report and the word FINAL indicates a break to occur when there is no more data. In this case FINAL refers to the end of the data file. When this condition arises, the report footings are to be printed.

In our sample program we want control headings and footings to print whenever there is a change in the salesperson number. The description of the input record (see Figure 9-4) shows that the data-name SALESPERSON has been used to describe salesperson number. There is one other control break which must also be specified. There is to be a footing printed at the very end of the report when every other line has been printed. In other words, one final line is to be written when there is nothing left to process. In a sense, the change from a situation where there are data to be processed to a situation where there are no data to be processed is a control break, which is specified by the word FINAL.

The REPORT SECTION to this point would then be:

```
REPORT SECTION
  RD  TOY-SALES-REPORT
      CONTROLS ARE FINAL, SALESPERSON
```

The example uses only two control fields but you may specify as many controls as required by the application you are writing. The order in which you specify controls is important. The first control-name listed is treated as the major control, the second control-name as the first intermediate, and so on until the last control-name listed, which is considered the minor field. If you specify the controls in the wrong order, you will get headings and/or footings printed at points other than those expected.

The next entry is the PAGE LIMIT clause and its subparts:

```
REPORT SECTION,
  RD TOY-SALES-REPORT
      CONTROLS ARE FINAL, SALESPERSON
      PAGE LIMIT IS 60 LINES
      HEADING 2
      FIRST DETAIL 6
      LAST DETAIL 56
      FOOTING 59
```

The purpose of this clause is to specify where certain lines will appear on the page. To recap some of the requirements of the example program:

1. The report heading INTERNATIONAL TOYS, INC, is to appear on the second line of the report.
2. The report footing, reporting company-wide sales totals, is to appear on the 59th line of the page.

The PAGE LIMIT clause specifies the maximum number of lines that may be printed on a page. Since the 59th line of the page will contain the report footing, there will be at least 59 lines printed on some pages. The PAGE LIMIT could be stated as 59 lines or any number greater than 59 but less than the page size (usually ranging from 60 to 66 lines depending on the printer you use). In the sample program the major reason for exercising page control is to keep the report from printing past the end of a page. The phrases LIMIT IS or LIMITS ARE are not required but certainly add readability. We could have written:

```
PAGE LIMITS ARE 60 LINE
```

or

```
PAGE LIMIT IS 60 LINES
```

or

```
PAGE 60 LINES
```

The HEADING entry will specify the line on which the *first* heading printed would appear. There may be several different types of headings printed, but this statement is to specify where only the first will appear. The first heading in the example program is INTERNATIONAL TOYS, INC. and it is to be printed on the second line of the first page. The entry would be:

```
PAGE LIMIT IS 60 LINES
     HEADING 2
```

The HEADING 2 indicates that the heading will appear on line 2 of the page. Note the additional indentation is optional. You might have coded this entry:

```
A   B
     PAGE LIMIT IS 60 LINES HEADING 2
```

The FIRST DETAIL entry specifies the line where the first data line will be printed. The detail line is a data line. It is the line on the printer which shows the values of the various items in the report (type 1 sales, type 2 sales, etc.). In the toy program the detail line is the one which comes after the heading

```
INVOICE    CUSTOMER    TYPE1    TYPE2    ETC.
NUMBER     NUMBER      SALES    SALES
```

You must count all report and page heading lines and any blank lines to be skipped to arrive at the position of the first detail line. You may specify any line as the first detail line so long as it is greater than the HEADING line. In the INTERNATIONAL TOYS, INC. program, we want the the first detail line to appear after all the headings have been printed. The point where detail lines will be printed can be computed as follows:

Report heading appears on line	2
Next two page heading lines	+2
Skip one line	+1
	5

The next available line (line 6) will be the line where the first detail will be printed and will be so specified as:

```
PAGE LIMIT IS 60 LINES
     HEADING 2
     FIRST DETAIL 6
```

Again the indentation improves readability and we strongly recommend that you use it. However, the clause could be written:

```
PAGE LIMIT IS 60 LINES   HEADING  2   DETAIL 6
```

If you look at the layout of the report (Figure 9-6) you will notice that the FIRST DETAIL line starts on line 8, not line 6. On line 6 you will see the first

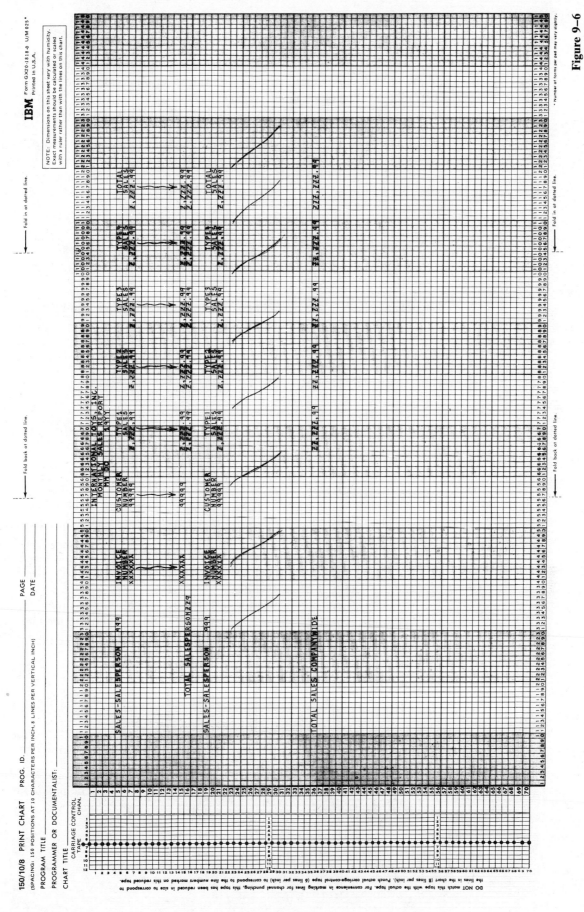

Figure 9–6
Report layout—toy company.

control heading, which starts SALES-SALESPERSON 001. This control heading will be printed only when there is a control break on salesperson number and it delays the printing of detail lines under those circumstances only. With the statement FIRST DETAIL 6 we are saying, in effect, ''put the first detail line on line 6 of every page unless a control heading must appear.''

The LAST DETAIL entry specifies where the last detail line is to appear on the page—not the last line, but the last detail or data line. You must decide where this line is to appear on the page and specify that no detail line is to appear after this point. In the toy program, you may compute the point where the last detail will appear:

Report footing appears on line	59
One line for last control footings	− 1
Skip one blank line between footings	− 1
	57

The next available line prior to line 57 (line 56) will be the last point where a detail line should appear. You would write the next entry then as:

```
PAGE LIMIT IS 60 LINES
     HEADING 2
     FIRST DETAIL 6
     LAST DETAIL 56
```

You may specify the LAST DETAIL anywhere prior to line 56 (but after line 6, where the first detail line appears, naturally). If you specify

```
FIRST DETAIL 25
LAST DETAIL  27
```

you would never print more than three detail lines per page. In addition, you would have headings and footings on the page. The programmer must decide, preferably with the help of the people who will use the report, what arrangement of lines is most useful and most aesthetically pleasing. For the purpose of our example problem, line 56 will suffice.

The FOOTING entry indicates the last line on which a footing may appear on any page of the report. The specifications dictate that the report footing be printed no later than the 59th line of the last page. For this reason we would add the following entry to the PAGE LIMIT clause:

```
PAGE LIMIT IS 60 LINES
     HEADING 2
     FIRST DETAIL 6
     LAST DETAIL 56
     FOOTING 59.
```

Note that the FOOTING clause ends with a period. This is because the RD entry is now complete. No other periods are allowed in the entry. The complete RD entry for the toy program is:

```
A    B
REPORT SECTION.
RD   TOY-SALES-REPORT
        CONTROLS ARE FINAL, SALESPERSON
        PAGE LIMIT IS 60 LINES
```

```
HEADING 2
FIRST DETAIL 6
LAST DETAIL 56
FOOTING 59.
```

There is another clause which can be used under the RD. This is the CODE clause. The CODE is used when you have more than one report being produced by your program and the report is to be printed off line. Off-line processing will use this code to see that this report is printed in the proper order and is not "mixed up" with lines from other reports. This clause will be used with very complex programs. Should you decide, after writing a few relatively simple REPORT WRITER programs, to develop a program which produces multiple reports, you may find this clause useful. We will not treat it in this text.

We have now described the report in general terms indicating where the various headings, data lines, and footings will appear without indicating specifically what any one of the lines will look like. A series of 01 entries after the RD entry will be used to describe the various lines of print.

SECTION 9
The 01 Entries in the REPORT WRITER

There may be many 01-level entries associated with a single RD entry. Each 01 may have, and usually will have, several lower-level entries describing the detail of a single line to be printed or a series of lines which are of similar type. The basic rules for assigning level numbers are the same as in other entries in the FILE SECTION and the WORKING-STORAGE-SECTION. The use of level 01 indicates a group description, level numbers 02-49 indicate elementary level descriptions, and each 02 or lower level may be further broken down by other level numbers of greater magnitude. For example,

```
01  REPORT-LINE
    02  REPORT-PARTS.
        03  ITEM-1          PICTURE X.
        03  ITEM-2          PICTURE X.
    02 etc.
```

Many of the clauses (COBOL reserved words) you have already studied may be used in the REPORT WRITER, and they perform the same function as in regular COBOL programming. These clauses are:

```
PICTURE
USAGE
BLANK WHEN ZERO
JUSTIFIED
VALUE
```

Some clauses which are used only in the REPORT SECTION are:

```
TYPE
LINE
COLUMN
```

```
GROUP

SOURCE

SUM
```

Each of these will be discussed in turn. Each serves a specific purpose in describing the exact characteristics of the line(s) to be written. Perhaps at this point we should list the specific type of things that might be important in describing a report line. Some may be stated in the form of questions:

What type of line is it?

Is it a heading? Footing?

Should it be reported when there is a control break(s)?

Where should the line appear on the page?

Should it follow on the next line or should lines be skipped?

Should it appear at the top of a page?

What items of data make up the line?

Is it made up of literals?

If not, where do the data making up each line come from?

In which column should I put each of the data-items?

In non-REPORT WRITER programs you handle many of these tasks in the PROCEDURE DIVISION. In REPORT WRITER programs, you handle them in the REPORT SECTION of the DATA DIVISION.

Each 01 that you write in the REPORT SECTION is the description of a report group: for example, one or more lines that are to be printed together as a group. In the FILE SECTION an 01 only describes one line to be written. Since headings and footings may consist of more than one line, the REPORT WRITER feature allows these items to be grouped.

Each 01 must answer the question "What type of line (or lines) is this?" This question is answered by the TYPE clause. The various TYPEs are:

```
01 TYPE IS REPORT HEADING.

01 TYPE IS PAGE HEADING.

01 TYPE IS CONTROL HEADING FINAL and/or data-name-1.

01 TYPE IS DETAIL.

01 TYPE IS CONTROL FOOTING FINAL and/or data-name-1.

01 TYPE IS PAGE FOOTING.

01 TYPE IS REPORT FOOTING.
```

Although we do not recommend their use, the foregoing entries have abbreviations: REPORT HEADING as RH, PAGE HEADING as PH, CONTROL HEADING as CH, DETAIL as DE, CONTROL FOOTING as CF, PAGE FOOTING as PF, and REPORT FOOTING as RF.

Note also that only two of the entries, CONTROL HEADING and CONTROL FOOTING, have variable entries. These data-items (FINAL, data-name-1, data-name-2, etc.) are used to control when the CONTROL HEADING and CONTROL FOOTING are printed. That is, a change in the value of the data-item specified will cause the CONTROL HEADING and/or the CONTROL FOOTING to be printed. When there are no more data to be read, it is a signal for FINAL, and the CONTROL HEADING and/or CONTROL FOOTINGS will be printed. More about this will be included in the PROCEDURE DIVISION entries.

If your report is to have a report heading then you must have the 01 TYPE IS REPORT HEADING entry. If you do not desire a report heading merely omit this entry. The same applies to each of the types. In the toy program we are going to use all of them except the PAGE FOOTING.

In addition to stating the TYPE, such as REPORT HEADING, you will also need to indicate where this type of line is to appear in the report. Usually the words themselves indicate the overall position of the line. A REPORT HEADING should come as the first item in the report and a REPORT FOOTING will be the last. However, in addition to knowing that a REPORT HEADING will come at the beginning, you need to specify on what line at the beginning of the report. This is done with the LINE NUMBER entry which is a part of the TYPE entry. The general form of the LINE NUMBER entry is:

$$\underline{\text{LINE}} \text{ NUMBER IS } \begin{Bmatrix} \text{integer-1[ON NEXT PAGE]} \\ \text{PLUS integer-2} \end{Bmatrix}$$

With the form LINE NUMBER IS integer you specify exactly where you want the line to appear on the page. If you had

    LINE NUMBER IS 5

the specified line will appear on line 5 of that page.

Generally the computer installation will define a computer output page as having 60 lines on which you can print. The actual size of the page is usually 66 lines (which is 11 inches long). The first 3 lines of the page are not used and the last 3 lines of the page are also skipped (with the use of a carriage control tape). When we have LINE NUMBER IS 5 it is with respect to the 60 available lines on which we may print. Recall that as part of the RD entry you have an entry PAGE LIMIT IS 60. The PAGE LIMIT IS 60 limits the number of lines that you want to print regardless of the computer center restrictions unless you attempt to print a greater number than is defined by the carriage control device of the printer. So long as you are under the computer center defined limits, there is no problem.

With the LINE NUMBER IS PLUS integer you specify that you want the line to appear the specified number of lines down from where the last line was printed. LINE NUMBER IS PLUS 3 indicates 3 lines down from the last printed material. The PLUS option is referred to as a relative numbering system. It is relative to where you were, rather than to a specific point on the page.

The use of the LINE NUMBER IS NEXT PAGE option is somewhat restricted. You may *not* use this option if the TYPE of the line being described is REPORT HEADING, PAGE HEADING, or PAGE FOOTING. When used with any other TYPE line it will cause the line to be printed on the next page. The position on the next page depends on the TYPE specified.

The report heading description is still not complete. The TYPE and LINE NUMBER have been described, but the question "What items of data make up this line?" remains to be answered. Our heading is to print the literal INTERNATIONAL TOYS, INC. centered on the page. In order to center these words on a 133 position print line, the literal must begin about column 56. In a regular COBOL program, you would begin by defining a FILLER of 55 spaces. In REPORT WRITER, this is not necessary. Any undefined positions will be padded with blanks. The entry to define this literal in our program will use the COLUMN clause, which has the general form:

    COLUMN NUMBER IS integer-1

For example:

```
COLUMN NUMBER IS 56.
```

We now have enough information to describe the REPORT HEADING.

Example 1

```
01   TYPE IS REPORT HEADING
     LINE NUMBER IS 2.
     02 COLUMN 56 PICTURE X(24)
        VALUE IS "INTERNATIONAL TOYS, INC.".
```

Notice that the use of the value clause is the same as in any other COBOL program. It simply spells out the literal to be used. Also, there is no definition of the 56 positions (including carriage control) which precede the literal or the 53 positions which follow it. Since they are undefined, they are assumed to be blank and will print out as spaces on the printer. Unfortunately, the COLUMN option is not allowed in the FILE-SECTION or WORKING-STORAGE SECTION.

It was not really necessary to describe the 02 level in this case, since there was only one data-item or literal on the line. The entry could have been handled exclusively at the 01 level as:

Example 2

```
01 TYPE IS REPORT HEADING
   LINE IS 2
   COLUMN 56
   PICTURE X(24) VALUE IS "INTERNATIONAL TOYS,INC.".
```

Notice in the preceding example (1) that the 01 and 02 entries both have periods after them. In Example 2 there is only one period at the end. All of the entry could have been placed on one line of code if it would fit. Example 3 is equivalent to Example 1 and Example 2 above.

Example 3

```
01   TYPE IS REPORT HEADING LINE IS 2 COLUMN 54
        PICTURE X(24) VALUE IS "INTERNATIONAL TOYS,INC.".
```

In addition to the report heading, we want our document to contain page headings. On the top of each page we wish to have the words (centered):

```
MONTHLY SALES REPORT
    MONTH, 19YR
```

For this two-line heading you need to know the month for which the report is being written and the year. Both the month and the year will be determined from the first input record from a variable known as PROCESSING-DATE (see Figure 9-4), which is moved to DATES in WORKING-STORAGE where MONTH and YEAR are described.

The date information is available only in the first input record so that after the first data record is read, the information is passed (MOVEd) to WORKING-STORAGE and saved there through the rest of the program. More about this when we get to the PROCEDURE DIVISION entries.

To begin the description of the page heading we have:

```
01 TYPE PAGE HEADING,
```

The LINE NUMBER is not specified since there are two lines in this heading. Each line will be described in separate 02-level entries, which will have the LINE NUMBER option. The first 02 presents very little problem since it is very similar to the REPORT HEADING entry seen earlier:

```
01   TYPE PAGE HEADING,
   02   LINE NUMBER IS 3
        COLUMN 56
        PICTURE A(20)
        VALUE IS "MONTHLY SALES REPORT",
```

The description of the second line of this page heading requires three data-items:

1. the literal ",19", the first part of the year data
2. the year, in numeric form
3. the month in alphabetic form, not numeric

The year will be read from the first input record. The "19" is a literal. The name of the month is not part of the input data. Only the numeric equivalent of the month is a part of the input record. In order to convert the number to a month name, a table of alphabetic months should be coded in the WORKING-STORAGE SECTION as illustrated in Figure 9-7.

Thus, if the MONTH from the first data input is 2, then the variable MONTHTABLE (MONTH) will be ''FEBRUARY''.

With this information we can code the entry for the second part of the page heading as:

```
02   LINE IS PLUS 1,
   03   COLUMN 57   PICTURE X(9)   SOURCE IS
        MONTHTABLE (MONTH),
   03   COLUMN 67 PICTURE X(4) VALUE IS ",19",
   03   COLUMN 71 PICTURE 99 SOURCE IS YEAR,
```

Note the first 03 is coded:

```
03   COLUMN 57 PICTURE X(9) SOURCE IS MONTHTABLE (MONTH),
```

which incorporates a new clause, SOURCE IS.

The SOURCE IS clause is similar to the VALUE IS clause except the SOURCE IS clause causes the variable information to be moved from the data-name that follows the clause to the PICTURE (in this case X(9)) that precedes it. The VALUE IS transfers information only once and is constant whereas the SOURCE IS clause will cause whatever variable information that is stored to be moved. When the

Figure 9–7
Table of month names.

```
01  MONTHS-OF-THE-YEAR.
    02 ALL-THE-MONTHS.
       03 FILLER PIC A(9) VALUE '  JANUARY'.
       03 FILLER PIC A(9) VALUE ' FEBRUARY'.
       03 FILLER PIC A(9) VALUE '    MARCH'.
       03 FILLER PIC A(9) VALUE '    APRIL'.
       03 FILLER PIC A(9) VALUE '      MAY'.
       03 FILLER PIC A(9) VALUE '     JUNE'.
       03 FILLER PIC A(9) VALUE '     JULY'.
       03 FILLER PIC A(9) VALUE '   AUGUST'.
       03 FILLER PIC A(9) VALUE 'SEPTEMBER'.
       03 FILLER PIC A(9) VALUE '  OCTOBER'.
       03 FILLER PIC A(9) VALUE ' NOVEMBER'.
       03 FILLER PIC A(9) VALUE ' DECEMBER'.
    02 MONTHLIST REDEFINES ALL-THE-MONTHS.
       03 MONTHTABLE OCCURS 12 TIMES PIC A(9).
```

subscript MONTH [MONTHTABLE (MONTH)] has a different value, then the new month name would be transferred to the PICTURE X(9). It is as if the value of the item is a function of where the SOURCE IS variable is pointing.

The second 03 is:

```
03  COLUMN 67 PICTURE X(4) VALUE IS ", 19".
```

The value stored in the PICTURE X(4) will be ", 19" and will not change as the program runs.

The third 03 is:

```
03  COLUMN 71 PICTURE 99 SOURCE IS YEAR.
```

The value to be stored in the PICTURE 99 is a function of what is stored in the variable YEAR. If the value of the variable YEAR should change then the value of this item would also change.

The COLUMN part of each entry indicates where the information is to be written across the line. The columns not specified will automatically be blank.

This completes the definition of the page heading. The complete entry looks like:

```
01  TYPE PAGE HEADING.
    02 LINE IS 3 COLUMN 56
       PICTURE A(20)
       VALUE 'MONTHLY SALES REPORT'.
    02 LINE IS PLUS 1.
       03 COLUMN 57 PIC X(19)
          VALUE 'SALES-SALESPERSON'.
       03 COLUMN 67 PIC X(4)
          VALUE ', 19'.
       03 COLUMN 71 PIC 99
          SOURCE IS YEAR.
```

Up to this point we have described the report heading and the page heading. Before the actual data are printed in our toy program we desire some additional heading lines, primarily for column headings. These are:

```
SALES-SALESPERSON ...nnn INVOICE CUSTOMER TYPE1 TYPE2 etc.
                         NUMBER   NUMBER   SALES SALES
```

We want this heading to be printed before any data lines are written and also before the detail for each new salesperson. Whenever the data change from one salesperson to another, the heading needs to be printed. This requires that the data be in sequence (sorted) before we run this program. The data could be sorted by hand, by a card sorter, by a utility package, or by the COBOL SORT procedure described in Chapter 8.

This column heading is controlled by a change in the data-name SALESPERSON or by beginning the report. It is therefore a CONTROL HEADING and you would have the following entry.

```
01   TYPE CONTROL HEADING SALESPERSON.
```

The phrase TYPE CONTROL HEADING indicates the type of line to be written. The phrase SALESPERSON specifies the name of the control field. Any time there is a change in this control field, a new control heading will be written. Anytime you have a TYPE CONTROL HEADING or a TYPE CONTROL FOOTING, you must also specify the name of the field on which the control breaks.

You may have more than one control heading and/or more than one control footing in a report. If you do, you must place the descriptions for control headings in descending order of importance, from major to minor. Conversely, you must describe control footings in ascending order, from minor to major.

The complete description for the two-line control headings in the example program is given in Figure 9-8.

In Figure 9-8 there is only one SOURCE IS entry on the line descriptions. This is:

```
03   COLUMN 30 PICTURE 999 SOURCE IS SALESPERSON.
```

This means the salesperson's number will come from the data-name SALES-PERSON, which in this case is a part of the input record.

Figure 9–8
CONTROL HEADING entry.

```
01 TYPE CONTROL HEADING SALESPERSON.
   02 LINE IS PLUS 3.
      03 COLUMN 10  PIC X(19)  VALUE 'SALES-SALESPERSON'.
      03 COLUMN 30  PIC 999    SOURCE SALESPERSON.
      03 COLUMN 39  PIC X(7)   VALUE 'INVOICE'.
      03 COLUMN 53  PIC X(8)   VALUE 'CUSTOMER'.
      03 COLUMN 68  PIC X(5)   VALUE 'TYPE1'.
      03 COLUMN 80  PIC X(5)   VALUE 'TYPE2'.
      03 COLUMN 92  PIC X(5)   VALUE 'TYPE3'.
      03 COLUMN 104 PIC X(5)   VALUE 'TYPE4'.
      03 COLUMN 115 PIC X(5)   VALUE 'TOTAL'.
   02 LINE IS PLUS 1.
      03 COLUMN 40  PIC X(6)   VALUE 'NUMBER'.
      03 COLUMN 54  PIC X(6)   VALUE 'NUMBER'.
      03 COLUMN 68  PIC X(5)   VALUE 'SALES'.
      03 COLUMN 80  PIC X(5)   VALUE 'SALES'.
      03 COLUMN 92  PIC X(5)   VALUE 'SALES'.
      03 COLUMN 104 PIC X(5)   VALUE 'SALES'.
      03 COLUMN 115 PIC X(5)   VALUE 'SALES'.
```

SECTION 10
Developing Totals—Manual Methods and the Sum Clause

The INTERNATIONAL TOYS program requires the printing of a detail line listing certain important information about each of the input records processed. There will be one of these detail lines written for each input record. Really these detail lines represent the basic data for the report. All the other headings and footing lines are just to make the report more readable and to present the information in a more understandable form.

In the CONTROL HEADING entry, provision was made for appropriate headings for the information to be reported. These items of information are:

invoice number

customer number

type1 sales

type2 sales

type3 sales

type4 sales

total sales (per invoice for all types of toys)

All these data-items, except the invoice total, are available in the input record. In order to accumulate the invoice total, the four types of sales must be added together. There is a feature of the REPORT WRITER that provides for automatic accumulation of totals, but this feature (the SUM clause) may be used only when the TYPE of line being described is CONTROL FOOTING. Since the detail line does not meet this requirement, provision must be made in the PROCEDURE DIVISION simply to add the appropriate fields together as each record is read. This may be accomplished using either an ADD or COMPUTE statement. The receiving field of the computation will then be available to the REPORT WRITER as the SOURCE of the invoice total. In the sample program, an area called DETAIL-LINE-TOTAL with a PICTURE of 9(7)V99 is defined in the WORKING-STORAGE SECTION.

In the REPORT SECTION we describe the lines to be printed. In the PROCEDURE DIVISION we will issue the commands that read the data and cause the report to be printed.

Keep in mind that headings and footings are printed by the REPORT SECTION whereas the data to be read and the detail lines written are controlled by the PROCEDURE DIVISION. This distinction will be developed more fully later in the chapter.

The entry to define the detail line may now be written.

```
01  LINE-OF-DATA TYPE IS DETAIL LINE PLUS 1.
     02 COLUMN 39 PIC X(6)   SOURCE IS INVOICE.
     02 COLUMN 54 PIC 9(5)   SOURCE IS CUSTOMER.
     02 TYPE1-DETAIL COLUMN 64   PIC ZZ,ZZZ.99
             SOURCE IS TYPE1.
     02 TYPE2-DETAIL COLUMN 76   PIC ZZ,ZZZ.99
             SOURCE IS TYPE2.
     02 TYPE3-DETAIL COLUMN 88   PIC ZZ,ZZZ.99
             SOURCE IS TYPE3.
     02 TYPE4-DETAIL COLUMN 100 PIC ZZ,ZZZ.99
             SOURCE IS TYPE4.
     02 LINE-TOTAL COLUMN 111      PIC ZZ,ZZZ.99
             SOURCE DETAIL-LINE-TOTAL.
```

You will notice that, for the first time, some of the entries have been assigned names. The `01` entry has a record-name `LINE-OF-DATA`. This is programmer-created. Note that none of the previous `01` entries had a record-name but they could have, had we so desired. The reason for adding names is to be able to refer to this particular line whenever we desire to do so in the `PROCEDURE DIVISION`. The third `02` entry:

```
02   TYPE1-DETAIL COLUMN  64   PICTURE ZZ,ZZZ,99
             SOURCE IS TYPE1,
```

has an element-name `TYPE1-DETAIL`. We could have added element-names to all of the `02`'s, `03`'s, etc. in the previous report heading and page heading. The reason for using the element-name in this case is that we will have reason to refer to this data-item either in the `REPORT SECTION` or in the `PROCEDURE DIVISION`. The reason `TYPE1-DETAIL,TYPE2-DETAIL`, `TYPE3-DETAIL`, `TYPE4-DETAIL`, and `LINE-TOTAL` were assigned names is that the information reported in these positions in the detail line are to be used again. They are to be totaled so that each salesperson's total sales may be reported.

The detail line will be printed for each invoice number. If saleperson number 1 had nine sales, he or she would have nine invoices and nine detail lines detailed in the report. Following these lines would be the salesperson's total line:

```
TOTAL SALESPERSON 1   3,770,54  226,93  3,840,33 etc.
```

This line is called a *control footing* because it is controlled by a change in the value of the data-item `SALESPERSON`. For each salesperson we should have:

1. column headings (`TYPE IS CONTROL HEADING`)
2. all detail lines for this salesperson (`TYPE IS DETAIL`)
3. totals for this sales person (`TYPE IS CONTROL FOOTING`)

The control footing, printed on the occurrence of any change in the salesperson number, consists of a series of totals, one for each type of sale and one for the total of all invoices since the previous control break. In order to accumulate these totals, the `SUM` clause will be used.

The `SUM` clause, which may be used only with a `TYPE CONTROL FOOTING` description, has the following general form:

```
SUM  data-name-1, data-name-2, etc.
```

For example:

```
02   TYPE1-TOTAL COLUMN 63 PICTURE ZZ,ZZZ,99 SUM TYPE1,
```

When you list one or more data-names after the word `SUM`, these data-items will be added to an accumulator each time the data-name is changed. On any control break where the control footing (of which the `SUM` clause is a part) is written, the accumulator will be reset to zero after it is written and the process will be started again. To illustrate, the toy program requires a control footing (each time there is a change in salesperson number), which will reflect the total sales for a particular salesperson by type of sale and in total. The detail of this information is described in the entry having the data-name `LINE-OF-DATA` and including the data-items called `TYPE1-DETAIL`, `TYPE2-DETAIL`, `TYPE3-DETAIL`, `TYPE4-DETAIL`, and `LINE-TOTAL`. The first total to be developed is to be composed of all the individual amounts in `TYPE1-DETAIL` since the last control break. The second total is to be the sum of all the TYPE2-DETAILS since the last break, and so on. In order to write the entry, it is first necessary to write the TYPE statement. It is:

```
01  TYPE CONTROL FOOTING SALESPERSON.
```

Note that in the CONTROL FOOTING entry it is necessary to state what the control field is (SALESPERSON in this case). It is also necessary that the data-name stated be included in the CONTROLS ARE clause of the RD. The entry to describe the line which follows the detail lines is:

```
01  TYPE CONTROL FOOTING SALESPERSON LINE PLUS 1.
    02 COLUMN 17 PIC X(22) VALUE 'TOTAL SALESPERSON'.
    02 COLUMN 34 PIC ZZZ SOURCE SALESPERSON-OLD.
    02 TYPE1-TOTAL COLUMN 63 PIC ZZZ,ZZZ.99 SUM TYPE1.
    02 TYPE2-TOTAL COLUMN 75 PIC ZZZ,ZZZ.99 SUM TYPE2.
    02 TYPE3-TOTAL COLUMN 87 PIC ZZZ,ZZZ.99 SUM TYPE3.
    02 TYPE4-TOTAL COLUMN 99 PIC ZZZ,ZZZ.99 SUM TYPE4.
    02 TOTAL-TOTAL COLUMN 110 PIC Z,ZZZ,ZZZ.99
           SUM DETAIL-LINE-TOTAL.
```

Once again, the entries have been assigned names because the program must develop a grand total of all sales. This will be done by adding the totals just described (TYPE1-TOTAL, etc.) to another accumulator each time the line described above is written. This will be effected through the description of the next CONTROL FOOTING, which will look like:

```
01  TYPE CONTROL FOOTING FINAL.
    02 LINE IS 59.
        03 COLUMN 10 PIC X(23) VALUE 'TOTAL SALES
 =             COMPANYWIDE'.
        03 COLUMN 62 PIC Z,ZZZ,ZZZ.99 SUM TYPE1-TOTAL.
        03 COLUMN 74 PIC Z,ZZZ,ZZZ.99 SUM TYPE2-TOTAL.
        03 COLUMN 86 PIC Z,ZZZ,ZZZ.99 SUM TYPE3-TOTAL.
        03 COLUMN 98 PIC Z,ZZZ,ZZZ.99 SUM TYPE4-TOTAL.
        03 COLUMN 109 PIC Z,ZZZ,ZZZ.99 SUM TOTAL-TOTAL.
```

The difference between this control footing and the previous one is that they are keyed by different controls. The first will print each time there is a change in the salesperson number. The second, shown above with the control listed as FINAL, will print only when the report is completed and all other lines printed. The FINAL control break is caused by a particular PROCEDURE DIVISION instruction which will be discussed later. You will notice that the SUM statements in the last control footing accumulate the total of some data-items that are themselves created by SUM statements in the first control footing. This is permissible. The data elements SUMmed may appear anywhere in the DATA DIVISION. But remember the SUM statement may be used only in a TYPE CONTROL FOOTING description.

SECTION 11
FILE SECTION Entries in the
ENVIRONMENT DIVISION

The special REPORT WRITER DATA DIVISION ENTRIES are now complete. The RD has been written to reflect the general attributes of the report and a series of associated 01 entries show the specific nature of each report line or each set of lines. The RD does not describe a *file,* however. But it is still necessary to write a FILE SECTION entry to describe the physical file on which the report will be written. In addition to the clauses you have used before in FD entries, you will have one which has not been discussed in the earlier chapters because it is used only in conjunction with the REPORT WRITER feature. This is the REPORT IS clause. The purpose of this clause is to identify a given report-name (the name assigned in the RD entry) as being the report to be written on the file described. For our program:

```
FD   PRINTED-OUTPUT
     RECORD CONTAINS 133 CHARACTERS
     LABEL RECORDS ARE OMITTED
     REPORT IS TOY-SALES-REPORT.
```

The last line, REPORT IS TOY-SALES-REPORT, ties the various lines which the REPORT SECTION described to the output file PRINTED-OUTPUT. This FD entry for the REPORT WRITER does not have any 01 entries with it to describe a line of output because the lines are described in the REPORT SECTION under the RD entries.

Finally, as always, the DATA DIVISION FD must be tied back to an ENVIRON-MENT DIVISION entry. For our program this would be:

```
INPUT-OUTPUT SECTION.
FILE-CONTROL.
     SELECT INPUT-RECORD ASSIGN TO INFILE.
     SELECT PRINTED-OUTPUT ASSIGN TO PRINTER.
```

SECTION 12
PROCEDURE DIVISION Entries

Most of the features of REPORT WRITER are found in the DATA DIVISION. Most of the actual writing of lines is handled by the REPORT WRITER and does not require action on the part of the programmer. Actually, there are only four PROCEDURE DIVISION commands which the REPORT WRITER uses. They are:

USE AFTER REPORTING identifier (used in conjunction with DECLARATIVES discussed below)

INITIATE report-name-1, report-name-2, etc.

GENERATE identifier (detail-line-name)

TERMINATE report-name-1, report-name-2, etc.

DECLARATIVES

DECLARATIVES are specialized statements that are invoked automatically when certain specific kinds of conditions are encountered. The use of DECLARATIVES is not limited to REPORT WRITER applications but, because such applications represent a major use for declaratives, we will discuss:

- the general characteristics of DECLARATIVES;
- using DECLARATIVES to suppress reporting of certain REPORT WRITER lines;
- using DECLARATIVES in non-REPORT WRITER situations.

DECLARATIVES are regular COBOL statements that are executed only when specific conditions are encountered during execution of the program. These statements must be included in a special DECLARATIVES section, which *must* be the first section in the PROCEDURE DIVISION of the program. Each DECLARATIVE (each set of statements relating to a special set of conditions) must be in a separate SECTION of code. The general format of the DECLARATIVE section is:

```
PROCEDURE DIVISION.
DECLARATIVES.
section-name SECTION.   {USE BEFORE REPORTING identifier.}
                        {other non-report-writer statements.}
paragraph-name.
     {sentences        }
     {SUPPRESS PRINTING}
· · · · · · · · · · · · · · · · ·
END DECLARATIVES.
```

Suppose that you may have a situation in which there are "empty sets" in the data to be reported. In the toy reporting problem we are working with, for example, there may be salespeople who have no sales during a reporting period (because of vacations, for example) and, even though we want to report zero sales for these people on the detail line, it doesn't make much sense to also report that their total sales are also zero. We may use DECLARATIVES to suppress the printing of the control footing which reports total sales. Recall the DATA DIVISION entry which defined this line:

```
01   TYPE CONTROL FOOTING SALESPERSON LINE PLUS 1.
     02 COLUMN 17 PIC X(22) VALUE 'TOTAL SALESPERSON'.
     02 COLUMN 34 PIC ZZZ.................
               0
               0
               0
     02 TOTAL-TOTAL COLUMN 110 PIC Z,ZZZ,ZZ.99
          SUM DETAIL-LINE-TOTAL.
```

To use the declaratives we must identify the control footing so we will provide a data-name for the line:

```
01   SALESPERSON-TOTAL TYPE CONTROL FOOTING
          SALESPERSON LINE PLUS 1.
     02 COLUMN 17 PIC X(22) VALUE 'TOTAL SALESPERSON'.
     02 COLUMN 34 PIC ZZZ.................
               0
               0
               0
     02 TOTAL-TOTAL COLUMN 110 PIC Z,ZZZ,ZZ.99
          SUM DETAIL-LINE-TOTAL.
```

Next the DECLARATIVES section of the PROCEDURE DIVISION will be written:

```
PROCEDURE DIVISION.
DECLARATIVES.
DELETE-ZERO-TOTALS SECTION.
    USE BEFORE REPORTING SALESPERSON-TOTAL.
CONDITIONS-FOR-NOT-REPORTING.
    IF TOTAL-TOTAL IS EQUAL TO ZERO
        SUPPRESS PRINTING
END DECLARATIVES.
```

Notice that the USE BEFORE REPORTING clause appears immediately after the section heading. This verb does not appear in the formal logic sequence of your program, but it operates as if it is included within that section of the code that causes a total line (the one we have named SALESPERSON-TOTAL) to print. Each time SALESPERSON-TOTAL is to be printed, the logic included in the section DELETE-TOTALS SECTION will be executed. All statements other than the USE BEFORE REPORTING statement must be grouped under a separate paragraph heading or a group of separate paragraph headings. The SUPPRESS PRINTING clause is a special-purpose clause for use with the REPORT WRITER feature. As its name implies, it suppresses the print line named in the USE BEFORE REPORTING statement if all conditions included in the sentence in which it appears are met.

You may use multiple DECLARATIVES but each must be included in a separately named SECTION and the END DECLARATIVES statement must follow the last one. You may incorporate any COBOL statements which are necessary to achieve your programming objective—there is no limit to the length of the SECTION. When used in conjunction with REPORT WRITER the USE BEFORE REPORTING clause must be included with in the DECLARATIVE. There are, however, other non-REPORT WRITER uses for DECLARATIVES.

Using DECLARATIVES *for* INVALID KEY *and End of File*

In the general format for DECLARATIVES given before, the non-REPORT WRITER entries were grouped together so we could devote our attention to REPORT WRITER topics. You may use the DECLARATIVES to specify procedures to be followed in the event an error condition is encountered during I/O operations. Indeed, if you fail to include required INVALID KEY or AT END clauses, you *must* include one or more DECLARATIVES incorporating USE statements. The complete general format for DECLARATIVES is:

```
PROCEDURE DIVISION.
DECLARATIVES.
section-name SECTION.
    USE BEFORE REPORTING identifier
```

$$\text{USE \underline{AFTER} STANDARD} \begin{Bmatrix} \underline{\text{EXCEPTION}} \\ \underline{\text{ERROR}} \end{Bmatrix} \underline{\text{PROCEDURE}} \begin{Bmatrix} \text{file-name-1} \\ \text{[file-name-n]} \\ \underline{\text{INPUT}} \\ \underline{\text{OUTPUT}} \\ \underline{\text{I/O}} \end{Bmatrix}$$

Procedures included under a DECLARATIVES section which includes a USE AFTER ERROR (or EXCEPTION) clause would be executed if an error condition were encountered:

• in a file	if you specify a file-name
• in any of several files	if you specify more than one file
• in any file OPENed as INPUT	if you specify INPUT in the USE statement
• in any file OPENed as OUTPUT	if you specify OUTPUT in the USE statement
• in any file OPENed as I/O	if you specify I/O in the USE statement.

For example:

```
PROCEDURE DIVISION,
DECLARATIVES,
DELETE-FAILURE SECTION,
    USE AFTER ERROR PROCEDURE ON EMPLOYEE-MASTER,
INACTIVE-RECORD-ON-DELETE,
    DISPLAY 'NO RECORD FOR EMPLOYEE ' WS-EMPLOYEE-NUMBER
            ' ON ATTEMPT TO DELETE RECORD',
END-OF-FILE SECTION,
    USE AFTER EXCEPTION PROCEDURE ON INPUT,
END-OF-FILE-CONDITION,
    DISPLAY 'END OF FILE ERROR CONDITION',
    DISPLAY EMPLOYEE-NUMBER OF INPUT-RECORD-SAVED,
    CLOSE INFILE OUTFILE PRINTFILE,
    STOP RUN,
END DECLARATIVES,
```

Other REPORT WRITER PROCEDURE DIVISION *Commands*

The INITIATE command starts the automatic features of the report. All summation counters are initialized at zero. All report headings, page headings, and control headings are printed. Report-name-1 is the name of the report given in the RD entry—TOY-SALES-REPORT for the toy program. You may specify a series of report names if your program produces several reports.

The DETAIL lines are written with the GENERATE statement. To illustrate the use of the INITIATE, GENERATE, and TERMINATE commands let's look at part of the PROCEDURE DIVISION of the toy program.

```
PROCEDURE DIVISION,
START-UP,
    OPEN INPUT INPUT-RECORD, OUTPUT PRINTED-OUTPUT,
    READ INPUT-RECORD, AT END MOVE 6 TO STOP-SWITCH,
    MOVE PROCESSING-DATE TO DATES,
    INITIATE TOY-SALES-REPORT,
```

Notice that there are three regular COBOL statements before the INITIATE statement.

```
OPEN INPUT INPUT-RECORD, OUTPUT PRINTED-OUTPUT,
```

opens the files to be used in the program. This statement is the same as in a non-REPORT WRITER program and is necessary because the INITIATE statement does not OPEN files. The files opened are defined in the FD's. Note that RD names are *not* opened.

READ INPUT-RECORD, AT END MOVE 6 TO STOP-SWITCH, accesses a single input record. The reason that this statement appears before the INITIATE command is that certain information to be used in the headings is available to the REPORT WRITER when the first record is accessed.

You may recall that when the page heading description was written, we specified the SOURCE of the date information to be written as MONTH and YEAR. These fields do not appear as part of the input record description but as a part of WORKING-STORAGE. The reason for handling these items in this particular way is to avoid including the current date with every input record. In this way, the date need appear only on the first input record. The MOVE then makes the information available in the form specified in the page heading description.

```
INITIATE TOY-SALES-REPORT
```

causes all headings to be readied for printing. The actual writing of the line does not occur until either a detail line is generated or the report is terminated. Once you have written an INITIATE command, you may consider the headings written. It is the GENERATE statement that actually causes a detail line to be written. If any control breaks occur, a set of control footings (if any have been specified) for any previously generated detail lines will be written and a set of headings (if any have been specified) for the detail line causing the break will be written before the actual printing of the detail line takes place.

Now let's look at the rest of the PROCEDURE DIVISION.

```
PROCEDURE DIVISION.
START-UP.
    OPEN INPUT INPUT-RECORD OUTPUT PRINTED-OUTPUT.
    READ INPUT-RECORD AT END MOVE 6 TO STOP-SWITCH.
    INITIATE TOY-SALES-REPORT.
    PERFORM REPORT-ROUTINE
        UNTIL STOP-SWITCH > 1.
    TERMINATE TOY-SALES-REPORT.
    CLOSE INPUT-RECORD PRINTED-OUTPUT.
    STOP-RUN.
REPORT-ROUTINE.
    ADD TYPE1 TYPE2 TYPE3 TYPE4 GIVING DETAIL-LINE-TOTAL.
    GENERATE LINE-OF-DATA.
    MOVE SALESPERSON TO SALESPERSON-OLD.
    READ INPUT-RECORD AT END MOVE 8 TO STOP-SWITCH.
```

Having read the first record and effectively caused the report heading, page heading, and control headings to be printed, the first command in the second paragraph (REPORT-ROUTINE) adds the four types of sales together giving DETAIL-LINE-TOTAL, which is a SOURCE item for the DETAIL line.

The second command is to generate the DETAIL line by specifying:

```
GENERATE LINE-OF-DATA.
```

The third command saves the salesperson's number for the printing of the footing line if there should happen to be a change in the salesperson's number with the next read. This command is:

```
MOVE SALESPERSON TO SALESPERSON-OLD.
```

The fourth command is another read statement. It reads another record and the REPORT WRITER takes over and automatically checks to see if there is a change in the salesperson number. If no change in number is found, then the next command transfers control back to this same paragraph and the process is repeated. The data fields are added and the record (detail line) is written unless there is a change in salesperson number.

When there is a change in salesperson number, then the REPORT WRITER takes over and automatically prints the footings (control footings) and the new headings for the next salesperson. From this point, control is returned to the next command, which starts the process over again unless there are no more records in the file. In that case, the a "switch" is set, which causes the procedure being performed to be exited, returning control to the TERMINATE command. The TERMINATE statement is logically similar to the CLOSE statement but, as you can see, does not replace it. TERMINATE causes the printing of any control footings and report footings but does not CLOSE the file. These procedures are handled by the REPORT WRITER and require only the TERMINATE command. As in the INITIATE clause, the report name is the name of the RD entry.

Files are then closed and processing is terminated.

The REPORT WRITER feature makes the writing of reports much easier (assuming that the data are sorted) than would comparable statements in regular COBOL, which would require code to test the various fields for changes in variables and PERFORM the various headings, detail lines, and footings. Admittedly, the REPORT WRITER is designed for this type of special report and not for all computer programs. However, when the report desired is of the above nature, it is best to use the REPORT WRITER.

SECTION 13
Sample COBOL Program

The following program (Figure 9-9) is the Toy Company Problem discussed throughout the chapter. Input data for the program is presented in Figure 9-10 and the output appears as Figure 9-11. In order to get a good understanding of the REPORT WRITER we advise studying this program and if time permits, entering and running it.

Figure 9–9
Sample program.

```
IDENTIFICATION DIVISION.
PROGRAM-ID. TOY-SALES-REPORT.
AUTHOR. MELISSA JONES.
INSTALLATION. HIGH TECH.
DATE COMPLIED.
REMARKS.
THIS IS A DEMONSTRATION PROGRAM FOR THE REPORT WRITER.
ENVIRONMENT DIVISION.
CONFIGURATION SECTION.
SOURCE-COMPUTER.
        IBM-370.
OBJECT-COMPUTER.
    IBM-370.
INPUT-OUTPUT SECTION.
FILE-CONTROL.
        SELECT INPUT-RECORD ASSIGN TO INFILE.
        SELECT PRINTED-OUTPUT ASSIGN TO PRINTER.
```

Figure 9–9 (continued)

```
DATA DIVISION.
FILE SECTION.
FD  INPUT-RECORD
    LABEL RECORDS ARE OMITTED
    DATA RECORD IS SALES-INFORMATION.
01  SALES-INFORMATION.
    02 SALESPERSON              PIC 999.
    02 INVOICE                  PIC X(6).
    02 TYPE1                    PIC 9(5)V99.
    02 TYPE2                    PIC 9(5)V99.
    02 TYPE3                    PIC 9(5)V99.
    02 TYPE4                    PIC 9(5)V99.
    02 CUSTOMER                 PIC 9(5).
    02 PROCESSING-DATE          PIC 9999.
    02 FILLER                   PIC X(34).
FD  PRINTED-OUTPUT
    RECORD CONTAINS 133 CHARACTERS
    LABEL RECORDS ARE OMITTED
    REPORT IS TOY-SALES-REPORT.
WORKING-STORAGE SECTION.
01  DATES.
    02 MONTH                    PIC 99 VALUE 1.
    02 YEAR                     PIC 99 VALUE 1.
01  MONTHS-OF-THE-YEAR.
    02 ALL-THE-MONTHS.
       03 FILLER PIC A(9) VALUE '  JANUARY'.
       03 FILLER PIC A(9) VALUE ' FEBRUARY'.
       03 FILLER PIC A(9) VALUE '    MARCH'.
       03 FILLER PIC A(9) VALUE '    APRIL'.
       03 FILLER PIC A(9) VALUE '      MAY'.
       03 FILLER PIC A(9) VALUE '     JUNE'.
       03 FILLER PIC A(9) VALUE '     JULY'.
       03 FILLER PIC A(9) VALUE '   AUGUST'.
       03 FILLER PIC A(9) VALUE 'SEPTEMBER'.
       03 FILLER PIC A(9) VALUE '  OCTOBER'.
       03 FILLER PIC A(9) VALUE ' NOVEMBER'.
       03 FILLER PIC A(9) VALUE ' DECEMBER'.

    02 MONTHLIST REDEFINES ALL-THE-MONTHS.
       03 MONTHTABLE OCCURS 12 TIMES PIC A(9).
01  DETAIL-LINE-TOTAL           PIC 9(7)V99 VALUE ZERO.
01  SALESPERSON-OLD             PIC 999 VALUE ZERO.
01  STOP-SWITCH                 PIC 9   VALUE ZERO.
REPORT SECTION.
RD  TOY-SALES-REPORT
    CONTROLS ARE FINAL, SALESPERSON
    PAGE LIMIT IS 60 LINES
    HEADING 2
    FIRST DETAIL 6
    LAST DETAIL 56
    FOOTING 59.
01  TYPE REPORT HEADING LINE IS 2.
    02 COLUMN 54 PIC X(24) VALUE 'INTERNATIONAL TOYS, INC.'.
01  TYPE PAGE HEADING.
    02 LINE IS 3 COLUMN 56
       PIC A(20) VALUE 'MONTHLY SALES REPORT'.
    02 LINE IS PLUS 1.
       03 COLUMN 57 PIC X(19) SOURCE IS MONTHTABLE (MONTH).
       03 COLUMN 67 PIC X(4) VALUE ', 19'.
       03 COLUMN 71 PIC 99 SOURCE IS YEAR.
01  TYPE CONTROL HEADING SALESPERSON.
    02 LINE IS PLUS 3.
       03 COLUMN 10  PIC X(19) VALUE 'SALES-SALESPERSON'.
       03 COLUMN 30  PIC 999    SOURCE SALESPERSON.
       03 COLUMN 39  PIC X(7)   VALUE 'INVOICE'.
       03 COLUMN 53  PIC X(8)   VALUE 'CUSTOMER'.
       03 COLUMN 68  PIC X(5)   VALUE 'TYPE1'.
       03 COLUMN 80  PIC X(5)   VALUE 'TYPE2'.
       03 COLUMN 92  PIC X(5)   VALUE 'TYPE3'.
       03 COLUMN 104 PIC X(5)   VALUE 'TYPE4'.
       03 COLUMN 115 PIC X(5)   VALUE 'TOTAL'.
```

Figure 9-9 (continued)

```
            02 LINE IS PLUS 1.
               03 COLUMN 40  PIC X(6)  VALUE 'NUMBER'.
               03 COLUMN 54  PIC X(6)  VALUE 'NUMBER'.
               03 COLUMN 68  PIC X(5)  VALUE 'SALES'.
               03 COLUMN 80  PIC X(5)  VALUE 'SALES'.
               03 COLUMN 92  PIC X(5)  VALUE 'SALES'.
               03 COLUMN 104 PIC X(5)  VALUE 'SALES'.
               03 COLUMN 115 PIC X(5)  VALUE 'SALES'.
     01  LINE-OF-DATA TYPE IS DETAIL LINE PLUS 1.
         02 COLUMN 39 PIC X(6) SOURCE IS INVOICE.
         02 COLUMN 54 PIC 9(5) SOURCE IS CUSTOMER.
         02 TYPE1-DETAIL COLUMN 64  PIC ZZ,ZZZ.99
                 SOURCE IS TYPE1.
         02 TYPE2-DETAIL COLUMN 76  PIC ZZ,ZZZ.99
                 SOURCE IS TYPE2.
         02 TYPE3-DETAIL COLUMN 88  PIC ZZ,ZZZ.99
                 SOURCE IS TYPE3.
         02 TYPE4-DETAIL COLUMN 100 PIC ZZ,ZZZ.99
                 SOURCE IS TYPE4.
         02 LINE-TOTAL COLUMN 111   PIC ZZ,ZZZ.99
                 SOURCE DETAIL-LINE-TOTAL.
     01 TYPE CONTROL FOOTING SALESPERSON LINE PLUS 1.
         02 COLUMN 17 PIC X(22) VALUE 'TOTAL SALESPERSON'.
         02 COLUMN 34 PIC ZZZ SOURCE SALESPERSON-OLD.
         02 TYPE1-TOTAL COLUMN 63  PIC ZZZ,ZZZ.99 SUM TYPE1.
         02 TYPE2-TOTAL COLUMN 75  PIC ZZZ,ZZZ.99 SUM TYPE2.
         02 TYPE3-TOTAL COLUMN 87  PIC ZZZ,ZZZ.99 SUM TYPE3.
         02 TYPE4-TOTAL COLUMN 99  PIC ZZZ,ZZZ.99 SUM TYPE4.
         02 TOTAL-TOTAL COLUMN 110 PIC Z,ZZZ,ZZZ.99
                 SUM DETAIL-LINE-TOTAL.
     01 TYPE CONTROL FOOTING FINAL.
         02 LINE IS 59.
               03 COLUMN 10  PIC X(23) VALUE 'TOTAL SALES COMPANYWIDE'.
               03 COLUMN 62  PIC Z,ZZZ,ZZZ.99 SUM TYPE1-TOTAL.
               03 COLUMN 74  PIC Z,ZZZ,ZZZ.99 SUM TYPE2-TOTAL.
               03 COLUMN 86  PIC Z,ZZZ,ZZZ.99 SUM TYPE3-TOTAL.
               03 COLUMN 98  PIC Z,ZZZ,ZZZ.99 SUM TYPE4-TOTAL.
               03 COLUMN 109 PIC ZZ,ZZZ,ZZZ.99 SUM TOTAL-TOTAL.
PROCEDURE DIVISION.
START-UP.
    OPEN INPUT INPUT-RECORD OUTPUT PRINTED-OUTPUT
    READ INPUT-RECORD AT END MOVE 6 TO STOP-SWITCH.
    MOVE PROCESSING-DATE TO DATES.
    INITIATE TOY-SALES-REPORT.
    PERFORM REPORT-ROUTINE UNTIL STOP-SWITCH > 1.
    TERMINATE TOY-SALES-REPORT.
    CLOSE INPUT-RECORD PRINTED-OUTPUT.
    STOP RUN.
REPORT-ROUTINE.
    ADD TYPE1 TYPE2 TYPE3 TYPE4 GIVING DETAIL-LINE-TOTAL.
    GENERATE LINE-OF-DATA.
    MOVE SALESPERSON TO SALESPERSON-OLD.
    READ INPUT-RECORD AT END MOVE 8 TO STOP-SWITCH.
```

Figure 9–10
Input data for report program.

```
001F35008001633000024560045530000155305600000183
001F35115005555350000000055300000074530560003
001F35077000245600035760045500000045300560006
001F35045006652400005630004553000002530056007
001F35019008937100045600078630000058530056013
001F35101000145300015500055530000015500560014
001F35028007530800024530055530500002553056017
001F35080002555300024680002453000000255056019
001F35132004452400000000000025500045450560020
002F35088004455300354430045200000015500560001
002F35044000000000005302004550000005530056004
002F35066000245500015530024530000005560560004
002F35133006522200222500002145000002230560004
002F35121005332400053000000000000058056009
002F35110000145500041480096696000153005600012
002F35081005555350001456005458300000453056014
002F35007000627100011530002530000455305600015
002F35146003545800055005000384200000255056015
002F35018001679300002463002233000015830560016
002F35027007894500003542005553000004553056016
002F35103000453000021530045530000055305600016
002F35056005225800097500075433000066005600017
003F35017005193700002250055320000458605600002
003F35116005555500015500005423000005770560004
003F35016006756000053030055300000078840560005
003F35026000000100045300045553000021550560005
003F35085005553210002450004500200000255056005
003F35043009622400045300045530000215505600006
003F35006000333500002553002100200078850560010
003F35123000000000025530000080000245056012
003F35106000145300015300055305000002505600017
004F35073000225600025530003558600015600560001
004F35114005530500055000077300000085300560001
004F35005000868100024530032553000025530560005
004F35042007855400002453004553000001563056005
004F35052003366900015300045600000015300560005
004F35056003224400048040053006000035056006
004F35111000145500052260075353000027530560006
004F35087003515800045860055300000155005600007
004F35015000973500030550054533000025530560008
004F35025009635200153020055330000058300560008
004F35120005585500045530000000006545056008
004F35139001252200450050002155000015505600009
004F35145003248600743200002453000002150560010
004F35095002585500024580075500000074500560012
004F35054003345700015300085302000025005600013
004F35062000344500014570001453000002550550013
004F35099002456000155000155530000250056013
004F35082005322400022560075200000022505600015
004F35130007444500025830002455000245505600018
004F35059006554200048600002530000058005600020
004F35107002453000155000455000000325056020
005F35072001235500021550014850000553056002
005F35111005523600000000088521000753005600002
005F35004009501500215300303560002563056005
005F35078005423500045860050025000455005600005
005F35134006522300220050022553000025305600005
005F35014000196600065410024753000022530560006
005F35024007508200155000053302000155305600006
005F35090005552500054750085300001550056006
005F35146005548550055300000556300000215056006
005F35119005223600323580012500000852005600007
005F35142004555500055200000215500025305600007
005F35144005563500035300024530000045305600007
005F35050002337800021530077530000155005600008
005F35086003245600025580045500000253005600008
005F35091005456300354560045300000153005600008
005F35094001556300000022005530000078305600010
005F35098002456000155300256300000245056011
005F35124004523200024550056530000025705600011
005F35060008652200014560002453000002205600014
005F35067000214500045750045330000024505600014
005F35100000245000015500045530000253005600014
005F35126007553200025500053000000256056014
005F35129004553200021530022553000055505600017
005F35041008865400045300045300000155305600019
006F35030018852000225300255330000055305600003
006F35048006674400015300071200000155005600004
006F35076002223500583040002155000530005600004
006F35055130002445000145300126930000255005600004
006F35140004553300752000021485000021405600004
006F35040001234500156300054530000155505600007
006F35049002255600014300078530000015530560007
006F35137004553300025530021553000021505600007
006F35013001152200025630043005000025505600009
006F35039007651800025540045500000055305600011
006F35096005554200034560045555000752005600012
006F35092002556300075521004550000057305600015
006F35102000155300015530045305000055350560015
006F35127008785500021550013447000325505600015
006F35105000214500001450005520000007420056019
006F35147-0554760075300007858300000255056019
```

Figure 9–10 (continued)

```
007F35051003477600015300048630000155005600I
007F350840032458000245800855300000253056001
007F35002007919500025630002530000255005600S
007F351350055223000554500245500000255056003
007F35074000215500024580002455000720005600S
007F35089004553200133580075500000015500560OS
007F35012003608600024450025300000000005600G
007F35141005552400543200055530000025505600G
007F35136004533200024550025530000025500560O7
007F35075000036950096530000214500055500560O8
007F350970003456000255300455300007686056010
007F350380000058000545300455300002565056012
007F35125002553300021530055300000255005601B
007F350570054565000863000964300007300560IS
007F35061008875500045860001453000000005601S
007F350790032445000458600453060000255056016
007F35063000245600057600015300002550560IB
007F350230063677001553000444000001553056020
008F35001000300100025630030245000255305600I
008F350700000000000156500885500000256056005
008F351170085555000455200452000004500056005
008F350580085554000486000024660000025705600Z
008F35064000244500015500004758000024505600Z
008F35011008350200024550045300000255005600B
008F35112000445600021560055530000015500560O8
008F35138000000000545300021550000215056008
008F351430055535007520000255330000245056008
008F35053004435500021450055300000245056010
008F3503700875330086314004550000055630560I3
008F350830063324000258300453200000225056016
008F350930024563000225005530000055305601G
008F351080002155000255300455000003005056016
008F35128005544500021550013235000555705601B
008F350220036741000443000253000001253056018
008F35104000145500045300047850000000505601B
009F35071000000000045500043060000255056004
009F3501000068900024630054530000253005600S
009F351090002155000245300696796000415305600S
009F351180055555000558500542300000453005600B
009F350860074566000256300530020005533056016
009F350210029039000456300000000001556056019
009F351310054552000000000345600044230560IS
010F35047008632400045300078850000155305600S
010F35020009125000024530000245000458505600G
010F35046005744400025300045530000553305600G
010F35068000214500057830055330000255005600G
010F35151003255300045300004550000002550560O7
010F351480035458005520800585220000553056007
010F35150005455500045000005530000021405600Z
010F35152003256300753000055300000002550560O9
010F350290014563000245300550030007882056010
010F3512200545530001560000000200004530560I0
010F35009000602100014530013300000258305601B
010F3505500033680002530008630000025005601G
010F35149005552400585500085233000024505601B
//
```

```
                    INTERNATIONAL TOYS, INC.
                       MONTHLY SALES REPORT
                         JANUARY , 19 83
```

SALES-SALESPERSON 001

INVOICE NUMBER	CUSTOMER NUMBER	TYPE1 SALES	TYPE2 SALES	TYPE3 SALES	TYPE4 SALES	TOTAL SALES
F35008	05600	163.30	24.56	455.30	15.53	658.69
F35115	05600	555.35	.00	553.00	74.53	1,182.88
F35077	05600	24.56	35.76	455.00	45.30	560.62
F35045	05600	665.24	56.30	455.30	25.30	1,202.74
F35019	05601	893.71	45.60	786.30	58.53	1,784.14
F35101	05601	14.53	15.50	555.30	15.50	600.83
F35028	05601	753.08	24.53	555.05	25.53	1,356.19
F35080	05601	255.53	24.68	24.53	2.55	307.29
F35132	05602	445.24	.00	2.55	45.45	493.24
TOTAL SALESPERSON 1		3,770.54	226.93	3,840.33	308.22	8,146.02

SALES-SALESPERSON 002

INVOICE NUMBER	CUSTOMER NUMBER	TYPE1 SALES	TYPE2 SALES	TYPE3 SALES	TYPE4 SALES	TOTAL SALES
F35088	05600	445.53	354.43	452.00	15.50	1,267.46
F35044	05600	.00	53.02	455.00	55.30	563.32
F35066	05600	24.55	15.53	245.30	5.56	290.94
F35133	05600	652.22	222.50	21.45	2.23	898.40
F35121	05600	533.24	52.42	.58	.58	586.82
F35110	05601	14.53	41.48	966.96	15.30	1,038.29
F35081	05601	555.35	14.56	545.83	4.53	1,120.27
F35007	05601	62.71	11.53	25.30	45.53	145.07
F35146	05601	354.58	550.05	38.42	2.55	945.60
F35018	05601	167.93	24.63	223.30	15.83	431.69
F35027	05601	789.45	35.42	555.30	45.53	1,425.70
F35103	05601	45.30	21.53	455.30	55.30	577.43
F35056	05601	522.58	97.50	754.33	6.60	1,391.01
TOTAL SALESPERSON 2		4,167.99	1,495.18	4,738.49	270.34	10,672.03

SALES-SALESPERSON 003

INVOICE NUMBER	CUSTOMER NUMBER	TYPE1 SALES	TYPE2 SALES	TYPE3 SALES	TYPE4 SALES	TOTAL SALES
F35017	05600	519.37	2.25	553.20	45.86	1,120.68
F35116	05600	555.55	155.00	542.30	5.77	1,258.62
F35016	05600	675.60	53.03	553.00	78.84	1,360.47
F35026	05600	-.01	45.30	455.30	21.55	522.39
F35085	05600	553.21	24.50	450.02	2.55	1,030.28
F35043	05600	962.24	45.30	455.30	21.55	1,484.39
F35006	05601	33.35	25.53	210.02	78.85	347.75
F35123	05601	.00	25.30	.08	2.45	28.06
F35106	05601	14.53	15.30	553.05	.25	583.13
TOTAL SALESPERSON 3		3,313.86	391.74	3,772.50	257.67	7,735.77

SALES-SALESPERSON 004

INVOICE NUMBER	CUSTOMER NUMBER	TYPE1 SALES	TYPE2 SALES	TYPE3 SALES	TYPE4 SALES	TOTAL SALES
F35073	05600	22.56	25.50	355.86	15.60	419.52
F35114	05600	553.05	55.00	773.00	85.30	1,466.35
F35005	05600	86.81	24.53	325.53	25.53	462.40

Figure 9-11

Output from sample program.

MONTHLY SALES REPORT
JANUARY , 19 83

INVOICE NUMBER	CUSTOMER NUMBER	TYPE1 SALES	TYPE2 SALES	TYPE3 SALES	TYPE4 SALES	TOTAL SALES
F35042	05600	785.54	24.53	455.30	15.63	1,281.00
F35052	05600	336.69	15.30	456.00	15.30	823.29
F35056	05600	322.44	48.04	530.06	.35	900.89
F35111	05600	14.55	52.26	753.53	27.53	847.87
F35087	05600	351.58	45.86	553.00	15.50	965.94
F35015	05600	97.35	30.55	545.33	25.53	698.76
F35025	05600	963.52	153.02	555.33	58.30	1,730.17
F35120	05600	558.55	45.53	.00	65.45	669.53
F35139	05600	125.22	450.05	21.55	1.55	598.37
F35145	05601	324.86	743.20	24.53	2.15	1,094.74
F35095	05601	258.55	24.58	755.00	74.50	1,112.63
F35054	05601	334.57	15.30	853.02	2.50	1,205.39
F35062	05501	34.45	14.57	14.53	2.55	66.10
F35099	05601	24.56	15.50	155.53	2.50	198.09
F35082	05601	532.24	22.56	752.00	2.25	1,309.05
F35130	05601	744.45	25.83	24.55	24.55	819.38
F35059	05602	655.42	48.60	25.30	5.80	735.12
F35107	05602	24.53	15.50	455.00	3.25	498.28
		7,151.49	1,895.81	8,383.95	471.62	17,902.87

TOTAL SALESPERSON 4

SALES-SALESPERSON 005

INVOICE NUMBER	CUSTOMER NUMBER	TYPE1 SALES	TYPE2 SALES	TYPE3 SALES	TYPE4 SALES	TOTAL SALES
F35072	05600	123.55	21.55	14.85	5.53	165.48
F35111	05600	552.36	.00	885.21	75.30	1,512.87
F35004	05600	950.15	21.53	303.56	25.63	1,300.87
F35078	05600	542.35	45.86	500.25	45.50	1,133.96
F35134	05600	652.23	220.01	225.53	2.53	1,100.34
F35014	05600	19.66	65.41	247.53	22.53	355.13
F35024	05600	750.82	155.00	533.02	15.53	1,454.37
F35090	05600	555.25	54.75	853.00	15.50	1,478.50
F35146	05600	554.85	50,553.00	556.30	2.15	51,666.30
F35119	05600	522.36	323.58	125.00	85.20	1,056.14
F35142	05600	455.55	552.00	21.55	2.53	1,031.63
F35144	05600	556.35	535.30	245.30	4.53	1,341.48
F35050	05600	233.78	21.53	775.30	15.50	1,046.11
F35086	05600	324.56	25.58	455.00	25.30	830.44
F35091	05601	545.63	354.56	453.00	15.30	1,368.49
F35094	05601	155.63	.22	553.00	78.30	787.15
F35098	05601	24.56	15.53	256.30	2.45	298.84
F35124	05601	452.32	24.55	565.30	2.57	1,044.74
F35060	05601	865.22	14.56	24.53	.22	904.53
F35067	05601	21.45	45.75	453.30	2.45	522.95
F35100	05601	24.50	15.50	455.30	25.30	520.60
F35126	05601	755.32	25.50	530.00	2.56	1,313.38
F35129	05601	455.32	21.53	225.53	55.55	757.93
F35041	05601	886.54	45.30	453.00	15.53	1,400.37
		10,980.31	53,158.14	9,710.66	543.49	74,392.60

TOTAL SALESPERSON 5

Figure 9–11 (continued)

MONTHLY SALES REPORT
JANUARY ,19 83

SALES-SALESPERSON 006

INVOICE NUMBER	CUSTOMER NUMBER	TYPE1 SALES	TYPE2 SALES	TYPE3 SALES	TYPE4 SALES	TOTAL SALES
F35003	05600	188.52	22.53	255.33	5.53	471.91
F35048	05600	667.44	15.30	712.00	15.50	1,410.24
F35076	05600	222.35	583.04	21.55	53.00	879.94
F35513	05600	24.45	14.53	126.93	25.50	191.41
F35140	05600	455.33	752.00	214.85	2.14	1,424.32
F35040	05600	123.45	156.30	545.30	15.55	840.60
F35049	05600	225.56	14.30	785.30	15.53	1,040.69
F35137	05600	455.33	25.53	215.53	2.15	698.54
F35013	05600	115.22	25.63	430.05	2.55	573.45
F35039	05601	765.18	25.45	455.00	55.30	1,300.93
F35096	05601	555.42	34.56	455.55	75.20	1,120.73
F35092	05601	255.63	755.21	455.00	5.73	1,471.57
F35102	05601	15.53	15.50	453.05	55.35	539.43
F35127	05601	878.55	21.55	134.47	32.55	1,067.12
F35105	05601	21.45	14.50	552.00	74.20	662.15
F35147	05601	554.76	753.00	785.83	2.55	2,096.14
TOTAL SALESPERSON 6		5,524.17	3,228.93	6,597.74	438.33	15,789.17

SALES-SALESPERSON 007

INVOICE NUMBER	CUSTOMER NUMBER	TYPE1 SALES	TYPE2 SALES	TYPE3 SALES	TYPE4 SALES	TOTAL SALES
F35051	05600	347.76	15.30	486.30	15.50	864.86
F35084	05600	324.58	24.58	855.30	2.53	1,206.99
F35002	05600	791.95	25.63	25.30	25.50	868.38
F35135	05600	552.23	55.45	245.50	2.55	855.73
F35074	05600	21.55	24.58	24.55	72.00	142.68
F35089	05600	455.32	133.58	755.00	15.50	1,359.40
F35012	05600	360.86	24.45	253.00	.00	638.31
F35141	05600	555.24	543.20	555.30	2.55	1,656.29
F35136	05600	453.32	24.55	255.30	25.50	758.67
F35075	05600	36.95	965.30	21.45	55.50	1,079.20
F35097	05601	34.56	25.53	455.30	76.86	592.25
F35038	05601	.58	54.53	455.30	25.65	536.06
F35125	05601	255.33	21.53	553.00	25.50	855.36
F35057	05601	545.65	86.30	964.30	7.30	1,603.55
F35061	05601	887.55	45.86	14.53	.00	947.94
F35079	05601	324.45	45.86	453.06	2.55	825.92
F35063	05601	24.56	57.60	15.30	2.55	100.01
F35023	05602	636.77	155.30	444.00	15.53	1,251.60
TOTAL SALESPERSON 7		6,609.21	2,329.13	6,831.79	373.07	16,143.20

SALES-SALESPERSON 008

INVOICE NUMBER	CUSTOMER NUMBER	TYPE1 SALES	TYPE2 SALES	TYPE3 SALES	TYPE4 SALES	TOTAL SALES
F35001	05600	30.01	25.63	302.45	25.53	383.62
F35070	05600	.00	15.65	885.50	2.56	903.71
F35117	05600	855.55	45.52	452.00	45.00	1,398.07
F35058	05600	855.54	48.60	24.66	2.57	931.37
F35064	05600	24.45	15.50	47.58	2.45	89.98

Figure 9-11 (continued)

MONTHLY SALES REPORT
JANUARY , 19 83

INVOICE NUMBER	CUSTOMER NUMBER	TYPE1 SALES	TYPE2 SALES	TYPE3 SALES	TYPE4 SALES	TOTAL SALES
F35011	05600	835.02	24.55	453.00	25.50	1,338.07
F35112	05600	44.56	21.56	555.30	15.50	636.92
F35138	05600	.00	545.30	21.55	2.15	569.00
F35143	05600	555.35	752.00	255.33	2.45	1,565.13
F35053	05601	443.55	21.45	553.00	2.45	1,020.45
F35037	05601	875.33	863.14	455.00	55.63	2,249.10
F35083	05601	633.24	25.83	453.20	2.25	1,114.52
F35093	05601	245.63	2.25	553.00	55.30	856.18
F35108	05601	21.55	25.53	455.00	30.05	532.13
F35128	05601	554.45	21.55	132.35	55.57	763.92
F35022	05601	367.41	44.30	253.00	12.53	677.24
F35104	05601	14.55	45.30	478.50	.05	538.40
TOTAL SALESPERSON 8		6,356.19	2,543.66	6,330.42	337.54	15,567.81

SALES-SALESPERSON 009

INVOICE NUMBER	CUSTOMER NUMBER	TYPE1 SALES	TYPE2 SALES	TYPE3 SALES	TYPE4 SALES	TOTAL SALES
F35071	05600	.00	45.50	430.06	2.55	478.11
F35010	05600	68.90	24.63	545.30	25.30	664.13
F35109	05600	21.55	24.53	696.96	41.53	784.57
F35118	05600	555.55	55.85	542.30	45.30	1,199.00
F35086	05601	745.66	25.63	530.02	55.33	1,356.64
F35021	05601	290.39	45.63	.00	15.56	351.58
F35131	05601	545.52	.00	34.56	44.23	624.31
TOTAL SALESPERSON 9		2,227.57	221.77	2,779.20	229.80	5,458.34

SALES-SALESPERSON 001

INVOICE NUMBER	CUSTOMER NUMBER	TYPE1 SALES	TYPE2 SALES	TYPE3 SALES	TYPE4 SALES	TOTAL SALES
F35047	05600	863.24	45.30	788.50	15.53	1,712.57
TOTAL SALESPERSON 1		863.24	45.30	788.50	15.53	1,712.57

SALES-SALESPERSON 010

INVOICE NUMBER	CUSTOMER NUMBER	TYPE1 SALES	TYPE2 SALES	TYPE3 SALES	TYPE4 SALES	TOTAL SALES
F35047	05600	863.24	45.30	788.50	15.53	1,712.57
F35020	05600	912.50	24.53	2.45	45.85	985.33
F35046	05600	574.44	25.30	455.30	55.30	1,110.34
F35068	05600	21.45	57.83	553.30	2.55	635.13
F35151	05600	325.53	453.00	455.00	2.55	1,236.08
F35148	05600	354.58	552.08	585.22	5.53	1,497.41
F35150	05600	545.55	450.00	553.00	2.14	1,550.69
F35152	05601	325.63	753.00	553.00	.00	1,631.63
F35029	05601	145.63	24.53	550.03	78.82	799.01
F35122	05601	545.53	15.60	.02	4.53	565.68
F35009	05601	60.21	14.53	133.00	25.83	233.57
F35055	05601	33.68	25.30	863.30	2.50	924.78
F35149	05601	555.24	585.50	852.33	2.45	1,995.52
TOTAL SALESPERSON 10		5,263.21	3,026.50	6,344.45	243.58	14,877.74

| TOTAL SALES COMPANYWIDE | | 56,227.78 | 68,563.09 | 60,118.03 | 3,489.1 | 188,398.09 |

Figure 9–11 (continued)

Questions and Exercises

I. Questions

1. What are control breaks?
2. What are the differences between headings, footings, and detail lines?
3. How does the REPORT WRITER use the DATA DIVISION to accomplish what is done in the PROCEDURE DIVISION in other COBOL programs?
4. What is the function of the PAGE LIMIT entry?
5. Identify the uses for the following clauses: TYPE, LINE, COLUMN, GROUP, SOURCE, and SUM.
6. There are three types of headings which are handled by the REPORT WRITER feature.
   a. What are the three types of headings?
   b. In what division of a COBOL program are these headings defined?
   c. What COBOL statement(s) is used to define each of these headings?
7. There are three types of footings which are handled by the REPORT WRITER feature.
   a. What are the three types of footings?
   b. In what division of a COBOL program are these footings defined?
   c. What COBOL statement(s) is used to define each of these footings?
8. What special rules apply to the use of REPORT SECTION?
9. What REPORT WRITER phrase(s) must be used to control page size (number of lines per page)?
10. To what does the CONTROLS ARE clause refer?
11. Discuss the terms "major control break," "intermediate control break," and "minor control break."

II. Exercises and Problems

1. Write a COBOL program using the REPORT WRITER feature as follows:
   a. You are given a file (RAIN-FILE), which contains information on the monthly rainfall amounts for January through December for the years 1918 through 1976 for all of the counties (parishes) in your state. The input data contain the name of the county and 12 rainfall amounts. The output from the program should be written on a 50-line page with headings on lines 3 and 4 and footings on line 49. The report should write totals after each county and after all of the counties (of the amount of rain per month). Give the RD entry to accomplish this task.
   b. Provide the 01 entry to describe a report heading which is to appear on line 3 of the printed report. Any suitable title will be satisfactory.
   c. On each page of the printed report (near the top) will be a page heading to indicate what the data actually represents. For example, NAME OF COUNTY, JANUARY FEBRUARY MARCH...etc. Give the 01 TYPE entry for this heading, which is controlled by the name of the county.
   d. The data line should contain the name of the county, the 12 monthly figures and the total for that year. Give the 01 TYPE entry to describe this line.

e. After all of the years are listed for one county, a total line for the county should be printed. The totals should represent the total amount of rain for each month as well as for the total number of years. Give the 01 TYPE entry to describe this total line.

f. After the list for all of the counties in the state is complete a grand-total line is desired. This grand-total line should contain the total amount of rain in all of the January months (all years and all counties) and similar totals for each of the rest of the months as well. Give the 01 TYPE entry to describe this line.

2. Use the COBOL REPORT WRITER feature to list the records contained in the customer master file. List only the customer number, customer name, balance, and credit limit. Put appropriate headings on the report. Total the customer's balances and print this total at the end of the listing.

3. Use the COBOL REPORT WRITER feature to list the records contained in the invoice master file (after it has been sorted in customer number sequence) to list the invoices to the line printer. The output line should include the following fields:

- invoice number
- customer number
- transaction type (decoded)
- invoice date
- invoice amount

Provide a total for each customer when the customer number changes. Also print a total for charge sales, cash sales, payments, and credit memos at the end of the report.

10

On-line Transaction Processing

Until very recently most processing of data took place in the batch mode, in which transactions are accumulated for a period of time and then processed in a "batch." As the costs of computing equipment have continued to decrease and as user and equipment sophistication levels have risen, businesses have begun to process more data as the transactions occur (transaction processing). Typically these transactions are captured at the site where they occur (often remote from the CPU).

There are a number of innovations that allow us to process data as they occur. Some of these innovations, such as terminal devices, time-sharing CPUs, and data-communications devices such as modems and multiplexors, are hardware oriented. Others, such as improvements in operating systems, communications software, transaction-processing software, and enhancements to programming languages (all of which allow us to process these transactions as they occur), are software oriented.

The focus of this chapter is on the software enhancements to COBOL that allow the use of COBOL plus terminals to process data in a transaction oriented fashion. Such operations are highly machine dependent. For example, IBM systems use an operating system enhancement called CICS to implement terminal oriented program development and the use of COBOL in that environment necessarily requires that you follow the CICS rules. The illustrations here use the DEC VAX system to present on-line concepts. There may be slight differences in the way on-line transaction processing is handled by different computer systems but you may expect the basic concepts to be similar. The purpose here is to provide you with a basic orientation in data communications using the COBOL language. For more thorough coverage of the material you may want to consult one of the excellent texts in this field of data processing.

SECTION 1
Menus and Screens

A key consideration in transaction oriented processing is the simplification of the use of the user-developed, computer-based software. The reason that simplification is so important in this type of applications is that the users are typically not data processors and so may be expected to be relatively naive concerning computers and computer operations. The process of using computer software through a terminal at a remote site must be made as simple as possible. Such simplification requires that the program developer consider the user at all times and utilize techniques in the programs that make the system easier to use. Incorporation of menus, submenus, and screens tend to provide some of the desired simplification.

A system menu is simply a listing of the processing choices that a user has for the system he or she is operating. The choices are listed sequentially on the video device and the user is asked to select an option from the list (menu) of choices available. Consider the menu of a fictional accounts payable system as presented in Figure 10-1. This menu, and the submenus that are discussed later, are a part of the illustrative program that is developed in this chapter.

Notice that in this menu there are 10 choices that the user may make. The user is also directed, by the last line in the menu, to choose one of the processing options that are available. For example: if the user wants to process some activity related to the chart of accounts, then the choice "2" would be entered and the program driving the menus would cause the program that maintains the chart of accounts file to be CALLed and executed.

The menu (submenu) for the chart of accounts maintenance will now appear on the screen (see Figure 10-2). Again the user has choices that can be made from this submenu. Notice that the choices that are presented in the submenu are organized in a fairly logical sequence. If the user wanted to add an account to the chart of accounts file, then he or she would select a "1" from the menu and the data entry

Figure 10-1
Main menu for an accounts payable system.

```
***********************************************
*  ACCOUNTS PAYABLE MASTER MENU               *
***********************************************
*01 VENDOR MAINTENANCE                        *
*02 CHART OF ACCOUNTS MAINTENANCE             *
*03 INVOICE ENTRY & MAINTENANCE               *
*04 REPORTS MENU                              *
*05 INVOICE SELECTION FOR PAYMENT             *
*06 PRINT CHECKS                              *
*07 POST INVOICES                             *
*08 PRINT ACCOUNT ACTIVITY                    *
*09 RECONCILE CHECKS                          *
*10 END IT ALL                                *
*02 CHOOSE ONE!                               *
***********************************************
```

Figure 10-2
Chart of accounts maintenance submenu.

```
*********************************************
*  CHART OF ACCOUNT MAINTENANCE             *
*********************************************
*  1 ADD AN ACCOUNT                         *
*  2 CHANGE AN ACCOUNT                       *
*  3 DISPLAY AN ACCOUNT                      *
*  4 DELETE AN ACCOUNT                       *
*  5 PRINT CHART OF ACCOUNTS                 *
*  6 RETURN TO MAIN MENU                     *
*  □ CHOOSE ONE!                            *
*********************************************
```

Figure 10–3
Data-entry screen for chart of
accounts.

```
*****************************************************
*            CHART  OF  ACCOUNTS  ADDITIONS         *
*****************************************************
*ACCOUNT NUMBER:▓_____ACCT IND:                   *
*ACCT-NAME:                                         *
*BALANCES:                    OKAY Y/N?             *
*                                                   *
*****************************************************
```

screen for entry of an item into the chart of accounts appears on the video terminal
(see Figure 10-3). Notice that this screen requires that we fill in the blanks on the
screen just as we would fill in the blanks on a paper form.

Observe also in Figure 10-3 that there is a series of dashes in the account
number field. The line of dashes indicates the number of characters that can be
entered into the field. There is also a square block at the beginning of the field.
This square block indicates the position of the cursor. The purpose of the cursor is
to prompt or point the user to the position on the form where data are currently to
be entered. In this example (although you cannot see it), the square block blinks in
the account number field indicating that the user is to enter the ACCT #.

Figure 10-4 shows the account number being entered. Notice two things in this
illustration:

1. The cursor has moved as the data were entered from the terminal keyboard.
2. There is room in the account number field to accommodate a larger value.

The user, at this point, usually enters the data from this field to the program by
depressing the ENTER key on his or her terminal. The cursor then moves to the
next field and prompts the user to enter the ACCT IND field (account indicator—
which allows you to group accounts for presentation purposes [see Figure 10-5]).
After the ACCT IND field is entered then the user enters the next field, ACCT NAME
(Figure 10-6), after which prompts are given to enter the other items of information (Figure 10-7) until all the data are entered.

Figure 10–4
Data entry of account number.

```
*****************************************************
*            CHART  OF  ACCOUNTS  ADDITIONS         *
*****************************************************
*ACCOUNT NUMBER:124-5___ACCT IND:                   *
*ACCT-NAME:                                         *
*BALANCES:                    OKAY Y/N?             *
*                                                   *
*****************************************************
```

Figure 10–5
Data entry of account indicator
(continued).

```
*****************************************************
*            CHART  OF  ACCOUNTS  ADDITIONS         *
*****************************************************
*ACCOUNT NUMBER:124-5___ACCT IND:CA                 *
*ACCT-NAME:                                         *
*BALANCES:                    OKAY Y/N?             *
*                                                   *
*****************************************************
```

Figure 10–6
Data entry of account name.

```
*****************************************************
*            CHART  OF  ACCOUNTS  ADDITIONS         *
*****************************************************
*ACCOUNT NUMBER:124-5___ACCT IND:CA                 *
*ACCT-NAME:    BUILDINGS                            *
*BALANCES:                    OKAY Y/N?             *
*                                                   *
*****************************************************
```

Figure 10–7
Data entry of account balance.

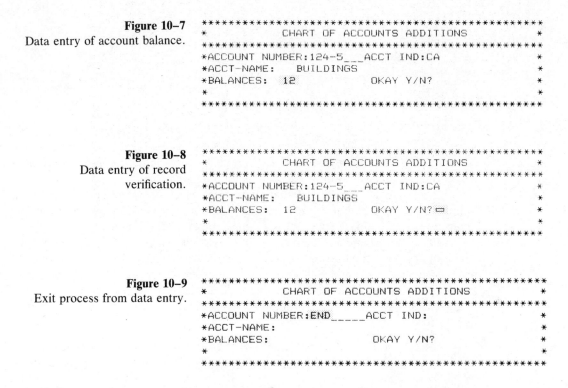

```
**********************************************************
*               CHART  OF  ACCOUNTS  ADDITIONS           *
**********************************************************
*ACCOUNT NUMBER:124-5___ACCT IND:CA                      *
*ACCT-NAME:     BUILDINGS                                *
*BALANCES:   12              OKAY Y/N?                    *
*                                                        *
**********************************************************
```

Figure 10–8
Data entry of record
verification.

```
**********************************************************
*               CHART  OF  ACCOUNTS  ADDITIONS           *
**********************************************************
*ACCOUNT NUMBER:124-5___ACCT IND:CA                      *
*ACCT-NAME:     BUILDINGS                                *
*BALANCES:   12              OKAY Y/N? ▭                 *
*                                                        *
**********************************************************
```

Figure 10–9
Exit process from data entry.

```
**********************************************************
*               CHART  OF  ACCOUNTS  ADDITIONS           *
**********************************************************
*ACCOUNT NUMBER:END_____ACCT IND:                        *
*ACCT-NAME:                                              *
*BALANCES:                   OKAY Y/N?                    *
*                                                        *
**********************************************************
```

After all the data are entered, the screen prompts the user as to whether or not the data that have been entered are correct (Figure 10-8). One of the advantages of the terminal as a data-entry device is that corrections are made at the point at which data are entered into the system. There are a number of ways in which this can be done. Usually, we would set up procedures in the program to allow the user to enter an identification number of a field (or fields) to be corrected and correct that field. In this illustrative program we are using such a small number of fields that it doesn't make sense to incorporate the identification numbers for each field. Our program requires the user to reenter all the data. Figure 10-9 shows how the user escapes the data-entry process. In this case, by entering the word END in the ACCT # field. After the entry of the word END, the program displays the submenu depicted in Figure 10-2. The user may then select any other chart of accounts maintenance activity desired. Notice that one of the entries in the menu in Figure 10-2 is a choice to return to the main menu. The master menu also has a choice to end the process and to exit to the operating system.

The following sections of this chapter describe the COBOL programs used in the process just described.

SECTION 2
The MASTER MENU Program (APMENU)

The computer system we are using for this illustration requires one of two approaches to accomplish what we have done in our examples. One is the so-called "native" mode and the other is a group of CALLs to the runtime library (RTL). In this chapter the emphasis is on the CALL method. It is important to understand the differences between these two methods, so we will discuss both methods briefly prior to getting into the construction of the programs in order for you to see why the CALL method was chosen.

In the native mode the various instruments used have to be defined. For example, the terminal used has to be defined in the SPECIAL-NAMES paragraph as follows:

```
SPECIAL-NAMES,
      SYMBOLIC CHARACTERS VT100C IS 97,
      SYMBOLIC CHARACTERS ESCAPE-CHARACTER IS 28,
```

In the preceding example the type of terminal we used, a DEC VT100, is defined and, in the second statement, the value of the cursor character is defined. The values assigned here are good *only* for the DEC VT100C and for the DEC-VAX VMS operating system. So if you are using a different terminal or a different operating system you would be obliged to consult the COBOL user's manual for the operating system in use and the specifications for the terminal in use. All this work is contradictory to the generalizable characteristics of COBOL. You would then need to code some additional definitions in the DATA DIVISION in order to refer to these items in the PROCEDURE DIVISION. An example of this is as follows:

```
01  DEVICE-TYPE       PIC X,
      88 VT100 VALUE VT100C,
```

Movement of the cursor on the screen can then be handled as follows in the native mode:

```
ESC [line #;column-number f.]
```

This statement, when coupled with the characters in the SPECIAL-NAMES SECTION of the ENVIRONMENT DIVISION, causes the cursor to "HOME UP," that is, to move to the upper-left-hand side of the video display terminal. Again, in order to use native mode you must either memorize the characters that cause cursor movements of certain types ("#" and "f" in our case for the uppermost row in the leftmost column) or you must look them up. The same procedure can be accomplished with a CALL to the RTL without having to define special characters or to remember the special sequence of characters required in the native mode.

Run-Time Library Calls

Consider the following statement, available on DEC-VAX systems, which causes a HOME UP.

```
CALL "SCR$SET_CURSOR" USING BY VALUE 1,1,
```

This statement tells the RTL to position the cursor to line 1 position 1 of the video screen, just as in the example for native mode. The procedure "SCR$SET_CURSOR" has been defined in the RTL of the DEC-VAX/VMS operating system, so if you transport your program to a machine using a different operating system you will have to recode this, and other similar lines. In other words, these instructions are extremely machine dependent—again neutralizing one of the strengths of the COBOL language. However, the RTL call is still easier to use than the native mode.

There are a number of other operations that are necessary in the use of video form control operations. One of these is the "CLEAR SCREEN" function. The CALL to the RTL that will blank the video screen and move the cursor to the home up position is as follows:

```
CALL "SCR$ERASE_PAGE" USING BY VALUE 1,1,
```

The USING BY VALUE 1,1 phrase in the CALL statement passes the line number and column number to the CALLed procedure stating where on the video screen you wish to position the cursor.

Horizontal and vertical positioning of the cursor is accomplished by use of the CALL "SCR$SET_CURSOR" USING BY VALUE x,y command, where x is the line number and y is the position number within line x. For example, to position the cursor to line 5 position 20, the following CALL command would be used.

```
CALL "SCR$SET_CURSOR" USING BY VALUE 5,20,
```

DISPLAY *and* ACCEPT *Statements*

The DISPLAY and ACCEPT statements are used to "paint" information on the screen and retrieve data from terminal devices. The use of these two statements is similar to their use in batch systems and is illustrated here by reference to the sample programs.

The Main Menu Program

The program for displaying the master menu on the video screen is shown in its entirety in Figure 10-10. The following explanations will make use of portions of the program as they are required.

Notice that there is nothing in the IDENTIFICATION or ENVIRONMENT DIVISIONs that is different than for batch programs. The PROCEDURE DIVISION, however, may contain statements that are not familiar to you at this point. You may want to review or refer to Chapter 7 as you read through the material here, since many of the statements are covered in more detail in that chapter.

000-MAIN.

000-MAIN controls the other modules in the program. The statements in this module are as follows:

```
PERFORM 800-PAINT-MENU
PERFORM 200-GET-ANSWER
GO TO 000-MAIN,
```

The first PERFORM statement causes the program to execute the module that "paints" or displays the master menu on the video display device. The terms "paint," "screen painting," and "form painting" are commonly used to describe the process of displaying data on a monitor, and we will follow that convention throughout the chapter.

The next statement

```
PERFORM 200-GET-ANSWER,
```

causes the program to execute the module that processes the user's menu selection. The PERFORMed procedure (200-GET-ANSWER) also causes the program to CALL the program appropriate to the user's choice of menu item from the library for execution.

Figure 10–10
Program for painting the master
menu.

```
IDENTIFICATION DIVISION.
PROGRAM-ID. APMENU.
AUTHOR. CSIMPSON.
INSTALLATION. GRAMBLING STATE UNIVERSITY.
ENVIRONMENT DIVISION.
CONFIGURATION SECTION.
SOURCE-COMPUTER. VAX-11.
OBJECT-COMPUTER. VAX-11.
DATA DIVISION.
WORKING-STORAGE SECTION.
01 H1.
        05  FILLER PIC X(40) VALUE ALL "*".
01   H2.
        05  FILLER PIC X(40) VALUE
        "* ACCOUNTS PAYABLE MASTER MENU          *".
01   H3.
        05  FILLER PIC X(40) VALUE
        "*01 VENDOR MAINTENANCE                  *".
01   H4.
        05  FILLER PIC X(40) VALUE
        "*02 CHART OF ACCOUNTS MAINTENANCE       *".
01   H5.
        05  FILLER PIC X(40) VALUE
        "*03 INVOICE ENTRY & MAINTENANCE         *".
01   H6.
        05  FILLER PIC X(40) VALUE
        "*04 REPORTS MENU                        *".
01   H7.
        05  FILLER PIC X(40) VALUE
        "*05 INVOICE SELECTION FOR PAYMENT       *".
01   H8.
        05  FILLER PIC X(40) VALUE
        "*06 PRINT CHECKS                        *".
01   H9.
        05  FILLER PIC X(40) VALUE
        "*07 POST INVOICES                       *".
01   H10.
        05  FILLER PIC X(40) VALUE
        "*08 PRINT ACCOUNT ACTIVITY              *".
01   H11.
        05  FILLER PIC X(40) VALUE
        "*09 RECONCILE CHECKS                    *".
01   H12.
        05  FILLER PIC X(40) VALUE
        "*10 END IT ALL                          *".
01   H13.
        05  FILLER PIC X(40) VALUE
        "*       CHOOSE ONE!                     *".
01  ANSWER PIC 99 VALUE ZEROS.
PROCEDURE DIVISION.
000-MAIN.
        PERFORM 800-PAINT-MENU.
        PERFORM 200-GET-ANSWER.
        GO TO 000-MAIN.
200-GET-ANSWER.
        CALL "SCR$SET_CURSOR" USING BY VALUE 14,2.
        ACCEPT ANSWER.
        GO TO CALL-1
                CALL-2
                CALL-3
                CALL-4
                CALL-5
                CALL-6
                CALL-7
                CALL-8
                CALL-9
                CALL-10
                              DEPENDING ON ANSWER.
        GO TO 000-MAIN.
CALL-1.
        GO TO 000-MAIN.
CALL-2.
        CALL "AP2".
        GO TO 000-MAIN.
CALL-3.
        GO TO 000-MAIN.
CALL-4.
        GO TO 000-MAIN.
CALL-5.
        GO TO 000-MAIN.
CALL-6.
        GO TO 000-MAIN.
CALL-7.
        GO TO 000-MAIN.
CALL-8.
        GO TO 000-MAIN.
CALL-9.
        GO TO 000-MAIN.
CALL-10.
        STOP RUN.
```

Figure 10–10 (continued)

```
800-PAINT-MENU.
          CALL "SCR$ERASE_PAGE" USING BY VALUE 1,1.
          CALL "SCR$SET_CURSOR" USING BY VALUE 1,1.
          DISPLAY H1 WITH NO ADVANCING.
          CALL "SCR$SET_CURSOR" USING BY VALUE 2,1.
          DISPLAY H2 WITH NO ADVANCING.
          CALL "SCR$SET_CURSOR" USING BY VALUE 3,1.
          DISPLAY H1 WITH NO ADVANCING.
          CALL "SCR$SET_CURSOR" USING BY VALUE 4,1.
          DISPLAY H3 WITH NO ADVANCING.
          CALL "SCR$SET_CURSOR" USING BY VALUE 5,1.
          DISPLAY H4 WITH NO ADVANCING.
          CALL "SCR$SET_CURSOR" USING BY VALUE 6,1.
          DISPLAY H5 WITH NO ADVANCING.
          CALL "SCR$SET_CURSOR" USING BY VALUE 7,1.
          DISPLAY H6 WITH NO ADVANCING.
          CALL "SCR$SET_CURSOR" USING BY VALUE 8,1.
          DISPLAY H7 WITH NO ADVANCING.
          CALL "SCR$SET_CURSOR" USING BY VALUE 9,1.
          DISPLAY H8 WITH NO ADVANCING.
          CALL "SCR$SET_CURSOR" USING BY VALUE 10,1.
          DISPLAY H9 WITH NO ADVANCING.
          CALL "SCR$SET_CURSOR" USING BY VALUE 11,1.
          DISPLAY H10 WITH NO ADVANCING.
          CALL "SCR$SET_CURSOR" USING BY VALUE 12,1.
          DISPLAY H11 WITH NO ADVANCING.
          CALL "SCR$SET_CURSOR" USING BY VALUE 13,1.
          DISPLAY H12 WITH NO ADVANCING.
          CALL "SCR$SET_CURSOR" USING BY VALUE 14,1.
          DISPLAY H13 WITH NO ADVANCING.
          CALL "SCR$SET_CURSOR" USING BY VALUE 15,1.
          DISPLAY H1 WITH NO ADVANCING.
```

The next statement

```
GO TO 000-MAIN.
```

is, unfortunately, not in keeping with the kind of programming structures that we like to see. However, as we discussed in Chapter 2, the term "structured programming" is not strictly equivalent to "GO TOless programming." You may also recall that COBOL does not directly implement the CASE construct. The logic in this program is a good example of the CASE structure. In order to implement the logic and to assure that the code is uncluttered we, reluctantly, but with justification, introduce an unconditional branch.

200-GET-ANSWER

The logic in this module is as follows:

```
CALL "SCR$SET_CURSOR" USING BY VALUE 14,2.
ACCEPT ANSWER.
GO TO CALL-1
          CALL-2
          CALL-3
          CALL-4
          CALL-5
          CALL-6
          CALL-7
          CALL-8
          CALL-9
          CALL-10
               DEPENDING ON ANSWER.
```

The statement

```
CALL "SCR$SET_CURSOR" USING BY VALUE 14,2.
```

CALLs (from the RTL) the routine necessary to move the cursor to line 14 position 2. Notice from Figure 10-1 that line 14 position 2 is the point on the menu screen at which the user is asked to make a choice of menu items. Also observe that the cursor displayed in Figure 10-1 is sitting in the main menu on line 14 position 2.

The next statement

```
ACCEPT ANSWER.
```

ACCEPTs keyboard input from the terminal device when the ENTER key is depressed. In this case, it should be a value from 01 through 10.

The GO TO...DEPENDING ON... statement, which provides for an indirect implementation of the CASE construct, uses the value of ANSWER to determine the next statement to be executed in the program. Recall from Chapter 7 that the next statement to be executed will be the first statement in the paragraph named CALL-1 if the value of ANSWER is 01 or of CALL-2 if the value of ANSWER is 02 or of CALL-3 if the value of ANSWER is 03 and so forth. These program segments are presented for purposes of illustration. We have not included code for the paragraphs CALL-1, CALL-2, etc. because the details of procedures to be performed do not contribute to the illustration of concepts introduced here. In a program written for purposes other than illustration, the paragraph-names would be more descriptive of the functions performed and would also refer to a section of the system specifications.

If the value of ANSWER is not in the range 01 to 10 the PERFORM statement that is in control (PERFORM 200-GET ANSWER) is completed and the logic branches back to the unconditional branch statement that we reluctantly included (GO TO 000-MAIN). The process is then started all over again: the screen will be repainted and the process of selecting a menu item can continue.

CALL-1, CALL-2, *etc.*

The paragraphs CALL-1, CALL-2, and so forth, serve the purpose of CALLing the appropriate program from the library of programs available to the user, based on the user's choice from the menu. If the user selects the value 02 from the menu, this means that he or she wants to maintain chart of accounts data. If, however, that really was not what the user wanted to do, then the CALLed program should provide for easy exit from it back to the main menu. Such an exit process is provided in our example programs.

The main menu program (APMENU) will then CALL the program AP2 from the user's library of programs. It is necessary to remember that in order to successfully compile, link, and execute a program with CALL statements in it, the library must contain these programs in the form of previously compiled programs.

800-PAINT-MENU.

The module 800-PAINT-MENU causes the actual menu to be DISPLAYed on the video screen.

The first statement in the module

```
CALL "SCR$ERASE_PAGE" USING BY VALUE 1,1,
```

causes the computer to erase whatever information is on the screen and to position the cursor to the home position.

The next pair of statements and all subsequent pairs of statements in this module position the cursor to the specified line and column on the screen and then DISPLAY the information from the WORKING-STORAGE SECTION on the screen.

As a result of executing this module, the screen, as depicted in Figure 10-1, is painted on the user's video terminal.

SECTION 3
The Chart of Accounts Maintenance Submenu

After the user selects a value of 02 from the main menu, the program AP2 (see Figure 10-11) is CALLed from the library. The next thing the user sees on the video terminal is the submenu as depicted in Figure 10-2.

The logic required to present this screen is contained in paragraph 600-PAINT-MENU. This logic is very similar to that presented in the 800-PAINT-MENU module of the main menu program.

From the menu shown in Figure 10-2 the user can make a number of choices about what he or she wants to do to the chart of accounts file. If the user desires to add a record to the CHART-MASTER then 1 will be selected from the submenu. If the user wants to change a record in the submenu then 2 will be selected, and so forth. For purposes of illustration we have included the code for only the first option on the menu, an addition to the chart of accounts. The reader is asked to complete this logic as a requirement of Exercise 10-1.

Figure 10-11

Program to maintain chart of accounts.

```
IDENTIFICATION DIVISION.
PROGRAM-ID. AP2.
AUTHOR. CSIMPSON.
INSTALLATION.  GRAMBLING STATE UNIVERSITY.
ENVIRONMENT DIVISION.
CONFIGURATION SECTION.
SOURCE-COMPUTER. VAX-11.
OBJECT-COMPUTER. VAX-11.
INPUT-OUTPUT SECTION.
FILE-CONTROL.
        SELECT CHART-MASTER ASSIGN TO "COAMAST.DAT"
                ORGANIZATION IS INDEXED
                ACCESS MODE IS DYNAMIC
                RECORD KEY IS ACCOUNT-NUMBER.
DATA DIVISION.
FILE SECTION.
        COPY "CHARTFD.COB".
WORKING-STORAGE SECTION.
01  LINE-NO                PIC 99 VALUE 05.
01  COL-NO                 PIC 99 VALUE 12.
01  REV                    PIC 9 USAGE COMP VALUE 2.
01  MONEY-IN               PIC S9(08) VALUE ZEROS.
01  MONEY-INX REDEFINES MONEY-IN PIC X(08).
01  ANSWER                 PIC 9.
01  XANSWER                PIC X.
01  I                      PIC 99 VALUE ZEROS.
01  SUB                    PIC 99 VALUE ZEROS.
01  S1  PIC X(39) VALUE ALL "*".
01  S2  PIC X(39) VALUE
        "* CHART OF ACCOUNT MAINTENANCE          *".
01  S3  PIC X(39) VALUE
        "* 1 ADD AN ACCOUNT                      *".
01  S4  PIC X(39) VALUE
        "* 2 CHANGE AN ACCOUNT                   *".
01  S5  PIC X(39) VALUE
        "* 3 DISPLAY AN ACCOUNT                  *".
01  S6  PIC X(39) VALUE
        "* 4 DELETE AN ACCOUNT                   *".
01  S7  PIC X(39)
        VALUE "* 5 PRINT CHART OF ACCOUNTS           *".
01  S8  PIC X(39) VALUE
        "* 6 RETURN TO MAIN MENU                 *".
01  S9  PIC X(39) VALUE
        "*   CHOOSE ONE!                         *".
01  L1  PIC X(50) VALUE ALL "*".
01  L2  PIC X(50) VALUE
        "*            CHART OF ACCOUNTS DISPLAY            *".
01  L3  PIC X(50) VALUE
        "*            CHART OF ACCOUNTS CHANGES            *".
01  L4  PIC X(50) VALUE
        "*            CHART OF ACCOUNTS ADDITIONS          *".
```

Figure 10–11 (continued)

```
01  L5.
    05  FILLER          PIC X(16) VALUE "*ACCOUNT NUMBER: ".
    05  FILLER          PIC X(08) VALUE ALL " ".
    05  FILLER          PIC X(09) VALUE "ACCT-IND: ".
    05  FILLER          PIC X(16) VALUE SPACES.
    05  FILLER          PIC X(01) VALUE "*".
01  L6.
    05  FILLER          PIC X(11) VALUE "*ACCT-NAME: ".
    05  L6-ACCOUNT-NAME PIC X(35).
    05  FILLER          PIC X(04) VALUE "   *".
01  L7.
    05  FILLER          PIC X(11) VALUE "*BALANCES:  ".
    05  FILLER          PIC X(14) VALUE SPACES.
    05  FILLER          PIC X(09) VALUE "OKAY Y/N?".
    05  FILLER          PIC X(15) VALUE SPACES.
    05  FILLER          PIC X(01) VALUE "*".
01  L8.
    05  FILLER          PIC X(02) VALUE "* ".
    05  L8-BAL1         PIC ZZZZZZ.99CR.
    05  FILLER          PIC X(01) VALUE SPACES.
    05  L8-BAL2         PIC ZZZZZZ.99CR.
    05  FILLER          PIC X(01) VALUE SPACES.
    05  L8-BAL3         PIC ZZZZZZ.99CR.
    05  FILLER          PIC X(01) VALUE SPACES.
    05  L8-BAL4         PIC ZZZZZZ.99CR.
    05  FILLER          PIC X(01) VALUE "*".
01  TABLE-DATA.
    05  FILLER PIC X(26) VALUE "CAFALINWSACSSEAEOECEFEOITE".
01  ACCOUNT-CODES REDEFINES TABLE-DATA.
    05  ACCOUNT-CODE OCCURS 13 TIMES PIC XX.
01  EOF-SW      PIC X(01) VALUE SPACES.
01  VALID-SW    PIC X(01) VALUE SPACES.
01  ENTRY-FOUND-SWITCH PIC X(03).
    88  ENTRY-FOUND   VALUE "YES".
    88  END-OF-TABLE VALUE "END".
PROCEDURE DIVISION.
000-MAIN.
    OPEN I-O CHART-MASTER.
100-HANDLE-REQUEST.
    PERFORM 500-DISPLAY-MENU.
    CALL "SCR$SET_CURSOR" USING BY VALUE 10,3.
    ACCEPT ANSWER.
    GO TO   210-ADD-AN-ACCOUNT
            220-CHANGE-AN-ACCOUNT
            230-DISPLAY-AN-ACCOUNT
            240-DELETE-AN-ACCOUNT
            250-PRINT-ACCOUNTS
            260-RETURN-TO-MAIN
                DEPENDING ON ANSWER.
    GO TO 100-HANDLE-REQUEST.
210-ADD-AN-ACCOUNT.
    MOVE SPACES TO ENTRY-FOUND-SWITCH.
    PERFORM 600-DISPLAY-FORM.
    CALL "SCR$SET_CURSOR" USING BY VALUE 4,17.
    ACCEPT ACCOUNT-NUMBER.
    IF ACCOUNT-NUMBER = "END"
        GO TO 100-HANDLE-REQUEST.
    PERFORM 650-CHECK-FOR-ACCOUNT.
211-RETRY-INDICATOR.
    CALL "SCR$SET_CURSOR" USING BY VALUE 5,52.
    DISPLAY "                    " WITH NO ADVANCING.
    CALL "SCR$SET_CURSOR" USING BY VALUE 4,34.
    ACCEPT ACCOUNT-INDICATOR.
    MOVE SPACES TO ENTRY-FOUND-SWITCH.
    PERFORM 700-SEARCH-CODE
        UNTIL ENTRY-FOUND
        OR END-OF-TABLE.
    IF ENTRY-FOUND
        NEXT SENTENCE
    ELSE
        GO TO 211-RETRY-INDICATOR.
    CALL "SCR$SET_CURSOR" USING BY VALUE 5,15.
    ACCEPT ACCOUNT-NAME.
    PERFORM 212-ACCEPT-BALANCES
        VARYING SUB
            FROM 1 BY 1
                UNTIL SUB > 12.
REACCEPT-ANSWER.
    CALL "SCR$SET_CURSOR" USING BY VALUE 6,41.
    ACCEPT XANSWER.
    IF XANSWER = "N"
        NEXT SENTENCE
    ELSE
        IF XANSWER = "Y" PERFORM 750-WRITE-RECORD
            GO TO 210-ADD-AN-ACCOUNT.
    GO TO REACCEPT-ANSWER.
212-ACCEPT-BALANCES.
    MOVE ZEROS TO ACCOUNT-BALANCES (SUB).
    CALL "SCR$SET_CURSOR" USING BY VALUE 6,13.
    DISPLAY SUB.
    CALL "SCR$SET_CURSOR" USING BY VALUE 6,17.
    ACCEPT MONEY-INX.
    INSPECT MONEY-INX REPLACING ALL " " BY "0".
    DIVIDE MONEY-IN BY 100 GIVING ACCOUNT-BALANCES (SUB).
```

Figure 10-11 (continued)

```
220-CHANGE-AN-ACCOUNT.
        EXIT.
230-DISPLAY-AN-ACCOUNT.
        EXIT.
240-DELETE-AN-ACCOUNT.
        EXIT.
250-PRINT-ACCOUNTS.
        EXIT.
260-RETURN-TO-MAIN.
        EXIT PROGRAM.
500-DISPLAY-MENU.
        CALL "SCR$ERASE PAGE" USING BY VALUE 1, 1.
        CALL "SCR$SET_CURSOR" USING BY VALUE 1, 1.
        DISPLAY S1 WITH NO ADVANCING.
        CALL "SCR$SET_CURSOR" USING BY VALUE 2, 1.
        DISPLAY S2 WITH NO ADVANCING.
        CALL "SCR$SET_CURSOR" USING BY VALUE 3, 1.
        DISPLAY S1 WITH NO ADVANCING.
        CALL "SCR$SET_CURSOR" USING BY VALUE 4, 1.
        DISPLAY S3 WITH NO ADVANCING.
        CALL "SCR$SET_CURSOR" USING BY VALUE 5, 1.
        DISPLAY S4 WITH NO ADVANCING.
        CALL "SCR$SET_CURSOR" USING BY VALUE 6, 1.
        DISPLAY S5 WITH NO ADVANCING.
        CALL "SCR$SET_CURSOR" USING BY VALUE 7, 1.
        DISPLAY S6 WITH NO ADVANCING.
        CALL "SCR$SET_CURSOR" USING BY VALUE 8, 1.
        DISPLAY S7 WITH NO ADVANCING.
        CALL "SCR$SET_CURSOR" USING BY VALUE 9, 1.
        DISPLAY S8 WITH NO ADVANCING.
        CALL "SCR$SET_CURSOR" USING BY VALUE 10, 1.
        DISPLAY S9 WITH NO ADVANCING.
        CALL "SCR$SET_CURSOR" USING BY VALUE 11, 1.
        DISPLAY S1 WITH NO ADVANCING.
600-DISPLAY-FORM.
        CALL "SCR$ERASE PAGE" USING BY VALUE 1, 1.
        CALL "SCR$SET_CURSOR" USING BY VALUE 1, 1.
        DISPLAY L1 WITH NO ADVANCING.
        CALL "SCR$SET_CURSOR" USING BY VALUE 2, 1.
        IF ANSWER = 1
                DISPLAY L4 WITH NO ADVANCING
        ELSE
                IF ANSWER = 2
                        DISPLAY L3 WITH NO ADVANCING
        ELSE
                IF ANSWER = 3
                        DISPLAY L2 WITH NO ADVANCING.
        CALL "SCR$SET_CURSOR" USING BY VALUE 3, 1.
        DISPLAY L1 WITH NO ADVANCING.
        CALL "SCR$SET_CURSOR" USING BY VALUE 4, 1.
        DISPLAY L5 WITH NO ADVANCING.
        CALL "SCR$SET_CURSOR" USING BY VALUE 5, 1.
        DISPLAY L6 WITH NO ADVANCING.
        CALL "SCR$PUT_SCREEN"
                USING  L6-ACCOUNT-NAME, LINE-NO, COL-NO, REV.
        CALL "SCR$SET_CURSOR" USING BY VALUE 6, 1.
        DISPLAY L7 WITH NO ADVANCING.
        CALL "SCR$SET_CURSOR" USING BY VALUE 7, 1.
        DISPLAY L8 WITH NO ADVANCING.
        CALL "SCR$SET_CURSOR" USING BY VALUE 8, 1.
        DISPLAY L1 WITH NO ADVANCING.
650-CHECK-FOR-ACCOUNT.
        READ CHART-MASTER
                INVALID KEY
                        CALL "SCR$SET_CURSOR" USING BY VALUE 5, 52
                        DISPLAY "WE WILL ADD RECORD" ACCOUNT-NUMBER
                        WITH NO ADVANCING
                        MOVE "X" TO VALID-SW.
        IF VALID-SW = " "
                DISPLAY "THIS IS A DUPLICATE RECORD"
                DISPLAY "PRESS ANY KEY TO CONTINUE"
                ACCEPT XANSWER
                GO TO 100-HANDLE-REQUEST.
        MOVE " " TO VALID-SW.
700-SEARCH-CODE.
        ADD 1 TO I.
        IF ACCOUNT-INDICATOR = ACCOUNT-CODE (I)
                MOVE "YES" TO ENTRY-FOUND-SWITCH.
        IF I = 13
                MOVE "END" TO ENTRY-FOUND-SWITCH.
750-WRITE-RECORD.
        WRITE CHART-RECORD
                INVALID KEY
                DISPLAY "THIS SHOULD NOT HAPPEN, BUT--"
                DISPLAY "YOU HAVE A DUPLICATE RECORD  "
                DISPLAY "PRESS ANY KEY TO CONTINUE    "
                ACCEPT XANSWER
                GO TO 100-HANDLE-REQUEST.
```

`100-HANDLE-REQUEST,`

The logic in `100-HANDLE-REQUEST` `ACCEPT`s an `ANSWER` from the terminal user and goes to the module selected, based on the value of `ANSWER`. The only `ANSWER`s allowed are 1, 2, 3, 4, 5, and 6. If a value is entered other than one of these numbers, the logic directs that the submenu be redisplayed and the user gets another chance to enter the desired selection. If the user has entered the program by mistake, then the menu provides the user with the option to return to the main menu before anything is done by selecting item 6.

`210-ADD-AN-ACCOUNT,`

The logic for `210-ADD-AN-ACCOUNT` is presented as Figure 10-11. The first statement resets an edit "switch" that is used to check the account indicator to see if it is valid.

The next statement, `PERFORM 600-DISPLAY-FORM`, causes the execution of the module that paints the data entry form on the screen.

The next two statements

```
CALL "SCR$SET_CURSOR" USING BY VALUE 4,17,
ACCEPT ACCOUNT-NUMBER,
```

position the cursor at the point on the form where the ACCOUNT NUMBER is to be entered and `ACCEPT`s the ACCOUNT-NUMBER into the record area.

The next statement checks for the value `END`. If that value is encountered, there is an exit from the `210-ADD-AN-ACCOUNT` routine and a return to the module that paints the AP2 submenu.

The `PERFORM 650-CHECK-FOR-ACCOUNT` statement `PERFORM`s the module that `READ`s the `CHART-MASTER` and checks for the presence or absence of a record. If a record is not present then the record can be added to the file. If the record is present then the record cannot be added to the file, because it would be a duplicate record. In this particular case we use the `INVALID KEY` clause to handle the "good" condition—having no record on the file when we try to add one. When we get an `INVALID KEY` return we go ahead and process the addition of the record. If, on the other hand, we get no invalid key indication, we consider this to be a "bad" result—trying to add a record that already exists—and we `DISPLAY` an error message and abort the attempt to add.

The logic

```
211-RETRY-INDICATOR,
    CALL "SCR$SET_CURSOR" USING BY VALUE 4,31,
    ACCEPT ACCOUNT-INDICATOR,
    PERFORM 700-SEARCH-CODE
        UNTIL ENTRY-FOUND
        OR END-OF-TABLE,
    IF ENTRY-FOUND
        NEXT SENTENCE
    ELSE
        GO TO 211-RETRY-INDICATOR,
```

`ACCEPT`s the `ACCOUNT-INDICATOR` and checks to see if it is one of the 13 valid account indicators contained in a table. If so, the logic proceeds, if not, the user is directed back to the point on the screen where the account indicator is to be reentered.

The next two statements in the module position the cursor to line 5 position 15 and `ACCEPT`s the `ACCOUNT NAME` data.

The next group of statements ACCEPTs balances for the 12 months of the year by PERFORMing 212-ACCEPT-BALANCES.

The next portion of this module

```
CALL "SCR$SET_CURSOR" USING BY VALUE 6,41,
ACCEPT XANSWER,
IF XANSWER = "N"
    NEXT SENTENCE
ELSE
    IF XANSWER = "Y"
        PERFORM 750-WRITE-RECORD
        GO TO 210-ADD-AN-ACCOUNT,
```

positions the cursor to line 6 position 41 and accepts the value "Y" or "N". If the value of XANSWER is Y then the record is written to disc. If the answer is N or anything else the module returns the user to the submenu.

SECTION 4
Questions and Exercises

I. Questions

1. What is a terminal?
2. What is transaction oriented processing?
3. What is a menu as it relates to on-line data processing?
4. What is a submenu and why is one used?
5. What is a cursor?
6. Why is the DISPLAY statement used with the NO ADVANCING option in the chapter exercise?
7. How is the CASE structure implemented in the example program in this chapter?

II. Programming Exercises

1. Complete the example program used in this chapter to include:
   a. changes
   b. displays
   c. deletions
   d. a listing of the chart of accounts after changes and deletions.
   e. Change the logic in the 210-ADD-AN-ACCOUNT module to allow the user to correct a response to the question regarding whether or not the data entered are correct. In the present logic the user is returned to the beginning of the form if either N or any value but Y is entered.
   f. Change the program to allow the user to retry the answer if a value other than N or Y is entered.
2. Refer to the indexed customer master file created in Exercise II-3 of Chapter 4. Write a COBOL program that uses this file as input to accomplish the following operations from a terminal:

   • add customers to the customer master file
   • display a specific customer on the user terminal

- delete a specific customer from the file
- change any field in the customer master file with the exception of the customer number field [key field]

Use a submenu to provide for the selection of item(s) to selected from among these operations.

3. Refer to the indexed personnel master file created in the exercises in Chapter 4. Write a COBOL program that will perform the following operations:

- add personnel records to the file
- display an employee
- delete a specific employee
- change any field in a record except social security number.

Use a submenu on the terminal to allow selection of the operation(s) to be executed from the list of operations.

11

Table-Handling Concepts and Techniques

Tables are frequently used in business applications. Tables in these applications are used for three primary purposes:

1. encoding data and decoding coded data
2. temporary storage of accumulated data
3. retrieving table values based on other values

Data are frequently coded to save storage space on mass storage devices. When reports are needed, the coded information may be displayed in noncoded form on whatever output medium is desired. Values may be temporarily stored in a table based on an index or relative value. For example, if an input record contains a division code and sales values, among other values, the division code may be used as the basis for adding the sales value to the table in the appropriate position and then printing the total sales for each division at the end of the input process.

Data that are necessary for further calculations can be retrieved from a table based on the value of input data-items. The data-items are used as the reference points for retrieving the table-item needed in some way within the program. For example, in the often-used payroll problem, the employee's paycheck amount will be calculated from a number of variables such as rate of pay, hours worked, number of dependents, and amount of insurance.

The way in which a table is used may dictate the table-processing techniques used in the COBOL program.

Table Terms and Concepts

Prior to consideration of different table-handling and creation techniques, a number of terms related to table concepts should be defined. The following definitions will apply in this chapter:

Term	Definition
Table	a collection of items
Table entry	an individual item stored in a table
Table argument	value stored in table that is used to retrieve a data-item (table function) from the table
Search argument	value, usually from input record, used to match the table argument in order to retrieve a data-item from the table.
Table function	data-items stored in the table that are being retrieved usually for use in decoding data.
Subscripts	relative position value vis-à-vis the beginning of the table.

Figure 11-1 illustrates the preceding terms.

The set of items illustrated in Figure 11-1 composes a table: the product classification table. Each line in the table is a table entry. The first column of the table, "product classification code," is the table argument. The table has three table functions:

- product classification name
- product classification cost
- unit of measure

Two terms, *subscripts* and *search arguments,* remain to be discussed. The subscript is the relative position of an entry in a table. For example: product classification code 04 is the first entry in the table—therefore, the subscript value that refers to this entry is 1; product classification code 06 entry is the second table entry *relative to the beginning of the table*—therefore, its subscript is 2; and so forth for each entry in the table. The maximum subscript value is the same as the number of entries in the table and the minimum subscript value in COBOL is 1. This minimum subscript value may differ from that of other languages, such as BASIC.

A search argument is probably most easily defined through the use of an illustration.

Suppose that you have an input record with the following format:

Input Columns	Content
1–2	record code
3–7	vendor code
8–10	quantity
11–12	product classification code

Figure 11–1
Illustration of table terms.

Product Classification Code	Product Classification Name	Product Classification Cost	Unit of Measure
04	cattle	.57	pound→ Table entry
06	hogs	.37	pound→ Table entry
08	sheep	.22	pound→ Table entry
11	hay	1.22	bale——→Table entry
22	grain	3.25	bushel→ Table entry

Table argument ↑

Table functions

Further assume that you have an output report requirement as follows:

Output Columns	Content
1–3	blank
4–10	product classification name
11	blank
12–14	quantity
15	blank
16–19	product cost
20	blank
21–25	unit of measure
26	blank
27–32	total cost

As you can see, quantity comes from the input record and can be moved directly to the output record. However, product classification name, product cost, and unit of measure are not contained in the input record and must be moved to the output report from some other source. If we have a table of values such as the one in Figure 11-1 and that table is accessible to the program, then we have a source for these missing variables. Total cost is calculated from input data (quantity) and table data (product cost).

The issue of greatest importance to us is the way in which the input data and the table data are related. They are related through the use of the table argument and the search argument. The search argument is compared to the table argument repeatedly until there is a match or until all the table entries have been exhausted in the comparison process.

The items moved from the table to the output report (product classification name, product cost, and unit of measure) are table functions. A subscript (relative position indicator) is required to extract data from the table.

Table argument codes can be implied in some tables. The most common example of this is a month table, in which the code for the month implies the month's relative position in the table. Figure 11-2 illustrates this concept. In Figure 11-2, "month code" is the table argument and "month name" is the table function. In this particular case, the subscript and table argument are equal. In almost all programming operations using a table of this type, the inclusion of the month code is redundant since the code also reflects the table entry's relative position in the

Figure 11–2
Month table.

Month Code	Month Name
01	January
02	February
03	March
04	April
05	May
06	June
07	July
08	August
09	September
10	October
11	November
12	December

table. When this situation occurs, the table argument need not be included as part of the table entry. There are other situations in which the table argument can be calculated so that it need not be included in the table.

SECTION 2
Classification of Tables

There are almost as many ways to classify tables as there are people writing on the subject. The means of classification that we enumerate here are commonly used in the COBOL user community.

Internal versus External Tables

Tables are classified as internal or external, based on the COBOL program's perspective. If the table is incorporated within the program it is said to be an internal table. If the the table resides on an I/O device and is retrieved from that device, then the table is considered to be an external table.

Internal tables may be further classified as "hard coded" or "input loaded." A hard-coded table's entries are coded within the COBOL program's DATA DIVISION. An input-loaded table's entries are read from some I/O device and temporarily stored in the COBOL program's DATA DIVISION. Changes to the data included in a hard-coded table require that changes be made to the VALUE clauses that constitute a part of the table definition. Similar changes to an input-loaded table are effected (as the name implies) by READing or ACCEPTing new data into the table. No change to the program code itself is required in the case of an input-loaded table.

External tables generally use the file-handling techniques described in previous chapters, particularly those that deal with imbedded pointers. External tables may also use some data structures, such as B and B+ trees, that are not implemented with facility in COBOL. Also, stacks and queues are table types that are not manipulated with any degree of facility in COBOL. Therefore, this chapter focuses only on internal table concepts.

Static versus Volatile Tables

Tables may be classified further as static or volatile. This classification is based on the relative frequency of updating entries in a table. Tables that have infrequent updates are static tables and tables that have frequent updates are volatile tables.

Establishing the expected volatility of a table helps the program designer determine whether to use an external or internal table and, in the case of internal tables, whether to use in input-loaded or hard-coded table. Generally, a static table is usually internal and hard coded. In the case of Figure 11-2, it is not likely that the months of the year will change. On the other hand, the table illustrated in Figure 11-1 is likely to be an input-loaded internal table—internal because of the amount of data involved, and input loaded because the cost function is very likely to change. Certainly, in this case a programmer would not want to change the DATA DIVISION entries and recompile the program every time the cost data changed.

Table Organization Methods

Tables are usually organized in one or more of the following ways:

1. sequentially
2. randomly
3. usage frequency
4. relatively (direct)

Sequential Table Organization

Sequential table organization is based on the value of the table argument for each of the table entries. The data entries in Figure 11-1 and 11-2 are arranged in sequence on the value of the table argument, therefore they constitute sequential tables. If the data entries for Figure 11-2 were rearranged as in Figure 11-3, the table would be a randomly organized table. (There is no specific order based on the value of the table arguments.)

Figure 11–3
Randomly organized table.

Product Classification Code	Product Classification Name	Product Class. Cost	Unit of Measure
04	cattle	.57	pound
06	hogs	.37	pound
22	grain	3.25	bushel
11	hay	1.22	bale
08	sheep	.22	pound

The table in Figure 11-4 illustrates a usage-frequency table organization, assuming that the items contained in the table were arranged in the table based on their frequency of retrieval from the table. You may assume that a study of inventory movements has indicated that the record for hay is the most commonly accessed record, that the record for grain is second, and so on.

Figure 11–4
Usage frequency table organization.

Product Classification Code	Product Classification Name	Product Class. Cost	Unit of Measure
11	hay	1.22	bale
22	grain	3.25	bushel
04	cattle	.57	pound
06	hogs	.37	pound
08	sheep	.22	pound

The rationale behind this organization method is that time spent searching for an item in the table is minimized.

Positional Organization

The table data contained in Figure 11-2 can also be considered to be organized relatively. A relatively organized table must be arranged in ascending sequence on the value of the table argument and the table argument must be equal to the table entry's relative entry position. In other words, the table arguments must begin with a value of 1 and be incremented by 1 until the end of the table is reached. Otherwise, some conversion routine must be used to convert the table argument to such a set of relative values.

Levels of Tables (Dimensions)

Tables may also be classified based on the number of levels that exist within the table structure. The current maximum number of levels available in COBOL is three. COBOL 8x will allow a much higher limit—seven. We do not envision that this will be used to any great extent in COBOL programs, because most programmers have enough difficulty keeping up with three-level tables. You will see the reasons for these difficulties in subsequent sections of this chapter.

The number of levels (dimensions) of a table is determined by the number of table arguments that the table has. The table presented in Figure 11-1 is a one-dimension table because there is only one table argument—product classification code.

If we add another table argument (region) to the table presented in Figure 11-1, we will derive a two-dimension table as indicated in Figure 11-5.

Figure 11–5
Two-dimension table.

Product Classification Code	Product Classification Name	Product Class. Cost	Unit of Measure
Region 1			
11	hay	1.22	bale
22	grain	3.25	bushel
04	cattle	.57	pound
06	hogs	.37	pound
08	sheep	.22	pound
Region 2			
11	hay	1.25	bale
22	grain	3.24	bushel
04	cattle	.59	pound
06	hogs	.40	pound
08	sheep	.21	pound
	o		
	o		
	o		

Because the table now contains two table arguments, the retrieval process uses two search arguments—one for region and one for product classification code.

In becoming a two-dimension table, the table has become poorly constructed. The table functions (product classification name and unit of measure) do not change for a particular product: they are repeated from one region to the other, so the table contains redundant data. In properly constructed tables redundant data are minimized. This particular problem can be avoided by constructing another table that contains product classification name and unit of measure.

SECTION 3
Table-Retrieval Methods

The way in which data are retrieved from a table is referred to as the *retrieval method,* or as the *table search method.* The retrieval or search methods discussed in this chapter are:

1. serial search
2. serial search with early exit
3. binary search
4. relative retrieval

Serial Search of a Table

A serial search compares the value of the search argument to the value of each table argument in the table being searched. When the value of the search argument is equal to the value of the table argument, the table function(s) for this table entry may be retrieved. This is referred to as a "hit."

A sequential search does not necessarily require that the data be ordered in any particular way, since the comparison of search argument with table argument proceeds from entry to entry, until either a "hit" occurs or the table is exhausted. If a serial search with early exit is attempted, the file must be ordered on the basis of the table argument as is discussed in the next section.

If the comparison of search argument proceeds from the beginning of the table to the end of the table without a matching table argument being found, the search has failed and, typically, some indication of an error condition is displayed (or printed).

Assume that the table in Figure 11-1 is to be searched for a record having a product classification code of 08. Program logic using a serial search will proceed as follows:

Step	Action	Result	Action
1	compare 08 : 04	unequal	proceed to step 2
2	compare 08 : 06	unequal	proceed to step 3
3	compare 08 : 08	equal	exit process

Figure 11-6 shows the results of these comparisons.

Figure 11–6
Results of search of
single-dimension table.

Product Classification Code	Product Classification Name	Product Class. Cost	Unit of Measure
04 <08	cattle	.57	pound
06 <08	hogs	.37	pound
08 =08	sheep	.22	pound
11	hay	1.22	bale
22	grain	3.25	bushel

Figure 11–7
Search failure for
single-dimension table.

Product Classification Code	Product Classification Name	Product Class. Cost	Unit of Measure
04 <07	cattle	.57	pound
06 <07	hogs	.37	pound
08 >07	sheep	.22	pound
11 >07	hay	1.22	bale
22 >07	grain	3.25	bushel

When the equal comparison results in the search process, then one or more of the table functions for that specific entry are retrieved.

Let us now take a search argument for which there is no corresponding table argument and see what happens. Assume an input search argument equals 07. Figure 11-7 illustrates the results of this search.

Notice that the search argument is compared to each of the table entries for the product classification codes in the table. In all of the comparisons the result of the comparison is unequal, therefore there is no "hit" in the table.

Serial Search with Early Exit

It is easy to see that all comparisons—except the first, in which the table argument is greater than the search argument—are unnecessary. Since the table is in sequence, once a "greater than" comparison is reached, all subsequent comparisons will have the same result. We may use this observation to improve the efficiency of a sequential search. If the table is not in sequence based on the search argument, the entire table must be searched in order to conclude that the record sought is missing. But, if the table is sequenced (or ordered, or sorted) then the first "greater than" condition indicates conclusively that the record sought is not in the table, and the search may be abandoned. This process of abandoning the search process at this point is referred to as early exit. Early exit will result in greater efficiency when searching large tables than it does in this particular example.

Binary Table Search

When a table is large, the amount of time required to search that table sequentially can become significant. Generally, when a table contains more than 25 entries, binary search techniques should be used to reduce the number of compares in the search process.

Let us expand our example table a bit (although not to more than 25 entries) to illustrate the way a binary search process works. This expansion is contained in Figure 11-8.

The first requirement of a binary search is that the table entries be arranged in sequence (ascending or descending) on the value of the table argument.

The steps necessary to search the table in a binary process using a search argument of 37:

1. Select midpoint of the table (fifth item).
2. Compare search argument and table argument—37:22.
   a. If equal compare results, this is a hit.

Figure 11–8
Binary table search.

Product Classification Code	Product Classification Name	
04	cattle	
06	hogs	
08	sheep	
11	hay	
22	grain	← First compare < 37 ⌐
37	tractors	← Final compare
39	implements	← Third compare
44	fuels	← Second compare ←
66	fencing	
77	seed	

    b. If table argument is < search argument proceed one-half up in table. One half of the table items are eliminated at this point.

    c. If table argument is > search argument, proceed one-half down in table. One half of the table items are eliminated at this point.

  3. Proceed in this manner until a match is found or until entries in table are exhausted.

The number of compares needed to retrieve the table item in the example is four. The maximum number of compares required to retrieve an entry from a table is a function of the powers of 2—hence the name "binary search." (I.e., a maximum of 4 compares can search up to 16 [not inclusive] items in a table; 5 compares, up to 32, 6 compares, up to 64, etc.)

Relative Retrieval of Table Entries

Direct retrieval methods retrieve table data based on the relative position of entries in the table. Consider an example based on the data in Figure 11-2.

Month Code	Month Name	
01	January	
02	February	
03	March	
04 ←	April	⌐
05	May	
06	June	
07	July	→ Search argument = 04
08	August	direct retrieval "April"
09	September	
10	October	
11	November	
12	December	

If the input record contains a month code that needs to be decoded and that coded value is 04, then the program can directly retrieve the function (month name) directly as the fourth table entry relative to the beginning of the table.

SECTION 4
Processing Table Data in COBOL

Table Construction

The first step in the implementation of the table retrieval process is the establishment of the table (or an area in memory for the table) in the program.

As we have discussed in the preceding sections, the table may be constructed in memory as an input-loaded table or as a hard-coded table. First we will examine the hard-coded process.

We will use the previous illustrations in the discussion which follows. Figure 11-9 contains the month table as a hard-coded table. Figure 11-10 contains the product classification table as a hard-coded table of multiple functions.

The items included in Figure 11-9 are said to be hard-coded because they are physically part of the DATA DIVISION of a program. The first part of the table construction process is to create 12 separate items with data values assigned via the VALUE clause. Each of the data-items must contain exactly the same number of characters.

The next step is to impose a different way of referencing these data on the table values. This is accomplished with the REDEFINES clause. In our example, the REDEFINES clause tells the COBOL compiler to back up to the previous level number of the same value as the REDEFINES clause's level number, to rename this entry and divide the area into the number of areas described in the OCCURS clause and assign a PICTURE value as specified.

The product classification table is slightly more complex, since it consists of multiple table functions. Information such as that included in the product classification example is not likely to be hard-coded because of the volatility of the data contained in the table. We are using the example to illustrate the inclusion of a table with multiple table functions as a hard-coded table. Figure 11-10 includes line numbers for the code that are referenced in the discussion that follows.

The first six lines in Figure 11-10 define the values to be included within the table. Care should be taken to ensure that the various items within each entry will occupy the same (and correct) position from table entry to table entry.

Line number 7 superimposes the table structure from lines 9 through 13 over the data values assigned through VALUE clauses in lines 2 through 6. Coding line 8 specifies the number of entries the table will contain. Lines 9 through 13 divide each entry in the table as indicated.

Figure 11–9
Hard-coded month table.

```
01   MONTH-VALUES.
     05   FILLER        PIC X(9)  VALUE "JANUARY  ".
     05   FILLER        PIC X(9)  VALUE "FEBRUARY ".
     05   FILLER        PIC X(9)  VALUE "MARCH ".
     05   FILLER        PIC X(9)  VALUE "APRIL ".
     05   FILLER        PIC X(9)  VALUE "MAY ".
     05   FILLER        PIC X(9)  VALUE "JUNE ".
     05   FILLER        PIC X(9)  VALUE "JULY ".
     05   FILLER        PIC X(9)  VALUE "AUGUST ".
     05   FILLER        PIC X(9)  VALUE "SEPTEMBER".
     05   FILLER        PIC X(9)  VALUE "OCTOBER ".
     05   FILLER        PIC X(9)  VALUE "NOVEMBER ".
     05   FILLER        PIC X(9)  VALUE "DECEMBER ".
01   MONTH-TABLE        REDEFINES MONTH-VALUES.
     05   MONTHS        OCCURS 12 TIMES
                        PIC X(9).
```

Figure 11–10
Hard-coded table—multiple functions.

Line of Code
↓

```
1. 01 PRODUCT-VALUES,
2.     05   FILLER PIC X(17) VALUE "04CATTLE057POUND ",
3.     05   FILLER PIC X(17) VALUE "06HOGS 037POUND ",
4.     05   FILLER PIC X(17) VALUE "08SHEEP 022POUND ",
5.     05   FILLER PIC X(17) VALUE "11HAY 122BALE ",
6.     05   FILLER PIC X(17) VALUE "22GRAIN 325BUSHEL",
7. 01 PRODUCT-CLASS-TABLE REDEFINES PRODUCT-VALUES,
8.     05   PRODUCT-CLASS-ENTRY OCCURS 5 TIMES,
9.          10   PRODUCT-CLASS-CODE    PIC X(02),
10.         10   PRODUCT-CLASS-NAME    PIC X(06),
11.         10   PRODUCT-COST          PIC 9V99,
12.         10   PRODUCT-UNIT-MEASURE PIC X(06),
```

The essential problem with hard-coded tables is that each time the data are changed the program must be changed and recompiled. In the month table example it is not likely that a new month will be added to the selection of months available, therefore, it is a good example of an appropriate use of hard-coding.

The product classification table is not a good hard-coded candidate due to the volatility of the data contained in the table.

Input-Loaded Table

The creation of a hard-coded table requires that you code entries only in the DATA DIVISION. The creation of an input-loaded table requires DATA DIVISION and PROCEDURE DIVISION entries. The DATA DIVISION entries create a place to store the data and the PROCEDURE DIVISION entries place the table entries into the appropriate table area. Figure 11-11 represents the DATA and PROCEDURE DIVISION entries to implement an input-loaded table.

Figure 11–11
DATA DIVISION and PROCEDURE DIVISION entries to create an entry-loaded table.

```
01     PRODUCT-CLASS-TABLE,
       05 PRODUCT-CLASS-ENTRY OCCURS 25 TIMES
              INDEXED BY PRODUCT-INDEX,
          10   PRODUCT-CLASS-CODE       PIC X(02),
          10   PRODUCT-CLASS-NAME       PIC X(06),
          10   PRODUCT-COST             PIC 9V99,
          10   PRODUCT-UNIT-MEASURE     PIC X(06),
                           o
                           o
                           o
PROCEDURE DIVISION,
                 o
                 o
                 o
       READ PRODUCT-TABLE-FILE
              AT END MOVE "X" TO EOT-SW,
       PERFORM 100-LOAD-PRODUCT-TABLE
              VARYING PRODUCT-INDEX
              FROM 1 BY 1
              UNTIL EOT-SW = "X",
                 o
                 o
                 o
```

Figure 11–11 (continued)

```
100-LOAD-PRODUCT-TABLE.
    IF PRODUCT-INDEX > 25
        MOVE "X" TO EOT-SW
        DISPLAY "ATTEMPT TO OVERLOAD TABLE"
    ELSE
        MOVE PT-PRODUCT-CLASS-CODE
            TO PRODUCT-CLASS-CODE (PRODUCT-INDEX)
        MOVE PT-PRODUCT-CLASS-NAME
            TO PRODUCT-CLASS-NAME (PRODUCT-INDEX)
        MOVE PT-PRODUCT-COST
            TO PRODUCT-COST (PRODUCT-INDEX)
        MOVE PT-PRODUCT-UNIT-MEASURE
            TO PRODUCT-UNIT-MEASURE (PRODUCT-INDEX).
    READ PRODUCT-TABLE-FILE
        AT END MOVE "X" TO EOT-SW.
```

The DATA DIVISION entries reserve the necessary memory locations, name the group and elementary items, and set up the necessary subscript— PRODUCT-INDEX. The PROCEDURE DIVISION entries read the tables records from an input file and load the table entries into the table area. This is a very simple, straightforward, and often-used programming technique.

Because of the lack of facility of the COBOL language for handling external tables, they are not covered in this text other than as may be implied from the chapter on relative files (Chapter 6).

Data Retrieval from Tables

Data retrieval from tables may be accomplished in a fairly straightforward manner. The product classification table will be used to illustrate data retrieval using the following verbs:

1. PERFORM VARYING
2. SEARCH
3. SEARCH ALL

A fourth method, direct retrieval, will be illustrated using the month table data.

Sequential Table Search Using PERFORM VARYING

Figure 11-12 presents the COBOL code to sequentially search the product classification table.

Figure 11–12
Partial program illustrating
sequential table search.

```
DATA DIVISION.
FILE SECTION.
    o
    o
    o
FD  SALE-FILE
    LABEL RECORDS ARE STANDARD.
01  SALE-RECORD.
    05  SR-RECORD-CODE        PIC X(02).
    05  SR-VENDOR-CODE        PIC X(05).
    05  SR-QUANTITY           PIC 9(03).
    05  SR-PRODUCT-CODE       PIC X(02).
    o
    o
    o
```

Figure 11–12 (continued)

```
FD    PRODUCT-TABLE-FILE
      LABEL RECORDS ARE STANDARD,
01    PRODUCT-TABLE-RECORD,
      05   PT-PRODUCT-CLASS-CODE        PIC X(02),
      05   PT-PRODUCT-CLASS-NAME        PIC X(07),
      05   PT-PRODUCT-COST              PIC 9V99,
      05   PT-PRODUCT-UNIT-MEASURE      PIC X(05),
      o
      o
      o

WORKING-STORAGE SECTION,
      o
      o
      o
01    WS-HIT-SW                 PIC X(01),
01    WS-SUBSCRIPT              PIC S9(2),
01    WS-EOT-SW                 PIC X(01) VALUE SPACES,
01    WS-ERROR-SW               PIC X(01) VALUE SPACES,
      o
      o
      o
01    DETAIL-LINE,
      05   FILLER               PIC X(03) VALUE SPACES,
      05   DL-PRODUCT-NAME      PIC X(07),
      05   FILLER               PIC X(01) VALUE SPACES,
      05   DL-QUANTITY          PIC 9(03),
      05   FILLER               PIC X(01) VALUE SPACES,
      05   DL-PRODUCT-COST      PIC Z,99,
      05   FILLER               PIC X(01) VALUE SPACES,
      05   DL-UNIT              PIC X(05),
      05   FILLER               PIC X(01) VALUE SPACES,
      05   DL-TOTAL-COST        PIC ZZZ,99,
      o
      o
      o
01    PRODUCT-CLASS-TABLE,
      05   PRODUCT-CLASS-ENTRY OCCURS 25 TIMES,
           10   PRODUCT-CLASS-CODE       PIC X(02),
           10   PRODUCT-CLASS-NAME       PIC X(06),
           10   PRODUCT-COST             PIC 9V99,
           10   PRODUCT-UNIT-MEASURE     PIC X(05),
      o
      o
      o
PROCEDURE DIVISION,
      o
      o
      o
      READ PRODUCT-TABLE-FILE
          AT END MOVE "X" TO WS-EOT-SW,
      PERFORM 100-LOAD-PRODUCT-TABLE
          VARYING WS-SUBSCRIPT
               FROM 1 BY 1
          UNTIL WS-EOT-SW = "X",
      o
      o
      o
      MOVE " " TO WS-HIT-SW,
```

Figure 11–12 (continued)

```
                          PERFORM 600-SEARCH-FOR-PRODUCT
                              VARYING WS-SUBSCRIPT
                              FROM 1 BY 1
                              UNTIL WS-HIT-SW = "X".
                  o
                  o
                  o
     600-SEARCH-FOR-PRODUCT.
         IF WS-SUBSCRIPT > 25
                 MOVE "X" TO WS-HIT-SW
                 MOVE "X" TO WS-ERROR-SW
             ELSE
                 IF SR-RECORD-CODE =
                         PRODUCT-CLASS-CODE (WS-SUBSCRIPT)
                     MOVE "X" TO WS-HIT-SW
                     MOVE PRODUCT-CLASS-NAME (WS-SUBSCRIPT)
                         TO DL-PRODUCT-NAME
                     MOVE PRODUCT-COST (WS-SUBSCRIPT)
                         TO DL-PRODUCT-COST
                     MOVE PRODUCT-UNIT-MEASURE (WS-SUBSCRIPT)
                         TO DL-UNIT
                     COMPUTE DL-TOTAL-COST =
                         PRODUCT-COST (WS-SUBSCRIPT) *
                             SR-QUANTITY.
```

The DATA DIVISION entries are essentially the same as the example from Figure 11-11.

The statement

```
     MOVE " " TO WS-HIT-SW.
```

is used to reset the switch that is turned on when an entry is found or when all entries have been searched and a corresponding table argument cannot be found.

The PERFORM VARYING statement is the statement that causes the table to be sequentially searched. This statement is sometimes referred to as the "search driver."

```
     PERFORM 600-SEARCH-FOR-PRODUCT
             VARYING WS-SUBSCRIPT
             FROM 1 BY 1
             UNTIL WS-HIT-SW = "X".
```

The first part of the PERFORM statement indicates the module that is to be PERFORMed in this example, 600-SEARCH-FOR-PRODUCT. The next line VARYING WS-SUBSCRIPT indicates the subscript to be used. The next phrase, FROM 1 BY 1, indicates the initial value of the subscript (at 1) and what the rate of increase in the value of the subscript (in this case +1). The last line of the statement, UNTIL WS-HIT-SW = "X", indicates the condition that stops the execution of the search paragraph.

The 600-SEARCH-FOR-PRODUCT module is where the comparison of the search argument, SR-RECORD-CODE, and the table argument, PRODUCT-CLASS-CODE (WS-SUBSCRIPT), takes place.

As can be seen in Figure 11-12 there is only one statement in the program module, the IF statement. The first part of the statement checks the table limit to see if it has been exceeded. If so, the WS-HIT-SW is turned on to effect the end of the search process. The error switch is also turned on to indicate to some other part of the program that the item was not in the table.

The second part of the IF statement, the ELSE part, compares the search argument and the table argument. If the compare is equal, and the search argument is found, then the table function(s) are moved out of the table to the print line and total cost is calculated.

Sequential Search with Early Exit

The same problem may be used to illustrate the early exit process. Figure 11-13 shows the PROCEDURE DIVISION entries to accomplish early exit in the search paragraph. Remember, in order for early exit from the search process to work, the entries in the table must be in ascending or descending sequence on the value of table argument.

Figure 11–13
Early exit from sequential search.

```
600-SEARCH-FOR-PRODUCT.
    IF SR-RECORD-CODE < PRODUCT-CLASS-CODE (WS-SUBSCRIPT)
        MOVE "X" TO WS-HIT-SW
        MOVE "X" TO WS-ERROR-SW
    ELSE
        o
        o
        o
```

This change causes the COBOL program to stop the table search when the search argument becomes less than the table argument. If the table is in ascending sequence, any time the search argument becomes less than the table argument, the item that is being searched for is not in the table and the search process may be terminated.

This process is not entirely correct. What happens if we get to the end of the table and the item still has not been retrieved? The program will fail. To repair this damage requires two minor adjustments. The adjusted sequential search with early exit is as follows:

```
PERFORM 600-SEARCH-FOR-PRODUCT
    VARYING WS-SUBSCRIPT
    FROM 1 BY 1
    UNTIL WS-HIT-SW = "X"
    OR EOT-SW = "X".
    o
    o
    o
600-SEARCH-FOR-PRODUCT.
    IF WS-SUBSCRIPT > 25
        MOVE "X" TO WS-HIT-SW
        MOVE "X" TO WS-ERROR-SW
    ELSE
        IF SR-RECORD-DODE <
            PRODUCT-CLASS-CODE (WS-SUBSCRIPT)
            MOVE "X" TO WS-HIT-SW
            MOVE "X" TO WS-ERROR-SW
    ELSE
        IF SR-RECORD-CODE =
            PRODUCT-CLASS-CODE (WS-SUBSCRIPT)
        o
        o
        o
```

This code is very simple and should cause no problems in handling other similar search processes. Remember, however, that each programming situation is different and will require that you adjust the logic of your program according to some specific situation.

The SEARCH **Statement**

The same process just achieved can be accomplished with much greater ease with the use of the SEARCH statement.

In order to use the SEARCH statement the DATA DIVISION statements for the table must include an index. Figure 11-12 shows that the index, PRODUCT-INDEX, is included with the table entries, so our program meets this requirement. If we use the same example that we have previously used we may now substitute the SEARCH verb for the PERFORM VARYING statement and drive the search paragraph with the SEARCH verb. The new coding to achieve this is as follows:

```
SET PRODUCT-INDEX TO 1,
SEARCH PRODUCT-CLASS-ENTRY
     AT END MOVE "X" TO EOF-SW
WHEN
     PRODUCT-CLASS-CODE (PRODUCT-INDEX) = SR-RECORD-CODE
     MOVE "X" TO WS-HIT-SW
     MOVE PRODUCT-CLASS-NAME (PRODUCT-INDEX)
          TO DL-PRODUCT-NAME
     o
     o
     o
```

The SET statement initializes the index to 1, which is where the search starts relative to the beginning of the table. The SEARCH statement directs which table is to be searched. Notice, however, the table name is not searched; the table entry name is searched (the data-item that has the OCCURS clause on it). The AT END option is encountered if the SEARCH proceeds to the end of the table without finding a corresponding table argument for the search argument. This is usually, but not always, an error condition. The WHEN clause tests the search argument against the table argument and if they are equal the table function(s) are used as required by the program.

The Binary Table Search—SEARCH ALL

The binary search requires some adjustments to both the DATA and PROCEDURE DIVISIONs in our sample program. The DATA DIVISION entries are as follows:

```
01  PRODUCT-CLASS-TABLE,
    05  PRODUCT-CLASS-ENTRY
        OCCURS 25 TIMES
        ASCENDING KEY PRODUCT-CLASS-CODE
        INDEXED BY PRODUCT-INDEX,
        10  PRODUCT-CLASS-CODE       PIC X(02),
        10  PRODUCT-CLASS-NAME       PIC X(06),
        10  PRODUCT-COST             PIC 9V99,
        10  PRODUCT-UNIT-MEASURE     PIC X(06),
    o
    o
    o
```

The difference between this example and the previous example is the addition of the

```
[ASCENDING ]
[DESCENDING] KEY
```

phrase. This clause is used to indicate whether the table that is to be searched has the table entries arranged in ascending or descending sequence based on the value of the table argument.

The PROCEDURE DIVISION entries are almost the same as they were in the previous example. The only difference is the inclusion of the ALL phrase and the omission of the SET statement. The amended PROCEDURE DIVISION entries for a binary search are:

```
SEARCH ALL PRODUCT-CLASS-ENTRY
     AT END MOVE "X" TO EOT-SW
WHEN
     PRODUCT-CLASS-CODE (PRODUCT-INDEX) = SR-RECORD-CODE
     MOVE "X" TO WS-HIT-SW
     MOVE PRODUCT-CLASS-NAME (PRODUCT-INDEX)
          TO DL-PRODUCT-NAME
        o
        o
        o
```

Direct Retrieval from a Table

The easiest method of retrieving data from a table is the direct retrieval method from a positionally organized table. The retrieval method requires that the table arguments be in relative record address sequence (or have the capability of simulating a relative address). The example for this type of search is displayed in Figure 11-14.

Figure 11–14
Direct retrieval from a table.

```
DATA DIVISION.
FILE SECTION.
FD   INPUT-FILE
          LABEL RECORDS ARE STANDARD.
01   INPUT-RECORD.
        o
        o
        o
        05   MONTH-CODE        PIC 9(02).
        o
        o
        o
     See Figure 11-2 for month table entries.
        o
        o
        o
PROCEDURE DIVISION.
        o
        o
        o
        MOVE MONTHS (MONTH-CODE) TO WS-MONTH-NAME.
```

Notice that only one statement is required in the PROCEDURE DIVISION to retrieve the name of the month from the month table. This coding is a little simplistic in that it does not provide for an error in the MONTH-CODE such that the MONTH-CODE should be in the range 01-12. If the MONTH-CODE is not in this range a subscript out of range error will occur and the program will "bomb off" the computer. The adjusted coding could be as follows:

```
IF MONTH-CODE < 01 OR > 12
    PERFORM MONTH-ERROR-ROUTINE
ELSE
    MOVE MONTHS (MONTH-CODE) TO WS-MONTHS-NAME.
```

Two-Dimension Tables

The following example illustrates the use of both two-dimension tables and temporary storage tables. The example program is exhibited in Figure 11-15. The sample problem assumes that we have an input file with the following format:

Columns	Content
1–2	district code
3–4	store code
5–13	daily sales total
14–19	date of sales

The purpose of the program is to read the input "daily sales file" and print a report of total sales for a month by store within a district. Such a report may appear as follows:

```
        MONTHLY SALES REPORT
DISTRICT STORE      TOTAL SALES
1        1          1,377,234.34
1        2          2,468,292.55
1        3          1,044,047.07
DISTRICT TOTAL      4,889,513.96
2        1          2,222,222.22
      o
      o
      o
```

Assume for this problem that there are six districts in this company and each district has a maximum of eight stores. Further assume that the input file is in no specific sequence: that is, the daily sales figures for a month for each of the stores are on the input file, and they are there in a random order.

Figure 11–15
Use of two-dimension and temporary storage tables.

```
DATA DIVISION.
FILE SECTION.
FD  SALES-FILE
    LABEL RECORDS ARE STANDARD.
01  SALES-RECORD.
    05   SR-DISTRICT              PIC 9(02).
    05   SR-STORE                 PIC 9(02).
    05   SR-SALES                 PIC 9(07)V99.
    05   SR-DATE                  PIC 9(06).
      o
      o
      o
      o
```

Figure 11–15 (continued)

```
WORKING-STORAGE SECTION.
01  DISTRICT-TOAL                  PIC 9(08)V99.
        o
        o
        o
01  SALES-TABLE.
    05  DISTRICTS OCCURS 6 TIMES.
        10  STORES OCCURS 8 TIMES.
            10 STORE-SALES PIC 9(08)V99.
        o
        o
        o
01  DETAIL-LINE.
    05  DL-DISTRICT                PIC 9(02).
    05  FILLER                     PIC X(03) VALUE SPACES.
    05  DL-STORE                   PIC 9(02).
    05  FILLER                     PIC X(03) VALUE SPACES.
    05  DL-SALES                   PIC Z,ZZZ,ZZZ.99.
    05  DL-STAR                    PIC X(01) VALUE SPACES.
        o
        o
        o
01  ROW-SUB                        PIC 9(02) VALUE ZEROS.
01  COL-SUB                        PIC 9(02) VALUE ZEROS.
        o
        o
        o
PROCEDURE DIVISION.
000 MAIN.
        OPEN INPUT SALES-FILE
            OUTPUT PRINT-FILE.
        PERFORM 100-INITIALIZE.
        PERFORM 300-READ-SALES-FILE.
        PERFORM 200-READ-AND-ACCUMULATE
                UNTIL EOF-SW = "X".
        PERFORM 400-PRINT-HEADINGS.
        PERFORM 450-PRINT-TABLE
            VARYING ROW-SUB
            FROM 1 BY 1
            UNTIL ROW-SUB > 6
            AFTER COL-SUB
            FROM 1 BY 1 UNTIL COL-SUB > 8.
        CLOSE SALES-FILE
             PRINT-FILE.
        STOP RUN.
100-INITIALIZE.
        MOVE ZEROS TO SALES-TABLE
                      ROW-SUB
                      COL-SUB
        o
        o
        o
200-READ-AND-ACCUMULATE.
        IF SR-DISTRICT < 01 OR > 06
            NEXT SENTENCE
        ELSE
            IF SR-STORE < 01 OR > 08
                NEXT SENTENCE
```

Figure 11–15 (continued)

```
                              ELSE
                                 ADD SR-SALES TO
                                    STORE-SALES (SR-DISTRICT SR-STORE)
                       .
                PERFORM 300-READ-SALES-FILE.
       300-READ-SALES-FILE.
            READ SALES-FILE
                AT END MOVE "X" TO EOF-SW.
       450-PRINT-TABLE.
            MOVE ROW-SUB TO DL-DISTRICT.
            MOVE COL-SUB TO DL-STORE.
            MOVE STORE-SALES (ROW-SUB COL-SUB)
                TO DL-SALES.
            ADD STORE-SALES (ROW-SUB COL-SUB)
                TO DISTRIC-TOTAL.
            WRITE PRINT-LINE FROM DETAIL-LINE AFTER 1.
            IF COL-SUB = 8
                MOVE SPACES TO DETAIL-LINE
                MOVE DISTRICT-TOTAL TO DL-SALES
                MOVE "*" TO DL-STAR
                WRITE PRINT-LINE FROM DETAIL-LINE AFTER 1
                MOVE ZEROS TO DISTRICT-TOTAL
                MOVE " " TO DL-STAR
                       .
```

This is the essential logic necessary to illustrate the problem as described. Let us now examine each DIVISION's entries and see what we have accomplished.

First, the DATA DIVISION entries for the two-dimension table need to be explained (specifically the table construction entries).

```
01  SALES-TABLE.
    05  DISTRICTS OCCURS 6 TIMES
```

OR

```
10  STORES OCCURS 8 TIMES.
    15  STORE-SALES PIC 9(08)V99.
```

These entries create the following matrix:

Sales Table

	S 1	S 2	S 3	S 4	S 5	S 6	S 7	S 8
District (1)								
District (2)								
District (3)								
District (4)								
District (5)								
District (6)								

The name of the table or matrix is SALES-TABLE. This matrix consists of six rows which are named DISTRICTS. Each row consists of eight columns, which are named STORES. We have chosen to give each item in the matrix (we didn't have to) the name STORE-SALES and, further, to assign a PIC of 9(08)V99 to each of the cells in the matrix.

To address an individual cell in the matrix requires two subscripts: one subscript for the row number and one subscript for the column number in the row. Also required is the cell name. In order, for example, to refer to the sales for the fifth store in district 2, we would refer to STORE-SALES (2 5).

The next process required in our exposition is the examination of the PROCEDURE DIVISION entries.

000-MAIN

The statements included in this paragraph are as follows:

```
OPEN INPUT SALES-FILE
     OUTPUT PRINT-FILE.
PEFORM 100-INITIALIZE.
PERFORM 300-READ-SALES-FILE
PERFORM 200-READ-AND-ACCUMULATE
     UNTIL EOF-SW = "X".
PERFORM 400-PRINT-HEADINGS.
PERFORM 450-PRINT-TABLE
     VARYING ROW-SUB
     FROM 1 BY 1
     UNTIL ROW-SUB > 6
     AFTER COL-SUB
     FROM 1 BY 1
     UNTIL COL-SUB > 8
```

The first three statements really do not require any explanation. The fourth statement

```
PERFORM 200-READ-AND-ACCUMULATE
     UNTIL EOF-SW = "X".
```

is the statement that PERFORMS the reading of SALES-RECORDS from the SALES-FILE and adding the daily sales figures for the month to the monthly sales totals in the DATA DIVISION table.

The module 400-PRINT-HEADINGS causes one heading to be printed (we are obviously assuming a one-page report).

The statement

```
PERFORM 450-PRINT-TABLE
     VARYING ROW-SUB
     o
     o
     o
```

is the statement that causes the table to be printed out to the line print or display device. The structure of this statement is important. It causes the variation of the row and column subscripts in the sequence appropriate to retrieve the monthly sales totals from the table as desired.

This statement causes the following values to be generated for `ROW-SUB` and `COL-SUB`.

```
ROW-SUB          COL-SUB
1                   1
1                   2
1                   3
1                   4
1                   5
1                   6
1                   7
1                   8
2                   1
2                   2
              o
              o
              o
6                   8
```

The `CLOSE` and `STOP` statements do not require explanation at this time.

100-INITIALIZE

The statements in `100-INITIALIZE` are used to set initial values to data areas in the `WORKING-STORAGE SECTION` of the `DATA DIVISION`. The part of this paragraph that is of importance to us is the:

```
MOVE ZEROS TO SALES-TABLE.
```

This statement initializes all the elements in the table to zeros. This may not work on some computer systems and the following logic will have to be substituted:

```
PERFORM 110-INITIALIZE-TABLE
        VARYING ROW-SUB FROM 1 BY 1
        UNTIL ROW-SUB > 6
        AFTER COL-SUB FROM 1 BY 1
        UNTIL COL-SUB > 8
     o
     o
     o
110-INITIALIZE.
        MOVE ZEROS TO STORE-SALES (ROW-SUB COL-SUB)
```

This logic manipulates the subscripts as indicated above such that each of the `STORE-SALES` cells in the `SALES-TABLE` are initialized to zero.

200-READ-AND-ACCUMULATE

This is the paragraph in which the accumulation of daily sales values from the input sales file are added to the appropriate cell in the `SALES-TABLE`.
The phrase

```
IF SR-DISTRICT < 01 OR > 06
   NEXT SENTENCE
```

checks the district value in the input record to see if it is not legitimate; if it is not, the record is dropped from processing (this record dropping is not a likely technique in "real-world" programming).

The next phrase

```
ELSE
     IF SR-STORE < 01 OR > 08
          NEXT SENTENCE
```

checks the store code in the input record to see if it is in the proper range. If it is not, the record is not processed.

The last phrase in the sentence

```
ELSE
     ADD SR-SALES TO STORE-SALES (SR-DISTRICT SR-STORE)
```

causes the sales value in the input record to be added to the SALES-TABLE cell STORE-SALES (SR-DISTRICT SR-STORE). Remember that the rows in the table represent districts and the columns represent stores within the district: therefore, we can use the input district and store codes as subscripts to access the appropriate cell within the table.

450-PRINT-TABLE

The 450-PRINT-TABLE paragraph causes the data to be moved from the SALES-TABLE based on the value of the subscripts ROW-SUB and COL-SUB. Each line is printed as it is encountered.

The IF statement in the paragraph is used to check to see if we have printed the last store in the district. If we have, then we can print the total for this district.

The print format, as described above, causes the output to print straight down the page. A few simple changes may be made to the program logic to cause the output to be printed in matrix form. That is, as follows:

Monthly Sales Report

District	Store 1	Store 2	Store 3...	Total	
1	2	3	4	5	6

The first area of change is to the DETAIL-LINE in the DATA DIVISION. This may be recoded as follows:

```
01 DETAIL-LINE.
     05   DL-DISTRICT          PIC 9(02).
     05   DL-STORES OCCURS 8 TIMES.
          10   FILLER          PIC X(02).
          10   DL-SALES        PIC Z,ZZZ,ZZZ.99.
     05   FILLER               PIC X(02) VALUE SPACES.
     05   DL-TOTAL             PIC ZZ,ZZZ,ZZZ.99.
```

This print line must be structured in a manner similar to this to cause the proper printing of the report from the print module in the program.

The 450-PRINT-TABLE paragraph is changed as follows:

```
450-PRINT-TABLE.
     MOVE ROW-SUB TO DL-DISTRICT.
```

```
          MOVE STORE-SALES (ROW-SUB COL-SUB TO DL-SALES
          (COL-SUB).
          ADD STORE-SALES (ROW-SUB COL-SUB) TO DISTRICT-TOTAL.
          IF COL-SUB = 8
              MOVE DISTRICT-TOTAL TO DL-TOTAL
              WRITE PRINT-LINE FROM DETAIL-LINE AFTER 1
              MOVE ZEROS TO DISTRICT-TOTAL.
```

This logic now creates the matrix-type printout that was just described. Notice that this logic requires that we print a line only when the column subscript is equal to 8. The reason this is handled this way is that without this logic the program would cause 8 lines to be printed for each district, and that was not what was desired.

Three-Dimension Tables

Let us now expand our two-dimension problem, as described before, into a three-dimension table problem.

We will use essentially the same input file, output file, and program logic to describe this problem.

Assume that we have accumulated daily sales records for a month in a company's sales file. The input record format is as follows:

Columns	Content
1–2	region code
3–4	district code
5–6	store code
7–15	daily sales total
16–21	date of sale

The desired output is a report of sales similar to the sales report described above, except that the company is divided into three regions of six districts each, with each district having a maximum of eight stores.

The partial program that accomplishes this output is depicted in Figure 11-16.

Figure 11–16
Three-dimension table-handling program.

```
DATA DIVISION.
FILE SECTION.
FD SALES-FILE
          LABEL RECORDS ARE STANDARD.
01   SALES-RECORD.
          05   SR-REGION         PIC 9(02).
          05   SR-DISTRICT        PIC 9(02).
          05   SR-STORE          PIC 9(02).
          05   SR-SALES          PIC 9(07)V99.
          05   SR-DATE           PIC 9(06).
          o
          o
          o
WORKING-STORAGE SECTION.
01   SALES-TABLE.
          05   REGIONS OCCURS 3 TIMES.
               10   DISTRICTS OCCURS 6 TIMES
                    15   STORES OCCURS 8 TIMES.
                         20   STORE-SALES PIC 9(08)V99.
          o
          o
          o
```

Figure 11-16 (continued)

```
01    DETAIL-LINE.
      05   DL-REGION            PIC 9(02).
      05   FILLER               PIC X(02) VALUE SPACES.
      05   DL-DISTRICT          PIC 9(02).
      05   DL-STORES            OCCURS 8 TIMES.
           10   FILLER          PIC X(02).
           10   DL-SALES        PIC ZZ,ZZZ,ZZZ.99.
      o
      o
      o

PROCEDURE DIVISION.
000-MAIN.
      OPEN INPUT SALES-FILE
           OUTPUT PRINT-FILE.
      PERFORM 100-INITIALIZE.
      PERFORM 300-READ-SALES-FILE.
      PERFORM 200-READ-AND-ACCUMULATE
           UNTIL EOF-SW = "X".
      PERFORM 400-PRINT-HEADINGS.
      PERFORM 450-PRINT-TABLE
           VARYING REGION-SUB
           FROM 1 BY 1 UNTIL REGION SUB > 3
           AFTER ROW-SUB
                FROM 1 BY 1 UNTIL ROW-SUB > 6
                AFTER COL-SUB
                     FROM 1 BY 1 UNTIL COL-SUB > 8
                .
      CLOSE SALES-FILE
            PRINT-FILE.
      STOP RUN.
      o
      o
      o

200-READ-AND-ACCUMULATE.
      IF SR-REGION < 01 OR > 3
           NEXT SENTENCE
      ELSE
           IF SR-DISTRICT < 1 OR > 6
                NEXT SENTENCE
           ELSE
                IF SR-STORE < 1 OR > 8
                     NEXT SENTENCE
                ELSE
                ADD SR-SALES TO
                STORE-SALES  (SR-REGION SR-DISTRICT SR-STORE)
           .
      PERFORM 300-READ-SALES-FILE.
      o
      o
      o

450-PRINT-TABLE.
      MOVE STORE-SALES (REGION-SUB ROW-SUB COL-SUB)
           TO DL-SALES (COL-SUB).
      IF COL-SUB = 8
           MOVE REGION-SUB TO DL-REGION
           MOVE ROW-SUB TO DL-DISTRIC
           WRITE PRINT-LINE FROM DETAIL-LINE AFTER 1
           .
```

DATA DIVISION *Entries for Three-Dimension Tables*

The SALES-TABLE entries create a three-dimension table as illustrated in Figure 11-17:

The DATA DIVISION entries created a table that consists of three regions divided into six districts each of which are divided into eight stores.

To refer to sales for a specific store requires three subscripts. For example, STORE-SALES (2 1 3) refers to the sales for the third store in the first district of region 2.

The PERFORM VARYING statement is the same as the previous example except that there is one additional AFTER clause. This PERFORM causes the subscripts to be created as follows:

```
1,1,1; 1,1,2; 1,1,3; 1,1,4; 1,1,5; 1,1,6; 1,1,7; 1,1,8;
1,2,1; 1,2,2;...
                  .
                  .
                  .
3,6,1.........................................  3,6,8
```

This will cause the data to be removed from the table and printed in a matrix similar to that presented in the previous example.

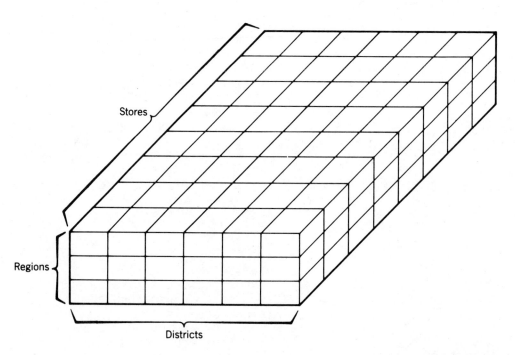

Figure 11–17
Illustration of store sales table
in three dimensions.

SECTION 5
Questions and Problems

I. Questions

1. Define the following terms:
   a. table
   b. table entry
   c. table argument
   d. search argument
   e. table function
   f. subscript
   g. multiple level table

2. Develop a table that you can use to illustrate the terms from Question 1.

3. How may tables be classified? Illustrate the differences between the methods of classification, verbally or pictorially.

4. What are the four basic ways of organizing tables that are listed in Chapter 11? Illustrate each of these organizational methods.

5. What is the highest number of levels that can be provided for under the current version of COBOL? What is the number under COBOL 8x?

6. What are the basic retrieval methods used to retrieve data from a table? Is the method used for data retrieval related in any way to the organizational method? If so, how?

7. Why is the term "early exit" used in connection with table-retrieval methods? What does it mean? What are the benefits of using an early exit procedure?

8. When would you use a binary search? What are the advantages to using a binary search?

9. Are there any restrictions to using a binary search? If so, what are they? If not, how is this possible?

10. Can you see any dangers to using a relative retrieval method? What are they?

11. What is an "input-loaded" table? Why would such a table be used?

12. Consider the following WORKING-STORAGE SECTION entries:

```
01   EXAMPLE-TABLE.
     05   TABLE-FUNCTION1 OCCURS 10 TIMES PIC X(5).
     05   TABLE-FUNCTION2 OCCURS 10 TIMES PIC X(20).
```

   a. Is this a multiple-level table?
   b. Draw a memory layout to illustrate the way data are stored in the table.

13. Consider the following WORKING-STORAGE SECTION entries:

```
01   EXAMPLE-TABLE
     05   TABLE-ENTRIES OCCURS 10 TIMES.
          10   TABLE-FUNCTION1 PIC X(5).
          10   TABLE-FUNCTION2 PIC X(20).
```

   a. How is this table different from the table presented in Question 12?
   b. Draw a memory layout to illustrate the way data are stored in the table.
   c. Which method of the two illustrated do you think you prefer? Why?

14. Consider the following entries:

```
01  EXAMPLE-TABLE,
    05  FUNCTION1 OCCURS 5 TIMES,
        10 FUNTION2 OCCURS 10 TIMES PIC X(07),
01  SUB1 PIC 9(02) USAGE COMP,
01  SUB2 PIC 9(02) USAGE COMP,


    PERFORM TABLE-SEARCH
        VARYING SUB1 FROM 1 BY
            UNTIL SUB1 > 5
    AFTER
        SUB2 FROM 1 BY 1
            UNTIL SUB2 > 10,
```

Indicate the values of SUB1 and SUB2 as the TABLE-SEARCH paragraph is PERFORMed.

II. Programming Problems

1. Your Advanced COBOL professor has given an exam and graded it. He or she has further created a record that contains the following data:

Columns	Content
1–9	student number
10–29	student name
30–31	percent correct answers
32	student classification code (1–5)

Your professor needs the following output:

a. A listing that contains:

the student's number

the student's name

the student's letter grade

(based as follows):

90–100% = A
80–89 = B
70–79 = C
60–69 = D
below 60 = F

decoded student classification:

1 = freshman
2 = sophomore
3 = junior
4 = senior
5 = graduate student

b. A printout of the count of the number of A's, B's, C's, D's, and F's.

c. Determine and print the average A score, B score, C score, D score, F score.

2. Consider the following single dimension array values: 1, 12, 374, 8, 4, 99, 324, 687, 44, 55. Write a COBOL program that will:

a. determine and print the highest number from the array.

b. determine and print the lowest number from the array.

3. Write a COBOL program that will grade any multiple-choice exam of up to 25 questions. The input format is as follows:

Columns	Content
1–9	student number
10–34	**answers**

Note: The first record in the file is the answer record and has a student number of 000000000. A report is to be printed in the following basic form:

```
STUDENT    Q   Q   Q   Q   Q   Q  ...   Q   GRADE
NUMBER     1   2   3   4   5   6        25

000000000  A   C   D                    B
EXAM ANS.

001010001  C   A   D                    B
           X   X                             65
                   o
                   o
                   o

HIGH SCORE: 100
LOW SCORE:   55
AVG. SCORE:  73.8
```

4. A sales summary program is to be printed for the XYZ Retail Corporation. The following applies:

Program name: sales summary report

Input file: sales-file

Note: The file is not in any order on any key field. The file contains one record for each district within each division within each region for each day of a specific month.

Record layout:

Columns	Content
1–2	region (highest region # is 04)
3–4	division (highest division # is 12)
5–6	district (highest district # is 3)
7–14	sales amount (dollars only)
15–20	date of sale

Report layout:

XYZ Company

Divisions

Regions	1	2	3	...	12
1	XXX	XXX	XXX	XXX	
2					
3					
4					

Processing notes:

a. The sales are to be accumulated randomly from the input file into a sales table and printed after all sales have been accumulated.

b. The previously stipulated format is a guide only; the student is free to design the format to his or her own desire, provided that the total sales for all divisions in a region are printed on the same line. (If your printout runs down the page 12 lines for a specific region, you have a programming logic error.)

5. Expand Problem 4 to print a sales report for each district within each division within each region.

   Note: This is a three-level table problem.

6. The Odessa Trucking Company needs a COBOL program that will rate and print the charges for each customer shipment.

   The company is a small regional trucking company that serves three zones and most of the shipments are for less than 60 pounds, although occasional shipments exceed this weight.

   The charge for a shipment is determined by the zone a shipment is shipped to times the weight of the shipment. The following table is to be used to rate a shipment:

Weight (in pounds)	Zone 1	2	3
0–10	5.00	8.00	11.00
11–20	7.00	10.00	13.00
21–30	9.00	12.00	15.00
31–40	11.00	14.00	17.00
41–50	13.00	16.00	19.00
51–60*	15.00	18.00	21.00

* Over 60 = 60-lb. rate plus $2 for each additional 10 lb. or fraction.

7. The Grambling–Auburn Airline Company has one plane that flies (when able) each morning from Grambling to Auburn and then returns from Auburn that afternoon (more or less). The plane is divided into two sections: First Class (4 rows—administrators) and Peasant Class (10 rows—professors, associates, assistants, and instructors). Each section is divided into smoking and no smoking (chewers and dippers are not allowed in First Class). There are 4 seats per row (LW LA RA RW)

   LW left window
   LA left aisle
   RA right aisle
   RW right window

   Flight reservations are accepted on a week-by-week basis. (Monday through Sunday). If a passenger wants to schedule a flight past this point in time he or she is told to call back next week.

   Write a COBOL program that will do the following:

   a. Present a menu that allows for the selection of seats, displays seats assigned, and supplies a printout of each or one of the flights.

b. Let a potential tree-topper (passenger) select smoking or no smoking, window or aisle, First Class or Peasant Class, and state his or her name.

c. After the passenger has specified his or her choices, then the program should assign the passenger a seat, if possible. If not, the program should specify that the parameters specified are not possible and go back to the seat-selection process. Please note that in the recorded history of this airline, no flight has ever been sold out.

d. For the seat-assignment display, determine which flight and which day the flight is for, then display all the passenger names on the screen (14 x 80).

e. For the printout process, determine if a particular flight or all flights are to be printed and then print as specified on the line printer.

APPENDIX **A**

ANSI Standard COBOL Format with IBM Extensions

IDENTIFICATION DIVISION—BASIC FORMATS

$$\left\{\begin{array}{l}\underline{\text{IDENTIFICATION DIVISION}}.\\ \underline{\text{ID DIVISION}}.\end{array}\right\}$$

<u>PROGRAM-ID</u>. *program-name*.

<u>AUTHOR</u>. [*comment-entry*]. . .

<u>INSTALLATION</u>. [*comment-entry*] . . .

<u>DATE-WRITTEN</u>. [*comment-entry*] . . .

<u>DATE-COMPILED</u>. [*comment-entry*] . . .

<u>SECURITY</u>. [*comment-entry*] . . .

<u>REMARKS</u>. [*comment-entry*] . . .

ENVIRONMENT DIVISION—BASIC FORMATS

<u>ENVIRONMENT DIVISION</u>.

<u>CONFIGURATION SECTION</u>.

<u>SOURCE-COMPUTER</u>. *computer-name*.

<u>OBJECT-COMPUTER</u>. *computer-name* [<u>MEMORY</u> SIZE *integer* $\left\{\begin{array}{l}\underline{\text{WORDS}}\\ \underline{\text{CHARACTERS}}\\ \underline{\text{MODULES}}\end{array}\right\}$]

[<u>SEGMENT-LIMIT IS</u> *priority-number*].

---

[1] Reprinted by permission of International Business Machines Corporation. Items printed on a shaded background are IBM's extensions to ANS COBOL.

317

SPECIAL-NAMES. [*function-name* IS *mnemonic-name*] . . .

   [CURRENCY SIGN IS *literal*]

   [DECIMAL-POINT IS COMMA].

INPUT-OUTPUT SECTION.

FILE-CONTROL.

  {SELECT [OPTIONAL] *file name*

  ASSIGN TO [*integer-1*] *system-name-1* [*system-name-2*] . . .

$$\left[\text{FOR MULTIPLE} \begin{Bmatrix} \text{REEL} \\ \text{UNIT} \end{Bmatrix}\right]$$

$$\text{RESERVE} \begin{Bmatrix} \text{NO} \\ \textit{integer-1} \end{Bmatrix} \text{ALTERNATE} \begin{bmatrix} \text{AREA} \\ \text{AREAS} \end{bmatrix}$$

$$\begin{Bmatrix} \text{FILE-LIMIT IS} \\ \text{FILE-LIMITS ARE} \end{Bmatrix} \begin{Bmatrix} \textit{data-name-1} \\ \textit{literal-1} \end{Bmatrix} \underline{\text{THRU}} \begin{Bmatrix} \textit{data-name-2} \\ \textit{literal-2} \end{Bmatrix}$$

$$\left[\begin{Bmatrix} \textit{data-name-3} \\ \textit{literal-3} \end{Bmatrix} \underline{\text{THRU}} \begin{Bmatrix} \textit{data-name-4} \\ \textit{literal-4} \end{Bmatrix}\right] . . .$$

$$\text{ACCESS MODE IS} \begin{Bmatrix} \text{SEQUENTIAL} \\ \text{RANDOM} \end{Bmatrix}$$

PROCESSING MODE IS SEQUENTIAL

ACTUAL KEY IS *data-name*

NOMINAL KEY IS *data-name*

RECORD KEY IS *data-name*

$$\text{TRACK-AREA IS} \begin{Bmatrix} \textit{data-name} \\ \textit{integer} \end{Bmatrix} \text{CHARACTERS}$$

$$\text{TRACK-LIMIT IS } \textit{integer} \begin{bmatrix} \text{TRACK} \\ \text{TRACKS} \end{bmatrix} \} . . .$$

I-O-CONTROL.

$$\text{RERUN ON } \textit{system-name} \text{ EVERY} \begin{bmatrix} \textit{integer} \text{ RECORDS} \\ \text{[END OF]} \begin{Bmatrix} \text{REEL} \\ \text{UNIT} \end{Bmatrix} \end{bmatrix} \text{OF } \textit{file-name}$$

$$\text{SAME} \begin{bmatrix} \text{RECORD} \\ \text{SORT} \end{bmatrix} \text{AREA FOR } \textit{file-name-1} \{\textit{file-name-2}\} . . .$$

MULTIPLE FILE TAPE CONTAINS *file-name-1* [POSITION *integer-1*]

  [*file-name-2* [POSITION *integer-2*]] . . .

APPLY WRITE-ONLY ON *file-name-1* [*file-name-2*] . . .

APPLY <u>CORE-INDEX</u> ON *file-name-1* [*file-name-2*] . . .

APPLY <u>RECORD-OVERFLOW</u> ON *file-name-1* [*file-name-2*] . . .

APPLY <u>REORG-CRITERIA</u> TO *data-name* ON *file-name*. . .

NOTE: **Format 2 of the** RERUN **Clause (for Sort Files) is included with Formats for the** SORT **feature.**

DATA DIVISION—BASIC FORMATS

<u>DATA</u> <u>DIVISION</u>.

<u>FILE</u> <u>SELECTION</u>.

<u>FD</u> *file-name*

<u>BLOCK</u> CONTAINS [*integer-1* <u>TO</u>] *integer-2* $\begin{Bmatrix} \text{CHARACTERS} \\ \underline{\text{RECORDS}} \end{Bmatrix}$

<u>RECORD</u> CONTAINS [*integer-1* <u>TO</u>] *integer-2* CHARACTERS

<u>RECORDING</u> MODE IS *mode*

<u>LABEL</u> $\begin{Bmatrix} \underline{\text{RECORD}} \text{ IS} \\ \underline{\text{RECORDS}} \text{ ARE} \end{Bmatrix}$ $\begin{Bmatrix} \underline{\text{OMITTED}} \\ \underline{\text{STANDARD}} \\ \textit{data-name-1} \text{ [}\textit{data-name-2}\text{] . . . [}\underline{\text{TOTALING}}\text{ AREA} \\ \qquad \text{IS } \textit{data-name-3} \underline{\text{ TOTALED}} \text{ AREA IS } \textit{data-name-4}\text{]} \end{Bmatrix}$

<u>VALUE</u> <u>OF</u> *data-name-1* IS $\begin{Bmatrix} \textit{literal-1} \\ \textit{data-name-2} \end{Bmatrix}$ [*data-name-3* IS $\begin{Bmatrix} \textit{literal-2} \\ \textit{data-name-4} \end{Bmatrix}$] . . .

<u>DATA</u> $\begin{Bmatrix} \underline{\text{RECORD}} \text{ is} \\ \underline{\text{RECORDS}} \text{ ARE} \end{Bmatrix}$ *data-name-1* [*data-name-2*]. . . .

NOTE: **Format for the** REPORT **Clause is included with Formats for the** REPORT WRITER **feature.**

01-49 $\begin{Bmatrix} \textit{data-name-1} \\ \underline{\text{FILLER}} \end{Bmatrix}$

<u>REDEFINES</u> *data-name-2*

<u>BLANK</u> WHEN <u>ZERO</u>

$\begin{Bmatrix} \underline{\text{JUSTIFIED}} \\ \underline{\text{JUST}} \end{Bmatrix}$ RIGHT

$\begin{Bmatrix} \underline{\text{PICTURE}} \\ \underline{\text{PIC}} \end{Bmatrix}$ IS *character string*

[<u>SIGN</u> IS] $\begin{Bmatrix} \underline{\text{LEADING}} \\ \underline{\text{TRAILING}} \end{Bmatrix}$ [<u>SEPARATE</u> CHARACTER] (Version 3 & 4)

$\begin{Bmatrix} \underline{\text{SYNCHRONIZED}} \\ \underline{\text{SYNC}} \end{Bmatrix}$ $\begin{bmatrix} \underline{\text{LEFT}} \\ \underline{\text{RIGHT}} \end{bmatrix}$

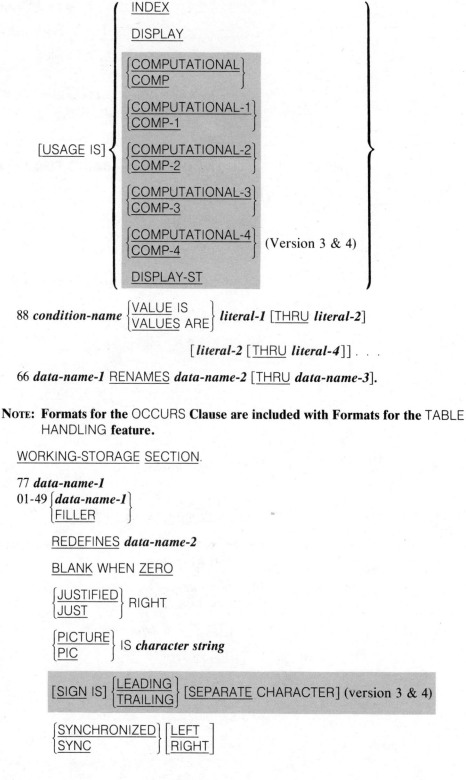

[USAGE IS]
$$\left\{\begin{array}{l}\underline{\text{INDEX}}\\\underline{\text{DISPLAY}}\\\left\{\begin{array}{l}\underline{\text{COMPUTATIONAL}}\\\underline{\text{COMP}}\end{array}\right\}\\\left\{\begin{array}{l}\underline{\text{COMPUTATIONAL-1}}\\\underline{\text{COMP-1}}\end{array}\right\}\\\left\{\begin{array}{l}\underline{\text{COMPUTATIONAL-2}}\\\underline{\text{COMP-2}}\end{array}\right\}\\\left\{\begin{array}{l}\underline{\text{COMPUTATIONAL-3}}\\\underline{\text{COMP-3}}\end{array}\right\}\\\left\{\begin{array}{l}\underline{\text{COMPUTATIONAL-4}}\\\underline{\text{COMP-4}}\end{array}\right\}\text{(Version 3 \& 4)}\\\underline{\text{DISPLAY-ST}}\end{array}\right\}$$

88 *condition-name* $\left\{\begin{array}{l}\underline{\text{VALUE}}\text{ IS}\\\underline{\text{VALUES}}\text{ ARE}\end{array}\right\}$ *literal-1* [<u>THRU</u> *literal-2*]

[*literal-2* [<u>THRU</u> *literal-4*]] . . .

66 *data-name-1* <u>RENAMES</u> *data-name-2* [<u>THRU</u> *data-name-3*].

NOTE: **Formats for the** OCCURS **Clause are included with Formats for the** TABLE HANDLING **feature.**

<u>WORKING-STORAGE</u> <u>SECTION</u>.

77 *data-name-1*
01-49 $\left\{\begin{array}{l}\textit{data-name-1}\\\underline{\text{FILLER}}\end{array}\right\}$

<u>REDEFINES</u> *data-name-2*

<u>BLANK</u> WHEN <u>ZERO</u>

$\left\{\begin{array}{l}\underline{\text{JUSTIFIED}}\\\underline{\text{JUST}}\end{array}\right\}$ RIGHT

$\left\{\begin{array}{l}\underline{\text{PICTURE}}\\\underline{\text{PIC}}\end{array}\right\}$ IS *character string*

[<u>SIGN</u> IS] $\left\{\begin{array}{l}\underline{\text{LEADING}}\\\underline{\text{TRAILING}}\end{array}\right\}$ [<u>SEPARATE</u> CHARACTER] (version 3 & 4)

$\left\{\begin{array}{l}\underline{\text{SYNCHRONIZED}}\\\underline{\text{SYNC}}\end{array}\right\}$ $\left[\begin{array}{l}\underline{\text{LEFT}}\\\underline{\text{RIGHT}}\end{array}\right]$

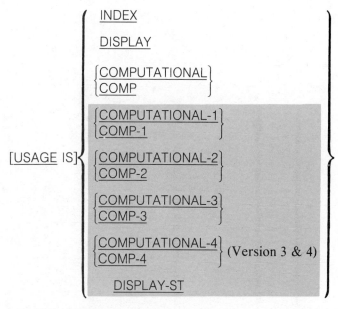

VALUE IS *literal*

88 *condition-name* $\left\{ \begin{array}{l} \underline{VALUE} \ IS \\ \underline{VALUES} \ ARE \end{array} \right\}$ *literal-1* [THRU *literal-2*]

     [*literal-3* [THRU *literal-4*]] . . .

66 *data-name-1* RENAMES *data-name-2* [THRU *data-name-3*].

NOTE: Formats for the OCCURS **Clause are included with Formats for the** TABLE HANDLING **feature.**

LINKAGE SECTION.

77 *data-name-1*

01-49 $\left\{ \begin{array}{l} data\text{-}name\text{-}1 \\ \underline{FILLER} \end{array} \right\}$

    REDEFINES *data-name-2*

    BLANK WHEN ZERO

    $\left\{ \begin{array}{l} \underline{JUSTIFIED} \\ \underline{JUST} \end{array} \right\}$ RIGHT

    $\left\{ \begin{array}{l} \underline{PICTURE} \\ \underline{PIC} \end{array} \right\}$ IS *character string*

    [SIGN IS] $\left\{ \begin{array}{l} \underline{LEADING} \\ \underline{TRAILING} \end{array} \right\}$ [SEPARATE CHARACTER] (Version 3 & 4)

    $\left\{ \begin{array}{l} \underline{SYNCHRONIZED} \\ \underline{SYNC} \end{array} \right\}$ $\left[\begin{array}{l} \underline{LEFT} \\ \underline{RIGHT} \end{array} \right]$

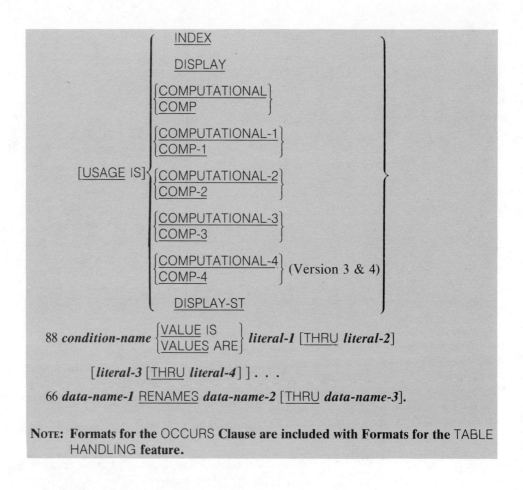

88 *condition-name* $\begin{Bmatrix} \underline{VALUE} \text{ IS} \\ \underline{VALUES} \text{ ARE} \end{Bmatrix}$ *literal-1* [<u>THRU</u> *literal-2*]

[*literal-3* [<u>THRU</u> *literal-4*]] . . .

66 *data-name-1* <u>RENAMES</u> *data-name-2* [<u>THRU</u> *data-name-3*].

NOTE: **Formats for the** OCCURS **Clause are included with Formats for the** TABLE HANDLING **feature.**

PROCEDURE DIVISION—BASIC FORMATS

$\begin{Bmatrix} \underline{PROCEDURE} \ \underline{DIVISION}. \\ \underline{PROCEDURE} \ \underline{DIVISION} \ \underline{USING} \ identifier\text{-}1 \ [identifier\text{-}2] \ . \ . \ . \ . \end{Bmatrix}$

ACCEPT **Statement**

FORMAT 1

FORMAT 2 (Version 4)

ADD **Statement**

FORMAT 1

$$\text{ADD} \begin{Bmatrix} \textit{identifier-1} \\ \textit{literal-1} \end{Bmatrix} \begin{bmatrix} \textit{identifier-2} \\ \textit{literal-2} \end{bmatrix} \ldots \underline{\text{TO}}\ \textit{identifier-m}\ [\underline{\text{ROUNDED}}]$$

$$[\textit{identifier-n}\ [\underline{\text{ROUNDED}}]]\ldots[\text{ON}\ \underline{\text{SIZE}}\ \underline{\text{ERROR}}\ \textit{imperative-statement}]$$

FORMAT 2

$$\text{ADD} \begin{Bmatrix} \textit{identifier-1} \\ \textit{literal-1} \end{Bmatrix} \begin{Bmatrix} \textit{identifier-2} \\ \textit{literal-2} \end{Bmatrix} \begin{bmatrix} \textit{identifier-3} \\ \textit{literal-3} \end{bmatrix} \ldots \underline{\text{GIVING}}$$

$$\textit{identifier-m}\ [\underline{\text{ROUNDED}}]\ [\text{ON}\ \underline{\text{SIZE}}\ \underline{\text{ERROR}}\ \textit{imperative-statement}]$$

FORMAT 3

$$\text{ADD} \begin{Bmatrix} \underline{\text{CORRESPONDING}} \\ \underline{\text{CORR}} \end{Bmatrix} \textit{identifier-1}\ \underline{\text{TO}}\ \textit{identifier-2}\ [\underline{\text{ROUNDED}}]$$

$$[\text{ON}\ \underline{\text{SIZE}}\ \underline{\text{ERROR}}\ \textit{imperative-statement}]$$

ALTER Statement

$$\underline{\text{ALTER}}\ \textit{procedure-name-1}\ \underline{\text{TO}}\ [\underline{\text{PROCEED}}\ \underline{\text{TO}}]\ \textit{procedure-name-2}$$

$$[\textit{procedure-name-3}\ \underline{\text{TO}}\ [\underline{\text{PROCEED}}\ \underline{\text{TO}}]\ \textit{procedure-name-4}]\ldots$$

CALL Statement

FORMAT 1

$$\underline{\text{CALL}}\ \textit{literal-1}\ [\underline{\text{USING}}\ \textit{identifier-1}\ [\textit{identifier-2}]\ldots]$$

FORMAT 2 (Version 4)

$$\underline{\text{CALL}}\ \textit{identifier-1}\ [\underline{\text{USING}}\ \textit{identifier-2}\ [\textit{identifier-3}]\ldots]$$

CANCEL Statement (Version 4)

$$\underline{\text{CANCEL}} \begin{Bmatrix} \textit{literal-1} \\ \textit{identifier-1} \end{Bmatrix} \begin{bmatrix} \textit{literal-2} \\ \textit{identifier-2} \end{bmatrix} \ldots$$

CLOSE Statement

FORMAT 1

$$\underline{\text{CLOSE}}\ \textit{file-name-1} \begin{bmatrix} \underline{\text{REEL}} \\ \underline{\text{UNIT}} \end{bmatrix} [\text{WITH} \begin{Bmatrix} \underline{\text{NO REWIND}} \\ \underline{\text{LOCK}} \end{Bmatrix}]$$

$$[\textit{file-name-2} \begin{bmatrix} \underline{\text{REEL}} \\ \underline{\text{UNIT}} \end{bmatrix} [\text{WITH} \begin{Bmatrix} \underline{\text{NO REWIND}} \\ \underline{\text{LOCK}} \end{Bmatrix}]]\ldots$$

FORMAT 2

$$
\underline{\text{CLOSE}}\ \textit{file-name-1}\ [\text{WITH}\ \left\{\begin{array}{l}\underline{\text{NO}}\ \underline{\text{REWIND}}\\ \underline{\text{LOCK}}\\ \underline{\text{DISP}}\end{array}\right\}\ ]
$$

$$
[\ \textit{file-name-2}\ [\text{WITH}\ \left\{\begin{array}{l}\underline{\text{NO}}\ \underline{\text{REWIND}}\\ \underline{\text{LOCK}}\\ \underline{\text{DISP}}\end{array}\right\}\ ]]\ .\ .\ .
$$

FORMAT 3

$$
\underline{\text{CLOSE}}\ \textit{file-name-1}\ \left\{\begin{array}{l}\underline{\text{REEL}}\\ \underline{\text{UNIT}}\end{array}\right\}\ [\text{WITH}\left\{\begin{array}{l}\underline{\text{NO}}\ \underline{\text{REWIND}}\\ \underline{\text{LOCK}}\\ \underline{\text{POSITIONING}}\end{array}\right\}\ ]
$$

$$
[\ \textit{file-name-2}\ \left\{\begin{array}{l}\underline{\text{REEL}}\\ \underline{\text{UNIT}}\end{array}\right\}\ [\text{WITH}\left\{\begin{array}{l}\underline{\text{NO}}\ \underline{\text{REWIND}}\\ \underline{\text{LOCK}}\\ \underline{\text{POSITIONING}}\end{array}\right\}\ ]]\ .\ .\ .
$$

COMPUTE Statement

$$
\underline{\text{COMPUTE}}\ \textit{identifier-1}\ [\underline{\text{ROUNDED}}] = \left\{\begin{array}{l}\textit{identifier-2}\\ \textit{literal-1}\\ \textit{arithmetic-expression}\end{array}\right\}
$$
$$
[\text{ON}\ \underline{\text{SIZE}}\ \underline{\text{ERROR}}\ \textit{imperative-statement}]
$$

DECLARATIVE Section

$\underline{\text{PROCEDURE}}\ \underline{\text{DIVISION}}.$

$\underline{\text{DECLARATIVES}}.$

$\{\textit{section-name}\ \underline{\text{SECTION}}.\ \underline{\text{USE}}\ \textit{sentence.}$

$\{\textit{paragraph-name}.\ \{\textit{sentence}\}\ .\ .\ .\}\ .\ .\ .\}\ .\ .\ .$
$\underline{\text{END}}\ \underline{\text{DECLARATIVES}}.$

DISPLAY Statement

$$
\underline{\text{DISPLAY}}\ \left\{\begin{array}{l}\textit{literal-1}\\ \textit{identifier-1}\end{array}\right\}\left[\begin{array}{l}\textit{literal-2}\\ \textit{identifier-2}\end{array}\right]\ .\ .\ .\ [\underline{\text{UPON}}\left\{\begin{array}{l}\text{CONSOLE}\\ \text{SYSPUNCH}\\ \text{SYSOUT}\\ \textit{mnemonic-name}\end{array}\right\}\ ]
$$

DIVIDE Statement

FORMAT 1

$$
\underline{\text{DIVIDE}}\ \left\{\begin{array}{l}\textit{identifier-1}\\ \textit{literal-1}\end{array}\right\}\ \underline{\text{INTO}}\ \textit{identifier-2}\ [\underline{\text{ROUNDED}}]
$$
$$
[\text{ON}\ \underline{\text{SIZE}}\ \underline{\text{ERROR}}\ \textit{imperative-statement}]
$$

FORMAT 2

$$\underline{\text{DIVIDE}} \left\{ \begin{array}{l} \textit{identifier-1} \\ \textit{literal-1} \end{array} \right\} \left\{ \begin{array}{l} \underline{\text{INTO}} \\ \underline{\text{BY}} \end{array} \right\} \left\{ \begin{array}{l} \textit{identifier-2} \\ \textit{literal-2} \end{array} \right\} \underline{\text{GIVING}} \; \textit{identifier-3}$$

$$[\underline{\text{ROUNDED}}] \; [\underline{\text{REMAINDER}} \; \textit{identifier-4}] \; [\text{ON} \; \underline{\text{SIZE}} \; \underline{\text{ERROR}} \; \textit{imperative-statement}]$$

ENTER **Statement**

$$\underline{\text{ENTER}} \; \textit{language-name} \; [\textit{routine-name}].$$

ENTRY **Statement**

$$\underline{\text{ENTRY}} \; \textit{literal-1} \; [\underline{\text{USING}} \; \textit{identifier-1} \; [\textit{identifier-2}] \; . \; . \; .]$$

EXAMINE **Statement**

FORMAT 1

$$\underline{\text{EXAMINE}} \; \textit{identifier} \; \underline{\text{TALLYING}} \left\{ \begin{array}{l} \underline{\text{UNTIL}} \; \underline{\text{FIRST}} \\ \underline{\text{ALL}} \\ \underline{\text{LEADING}} \end{array} \right\} \; \textit{literal-1}$$

$$[\underline{\text{REPLACING}} \; \text{BY} \; \textit{literal-2}]$$

FORMAT 2

$$\underline{\text{EXAMINE}} \; \textit{identifier} \; \underline{\text{REPLACING}} \left\{ \begin{array}{l} \underline{\text{ALL}} \\ \underline{\text{LEADING}} \\ \underline{\text{FIRST}} \\ \underline{\text{UNTIL}} \; \underline{\text{FIRST}} \end{array} \right\} \; \textit{literal-1} \; \underline{\text{BY}} \; \textit{literal-2}$$

EXIT **Statement**

$$\textit{paragraph-name.} \; \underline{\text{EXIT}} \; [\underline{\text{PROGRAM}}].$$

GOBACK **Statement**

$$\underline{\text{GOBACK}}.$$

GO TO **Statement**

FORMAT 1

$$\underline{\text{GO}} \; \underline{\text{TO}} \; \textit{procedure-name-1}$$

FORMAT 2

$$\underline{\text{GO}} \; \underline{\text{TO}} \; \textit{procedure-name-1} \; [\textit{procedure-name-2}] \; . \; . \; . \; \underline{\text{DEPENDING}} \; \text{ON} \; \textit{identifier}$$

FORMAT 3

$$\underline{\text{GO}} \; \underline{\text{TO}}.$$

IF **Statement**

$$\underline{\text{IF}} \; \textit{condition} \; \text{THEN} \left\{ \begin{array}{l} \textit{statement-1} \\ \underline{\text{NEXT}} \; \underline{\text{SENTENCE}} \end{array} \right\} \left\{ \begin{array}{l} \underline{\text{ELSE}} \\ \underline{\text{OTHERWISE}} \end{array} \right\} \left\{ \begin{array}{l} \textit{statement-2} \\ \underline{\text{NEXT}} \; \underline{\text{SENTENCE}} \end{array} \right\}$$

MOVE **Statement**

FORMAT 1

$$\underline{MOVE} \begin{Bmatrix} \textit{identifier-1} \\ \textit{literal-1} \end{Bmatrix} \underline{TO} \ \textit{identifier-2} \ [\textit{identifier-3}] \ . \ . \ .$$

FORMAT 2

$$\underline{MOVE} \begin{Bmatrix} \underline{CORRESPONDING} \\ \underline{CORR} \end{Bmatrix} \textit{identifier-1} \ TO \ \textit{identifier-2}$$

MULTIPLY **Statement**

FORMAT 1

$$\underline{MULTIPLY} \begin{Bmatrix} \textit{identifier-1} \\ \textit{literal-1} \end{Bmatrix} \underline{BY} \ \textit{identifier-2} \ [\underline{ROUNDED}]$$
$$[ON \ \underline{SIZE} \ \underline{ERROR} \ \textit{imperative-statement}]$$

FORMAT 2

$$\underline{MULTIPLY} \begin{Bmatrix} \textit{identifier-1} \\ \textit{literal-1} \end{Bmatrix} \underline{BY} \begin{Bmatrix} \textit{identifier-2} \\ \textit{literal-2} \end{Bmatrix} \underline{GIVING} \ \textit{identifier-3}$$
$$[\underline{ROUNDED}] \ [ON \ \underline{SIZE} \ \underline{ERROR} \ \textit{imperative-statement}]$$

NOTE **Statement**

$$\underline{NOTE} \ \textit{character string}$$

OPEN **Statement**

FORMAT 1

$$\underline{OPEN} \ [\underline{INPUT} \ \{\textit{file-name} \begin{bmatrix} \underline{REVERSED} \\ WITH \ \underline{NO} \ REWIND \end{bmatrix} \} \ . \ . \ .]$$
$$[\underline{OUTPUT} \ \{\textit{file-name} \ [WITH \ \underline{NO} \ REWIND] \} \ . \ . \ .]$$
$$[\underline{I\text{-}O} \ \{\textit{file-name}\} \ . \ . \ .]$$

FORMAT 2

$$\underline{OPEN} \ [\underline{INPUT} \ \{\textit{file-name} \begin{bmatrix} \underline{REVERSED} \\ WITH \ \underline{NO} \ REWIND \end{bmatrix} \begin{bmatrix} \underline{LEAVE} \\ \underline{REREAD} \\ \underline{DISP} \end{bmatrix} \} \ . \ . \ .]$$
$$[\underline{OUTPUT} \ \{\textit{file-name} \ [WITH \ \underline{NO} \ REWIND] \begin{bmatrix} \underline{LEAVE} \\ \underline{REREAD} \\ \underline{DISP} \end{bmatrix} \} \ . \ . \ .]$$
$$[\underline{I\text{-}O} \ \{\textit{file-name}\} \ . \ . \ .]$$

PERFORM **Statement**

FORMAT 1

$$\underline{PERFORM} \ \textit{procedure-name-1} \ [\underline{THRU} \ \textit{procedure-name-2}]$$

FORMAT 2

$$\underline{PERFORM} \ \textit{procedure-name-1} \ [\underline{THRU} \ \textit{procedure-name-2}] \begin{Bmatrix} \textit{identifier-1} \\ \textit{integer-1} \end{Bmatrix} \underline{TIMES}$$

FORMAT 3

PERFORM *procedure-name-1* [THRU *procedure-name-2*] UNTIL *condition-1*

FORMAT 4

PERFORM *procedure-name-1* [THRU *procedure-name-2*]

VARYING $\begin{Bmatrix} \textit{index-name-1} \\ \textit{identifier-1} \end{Bmatrix}$ FROM $\begin{Bmatrix} \textit{index-name-2} \\ \textit{literal-2} \\ \textit{identifier-2} \end{Bmatrix}$ BY $\begin{Bmatrix} \textit{literal-3} \\ \textit{identifier-3} \end{Bmatrix}$ UNTIL *condition-1*

AFTER $\begin{Bmatrix} \textit{index-name-4} \\ \textit{identifier-4} \end{Bmatrix}$ FROM $\begin{Bmatrix} \textit{index-name-5} \\ \textit{literal-5} \\ \textit{identifier-5} \end{Bmatrix}$ BY $\begin{Bmatrix} \textit{literal-6} \\ \textit{identifier-6} \end{Bmatrix}$ UNTIL *condition-2*

AFTER $\begin{Bmatrix} \textit{index-name-7} \\ \textit{identifier-7} \end{Bmatrix}$ FROM $\begin{Bmatrix} \textit{index-name-8} \\ \textit{literal-8} \\ \textit{identifier-8} \end{Bmatrix}$ BY $\begin{Bmatrix} \textit{literal-9} \\ \textit{identifier-9} \end{Bmatrix}$ UNTIL *condition-3*

READ **Statement**

READ *file-name* RECORD [INTO *identifier*]

$\begin{Bmatrix} \text{AT END} \\ \text{INVALID KEY} \end{Bmatrix}$ *imperative-statement*

REWRITE **Statement**

REWRITE *record-name* [FROM *identifier*] [INVALID KEY *imperative-statement*]

SEEK **Statement**

SEEK *file-name* RECORD

START **Statement**

FORMAT 1

START *file-name* [INVALID KEY *imperative-statement*]

FORMAT 2 (Version 3 & 4)

START *file-name*

USING KEY *data-name* $\begin{Bmatrix} \text{EQUAL TO} \\ = \end{Bmatrix}$ *identifier*

[INVALID KEY *imperative-statement*]

STOP **Statement**

STOP $\begin{Bmatrix} \text{RUN} \\ \textit{literal} \end{Bmatrix}$

SUBTRACT **Statement**

FORMAT 1

$$\text{\underline{SUBTRACT}} \begin{Bmatrix} \textit{identifier-1} \\ \textit{literal-1} \end{Bmatrix} \begin{bmatrix} \textit{identifier-2} \\ \textit{literal-2} \end{bmatrix} \ldots \text{\underline{FROM}} \ \textit{identifier-m} \ [\text{\underline{ROUNDED}}]$$

$$[\textit{identifier-n} \ [\text{\underline{ROUNDED}}]] \ \ldots \ [\text{ON} \ \text{\underline{SIZE}} \ \text{\underline{ERROR}} \ \textit{imperative-statement}]$$

FORMAT 2

$$\text{\underline{SUBTRACT}} \begin{Bmatrix} \textit{identifier-1} \\ \textit{literal-1} \end{Bmatrix} \begin{bmatrix} \textit{identifier-2} \\ \textit{literal-2} \end{bmatrix} \ldots \text{\underline{FROM}} \begin{Bmatrix} \textit{identifier-m} \\ \textit{identifier-m} \end{Bmatrix} \text{\underline{GIVING}} \ \textit{identifier-}$$

$$[\text{\underline{ROUNDED}}] \ [\text{ON} \ \text{\underline{SIZE}} \ \text{\underline{ERROR}} \ \textit{imperative-statement}]$$

FORMAT 3

$$\text{\underline{SUBTRACT}} \begin{Bmatrix} \text{\underline{CORRESPONDING}} \\ \text{\underline{CORR}} \end{Bmatrix} \textit{identifier-1} \ \text{\underline{FROM}} \ \textit{identifier-2} \ [\text{\underline{ROUNDED}}]$$

$$[\text{ON} \ \text{\underline{SIZE}} \ \text{\underline{ERROR}} \ \textit{imperative-statement}]$$

TRANSFORM **Statement**

$$\text{\underline{TRANSFORM}} \ \textit{identifier-3} \ \text{CHARACTERS} \ \text{\underline{FROM}} \begin{Bmatrix} \textit{figurative-constant-1} \\ \textit{nonnumeric-literal-1} \\ \textit{identifier-1} \end{Bmatrix}$$

$$\text{\underline{TO}} \begin{Bmatrix} \textit{figurative-constant-2} \\ \textit{nonnumeric-literal-2} \\ \textit{identifier-2} \end{Bmatrix}$$

USE **Sentence**

FORMAT 1

Option 1:

$$\text{\underline{USE}} \begin{Bmatrix} \text{\underline{BEFORE}} \\ \text{\underline{AFTER}} \end{Bmatrix} \text{STANDARD} \ [\text{\underline{BEGINNING}}] \begin{bmatrix} \text{\underline{REEL}} \\ \text{\underline{FILE}} \\ \text{\underline{UNIT}} \end{bmatrix}$$

$$\text{\underline{LABEL}} \ \text{\underline{PROCEDURE}} \ \text{ON} \begin{Bmatrix} \{\textit{file-name}\} \ldots \\ \text{\underline{OUTPUT}} \\ \text{\underline{INPUT}} \\ \text{\underline{I-O}} \end{Bmatrix}$$

Option 2:

$$\text{\underline{USE}} \begin{Bmatrix} \text{\underline{BEFORE}} \\ \text{\underline{AFTER}} \end{Bmatrix} \text{STANDARD} \ [\text{\underline{ENDING}}] \begin{bmatrix} \text{\underline{REEL}} \\ \text{\underline{FILE}} \\ \text{\underline{UNIT}} \end{bmatrix}$$

$$\text{\underline{LABEL}} \ \text{\underline{PROCEDURE}} \ \text{ON} \begin{Bmatrix} \{\textit{file-name}\} \ldots \\ \text{\underline{OUTPUT}} \\ \text{\underline{INPUT}} \\ \text{\underline{I-O}} \end{Bmatrix}$$

FORMAT 2

USE AFTER STANDARD ERROR PROCEDURE

$$\text{ON} \begin{Bmatrix} \{\textit{file-name}\} \ [\textit{file-name-2}] \ . \ . \ . \\ \underline{\text{INPUT}} \\ \underline{\text{OUTPUT}} \\ \underline{\text{I-O}} \end{Bmatrix}$$

[GIVING *data-name-1* [*data-name-2*]].

NOTE: Format 3 of the USE **Sentence is included in Formats for the** REPORT WRITER **feature.**

WRITE **Statement**

FORMAT 1

WRITE *record-name* [FROM *identifier-1*] [$\begin{Bmatrix} \underline{\text{BEFORE}} \\ \underline{\text{AFTER}} \end{Bmatrix}$ ADVANCING

$$\begin{Bmatrix} \textit{identifier-2} \ \text{LINES} \\ \textit{integer} \ \text{LINES} \\ \textit{mnemonic-name} \end{Bmatrix} \text{]} \ [\text{AT} \begin{Bmatrix} \underline{\text{END-OF-PAGE}} \\ \underline{\text{EOP}} \end{Bmatrix} \textit{imperative-statement}]$$

FORMAT 2

WRITE *record-name* [FROM *identifier-1*] AFTER POSITIONING $\begin{Bmatrix} \textit{identifier-2} \\ \textit{integer} \end{Bmatrix}$ LINES

$$[\text{AT} \begin{Bmatrix} \underline{\text{END-OF-PAGE}} \\ \underline{\text{EOP}} \end{Bmatrix} \textit{imperative-statement}]$$

FORMAT 3

WRITE *record-name* [FROM *identifier-1*] INVALID KEY *imperative-statement*

SORT—BASIC FORMATS

Environment Division Sort Formats

FILE-CONTROL PARAGRAPH—SELECT SENTENCE
SELECT **Sentence (for GIVING option only)**
   SELECT *file-name*

      ASSIGN TO [*integer-1*] *system-name-1* [*system-name-2*] . . .

        OR *system-name-3* [FOR MULTIPLE $\begin{Bmatrix} \underline{\text{REEL}} \\ \underline{\text{UNIT}} \end{Bmatrix}$]

        [RESERVE $\begin{Bmatrix} \textit{integer-2} \\ \underline{\text{NO}} \end{Bmatrix}$ ALTERNATE $\begin{bmatrix} \text{AREA} \\ \text{AREAS} \end{bmatrix}$].

SELECT **Sentence (for Sort Work Files)**

   SELECT *sort-file-name*

      ASSIGN TO [*integer*] *system-name-1* [*system-name-2*] . . .

I-O-CONTROL PARAGRAPH

<u>RERUN</u> **Clause**

<u>RERUN</u> <u>ON</u> *system-name*

SAME RECORD/SORT AREA **Clause**

<u>SAME</u> $\left\{ \begin{array}{l} \underline{RECORD} \\ \underline{SORT} \end{array} \right\}$ AREA FOR *file-name-1* {*file-name-2*} . . .

Data Division Sort Formats

SORT-FILE DESCRIPTION

<u>SD</u> *sort-file-name*

<u>RECORDING</u> MODE IS *mode*

<u>DATA</u> $\left\{ \begin{array}{l} \underline{RECORD} \text{ IS} \\ \underline{RECORDS} \text{ ARE} \end{array} \right\}$ *data-name-1* [*data-name-2*] . . .

<u>RECORD</u> CONTAINS [*integer-1* <u>TO</u>] *integer-2* CHARACTERS

[<u>LABEL</u> $\left\{ \begin{array}{l} \underline{RECORD} \text{ IS} \\ \underline{RECORDS} \text{ ARE} \end{array} \right\} \left\{ \begin{array}{l} \underline{STANDARD} \\ \underline{OMITTED} \end{array} \right\}$]. **(Version 4)**

Procedure Division Sort Formats

RELEASE **Statement**

<u>RELEASE</u> *sort-record-name* [<u>FROM</u> *identifier*]

RETURN **Statement**

<u>RETURN</u> *sort-file-name* RECORD [<u>INTO</u> *identifier*]

    AT <u>END</u> *imperative-statement*

SORT **Statement**

<u>SORT</u> *file-name-1* ON $\left\{ \begin{array}{l} \underline{DESCENDING} \\ \underline{ASCENDING} \end{array} \right\}$ KEY {*data-name-1*} . . .

[ON $\left\{ \begin{array}{l} \underline{DESCENDING} \\ \underline{ASCENDING} \end{array} \right\}$ KEY {*data-name-2*} . . .] . . .

$\left\{ \begin{array}{l} \underline{INPUT} \text{ PROCEDURE IS } section\text{-}name\text{-}1 \text{ [\underline{THRU} } section\text{-}name\text{-}2\text{]} \\ \underline{USING} \text{ } file\text{-}name\text{-}2 \end{array} \right\}$

$\left\{ \begin{array}{l} \underline{OUTPUT} \text{ PROCEDURE IS } section\text{-}name\text{-}2 \text{ [\underline{THRU} } section\text{-}name\text{-}4\text{]} \\ \underline{GIVING} \text{ } file\text{-}name\text{-}3 \end{array} \right\}$

REPORT WRITER—BASIC FORMATS

Data Division Report Writer Formats

NOTE: Formats that appear as Basic Formats within the general description of the Data Division are illustrated there.

FILE SECTION—REPORT **Clause**

$$\left\{ \begin{array}{l} \underline{REPORT} \ IS \\ \underline{REPORTS} \ ARE \end{array} \right\} report\text{-}name\text{-}1 \ [report\text{-}name\text{-}2] \ . \ .$$

REPORT SECTION
  REPORT SECTION.

RD *report-name*

WITH CODE *mnemonic-name*

$$\left\{ \begin{array}{l} \underline{CONTROL} \ IS \\ \underline{CONTROLS} \ ARE \end{array} \right\} \left\{ \begin{array}{l} \underline{FINAL} \\ identifier\text{-}1 \ [identifier\text{-}2] \ . \ . \ . \\ \underline{FINAL} \ identifier\text{-}1 \ [identifier\text{-}2] \ . \ . \ . \end{array} \right\}$$

$$\underline{PAGE} \left[\begin{array}{l} LIMIT \ IS \\ LIMITS \ ARE \end{array} \right] integer\text{-}1 \left\{ \begin{array}{l} \underline{LINE} \\ \underline{LINES} \end{array} \right\}$$

[HEADING *integer-2*]

[FIRST DETAIL *integer-3*]

[LAST DETAIL *integer-4*]

[FOOTING *integer-5*].

REPORT GROUP DESCRIPTION ENTRY

FORMAT 1

01 [*data-name-1*]

$$\underline{LINE} \ NUMBER \ IS \left\{ \begin{array}{l} integer\text{-}1 \\ \underline{PLUS} \ integer\text{-}2 \\ \underline{NEXT} \ \underline{PAGE} \end{array} \right\}$$

$$\underline{NEXT} \ \underline{GROUP} \ IS \left\{ \begin{array}{l} integer\text{-}1 \\ \underline{PLUS} \ integer\text{-}2 \\ \underline{NEXT} \ \underline{PAGE} \end{array} \right\}$$

$$
\text{TYPE IS} \begin{cases}
\begin{cases} \underline{\text{REPORT}} \text{ HEADING} \\ \underline{\text{RH}} \end{cases} \\[4pt]
\begin{cases} \underline{\text{PAGE}} \text{ HEADING} \\ \underline{\text{PH}} \end{cases} \\[4pt]
\begin{cases} \underline{\text{CONTROL}} \text{ HEADING} \\ \underline{\text{CH}} \end{cases} \begin{cases} \textit{identifier-n} \\ \underline{\text{FINAL}} \end{cases} \\[4pt]
\begin{cases} \underline{\text{DETAIL}} \\ \underline{\text{DE}} \end{cases} \\[4pt]
\begin{cases} \underline{\text{CONTROL}} \text{ FOOTING} \\ \underline{\text{CF}} \end{cases} \begin{cases} \textit{identifier-n} \\ \underline{\text{FINAL}} \end{cases} \\[4pt]
\begin{cases} \underline{\text{PAGE}} \text{ FOOTING} \\ \underline{\text{PF}} \end{cases} \\[4pt]
\begin{cases} \underline{\text{REPORT}} \text{ FOOTING} \\ \underline{\text{RF}} \end{cases}
\end{cases}
$$

USAGE **Clause.**

FORMAT 2

nn [*data-name-1*]
   LINE **Clause—See Format 1**
   USAGE **Clause.**

FORMAT 3

nn [*data-name-1*]
   <u>COLUMN</u> NUMBER IS *integer-1*
   <u>GROUP</u> INDICATE
   JUSTIFIED **Clause**
   LINE **Clause—See Format 1**
   PICTURE **Clause**

   $$\underline{\text{RESET}} \text{ ON} \begin{cases} \textit{identifier-1} \\ \underline{\text{FINAL}} \end{cases}$$

   BLANK WHEN ZERO **Clause**

   $$\underline{\text{SOURCE}} \text{ IS} \begin{cases} \underline{\text{TALLY}} \\ \textit{identifier-2} \end{cases}$$

   $$\underline{\text{SUM}} \begin{cases} \underline{\text{TALLY}} \\ \textit{identifier-3} \end{cases} \begin{bmatrix} \underline{\text{TALLY}} \\ \textit{identifier-4} \end{bmatrix} \dots [\underline{\text{UPON}} \textit{ data-name}]$$

   <u>VALUE</u> IS *literal-1*
   USAGE **Clause.**

FORMAT 4

> **01** *data-name-1*
>   BLANK WHEN ZERO **Clause**
>   COLUMN **Clause—See Format 3**
>   GROUP **Clause—See Format 3**
>   JUSTIFIED **Clause**
>   LINE **Clause—See Format 1**
>   NEXT GROUP **Clause—See Format 1**
>   PICTURE **Clause**
>   RESET **Clause—See Format 3**
>
> $\begin{Bmatrix} \text{SOURCE } \textbf{Clause} \\ \text{SUM } \textbf{Clause} \\ \text{VALUE } \textbf{Clause} \end{Bmatrix}$ **See Format 3**
>
>   TYPE **Clause—See Format 1**
>   USAGE **Clause.**

Procedure Division Report Writer Formats

GENERATE **Statement**

> GENERATE *identifier*

INITIATE **Statement**

> INITIATE *report-name-1* [*report-name-2*] . . .

TERMINATE **Statement**

> TERMINATE *report-name-1* [*report-name-2*] . . .

USE **Sentence**

> USE BEFORE REPORTING *data-name.*

TABLE HANDLING—BASIC FORMATS

Data Division Table Handling Formats

OCCURS **Clause**

FORMAT 1

> OCCURS *integer-2* TIMES
>
> $\left[\begin{Bmatrix} \underline{\text{ASCENDING}} \\ \underline{\text{DESCENDING}} \end{Bmatrix} \text{KEY IS } \textit{data-name-2} \left[\textit{data-name-3} . . . \right] \right] . . .$
>
> [INDEXED BY *index-name-1* [*index-name-2*] . . .]

FORMAT 2

> OCCURS *integer-1* TO *integer-2* TIMES [DEPENDING ON *data-name-1*]
>
> $\left[\begin{Bmatrix} \underline{\text{ASCENDING}} \\ \underline{\text{DESCENDING}} \end{Bmatrix} \text{KEY IS } \textit{data-name-2} \left[\textit{data-name-3} \right] . . . \right] . . .$
>
> [INDEXED BY *index-name-1* [*index-name-2*] . . .]

FORMAT 3

OCCURS *integer-2* TIMES [DEPENDING ON *data-name-1*]

$$\left[\begin{Bmatrix} \underline{\text{ASCENDING}} \\ \underline{\text{DESCENDING}} \end{Bmatrix} \text{KEY IS } \textit{data-name-2} \, [\textit{data-name-3}] \, . \, . \, .\right] \, . \, .$$

[INDEXED BY *index-name-1* [*index-name-2*] . . .]

USAGE Clause

[USAGE IS] INDEX

Procedure Division Table Handling Formats

SEARCH Statement

FORMAT 1

SEARCH *identifier-1* [VARYING $\begin{Bmatrix} \textit{index-name-1} \\ \textit{identifier-2} \end{Bmatrix}$]

[AT END *imperative-statement-1*]

WHEN *condition-1* $\begin{Bmatrix} \textit{imperative-statement-2} \\ \underline{\text{NEXT}} \, \underline{\text{SENTENCE}} \end{Bmatrix}$

[WHEN *condition-2* $\begin{Bmatrix} \textit{imperative-statement-3} \\ \underline{\text{NEXT}} \, \underline{\text{SENTENCE}} \end{Bmatrix}$] . . .

FORMAT 2

SEARCH ALL *identifier-1* [AT END *imperative-statement-1*]

WHEN *condition-1* $\begin{Bmatrix} \textit{imperative-statement-2} \\ \underline{\text{NEXT}} \, \underline{\text{SENTENCE}} \end{Bmatrix}$

SET Statement

FORMAT 1

SET $\begin{Bmatrix} \textit{index-name-1} \, [\textit{index-name-2}] \, . \, . \, . \\ \textit{identifier-1} \quad [\textit{identifier-2}] \quad . \, . \, . \end{Bmatrix}$ TO $\begin{Bmatrix} \textit{index-name-3} \\ \textit{identifier-3} \\ \textit{literal-1} \end{Bmatrix}$

FORMAT 2

SET *index-name-4* [*index-name-5*] . . . $\begin{Bmatrix} \underline{\text{UP}} \, \underline{\text{BY}} \\ \underline{\text{DOWN}} \, \underline{\text{BY}} \end{Bmatrix} \begin{Bmatrix} \textit{identifier-4} \\ \textit{literal-2} \end{Bmatrix}$

SEGMENTATION—BASIC FORMATS

Environment Division Segmentation Formats

OBJECT-COMPUTER PARAGRAPH
SEGMENT-LIMIT **Clause**
SEGMENT-LIMIT IS *priority-number*

Procedure Division Segmentation Formats

Priority Numbers

section-name <u>SECTION</u> [*priority-number*].

SOURCE PROGRAM LIBRARY FACILITY

COPY **Statement**

<u>COPY</u> *library-name* [SUPPRESS]

[<u>REPLACING</u> *word-1* <u>BY</u> $\begin{Bmatrix} word\text{-}2 \\ literal\text{-}1 \\ identifier\text{-}1 \end{Bmatrix}$ [*word-3* <u>BY</u> $\begin{Bmatrix} word\text{-}4 \\ literal\text{-}2 \\ identifier\text{-}2 \end{Bmatrix}$] . . .].

Extended Source Program Library Facility

BASIS **Card**

<u>BASIS</u> *library-name*

INSERT **Card**

<u>INSERT</u> *sequence-number-field*

DELETE **Card**

<u>DELETE</u> *sequence-number-filed*

DEBUGGING LANGUAGE—BASIC FORMATS

Procedure Division Debugging Formats

EXHIBIT **Statement**

<u>EXHIBIT</u> $\begin{Bmatrix} \underline{NAMED} \\ \underline{CHANGED} \ \underline{NAMED} \\ \underline{CHANGED} \end{Bmatrix}$ $\begin{Bmatrix} identifier\text{-}1 \\ nonnumeric\text{-}literal\text{-}1 \end{Bmatrix}$ $\begin{bmatrix} identifier\text{-}2 \\ nonnumeric\text{-}literal\text{-}2 \end{bmatrix}$ . . .

ON **(Count-Conditional) Statement**

Format 1

<u>ON</u> *integer-1* [<u>AND</u> <u>EVERY</u> *integer-2*] [<u>UNTIL</u> *integer-3*]

$\begin{Bmatrix} imperative\text{-}statement \\ \underline{NEXT} \ \underline{SENTENCE} \end{Bmatrix}$ $\begin{bmatrix} \underline{ELSE} \\ \underline{OTHERWISE} \end{bmatrix}$ $\begin{Bmatrix} statement \ . \ . \ . \\ \underline{NEXT} \ \underline{SENTENCE} \end{Bmatrix}$

Format 2 (Version 3 & 4)

<u>ON</u> $\begin{Bmatrix} integer\text{-}1 \\ identifier\text{-}1 \end{Bmatrix}$ [<u>AND</u> <u>EVERY</u> $\begin{Bmatrix} integer\text{-}2 \\ identifier\text{-}2 \end{Bmatrix}$] [<u>UNTIL</u> $\begin{Bmatrix} integer\text{-}3 \\ identifier\text{-}3 \end{Bmatrix}$]

$\begin{Bmatrix} imperative\text{-}statement \\ \underline{NEXT} \ \underline{SENTENCE} \end{Bmatrix}$ $\begin{bmatrix} \underline{ELSE} \\ \underline{OTHERWISE} \end{bmatrix}$ $\begin{Bmatrix} statement \ . \ . \ . \\ \underline{NEXT} \ \underline{SENTENCE} \end{Bmatrix}$

TRACE **Statement**

$$\begin{Bmatrix} \underline{READY} \\ \underline{RESET} \end{Bmatrix} \underline{TRACE}$$

Compile-Time Debugging Packet

DEBUG **Card**

> $\underline{DEBUG}$ *location*

FORMAT CONTROL—BASIC FORMATS

EJECT **Statement**

1	Area B
	$\underline{EJECT}$

SKIP1, SKIP2, SKIP3 **Statements**

1	Area B
	$\begin{Bmatrix} \underline{SKIP1} \\ \underline{SKIP2} \\ \underline{SKIP3} \end{Bmatrix}$

STERLING CURRENCY—BASIC FORMATS

Data Division Sterling Formats

Nonreport PICTURE **Clause**

$$\begin{Bmatrix} \underline{PICTURE} \\ \underline{PIC} \end{Bmatrix} \text{IS } 9\,[(n)] \text{ D } [8]\, 8D \begin{Bmatrix} 6[6] \\ 7[7] \end{Bmatrix} [[V]\, 9\,[(n)]] \ [\underline{USAGE} \text{ IS }] \ \underline{DISPLAY\text{-}ST}$$

Report PICTURE **Clause**

$$\begin{Bmatrix} \underline{PICTURE} \\ \underline{PIC} \end{Bmatrix} \text{IS}$$

[*pound-report-string*] [*pound-separator-string*] *delimiter shilling-report-string*
[*shilling-separator-string*] *delimiter pence-report-string* [*pence-separator-string*]
[*sign-string*] [$\underline{USAGE}$ IS] $\underline{DISPLAY\text{-}ST}$

PROGRAM PRODUCT INFORMATION—VERSION 4

TELEPROCESSING—BASIC FORMATS

Data Division Teleprocessing Formats

CD **Entry**

Format 1

> CD *cd-name* FOR INPUT

>> [[[SYMBOLIC QUEUE   IS *data-name-1*]

>> [SYMBOLIC SUB-QUEUE-1   IS *data-name-2*]

>> [SYMBOLIC SUB-QUEUE-2   IS *data-name-3*]

>> [SYMBOLIC SUB-QUEUE-3   IS *data-name-4*]

>> [MESSAGE DATE   IS *data-name-5*]

>> [MESSAGE TIME   IS *data-name-6*]

>> [SYMBOLIC SOURCE   IS *data-name-7*]

>> [TEXT LENGTH   IS *data-name-8*]

>> [END KEY   IS *data-name-9*]

>> [STATUS KEY   IS *data-name-10*]

>> [QUEUE DEPTH   IS *data-name-11*]]

>> [*data-name-1 data-name-2 . . . data-name-11*]].

Format 2

> CD *cd-name* FOR OUTPUT

>> [DESTINATION COUNT   IS *data-name-1*]

>> [TEXT LENGTH   IS *data-name-2*]

>> [STATUS KEY   IS *data-name-3*]

>> [ERROR KEY   IS *data-name-4*]

>> [SYMBOLIC DESTINATION   IS *data-name-5*].

Procedure Division Teleprocessing Formats

Message Condition

> [NOT] MESSAGE FOR *cd-name*

RECEIVE Statement

> RECEIVE *cd-name* { MESSAGE / SEGMENT } INTO *identifier-1*

>> [NO DATA *imperative-statement*]

SEND Statement

Format 1

> SEND *cd-name* FROM *identifier-1*

FORMAT 2

$$\underline{\text{SEND}}\ \textit{cd-name}\ [\underline{\text{FROM}}\ \textit{identifier-1}] \begin{Bmatrix} \text{WITH } \textit{identifier-2} \\ \text{WITH } \underline{\text{ESI}} \\ \text{WITH } \underline{\text{EMI}} \\ \text{WITH } \underline{\text{EGI}} \end{Bmatrix}$$

STRING MANIPULATION—BASIC FORMATS

STRING **Statement**

$$\underline{\text{STRING}} \begin{Bmatrix} \textit{identifier-1} \\ \textit{literal-1} \end{Bmatrix} \begin{Bmatrix} \textit{identifier-2} \\ \textit{literal-2} \end{Bmatrix} \dots \underline{\text{DELIMITED}} \text{ BY } \begin{Bmatrix} \textit{identifier-3} \\ \textit{literal-3} \\ \underline{\text{SIZE}} \end{Bmatrix}$$

$$\left[\begin{Bmatrix} \textit{identifier-4} \\ \textit{literal-4} \end{Bmatrix} \begin{Bmatrix} \textit{identifier-5} \\ \textit{literal-5} \end{Bmatrix} \dots \underline{\text{DELIMITED}} \text{ BY } \begin{Bmatrix} \textit{identifier-6} \\ \textbf{\textit{literal-6}} \\ \underline{\text{SIZE}} \end{Bmatrix} \right] \dots$$

$$\underline{\text{INTO}}\ \textit{identifier-7}\ [\text{WITH } \underline{\text{POINTER}}\ \textit{identifier-8}]$$

$$[\text{ON } \underline{\text{OVERFLOW}}\ \textit{imperative-statement}]$$

UNSTRING **Statement**

$$\underline{\text{UNSTRING}}\ \textit{identifier-1}$$

$$[\underline{\text{DELIMITED}} \text{ BY } [\underline{\text{ALL}}] \begin{Bmatrix} \textit{identifier-2} \\ \textit{literal-2} \end{Bmatrix} [\text{OR } [\underline{\text{ALL}}] \begin{Bmatrix} \textit{identifier-3} \\ \textit{literal-3} \end{Bmatrix}] \dots]$$

$$\underline{\text{INTO}}\ \textit{identifier-4}\ [\underline{\text{DELIMITER}} \text{ IN } \textit{identifier-5}]$$

$$[\underline{\text{COUNT}} \text{ IN } \textit{identifier-6}]$$

$$[\textit{identifier-7}\ [\underline{\text{DELIMITER}} \text{ IN } \textit{identifier-8}]$$
$$[\underline{\text{COUNT}} \text{ IN } \textit{identifier-9}]]\ \dots$$

$$[\text{WITH } \underline{\text{POINTER}}\ \textit{identifier-10}]$$

$$[\underline{\text{TALLYING}} \text{ IN } \textit{identifier-11}]$$

$$[\text{ON } \underline{\text{OVERFLOW}}\ \textit{imperative-statement}]$$

VSAM FORMATS (OS/VS COBOL Only)

Environment Division—File-Control Entry

FORMAT 1—Sequential VSAM **Files**

$$\underline{\text{FILE-CONTROL}}.$$
$$\{\underline{\text{SELECT}}\ [\underline{\text{OPTIONAL}}]\ \textit{file-name}$$
$$\underline{\text{ASSIGN}} \text{ TO } \textit{system-name-1}\ [\textit{system-name-2}]\ \dots$$
$$[\underline{\text{RESERVE}}\ \textit{integer} \begin{bmatrix} \text{AREA} \\ \text{AREAS} \end{bmatrix}]$$
$$[\underline{\text{ORGANIZATION}} \text{ IS } \underline{\text{SEQUENTIAL}}]$$
$$[\underline{\text{ACCESS}} \text{ MODE IS } \underline{\text{SEQUENTIAL}}]$$
$$[\underline{\text{PASSWORD}} \text{ IS } \textit{data-name-1}]$$
$$[\underline{\text{FILE}}\ \underline{\text{STATUS}} \text{ IS } \textit{data-name-2}].\ \}\ \dots$$

FORMAT 2—Indexed VSAM Files

FILE-CONTROL.

  {SELECT *file-name*

  ASSIGN TO *system-name-1* [*system-name-2*] . . .

  [RESERVE *integer* $\begin{Bmatrix} \text{AREA} \\ \text{AREAS} \end{Bmatrix}$]

  ORGANIZATION IS INDEXED

  [ACCESS MODE IS $\begin{Bmatrix} \text{SEQUENTIAL} \\ \text{RANDOM} \\ \text{DYNAMIC} \end{Bmatrix}$]

  RECORD KEY IS *data-name-3*

  [PASSWORD IS *data-name-1*]

  [FILE STATUS IS *data-name-2*]. } . . .

Environment Division—I-O-Control Entry

I-O-CONTROL.
  [RERUN ON *system-name* EVERY *integer* RECORDS
    OF *file-name-1*] . . .
  [SAME [RECORD] AREA
    FOR *file-name-2* [*file-name-3*] . . .] . . .

Data Division

LABEL RECORDS **Clause**

  LABEL $\begin{Bmatrix} \text{RECORD IS} \\ \text{RECORDS ARE} \end{Bmatrix}$ $\begin{Bmatrix} \text{STANDARD} \\ \text{OMITTED} \end{Bmatrix}$

NOTE: Other Data Division clauses have the same syntax for VSAM files that they have for other files.

Procedure Division

CLOSE **Statement**

  CLOSE *file-name-1* [WITH LOCK]
       [*file-name-2* [WITH LOCK]] . . .

DELETE **Statement**

  DELETE *file-name* RECORD
    [INVALID KEY *imperative-statement*]

OPEN **Statement**

  OPEN $\begin{Bmatrix} \text{INPUT} & \textit{file-name-1} \text{ [\textit{file-name-2}] . . .} \\ \text{OUTPUT} & \textit{file-name-1} \text{ [\textit{file-name-2}] . . .} \\ \text{I-O} & \textit{file-name-1} \text{ [\textit{file-name-2}] . . .} \\ \text{EXTEND} & \textit{file-name-1} \text{ [\textit{file-name-2}] . . .} \end{Bmatrix}$ . . .

READ **Statement**

FORMAT 1

READ *file-name* [NEXT] RECORD [INTO *identifier*]
[AT END *imperative-statement*]

FORMAT 2

READ *file-name* RECORD [INTO *identifier*]
[INVALID KEY *imperative-statement*]

REWRITE **Statement**

REWRITE *record-name* [FROM *identifier*]
[INVALID KEY *imperative-statement*]

STATE **Statement**

START *file-name* [KEY IS $\begin{Bmatrix} \text{EQUAL TO} \\ = \\ \text{GREATER THAN} \\ > \\ \text{NOT LESS THAN} \\ \text{NOT} < \end{Bmatrix}$]

[INVALID KEY *imperative-statement*]

USE **Sentence**

USE AFTER STANDARD $\begin{Bmatrix} \text{EXCEPTION} \\ \text{ERROR} \end{Bmatrix}$ PROCEDURE

ON $\begin{Bmatrix} \textit{file-name-1} \text{ [\textit{file-name-2}]} \dots \\ \text{INPUT} \\ \text{OUTPUT} \\ \text{I-O} \\ \text{EXTEND} \end{Bmatrix}$

WRITE **Statement**

WRITE *record-name* [FROM *identifier*]
[INVALID KEY *imperative-statement*]

MERGE FACILITY FORMATS (OS/VS COBOL Only)

Environment Division—Input-Output Section

FILE-CONTROL **Entry**

FILE-CONTROL.
  {SELECT *file-name*
  ASSIGN TO *system-name-1* [*system-name-2*] . . . .} . . .

I-O-CONTROL **Entry**

I-O-CONTROL.

SAME $\begin{Bmatrix} \text{SORT} \\ \text{SORT-MERGE} \\ \text{RECORD} \end{Bmatrix}$ AREA FOR *file-name-1* [*file-name-2*] . . .

Data Division—Merge File Description Entry

SD *merge-file-name*

   [RECORD CONTAINS [*integer-1* TO] *integer-2* CHARACTERS]

   [DATA $\begin{Bmatrix} \text{RECORD IS} \\ \text{RECORDS ARE} \end{Bmatrix}$ *data-name-1* [*data-name-2*] . . .].

Procedure Division—Merge Statement

MERGE *file-name-1*

   ON $\begin{Bmatrix} \text{ASCENDING} \\ \text{DESCENDING} \end{Bmatrix}$ KEY *data-name-1* [*data-name-2*] . . .

   [ON $\begin{Bmatrix} \text{ASCENDING} \\ \text{DESCENDING} \end{Bmatrix}$ KEY *data-name-3* [*data-name-4*] . . .] . . .

   USING *file-name-2 file-name-3* [*file-name-4*] . . .

   $\begin{Bmatrix} \text{GIVING } \textit{file-name-5} \\ \text{OUTPUT PROCEDURE IS } \textit{section-name-1} \text{ [THRU } \textit{section-name-2}] \end{Bmatrix}$

B

A Rogues' Gallery of COBOL Features

Webster's Ninth New Collegiate Dictionary defines a *rogue* as: (1) a vagrant, tramp; (2) a dishonest or worthless person: scoundrel; (3) a mischievous person: scamp; (4) a horse inclined to shirk or misbehave; (5) an individual exhibiting a chance and usually inferior biological variation.

Perhaps the COBOL features included here are not as bad as some of those definitions suggest, but they really shouldn't be included in a well-designed, properly written program. The reason we discuss them is that they have been used rather extensively in the past and everyone may not agree with our assertion that use of these features is inappropriate. You may well find yourself involved in the maintenance of programs that incorporate one or more of these features, so we think it wise to review the basic characteristics of these ''rogues.''

SECTION 1
The GO TO Statements—Unconditional Branching

As you may have noted, some of the chapters in this book include a limited use of the unconditional GO TO statement. You may also recall that in each case there was a rather extensive apologia accompanying the use of this feature. Because we believe that a limited use of GO TO statements is not only justified but, in rare—repeat *rare*—cases, preferred, that apologia will appear again at the end of this section.

The general form of the unconditional branch is:

```
GO TO { procedure-name-1 }
```

For example:

```
GO TO PROCESS-NEXT-RECORD.
```

This statement may be combined with a conditional statement such as:

```
IF END-OF-PROCESSING-SWITCH > 4
    THEN GO TO WRAP-UP-PROCESSING
        ELSE
    PERFORM PROCESS-NEXT-RECORD.
```

The effect of an unconditional GO TO statement is to change the order of execution of instructions at the point the GO TO appears and to continue processing with the first statement of the paragraph or section named as procedure-name-1. It is clear that the GO TO is *not* a structured programming statement. Its use does not implement any of the basic structures discussed in Chapter 2.

The danger associated with the use of unconditional branches is that their use tends to defeat the objectives of structured programming. There are almost no circumstances in which the use of an unconditional GO TO is warranted. Those conditions do exist, however. For example, the case construct for structured programming can, at the present time, only be implemented using the GO TO ...DEPENDING ON... form of the GO TO statement (discussed in Chapter 7).

SECTION 2
The ALTER Statement

If you are unlucky enough to encounter the use of an ALTER, then your bad luck will be modified a bit should the program follow this approach. It should put you on guard just to see:

```
GO TO WRAPUP.
```

But if you should see:

```
GO TO.
```

then you know that somewhere in that program is an ALTER statement that will change the order of execution of the program, not in a foreseeably logical manner, but on the basis of the form of the data.

It is our fond hope that in your many years of dealing with COBOL programs, you never (never, never) encounter an ALTER statement.

The ALTER statement richly deserves billing in this rogues' gallery. The only reason it is relegated to Section 2 is that its use depends on prior use of the GO TO. In short, its use is a compound programming crime. You should never use it. However, you may be called upon to maintain a program written by someone who did use it.

The ALTER statement allows the programmer to provide "flexibility" in transferring from one paragraph to another within the program. A GO TO statement is an unconditional transfer because when one is found in the program, control is immediately transferred to the paragraph that is specified after the GO TO.

The function of the ALTER statement is to change the name of the paragraph that follows the words GO TO, so that control will be passed to a desired point.

The general form of the ALTER statement is:

```
ALTER paragraph-name TO PROCEED TO new-paragraph-name.
```

For example,

```
ALTER PARAGRAPH1 TO PROCEED TO PARAGRAPH-X.
```

The `ALTER` statement is used in connection with a paragraph that has only one statement in it, which is a `GO TO` statement. The paragraph itself will have any name that you desire. Consider:

```
TRANSFER.
    GO TO DESIRED-POINT.
```

In a normal program this statement would transfer control to the paragraph-name `DESIRED-POINT`. However, when we're using the `ALTER` command, the paragraph-name `DESIRED-POINT` merely holds the name of the paragraph where we want to go. The name of the paragraph got there by having previously been used in an `ALTER` statement.

```
ALTER TRANSFER TO PROCEED TO PARAGRAPH-1.
```

This effectively makes the `GO TO` statement in the paragraph `TRANSFER` now read:

```
TRANSFER.
    GO TO PARAGRAPH-1.
```

In the actual program the paragraph name will not change on the source listing. The logic of the transfer is changed during program execution.

You can have as many `ALTER` statements in your program as needed and each one will change the flow of the program. The `GO TO` statement being `ALTER`ed, however, must be in a paragraph by itself.

Consider the following figure, which contains part of a `PROCEDURE DIVISION` that used the `ALTER` statements. The program deals with various types of magazine subscriptions and their costs.

```
PROCEDURE DIVISION.
OPENING-PROCEDURE.
    OPEN INPUT INPUT-FILE, OUTPUT OUTPUT-FILE.
READ-DETAIL.
    READ INPUT-FILE AT END GO TO WRAPUP.
    IF PUBLICATION IS EQUAL TO "1" THEN
        MOVE "TODAYS LIFE" TO PERIODICAL
        MOVE "MONTHS" TO DAYS-MONTHS
        ALTER SIGNPOST TO PROCEED TO
            TODAYS-LIFE-SUBSCRIP
        GO TO HEADINGS.
    IF PUBLICATION IS EQUAL TO "2" THEN
        MOVE "THE EVENING PLANET" TO PERIODICAL
        MOVE "MONTHS" TO DAYS-MONTHS
        ALTER SIGNPOST TO PROCEED TO PLANET-SUBSCRIP
        GO TO HEADINGS.
    IF PUBLICATION IS EQUAL TO "3" THEN
        MOVE "SPORTSMANS JOURNAL" TO PERIODICAL
        MOVE "WEEKS" TO DAYS-MONTHS
        ALTER SIGNPOST TO PROCEED TO SPORTSMAN-SUBSCRIP
        GO TO HEADINGS.
    GO TO MOVE-DATA-PARAGRAPH.
```

```
HEADINGS.
    MOVE CORRESPONDING KEY-TO-PUBLICATION TO HEADING-1.
    WRITE LISTING FROM HEADING1 AFTER ADVANCING 3 LINES.
    MOVE SPACES TO LISTING.
    WRITE LISTING AFTER ADVANCING 1 LINES.
    GO TO READ-DETAIL.
MOVE-DATA-PARAGRAPH.
    MOVE CORRESPONDING SUBSCRIPTIONS TO DETAIL-LIST.
SIGNPOST.
    GO TO WRAPUP.
NOTE-ABOUT-SIGNPOST.
    NOTE *** THE PARAGRAPH ABOVE WILL BE ALTERED
             DEPENDING ON WHICH PUBLICATION IS BEING
             PROCESSED-ONLY IN EVENT OF ERROR WILL
             CONTROL TRANSFER TO WRAPUP ***.
WRAPUP.
    CLOSE INPUT-FILE OUTPUT-FILE.
    STOP RUN.
TODAYS-LIFE-SUBSCRIP.
    IF TERM OF SUBSCRIPTIONS = 12 MOVE 8.00 TO CHARGE.
    IF TERM OF SUBSCRIPTIONS = 24 MOVE 15.00 TO CHARGE.
    IF TERM OF SUBSCRIPTIONS = 36 MOVE 24.00 TO CHARGE.
    GO TO WRITIT.
PLANET-SUBSCRIP.
    IF DAYS-PER-WEEK = 1 GO TO SUNDAY-SCHEDULE.
    IF DAYS-PER-WEEK = 6 GO TO DAILY-SCHEDULE.
    MULTIPLY TERM OF SUBSCRIPTIONS BY 6.00 GIVING CHARGE.
    GO TO WRITIT.
SUNDAY-SCHEDULE.
    GO TO RATE1 RATE2 RATE3 RATE4 RATE5 RATE6
        DEPENDING ON TERM OF SUBSCRIPTIONS.
    MULTIPLY TERM OF SUBSCRIPTIONS BY 1.33 GIVING CHARGE.
    GO TO WRITIT.
RATE1.
    MOVE 1.50 TO CHARGE.
    GO TO WRITIT.
    MOVE CORRESPONDING SUBSCRIPTIONS TO DETAIL-LIST.
```

Notice that in the paragraph READ-DETAIL there are three ALTER statements. Each of these will change the transfer of control, depending on the type of magazine subscription being processed. When the program reaches the paragraph SIGNPOST, the GO TO statement inside GO TO WRAPUP will actually transfer control to some paragraph other than WRAPUP, because of the ALTER statements in the paragraph READ-DETAIL. If for some reason the SIGNPOST paragraph never was altered, then control would be passed to the paragraph WRAPUP and the program would end.

The paragraph SIGNPOST did not have to have a paragraph-name at the end of the GO TO statement. You could have had:

```
SIGNPOST.
    GO TO.
```

In this case, you must have altered the paragraph with the ALTER statement before SIGNPOST was executed. Some people prefer this type of statement because it tells the programmer that the place of transfer must be set somewhere else in the program. If you have to GO TO WRAPUP it is easy to believe this is where control will be passed when, in fact, the control will probably be going somewhere else. If you only have GO TO, then it is obvious that control transfer must have been previously set.

The ALTER statement may set more than one paragraph to be altered by specifying the additional paragraph-names to be changed. For example,

```
ALTER SIGNPOST TO PROCEED TO NEW-PLACE NEWPOINT TO PROCEED
            TO SECONDARY-POINT etc.
```

SECTION 3
The CORRESPONDING Option

COBOL compilers allow the use of an option with MOVE, ADD, and SUBTRACT statements, which appears in many programs but is somewhat controversial. Some authorities believe that the use of the CORRESPONDING option simplifies the coding process, whereas others believe that its disadvantages outweigh its advantages. Indeed, of three authors of this book, one encourages the use of the option, one discourages its use, and the third is totally indifferent.

The CORRESPONDING option allows a specified action to affect all like-named data-items in two or more groups. As an illustration, consider the following partial DATA DIVISION:

```
DATA DIVISION.
    FILE SECTION.
    FD INFILE
        o
        o
        o
    01  INPUT-RECORD.
        05  CUST-NAME        PIC X(20).
        05  ACCOUNT-NUMBER    PIC 9(05).
        05  BALANCE-CURRENT   PIC S9(05)V99.
        05  BALANCE-30        PIC S9(05)V99.
        05  BALANCE-60        PIC S9(05)V99.
        05  BALANCE-PAST-90   PIC S9(05)V99.
        05  BALANCE-TOTAL     PIC S9(07)V99.
        o
        o
        o
    WORKING-STORAGE SECTION.
    01  OUTPUT-FORMAT.
        05  CUSTOMER          PIC X(25) VALUE SPACES.
        05  ACCOUNT           PIC 9(05) VALUE ZEROS.
        05  BALANCE-TOTAL     PIC S9(09)V99 VALUE ZEROS.
        05  BALANCE-PAST-90   PIC S9(09)V99 VALUE ZEROS.
        05  BALANCE-60        PIC S9(09)V99 VALUE ZEROS.
        05  CRITICAL-AMT      PIC S9(09)V99 VALUE ZEROS.
        05  BALANCE-30        PIC S9(09)V99 VALUE ZEROS.
        05  BALANCE-CURRENT   PIC S9(09)V99 VALUE ZEROS.
```

If you want to MOVE, ADD, or SUBTRACT elementary items you usually have to do so one at a time, for example

```
ADD BALANCE-60 OF INPUT-RECORD TO BALANCE-60
    OF OUTPUT-FORMAT.
```

In this case qualification is necessary because BALANCE-60 is not a unique data-name.

The general format of the MOVE statement with the CORRESPONDING option is:

MOVE $\begin{Bmatrix} \text{CORRESPONDING} \\ \text{CORR} \end{Bmatrix}$ identifier-1 TO identifier-2.

In the case of our example, the statement

```
MOVE CORRESPONDING INPUT-RECORD TO OUTPUT-FORMAT.
```

is precisely equivalent to

```
MOVE BALANCE-CURRENT OF INPUT-RECORD
    TO BALANCE-CURRENT OF OUTPUT-FORMAT.
MOVE BALANCE-30 OF INPUT-RECORD
    TO BALANCE-30 OF OUTPUT-FORMAT.
MOVE BALANCE-60 OF INPUT-RECORD
    TO BALANCE-60 OF OUTPUT-FORMAT.
MOVE BALANCE-PAST-90 OF INPUT-RECORD
    TO BALANCE-PAST-90 OF OUTPUT-FORMAT.
```

Clearly, the CORRESPONDING option saves a lot of writing, but it may be a mixed blessing. Because the customer name field and the customer account field do not have corresponding names (CUST-NAME NOT = CUSTOMER and ACCOUNT-NUMBER NOT = ACCOUNT) these data were not moved. Obviously we could have made the names equivalent in each group and all items in the input would be MOVEd. We will remind you of this failure of correspondence when we discuss the ADD and SUBTRACT with the CORRESPONDING option below.

The general form of the ADD CORRESPONDING is:

ADD $\begin{Bmatrix} \text{CORRESPONDING} \\ \text{CORR} \end{Bmatrix}$ identifier-1 TO identifier-2 (ROUNDED).

The general form of the SUBTRACT CORRESPONDING is:

SUBTRACT $\begin{Bmatrix} \text{CORRESPONDING} \\ \text{CORR} \end{Bmatrix}$ identifier-1 FROM identifier-2 (ROUNDED).

The effect of these instructions is to ADD (or SUBTRACT) items whose data names are equivalent. For example,

```
ADD CORRESPONDING INPUT-RECORD TO OUTPUT-FORMAT.
```

This statement will add the value of the two data-items named BALANCE-30, store the result at BALANCE-30 OF OUTPUT-FORMAT, will add the value of the two data named BALANCE-CURRENT, store the result at BALANCE-CURRENT OF OUTPUT-FORMAT, and so on for all the like-named items. Now you may see why we assigned different variable names to customer's name and account number. As in any arithmetic operation, items must be defined with a numeric picture. The attempt to ADD or SUBTRACT CORRESPONDING when items with equivalent names are alphanumeric (as in the customer's name field) would prevent successful execution of your program. Furthermore, in most cases, we probably wouldn't want to add account numbers. But if you ADD CORRESPONDING, and the account number has the exact same name in each group (e.g., if we had assigned the name ACCOUNT in INPUT-RECORD rather than ACCOUNT-NUMBER as we did) then the addition of those two items will occur whether that was what was really intended or not. This is one of the pitfalls of the use of the CORRESPONDING option with ADD or SUBTRACT.

SUBTRACT CORRESPONDING is logically similar to ADD CORRESPONDING. In each, the receiving field is the correspondingly named elementary item in identifier-2. In the case of SUBTRACT CORRESPONDING, this is the data-name following the word FROM. The values of the corresponding fields defined in OUTPUT-FORMAT would be changed by execution of

```
SUBTRACT CORRESPONDING INPUT-RECORD FROM OUTPUT-RECORD.
```

SECTION 4
77-Level Entries in WORKING-STORAGE

You are not likely to see many "77 entries" (hereafter, we'll leave the quotes off and call them "77's" or "77" entries) since, for reasons that will become obvious, they aren't used very much.

Effectively, 77's are data-items that cannot be subdivided. For example, you often will use a WORKING-STORAGE item to indicate an end-of-file condition for a file. One way to do this is to define the items as 77's:

```
WORKING-STORAGE SECTION.
77 EOF-MASTER-FILE        PIC 9 VALUE ZEROS.
77 EOF-TRANSACTION-1      PIC 9 VALUE ZEROS.
77 EOF-TRANSACTION-2      PIC 9 VALUE ZEROS.
```

It is not an accident that these entries follow WORKING-STORAGE SECTION. One of the rules of the language (prior to COBOL 74) is that all 77's have to be grouped at the beginning of the WORKING-STORAGE SECTION.

You could achieve the same result by coding the entries:

```
01 EOF-MASTER-FILE        PIC 9 VALUE ZEROS.
01 EOF-TRANSACTION-1      PIC 9 VALUE ZEROS.
01 EOF-TRANSACTION-2      PIC 9 VALUE ZEROS.
```

and these entries could appear anywhere in the WORKING-STORAGE SECTION.

You could achieve the same result and provide superior documentation by coding:

```
01  END-OF-FILE-INDICATORS.
    05  EOF-MASTER-FILE       PIC 9  VALUE ZEROS.
    05  EOF-TRANSACTION-1     PIC 9  VALUE ZEROS.
    05  EOF-TRANSACTION-2     PIC 9  VALUE ZEROS.
```

As you can see, there is nothing particularly wrong with the use of 77 entries, but they lack flexibility and other methods are simply superior to them. There is no reason to clutter your program with 77's. Indeed, should you be called upon to maintain a program that incorporates these entries you may choose to redefine them as 01 entries or as elementary items under an 01 group item.

SECTION 5
88-Level Definition of Condition Names

The discussion of 88-level entries (hereafter called "88's") is, in our opinion, appropriately included in this rogues' gallery. These entries define conditions to be tested—but the actual definition takes place in the DATA DIVISION. Suppose that you have a file containing demographic data concerning the employees of the company. The file definition (in part) would look like this:

```
FD   EMPLOYEE-FILE
             o
             o
             o
01   EMPLOYEE-INFORMATION.
        05   EMPL-NAME        PIC X(30).
        05   MARITAL-STATUS   PIC XX.
        05   GENDER           PIC 9.
        05   EEOC-CODE        PIC XX.
```

Measuring compliance with the company affirmative action plan might require analysis of these codes. The test for marital status in the PROCEDURE DIVISION could take the following form:

```
IF MARITAL-STATUS = "S"
          PERFORM COUNT-SINGLES
ELSE
      IF MARITAL-STATUS = "M"
          PERFORM COUNT-MARRIED
ELSE
      PERFORM ERROR-STATUS-MARITAL.
```

The use of 88's allows the PROCEDURE DIVISION entries to be simplified somewhat, but introduces other difficulties.

Figure B-1 is a partial program for test of affirmative action using the 88-entry technique.

Notice that 88 entries may appear in either the FILE SECTION or the WORKING-STORAGE SECTION of the DATA DIVISION. In effect these entries equate a particular value of a data-item to the name specified in the 88-level entry. In the program in Figure B-1, for example, a value of 2 in the field defined as GENDER is equated with the condition-name MALE. Notice that the condition test in the PROCEDURE DIVISION is for the condition-name (IF MALE ...) rather than for the value of the field (IF GENDER IS EQUAL TO 2). The advantages of this treatment is that the meaning of the test is somewhat clearer (GENDER = 2 doesn't mean much when considered in isolation). The difficulty associated with the use of 88's is that it is more difficult to maintain complex programs when they are used. Suppose that our partial program was only a module of a rather large COBOL program. The phrase IF NATIVE-AMERICAN..., although descriptive in isolation, gives no clue as to where in the DATA DIVISION the condition-name NATIVE-AMERICAN is to be found.

The objections to the use of 88 entries can be overcome while maintaining their advantages by the use of descriptive symbolic names in non-88-type entries with value clauses.

```
01   DEMOGRAPHIC-DATA,
        05   FEMALE        PIC 9      VALUE 1,
        05   MALE          PIC 9      VALUE 2,
        05   MARRIED       PIC X      VALUE 'M',
        05   SINGLE        PIC X      VALUE 'S',
        05   NATIVE-AMERICAN .....................
                          o
                          o
                          o
                          o
     PROCEDURE DIVISION,
                          o
                          o
        IF GENDER = MALE..............
```

Figure B–1
Partial program illustrating the
use of 88-level entries.

```
IDENTIFICATION DIVISION.
PROGRAM-ID.
     TYPE88.
AUTHOR.
     NANCY MORRIS.
REMARKS.
     THIS PROGRAM ILLUSTRATES THE USE OF CONDITION NAMES
     ASSIGNED THROUGH '88' TYPE ENTRIES.
ENVIRONMENT DIVISION.
CONFIGURATION SECTION.
SOURCE-COMPUTER. IBM-4321.
OBJECT-COMPUTER. IBM-4321.
INPUT-OUTPUT SECTION.
FILE-CONTROL.
     SELECT EMPLOYEE-FILE
        ASSIGN TO EMPLOYEE.
DATA DIVISION.
FILE SECTION.
FD   EMPLOYEE-FILE
     LABEL RECORDS ARE STANDARD
     DATA RECORD IS EMPLOYEE-INFORMATION.
01   EMPLOYEE-INFORMATION.
     05 EMPL-NAME            PIC X(25).
     05 MARITAL-STATUS       PIC X.
        88 MARRIED                      VALUE 'M'.
        88 SINGLE                       VALUE 'S'.
     05 GENDER               PIC X.
        88 FEMALE                       VALUE 1.
        88 MALE                         VALUE 2.
     05 EEOC                 PIC XX.
        88 NATIVE-AMERICAN              VALUE 'NA'.
        88 SPANISH-SURNAME              VALUE 'SP'.
        88 BLACK                        VALUE 'BL'.
        88 ASIAN-PAC-ISLANDER           VALUE 'AS'.
        88 OCCIDENTAL                   VALUE 'OC'.
        88 OTHER                        VALUE 'OT'.
WORKING-STORAGE SECTION.
     01 END-OF-FILE-INDICATORS.
        05 EOF-EMPLOYEE-FILE    PIC X  VALUE 'N'.
           88 EMPTY                    VALUE 'Y'.
PROCEDURE DIVISION.
000-MAIN-PROCEDURE.
     PERFORM 100-HOUSEKEEPING.
     PERFORM 200-READ-RECORDS.
     PERFORM 300-EXAMINE-CHARACTERISTICS
        UNTIL EMPTY.
        *
        *
200-READ-RECORDS.
     READ EMPLOYEE-FILE, AT END MOVE 'Y' TO EOF-EMPLOYEE-FILE.
        *
        *
300-EXAMINE-CHARACTERISTICS.
     IF SINGLE PERFORM 210-COUNT-SINGLES
        ELSE
        IF MARRIED PERFORM 220-COUNT-MARRIED.

     IF FEMALE PERFORM 310-COUNT-WOMEN
        ELSE
        IF MALE PERFORM 320-COUNT-MEN.
     IF NATIVE-AMERICAN PERFORM 410-NATIVE
        ELSE
        IF SPANISH-SURNAME
        *
        *
        ELSE
        IF OTHER PERFORM 360-COUNT-OTHERS.
     PERFORM 200-READ-RECORDS.
```

SECTION 6
A Sample Program

The sample program in this section is for the purpose of illustrating the use of some of the rogue statements previously discussed. This is the way in which you may encounter these statements, and we believe that if you will try to follow the logic of this poorly designed and poorly structured program, all our assertions as to the inadvisablity of their use will be affirmed.

The program and data you see here are the same as the sample program in Chapter 7 except that this one violates virtually all the rules of proper programming. Take a look at the program at the end of Chapter 7 and contrast it with the one that follows. We believe that if you are not already an advocate of structured programming principles, you should be after such an exercise.

Inputs to the Sample Program

Figure B–2
Inputs to the sample program.

```
3      JULY 0387
OLIVER MCGILL    30 POSSUM TROT  KNOXVILLE, TENN.      15
JOHNSON CAIN     70126 EAGLE ST  PEAK, N.M.            26
AL TEUTSCHLAND   123 20TH PL     PANTHER CITY, TEX.    11
FRED WIMPLE      8215 HARMONY    IDAHO, IDA.           52
EDDIE GARCIA     1234 EASY ST    HAMMONDSBURG, PA.     52
JAI SUNG         2606 AVE G      HICKORY, N.C.         26
STIMSON CAMP     HWY 10 NORTH    SCURRY, OKLA.         15
1SEPTEMBER1587
JAMES TOWNWAY    245 GARRAR ST   WACO, TEXAS           12
ALICE ROARK      2914 RUGGLES    ITHICIA N.Y.          24
MARY RAGLAND     313 MAIN APT 2  OWENSBORO, KY         11
AMY CRUEZ        3114 OAKLAND    OAKFIELD, CALIF       36
2      JUNE 0787
SANDY PAPER      8854 HIGHWAY 41WASHINGTON, DC         011
PAUL SALEM       54 AVE D        BELLEVILLE ILL        016
ALEX MARTINDALE399 PEACE ST      WATERLOO IOWA         018
SUSAN CROW       108 CROW        SAGINAW MICHIGAN      012
GARY FRENCH      252 DORAN       DULUTH MINNESOTA      087
2      MAY 2487
BEN  BEENE       3414 RIDGE RD   HATTIESBURG, MS       101
JANE DURST       4105 NORTHBRIARMEMPHIS, TN            206
TOM SLOVACEK     28 APPLE ST     SILVER CITY, NM       156
BOB WOOD         289 HANCOCK     CINCINNATI, OHIO      521
1SEPTEMBER2988
SILVIA GEORGE    2704 D MAIN     DALLAS, TX            12
PETER GRAVES     89115 AVE A     SAN DIEGO, CALIF      24
```

The Sample Program

Figure B–3
Sample program.

```
IDENTIFICATION DIVISION.
PROGRAM-ID. ROGUES-GALLERY.
AUTHOR. CHERYL J. SIDNEY.
REMARKS.
    THE WORLD EMPIRE PUBLISHING COMPANY PUBLISHES TWO MAGAZINES
    TODAY'S LIFE AND SPORTSMAN'S JOURNAL AND A DAILY
    NEWSPAPER THE EVENING PLANET. SUBSCRIPTION RATES VARY BY
    PUBLICATION AND THE TERM OF THE SUBSCRIPTION.
ENVIRONMENT DIVISION.
CONFIGURATION SECTION.
SOURCE-COMPUTER.  IBM-3033.
OBJECT-COMPUTER.  IBM-3033.
INPUT-OUTPUT SECTION.
FILE-CONTROL.
    SELECT INPUT-FILE ASSIGN TO INFILE.
    SELECT OUTPUT-FILE ASSIGN TO PRINTER.
DATA DIVISION.
FILE SECTION.
```

Figure B–3 (continued)

```
FD    INPUT-FILE
      LABEL RECORDS ARE OMITTED.
01    KEY-TO-PUBLICATION.
      02 PUBLICATION      PICTURE X.
      02 MONTH            PICTURE X(9).
      02 DAYS             PICTURE 99.
      02 YEAR             PICTURE 99.
      02 FILLER           PICTURE X(66).
01    SUBSCRIPTIONS.
      02 NAME-SUB         PICTURE X(15).
      02 ADDRESS-SUB      PICTURE X(15).
      02 CITY-SUB         PICTURE X(20).
      02 TERM             PICTURE 99.
      02 DAYS-PER-WEEK    PICTURE 9.
      02 FILLER           PICTURE X(27).
FD    OUTPUT-FILE
      LABEL RECORDS ARE OMITTED.
01    LISTING             PICTURE X(133).
WORKING-STORAGE SECTION.
01    VALUEX              PICTURE S999 VALUE -1.
01    HEADING-1.
      02 FILLER           PICTURE X(36)          VALUE SPACES.
      02 PERIODICAL       PICTURE X(24)          VALUE SPACES.
      02 FILLER           PICTURE X(20)          VALUE SPACES.
      02 MONTH            PICTURE X(9)           VALUE SPACES.
      02 FILLER           PICTURE X              VALUE SPACES.
      02 DAYS             PICTURE Z9             VALUE ZEROES.
      02 FILLER           PICTURE X(4)           VALUE ', 19'.
      02 YEAR             PICTURE 99             VALUE ZEROES.
      02 FILLER           PICTURE X(35)          VALUE SPACES.
01    DETAIL-LIST.
      02 FILLER           PICTURE X(17)          VALUE SPACES.
      02 NAME-SUB         PICTURE X(15)          VALUE SPACES.
      02 FILLER           PICTURE X(10)          VALUE SPACES.
      02 ADDRESS-SUB      PICTURE X(15)          VALUE SPACES.
      02 FILLER           PICTURE X(10)          VALUE SPACES.
      02 CITY-SUB         PICTURE X(25)          VALUE SPACES.
      02 FILLER           PICTURE X(10)          VALUE SPACES.
      02 TERM             PICTURE 99             VALUE ZEROES.
      02 FILLER           PICTURE X              VALUE SPACE.
      02 DAYS-MONTHS      PICTURE X(6)           VALUE SPACE.
      02 CHARGE           PICTURE $ZZ.99.
      02 FILLER           PICTURE X(16)          VALUE SPACE.
PROCEDURE DIVISION.
OPENING-PROCEDURE.
      OPEN INPUT INPUT-FILE OUTPUT OUTPUT-FILE.
READ-DETAIL.
      READ INPUT-FILE, AT END GO TO WRAPUP.
      IF PUBLICATION IS EQUAL TO '1'
          MOVE 'TODAYS LIFE            ' TO PERIODICAL
          MOVE 'MONTHS' TO DAYS-MONTHS
          ALTER SIGNPOST TO PROCEED TO TODAYS-LIFE-SUBSCRIPTIONS,
              ELSE
      IF PUBLICATION IS EQUAL TO '2'
          MOVE 'THE EVENING PLANET     ' TO PERIODICAL
          MOVE 'MONTHS' TO DAYS-MONTHS
          ALTER SIGNPOST TO PROCEED TO PLANET-SUBSCRIPTIONS,
              ELSE
      IF PUBLICATION IS EQUAL TO '3'
          MOVE 'SPORTSMANS JOURNAL     ' TO PERIODICAL
          MOVE 'WEEKS' TO DAYS-MONTHS
          ALTER SIGNPOST TO PROCEED TO SPORTSMAN-SUBSCRIPTIONS,
              ELSE
              GO TO RUN-ON.
      MOVE CORRESPONDING KEY-TO-PUBLICATION TO HEADING-1.
      WRITE LISTING FROM HEADING-1 AFTER ADVANCING 1.
      MOVE SPACES TO LISTING.
      WRITE LISTING AFTER ADVANCING 1 LINES.
      GO TO READ-DETAIL.
RUN-ON.
      MOVE CORRESPONDING SUBSCRIPTIONS TO DETAIL-LIST.
SIGNPOST.
      GO TO WRAPUP.
NOTE-ABOUT-SIGNPOST.
      NOTE  *** THE PARAGRAPH ABOVE WILL BE ALTERED DEPENDING ON
                WHICH PUBLICATION IS BEING PROCESSED - ONLY IN
                EVENT OF ERROR WILL CONTROL TRANSFER TO WRAPUP ***
WRAPUP.
      CLOSE INPUT-FILE, OUTPUT-FILE.
      STOP RUN.
TODAYS-LIFE-SUBSCRIPTIONS.
      IF TERM OF SUBSCRIPTIONS = 12 MOVE 8.00 TO CHARGE,
          ELSE
      IF TERM OF SUBSCRIPTIONS = 24 MOVE 15.00 TO CHARGE,
          ELSE
      IF TERM OF SUBSCRIPTIONS = 36 MOVE 24.00 TO CHARGE,
      ELSE DISPLAY 'ERROR IN TERM', GO TO READ-DETAIL.
      GO TO WRITIT.
PLANET-SUBSCRIPTIONS.
      IF DAYS-PER-WEEK = 1 GO TO SUNDAY-SCHEDULE.
      IF DAYS-PER-WEEK = 6 GO TO DAILY-SCHEDULE.
      MULTIPLY TERM OF SUBSCRIPTIONS BY 6.00 GIVING CHARGE.
      GO TO WRITIT.
```

Figure B–3 (continued)

```
SUNDAY-SCHEDULE.
    GO TO RATE-1, RATE-2, RATE-3, RATE-4, RATE-5, RATE-6,
        DEPENDING ON TERM OF SUBSCRIPTIONS.
    MULTIPLY TERM OF SUBSCRIPTIONS BY 1.33 GIVING CHARGE.
    GO TO WRITIT.
DAILY-SCHEDULE.
    IF TERM OF SUBSCRIPTIONS IS LESS THAN 6
        MULTIPLY TERM OF SUBSCRIPTIONS BY 4.50 GIVING CHARGE
            OTHERWISE
            MULTIPLY TERM OF SUBSCRIPTIONS BY 4.00 GIVING CHARGE.
    GO TO WRITIT.
RATE-1.
    MOVE 1.50 TO CHARGE.
    MOVE CORRESPONDING SUBSCRIPTIONS TO DETAIL-LIST.
    GO TO WRITIT.
RATE-2.
    MOVE 2.95 TO CHARGE.
    GO TO WRITIT.
RATE-3.
    MOVE 4.25 TO CHARGE.
    GO TO WRITIT.
RATE-4.
    MOVE 5.80 TO CHARGE.
    GO TO WRITIT.
RATE-5.
    MOVE 6.75 TO CHARGE.
    GO TO WRITIT.
RATE-6.
    MOVE 8.00 TO CHARGE.
    GO TO WRITIT.
SPORTSMAN-SUBSCRIPTIONS.
    IF TERM OF SUBSCRIPTIONS = 15 MOVE 8.00 TO CHARGE,
        ELSE
    IF TERM OF SUBSCRIPTIONS = 26 MOVE 13.50 TO CHARGE,
        ELSE
    IF TERM OF SUBSCRIPTIONS = 52 MOVE 24.00 TO CHARGE,
        ELSE
    DISPLAY 'ERROR IN TERM', GO TO READ-DETAIL.
WRITIT.
    WRITE LISTING FROM DETAIL-LIST AFTER ADVANCING 1 LINES.
    GO TO READ-DETAIL.
```

Outputs from the Sample Program

```
          SPORTSMANS JOURNAL                         JULY   3, 1987

OLIVER MCGILL          30 POSSUM TROT      KNOXVILLE, TENN.        15 WEEKS $ 8.00
JOHNSON CAIN           70126 EAGLE ST      PEAK, N.M.              26 WEEKS $13.50
AL TEUTSCHLAND         123 20TH PL         PANTHER CITY, TEX.      11 WEEKS $13.50
FRED WIMPLE            8215 HARMONY        IDAHO, IDA.             52 WEEKS $24.00
EDDIE GARCIA           1234 EASYST         HAMMONDSBURG, PA.       52 WEEKS $24.00
JAI SUNG               2606 AVE G          HICKORY, N.C.           26 WEEKS $13.50
STIMSON CAMP           HWY 10 NORTH        SCURRY, OKLA.           15 WEEKS $ 8.00
          TODAYS LIFE                           SEPTEMBER 15, 1987

JAMES TOWNWAY          245 GARRAR ST       WACO, TEXAS             12 MONTHS$ 8.00
ALICE RORARK           2914 RUGGLES        ITHICA N.Y.             24 MONTHS$15.00
MARY RAGLAND           APT 2 313 MAIN      OWENSBORO, KY           11 MONTHS$15.00
AMY CRUEZ              3114 OAKLAND        OAKFIELD, CALIF         36 MONTHS$24.00
          THE EVENING PLANET                       JUNE   7, 1987

SANDY PAPER            8854 HIGHWAY 41     D.C.                    01 MONTHS$26.00
PAUL SALEM             54 AVE D            BELLEVILLE ILL          01 MONTHS$ 6.00
ALEX MARTINDALE        399 OEACE ST        WATERLOO IOWA           01 MONTHS$ 6.00
SUSAN CROW             108 CROW            SAGINAW MICHIGAN        01 MONTHS$ 6.00
GARY FRENCH            252 DORAN           DULUTH MINNESOTA        08 MONTHS$48.00
          THE EVENING PLANET                      MAY 24, 1987

BEN  BEENE             3414 RIDGE RD       HATTIESBURG, MS         10 MONTHS$ 2.00
JANE DURST             4105 NORTHBR        MEMPHIS, TN             20 MONTHS$20.00
TOM SLOVACEK           28 APPLE ST         SILVER CITY, NM         15 MONTHS$90.00
BOB WOOD               289 HANCOCK         CINCINNATI, OHIO        52 MONTHS$12.00
          TODAYS LIFE                           SEPTEMBER 29, 1988

SILVIA GEORGE          2704 D MAIN         DALLAS, TX              12 MONTHS$ 8.00
PETER GROVES           89115 AVE A         SAN DIEGO, CALIF        24 MONTHS$15.00
```

Figure B–4
Output from the sample
program.

C

File Status Key Values

File Status	Input/Output Statements	File Organization	Access Method	Meaning
00	all	all	all	successful
02	REWRITE WRITE	ind.	all	created duplicate alternate key
05	OPEN	all	all	optional file not present
13	READ	all	seq.	no next logical record (attend)
15	READ	all	seq.	optional file not present
16	READ	all	seq.	no valid next record (attend)
21	REWRITE	ind.	seq.	primary key changed after READ or START (invalid key)
21	WRITE	ind.	seq.	attempted nonascending key value (invalid key)
22	REWRITE	ind.	all	duplicate alternate key
22	WRITE	ind.,rel.	all	duplicate key
23	DELETE READ REWRITE START	ind.,rel.	ran.	record not in file
24	WRITE	ind.,rel.	all	boundary violation
25	READ	ind.,rel.	ran.	optional file not present
30	all	all	all	all other permanent errors
34	WRITE	seq.	seq.	boundary violation
90	READ	all	all	record locked by another user—record is available in record area.
91	OPEN	all	all	file locked by another program—record is not available
92	DELETE READ REWRITE START WRITE	all	all	record locked by another program
93	DELETE REWRITE	all	seq.	no previous READ or START
93	UNLOCK	all	all	no current record
94	CLOSE	all	all	file never opened or is already closed
94	OPEN	all	all	file already open, or closed with lock, or the current program's data description and/or relative location of an index key does not match the file's description of that index key
94	DELETE READ REWRITE START UNLOCK WRITE	all	all	file not open, or incompatible open mode
95	OPEN	all	all	no file space on device
97	OPEN	all	all	file not found
98	CLOSE	all	all	any other CLOSE error

D

Creating an Indexed File from a Sequential File

Creating an Indexed File from an Existing Sequential File Using the DEC-VAX Computer

The creation of an indexed file from an existing sequential file using system software for the VAX is a three-step process. The three steps are as follows:

1. EDIT/FDL: creates an FDL file to govern the conversion of the files.
2. CREATE/FDL: creates an empty file in which to put the data.
3. CONVERT: reads the input file and places the converted data in the output file. An example of this is included in Figure D-1.

This example takes as many default options through the utility package as is possible. In actual practice a user would more than likely answer the questions asked by the utility in a different manner.

At first look at Figure D-1, a student is likely to be put off and think that this is a complex process. It is not. This example took less than two minutes to complete.

Figure D-2 is a listing of the data in the sequential input file. Columns 1-9 were used as the key field. Note that the file is in no particular sequence. Figure D-3 is the indexed file created in the CONVERT process. Note that the records are in sequence.

```
$ edit/fdl
$_File:          indcr.fdl

                  Parsing Definition File

        DRA1:[SIMPSON]INDCR.FDL; will be created.

        Press RETURN to continue (^Z for Main Menu)

        (Add Delete Exit Help Invoke Modify Quit Set View)
        Main Editor Function                    (Keyword)[Help]          i

        (Add_Key Delete_Key Indexed Optimize
         Relative Sequential Touchup)
        Editing Script Title                    (Keyword)[-]             i

        Target disk volume Cluster Size (1-1Giga)[3]                     1

        Number of Keys to Define        (1-255)[1]   :

        (Line Fill Key Record Init Add)
        Graph type to display                   (Keyword)[Line]

        Number of Records that will be Initially Loaded
        into the File                       (0-1Giga)[-]                 1

        (Fast_Convert NoFast_Convert RMS_Puts)
        Initial File Load Method        (Keyword)[Fast]

        Number of Additional Records to be Added After
        the Initial File Load               (0-1Giga)[0]                 1

        Will Additional Records Typically be Added in
        Order by Ascending Primary Key (Yes/No)[No]

        Will Added Records be Distributed Evenly over the
        Initial Range of Pri Key Values (Yes/No)[No]                   yes

        Key  0 Load Fill Percent        (50-100)[100]

        (Fixed Variable)
        Record Format                           (Keyword)[Var]           f

        Record Size                     (1-32231)[-]                     7

        (Bin2 Bin4 Bin8 Int2 Int4 Int8 Decimal String)
        Key  0 Data Type                        (Keyword)[Str]

        Key  0 Segmentation desired     (Yes/No)[No]

        Key  0 Length                           (1-127)[-]               9

        Key  0 Position                         (0-118)[0]               1

        Key  0 Duplicates allowed       (Yes/No)[No]

        File Prolog Version                     (0_3)[3]

        Data Key Compression desired    (Yes/No)[Yes]

        Data Record Compression desired (Yes/No)[Yes]

        Index Compression desired       (Yes/No)[Yes]

PV-Prolog Version       3 KT-Key  0 Type      String EM-Emphasis Flatter ( 1)
DK-Dup Key  0 Values   No KL-Key  0 Length         9 KP-Key  0 Position       1
RC-Data Record Comp    0% KC-Data Key Comp        0% IC-Index Record Comp    0%
BF-Bucket Fill       100% RF-Record Format      Fixed RS-Record Size        127
```

Figure D–1
Example of VAX conversion of
a sequential file to an indexed
file.

```
LM-Load Method  Fast_Conv IL-Initial Load        1 AR-Added Records        1
     (Type 'FD' to Finish Design)
     Which File Parameter            (Mnemonic)[refresh]                fd

     Text for FDL Title Section      (1-126 chars)[null]
     : book test

     Data File file-spec             (1-126 chars)[null]
     : indfl.dat

     (Carriage_Return FORTRAN None Print)
     Carriage Control                        (Keyword)[Carr]

     Emphasis Used In Defining Default:      (      Flatter_files    )
     Suggested Bucket Sizes:                                          )
     Number of Levels in Index:              (      1      1      1 )
     Number of Buckets in Index:             (      2      2      2 )
     Pages Required to Cache Index:          (      2      2      2 )
     Processing Used to Search Index:        (     26     26    283 )

     Key  0 Bucket Size             (1-63)[1]

     Key  0 Name                 (1-32 chars)[null]
     :

     Global Buffers desired                  (Yes/No)[No]

     The Depth of Key  0 is Estimated to be No Greater
     than 1 Index levels, which is 2 Total levels.

      Press RETURN to continue (^Z for Main Menu)

     (Add Delete Exit Help Invoke Modify Quit Set View)
     Main Editor Function                    (Keyword)[Help]              e
```

Figure D–1 (continued)

```
     123456JOSEPH JOHN SCHWARTZWALDER    495 PLEASANT LANE       APT B
           MUSTANG DRAW       NM3598700000000000000000
     234567CATHERINE ROSS BROWNE         1589 REVLON PLACE
           HOLMESVILLE        OH1900700000000000000000
     111111PENELOPE P. SCHULTZ           8899 TOWER PARK         SUITE 5
           IRA                TX7780400000000000000000
     222222TIMOTHY WAYNE GARZA           ROUTE 5                 BOX 56
           PINEAPPLE          AL6700900000000000000000
     333333CLAUDIA L. ABKOWICZ           8743 CANNERY STREET
           MONTGOMERY         CA8176500000000000000000
```

Figure D–2
Sequential input file for the
conversion program.

```
     111111PENELOPE P. SCHULTZ           8899 TOWER PARK         SUITE 5
           IRA                TX7780400000000000000000
     123456JOSEPH JOHN SCHWARTZWALDER    495 PLEASANT LANE       APT B
           MUSTANG DRAW       NM3598700000000000000000
     222222TIMOTHY WAYNE GARZA           ROUTE 5                 BOX 56
           PINEAPPLE          AL6700900000000000000000
     234567CATHERINE ROSS BROWNE         1589 REVLON PLACE
           HOLMESVILLE        OH1900700000000000000000
     333333CLAUDIA L. ABKOWICZ           8743 CANNERY STREET
           MONTGOMERY         CA8176500000000000000000
```

Figure D–3
Indexed output file for the
conversion program.

APPENDIX **E**

Magnetic Tape Operations

SECTION 1
Characteristics of Magnetic Tape

A magnetic tape is a continuous strip of mylar plastic on which data may be recorded in the form of magnetic bits. Only one side of the tape is used for storing data. Reels of tape come in various lengths, of which 2400 feet is standard. Reels containing 1200, 600, and 250 feet are not uncommon. The standard width is one-half inch. One side of the tape is coated with a substance that can be magnetized in very small areas to represent data.

Tape-reading devices, not unlike the reel-to-reel devices used to record and play music on home stereo systems, are utilized to encode and decode bit patterns on magnetic computer tapes. These bit patterns are used to represent alphanumeric and special characters, which are the symbols of communication used in our culture.

Tape utilization has two special advantages: (1) relatively large amounts of data may be stored in a relatively small amount of space, and (2) this information can be written or read fairly rapidly as compared to speeds for cards or diskette.

A comparison of the characteristics of the now little-used punched card and magnetic tape may be useful in order to give you an idea of the relative capacity of magnetic tape. Then we will contrast magnetic tape with some more modern storage media. Up to 80 columns of information can be stored on a typical punched card. Each of these columns is referred to as a character, or byte, of information. Data cards come in boxes containing 2000 cards. The box of 2000 cards is about 8 inches wide, 15 inches long and 3½ inches high and weighs about 5 pounds. Depending on the tape density (characters per inch, which will be discussed later) you could put the information contained on 2000 cards (where all 80 columns on each card are completely punched), on 112 inches of tape (a little over 9 feet). Information from approximately 514,285 cards (each with 80 columns of information) can be recorded on one 2400-foot reel of tape. This is equivalent to approximately 257 boxes of cards (each box with 2000 cards and each card with 80 columns of information). A typical reel of tape is 10 inches in diameter and weighs four pounds. The 257 boxes of cards would be about 75 feet high and weigh in excess of a thousand pounds.

As indicated earlier, most data centers have eliminated the use of punched cards. Our "gee whiz" comparison of tape capacity to card capacity should, in the interest of fairness, be extended to compare tape storage to the successor medium, which is flexible disk. A typical flexible disk (if there can be said to be such a thing—in this case we will use a double-density double-sided 5½-inch disk as "typical") has a storage capacity of about one-half million bytes (500K). As we have seen, a 2400-foot reel of 1600-bpi tape will store about eight times as much. It is also many times heavier, takes up many times more space, costs four to five times as much, and is limited to sequential access. The improvements in technology that have recently taken place have effectively sounded the death knell for the use of magnetic tape as a major storage medium. There remain, however, as noted in the following list, many uses for which tape is uniquely suited: the physical shipment of data from place to place serves as one excellent example.

Other advantages associated with the use of magnetic tape are:

- Tape has increased storage capacity when compared with punched cards or low-volume magnetic disk.
- The medium itself (the tape) is much less expensive than disk space.
- The hardware used for accessing the tape (the tape drive) is much less expensive than similar rigid disk hardware. (This is not true for the lower-volume diskette or "floppy" disk drives.)
- In combination, the above advantages allow the use of magnetic tape for large-volume archival storage of data in circumstances where sequential access is acceptable.

There is at least one major disadvantage to the use of tape: the access method is sequential. If direct access to the data is desirable or essential then the use of magnetic tape is precluded. However, those conditions in which the use of sequential data is desirable or acceptable are relatively common and, although there is a clear-cut trend away from the use of tape in favor of disk devices, many data processing installations utilize magnetic tape extensively.

SECTION 2
How Data Are Stored on Tapes

When information is stored on a tape or on a disk, it is in the form of magnetic spots on the medium. A tape is divided into either seven or nine rows (tracks) on which spots can be magnetized. Most modern tapes are nine-track tapes. Figure E-1 represents a piece of tape and illustrates how the word COBOL would be stored on a seven-track tape and on a nine-track tape. There are a number of standard storage conventions available. The conventions that are used in Figure E-1 are the Binary Coded Decimal (BCD) code for seven-track tape and the Extended Binary Coded Decimal Interchange Code (EBCDIC) convention for nine-track tape. The binary equivalents of the alphabet and the decimal numbers in these two codes and in another common nine-bit code (the American Standard Code for Information Interchange—ASCII) are given in Figure E-2.

The only reason the seven- and nine-track tapes are discussed is so that you will be aware that computer tapes from one machine may or may not run on another even if the manufacturer is the same.

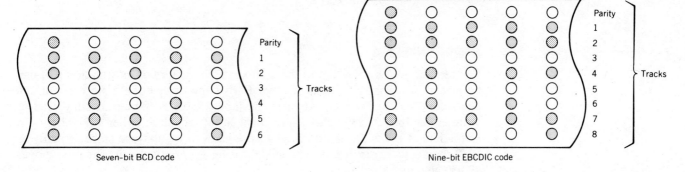

Figure E–1
Seven- and nine-track tape
character representation.

	Character	BCD	EBCDIC		ASCII	
Figure E–2 Three common tape-coding conventions.	A	110001	1100	0001	0100	0001
	B	110010	1100	0010	0100	0010
	C	110011	1100	0011	0100	0011
	D	110100	1100	0100	0100	0100
	E	110101	1100	0101	0100	0101
	F	110110	1100	0110	0100	0110
	G	110111	1100	0111	0100	0111
	H	111000	1100	1000	0100	1000
	I	111001	1100	1001	0100	1001
	J	100001	1101	0001	0100	1010
	K	100010	1101	0010	0100	1011
	L	100011	1101	0011	0100	1100
	M	100100	1101	0100	0100	1101
	N	100101	1101	0101	0100	1110
	O	100110	1101	0110	0101	1111
	P	100111	1101	0111	0101	0000
	Q	101000	1101	1000	0101	0001
	R	101001	1101	1001	0101	0010
	S	010010	1110	0010	0101	0011
	T	010011	1110	0011	0101	0100
	U	010100	1110	0100	0101	0101
	V	010101	1110	0101	0101	0110
	W	010110	1110	0110	0101	0111
	X	010111	1110	0111	0101	1000
	Y	011000	1110	1000	0101	1001
	Z	011001	1110	1001	0101	1010
	0	001010	1111	0000	0011	0000
	1	000001	1111	0001	0011	0001
	2	000010	1111	0010	0011	0010
	3	000011	1111	0011	0011	0011
	4	000100	1111	0100	0011	0100
	5	000101	1111	0101	0011	0101
	6	000110	1111	0110	0011	0110
	7	000111	1111	0111	0011	0111
	8	001000	1111	1000	0011	1000
	9	001001	1111	1001	0011	1001

Tape Density

The term *tape density* refers to the number of characters of information that can be placed in a specific length of tape. Early tape drives could store about 200 characters (bytes) per inch. Most of the tape drives in operation today read or write either 1600 or 3200 characters per inch (abbreviated either cpi or bpi—for characters or bytes per inch). The latest devices in regular use store as many as 6250 characters per inch and some models using laser optical units can record over 22,000 characters per inch.

Obviously, the greater the tape density, the larger the amount of data that can be stored on one reel of tape of a given length. As a general rule, the speed of access is a function of density (the greater the density, the faster the data can be read and written). A tape drive that turns at 18.75 inches per second can read 15,000 characters per second from an 800 cpi tape. However, the same drive (again turning at 18.75 inches per second) can read 30,000 characters per second if the density is 1600 characters per inch. As density increases and the tape speed increases, more data can be stored and in turn can be read or written faster. A tape drive that turns at 200 inches per second with a density of 1600 characters per inch can read or write 320,000 characters (bytes) per second.

SECTION 3
Blocking

When information is written on a tape, it is often written in blocks. These blocks may contain one record (the blocking factor is said to be "1") or several records taken as a group (a blocking factor of N—where N is the number of records per group).

The process of blocking causes the records to be strung together as a group before they are written. After each block is written there will still be a gap on the tape, but there will be fewer gaps if records are blocked than if records are not blocked. Blocking saves both space on the tape and time in reading and writing. When writing records one record at a time, the tape drive will write one record, slow down (leaving a gap), and stop. The tape drive will not place the second record on the tape until a write command is issued for the tape. The second write command will cause the second record to be written, then the tape drive to leave another gap, and will stop again. When using blocked records, the computer will retain a full block of records in the computer's memory and then write all at one time, as a single group, before leaving a gap on the tape. The tape drive will stop following the write of a block of records.

As the block size increases, the number of records that may be placed on a tape of a given density and length increases. However, there is a trade-off between the amount of internal storage that is required to hold the large blocks, the amount of time necessary to handle them, and the space savings on the tape.

The advantage of blocking records is in the time savings in transferring data to or from a tape unit. The time involved in waiting for a interrecord (or interblock) gap to pass by the read/write mechanism requires a wait on the part of the CPU. Blocking of records allows considerable reduction of this wait time.

Blocking of sequential records on disk allows similar processing time savings even though there will be no interrecord gap on disk. The time savings from blocking disk records arises from the fact that only one search is required in order to retrieve a block of N records, whereas retrieval of the same records, if unblocked, would require N searches.

If the data you are using are stored in blocked format, you must know the blocking factor in order to retrieve the records. Specification of record and block sizes are usually handled in the JCL external to your COBOL program and need not be specified in the program. However, there are a number of advantages to specifying this information in the DATA DIVISION. For example, if your company has subscribed to a service supplying accounting survey information (something like selected Securities Exchange Commission 10-K report data) and that data is sent to you on a nine-track magnetic tape, you would need to determine the record length (or range of record lengths if the records are of variable length) and the blocksize. Suppose the records are fixed length and blocked, twenty 1304-byte records to a block. You could document this in the FD for the file:

```
DATA    DIVISION.
FILE    SECTION.
FD      SEC-DATA-FILE
        RECORD FORMAT IS F
        RECORD LENGTH IS 1304 CHARACTERS
        BLOCK CONTAINS 26080 CHARACTERS
        LABEL RECORDS ARE STANDARD
        DATA RECORD IS SEC-RECORD.
```

The blocksize may also be specified:

```
BLOCK CONTAINS 20 RECORDS
```

SECTION 4
Tape Labels

Magnetic tape documentation may be augmented through the use of three different types of labels. External labels are simply paper stick-on labels that are affixed to the outside of the reel and on which you may write any important information. Sometimes only the volume number of the tape is written on the external label.

There are two types of internal labels. The header label appears at the beginning of the tape and includes all the general information about the tape that is known prior to the creation of a data file on the tape. For example, a header label might contain:

- the volume number (or serial number) of the reel of tape
- some designation of the ownership of the tape (XYZ Company or the University of Northern Idaho).
- the name of the file which is stored on the tape
- the record length, block size, and record format (fixed- or variable-length records, blocked or unblocked, etc.)
- the creation date
- the expiration date or retention period for the file

A trailer label will be appended to the end of a tape file and will contain information that may not be known until the creation of a file is complete. For example, a trailer label may contain such items as record counts or a count of the number of entries of a certain type that are contained on the file.

Tape-labeling standards are specific to certain types of hardware, so a label that is standard for an IBM machine may not be standard for a Burroughs computer.

Sometimes you may be called upon to access a tape that has nonstandard labels for the machine you are using. In such circumstances you should bypass the label processing through the appropriate job control language (or run control language) entries and specify that labels are not being consulted by including the following in the FD entry for the file:

```
LABEL RECORDS ARE OMITTED
```

The same entry is appropriate in those rare conditions in which you encounter data encoded on a tape that has no internal labels at all.

F

Characteristics of Disk Storage Devices

COBOL allows you to access different storage media with a high degree of "device independence." The way in which you code your COBOL program is relatively unaffected should you decide that the output from your program is to be stored on magnetic disk rather than, say, printed on paper by an impact printer. An obvious exception to this general rule is that you are constrained by the physical characteristics of a particular *class* of devices and by the requirements of the data organization of the file you are processing. For example, you would not attempt to access an indexed or random file if the storage medium is sequential (e.g., magnetic tape).

Because of the basic device independence of COBOL we have avoided discussion of the physical characteristics of specific media within the body of the text. We do think, however, that it is helpful in understanding some COBOL concepts to visualize the physical processes that take place when input or output instructions are executed. This appendix provides an overview of the physical characteristics of disk devices.

SECTION 1
Rigid Disk—A Single Surface View

Disk storage devices consist of one or more (usually more) disks, which are coated with a ferrous oxide substrate. Information may be stored in the form of magnetic spots. You may visualize these disks as being in the shape of a phonograph record, but without grooves. Indeed they have more of the appearance, and are based on the same physical principles, of the new video disks and audio disks that have appeared on the consumer market in the last few years. Figure F-1 models the single disk. The size of these disks ranges from about 5 inches in diameter to about 14 inches in diameter. Most are formed into "packs" of several surfaces ranging from two disks per pack to about twenty disks per pack. Typically the top surface and the bottom surface of a pack are not utilized because of

Figure F–1
Single magnetic disk surface.

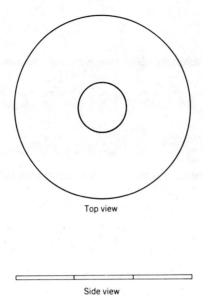

Top view

Side view

the higher risk of contamination of these surfaces: if you have a pack of 11 disks you would have a total of 20 surfaces on which data would actually be stored ([11 surfaces × 2 sides] − top − bottom = 20). Figure F-2 illustrates this concept using a pack of 11 disks. Discussion of the use of multiple recording surfaces is included in the next section of this appendix. First we will consider the way in which data are stored on any given surface.

Figure F–2
Disk of multiple surfaces.

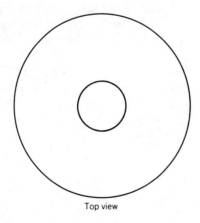

Top view

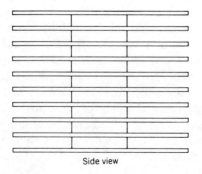

Side view

Appendix E outlines some of the common internal data representation conventions that are available for the storage of information in binary form. For example, the binary form of the alphabetic character C, using the EBCDIC convention, is 11000011. To store this information on disk the binary sequence would be placed in a "string" along a selected path on the surface of a disk. The disk surface, usually included as one of several in a pack, is loaded into a device (a drive) that spins the disks at a constant rate of speed. The drive incorporates one or more read/write servomechanisms, which are either in a fixed position in relation to the surface or which may be moved to a specific position over the surface. Figure F-3 illustrates this concept. The first figure shows the moveable read/write mechanism, in which the location of the data is dependent upon the physical movement of the read/write head. The second illustration is of the disk module, or so-called "Winchester", device which incorporates a number of fixed-position read/write mechanisms. In this of type device, the selection of the address of data is elec-

Figure F–3
Read/write mechanisms.

Circuitry

Moveable arm
with single
read/write head

Figure F–3 (continued)

Fixed multiple
Read/write
heads

Circuitry

tronic rather than mechanical. Disk modules are sealed and the read/write heads are an integral part of the pack. They are obviously superior in terms of data storage capacity per area, in resistance to surface contamination, and in speed of access. They are also measureably more expensive than those devices that utilize a moveable encoding mechanism. Since the module, or Winchester, devices are now commonly used and may be expected to increase in dominance over the next few years, we will use them in this discussion.

Returning to our example, in which we want to write the letter C to disk (you've probably guessed by now that before we're through we will write the word COBOL to disk). The computer's operating systems will select an unused area on the disk. This area may be addressed by the surface on which the data are to be stored (we are only dealing with one surface right now, so let's call it surface 1), and the relative distance from the edge of the disk. The disk surface may be visualized as a series of concentric circles (remember, the surface is smooth these are logical positions). Each concentric circle is "served" by a read/write mechanism so that each concentric circle is, in effect, an address. In a typical disk there will be about two hundred of these concentric circles (there may be fewer or more on any given type of module). Suppose we want to write on the middle of the disk surface (say the 99th read/write head), we now have an address for the data track 1 (the surface) and cylinder 99 (the relative distance from the edge of the disk). To complicate matters even more, some these devices support sets of read/write arrays (Figure F-4) so that each cylinder/track address may be further refined into a cylinder/track/sector address, which allows for faster retrieval or storage of the data on the disk. We will limit our review to the cylinder and track reference only.

Our track/cylinder (1/99) would have a capacity ranging from several thousand to several tens of thousands of bytes of data, depending on the device in use. For purposes of discussion, suppose our device has a capacity of 20,000 bytes per cylinder/track or 4,000,000 bytes per surface (20,000 × 200 cylinders) or, assuming our device has twenty useable surfaces, 80 million bytes per pack (4,000,000 × 20). In perspective, there are currently devices on the market that store upward of a half billion bytes per pack. So our 80-megabyte pack (1 million bytes = 1 megabyte) is a relatively limited one.

Your COBOL program, issuing an instruction to write the letter C to disk in EBCDIC code to address 1/99, would then cause the character string 11000011 to be stored on the first 1/20,000 of cylinder 99 of track 1 of disk pack X. Figure F-5 illustrates the storage of the word COBOL on the first 5/20,000 of the storage area.

Figure F–4
Segmentation of disk into logical sectors.

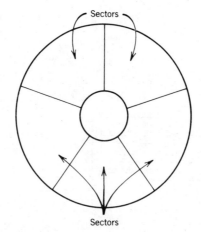

Figure F–5
Bit string for the letters
"COBOL" in EBCDIC code on
magnetic disk.

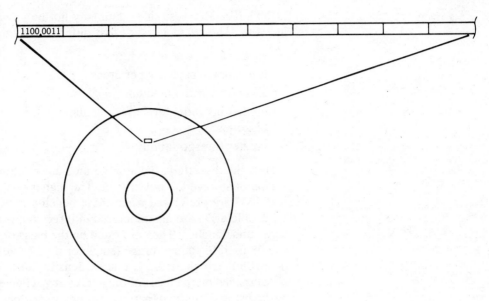

SECTION 2
Rigid Disk—Multiple Surfaces

Rigid disk will usually include the availability of multiple surfaces. This expands the storage capacity of these devices and allows similar speeds in the access to the data. The only addition to the logic of accessing these devices is that a specification of the surface (track) to be addressed must be made.

You may find the selection of terms for addressing a disk area confusing. Many people tend to think of the cylinder address as a "track" since it corresponds very roughly to the grooves on the familiar phonograph record. The terminology is an artifact of the transition from the once-dominant drum storage devices to disk storage. Since the drum storage device was, indeed, a cylinder—and a single cylinder at that—and since the areas accessed by read/write devices on the surface of the drum were called "tracks," the engineers who developed the early disk devices tended to carry this frame of reference forward to the new technology. Thus, they visualized the disk pack as being a collection of concentric drum-type cylinders, stacked one inside the other.

SECTION 3
Flexible Disk

The relatively recent appearance of flexible disks (or diskettes, or floppy disks) has provided a low-cost, high-volume, direct access capability storage medium that has almost completely replaced the punched card as a storage medium and, along with cost-per-character of storage reductions associated with the use of rigid disk, has contributed to the decline in the use of magnetic tape.

The physical storage of data on diskettes is similar to that of rigid disk. Since the diskettes has only one or two useable surfaces, there will be only one or two addresses equivalent to rigid disk track addresses. Flexible disks also have fewer "cylinder" addresses, since data may not be stored with as much density as in rigid disk. The characteristics that differentiate the "floppies" are:

- slower access/transfer rates
- less storage capacity per area
- less cost for the medium
- greater potential for surface contamination (although this is not as critical in diskettes)
- greater transportability

Thus the diskette is the storage medium of choice when speed of access and volume of storage are not critical. The higher-cost, higher-volume, faster-access rigid disks are preferable when these benefits outweigh the added costs.

Flexible disks are manufactured in three standard diameters—5¼ inches , 3½ inches and 8 inches. They are rated on the basis of whether both sides of the disk may be used for data storage (single or double sided) and the relative density of the medium (single density, double density, and "quad" density). They are further classified on the basis of the addressing schemes that are available for accessing data stored on them (hard sector or soft sector). Thus, if you plan to transport your data or programs from one installation to another, you may find that the devices that read and write flexible disks may differ from one location to another. There are 36 combinations that may be available to you (size × density × recording sides × sectoring = $3 \times 3 \times 2 \times 2 = 24$).

Index

Absence test, 56
ACCEPT statement, 175–177
  format 1, 175–176
  format 2, 175–177
  mainline module, 69
  master menu, 274, 277
  purpose, 13–14
ACCESS mode:
  checkwriter system, 129
  relative files, 151
  sequential file update, 61, 65–66
ACCESS MODE IS DYNAMIC, 150–153
ACCESS MODE IS RANDOM, 151–153
Account balance, data entry, 271–272
Account number tests, 56–57
ACCOUNT NUMBER, 281
ADD CORRESPONDING, 10, 348–349
ADD statement, 9–10
  REPORT WRITER, 250
Additions:
  pointers, 164
  transaction file, 58
ALL option, 178–180
Alternate key, checkwriter system 134–137
ALTER statement, 18, 344–347
ALTERNATE RECORD KEY:
  checkwriter system, 126–129
  inverted lists, 144–146
American National Standards Institute (ANSI),
  1
ANSWER, chart of accounts maintenance, 281
APMENU program, 272–278
Arithmetic statements, 9–12
ASCII, data storage, 362–363

ASSIGN statement, SORT statement, 211
AT END clause, 14–15, 17
  DECLARATIVES, 255
AT-INDEX, 194–195
ATTRIBUTE-RECORD, relative files, 165
ATTRIBUTES file, 168–169, 194
Audit/error list, 52
  indexed file update, 113, 115
Audit/error report:
  format, 64
  sequential file, 78
Audit reports, 57
AUTHOR paragraph, 5

BALANCE-30, 348
BALANCE-CURRENT, 348
Binary Coded Decimal code (BCD), 362
Binary table search, 292–293, 300–301
Bit strings, 370–371
Blank lines in programming, 30–31
BLOCK CONTAINS clause, 66
Blocking, 364–365

CALL statement, 20, 189–192
  control coupling
  MASTER MENU, 272, 277
  USING option, 191–192
CASE structure, 25
  extended grade example, 27–28
  GO TO DEPENDING ON statement,
    188–189
  implementation, 27–29
  master menu programming, 276
CHANGE procedure, master file, 72–73

Changes, transaction file, 58–59
Character testing, 55–56
Chart of accounts, 278–282
CHECK-LIST file, 127
CHECK-MASTER-FILE, 126–127, 129
Checkwriter system:
  000-CONTROL-CHECK-PRINT, 131–132
  100-HOUSEKEEPING, 132–133
  200-PRINT-CHECKS, 133–134
  230-WRITER-CHECK, 135
  232-STUB-TOTAL, 135–136
  233-WRITE-CHECK-RECORD, 136
  300-DISPLAY-TOTALS, 136
  800-READ-INVOICE, 136–137
  ENVIRONMENT DIVISION, 129–130
  file structure, 128–129
  flowchart, 126
  hierarchy chart, 128
  inputs and outputs, 137–138
  sample program, 139–143
  START verb, 134–137
CICS operating system enhancement, 269
Class test, 55
CLOSE statement, 13
Clustering, hashing, 160
COBOL (Common Business Oriented
    Language):
  ANSI standard formats, 317–341
  defined, 1
  history, 1–2
  language structure, 2–3
  program structure, 3–9
  rogues' gallery of features, 343–354
  separators, 2–3
  shorthand notation for statements, 21
  user-created words, 3
  words, 3
COBOL-8x, 1
COBOL-60, 1
COBOL-68, DELETE statements, 107–108
COBOL-74, 1
  DELETE statements, 107–108
CODE clause, REPORT WRITER, 243
Codes:
  modules, 26
  readability, 30–31
Cohesion in module design, 32, 34–36
Coincidental cohesion, 34
Collision, defined, 160–162
COLUMN clause, 245–246
Common coupling, 36
Communicational cohesion, 35
Compiler-directing statement, 4
COMPUTE statement, 10
  REPORT WRITER, 250
Condition names, 350–351
Conditional statement, 4
Conference on Data Systems Languages
    (CODASYL), 1
CONFIGURATION section, 5–6
Consistency test, 56
Content coupling, 36
Control breaks, 229–230
Control coupling, 37

CONTROL FOOTING, 244–245, 250–251
CONTROL HEADING, 244–245, 249
Control statements, transfer, 18–20
CONTROLS ARE clause, 252
CONTROLS, REPORT WRITER, 238
Copies, master file, 58
COPY feature, 192–194
CORRESPONDING option, 347–349
COUNT operation, 185
Coupling, 36–37

Data coupling, 37
DATA DIVISION:
  basic formats, 319–322
  binary search, 300–301
  checkwriter, 130
  CORRESPONDING option, 347–349
  coupling, 36
  88-level entries, 350
  format, 6–8
  internal *vs.* external tables, 288
  ISAM entries, 97
    updating, 101–104
  master menu, 273
  REPORT WRITER, 232–244
  sequential file processing, 66–67
  SORT program, 210, 219–220
  structure headers, 3–4
  table construction, 294–296
  table data retrieval, 298
  table handling, 300
  three-dimension tables, 310
  two-dimension table, 304–305
  UNSTRING command, 185
Data-entry screen, 271
Data-names, 3
DATA RECORD IS clause, 210
Data records, 149
Data retrieval, 296
Data storage, magnetic tapes, 362–363
Data validation, 55–57
  account number tests, 56–57
  audit reports, 57
  character testing, 55–56
  error listing, 57
  field testing, 56
DATE-COMPILED paragraph, 5
Date tests, 56
DATE-WRITTEN paragraph, 5
Debugging language, basic formats, 335–336
DECLARATIVES, 9, 254–255
  INVALID KEY, 255–256
DEC-VAX-11 system, 101
DEC VAX system:
  conversion of sequential file to indexed file,
    357–359
  on-line transaction processing, 269
DEC-VAX VMS operating, 273
DEC VT100, 273
DEC VT100C, 273
DELETE statement, 17
  relative files, 158–159
  updating indexed files, 107–108
  vendor master file, 72

Deletions:
   pointers, 164
   transaction file, 58–59
DELIMITED BY § §, 186
DELIMITER IN phrase, 185
DESTIN-DELIM, 185
DETAIL lines, 256–257
   REPORT WRITER, 231–232
Direct table retrieval, 301–302
Disk storage devices, 367–372
DISPLAY statement, 177–178
   master menu, 274
   output, 178
   purpose, 14
DISTRICTS, 304–305
DIVIDE BY option, 11
DIVIDE statement, 10–11
Division method of hashing, 160
Documentation:
   magnetic tape, 365–366
   structured programming, 26
DOWHILE statement, repetition structures, 24, 29
Driver program, 189
DYNAMIC ACCESS mode, 16–17, 129–130
   READ statement, 153
DYNAMIC WRITE, relative files, 155–156

EDIT statement, sequential file updating, 55
88-level entries, 350–351
EJECT feature, 198
ELSE statement, 18
Embedded pointers, 163
EMPLOYEE-MASTER file program, 168, 170
END DECLARATIVES, 255
END PROGRAM statement, 191
End-of-file processing, 59–60
ENVIRONMENT DIVISION:
   basic formats, 317–319
   checkwriter system, 129–130
   EJECT feature, 198
   FILE SECTION entries, 253
   format, 5–6
   ISAM, 96–97
     updating, 100–101
   master menu, 273
   paragraph headers, 4
   relative files, 150–151
   sequential file update, 61, 65–66
   SORT program, 211
   SORT statement, 210
   structure headers, 3–4
Error listing, 57
EXAMINE statement, 178–182
   REPLACING ALL option, 179
   REPLACING LEADING option, 180
   REPLACING-TALLY combination, 181–182
   REPLACING UNTIL FIRST option, 180
   TALLYING option, 181–182
EXIT PROGRAM statement, 191
Extended Binary Coded Decimal Interchange Code (EBCDIC), 362, 371
EXTEND in OPEN statement, 13
External coupling, 36

FD entries, 235
   format, 7
   sequential file processing, 66
Field testing, 56
FILE-CONTROL entries, 6
File description, *see* FD entries
File-names, 3
FILE SECTION, 6–7, 238
   88-level entries, 350
   ENVIRONMENT DIVISION, 253
   OUTPUT PROCEDURE, 219
   REPORT WRITER, 243–244
   sequential file processing, 66–67
   SORT program, 211
FILE STATUS clause, 101
   key values, 355–356
File structure, 94–95
   checkwriter system, 128–129
FILLER, record description entry, 245
FINAL control break, 252
FINAL reserved word, 238–239
FIRST DETAIL entry, 240, 242
Flexible disks, 371–372
Flowcharts:
   checkwriter system, 126
   indexed file creation, 96
   indexed file update, 95
   SORT program, 224
FOOTING entry, 242
Footings, REPORT WRITER, 230, 244
Format control, 336
Functional cohesion, 35–36

GENERATE statement, 256–257
GIVING option, 11
GO TO . . . DEPENDING ON statement, 17, 188–189
   CASE structure, 27–28
   master menu programming, 277
GO TOless programming, 275–276
GO TO statement, 18–19
   guidelines for, 26
   unconditional branching, 343–344

Hard-coded table, 294–295
Hashing:
   collision, 160–162
   division method, 160
   relative files, 159–162
HEADING entry, 240
Headings, REPORT WRITER, 230, 244
Hierarchy chart, 32–33
   checkwriter system, 128
HIGH-VALUES, 54

IBM systems:
   BLOCK CONTAINS clause, 66
   COBOL formats, 317–341
Identification, programming standards, 30–31
IDENTIFICATION DIVISION:
   basic formats, 317
   EJECT feature, 198
   format, 4–5

IDENTIFICATION DIVISION (*Continued*)
  master menu, 274
  paragraph headers, 4
IF statement, 17–19:
  table-handling, 307–308
  updating indexed files, 109
IFTHENELSE structure, 25
  selection structure implementation, 27–28
Imperative statement, 4
Indexed files, 95–96:
  created from sequential files, 357–359
  inverted lists, 144–146
  other applications, 125–146
Indexed sequential access methods, *see* ISAM
INDEXED-VENDOR-MASTER file, 96–97
Initialization:
  sequential file processing, 68–69
  table-handling, 306
INITIATE command, 256–258
INPUT:
  in OPEN statement, 13
  REPORT WRITER, 236–238, 261–262
Input-loaded table, 295–296
INPUT-OUTPUT instructions, 6, 12–17
INPUT PROCEDURE option, 216–218
Inputs:
  checkwriter system, 137–138
  indexed program, 110–111
  rogue's gallery, 352
  sequential file processing, 76–79
  SORT program, 208–209
  special statements, 201–202
Inquiry program:
  output, 167–168
  relative files, 166–168
INSPECT statement, 20, 183
INSTALLATION paragraph, 5
INTO phrase, 14
INVALID KEY, 17
  chart of accounts, 281
  DECLARATIVES, 255–256
  ISAM, 100
  relative files, 154–155
  REWRITE statement, 16
  START verb, 131
  updating indexed files, 108
  WRITE process, 136
Inverted lists, 129
  input, 146
  output, 146
  processing, 144–146
  relative files, 164–172
INVOICE-MASTER, 126, 128, 130
  invoice processing, 135
I-O-CONTROL paragraphs, 6
I-O, in OPEN statement, 13
ISAM, 93–122
  DATA DIVISION entries, 97, 101–104
  ENVIRONMENT DIVISION, 96–97, 100–101
  example problem, 95
  file structure, 94–95
  PROCEDURE DIVISION, 98–99
    updating, 105–110

program inputs and outputs, 110–115
  sample program, 116–122
  updating master file concepts, 99–100
IVM-VENDOR-NUMBER field, 97

Key field, 52–53, 96
Key values, file status, 355–356

LABEL RECORD clause, 67
LAST DETAIL entry, 242
LAST-NAME field, 185
LEADING option, 178–180
LIMIT IS phrase, 239–240
Limit test, 56
LIMITS ARE phrase, 239–240
Line control, 231
LINE NUMBER entry, 245, 247
LINKAGE SECTION, 6
Linked lists, 163
Logical cohesion, 34
Logical statements, 17–18
LOW-VALUES, 54

Magnetic tape:
  blocking, 364–365
  data storage, 362–363
  density, 364
  documentation, 365–366
  operations, 361–366
Main menu, 270
Master file, 51–52
  indexed update listing, 116–122
  indexed vendor, 110, 112–113
  maintenance, 54–57
  new vendor sample program, 77
  record layout, 62–63
  retention cycle, 53
  transaction file and, 58–59
  updated, 52
  ISAM, 99–100
MASTER MENU program, 272–278
Menus, 270–272
Merge facility formats, 340–341
Modules:
  200-UPDATE-MASTER-FILE, 69–70
  210-COMPARE-KEYS, 70
  220-ADD-MASTER, 70–71
  230-COPY MASTER, 71
  240-DELETE MASTER, 72
  250-CHANGE-MASTER, 72
  300-PRINT-AUDIT, 72
  audit report print, 73–74
  cohesion, 32, 34–36
  coupling, 36–37
  ISAM
    PROCEDURE DIVISION entries, 105–110
  main menu program, 274–278
mainline, 67
  PROCEDURE DIVISION, checkwriter system, 131–134
  READ procedure-master file, 75
  READ procedure-transactions file, 76
  span of control, 37
  structured programming, 26

top-down design, 32
totals print procedure, 74
well-designed, 31–37
wrap-up, 34–35
Modulus 11 check digits, 56–57
MONTH, 229–230, 246–247
Month code, 287
MOVE 51 command, 69
MOVE LOW-VALUES statement, 69
MOVE statement, 20–21
MOVE ZEROS statement, 69
Multilinked lists, 163
Multiple-surface disks, 368–369
MULTIPLY statement, 11–12

Nested driver program, 190
Nested program structures, 25
New page feature, 198
NEXT SENTENCE, 18
NO REWIND option, 13

OCCURS clause, 294
OLD-VENDOR-MASTER-FILE, 67
ON ASCENDING KEY clause, 212–213
ON DESCENDING KEY clause, 212–213
On-line transaction processing, 269–282
ON OVERFLOW clause, 185
ON SIZE ERROR, 10, 17
OPEN statement, 12–13
  relative files, 151–152
ORGANIZATION clause:
  ISAM, 97
  sequential file update, 61, 65–66
ORGANIZATION IS RELATIVE clause,
  150
OUTPUT:
  in OPEN statement, 13
  REPORT WRITER, 234–235, 263–266
  SORT program, 222
    selected records, 224
OUTPUT PROCEDURE, 218–221
Outputs:
  checkwriter system, 137–138
  sequential file processing, 76–79
Overflow area, 161

Page control, 230–231
PAGE FOOTING, 244–245
PAGE HEADING, 244–245
PAGE LIMIT clause, 239
Painting, master menu, 275–276
Paragraph headers, 4
Paragraph-names, 3
Passes, master file, 58
PERFORM statement, 19–20
  checkwriter system, 134
  mainline module, 69
  master menu programming, 277
  PROCEDURE DIVISION, 68
  repetition structures, 29
PERFORM . . . UNTIL statement, 18
PERFORM VARYING, 296–298
  table-handling, 300
PHONE number, COPY feature, 193

PICTURE, 247–249
  ISAM updating, 101
PICTURE value, 294
POINTER phrase, 185
Pointers, 162–164
  alphabetic sequence, 163
  embedded, 163
Positional organization, 289–290
Preprinted check form, 127
Preprinted statement form, 148
Presence test, 56
PREVIOUS-KEY, 54
Primary clustering, 160
Primary data area, 94
Prime data area, 94
Prime number division, 160–161
Procedural cohesion, 35
PROCEDURE DIVISION:
  alternate statements, 130–131
  basic formats, 322–329
  binary search, 300–301
  checkwriter system sample entries, 131–134
  EXAMINE statement, 178–182
  format, 8–9
  GO TO statements, 18–19
  input-loaded table, 295–296
  ISAM, 98–99
    updating, 105–110
  master menu, 273–278
  OUTPUT-FILE, 213–214
  paragraph headers, 4
  READ NEXT statement, 131
  relative files, 151–159
  REPORT WRITER:
    commands, 253–258
    line printing, 232
    SUM clause, 250–251
    tasks, 244
  sequence structures, 26
  sequential file, 67–76
  sequential search, 299–300
  SORT data, 207–208
  SORT program, 210–211, 219–224
    INPUT PROCEDURE, 217–218
  START verb, 130–131
  structure headers, 3–4
  two-dimensional table, 304–305
PRODUCT-CLASS-CODE, 298
PRODUCT-INDEX, 296, 300
PROGRAM-ID, defined, 5
Programming standards, 30–31
Programming structure:
  sample with structured concepts, 38
  sample with unstructured code, 39
Program-names, 3
Program objectives, 23–24
Program structure, 24–25
Pump priming operation, 105
  checkwriter system, 132–133

RANDOM access option, 101
Randomly organized tables, 289
RANDOM READ statement, 152–153
RANDOM WRITE relative files, 155–156

Range test, 56
READ-DETAIL paragraph, ALTER
    statements, 346
READ NEXT statement, 131
READ procedure:
    master file, 75
    transactions file, 76
READ statement:
    DYNAMIC ACCESS MODE, 153
    sequential access in relative files, 152
READ statement (I-O), 15
READ statement (sequential), 14–15
READ-TRANSACTION statements, ISAM,
    110
Read/write mechanisms, 369
Reasonableness test, 56
RECORD CONTAINS clause, 66, 194
Record description entries, 7–8
RECORD KEY:
    ISAM, 97, 101
        updating, 101–102
    relative files, 165
Record-names, 3
Record verification, 272
REDEFINES clause, 294
RELATIVE access mode, 16–17
Relative files, 149–150
    collision, 160–162
    ENVIRONMENT DIVISION, 150–151
    hashing, 159–162
    inputs example, 165–166
    inquiry program, 166–168
    inverted list, 164–172
    pointers, 162–164
    PROCEDURE DIVISION, 151–159
    updating program, 169, 171–172
RELATIVE KEY, 150
    DELETE statement, 159
Relative position number, 159
Relative retrieval of table entries, 293
RELEASE statement, INPUT PROCEDURE,
    216–218
Repetition structures, implementation, 29
REPLACING option, 178–180
    COPY feature, 193
Report descriptions (RDs), 235, 238
REPORT FOOTING, 230, 244
REPORT HEADING, 230, 244
    examples, 246
Report layouts, 240–241
REPORT SECTION, 6, 232–235, 239
REPORT WRITER, 6, 229–266
    01 entries, 243–249
    basic formats, 331–333
    control breaks, 229–230
    DECLARATIVES, 254–256
    detail lines, 231–232
    ENVIRONMENT DIVISION, FILE
        SECTION entries, 253
    input data, 261–262
    input, 236–238
    line control, 231
    manual methods, 250–252

page control, 230–231
PROCEDURE DIVISION entries, 253–258
sample program, 258–266
SUM clause, 250–252
totaling, 231
Retention cycle, 53
Retrieval method, 291
RETURN command, 221
RETURN INTO statement, 221
REWIND option, 13
REWRITE statement, 16
    relative files, 156–158
    updating indexed files, 109
Rigid disks, 367–371
    multiple surfaces, 371
    see also Flexible disks
Rogues' gallery, 343–354
    sample programs, 352–354
ROUNDED option, 10
Runtime library, 272–274

SALES-TABLE, 304–306
    three dimensional, 310
Screens, 270–272
SD entry, 210
SEARCH, 195–198
    table-handling, 300
SEARCH ALL, 195–198, 300–301
Search arguments, 286
Search failure for single dimension table,
    291–292
Secondary clustering, 160
Section headers, 3–4
Section-names, 3
SECURITY paragraph, 5
Segmentation, basic formats, 334–335
SELECT statement and SORT statement, 211
Selection structures, 25
    implementation, 27–29
Separators, 2–3
Sequence checking, 54–55
Sequenced data, 207–210
Sequence structures, 25–26
SEQUENTIAL access mode, 16–17
Sequential cohesion, 35
Sequential file processing:
    DATA DIVISION entries, 66–67
    end-of-file processing, 59–60
    indexed files from, 357–359
    inputs and outputs, 76–79
    PROCEDURE DIVISION entries, 67–76
    processing, 51–87
        requirements, 52–54
    sample program, 80–87
    sequence checking, 54–55
    sorted, 95–96
    updating, 51–52
        concepts, 60–61
        ENVIRONMENT DIVISION entries, 65
        program design, 61–64
        structure diagram, 62
SEQUENTIAL MASTER file, 96–97
Sequential table organization, 289

Sequential table search
  early exit, 295–300
    PERFORM VARYING, 296–298
Serial search of a table, 291–292
SET statement, 21, 195–198
77 entries, 349
Shorthand notation, program structures, 31
Sign test, 56
SIGNPOST, 346
Simple sequence structures, 25
Single magnetic disk surface, 368
Single-dimension table, 291–292
SIZE ERROR option, 10
SORT, 207–227
  basic formats, 329–331
  DATA DIVISION, 219–220
  INPUT PROCEDURE option, 216–218
  inputs, 208–209
  OUTPUT PROCEDURE, 218–224
  output program, 222
  PROCEDURE DIVISION, 207–208, 219–224
  process, 224–225
  sample, 225–227
  SD entry, 210
  selected records, 223
  SELECT statement, 211
  sequential file, 53
  USING and GIVING options, 215
SORT DESCRIPTION entry, 210
Sort-work files, 224
SOURCE IS clause, 247–249
Source program library facility, 335
Spaghetti programming, 39
SPECIAL-NAMES paragraph, 273
Special statements, 175–202
  sample programs, 199–202
SR-RECORD-CODE, 298
Stamp coupling, 37
START statement, 16–17
  relative files, 154–155
START verb, 130–131
  alternate key, 134–137
  sample entries, 131–132
Sterling currency, basic formats, 336
STOP statement, 17
STRING program, 187
STRING statement, 186–187
  basic formats, 338
Structured programming, 276
  guidelines, 25–26
  sequential file update, 61–64
Structured Programming Concepts, 2
Sub menus, 270
Subprogram, 189
Subscription program, 189
Subscripts, 286
SUBTRACT statement, 12
SUBTRACT CORRESPONDING, 348–349
SUM clause, 250–252
SUPERCODE, 32
SUPPRESS PRINTING clause, 255
Systems flowchart, *See* Flowcharts

Table classification, 288–290
Table construction, 294–295
Table-handling, 284–310
  basic formats, 333–334
  binary search, 300–301
  data retrieval, 296
  dimension levels, 290
  direct retrieval, 301–302
  internal *vs.* external, 288
  organization methods, 289
  relative retrieval, 293
  search failures, 289–293
  static *vs.* volatile, 288
  temporary storage, 302–308
  three-dimensional, 308–310
  two-dimensional, 302–308
Table-retrieval methods, 291–294
Table search method, 291
Table terms and concepts, 284–288
TALLY option, 181–182
  UNSTRING command, 185
Tape character representation, 363
Tape-coding conventions, 362–363
  disk storage devices, 369–370
Tape density, 364
Tape labels, 365–366
Teleprocessing, basic formats, 336–338
Temporal cohesion, 34
Temporary storage tables, 302–308
TERMINATE commands, 256–258
Three-dimension tables, 308–310
THROUGH option, 212
Top-down program design, 26, 32
Totaling—subtotals and grand totals, 231
Transaction file, 51
  master file and, 58–59
  record layout, 63
Two-dimension tables, 290, 302–308

Unconditional branching, 343–344
UNSTRING command, 183–186
  illustration, 184–185
  inputs and outputs, 186
UNTIL option, repetition structures, 29
UNTIL FIRST option, 178
Updating:
  disposition of file activities, 79
  distribution of activities, 113–114
  illustration of concepts, 60–61
  indexed files, 99–110
  relative files, 163–164
    program, 169, 171–172
  sequential files, 51–52
  structured program design, 61–64
Usage frequency table organization, 289
USE AFTER ERROR, 254–255
USE BEFORE REPORTING clause, 254–255
User-created words, 3
USING option, 191–192

VALUE clause, 195–198
  table classification, 288
  table construction, 294

VALUE IS clause, 247–249
Variable-length records, 194–195
VENDOR-AUDIT-ERROR-LIST report,
  67
VENDOR-MASTER-FILE, 126, 128
VENDOR-TRANSACTION-FILE, 67
Virtual storage access methods (VSAM), 93
  formats, 338–340
Visual table of contents (VTOC), 32–34
  checkwriter system, 128
  span of control, 37

WHEN clause, 196
WORKING-STORAGE SECTION, 6
  88-level entries, 350

OUTPUT PROCEDURE, 219
purpose, 8
relative files, 150–151
REPORT HEADING, 246
REPORT WRITER, 231, 235, 243–249
sequence checking, 54
sequential file processing, 66–67
77-level entries, 349
VALUE clauses, 196–198
WRITE, 15
ISAM, 99
nonsequential, 16
relative files, 155

YEAR, 230, 246–247

FOOTING	LINKAGE	POINTER
FOR	LOCK	POSITION
FREE	LOW-VALUE	POSITIONING
FROM	LOW-VALUES	POSITIVE
GENERATE	LOWER-BOUND	PREPARED
GIVING	LOWER-BOUNDS	PRINTING
GO	MASTER-INDEX	PRINT-SWITCH
GOBACK	MEMORY	PRIORITY
GREATER	MERGE	PROCEDURE
GROUP	MESSAGE	PROCEDURES
HEADING	MODE	PROCEED
HIGH-VALUE	MODULES	PROCESS
HIGH-VALUES	MORE-LABELS	PROCESSING
HOLD	MOVE	PROGRAM
I-O	MULTIPLE	PROGRAM-ID
I-O-CONTROL	MULTIPLY	QUEUE
ID	NAMED	QUOTE
IDENTIFICATION	NATIVE	QUOTES
IF	NEGATIVE	RANDOM
IN	NEXT	RANGE
INDEX	NO	RD
INDEX-n	NOMINAL	READ
INDEXED	NOT	READY
INDICATE	NOTE	RECEIVE
INITIAL	NSTD-REELS	RECORD
INITIATE	NUMBER	RECORD-OVERFLOW
INPUT	NUMERIC	RECORDING
INPUT-OUTPUT	NUMERIC-EDITED	RECORDS
INSERT	OBJECT-COMPUTER	REDEFINES
INSPECT	OBJECT-PROGRAM	REEL
INSTALLATION	OCCURS	REFERENCES
INTO	OF	RELATIVE
INVALID	OFF	RELEASE
IS	OH	REMAINDER
JUST	OMITTED	REMARKS
JUSTIFIED	ON	REMOVAL
KEY	OPEN	RENAMES
KEYS	OPTIONAL	REORG-CRITERIA
LABEL	OR	REPLACING
LABEL-RETURN	ORGANIZATION	REPORT
LAST	OTHERWISE	REPORTING
LEADING	OUTPUT	REPORTS
LEAVE	OV	REREAD
LEFT	OVERFLOW	RERUN
LENGTH	PAGE	RESERVE
LESS	PAGE-COUNTER	RESET
LIBRARY	PERFORM	RETURN
LIMIT	PF	RETURN-CODE
LIMITS	PH	REVERSED
LINAGE	PIC	REWIND
LINAGE-COUNTER	PICTURE	REWRITE
LINES	PLUS	RF